The Survival
of Ethiopian Independence

Lund Studies in International History.
Editors: Göran Rystad and Sven Tägil

SCANDINAVIAN UNIVERSITY BOOKS
Denmark, MUNKSGAARD, *Copenhagen*
Norway, UNIVERSITETSFORLAGET, *Oslo, Bergen, Tromsö*
Sweden, ESSELTE STUDIUM, *Stockholm, Gothenburg, Lund*

Lund Studies in International History 7

The Survival
of Ethiopian Independence

Sven Rubenson

Professor of History
Addis Ababa University

HEINEMANN LONDON · IBADAN · NAIROBI · LUSAKA

IN ASSOCIATION WITH
ESSELTE STUDIUM &
ADDIS ABABA UNIVERSITY PRESS

Heinemann Educational Books Ltd
48 Charles Street, London W1X 8AH
P.M.B. 5205 Ibadan · P.O. Box 45314 Nairobi
P.O. Box 3966 Lusaka
EDINBURGH MELBOURNE TORONTO AUCKLAND
SINGAPORE HONG KONG KUALA LUMPUR NEW DELHI KINGSTON

For Scandinavian orders
Esselte Studium
S-11285 Stockholm, Sweden

For Ethiopian orders
Addis Ababa University Press
P.O. Box 1176, Addis Ababa, Ethiopia

ISBN 0 435 94240 9 (cased) (Heinemann Educational Books)
ISBN 0 435 94241 7 (paper)
ISBN 91–24–26 461–X (Esselte Studium)

Maps drawn by Peter McClure

Set in 10 on 11 pt. Baskerville

Printed in Great Britain by
Richard Clay (The Chaucer Press), Ltd.,
Bungay, Suffolk

To Britta

Contents

List of maps, documents, and illustrations ix

Preface xi

Introduction 1

I   *A survey of sources* 7
Documentary materials (p. 7). The voice of the Ethiopians
(p. 13). Reports, narratives, and memoirs by Europeans (p. 16).
Ethiopian chronicles (p. 20)

II *Prospects and first contacts* 29
The coming of a new era (p. 29). The Ethiopian polity (p. 30).
Valentia's contacts with Welde Sillasē: strategy, trade, or
assistance (p. 36). Salt's second visit (p. 43). Welde Sillasē's
letter to George III: his priorities (p. 49). Communication
problems and their consequences (p. 52)

III *Increasing pressures and sporadic responses* 55
The end of isolation (p. 55). Sebagadis and the Ali/Coffin
mission (p. 58). Wibē: CMS missionaries and French
businessmen at Adwa (p. 68). Antoine d'Abbadie's mission
(p. 76). The courting of Wibē by Combes and Lefebvre (p. 82).
The Wibē–Ali conflict of 1842: Orthodoxy or Islam, Tigrē or
Yejju (p. 90). Blondeel's projects (p. 99). Increasing conflict in
the north (p. 102). The Schimper/De Jacobis 'protectorate'
(p. 109). Egyptian foothold on the coast: Wibē's reaction (p. 115).
Plowden and Rolland: Wibē disillusioned, Ali indifferent (p. 120).
An Ethiopian emissary: Jerusalem and Cairo (p. 131). The end
of the *Zemene Mesafint*: an Ethiopian affair (p. 136). Eritrea
conceived (p. 140). The initial promise of Shewa (p. 144). Rochet
and Krapf at the court of Sahle Sillasē (p. 148). The Anglo-
Ethiopian treaty (p. 152). Rochet's fraud (p. 159). The legacy of
suspicion in Shewa (p. 164). Summary (p. 165)

IV *Unification and an active foreign policy*   172

Tēwodros—unifier, restorer, modernizer (p. 172). Missionaries
and craftsmen (p. 174). Tēwodros and Plowden: sovereignty and
reciprocity (p. 180). Nigusē and the Catholics: the prospect of
two Ethiopian states (p. 189). Tēwodros and the Turks: war or
peace (p. 208). Ethiopia and Europe: shattered expectations
(p. 223). Tēwodros and Britain: the defiance of the defeated
(p. 239). The significance of Tēwodros and Meqdela (p. 269)

V *Trials of strength with Egypt and Italy*   288

The Bogos crisis (p. 288). Greater Egypt (p. 310). The battles of
Gundet and Gura (p. 318). Negotiations in the aftermath of
Gura (p. 329). The Gordon negotiations (p. 335). The Adwa peace
treaty (p. 347). The main source of strength (p. 362). Massawa
to Metemma (p. 378). The treaty of Wiçhalē (p. 384). Adwa:
the seal of victory (p. 399)

Conclusion   407

Abbreviations   411

Note on Transliteration   413

Glossary   415

Bibliography   417

Index   428

Maps, Documents, and Illustrations

Maps

1 Ethiopia in the first half of the nineteenth century   31
2 Tigrē and Simēn from Welde Sillasē to Wibē   39
3 Ethiopia under Tēwodros   216
4 The Egyptian attacks in the north   291
5 The threat of encirclement and Minīlik's definition of Ethiopian
    territory in 1891   316
6 Disputed territories and solutions proposed by British Vice-consul
    Wylde and General Gordon   339
7 The Italian attack   387

Documents

1 Letter from Welde Sillasē to George III   49
    Public Record Office, London, FO 1/1, fol. 73
2 Letter from Sebagadis to George IV   60
    Public Record Office, London, FO 1/2, fol. 6
3 The Franco-Shewan 'treaty' of 1843   facing 160
    Archives du Ministère des Affaires Étrangères, Paris, Traités,
    Éthiopie
4 The Adwa peace treaty of 1884 with Egypt   357
    Public Record Office, London, FO 93/2/2
5 Letter from Minīlik to Khedive Ismail   373
    The National Archives, Cairo, Soudan Carton 5/2/7

Illustrations (between pages 84 and 85)

1 Ancient architectural stele at Aksum
2 The monastery of Debre Bīzēn in Eritrea
3 Massawa
4 Salt plain in the Danakil desert
5 The palace grounds of the imperial city of Gonder
6 Crumbling castles in Gonder
7 The castle of Fasīledes
8 King Tēwodros *from* G. Lejean, *Théodore II. Le nouvel empire
Abyssinie*

9 Abune Selama *from* Henry A. Stern, *Wanderings among the Falashas in Abyssinia*
10 The Meqdela massif with the Islamgē saddle and the peak of Sillasē to the right
11 One of Tēwodros's mortars on its way to Meqdela in 1867–68 *from* H. Rassam, *Narrative of the British Mission to Theodore*
12 At rest on Meqdela (Islamgē saddle) a century later
13 Meqdela from the north
14 Bridge over the Mereb, *c*. 1890. EFS Archives, Stockholm
15 Amba Alagē, the southern limit of the Italian penetration in 1895
16 Yohannis IV. Photograph by the author of a painting in the governor's residence at Meqele
17 Minīlik II. EFS Archives, Stockholm
18 The Adwa battlefield
19 Nineteenth-century Ethiopian seals. Archives du Ministère des Affaires Étrangères and Bibliothèque Nationale, Paris, and Public Record Office, London

Preface

Before this book goes to press, I wish to thank all those whose encouragement and assistance have made it possible for me to complete the task. Many have been involved in Ethiopia and Sweden over a period of five years or more and I cannot hope to mention all individually. I trust that all friends who have had anything to do with *The Survival of Ethiopian Independence* will feel that they are included in the following words.

Archives, libraries, and private individuals who have placed manuscript materials at my disposal have been acknowledged in the bibliography, and colleagues who in special cases have shared their materials with me are mentioned in the appropriate footnotes. The sketch-maps by General C. G. Gordon and Vice-consul A. B. Wylde and the facsimile reproductions of documents from the Foreign Office Records are published by permission of the Controller of Her Majesty's Stationery Office, London. For the other two facsimile reproductions I am indebted to the chief archivists of the Archives diplomatiques du Ministère des Affaires Étrangères, Paris, and the National Archives in Cairo, respectively.

To my Addis Abeba colleagues in the field of nineteenth-century Ethiopian history, Dr Donald Crummey and Dr Richard Caulk, I am indebted for many useful suggestions and comments. Dr Getachew Haile and Dr Merid Wolde Aregay have translated Gi'iz documents for me and checked some of my Amharic translations. For work on Arabic and Turkish documents I am indebted in particular to Dr Samir Ghabbour, Cairo, Mr Senot Khalil, Addis Abeba, and Professor Cenghiz Orhonlu, Istanbul. Professors Birgitta Odén and Sven Tägil, Lund, have both read the manuscript *in toto* and provided valuable comment and much encouragement in my work. I also owe much to Mrs Innes Marshall, general editor of the Addis Ababa University Press, for her expert advice, encouragement and assistance with the text.

Without the financial support of a generous grant from *The Tri-Centennial Fund of the Bank of Sweden* it would have been impossible for me to undertake the research and set aside the time necessary for the writing of this book. I therefore ask the board to accept my sincere thanks, and include in this thanks also Professors Jerker Rosén and Birgitta Odén who took the courageous step of recommending my application.

Last but not least, I want to acknowledge the share of my wife in the successful completion of the research and writing of this book. Without her moral support, patience, and willingness to sacrifice I would not have been able to carry out the work.

PREFACE

The Survival of Ethiopian Independence has been completed for the one-hundredth anniversary of the Ethiopian victories of Gundet and Gura. *Then* it was Ethiopia's survival as an independent state that was at stake. *Today* the Ethiopians are facing new and perplexing problems of equal magnitude. For someone who has been allowed to spend a quarter of a century with the Ethiopians and who, like myself, has received inspiration and joy from his association with them, it is only natural to desire and hope that they will show the inner strength to surmount their present problems with the same ultimate success as they defended their independence a century ago.

S.R.

Introduction

How did it happen that Ethiopia, as the only old state in Africa, preserved its independence throughout the era of European colonization? Why did Ethiopia alone survive the 'Scramble for Africa' as a free nation? This is a fundamental issue in the modern history of Ethiopia. From the fact of 'the survival' derives much of Ethiopia's unique position in the community of African nations of the twentieth century. Independence delayed the introduction and tempered the impact of European political and economic forces in the country, at the same time as it created a leadership role for Ethiopia in the first decades of the African decolonization era.

Ethiopia has a long history of national survival, and it is tempting to seek an overall explanation for a number of really very different expressions of national self-preservation. This is what Arnold J. Toynbee does when he concludes that the peculiarities of Ethiopia (or Abyssinia),[1] *inter alia,*

> the survival of her political independence in the midst of an Africa under European dominion, the survival of her Monophysite Christianity in the borderland between Islam and paganism, the survival of her Semitic language between the Hamitic and Nilotic language-areas . . . derive from the same cause: that is, from the virtual impregnability of the highland-fastness . . . This is the explanation of Abyssinian survival-power.[2]

Though he places 'the national spirit based upon the legendary foundation and the common faith' alongside with 'physical impregnability' as one of two

1 Ethiopia and Abyssinia have been used as synonyms by Ethiopians and foreigners alike for almost 2,000 years of recorded history. When a distinction is made by European writers, Abyssinia is normally used (as by Toynbee) for the Christian and Semitic-speaking population of the northern and central highlands of present Ethiopia, while Ethiopia is used for the modern state. For the purposes of this study I have found no reason to differentiate between the two.

2 *A Study of History* (London, 1934–61), Vol. II, p. 365.

factors behind the survival of Ethiopia, J. Spencer Trimingham emphasizes the overall importance of the physical features of the country:

> It was this impregnability of the highlands which enabled Abyssinian Christianity to survive the successive dangers of an Islamic domination by nomadic tribes, the outpost tentacles of the Ottoman military power, the locust-like invasion of the Galla, the designs of the emergent totalitarian state of Egypt under Muḥammad 'Alī and his successors . . . the threat of the Baqqāra Arabs under Mahdism, and, finally, the menace of Western imperialism which was imposing itself over the whole of Africa.[3]

It is not my intention to deny the importance of geographical factors in the history of Ethiopia generally, only to question the thesis that they played a decisive role in saving the country from nineteenth-century European imperialism. In fact, it would be strange if the contrast between the highlands, with their 2,000 years or more of settled agriculture, and the surrounding deserts or semi-deserts had not contributed to the feeling of separateness which is one of the basic elements of a national consciousness. But that is an altogether different matter. It is also evident that the institution of the monarchy with its legendary roots in Old Testament times and the common faith, traditions, and culture of an ancient Christian church were valuable assets in the formation of a national and political consciousness essential to survival. It is an altogether different matter, again, to accept these factors as a full and sufficient explanation of anything as specific and exceptional as Ethiopia's successful struggle against European imperialism.

In a paper read at the Leverhulme African Inter-Collegiate Conference in History at Salisbury in September 1960,[4] I made a first attempt to outline an answer to the question of Ethiopia's survival in terms of the events of the actual period. I proposed that the relevant factors belonged to three categories: firstly, the diplomatic, political, and military conditions on the European (and the Turkish–Egyptian) side; secondly, the actual political and military conditions on the Ethiopian side; thirdly, the serious and repeated miscalculations of Ethiopia's strength by its 'protectors' and invaders.

The first two of these categories are obvious, and my contribution was only a shift of emphasis. I submitted that 'from the point of view of Ethiopian history, it is far more important to investigate the conditions in Ethiopia which enabled it to withstand the political and military attacks on its independence, than to deal with various European factors forwarding or hampering the advance of colonialism in the area'.[5] This proposition was much less of a truism fifteen years ago than it is today. The reorientation of nineteenth- and twentieth-century African history away from the traditional focus on European activities towards the study of the attitudes and activities of the Africans themselves has almost entirely taken place since 1960. The debate whether there really was or

---

3   *Islam in Ethiopia* (Oxford, 1952), p. 145.
4   'Some Aspects of the Survival of Ethiopian Independence in the Period of the Scramble for Africa', *Historians in Tropical Africa* (Salisbury, 1960), and *University College Review* (Addis Abeba, 1961), pp. 8–24. Page references in the following relate to the latter publication.
5   ibid., p. 9.

was not a 'scramble *for* Africa' by the Powers has receded, and the issues of the African experience of the 'scramble *in* Africa', and what the Africans did about it, have received more attention. This could be exemplified in many ways. To mention the recently published volume *Protest and Power in Black Africa*[6] is only one.

The change of emphasis does not mean, of course, that the international politics of the time with the alignments and rivalries of the powers as well as the political and military strength and the economic resources of the foreign governments involved were not important. The same is true about the more or less skilful handling of negotiations and military encounters with Ethiopia by the foreigners directly involved. But these factors must be viewed also from the Ethiopian angle. At the time, each country involved with Ethiopia presented its case. The British explained the almost unbelievable success of their Abyssinian expedition in 1867–68 in terms of the careful planning of the campaign and the skill with which it was carried out. American officers who participated in the Ethio-Egyptian war of 1875–76 accounted for the Egyptian defeat in terms o the rivalries among the officers of Khedive Ismail and other weaknesses on the Egyptian side. The Italian defeat at Adwa in 1896 was analysed in terms of the weakness of Francesco Crispi's government at home, the conflicting philo-Shewan and philo-Tigrean policies of Pietro Antonelli and his opponents, and the military blunders or bad luck of General Baratieri. The French blamed the British for their difficulties and set-backs, and the Italians blamed the French. The role of the Ethiopian people and their leaders seemed at most to have been marginal.

Later historical literature has made few changes in this pattern. Official histories such as G. Douin, *Histoire du règne du Khédive Ismaïl*, and the monumental work of the Comitato per la documentazione dell'opera dell'Italia in Africa called *L'Italia in Africa: Etiopia–Mar Rosso*[7] are bound to present the Egyptian and Italian side of the story. Thomas E. Marston, *Britain's Imperial Role in the Red Sea Area 1800–1878*, and Georges Malécot, 'Les voyageurs français et les relations entre la France et l'Abyssinie de 1835 à 1870'[8] likewise stress European action. But also the standard works of Ethiopian history of the 1920s, E. A. Wallis Budge, *A History of Ethiopia*, and J. B. Coulbeaux, *Histoire politique et religieuse de l'Abyssinie*,[9] though not devoted to the history of British or French relations with Ethiopia, show how easy it was (and is) to fall into the trap of writing European history instead of Ethiopian as soon as Europeans are involved in the story told.

This does not necessarily mean that accounts such as these are biased against Ethiopia, only that their emphasis is on non-Ethiopian aspects. The degree of objectivity or lack of objectivity exercised by the historians of European–African relations in the past will inevitably be tested case by case as will, evidently, the results of the new African historiography. Scholarly historians who have taken up Afro-European relations as an aspect of *African* history, while exposing

6 Robert I. Rotberg and Ali A. Mazrui, eds, *Protest and Power in Black Africa* (New York, 1970)
7 Cairo, 1936–51, and Rome, 1958–, respectively.
8 Hamden, 1961, and *RFHO*, LVIII (1971), respectively.
9 London, 1928, and Paris, 1929, respectively.

whatever bias they may have discovered in others, certainly do not presume to be infallible themselves. Many new structures or attempted reconstructions will crumble. But what has come to stay is *an African approach* to these relations and the conviction that it is as legitimate as the European approach.

It is not, as I have already indicated, primarily a question of bias against the African partner in the historical relationship. In 1935 Ernest Work wrote a strongly *pro-Ethiopian* diplomatic history of the partition period. Its very title, *Ethiopia: A Pawn in European Diplomacy*, nevertheless indicates the role of object, rather than subject, assigned to the central figure in the play. To answer the question whether Ethiopia was merely an object, albeit a little more difficult for the imperialists to handle than many others in Africa, it is necessary to focus one's attention on the Ethiopian side in the confrontations of the period, to read the Ethiopian documents and to give them precedence as expressions of the Ethiopian viewpoint. This is stressing the obvious, but there may still be some merit in doing it.

In the last few years a more Ethiopian approach to nineteenth-century Ethiopian history has fortunately emerged, less conspicuous probably than in African history in general, but nevertheless real. I refer here to articles or books by a new generation of Ethiopian historians—Mordechai Abir, Aleme Eshete, Richard Caulk, Donald Crummey, Kofi Darkwah, Harold Marcus, Richard Pankhurst, Zewde Gabre-Sellassie, and others, who have dealt with a number of aspects of this formative period in Ethiopian history. Some of their writings provide important insights into the background of the survival of Ethiopian independence and will be cited in the following.

It is clearly impossible to provide within the covers of one book a comprehensive analysis of both the foreign relations of Ethiopia in the nineteenth century and the unification and consolidation process which lies behind its survival as an independent state through the era of European colonialism. That process is obviously a decisive factor for the outcome but I have dealt with it only as it is related to the foreign pressures and how they were met. My early impression, i.e. that the miscalculations of Ethiopia's potential by her would-be protectors and invaders played a decisive role, has been strengthened. The unification and political consolidation of Ethiopia and the diplomatic awareness and activity of her rulers seem to have kept well ahead of all outside expectations during the last three decades of the nineteenth century. This gave Ethiopia the advantage of entering into diplomatic negotiations and military conflict stronger than her opponents supposed her to be. How it happened and why the Europeans and the Egyptians missed the point is the main theme of this study.

For the first three-quarters of the century, I have attempted to cover all foreign contacts of any importance in order to establish where the initiatives came from and what contribution they made to the formation of an active Ethiopian foreign policy. Comprehensive studies of the reigns of Yohannis and Minīlik have recently been made by Zewde Gabre-Sellassie, 'The Process of Re-unification of the Ethiopian Empire 1868–1889', and Richard Caulk, 'The Origins and Development of the Foreign Policy of Menelik II, 1865–1896'.[10]

10 PhD dissertations, Oxford, 1971, and London, 1966, respectively.

In the hope that their results will soon appear in print and supplement the biography of Minilik by Harold G. Marcus which has just been published,[11] I have discontinued the detailed analysis of Ethio-European contacts with the Ethiopian victories in the war of 1875–76.

The main lines of the diplomatic and military confrontation with Italy have, however, been included in the last chapter on the basis of earlier publications because of the importance of this conflict as the final test of the determination and ability of the Ethiopian people to defend themselves. The history of the closing stage of Ethiopia's struggle for survival, moreover, provides an excellent example of the difference between a Euro-centred approach to 'one of the most controversial subjects in the history of the African continent'[12] and my own attempts to see and interpret the historical confrontation as one between two *essentially* equal partners.

11   *The Life and Times of Menelik II: Ethiopia 1844–1913* (Oxford, 1975).
12   Carlo Giglio, 'Article 17 of the Treaty of Uccialli', *JAH*, VI, 2 (1965), p. 221.

I

A Survey of Sources

The source materials for a study of nineteenth-century Ethiopian history are many and varied. A detailed survey and evaluation of them all would take us too far without answering any immediate purpose. The specific sources of greatest importance for the content and conclusions of the following chapters have been dealt with in their proper context. This is the case with a number of original letters from Ethiopian rulers and particularly the treaty texts of 1843, 1884, and 1889 and certain documents which reveal the history of their genesis. What follows here is a general survey to acquaint the reader with the types of sources consulted and some of the problems involved in their use.

Documentary Materials

In a study where diplomatic relations play the central role, the diplomatic archives must necessarily claim first attention. Their utilization, however, presents several problems. The first observation is that documents relating to Ethiopia are widely scattered and sparsely published. In Ethiopia itself there are no organized central archives open to researchers. Some of the government papers from the nineteenth century are now preserved in the archives of the Ministry of Pen, albeit on a very limited scale. Occasional documents or small collections have also been preserved in churches and monasteries as well as in the hands of private persons, but the work of tracing these documents for the purpose of historical research has only just begun. No collections of nineteenth-century documents have been published in Ethiopia, and the occasional documents which appear copied into chronicles or other Ethiopian works can often be traced to European sources.

A number of reasons can be given for the scarcity of original documents on the Ethiopian side, some of them external. Emperor Tēwodros's archives were lost in 1868 when the British army burnt the buildings on Meqdela after the Emperor's suicide. That a collection had existed is obvious from the fact that the

British envoy Hormuzd Rassam, who was a captive there for two years, speaks of the chronicler Debtera Zeneb as 'the keeper of the royal archives'.[1] Some letters were carried off to England by members of the British army, but very few have turned up in any public archives there. Parts of Emperor Yohannis's archives suffered a similar fate after the battle of Metemma in 1889, in which he lost his life. To prove that the Emperor had fallen, Khalifa Abdallahi sent some captured letters from Queen Victoria and Salisbury to London.[2] My research in the Khartoum archives, however, has revealed no traces of Yohannis's papers. Emperor Minīlik's archives, finally, were, at least in part, preserved in Addis Abeba until the Italian occupation. Important collections were then taken to Italy. Some papers have been restored; others were probably destroyed; others again, including original letters from King Umberto to Emperor Minīlik, with Amharic minutes and archival directions in the margins, are now in the archives of the former Ministero dell'Africa Italiana in Rome.[3]

The result of this situation is that Ethiopia's relations with foreign powers must be approached mainly through the archives of these powers. The richest in material for the whole period are the British and French archives, especially the Foreign Office Records at the Public Record Office and the India Office Records at the India Office Library in London, and the Archives du Ministère des Affaires Étrangères in Paris. From 1885 until the end of the century, the Archivio Storico dell'ex Ministero dell'Africa Italiana becomes the most important, with interesting supplementary material in such deposits as *Fondo Crispi* in the Archivio Centrale dello Stato. Some other government archives containing Ethiopian materials for this period are the Politisches Archiv des Auswärtigen Amts, Bonn, and the Deutsches Zentralarchiv, Potsdam; the Haus-, Hof- und Staatsarchiv (now Österreichisches Staatsarchiv), Vienna; the Archive of Russia's Foreign Policy, Moscow; the Archives du Ministère des Affaires Étrangères and Archives des Palais Royaux, Brussels; the archives of the Sublime Porte, Istanbul; the National Archives, Cairo; and the Central Records Office, Khartoum.[4] While the Belgian, German, Austrian, Russian, and Turkish archives mainly show the attitudes of these powers to the British, French, and Italian activities, they also contain evidence of direct contacts from time to time. The Egyptian, Sudanese, and former Aden archives, on the other hand, are particularly valuable because of primary source material for the Ethiopian side of the story: Aden mainly for the years 1840–70, Cairo for 1870–82, and Khartoum for 1885–98.

A good deal of the British and Italian documents were published at an early date in the Parliamentary Papers of the respective governments, the so-called Blue Books and Libri Verdi. The French government was less generous with information, and very few documents referring to Ethiopia have found their way

1 Hormuzd Rassam, *Narrative of the British Mission to Theodore* (London, 1869), Vol. II, p. 192. See also below, p. 22.
2 F. R. Wingate, *Mahdiism and the Egyptian Sudan* (London, 1891), pp. 444, 448.
3 See, for instance, ASMAI 36/2–21 *bis*.
4 I have not had the opportunity to consult the archives in Moscow, but the Soviet government has kindly provided me with some important documents from 1870 onwards in microfilm.

into the Livres Jaunes. The same is true about the collections of diplomatic documents published in the twentieth century, such as *Die Grosse Politik* and *Documents diplomatiques français 1871–1914*. The important exception is the recent documentary volumes of *Etiopia–Mar Rosso* in the series *L'Italia in Africa* published by the Comitato per la documentazione dell'opera dell'Italia in Africa. These contain almost everything of importance not already published in the Documenti Diplomatici of the Atti Parlamentari. The work so far covers 1859–89.

The diplomatic material of the British and Italian governments can be used in a third form, the so-called Confidential Papers or Confidential Print, and the Serie Confidenziale, respectively. Occasional reports, memoranda, or collections of documents, printed for internal confidential use will be found in many other archives, but the Confidential Papers of the British government in particular are on a completely different scale. The Foreign Office alone printed 10,000 such papers from 1850 to 1910, and the Colonial Office 2,500 up to 1916.[5] Some are brief memoranda of a page or two, but others are big volumes of as many as a thousand pages. The Foreign Office list of these papers contains fifty-four items on Ethiopia from 1854 to 1896, the most comprehensive with no less than 1,280 documents plus a number of enclosures. The Italian series on Ethiopia, no. 94, contains about twenty volumes of chronologically arranged documents covering 1862–1914.

Because of the limited circulation of the Confidential Papers and their character of internal working papers, much more could be—indeed often had to be—included than in the Parliamentary Papers. A comparison between, for instance, the Blue Book on Tēwodros's reign, *Correspondence respecting Abyssinia 1846–1868*, and the two volumes of Confidential Print with the same title (FO 401/1 and FO 401/2), shows that about 40 per cent of the documents printed for the use of the Foreign Office also reached Parliament. This is an unusually high proportion, which most probably reflects both the general interest of the British public in the fate of the European captives in Ethiopia and the pressure on the British government to explain how matters had reached such an *impasse*. On the other hand, the collection of correspondence relating to the important peace treaty of 1884, the so-called Hewett treaty, has been reduced from forty-three pages in the Confidential Print (FO 401/6) to eight pages in the Parliamentary Papers. On many issues, of course, no papers reached Parliament at all. The Foreign Office Confidential Papers, on the other hand, have a very good coverage of the correspondence relating to Ethiopia, including in some cases minutes, working memoranda, and private letters, from about 1850 onwards, even if no regular series with consecutive issues on the *Affairs of Abyssinia* (FO 401) was created until 1905. Before that the correspondence about Ethiopia was mostly issued in *Affairs of Egypt* (FO 407) and in *Red Sea and Somali Coast*, or *North-East Africa and the Soudan* (both FO 403), unless there was special reason for a separate collection of papers on Ethiopia.

The main advantage of the Confidential Papers, besides the practical one of

5   *List of Confidential Papers relating to Foreign Affairs arranged in order of Countries Nos 1 to 10,000* (London, n.d.); *List of Colonial Office Confidential Print to 1916* (London, 1965).

being easier to handle and refer to than the files of original correspondence, is that the original correspondence in the *Abyssinia* files (FO 1) has in the Confidential Print been supplemented by correspondence relating to Ethiopia from the files of other countries and other relevant materials. It therefore serves as an obvious and most useful starting-point from which to approach the British archival materials on Ethiopia. Although the Confidential Papers give no references to the original files, the Public Record Office materials are so well organized that there is no difficulty in passing on to the original correspondence on important points and checking if anything significant has been omitted.

While the geographical dispersal of the Ethiopian documents proves the manifold foreign contacts of the Ethiopian rulers, the treatment of the documents in the various archives indicates that difficulties were caused by the questions of the international status of Ethiopia and its rulers, and of proper channels of communication with the latter. With the exception of the British consuls Walter Plowden and Duncan Cameron, 1848–68, no regular diplomatic or consular representatives were posted to Ethiopia until after the battle of Adwa. The main task of French and British consular representatives at Massawa was to observe trade prospects and political conditions in Ethiopia, but their position vis-à-vis Ethiopia on one hand and Turkey/Egypt on the other was often ambiguous.[6]

British correspondence with Ethiopia occasionally passed from the India Office via Bombay and Aden, but usually from the Foreign Office through the consul general at Cairo or by special envoys. Among the India Office Records it is the *Secret Letters from Aden,* beginning in 1842 (re-named *Political and Secret* in 1875), and the *Abyssinia Original Correspondence* files for 1867–71 that contain most of value. For the issues dealt with in this study, the Foreign Office Records are, however, the main source. Besides *Abyssinia,* FO 1, which starts with 1808, it is *Turkey,* FO 78, that is of greatest importance until replaced in 1885 by *Italy,* FO 45. From this year until 1897 the *Abyssinia* files were even discontinued. For anyone who wants to understand the Ethiopian side of the story, the volumes of *Royal Letters* in FO 95 are also of primary importance. No one would expect these volumes, at first sight dedicated exclusively to letters on the births, deaths, and marriages in Queen Victoria's and other royal families, to contain anything of political importance for Africa. But to the surprise of both the archivists—this was in 1953—and myself, a few letters from the sovereigns of exotic lands were found at the end of almost every one of the yearly volumes of the second half of the nineteenth century. Ethiopian rulers are well represented with more than twenty-five important original letters for the crucial period in Ethio-British relations from 1862 to 1887.

In the archives of the Ministère des Affaires Étrangères in Paris the most important series for Ethiopian materials are *Mémoires et Documents, Afrique, Abyssinie* and *Mer Rouge; Correspondance politique,* [*Egypte*], *Massouah;* and *Correspondance commerciale, Massouah.* The two series of *Mémoires et Documents,* which begin with 1838 and 1839 respectively, and the other two, which begin with

6   See below, pp. 109, 119–21.

1840, all run parallel, and continue uninterrupted by the Italian claims to handle the foreign affairs of Ethiopia from 1889 to 1896. The main principle seems to have been to place all documents related to special missions or envoys to Ethiopia in *Mémoires et Documents*, and this is where we find both the most comprehensive reports and the largest number of original letters from Ethiopia. The regular reporting by diplomatic and consular representatives is found in the *Correspondance* files. In addition to the collections at Quai d'Orsay, materials on Ethiopia are found in the archives of the Ministère de la Marine and the former Ministère de la France d'Outre Mer (now Section Outre-Mer, Archives Nationales), the latter having inherited the archives of the Ministère des Colonies, which until 1894 was combined alternately with the Ministries of the Marine and of Commerce and Industry.

The Italian diplomatic materials concerning Ethiopia are heavily concentrated in the Archivio Storico of the former Ministero dell'Africa Italiana (ASMAI). This is due to the fact that the nineteenth-century African archives in the Ministry of Foreign Affairs were transferred to the Ministry of Colonies, later the Ministry of Italian Africa. They have now been returned to the Ministry of Foreign Affairs, but form a separate collection there. The most important among the documents which were not transferred are the originals of the treaties between the Ethiopian rulers and Italy. They are found in the Archivio Storico of the Ministero degli Affari Esteri (ASMAE). The files in ASMAI of greatest importance for the period up to 1896 are *Etiopia, Posiz.* 36; *Eritrea, Posiz.* 1–3, 7–8, and 14; and *Conferenze internazionale e Congressi, Posiz.* 155. Some of the government papers which one would have expected to find in either ASMAI or ASMAE are found in Crispi's private archives, *Fondo Crispi* in Archivio Centrale dello Stato.

The materials concerning Ethiopia in the National Archives, Cairo, are distributed in the first place by language between the Turkish/Arabic and the French archives. Though there is an *Abyssinie: Dossier Général*, the French documents from or on Ethiopia are mostly included under *Soudan, Soudan et Afrique Orientale*, or *Soudan et Afrique Equatoriale*. A number of very important Arabic and Amharic letters from Ethiopia are found in a box of miscellaneous documents classified as *Bahr Barra* (Carton 19). These go as far back as 1842. Other documents are found in boxes listed simply as *Maia Sanieh* (the Cabinet) or *Abdin* (the Palace). Much material is duplicated in the registers (or letter-books) of supreme orders, and of letters and telegrams, both dispatched and received. The items on Ethiopia are not easy to locate, and in some cases I have been obliged to refer to the extracts published by G. Douin in *Histoire du règne du Khédive Ismaïl* without being able to check them.

The Khartoum archives are a great deal more manageable, and the documents from the Mahdia have been carefully examined over the past twenty years.[7] The correspondence between the khalifa and his generals on one hand and Yohannis, Minīlik, and other Ethiopians on the other includes a number of

7 P. M. Holt, 'The Archives of the Mahdia', *SNR*, XXXVI, 1 (1955), pp. 71–80; G. N. Sanderson, 'Contributions from African Sources to the History of European Competition in the Upper Valley of the Nile', *JAH*, III, 1 (1962), pp. 69–90.

original letters in Amharic and Arabic from the Ethiopian side. The most important series here is *Mahdia* 1/55, earlier no. 1/34.

The collections of the Turkish archives, on the other hand, are immense. I have been able to consult only the archives of the Ministry of Foreign Affairs, Hariciye Nezareti Arşivi, and Egyptian (*Misir*) volumes of the *Irade* collection in the Prime Minister's archives, Başbakanlik Arşivi Genel Müdürlügü, both at the Sublime Porte in Istanbul, the former mainly in French, the latter in Turkish. To judge from what I have found there, however, the documents on Ethiopia are not very numerous. Both the identification, in Turkish claims, of Ethiopia with an Ottoman province of Habeshistan, and the growing autonomy of Egypt in foreign affairs, are reflected in the ways documents concerning Ethiopia have been dealt with. In the archives of the Ministry of Foreign Affairs, for instance, there is a file for Abyssinia, but most of the documents on Ethiopia are nevertheless found in the Egypt series.

The archives of the German Foreign Office, Auswärtiges Amt, are now divided between Politisches Archiv des Auswärtigen Amts, Bonn, and Deutsches Zentralarchiv, Potsdam. A very large portion were captured and microfilmed in the USA and Great Britain before being returned to West Germany.[8] The documents of the Political Department were coded I, later IA, IB, A, etc. Files of Ethiopian documents began as early as 1858, but unfortunately the first volume, though listed after World War II as preserved at DZA, could not be located there in March 1971. A new series for *Abessinien* was started in 1872, followed in 1886 by *Italienische Besitzungen in Afrika, Massaua*, and in 1889 by *Italienisches Protektorat über Abessinien*, etc. These materials are in the Bonn archives. A number of other files both there and at Potsdam contain Ethiopian materials as well. In comparison with Bonn and Potsdam, the collections preserved in the Bundesarchiv, Koblenz, and Geheimes Staatsarchiv, Berlin-Dahlem, are of little significance for nineteenth-century Ethiopia.

In the Haus-, Hof- und Staatsarchiv, now Österreichisches Staatsarchiv, Vienna, the earliest documents, referring to an Ethiopian mission in 1872, are found in the *Politisches Archiv VIII, England*. From 1885 to 1890, most of the material was filed in PA XXXI, *Ägypten, Italien im Roten Meer*, and thereafter in the Italy series.

As early as 1840, the interest of the first Belgian consul in Egypt, Édouard Blondeel, resulted in both a special colonization file and a file for Ethiopia in the *Afrique* series, AF–4, *Abyssinie*, at the Belgian Ministère des Affaires Étrangères. The first *Abyssinie* file continues with sporadic documents until 1902. Occasional documents are found in others of the AF files, such as *Égypte* and *Colonies italiennes*. Correspondence with Egypt and Italy as well as other European governments on Ethiopian matters is mostly filed in the *Correspondance politique* series. Of special interest are the files of *Acte Général de Bruxelles*, where the views of all the interested European governments about the Italian protectorate claims are aired. Important documents on 'the Minīlik incident'

---

8   F. Epstein, *Guide to Captured German Documents* (New York, 1952); *A Catalogue of Files and Microfilms of the German Foreign Ministry Archives 1867–1920* (Oxford, 1959); *Übersicht über die Bestände des Deutschen Zentralarchivs Potsdam* (Berlin, 1957).

at the Brussels conference and on the projected lease of Eritrea to Leopold II
after the battle of Adwa are also found in the Archives des Palais Royaux,
Brussels.

The problems of locating the Ethiopian materials in the various archives,
though considerable, are not much different from those encountered by historians
consulting more or less well organized archives in general. Probably the degree
of confusion is somewhat higher, the proportion of letters that disappeared,
were misplaced, or went unanswered greater. At the beginning of the period
this was at least partly due to the irregularity of the contacts. At the end, it was
one of the consequences of Italy's claim that it was entitled to handle Ethiopia's
foreign relations. The stand taken by the British government on this issue explains, for instance, why a letter from Minīlik to Victoria in 1893 went unanswered. Why it should appear *without any translation* from Amharic among the
Royal Letters for *1874–75* is more difficult to explain.[9]

Second in importance only to the government archives are those of the
various missionary societies with activities in Ethiopia in the nineteenth century: the Church Missionary Society (CMS), the Chrischona (or Pilgrim)
Mission, the Congrégation de la Mission (Lazarists), and the Swedish Evangelical Mission (SEM), to mention some of the most important. The CMS
archives are very rich and easy to consult. For the Chrischona Mission, the best
collection is *C. F. Spittler Privat-Archiv 653*, preserved in the Staatsarchiv des
Kantons Basel-Stadt.[10] The correspondence of the Lazarist missionaries was
directed to their headquarters in France as well as to the Sacra Congregazione
de Propaganda Fide in Rome, where correspondence of other Catholic missionaries as well as a few original letters from Ethiopian rulers are also found. The
archives of Evangeliska Fosterlands-stiftelsen (The Swedish Evangelical Mission), deposited in Stockholms Stadsarkiv, are very rich in material on Eritrea
in particular. A tremendous amount of missionary correspondence has been
published in the journals of the various missionary organizations, *Church
Missionary Record, Annales de la Congrégation de la Mission, Missionstidning*, etc., but
there are of course always questions that can be answered only by consulting
the archival materials.

The Voice of the Ethiopians

For much of African history, the alternative sources to the accounts and explanations presented by consuls, missionaries, and other Europeans on the spot
are oral traditions. The fact that most of Ethiopia's political and ecclesiastical
leaders were literate provides the student of Ethiopian history with the oppor-

9   FO 95/733.
10 I am very grateful to Dr Donald Crummey and the Rev. Gustav Arén for sharing with me
    their notes and microfilms of the Spittler collection and of materials from the Archiv der
    Basler Mission respectively. For further information on missionary sources, see Donald
    Crummey, *Priests and Politicians* (Oxford, 1972), pp. 152–6, and 'Missionary Sources and
    their Contribution to our Understanding of Ethiopian History 1830–1868', *Rural Africana*,
    11 (1970).

tunity to check in black and white what the representatives of this African people actually said in the negotiations with the Europeans.

The real problem and challenge in utilizing the European diplomatic archives for a study of Ethiopian history does not lie in locating the documents nor in deciding when a published, a confidentially printed, or an original document must be used. It is easy to check the printed translation of an Amharic document with the unprinted translation, and find the eventual discrepancies or omissions. This is, however, where the search for the truth has almost without exception stopped. It need not have been so. From the point of view of a correct appreciation of Ethiopia's relations with foreign powers, it is deplorable that historians have so far almost completely ignored the Amharic originals. With the exception of the Wiçhalē treaty of 1889, this is the case also with documents as important as treaty texts. Not only have the politicians refused to consider the Amharic versions, or seemingly remained ignorant of the discrepancies; historians also have by and large taken the same line. Thus secondary texts which guided nineteenth-century European governments in their policies, and which may in many cases be a satisfactory basis for the writing of European colonial history, have become the ultimate source for the European historian in Ethiopian history as well.

My first contacts with the Amharic originals revealed to me how unsatisfactory many of the translations are. In some cases they can hardly be called translations at all. Whether made by Ethiopians with a weak knowledge of English, French, or Italian, or, more often, by Europeans with an equally poor understanding of Amharic, they not only misled European governments at the time about the positions, plans, and requests of the rulers of Ethiopia, but they have misled historians as well. Even in cases where both a correct and an incorrect translation exist in the files, historians seem to have taken it for granted that the version used by the European government in question at the time must be the correct one. This is in my view the only really crucial area where there is at present no substitute for the files of original correspondence. Because the Ethiopian documents are so few compared with all the reports by foreigners, and because they alone can really be regarded as primary sources for the Ethiopian side of the story, it is essential that they are allowed to speak. It is my hope that this study will in its entirety prove this point, but a few examples may not be out of place in this context.

In 1828 the Englishman William Coffin arrived in London as the bearer of a letter from Dejjazmach Sebagadis to George IV. This ruler of Tigrē has always been presented as one of the first, relatively speaking, open-minded, modern rulers of Ethiopia, 'an educated, travelled and enlightened man' who turned away from the 'sordid and dangerous politics' of central Ethiopia towards the coast and what could be gained by opening the country to foreign influences.[11] To what extent this view is correct must be discussed elsewhere.[12] But the statement 'I hope you will take the Port Massowen and give it up to us or keep it in Your Majesty's Possession . . .', allegedly contained in the above-mentioned

11   Stephen H. Longrigg, *A Short History of Eritrea* (Oxford, 1945), p. 81.
12   See below, p. 58–63.

letter, cannot be quoted as proof that he 'for the first time in the modern era . . . seriously attempted to breach the wall of isolation around Ethiopia and create a bridge to Christian Europe'.[13] Sebagadis's letter, the only one he ever wrote to any European monarch, does not even mention Massawa or the coast.[14] The statement appears in an English document signed by Coffin. A poor but faithful translation of the Amharic letter made in 1829 has been ignored.[15]

In 1849 a genuine, sealed letter from Dejjazmach Wibē Hayle Maryam to Queen Victoria was forwarded by Consul Walter Plowden, accompanied by a translation in Plowden's own hand. The consul adds a 'recently' about the occupation of Massawa (in 1557) by the Turks, strengthens the insistence that the Turks should not set foot on the mainland, and questions the right of the Turks even to the island of Massawa itself, without this being in the original letter at all.[16]

The problem is indicated by the treatment of Emperor Yohannis's letter to Queen Victoria of 13 August 1872. A comparison of the text in the Confidential Print with the English version in the *Abyssinia* original correspondence reveals no omissions. Even the addition at the end of the letter, 'Translated by the King's Interpreter to General J. C. Kirkham . . .', is reproduced. There are no minutes indicating that the Amharic letter was ever translated in England. The English version was, quite naturally and in good faith, accepted as Yohannis's message to Victoria. After all, it was quite expensive to get an Amharic letter translated, and the British government did not at the time have the slightest interest in any correspondence with Ethiopian princes.[17] But the English translation omits a fairly long and very important portion at the end of the Amharic original, in which Yohannis accuses the Catholic missionaries of having incited the people not to pay taxes to him, on the grounds that they were Catholics and under the protection of the French consul at Massawa.[18]

The instances of additions, mistranslations, and omissions are numerous and, of course, not limited to the documents preserved in the British archives, though I have chosen my three examples from there. Other discrepancies of this kind will be dealt with in the text or in footnotes in the following chapters. Sometimes those found in the correspondence are of little significance, because the matters dealt with are of marginal importance. The most serious of all the discrepancies are obviously those that exist between the Amharic and English, French, or Italian versions of treaty texts. In the case of the Wichalē treaty, the existence of two texts and the difference between the Amharic and Italian versions of Article XVII have been well known to European scholars interested in Ethiopian history practically since the treaty was signed. The article received much politically motivated comment at the time, and the fact of the discrepancy

13 Mordechai Abir, *Ethiopia: The Era of the Princes* (London, 1968), p. 35, quoting FO 1/2, fols 1–2, Sebagadis to George IV, 24 Apr. 1827, Coffin's version.
14 FO 1/2, fol. 6, Amharic original.
15 ibid., fol. 9, translation by Samuel Lee.
16 FO 1/5, fols 310–11, Wibē to Victoria, n.d. See below, pp. 123–4.
17 FO 1/28 contains several minutes to this effect. See below, pp. 283–4.
18 FO 95/731, no. 143; FO 1/27B, fols 8– 2, 57–8. See below, pp. 298–300.

has been continuously mentioned in the historical literature, but no serious attempts were really made to penetrate the significance of the existence of the two versions until my article 'The Protectorate Paragraph of the Wiçhalē treaty' appeared in 1964.[19] In all other cases, the Amharic texts have simply been ignored by historians. Whatever the reasons for this may have been, the result has been a less complete and less accurate view of the relations between Ethiopia and European governments than we would otherwise have had. In this respect, the Rochet d'Héricourt 'agreement' with Sahle Sillasē of Shewa in 1843, the so-called Hewett treaty of 1884, and the forerunners of the Wiçhalē treaty are of particular importance.[20]

Reports, Narratives, and Memoirs by Europeans

Other published correspondence, reports, narratives, and memoirs have been consulted on many points, but I certainly make no claim to have covered all the ground. Among the journals used, I think *Mittheilungen aus Justus Perthes, Geographischer Anstalt von A. Petermann, Bulletin de la Société de géographie*, and *Le Tour du Monde* should be mentioned in particular. Some of the material first published in scholarly and mission journals reappears in the narratives and memoirs published as books by many of the actors on or observers of the Ethiopian scene.

The value of all these sources, including the reporting in the diplomatic correspondence, obviously varies tremendously with the knowledge and personalities of the authors, the character of their involvement with Ethiopia, their opportunities of observing the events, and their motives for writing about them.[21] Although there are many borderline cases between the various categories, it is probably useful to note that the Europeans who reported on Ethiopia in the nineteenth century belonged to the following categories: government representatives, missionaries, explorers (both scientific and commercial, and including amateurs), and, finally, people who came to the country to make their future there, with no obligations to anyone in Europe.

In general, the government representatives are fairly easy to deal with as informants, unless or until they proved unsuccessful in some way or other, and felt the need to cover up or explain away unpleasant facts. There are many instances of this, from the failure of Henry Salt to reach Gonder in 1810 with the letter and presents of George III,[22] to the failure of General Oreste

19 Sven Rubenson, 'The Protectorate Paragraph of the Wiçhalē Treaty, *JAH*, V, 2 (1964), pp. 243–83. For a survey of the literature, see pp. 251–8, with references. See also below, pp. 385–94.
20 See below, pp. 159–63, 356–60, 379, 382.
21 It is not possible in this study to deal with the background of individual informants save in exceptional cases. The need for research on less-known travellers is recognized, as indicated in the case of Edmond Combes and Maurice Tamisier by Richard Pankhurst, 'The Saint Simonians and Ethiopia', *Proceedings of the Third International Conference of Ethiopian Studies* (Addis Abeba, 1969), pp. 169–223. For an introduction to the French travellers in general, see Georges Malécot, 'Les voyageurs français et les relations entre la France et l'Abyssinie de 1835 à 1870', *RFHO*, LVIII (1971), pp. 137–82, 279–352.
22 See below, pp. 46–8.

Baratieri to beat the Ethiopian army at Adwa in 1896. Though always present, the element of self-defence becomes more sophisticated as the number of observers and the risks of being exposed increase. It is very conspicuous in the reports and memoirs of some of Tēwodros's European captives, for example D. C. Cameron and Hormuzd Rassam, while Henry Blanc and W. F. Prideaux, whose positions were less exposed, are more straightforward.[23]

But Europe was far away, and in Ethiopia, as elsewhere in Africa, there was much scope for private initiative. Several of those who represented European governments as consuls or special envoys were people who had first gone to Ethiopia on their own and who offered their services after they had established contacts with Ethiopian rulers. This was the case with, for instance, Henry Salt and Walter Plowden among the British. Among the diplomatically active Frenchmen and Italians, there were several who first arrived in Ethiopia as members of scientific expeditions, for example Antoine d'Abbadie, Théophile Lefebvre, Pietro Antonelli, and Ferdinando Martini. In most cases, their attitudes were no different from those of the more regular diplomats. The most outstanding example on the Ethiopian scene of the European who used government appointments to further private interests is Werner Munzinger. He came to northern Ethiopia as an independent Swiss scholar and businessman, and ended up as an Egyptian governor general, after having been the official consular representative of both France and England at Massawa.[24] Around 1870 his power and influence were so great that a Swedish missionary could write from Massawa: 'His private person and name [alone] here count as much, yes, more than the [combined] names of the nations England and France, whose representative he has been.'[25] It goes without saying that information coming from as active and versatile a person as Munzinger can be evaluated only from case to case.

Because of their involvement in the political and diplomatic issues, the representatives of European governments were often better informed than the missionaries and people with purely scientific interests. On the other hand, the latter were often more detached and objective about the information they could provide on political matters. It should be noted, however, that several of the leading missionaries, particularly the Catholics G. De Jacobis, G. Sapeto, J. M. Touvier, and G. Massaja, but also the Protestant J. L. Krapf, were deeply involved in political and diplomatic matters on various occasions.[26] During the reign of Tēwodros, a group of craftsmen-missionaries from Chrischona accepted direct employment with the King. Although they were certainly not uncritical about the actions of their master, it is not difficult to sense the dif-

23 Rassam, *British Mission*; H. Blanc, *A Narrative of Captivity in Abyssinia* (London, 1868). Cameron published no memoirs, but has a long report in FO 1/26, fols 247–53. Prideaux's account of the mission is printed in C. R. Markham, *A History of the Abyssinian Expedition* (London, 1869), pp. 90–127.
24 Werner Munzinger, *Ostafrikanische Studien* (Schaffhausen, 1864); J. V. Keller-Zschokke, *Werner Munzinger-Pascha. Sein Leben und Wirken* (Aarau, 1891). See also below, pp. 277–8, 285, 292–7
25 *MT*, 1870, pp. 62–3, Englund, 12 Apr. or 13 May 1870.
26 Recent studies dealing with this matter include Crummey, *Priests*, and Aleme Eshete, *La Mission Catholique Lazariste en Éthiopie* (Paris, n.d. [1970], mimeographed).

ference in attitude between, for instance, Theophilus Waldmeier of this group and the Felasha missionary Henry Stern.[27] For obvious reasons, the missionaries of the Swedish Evangelical Mission were the least involved: '. . . as they have no Consul to bother them they set about their affairs in a quiet manner'.[28] An important aspect of the missionary sources is that the distribution of the missionaries throughout the country, their many years of residence, and knowledge of the languages of the people, made it possible for them to provide information not available from other informants.

Whether they actually involved themselves in political matters or not, both individual explorers and scientific expeditions have in their reports and narratives provided much material of historical interest. The first traveller's accounts of Ethiopia in the nineteenth century are Henry Salt's narratives of his visits to Tigrē in 1805 and 1810 respectively. The first was published by Lord Valentia,[29] and the second, which in fact describes an official mission, by Salt himself.[30] Reports to the Foreign Office and two small collections of letters among the Aberdeen Papers in the British Museum, mainly from Ethiopians to Salt and between Valentia, Salt, and Nathaniel Pearce, provide valuable opportunities to check the narratives.[31]

Other important informants in this category are the well-known German scholar Eduard Rüppell, who visited Ethiopia in 1832–33,[32] the two French–Irish brothers Antoine and Arnauld d'Abbadie, who both spent many years (1838–48) in the country,[33] Théophile Lefebvre and P. V. Ferret and J.-G. Galinier, who led French scientific expeditions between 1839 and 1843,[34] and C. F. X. Rochet d'Héricourt, who made two trips to Shewa about the same time, and a later one to Gonder.[35] There are scores of others. These names have all been chosen from the first half of the century because it is during this period

27 Theophil Waldmeier, *Erlebnisse in Abessinien in den Jahren 1858 bis 1868* (Basel, 1869); Henry A. Stern, *The Captive Missionary: being an Account of the Country and People of Abyssinia* (London, 1868).

28 A. B. Wylde, *'83 to '87 in the Soudan* (London, 1888), Vol. II, p. 1. Wylde was himself a British vice-consul for the Red Sea, involved in Ethiopian affairs in the 1870s and 1880s.

29 Viscount Valentia, *Voyages and Travels to India, Ceylon, the Red Sea, Abyssinia, and Egypt, in the years 1802, 1803, 1804, 1805, and 1806* (London, 1809), Vol. II, pp. 451–510; Vol. III, pp. 1–241.

30 Henry Salt, *A Voyage to Abyssinia* (London, 1814).

31 BM, Add. 19343 and 19347. Except where his own interests dictate otherwise, Salt gives the impression of being a reasonably reliable source. His editing has not eliminated contradictory statements nor such errors as eight days in a week or Easter Day on a Thursday (Salt, *Voyage*, pp. 234, 257, 367–8).

32 Eduard Rüppell, *Reise in Abyssinien* (Frankfurt am Main, 1838–40).

33 Arnauld d'Abbadie, *Douze ans dans la Haute-Éthiopie* (Paris, 1868). Only the first volume of what was planned to be a larger work was ever published. See Roger Izarn, 'Les documents Arnauld d'Abbadie', *Proceedings of the Third International Conference of Ethiopian Studies*, pp. 155–68, for information on the manuscript material.

34 T. Lefebvre and others, *Voyage en Abyssinie exécuté pendant les années 1839, 1840, 1841, 1842, 1843* (Paris, 1845–51); P. V. Ferret and J.-G. Galinier, *Voyages en Abyssinie dans les provinces du Tigré, du Samen et de l'Amhara* (Paris, 1847).

35 C. F. X. Rochet d'Héricourt, *Voyage sur la côte orientale de la Mer Rouge, dans le pays d'Adel et le Royaume de Choa* (Paris, 1841); idem, *Second voyage sur les deux rives de la Mer Rouge, dans le pays des Adals et le Royaume de Choa* (Paris, 1846).

that their information is of greatest relative importance. Later the diplomatic archives in most cases provide sufficient materials for double-checking dubious statements.

The last and most heterogeneous group of informants is made up of those who came to Ethiopia with no obligations to anyone in Europe, or who more or less cut the ties and entered the service of the Ethiopian rulers, or settled down in the country to earn their living on their own. They are the ones who would today be classified as mercenaries, settlers, or 'experts'. Because they often represent a more Ethiopian outlook, they are significant as a means of counter-balancing the more strictly European viewpoints in the source materials in general.

Nathaniel Pearce and William Coffin, who came to Ethiopia with Henry Salt and entered the service of Ras Welde Sillasē of Tigrē, are the two earliest representatives of this group. Pearce does not seem to have had much choice. When he ran away from his employer to join Valentia at Mokha in 1805, he was according to his own story a 26-year-old sailor with a record of two desertions from the Royal Navy and two from East India ships, the last at Mokha, where he had become a Muslim. His prospects in India or England were gloomy indeed. Pearce made notes, and his memoirs covering 1810 to 1819 were published after his death in 1820.[36] Coffin contributed two chapters on a military campaign which was directed towards Gonder, and, while his account is somewhat confused, he may well have seen the city though he did not enter it.[37] Another early 'settler' was the botanist Wilhelm Schimper, who arrived in the 1830s and was deeply involved in political affairs in the 1840s.[38] Both he and Coffin lived for over forty years in the country.

The craftsmen-missionaries of Tēwodros's reign, who had much in common with the 'settler' group, have already been mentioned. Later representatives include such people as the British officer J. C. Kirkham, who came to Ethiopia with the British expedition in 1868, and died in the service of Yohannis eight years later, and Minīlik's best-known foreign adviser, the Swiss engineer Alfred Ilg.[39]

That persons deeply concerned in the events often adjusted their accounts to suit their own interests is nothing remarkable. But a word or two should probably be said about fiction writers and plagiarizers. Some cases are fairly simple. The French 'traveller' Émile Jonveaux, who describes personal experiences in Ethiopia during the last year of Tēwodros's reign, never set foot in Ethiopia. In fact, he admits this in a discreet phrase in the introductory letter to the reader.[40] In the preface to his book about a visit to Gonder in 1865, F. H. Apel, on the other hand, stresses that he had not written any book (*kein*

---

36   [N. Pearce], *The Life and Adventures of Nathaniel Pearce*, ed. J. J. Halls (London, 1831), Vol. I, pp. 1–36.
37   ibid., Vol. I, pp. 231–46.
38   See below, pp. 102–18, 125.
39   C. Keller, *Alfred Ilg, sein Leben und sein Wirken* (Frauenfeld, 1918). No biography of Kirkham exists. See below, pp. 277, 300, 332–3.
40   Émile Jonveaux, *Deux ans dans l'Afrique orientale* (Tours, 1871). See Joseph Tubiana, 'Le voyage d'Émile Jonveaux en Ethiopie: Effets récents d'une ancienne mystification', *JAH*, IV, 2 (1963), pp. 287–8. In the English edition (London, 1875), the admission is omitted.

Buch verfassen), but wanted only to record his experiences.[41] He relates conversations he had at Gonder with the Emperor, Abune Selama, Consul Cameron, and Reverend Stern, although the three latter were then prisoners on Amba Meqdela some 400 kilometres away.[42] While the interviews were clearly fictitious, much of the other contents of his book are plagiarized page up and page down from Guillaume Lejean's book on Tēwodros.[43]

In some cases, even people involved in the diplomatic relations used each other's reports without worrying too much about bringing them up to date. The Frenchman Auguste Bardel, for instance, who came to the court of Tēwodros and was employed by the Emperor as a courier to Paris in 1862, submitted to the French Government a seventy-page report on Ethiopia, including the 'actual' political situation, which was nothing but a translation of a 9-year-old report by the British consul, Walter Plowden.[44] The consequence is that defeated and even dead chiefs appear as contenders for supreme power, while the Emperor—whose emissary Bardel was—is mentioned only once in passing, as a minor chief who wanted to modernize his army. In a second report, the material from Plowden was exhausted, and Bardel made an attempt to describe Tēwodros's reign to date. It shows that the Frenchman had only the faintest ideas about the events of the years just preceding his mission, and could not distinguish between provinces as far apart as Tigrē and Shewa.[45] Bardel may have done the copying when he was at one time managing the consulate during the illness of Plowden's successor, but there were also reports that Plowden's Italian agent at Massawa, Raphael Baroni, after the consul's death had 'sold all Plowden's official correspondence with H.M. Government to so-called French Priests . . .' [46] Although Bardel was, perhaps, more careless than most informants, it is not difficult to detect other cases of borrowing in reports which pretended to be original.

Ethiopian Chronicles

The scarcity of documentary material from the Ethiopian side is in certain respects alleviated by the existence of the Ethiopian chronicles. For a closer

41 F. H. Apel, *Drei Monate in Abyssinien und Gefangenschaft unter König Theodorus II* (Zürich, 1866).
42 ibid., pp. 15–18, 65–71, 80–100.
43 Compare, for instance, Apel, *Drei Monate*, pp. 19–29, with G. Léjean, *Théodore II. Le nouvel empire d'Abyssinie* (Paris, n.d. [1865]), pp. 19–51. The dependence goes as far as Lejean's sometimes erratic transcription of many Amharic names and phrases: Menène–Menene for Menen, Tzoobèdje–Tsoobedje for Tewabech, and Goangoul, Kokobie, Beurrou, *oizoro*, etc.
44 AEMD, Afrique 61, fols 141–210, Bardel, '1er Rapport', 10 Mar. 1863, compared with FO 401/1, pp. 193–228, Plowden, 'Report', 9 Jul. 1854.
45 AEMD, Afrique 61, fols 211–21, Bardel, '2me Rapport', 10 Mar. 1863. It is an indication of the amount of textual criticism which remains to be done that the latest French work on the period (Malécot, 'Voyageurs', *RFHO*, LVIII, p. 327) describes the two reports with the statement: 'Il [Bardel] rédige également à l'intention du ministre un long et intéressant rapport sur l'état de l'Éthiopie.'
46 See below, pp. 224–5. For the story of the sale of the documents, see FO 1/13, fols 187–90, FO minutes, 17 May to 12 Jun. 1863; Kirwan Joyce, who reported this, was certainly rather a dubious character himself, but the fact remains that Bardel had got hold of the papers.

study of diplomatic relations, they are, however, of little immediate value, either because negotiations with foreigners were kept secret, or because the chroniclers did not regard them as important enough to record. For the possible motives behind the attitudes and actions of the Ethiopian rulers, however, the chronicles are very important supplementary sources. About the events on the Ethiopian side of campaigns and battles, they are in many cases our only sources, and in other cases they provide opportunities to check European secondary sources.

The chronicles of the Gonderine period were written in Gi'iz, but during the reign of Tēwodros Amharic was introduced for this type of literature. Because the centres of political and ecclesiastical power shifted so much during the century, a number of different and conflicting traditions have been preserved. The manuscripts were copied and recopied a good deal. Minor changes were made, and errors crept in, but re-editing was not the rule.

Chronicles for the first half of the century have been published by H. Weld Blundell and Carlo Conti Rossini. The former published portions of British Museum MS. Orient. 821, written by several different authors and covering from 1769 to 1830, followed by the last part of *Bibliothèque Nationale* MS. Ethiop. Abb. 118, covering 1830–40.[47] The author of the last portion of MS. Orient. 821 refers to himself as Abegaz Se'une from Shewa, and states that he finished the writing in 7344 after the creation of the world (1851/52).[48] The portion of MS. Ethiop. Abb. 118 published by Conti Rossini covers from 1800 to 1840.[49] For the first decade the manuscript is a copy of the same work as MS. Orient. 821, but then a different and much more detailed account follows for 1809–30. Though published first, Conti Rossini's translation, *La cronaca reale*, is superior to Weld Blundell's *Royal Chronicle* also in terms of accuracy. Even a cursory examination of the latter reveals that many of the errors regarding names and dates are not due to the Ethiopian chronicler but to the editor and translator. It is, for instance, confusing to find Welde Gebri'ēl campaigning in 1800 although he had died the year before, and 'Ras' Maru participating in the battle of Debre Abbay in 1831 though he had fallen at Koso Ber in 1827.[50] It is unnecessary, too, since in these cases even Weld Blundell's published Gi'iz text has the correct names Welde Sillasē and Mariyyē.[51]

The chronicles are dominated by the many political intrigues and campaigns of the feudal lords of the period. In spite of all the adulation of the princes involved, the chroniclers did not avoid recording also the negative aspects of their rule: ' . . . we will not absolve (omit) their devastation of countries, while we are recounting their exploits and good deeds. For thus is the rule for each man that the angel of life records his just deeds and the angel of death records

47   H. Weld Blundell, ed., *The Royal Chronicle of Abyssinia 1769–1840* (Cambridge, 1922).
48   ibid., pp. 103, 351.
49   Carlo Conti Rossini, ed., 'La cronaca reale abissina dall'anno 1800 all'anno 1840', *RRAL*, 5, XXV (1916), pp. 779–923.
50   Weld Blundell, *Chronicle*, pp. 461–2, 465, 485–6.
51   ibid., pp. 184, 198.

his sins.'[52] It would be a mistake, however, to regard the Gonder chronicles as purely didactic literature. There is much evidence that the authors had the ambition of keeping a correct record, for instance of all the appointments made at the court. At times, this was not an easy task, for Abegaz Se'une exclaims, 'We do not know what appointments were made, because not a single appointment was permanent . . .' Besides, people made appointments without having authority to do so. In other places, this author warns his readers that he is only passing on information received from others, that he was absent when certain events took place, or that there was no one to give him information because of the confusion at the court.[53]

In addition to *La cronaca reale*, Conti Rossini has translated and published some other Ethiopian texts of great importance for the first half of the nineteenth century, under the titles *Nuovi documenti per la storia d'Abissinia nel secolo XIX* and *Vicende dell'Etiopia e delle Missioni Cattoliche ai tempi di ras Ali, deggiàč Ubié e re Teodoro secondo un documento abissino*.[54] The latter, which covers the reign of Tēwodros as well, is a rather different kind of work from the chronicles, written by the Catholic priest Tekle Haymanot as a planned history of the beginning of the Catholic mission in its political context.

For Tēwodros's reign, three distinctly different chronicles are known and have been published. Of these, the one attributed to Debtera Zeneb is the most interesting. Only one manuscript of this chronicle is known.[55] It was brought to Europe by the missionary Martin Flad immediately after the fall of Meqdela in 1868, and handed over to the Berlin library.[56] Handwriting and other particulars clearly show its Ethiopian origin. The author is not mentioned in the manuscript, but both Enno Littmann, who published the text in 1902, and Theodor Nöldeke state that he was Zeneb, and this has been generally accepted by all scholars who have dealt with the problem.[57] Zeneb was well known to several foreigners. He was mentioned by Flad as Tēwodros's secretary or chancellor, by Rassam as 'the keeper of the royal archives', and by the missionary Waldmeier as a friend.[58] According to Flad, the Berlin manuscript is the only copy of Zeneb's work.[59] Flad was, in other words, of the opinion that he took the only existing copy out of the country when he left. Although a somewhat

52 ibid., p. 376.
53 ibid., pp. 437, 439, 470, 474, 478.
54 *RANL*, 8, II (1947), pp. 357–416, and *RRAL*, 5, XXV (1916), pp. 425–550.
55 Universitätsbibliothek Tübingen, former Preussischer Staatsbibliothek, MS. orient. quart. 478.
56 A. Dillmann, *Die Handschriften-Verzeichnisse der Königlichen Bibliothek zu Berlin* (Berlin, 1878), Dritter Band, p. II.
57 [Zeneb], *Ye-Tēwodros Tarīk*, edited and published in Amharic by E. Littmann, *The Chronicle of King Theodore of Abyssinia* (Princeton, 1902), p. v; T. Nöldeke, *Orientalische Skizzen* (Berlin 1892), p. 280. An Italian translation of this chronicle has been published by M. M. Moreno, 'La cronaca di re Teodoro attribuita al dabtarā "Zaneb"', *RSE*, II (1942), pp. 143–80.
58 J. M. Flad, *Zwölf Jahre in Abessinien* (Leipzig, 1887), Vol. I, p. 31; Spittler-Archiv, D 3/2, Flad to Gobat, 3 Dec. 1861; Rassam, *British Mission*, Vol. II, p. 192; Waldmeier, *Erlebnisse*, p. 10.
59 Dillmann, *Handschriften-Verzeichnisse*, p. 69.

later chronicler, Aleqa Welde Maryam, knew Zeneb personally,[60] no similarities between their chronicles indicate that he had seen Zeneb's work. Later Ethiopian historical writers seem also to have been ignorant of the contents of this earliest Tēwodros chronicle. The composition of Zeneb's chronicle is strictly annalistic, more so than the chronicles of the late Gonderine period. Apart from the somewhat legendary opening pages, the events are listed chronologically month by month, with many exact dates, and everything points to the conclusion that it was written very closely in time to the events recorded. The chronicler gives every impression of being well informed and accurate with his facts. Unfortunately the story ends with November 1859. The bias, where noticeable, is pro-Tēwodros, as might be expected in a chronicle by the King's secretary.

Aleqa Welde Maryam's Tēwodros chronicle presents the history of Tēwodros as preserved within the country. Many copies undoubtedly exist in Ethiopia, but no comparative study of them has been made. Two copies, identical in wording, were brought to Europe in the 1890s by C. Mondon-Vidailhet,[61] who published both the Amharic text and a French translation.[62] The author speaks of himself in the chronicle as a young man from Shewa province, who lived with Abune Selama in his captivity on Meqdela, and who assisted the bishop in his contacts with Minīlik in 1867.[63] Welde Maryam also informs us that his chronicle was written 'in the year of the creation of the world 7373' (1880/81).[64] Much of the material in this chronicle is different from Zeneb's also for the period covered by both, and there are a number of contradictions between the two. With regard to facts that can be checked, Welde Maryam is less reliable than Zeneb. The composition of the chronicle is not as tightly chronological as Zeneb's. The dates are vague and sometimes incorrect even for events which one might expect a Shewan writer to know, for instance the death of King Hayle Melekot and the escape of Minīlik from Meqdela.[65]

---

60 Welde Maryam, *Chronique de Théodros II, roi des rois d'Éthiopie*, ed. C. Mondon-Vidailhet (Paris, n.d. [1904]), p. 45. I will refer to this chronicle as well as Zeneb's by the name of the author, *Tēwodros*, and the page numbers of the printed Amharic texts, if nothing else is stated.

61 BN, Ethiop. 257 and 258. See M. Chaine, *Catalogue des Manuscrits Éthiopiens de la Collection Mondon-Vidailhet* (Paris, 1913), p. 43, for details. Mondon-Vidailhet visited Ethiopia twice in the period 1891–97, and spent altogether five years in the country. He gained the confidence of Emperor Minīlik, and was given the opportunity to have copies of all manuscripts he wanted.

62 See above, n. 60.

63 Welde Maryam, *Tēwodros*, p. 41.

64 ibid., p. 64.

65 ibid., pp. 11, 32. The date of Hayle Melekot's death is given as Friday, 30 Hidar. But this date (9 Dec. 1855) was first of all not a Friday, and secondly, another event which took place after the death of Hayle Melekot is dated Monday, 10 Hidar. The correct date is 30 Tiqimt (9 Nov. 1855), which is given by Minīlik's chronicler, Gebre Sillasē. The date given for Minīik's escape is 24 Senē 7358 after the creation of the world, i.e. 30 Jun. 1866. This is not a slip of the pen, since the writer also mentions the evangelist of the year, Mark, which is correct for 7358. Contemporary documentary material proves, however, that Minīlik fled from Meqdela one year earlier. Cf. Sven Rubenson, *King of Kings Tēwodros of Ethiopia* (Addis Abeba, 1966), pp. 53, n. 21, 81, with R. H. Kofi Darkwah, 'Emperor Theodore II and the kingdom of Shoa, 1855–1865', *JAH*, X, 1 (1969), pp. 105–15.

Finally, Welde Maryam is clearly biased against Tēwodros. The chronicle is nevertheless an important source for Tēwodros's reign, particularly for events in Shewa.

The third Tēwodros chronicle is strictly speaking not a chronicle at all. It is far removed from the normal annalistic style of the Ethiopian chronicle; the material is arranged by topics rather than chronologically. The author of this work is unknown. It was published in 1957–59 by Luigi Fusella.[66] It is a fairly late work, according to Fusella not earlier than Yohannis's reign.[67] In fact it is certainly still later, since Minīlik is called *aṭe* (emperor) in it.[68] The author was most probably from northern Ethiopia. He knew Tigriñña, and included material of clearly Tigrean origin.[69] Whether he was an eyewitness of any of the events described, as Fusella believes,[70] or not, is difficult to say. The general impression of this work is, in my view, not that of a straightforward account, but of a literary endeavour by a collector of oral tradition or a compiler. Its importance lies in the fact that it has largely preserved material other than the information given by Zeneb and Welde Maryam, in particular about the conflict with the foreigners and the last days of Tēwodros.

The published Ethiopian source material for the reigns of Tekle Gīyorgīs and Yohannis is meagre compared with the material for Tēwodros's time. Most of the early known chronicles are collected in MS. 72 of Collection Mondon-Vidailhet.[71] Folios 56–62, containing a Gi'iz text of a short chronicle, have been published with a French translation by M. Chaine.[72] The manuscript is dated 1887 Ethiopian calendar, which corresponds to 1894/95 Gregorian calendar. Chaine's statement that it is dated the same year as the published section on Yohannis closes, i.e. 1887 *Gregorian* calendar,[73] is due to the error of changing one of the dates to the Gregorian calendar, but not the other.

In addition to the date, the preface of the manuscript provides the names of two authors: Aleqa Lemlem from Mahdere Maryam for the first parts, and Aleqa Zeyohannis for the latter parts of the manuscript. It is also stated that at least Aleqa Lemlem wrote for 'Musē [Monsieur] Mondon', while both, or more probably only Aleqa Zeyohannis, wrote at Intotto.[74] Since the manuscript is a copy—there is no change of hand between the parts attributed to Lemlem and Zeyohannis respectively—the date and place could refer to the copying instead of the authorship.

A study of the texts soon reveals that we indeed have to do with two different

66 Luigi Fusella, ed., *Yaṭē Tēwodros Tarīk* (Rome, 1959). This was first published with an Italian translation, 'La cronaca dell'Imperatore Teodoro II di Etiopia in un manoscritto amarico', *Annali d'Istituto Universitario di Napoli*, n.s., VI–VIII (1957–59). I will refer to the separately published Amharic text of 1959.
67 ibid., Preface.
68 ibid., p. 13.
69 ibid., pp. 8, 11.
70 ibid., Preface.
71 BN, Ethiop. 259,
72 M. Chaine, 'Histoire du règne de Iohannes IV, Roi d'Éthiopie (1868–1889)', *RS*, 21 (1913), pp. 178–91.
73 BN, Ethiop. 259, fol. 1; cf. Chaine, *Catalogue*, p. 179.
74 BN, Ethiop. 259, fol. 1.

authors, different in both literary style and background. The first part has two sections: the history of the reign of Tekle Gīyorgīs, followed by a dirge (fols 5–14); and the history of the reign of Yohannis, also followed by a dirge (fols 15–41).[75] Although the presentation is chronological, with several precisely-given though not always accurate dates, the practice of the annalist of beginning each sentence or paragraph with a date is consistently applied only with regard to the years. The contents point to a man from Begēmdir, where Mahdere Maryam is situated, as the author.[76] In the section about Tekle Gīyorgīs, he gives the impression of having been a supporter of this ruler, which does not prevent him from showing sympathy also for his rival and successor Yohannis. In fact, the author must have been very close to Yohannis on some of his campaigns and at the state and church councils occasionally called by this emperor. On the other hand, there are no signs in Aleqa Lemlem's work of a bias in favour of Emperor Minīlik, nor any other indications that it was revised to suit new political conditions. On the contrary, the author states plainly—and in general correctly—in one case that Minīlik fled, in another that he asked mercy from Yohannis, in a third that his actions led to the new conflict in 1888, and so on.[77]

In the chronicle of Tekle Gīyorgīs, Yohannis is called Dejjazmach Kasa. In his own chronicle, he is mostly called *Janhoy* (His Majesty), as if he still ruled, and Minīlik is called *nigus* (king) and not *aṣē* (emperor) nor *Janhoy*.[78] In this respect Aleqa Lemlem shows more historical sense and independence than Ethiopian chroniclers have normally done. But this author is interesting also in other respects. He mentions a number of the proposals coming from the Italians and the Mahdists through correspondence or envoys, and the replies given.[79] One of Yohannis's most important letters to Queen Victoria, from 1887, is in fact copied almost *verbatim* into the chronicle.[80] Since there is also a separate copy of this letter in Mondon-Vidailhet's collection, and this is even closer to the original, it seems quite clear that Lemlem had either the original or a copy at his disposal.[81]

The second part of the manuscript contains Aleqa Zeyohannis's Yohannis chronicle, first in Amharic (fols 45–50) and then in Gi'iz (fols 56–62). It is this Gi'iz text that has been translated and published by M. Chaine. Between the two versions there is a short separate account of the war with the Mahdists up to 1887 (fols 53–4). Zeyohannis's chronicle is very simple in its composition.

---

75 Chaine describes the second as 'Histoire de l'avènement du roi Iohannes. Description des fêtes du couronnement' (*Catalogue*, pp. 43–4) although it is an account of the entire reign of Yohannis.

76 This includes minor details in connection with geographical definitions, for instance that the Emperor gave the land *beyond* the river Beshilo to Minīlik (fol. 24v.), and detailed knowledge of clerical appointments in what was then central Ethiopia (fol. 26).

77 BN, Ethiop. 259. fols 23v., 29r, 36v.

78 The one instance where Minīlik is called *aṣē*, fol. 25, is certainly a slip of the pen of the author or copyist.

79 BN, Ethiop. 259, fols 30–2.

80 ibid., fols 33–4. Cf. FO 95/748, no. 194.

81 BN, Ethiop. 282.

The events are recorded year by year, and in many cases dated only by the year of Yohannis's reign. There are no linguistic or other similarities between this chronicle and the longer one that can be used as evidence for direct relationship. Both the name of this chronicler, Zeyohannis, and the tenor of his work indicate a man from Tigrē.

Zeyohannis seems to know much more about the war with the Egyptians than with the Mahdists. In an account which lists the enemies of Ethiopia in terms of 'the children of Ammon and Moab, the Ishmaelites', it is remarkable to find the exact date, 7 Hidar 1868 (16 Nov. 1875 Gregorian calendar), and place, Gundet, of the first battle of the Egyptian war. It is indeed surprising to find that the chronicler's assertion, that the Emperor, on having heard about the coming of the Egyptians, prayed to God for three weeks before doing anything else, agrees with information from the Egyptian sources, which allow about twenty-seven days between the landing of the expeditionary force at Massawa and Yohannis's mobilization.[82] It must have taken about five or six days for a messenger to cover the distance between Massawa and Adwa, where the Emperor resided at this time.

In view of this, it is difficult to believe that the account of these events was written down fifteen to twenty years after they had happened. On the other hand, Zeyohannis's chronicle shows clear signs of revision, and possibly of the suppression of information which it was no longer opportune to disseminate. Not only is Minīlik throughout the chronicle called aṣē, but the conflicts and confrontations between him and his overlord are treated in such a manner that no blame should fall on any one, least of all on Minīlik.[83] It is probably because of such problems that the last two years of Yohannis's reign have been omitted altogether.

Additional material on the reigns of both Tēwodros and Yohannis is found in several other manuscripts, of which copies exist in Collection Mondon-Vidailhet. It is sufficient to mention MSS. Ethiop. 242, 244, and 260. These three are copies of the same chronicle of the kings of Ethiopia up to the beginning of the reign of Tēwodros. From 1855 to 1887, MS. 242 has a different and shorter text. All three praise Emperor Yohannis in terms which indicate that these parts were written during his reign. Unlike Lemlem's Yohannis chronicle in MS. 259, these manuscripts do not mention the often strained relations between Yohannis and Minīlik. In other ways, too, they are quite different from the chronicles in MS. 259. The contents indicate an author or authors from Gonder.

For Minīlik's life and reign, a detailed chronicle or biography was written by the Emperor's secretary and chancellor Gebre Sillasē. The official version of this work was published in French in 1930–31 by the French minister to Ethiopia, Maurice de Coppet, and in Amharic in 1966/67.[84] An earlier version of the

82 BN, Ethiop. 259, fols 46–7.
83 ibid., fol. 48r.
84 Guèbrè Sellassié, *Chronique du Règne de Ménélik II, roi des rois d'Éthiopie*, ed. Maurice de Coppet (Paris, 1930–31); Gebre Sillasē, *Tarīke Zemen ze-Dagmawī Minīlik, Niguse Negest ze-Ityopya* (Addis Abeba, 1966/67).

part up to 1890 is found in Mondon-Vidailhet's collection.[85] The difference lies mainly in the inclusion of additional material in the later version. A brief note at the beginning of the Mondon MS. states that this 'history of the Shewan kings' was written on Minīlik's own orders, and handed over to Mondon-Vidailhet by Gebre Sillasē in 1885, i.e. 1892/93 Gregorian calendar.

It is not so much a chronicle as a biography written with the all-too-obvious aim of justifying and praising Minīlik's actions, which are seen in the light of prophecies about his and Shewa's rise to prominence in Ethiopia. A typical instance of this is the account of Minīlik's escape from Meqdela in 1865, which ends with the statement that the history of Minīlik and Tēwodros agrees perfectly with that of David and Saul.[86] In his descriptions of the relations between Minīlik and Yohannis, Gebre Sillasē plays down the tension and conflict of Yohannis's reign. Foreign relations receive very little attention. That Yohannis kept Minīlik informed about the British–Egyptian peace mission in 1884 is mentioned,[87] but nothing is said about the negotiations leading to the Wichalē treaty.

The biography of Minīlik by Afewerq Gebre Īyesus is a little more rewarding as far as foreign relations are concerned.[88] As a student in Rome, Afewerq was for instance in a position to observe Ras Mekonnin's mission to Italy in 1889. What he writes in this connection, however, is more in the line of personal memoirs than of any official chronicle.[89] There are a number of other more or less contemporary but still unpublished Ethiopian accounts of the Minīlik period. The most interesting is probably a manuscript called *Ye-Galla Tarīk*, by Aṣme Gīyorgīs Gebre Mesih, which shows a critical attitude towards Minīlik's policies.[90]

Many other historical or partly historical manuscripts for the period remain to be studied. One of the manuscripts of the Gebre Mīka'ēl Girmu collection, recently acquired by the Institute of Ethiopian Studies in Addis Abeba, contains a detailed account of Ethiopian–Italian relations during the last decades of the nineteenth century, largely based, however, on Italian materials. More interesting from an Ethiopian point of view is a small manuscript which belonged to the late Qēs Badima Yalew, covering the reigns of Yohannis and Minīlik. It was copied in 1923/24 from one of the manuscripts of the great Ethiopian scholar Tayye Gebre Maryam, who had been commissioned by Minīlik to write the history of Ethiopia. For the period described in chapters 9 and 10—the only two included in the manuscript I have seen—Aleqa Tayye had access to much first-hand information. He seems to have written without reference to European sources also in passages dealing with foreign relations, for instance where he writes about the agreement between Yohannis and a person named *Yubēt*

---

85 BN, Ethiop. 261.
86 ibid., fol. 26.
87 ibid., fol. 82r.
88 Afewerq Gebre Īyesus, *Dagmawī Minīlik* (Rome, 1909).
89 ibid., p. 59.
90 National Library, Addis Abeba, MS. 47. For information on Aṣme Gīyorgīs personally, see Hiruy Welde Sillasē, *Ye-Hiywet Tarīk* (Addis Abeba, 1922/23), p. 55.

Admēral, ye-merkeb dejjazmach, better known among Europeans as Rear Admiral Sir William Hewett.[91]

With authors like Afewerq, Aṣme Gīyorgīs, and Tayye, the typical sources of Ethiopian history, that is, the annalistic, impersonal, and often anonymous chronicles, have disappeared in favour of more modern types of historical literature.

---

91   On Tayye Gebre Maryam, see the introduction by Taddesse Tamrat to Tayye Gebre Maryam, *Ye-Ītyopya Hizb Tarīk* (Addis Abeba, 1971/72, 8th edn), particularly pp. 20–7 The manuscript to which I am referring is additional to those described by Taddesse Tamrat, possibly an early draft of materials which Tayye intended to include in chapters 32 and 34 of his major, unfinished (or in part lost or hidden) work, *Ye-Ītyopya Tarīk*. It consists of fifty-two pages in Badima Yalew's own handwriting. For Hewett, see p. 25.

II

Prospects and First Contacts

The Coming of a New Era

Ethiopia's first contacts with Europe in the nineteenth century were not the result of Ethiopian but of European initiatives. One of the effects of Napoleon's unexpected invasion of Egypt in 1798 was an increased awareness, in France, Great Britain, and Russia, of the strategic importance of the Near and Middle East. A new era was born, and slowly but inevitably, it seems, the area became a battleground for European political and commercial adventurers, the more or less accredited 'consuls' of the nineteenth century. With, or just as often without, the official support of their respective governments, they laid their plans and prepared the ground. Eventually the situation led to the Suez Canal, the collapse of the Ottoman Empire, and European rule over most of the Near and Middle East.

Ethiopia was bound to be dragged into this development. Though it had long ago ceased to be a sea power or a mercantile nation, as it had been during the Aksumite period, it still had important interests to safeguard on its section of the Red Sea coast. Almost all its foreign trade passed through Massawa and a number of smaller and less important ports as far south as Zeyla.[1] Whatever other contacts Ethiopia had with the outside world, such as missions to bring bishops from Alexandria, pilgrimages to Jerusalem and Mecca, and occasional visits by foreigners who brought new ideas or new skills to the isolated country, these were also made either via the Red Sea coast or Nubia.

Neither the Ethiopians nor any of the other people in the Red Sea area had participated in any major international development since the interests of the Portuguese and the Turks had clashed there in the sixteenth century. In that conflict, Ethiopia had been the ally of Portugal. But as the European party gradually developed from a military ally into a spiritual mentor bent on re-

---

1 Abir, *Ethiopia*, pp. 5–26; Richard Pankhurst, 'The Trade of Northern Ethiopia in the Nineteenth and early Twentieth Centuries', *JES*, II, 1 (1964), pp. 49–159.

placing Orthodoxy by Roman Catholicism, the people rebelled and the ties were cut. The legacy of the Portuguese, or rather the Jesuits (Spanish and Portuguese), was in addition to the theological ferment mainly suspicion and hostility towards all Franks or *ferenj*, as everyone from Western Europe was called.

On the other hand, the sixteenth-century attempts to islamize the whole people and to make northern Ethiopia a province of the Ottoman Empire had also failed. The Turks were defeated and withdrew to the coast. But they held on to the little island of Massawa, and claimed suzerainty over an area which they called Habesh or Habeshistan.[2] Though they levied duties at the port, and at times gained some influence in the immediate neighbourhood of Arkiko on the mainland by allying themselves with local chiefs there, it was only occasionally that their presence really obstructed Ethiopian trade; still less did it pose any threat to the survival of the Ethiopian state.[3] Gradually the Ottoman government lost interest in the southern parts of the African coast. Habesh was officially renamed Sawakin and Jidda, though its earlier name, with its much wider implications, was also used.[4] Trade on the coast had declined. The revenue at Massawa no longer justified an Ottoman governor of the island. He was withdrawn and replaced by the *na'ib* (deputy) of Arkiko, a mainland chief of the Belew tribe who had long been a nominal vassal of the Porte and now became the *de facto* ruler of Massawa.[5] As for the Ethiopians, they lived in happy ignorance of any claims that they were Ottoman subjects. In their world view, there was no room even for the idea that their king of kings could be the vassal of any other man on earth.[6] In fact, Istanbul and Gonder were too far apart to engage in any serious struggle. There were many levels of authority in both states, and neither could at the beginning of the nineteenth century be called a vigorous polity. On the Red Sea coasts, issues and conflicts were local, almost parochial, in nature. It was into this vacuum that European nations and a reborn Egypt were to move, to challenge the very existence of the Ethiopian state. What were its prospects for survival?

The Ethiopian Polity

From many points of view, Ethiopia of 1800 was a weak state with serious internal problems and little visible cohesion. It was not, however, like many other areas of Africa, the home of a mere conglomeration of more or less closely affiliated tribes. The many centuries of settled agricultural life in the Ethiopian

2　Strictly speaking, the claim was limited to the African coastlands of the Red Sea, but since the Arabs called all Ethiopia *Bilad al-Habash* or *al-Habasha*, and the Ethiopians themselves also used Habesha or Habisha for their country and people, the mere use of this name implied or was understood to imply more extensive claims.

3　Trimingham, *Islam*, pp. 84–98; Abir, *Ethiopia*, p. 26.

4　Cengiz Orhonlu, 'Turkish archival sources on Ethiopia', *IV Congresso Internazionale di Studi Etiopici* (Rome, 1974), pp. 455–62.

5　Abir, *Ethiopia*, pp. 5–8; P. M. Holt, *A Modern History of the Sudan* (London, 1961), p. 25; Giglio, *Etiopia–Mar Rosso*, Vol. I, pp. 84–5.

6　See below, pp. 33–4.

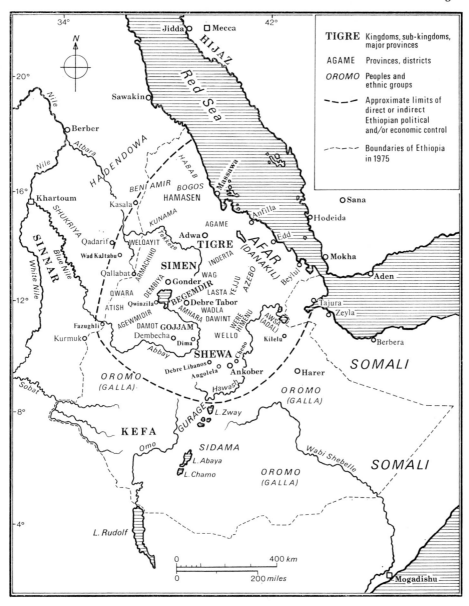

MAP 1 Ethiopia in the first half of the nineteenth century

highlands, the long history of the Ethiopian monarchy and the Christian church in the area, had weakened tribal structures in favour of a more regionally organized society. The politically and culturally dominating element in the region as a whole was the Christian and Semitic-speaking highland population who cultivated much of the plateau from the hinterland of Massawa roughly to the big bends of the Abbay and the Hawash. Within this area there remained, however, several pockets of Cushitic Agew, most of whom had been christianized but not linguistically assimilated.

More important from the political point of view were the Oromo or the Galla, as they are almost invariably called in both Ethiopian and European literature. The majority of these Cushitic tribes lived outside the Ethiopian state of the early nineteenth century, but some of their tribal federations had settled on the plains of Shewa in the south, as well as in the mountains and foothills along the eastern escarpment. Some had, in fact, penetrated into the very heartlands of Ethiopia east of Lake Ṭana. As they settled and turned to agriculture, a process of assimilation with the earlier Amharic-speaking population started. A Galla nobility emerged and through military service and intermarriage gained political influence on the level of the whole state, in spite of the fact that most of these Galla had accepted Islam rather than Christianity. Along the western border, a number of predominantly pagan Negroid population groups, e.g. the Kunama and the Barya, were also subject to the Ethiopian empire, and both along the Red Sea coast and east of the highlands there were nomadic Muslim tribes who lived in economic interdependence with the Ethiopians.[7]

While the process of assimilation and the long common history had created a certain sense of national identity, particularly in the highlands, there were also strong divisive forces at play, probably due as much to the difficult communications of a mountainous country and to the feudal character of the political system as to any purely ethnic factors. At the beginning of the nineteenth century, the authority of the central institutions, the monarchy and the church, was at a very low ebb. This is the period in Ethiopian history to which the Ethiopians have given the name *Zemene Mesafint*, 'the era of the princes (or judges)', so called because 'In those days there was no king in Israel: every man did that which was right in his own eyes'.[8]

The process of increasing regionalism and disintegration at the centre had set in about the middle of the eighteenth century. The last *niguse negest* (king of kings) to exercise any authority whatsoever of his own was Tekle Gīyorgīs Fiqir Segged. It was his fate to be enthroned and dethroned six times from 1789 to 1800, and to end his life in exile in Tigrē in 1817. Ethiopian tradition has nicknamed him *Fiṣṣamē Mengist* (the end of the government). His successors, Be'ide Maryam, Igwale Ṣiyon (Gwalu), Īyo'as, Gīgar, Īyasu, Sahle Dingil, and Yohannis, to mention just a few from the following decades, were mere puppets in the hands of regional governors and warlords. Deposed kings lived scattered

7 For further information on the ethnic, linguistic, and religious divisions in Ethiopia, see E. Ullendorff, *The Ethiopians* (Oxford, 1960), pp. 31–46, 97–135, and Trimingham, *Islam*, pp. 5–31, 147–224.
8 Judges 21:25.

at the courts of minor princes and in monasteries. Some were involved in intrigues to return to the throne; others seemed quite content to pass the remaining years of their lives far away from the centres of power.[9]

For the reigning king in the crumbling castles at the old capital of Gonder, there was still much empty glory; for he represented the 'glory of the kings', the *Kibre Negest*, from which the Ethiopian monarchy had drawn so much of its strength in the past.[10] As a descendant of Solomon and as *Siyyume Igzī'abihēr* (the elect of God), he was regarded as the source of all authority in the state.[11] In theory, he alone had the power of conferring ranks and governorships and of withdrawing them at will. In reality, he was powerless.

By the 1830s, the emperor had no military forces and almost no revenue. He governed the palace and lived on local income, fines and charity, toll from the Muslim merchants of Gonder, reportedly 300 Maria Theresa thalers (less than £100) in 1832, and, around 1840, 'a civil list of 100 £s per annum, and a trifling duty on all the butter imported into Gonder, the capital'.[12] This should be related to reports that, in addition to a tremendous amount of other wealth, the estate of a Tigrean vassal, Ras Welde Sillasē, in 1816 included 75,000 thalers, and that another nominal vassal, King Sahle Sillasē of Shewa, had in the early 1840s an annual income of 80,000–90,000 thalers and an expenditure of 10,000, which resulted in enormous hoards of silver.[13] There was indeed a dizzying gulf between the myth of the 'Niguse Negest of all the world if that declaration pleases', as the king-makers once addressed Tekle Gīyorgīs, and the real position of the shadow king at Gonder.[14] The strongest feelings of disgust and despair are voiced by the Ethiopian chronicler:

9   For this paragraph and those immediately following, see *inter alia* Conti Rossini, 'Cronaca', *RRAL*, 5, XXV, or Weld Blundell, *Chronicle, passim*; BN, Ethiop. 242, fols 82–3; [Pearce], *Life, passim*; Rüppell, *Reise*, Vol. II, pp. 369–403; d'Abbadie, *Douze ans*, particularly pp. 137–59. Though there are differences of opinion about the degree of disintegration and the causes of the decline of the Gonderine state, the many contemporary travellers in Ethiopia by and large confirm the dark picture drawn by the chroniclers. The issue is a very complex one and cannot be dealt with here, where my only aim is to give the reader a general idea of the internal conditions as a background to the response to foreign influences, which is the theme of this book. The most recent studies of the *Zemene Mesafint* are found in Abir *Ethiopia*, and Crummey, *Priests*, the former with an economic, the latter with a missionary and diplomatic emphasis. See also Rubenson, *Tēwodros*, pp. 17–25, and David Mathew *Ethiopia. The Study of a Polity, 1540–1935* (London, 1947), pp. 99–178.

10 C. Bezold, ed., *Kebra Nagast: die Herrlichkeit der Könige* (Munich, 1905).

11 This does not imply that any well-defined theories about the basis and functioning of authority existed. On the contrary, Arnauld d'Abbadie (*Douze ans*, pp. 110–11), after an attempt to explain this matter, concluded: 'On comprend . . . que les Éthiopiens disent qu'il est presque toujours aussi imprudent de vouloir préciser le premier moment de l'existence des grands pouvoirs, que de vouloir préciser le moment où l'âme entre dans le corps de l'homme.'

12 S. Gobat, *Journal of a Three Years' Residence in Abyssinia* (London, 1834), pp. 91, 96; Rüppell, *Reise*, Vol. II, p. 174; FO 1/3, fol. 150, Isenberg's notes on Wibē to Victoria, n.d. In prices at Gonder at the time, 300 thalers meant roughly 60 tons of grain (wheat or *ţef*), 30 horses, or 50–60 muskets of cheap quality. See Richard Pankhurst, *Economic History of Ethiopia 1800–1935* (Addis Abeba, 1968), pp. 349–50.

13 [Pearce], *Life*, Vol. II, pp. 95–6; W. C. Harris, *The Highlands of Aethiopia* (London, 1844), Vol. III, p. 28.

14 Weld Blundell, *Chronicle*, pp. 171, 447.

How is it that the kingdom has become contemptible to striplings and slaves? How is it that the kingdom is a laughing stock to the uncircumcized from the very beginning? How is it that the kingdom is the image of a worthless flower that children pluck in the autumn rains?[15]

The real rulers of Ethiopia were the regional governors, the *rases* and *dejjazmaches* of the various provinces. They kept the revenues of their provinces and commanded their own armies. The most powerful had made their positions hereditary, but popularity with the soldiers and connections with other families were often the decisive factors in the struggles for succession to the governorships. The aspiration of the most powerful governors was to become *ras* of the kingdom, or *ras bitwedded* (the favourite duke), and thereby guardian of the king of kings. The struggle for this supreme position, and the recurring attempts by feudal lords on all levels to increase their domains at the expense of their neighbours, caused a state of almost constant small-scale warfare. The awe in which the Solomonic dynasty had been held lingered on, and for several decades prevented attempts to usurp the throne itself; but as a symbol and a focus for national identity, the Gonderine monarchy had nothing more to offer.

The situation was further aggravated by developments in the Ethiopian church. Together with the monarchy, it had played an important role as a unifying factor and a mediator in political conflict. Though the clergy in many cases still acted as mediators, the doctrinal and structural unity of the church had all but disappeared. The growing intensity of the doctrinal disputes, primarily about the genesis of the nature of Christ, had resulted in warring factions who aligned themselves with various regional rulers, and fought each other with both spiritual and temporal means. The bishop or *abun* who was brought from Alexandria had a potentially very powerful position. But after the death of Abune Yosab in 1803, there were two long interregnums, and neither Qērilos (1816–30) nor Selama, who arrived only in 1841, was able to cope with the situation. They were caught up in the doctrinal confusion and political turmoil, as were the representatives of the most powerful Ethiopian office, that of the *içhegē*.[16] At the same time, the Wahhabi movement led to a revival of Islam in the Red Sea area, and increased the religious consciousness and commitment of the Muslim population in and around Ethiopia. More directly, the Gonderine state was affected by the emergence of Galla leadership at the court, since the Galla *rases* often had to fall back on their Muslim supporters in order to remain in power.[17]

The main political divisions during the first decades of the nineteenth century were Tigrē in the north; Simēn, Dembīya (Ye-Maru Qimis), Begēmdir, Amhara, Lasta, Yejju, and Wello in the centre; and Gojjam and Shewa in the south. Not all of these were politically on the same level, nor were they geographically stable. Particularly in the central parts, rebellions and shifting alliances caused many districts to change hands or gain a certain amount of autonomy for a

15   ibid., pp. 469–70; see also pp. 472 and 477.
16   Crummey, *Priests*, pp. 15–26.
17   For a useful summary of this aspect, see Trimingham, *Islam*, pp. 100–14.

while, only to lose it again. In the contacts with foreign powers, and in the struggle for unification and survival, three units played decisive roles: Begēmdir (Amhara), Shewa, and Tigrē.[18]

Among the regional princes, the governor of Begēmdir claimed precedence. From his residence at Debre Tabor he ruled the central Amhara lands, and the imperial capital Gonder was within his territories. In the 1770s, a powerful Yejju, Ali Gwangwil, known as Ali the Great, had emerged as king-maker and guardian, and six members of his originally Muslim and allegedly Galla family or dynasty followed him as *ras*. In the name of the emperor, they controlled all higher appointments, at least in theory. But their position between the largely Galla and Muslim population of Wello and Yejju, and the Christians of Gojjam and the Lake Tana region in general, was not easy. Nevertheless Ras Gugsa (1803–25) undoubtedly represented the unity of the Ethiopian state, such as it was, more than anyone else during the first quarter of the century, and even after his death Debre Tabor remained the leading political centre.[19] According-ing to Arnauld d'Abbadie, Ras Ali (II) Alula made the claim in the late 1830s that he had replaced the king of kings.[20] In 1849 he concluded a treaty with Great Britain, and signed as 'Alī, Niguse Habisha', but there is strong reason to believe that this was done to satisfy Consul Plowden rather than anything else.[21] In Ethiopian tradition he is never called *nigus*.

The province which had reached the highest degree of autonomy was Shewa. It was virtually an independent kingdom, known to have been governed since about 1700 by a line of rulers who claimed to be of the Solomonic dynasty. Sahle Sillasē (1813–47), the contemporary of Gugsa and Ali, had unilaterally declared himself *nigus*. This did not necessarily imply any claim to the throne at Gonder, and was, it seems, tacitly accepted by Ali, though it was opposed by the Gonder clergy. All observers agree that Sahle Sillasē had much firmer control over his territory than any of the other rulers. Via Awsa and Tajura, with which he normally had good relations, he could also carry on foreign trade and other contacts with the outside world independently of Gonder. His attempts to assert his independence in ecclesiastical matters, however, led to a profound crisis, and finally his excommunication by the *abun*.[22]

18 Begēmdir and Amhara are used both as names for specific provinces and for the whole central, mainly Amharic-speaking area. Begēmdir has a clearer political connotation: the provinces controlled directly or indirectly from Debre Tabor. It does not include Simēn, which during the last decades of the *Zemene Mesafint* was united with Tigrē. I shall generally use the term Begēmdir, since the term Amhara invites further confusion. Also, Shewa and Tigrē were terms used both for smaller units and for the provinces or sub-kingdoms of which they were part. Unless otherwise stated, I am referring to the larger unit.
19 D'Abbadie, *Douze ans*, pp. 183–90; Lefebvre, *Voyage*, Vol. I, pp. 356–64; Vol. II, pp. 122–31; W. C. Plowden, *Travels in Abyssinia and the Galla Country* (London, 1868), p. 38.
20 D'Abbadie, *Douze ans*, p. 402. See also p. 506 about the ambitions of Birru Goshu from Gojjam in this respect.
21 FO 93/2/1. See below, pp. 130–1.
22 For Shewa during this period, see Abir, *Ethiopia*, pp. 144–82, and Crummey, *Priests*, pp. 46–55. Lefebvre (*Voyage*, Vol. III, pp. 216–17) provides a brief and very critical description of Sahle Sillasē's rule; Harris (*Highlands*, *passim*) is more balanced, and Rochet (*Voyage*, pp. 284–6, 363) is full of praise.

The ties between Gonder and the third major unit, Tigrē, were closer. The caravan routes from central Ethiopia to the coast passed through Tigrē, and this necessitated some co-operation. The governors of Tigrē were normally appointed or sought confirmation of their offices from Gonder. They also involved themselves to a much higher degree than the Shewan rulers in the political intrigues and civil wars that took place in central Ethiopia. In Tigrē itself there was much political unrest and petty warfare as the ambitions and pretensions of the heads of the ruling families from the various sub-provinces clashed—Shirē, the district of Adwa and Aksum (also known as Tigrē), Tembēn, Inderta, Agamē, and Hamasēn aligning and realigning in attempts to control the sub-kingdom. From the beginning of the century until 1816, Ras Welde Sillasē from Tembēn and Inderta kept some order, and the same can be said of Dejjazmach Sebagadis of Agamē from about 1822 to 1831. But in 1831 Sebagadis's neighbour across the Tekkezē, Dejjazmach Wibē of Simēn, allied himself with Ras Mariyyē of Begēmdir to crush Sebagadis. They succeeded, and Tigrē came under the rule of Wibē. Because of his severity, and probably also because he was not a Tigrean himself, Wibē was unpopular with the local nobility, and there were frequent rebellions when he had problems elsewhere. Nevertheless, Wibē held on to Tigrē until the end of the *Zemene Mesafint*.[23]

This was the condition of the Ethiopian state which was called upon to face the external interference and aggression of the nineteenth century. There was not much in the situation that promised concerted action to safeguard the continued existence of an Ethiopian state. A national identity, vague and intangible as that concept must needs be in the circumstances, undoubtedly existed. Something of this is revealed even in the negative observation, 'they still nourish the delusion that they are a nation . . .'[24] How strong or widespread the consciousness of this identity was at the time, we do not know. What we do know is that the institutions which had in the past represented the national unity—the Solomonic dynasty and the church—had lost much of their direction and their own internal unity.

Valentia's Contacts with Welde Sillasē: Strategy, Trade, or Assistance

On 24 May 1804, the herald of the new era, Sir George Annesley, Viscount Valentia, arrived at Massawa to explore trade prospects with Abyssinia.[25] He came from India, and the main objective of his travel was allegedly scientific: the collection of geographical and botanical information for publication. His journey was not undertaken on behalf of the British government, though he nourished private hopes that it would be of some importance in the great struggle between France and Britain.[26]

23 Abir, *Ethiopia*, pp. 31–7. Conditions and events in Tigrē in the first half of the century are described in great detail by many of the travellers, among others Salt, Pearce, Lefebvre, Ferret and Galinier; and also in numerous reports from consular agents and missionaries.
24 FO 401/1, p. 196, Plowden to Clarendon, 9 Jul. 1854.
25 Valentia, *Voyages*, Vol. II, pp. 4, 47.
26 See Mathew, *Ethiopia*, pp. 109–16, for a brief introduction to the 'earnest, obscure and eccentric nobleman' Lord Valentia, and his young secretary and draughtsman, Henry Salt.

That he had a keen eye for commercial opportunities is evident from his whole account. It was only after his arrival in India that he made the plans and enlisted the support of the governor general of India 'for a voyage to the Red Sea . . . for the purpose of investigating the eastern shore of Africa, and making the necessary inquiries into the present state of Abyssinia'. These inquiries now expressly included an investigation of commercial opportunities, as might be expected in an undertaking which received the blessing of the British government in India.[27]

At Massawa, Valentia was at first well received by Na'ib Idris, 'a most excellent character'. He found that the Porte no longer exercised any direct authority there. Power and income were shared between the *na'ib* and his two brothers, the *sirdar* of the garrison at Massawa and the *dawla* of Arkiko. In Valentia's view, the trade was considerable, though probably decreasing.[28]

When Valentia paid his third visit to Massawa in March 1805, he decided to send his secretary and draughtsman Henry Salt into the country to establish contact with the Ethiopian court. The circumstances are not very clear. Valentia stated that his contact at Massawa, an Indian merchant called Currum Chund who was associated with the business of the *na'ib*, had frequently mentioned to him that the ruler of the Tigrē province, Ras Welde Sillasē, was anxious to hear from him. In response Valentia gave him a message, asking him to put it on paper and send it to the *ras*.[29] Whether Welde Sillasē's interest was genuine, induced, or simply imagined by Currum Chund is difficult to say. Valentia had asked the latter in August the year before about the possibilities of entering Ethiopia through Massawa and Currum Chund had reportedly replied that 'he would be answerable that the Nayib should place any one in the King's presence at Gondar in perfect safety'. The cost for finding horses, mules, guards, etc. would amount to 400 thalers.[30] For Currum Chund this was probably just another business opportunity which needed some prompting. He must have known that the amount mentioned was only a fraction of what Valentia would have to pay to get through. Less than a year later Salt was asked 1,000 thalers, excluding transport costs, and actually paid 500 before he got transport even as far as the escarpment, i.e. two to three days' journey instead of the month or more it would take to reach Gonder.[31]

By March 1805 Valentia also knew that Idris and his brothers were not easy people to deal with. In January he had been asked for a cash gift of 200 thalers after he had presented the *na'ib* with gunpowder worth 500. The *dawla* as his share claimed 1,000 thalers in anchorage for Valentia's two ships. This was in addition to the duties which were, however, 'in general moderate'. Valentia's reply was that 'English ships of war never paid anchorage here or any where

27 Valentia, *Voyages*, Vol. II, pp. 4–5.
28 ibid., Vol. II, pp. 45–7, 95–6, 248–50.
29 ibid., Vol. II, p. 336. Valentia says nothing about the content of this message.
30 ibid., Vol. II, p. 96.
31 ibid., Vol. II, p. 451.

else' and that he would cross over and burn Arkīko to the ground in retaliation for the 'insult'.[32]

It is not surprising, therefore, that Valentia began to think in terms of removing the *na'ib* or, as an alternative, bypassing Massawa. He reported that Currum Chund 'now spoke less cautiously of the political situation of Massowah, and acknowledged that it lies at the mercy of the King of Abyssinia', who could impose his will by cutting off all supplies from the mainland. 'In fact,' Valentia continued, 'Massowah is only of importance from being the port of Abyssinia, and were the trade to be turned into any other channel, it would sink into insignificance.' His interest was focused mainly on the bay of Zulla just south of Massawa to which he gave his own name Annesley: 'The trade that comes down from Abyssinia might easily be brought to the bottom of the bay . . . The distance would be less . . . and the facilities of embarkation would be equally good.'[33]

In June 1805 Currum Chund brought with him to Mokha a letter reportedly from Welde Sillasē. According to Valentia, it contained an invitation for him or his deputy to come to Tigrē.[34] Later Welde Sillasē told Salt that his coming was due to a mistake by Currum Chund, but even if the latter had probably taken some liberties in the matter, it is quite clear that the *ras* agreed that the British come, for he made arrangements for their transport and escort almost all the way from Arkīko.[35] Valentia immediately wrote to Welde Sillasē to announce the coming of Henry Salt who soon after sailed for Massawa again.[36] He failed, however, to send any letter to the *na'ib* this time, and was informed of his mistake in no uncertain terms: 'Very well.—But my friend understand that I am the gate of Abyssinia and that no person either goes there or returns except through me.' The mission would be forwarded for friendship's sake, not because they had come in a big ship. He was not impressed by Salt and his companions at all. They were 'like children without understanding'.[37] Salt had clearly run into difficulties with the *na'ib*, and it was only after much wrangling about the sums to be paid and after threatening to enter Abyssinia at some other point along the coast that he received permission to proceed.[38]

On 20 July he left Arkīko with his companions and was met the following day by the first escort and mules sent by Welde Sillasē. Though Salt reports many rivalries and conflicts between chiefs and local governors along his way, his trip

---

32 ibid., Vol. II, pp. 240–7. Valentia made this visit in two small ships, which were put at his disposal for the survey of the Red Sea coast by the Bombay government.

33 ibid., Vol. II, pp. 336, 338.

34 ibid., Vol. II, p. 406. The letter is not preserved with Valentia's reply in BM, Add. 19343, where one would expect to find it.

35 Valentia, *Voyages*, Vol. II, pp. 475, 490–3; Vol. III, p. 56.

36 BM, Add. 19343. fol. 38. [Valentia] to Welde Sillasē, n.d. This is an Arabic draft without Valentia's name, but it is absolutely clear from its contents that it was the letter sent to introduce Salt.

37 ibid., fols 38–9, Idris to Valentia, n.d., rec. 4 Aug. 1805; Valentia, *Voyages*, Vol. II, pp. 407–11.

38 BM, Add. 19343, fols 5–9, Salt to Valentia, 30 Jul. 1805; Valentia, *Voyages*, Vol. II, pp. 443–50.

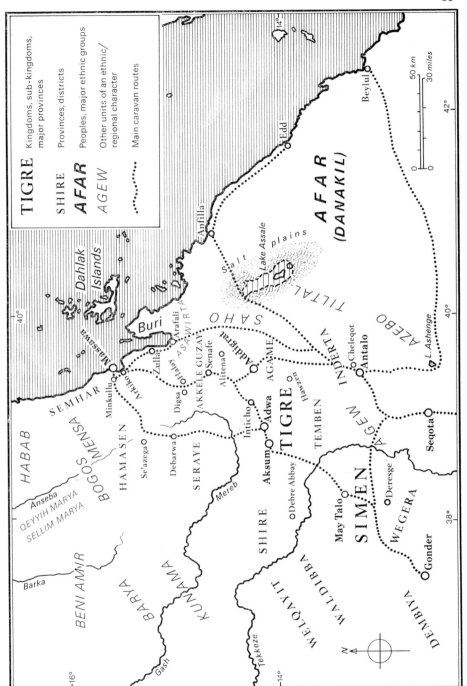

MAP 2 Tigrē and Simēn from Welde Sillasē to Wibē

39

went fairly smoothly and a little more than a month later, on 28 August 1805, he found himself at Antalo, Welde Sillasē's capital in southern Tigrē.[39]

Salt provided the *ras* with a copy of Valentia's letter, in case the original had been lost, and explained that the reason for his mission was 'an anxious desire to promote an intercourse of friendship between two such powerful countries as England and Abyssinia, the inhabitants of which were moreover of the same religion, and that if the Ras was inclined to form such a connection, to represent to him how much it might conduce to the interest of his country'. It would 'enable the Ras to supply himself at once with whatever commodities he might want' without paying excessive duties. According to Salt, the conversation turned to the question of the most convenient place for delivering the cargoes. Welde Sillasē did not share Salt's fear that the *na'ib* would be a serious obstacle, but when Salt suggested distant Beylul on the grounds that it was close to the capital of the *ras* (!), the latter offered to turn the trade to the Burī peninsula which belonged to him and which was in fact closer to Antalo than Massawa.[40] Salt's attempt to have one of his companions survey the road to Burī was, however, frustrated by Welde Sillasē.[41]

At a number of interviews Salt tried to pursue the matters further but with little success. There were problems about interpreters, intrigues, and suspicion. Salt did not trust the interpreter he had received, a merchant called Hajj Hammad, and accused him before the *ras*, who told Salt that the latter's agent in arranging the visit, Currum Chund, had 'been playing tricks' and had even written to tell the *ras* to beware of Salt and his party 'as dangerous persons'. Salt reports that Welde Sillasē repeatedly asked about his motives for coming to Ethiopia. At one point it was agreed that Salt should explain everything in writing, but if he did so he has not published this document in his account of the mission.[42] Salt continued to stress the economic benefits of an association with England, promising that all imports would be supplied at 50 per cent of the prevailing prices.[43] Even if the prices of the goods according to Valentia were more than doubled because of duties at both Mokha and Massawa and because of the high profits of the Indian merchants,[44] Salt cannot have seriously believed that British control of the trade would mean what he said to Welde Sillasē.

Probably Salt was less effective in explaining the commercial advantages to the *ras* than to the British public. Valentia's letter of introduction to Welde Sillasē had said nothing about trade. It contained strong expressions of friendship and an offer to provide Welde Sillasē with whatever assistance he might need, but the real message was a strong appeal to the *ras* to protect Salt and his companions and arrange for them to see the Emperor as quickly as possible.[45]

39 Valentia, *Voyages*, Vol. II, pp. 469–510; Vol. III, pp. 1–36.
40 ibid., Vol. III, pp. 38–40.
41 ibid., Vol. III, pp. 57, 114–17.
42 ibid., Vol. III, pp. 52–6, 62–4, 138–40.
43 ibid., Vol. III, p. 141.
44 ibid., Vol. III, p. 267; FO 1/1, fols 4–12, Valentia, 13 Sep. 1808, 'Observations on the Trade of the Red Sea'.
45 BM, Add. 19343, fol. 38, [Valentia] to Welde Sillasē, n.d.

This was an idea with which Welde Sillasē heartily disagreed. Salt had to give up all ideas of penetrating to the court at Gonder. The reigning Emperor, Gwalu or Igwale Ṣiyon, was not Welde Sillasē's choice for the throne. It was his chief opponent, Ras Gugsa, who had placed him there.[46]

Finally Welde Sillasē's commercial agent, Basha Abdallah at Adwa, who according to Salt was the head of all the Muslims in Tigrē and a very influential person, managed to bring about some kind of understanding. Letters and presents were prepared and on 10 October 1805 Salt started for the coast again.[47] As a substitute for an audience and a genuine letter from the Emperor to the King of England, Salt carried a letter written at Antalo in the name of the Emperor, but certainly without his knowledge.[48] This Valentia presented to the British government to be laid before the King as a letter from the Emperor, and in January 1807 he was received in audience by George III in recognition of the importance of his mission.[49] In his published account Valentia only mentioned that the letter contained a request by the Emperor for 'a person . . . who understood raising water, a medical man and a carpenter'.[50] In the discussions with the Foreign Office about a reply, Valentia reported that the Emperor in his letter had expressed the hope that George III would assist him in bringing peace to Ethiopia which was torn by rebellions, and further that British ships would 'trade direct with him without going to Mocha or Massowah'. Finally there was the request for a doctor, a carpenter, and a person 'who could raise water and carry it from one place to another'.[51] The request for someone who could construct a pump and an aqueduct sounds very genuine, and Valentia also mentioned that Welde Sillasē in another letter had promised to provide 'an ample allowance of villages' to support the three experts.[52]

The commercial programme on the other hand echoes Valentia's and Salt's own hopes and plans, and it is very likely that the request for military aid, *if actually made*, was no more than the accepted offer of assistance in the import of

---

46   Valentia, *Voyages*, Vol. III, pp. 41–4.
47   ibid., Vol. III, pp. 138–41, 150–4, 176.
48   ibid., Vol. III, pp. 154, 276. Note that Salt in this account calls it a letter 'delivered . . . by the Ras from his Sovereign' and Valentia 'The letter . . . for the King of Great Britain from the Emperor of Abyssinia', but in Salt's own book later it is a letter which the *ras* had sent 'in the name of the Emperor' (Salt, *Voyage*, p. 148). But when Lord Valentia felt he needed all the prestige the letter could give him, he spoke about Welde Sillasē as the 'Prime Minister of Abyssinia' and, probably in an attempt to confuse the Foreign Office, said that the letter was brought to Massawa by the 'Baharnegash or governor of Dixana' (FO 1/1, fol. 9, Valentia, 13 Sep. 1808). In the end the foreign secretary believed that it had come 'from the capital of Gonder' (FO 1/1, fols 49–50, Canning to Valentia, 6 Jan. 1809).
49   FO 1/1, fol. 3, Foreign Office minute, 13 Sep. 1808; fols 18–19, Valentia [to Canning], 20 Oct. 1808.
50   Valentia, *Voyages*, Vol. III, p. 276.
51   FO 1/1, fols 18–19, Valentia, 20 Oct. 1808.
52   ibid. One of the reasons why Welde Sillasē wanted to keep Pearce in the country was, according to Salt, that he could paint drawings for churches (Valentia, *Voyages*, Vol. III, p. 145).

firearms.[53] In a memorandum to the Foreign Office, Valentia stated that the assistance asked for by Ras Welde Sillasē was 'a supply of arms and ammunition', to which he added on his own responsibility 'a few pieces of light cannon and a few artillery men'.[54] But it is not clear at all that it was the Ethiopians who initiated the requests for arms. According to Pearce, writing from Adwa in 1809, the country was 'well-stocked' with firearms, 8,900 in Tigrē and a little over 1,000 in the Amhara provinces where, in Pearce's words, 'they are not fond of musquets'. The price had fallen from 60–70 thalers for a matchlock two years earlier to 30–45 thalers. This sounds more as if Pearce was warning Salt not to bring any arms than the opposite. A hint that the *ras* would like a double-barrelled gun cannot seriously be regarded as a request for firearms from a ruler with 8,900 already in his territory. And what Welde Sillasē 'particularly' wanted was 'a large looking-glass for his church'.[55]

On his arrival in London in 1806 Valentia had tried to win the support of the East India Company for his great plans to increase British trade in the Red Sea. There can be no doubt about Valentia's genuine interest in these commercial plans. He had, with the assistance of Salt, collected a considerable amount of valuable, though not always consistent, data on the trade: products, volume, prices, duties, profit margins, etc.[56] He made specific proposals. The island of Desē (which he called Valentia) might be purchased from the *na'ib* for a nominal sum and turned into a depot from which goods could be landed at Zulla without any duties being paid to the *na'ib*. If the latter co-operated, he would prevent 'the immediate ruin of Massowah as an independent state' but, as Valentia observed, 'its power is merely artificial, and depends only on the troops it is able to maintain, by the revenues arising from trade . . . and it will soon either become a barren sand, or sink again into the empire of Abyssinia'.[57] If the *na'ib* refused, this was no problem. An incident which had taken place at Valentia's last visit to Massawa was sufficient justification for taking the island from him against his will if necessary.[58]

Nevertheless, Valentia seems to have felt the need to justify his interest in the Red Sea trade by referring to other and higher motives than commercial profits. He stressed how the Abyssinians were exploited by the Indian merchants and the Muslim authorities at Mokha and Massawa, who raised the prices for

53 I have not been able to find the original letter referred to at the Public Record Office, the India Office Library, or the Royal Archives at Windsor Castle. It is, however, referred to in a letter to George III, published in A. Aspinall, ed., *The Later Correspondence of George III* (Cambridge, 1962–70), Vol. V, p. 161, as well as in King George's reply, of which a draft in Latin, dated December 1808, is preserved in IO, Home Miscellaneous Series, 456E.

54 FO 1/1, fol. 10, Valentia, 13 Sep. 1808. The passage about arms is clearly connected with Valentia's concern about forestalling the French by gaining an ally in Ethiopia.

55 BM, Add. 19347, fols 67–74, Pearce to Salt, 10 Jun. 1809. Though Pearce's figures may not be correct, the message seems clear to me. This does not exclude the possibility that Welde Sillasē had verbally asked Salt for arms in 1805, particularly if he hoped to get them as a gift, but it does indicate that he had no need for European contacts in order to obtain arms.

56 Valentia, *Voyages*, Vol. III, pp. 266–9; FO 1/1, fols 4–12, Valentia, 13 Sep. 1808.

57 Valentia, *Voyages*, Vol. III, p. 262.

58 ibid., Vol. III, pp. 296–8; FO 1/1, fol. 10, Valentia, 13 Sep. 1808.

Ethiopian consumers by an unnecessary 120 per cent.[59] He instructed Salt to draw a historical sketch of Abyssinia to be included in his book. Salt gave credit to the Ethiopians for having in the past 'resisted the open and formidable attacks of the Mahomedans, but likewise the more insidious attacks of the Romish church'. But he continued, 'At the present moment, however, the nation, with its religion is fast verging to ruin, the Galla and the Mussulmaun tribes around are daily becoming more powerful; and there is reason to fear that, in a short time, the very name of Christ may be lost among them.' In this situation Salt advocated that some of the interest and expenses directed towards the conversion of pagans should rather be channelled into a mission to save Christian Ethiopia and concluded, '. . . I am fully persuaded that there is no part of the world where European influence might be exerted with more beneficial effects than in Abyssinia'.[60]

As for the right to interfere, this was at the time an article of faith. Lord Valentia closed the memorandum in which he advocated 'gunboat diplomacy', a British trade monopoly, and profit margins of up to 400 per cent with the following grand statement: 'I have only to add that this may be done without the violation of one principle of right, and not only without loss, but with an incalculable profit.'[61]

Salt and Valentia did not, however, regard Ethiopia's Muslim neighbours as the real problem or danger to Ethiopia. This emerges quite clearly from their discussions about Massawa and other outlets on the coast. The all-important consideration was what European influences were to be exerted in the Middle East generally:

> The crescent of Mohammed no longer, indeed, forebodes danger to Christianity, but the equally terrible eagles of regenerated France threaten universal destruction to ancient establishments; and it is apparent, that their formidable master has more particularly formed his plans against the eastern Empire of England. It was for the fartherance of this object that Egypt was conquered; and it is a continuation . . . to cultivate the friendship of the Arab powers. Abyssinia is of infinitely more importance than these; but fortunately, France knew not that Abyssinia was accessible.

Valentia stressed that he came first, and so England had the opportunity of establishing relations with Abyssinia, 'which will for ever shut out the French; but if we should neglect the opportunity, they will profit by our folly . . .'[62]

Salt's Second Visit

When the East India Company in London showed no interest in Valentia's schemes, he sought out a private firm, Messrs W. and J. Jacob, who were willing to send a ship to Massawa. By stressing how disagreeable it would be if a British

59 FO 1/1, fol. 8, Valentia, 13 Sep. 1808.
60 Valentia, *Voyages*, Vol. III, pp. 256–8.
61 FO 1/1, fol. 12, Valentia, 13 Sep. 1808.
62 Valentia, *Voyages*, Vol. III, pp. 263–4.

ship visited Abyssinia without bringing a reply, Valentia secured an answer from King George to the letter from 'the King of Abyssinia'.[63] He selected Salt to carry the letter, drew up the list of royal presents and was consulted on the form and content of the letter as well as Salt's instructions.[64]

The instructions contained two important points. The envoy should use 'his utmost exertion to reach the court of Gonder and deliver His Majesty's Letters and Presents to the Emperor of Abyssinia in Person'. Likewise he should 'use his utmost exertion to ascertain the present state of the Abyssinian Trade, the Quantity, Quality and Value of the Emperor's Goods imported', etc. Salt should stress 'the desire of His Majesty to comply with the wishes of the Emperor to open a Trade between Abyssinia and His Majesty's Territories whether in India or in Europe' and the advantages of fixed customs duties to be paid on the landing of the goods only.[65]

The gifts were considerable, amounting to almost £2,000 worth of goods, including two light cannon and other arms and ammunition. The request for a doctor, a carpenter, and a man 'to raise water' was ignored and Valentia's attempts to get a few artillerymen to serve, or at least demonstrate, the cannon also failed.[66] The attitude with regard to craftsmen is somewhat puzzling. Pearce had written in 1806 that Welde Sillasē wanted carpenters and smiths.[67]

When Salt reached the Red Sea towards the end of 1809, he soon discovered that his earlier visit with Valentia had not been without consequences. But instead of facilitating the trade with Ethiopia, it had aggravated the situation. The *sharif* of Mecca had decided once again to send a representative of the Ottoman government to Massawa. Na'ib Idris and this new Turkish governor had written to the chieftains of the Dankali tribes around Anfilla and asked them to stop all transactions with the *ferenj* and their representative, a Somali trader named Yunus Bahralli. The Massawa authorities advised the chiefs to kill any person who arrived with goods belonging to the *ferenj* and divide the goods between themselves. Later Yunus had died under suspicious circumstances and Idris had sent two armed dows to Anfilla to seize his boat.[68] Since the main caravan route from Edd to northern Ethiopia followed the coast as far as Anfilla Bay it meant that communications from Edd would also be cut.[69]

Salt found, however, that Dankali chiefs as far north as the Burī peninsula were prepared to disregard the instructions of the *na'ib*. When he told them that he wanted a caravan for the interior from Anfilla Bay, it became evident that

63 FO 1/1, fols. 2, 26–27, Valentia [to Canning], 13 Sep. and 23 Nov. 1808.
64 ibid., fols 15–17, 26–7, 42–3, Valentia [to Canning], 2 Oct. and 23 Nov. 1808, 4 Jan. 1809.
65 ibid., fols 51–2, memorandum signed by Valentia and delivered to Salt 16 Jan. 1809. In his first draft Valentia had expressed the Emperor's desire for a 'free and direct trade' but the India Office decided that the Emperor had better not be specific about that (ibid., fols 35–8, draft of memorandum by Valentia, n.d.; fols 40–1, Dundas to Canning, 3 Jan. 1809).
66 ibid., fol. 10, Valentia, 13 Sep. 1808; fols 28–9, Valentia [to Canning], 14 Dec. 1808; fol. 30, Neville to Hammond, 15 Dec. 1808; fol. 57, Treasury to Hammond, 16 May 1809.
67 BM, Add. 19347, fols 11–14, Pearce to Valentia, 28 Feb. 1806.
68 FO 1/1, fol. 110, Idris and Uthman to the chieftains around Anfilla, n.d. (beginning of November 1809); fol. 112, Rudland to Salt, 20 Jan. 1810; fols 78–97, Salt to Smith, 4 Mar. 1811; Salt, *Voyage*, pp. 138–42.
69 Salt, *Voyage*, p. 139.

they were much more concerned about the possible implications of a clash between Welde Sillasē and his vassal Sebagadis. Above all they were displeased with Salt's earlier companion Pearce, who had recently made a visit to the coast to take up merchandise to the interior. According to the spokesman of the chiefs, Ali Goveta, Pearce had not delivered the promised gifts and had done him 'great mischief with the Ras'.[70] Pearce's version was somewhat different. He had regarded the demands for presents as unreasonable and had become so angry that he had shot the friend of one of the chiefs and barely escaped being killed. There is no question about the fact that 'gate-money' was extorted in various ways from merchants and other travellers. Pearce, however, contradicted himself by first telling Salt how he was gradually plundered and then bragging about the astonishment of the chiefs at Welde Sillasē's court over the amount of goods he had managed to get through. These he sold at a handsome profit and was rewarded in addition with a house and a piece of land from the brother of the *ras*.[71] Pearce's recklessness or at least unwillingness to accept customary procedures on the coast was, however, allowed to pass as a personal case. Salt had no problems communicating with Antalo from Anfilla, even though Pearce was reluctant to come to Anfilla to meet him.

Salt was very uncertain about what route to choose, but finally decided in favour of Massawa, largely because the Turkish governor, but not the *na'ib*, had been replaced by a more conciliatory person. He informed Welde Sillasē by sending up his companion William Coffin with a letter to Pearce, and when he arrived at Massawa, on 10 February 1810, an Ethiopian chief and Pearce were already there to escort him to the *ras*.[72] Though the authorities at Massawa were, understandably, anxious that as little trade as possible should evade them and therefore tried to bully the chiefs along the coast, it is evident that they had no power to prevent Welde Sillasē from making contact. In his report to the Foreign Office, Salt put down his success in entering Abyssinia through Massawa to 'a salutary terror of English resentment'.[73] Equally or more important was, no doubt, the fear of offending the ruler of Tigrē, who according to Salt had answered an attempt to detain some goods shortly before by a laconic: 'Send up the goods, or in a few days I will be with you', a threat which caused 'considerable alarm'.[74] There are many indications that the *na'ib*, at least, was more sensitive to pressures from the interior than from the sea and even moderated the imposts or duties rather than risk a conflict with his immediate neighbours.[75]

Salt expressed surprise that the Turkish governor made no attempt to prevent his taking the two cannon into the country. In return for suitable private presents, all the royal presents were exempted from duties, and low rates for the

70 ibid., pp. 144–9, 304.
71 FO 1/1, fol. 123, Pearce to Salt, 29 Dec. 1809; Salt, *Voyage*, pp. 314–20. See also BM, Add. 19347, fols 89–90, Pearce to Rudland, 10 Oct. 1809.
72 FO 1/1, fols 84–6, Salt, 4 Mar. 1811.
73 ibid., fol. 88, Salt, 4 Mar. 1811.
74 Salt, *Voyage*, p. 147.
75 See Valentia, *Voyages*, Vol. III, p. 261 and *passim*.

commercial goods as well as for anchorage were also arranged.[76] On 15 (or 16) March 1810 Salt received a hearty welcome at Welde Sillasē's court but was informed that there would be no journey to Gonder unless he was prepared to wait until after the rains (about seven months) and then accompany the *ras* himself on a planned campaign against Gugsa. Therefore Salt, with seeming indifference, handed over all the presents intended for the Emperor to the *ras*. There was a picture of the Virgin Mary, a beautiful marble table and a painted glass window for a church, gifts which caused much admiration. There were also the cannon.[77]

Having failed in his first task by not reaching the Emperor's court, Salt turned to the question of commercial opportunities for England in Ethiopia. He reported that Welde Sillasē always declared how anxious he was to maintain friendly relations with Great Britain and how strongly he desired to 'promote by every means in his power a commercial connection between Abyssinia and England, or India'. It was also Welde Sillasē who according to Salt pointed out the main difficulties: the unsettled state of the country which prevented the circulation of gold and other valuable articles, the ignorance and lack of interest in commercial transactions shown by the Christian Ethiopians, and finally the futility of Ethiopia's occupying the coast even if it could easily be done, as long as the Muslims controlled the islands and the sea. The latter course might actually leave Ethiopia worse off than before. Salt reported that he found the arguments unanswerable and had no instructions to propose a solution.[78] This seeming consensus that nothing could be done was, if we are to believe Salt, not reached without some argument. Salt had urged Welde Sillasē to do something about the political and administrative conditions in the country, and to occupy the coast or some point on the coast now that he had received arms and the moral support of the British. According to Salt, Welde Sillasē had told him not to worry about conditions on land but about the Turkish control of Massawa: 'Let the English take Massowa, however, and the command of the sea with their ships and I will take care all should be well regulated on shore.'[79] This may well have been too strong an expression of Welde Sillasē's views. Pearce reported his policy as: '. . . the English must settle Business with the Naybe by water and he [Welde Sillasē] will protect their goods by land'.[80]

On 30 April Salt was furnished with a letter in Gi'iz from Welde Sillasē to the King of England. This he delivered to the Foreign Office on his arrival in

76   Salt, *Voyage*, pp. 206–7, 214–15; FO 1/1, fol. 87, Salt, 4 Mar. 1811. The presents or bribes were not excessive: 200 thalers each for the Turkish governor and the *na'ib* were the two major posts (FO 1/1, fols 158–67, Salt's accounts).
77   FO 1/1, fols 89–90, Salt, 4 Mar. 1811; Salt, *Voyage*, pp. 261–6. Immediately on his arrival on the coast, Salt had asked the *ras* and Pearce to arrange for his onward journey to Gonder (FO 1/1, fol. 102, Salt to Welde Sillasē, 14 Oct. 1809; fols 104–7, Salt to Pearce, 13 Oct. 1809). Pearce had told him at Massawa that he would not be allowed to go to Gonder because of the enmity between Welde Sillasē and Gugsa, and Salt does not seem to have pressed for permission (Salt, *Voyage*, p. 265).
78   FO 1/1, fols 90–1, Salt, 4 Mar. 1811; Salt, *Voyage*, pp. 383–4.
79   FO 1/1, fols 200–2, Salt, 'Extract from original observations, April 1810'.
80   BM, Add. 19347, fols 89–90, Pearce to Rudland, 10 Oct. 1809.

London.[81] It was translated by a scholar in Scotland, Dr Alexander Murray, whom Salt recommended for the task as someone with 'a perfect knowledge' of the language.[82] The result turned out to be embarrassing for Salt. Welde Sillasē thanked George III for the presents *he* had received, declared that Salt did not go to Gonder because the King there was unorthodox and implied that he hoped to use some of the gifts of the King of England to fight the guardian of his own sovereign.[83]

Salt produced a memorandum of the contents of the letter, made at Antalo immediately after the letter had been explained to him with Pearce as interpreter. According to this, Welde Sillasē acknowledged the presents 'as received in trust' and declared that he could not permit Salt to go to Gonder because he was at war with Ras Gugsa.[84] Salt gave further explanations, stating that Welde Sillasē had assured him that he intended to maintain and strengthen Gwalu on the throne on condition that he would return to the true faith which seemed extremely likely. As for the presents, those 'designed for the King' had been delivered to Welde Sillasē *in trust*. The simplest explanation was that Dr Murray had made a mistake in the translation, but shifting his ground with the utmost ease, Salt continued: '. . . even if I had entertained doubts of his sincerity . . . what other mode of proceeding could I have adopted? The political situation of the Country was clearly stated by me long before I left England, and I never conceived, unless the situation of affairs should have materially altered that I could have communication with any other person than the Ras . . .'[85]

In his published narrative, Salt even advocated the setting up of a separate Tigrean kingdom under 'a branch of the royal family . . . on the throne at Axum', and a few years later he welcomed the news that Welde Sillasē had established the deposed Emperor, Tekle Gīyorgīs, on the throne at Aksum 'and thus one of the great objects that we have looked to is accomplished'.[86] Thus he was either quite insincere when he accepted his instructions or had rationalized his failure to reach Gonder. But the foreign secretary had been changed in the meantime, and although it took time, Salt was ultimately rewarded for

---

81 FO 1/1, fol. 71, Salt to Smith, n.d., (rec. 25 Feb. 1811); fol. 73, Welde Sillasē to George III, n.d. For the date of Welde Sillasē's letter, see FO 1/1, fol. 91, Salt, 4 Mar. 1811, and Salt, *Voyage*, pp. 365–76. Salt has mixed up his dates badly. In the Foreign Office report he gives 29 April as the date when he received the letter. In his published narrative, however, which is much more detailed, Salt describes the last day of Lent under 25 April, followed by Easter Day and the audience on *27 April* during which the letter was handed over. This is impossible since it makes Easter Day fall on a Thursday. The correct date for Ethiopian Easter that year was 29 April which leads to 30 April for the audience.

82 FO 1/1, fol. 71, Salt to Smith, n.d.

83 ibid., fol. 73, Welde Sillasē to George III, n.d.; for translation, see fols 155–6.

84 ibid., fol. 186, Salt, memorandum, 29 Apr. 1810 (*sic*).

85 ibid., fols 180–5, Salt to Smith, 2 Apr. 1811. As soon as Salt saw the translation, he wrote to Murray and asked him to revise it. This Murray did but not in time for Salt to have it when he was called upon to explain the matter. The revision, in fact, did not change the important statements. Nevertheless, Salt later showed it to Smith in the hope, presumably, that Murray's own opinions about conditions in Ethiopia would support his case. See J. J. Halls, *The Life and Correspondence of Henry Salt* (London, 1834), Vol. I, pp. 246–60.

86 Salt, *Voyage*, p. 496; Halls, *Salt*, Vol. I, p. 437, Salt to Valentia, 26 Jan. 1816.

having acted 'with great Diligence and Zeal'.[87] He received £2,000 which brought the cost of his mission to about £7,000,[88] and in 1815 he was appointed British consul general in Egypt. In addition to Pearce, a second Englishman, William Coffin, remained behind in Ethiopia but there were no serious attempts to develop closer relations for fifteen years.

Salt's visits to Tigrē in 1805 and 1810 and his negotiations there are significant in several ways. Many of the issues and problems that would plague Ethiopia's relations with the outside world throughout the century are discernible in these first contacts.

On the European side the main underlying motive is fairly clear and not surprising: the promotion of trade with as high profits as possible and, preferably, no engagements. If this called for the unification and pacification of Ethiopia and the elimination of all Turkish influence on the coast, it was the obvious duty of the 'Prime Minister' of Ethiopia, Ras Welde Sillasē, to do something about it. Nowhere is this more clearly stated than in Salt's 'original observations', where he expressed the conviction that Welde Sillasē could subdue the *na'ib* whenever he liked, and continued: 'Should this be effected and Massowah or some Island on the coast be *put into the hands of the English* . . .'[89]

The strategic aspects were secondary in the sense that they were ultimately caused by concern for the commercial empire of India. Here the rivalry between France and Great Britain initiated the development and would play a dominant role throughout the century. The third of the driving forces in the opening up and eventual partition of Africa, the humanitarian or missionary motive, was expressed in the stereotyped phrase that 'legal trade . . . would also have the very important effect of putting an end to the exportation of slaves' and as a very general call for assistance to the Orthodox church in the country in its contest with Islam. As a concrete step Valentia and Salt advocated support in the question of obtaining a new *abun* or bishop from Egypt, 'going out under British protection'.[90] Of greater significance for future European missionary activity were the contacts and co-operation which developed between the first travellers to Ethiopia and the British and Foreign Bible Society.[91]

It should be remembered, however, that Lord Valentia's standing with the British government left much to be desired, and neither the government nor the India Office Board was more than lukewarm about the whole Abyssinian scheme. It is therefore quite understandable that Valentia and Salt attempted to generate interest and remove eventual objections by presenting as much of their plans as possible in the form of initiatives and requests from the Ethiopian rulers. This was to become almost a standard feature of European–Ethiopian relations for decades to come.

87   FO 1/1, fol. 217, Wellesley to Canning, 18 Feb. 1812.
88   ibid., fol. 225, memorandum, 9 Apr. 1812.
89   ibid., fol. 200, Salt, April 1810 (my emphasis).
90   Valentia, *Voyages*, Vol. III, pp. 256–7, 266. Abune Yosab died in 1803 and his successor Merqorēwos in 1808 after a few months in the country, and therefore the problem was acute at both of Salt's visits. See Valentia, *Voyages*, Vol. II, p. 96; Salt, *Voyage*, p. 218; Weld Blundell, *Chronicle*, pp. 474, 476.
91   See below, p. 55.

Welde Sillasē's Letter to George III: His Priorities

As we have seen, there are some indications in Salt's reports that Welde Sillasē had views of his own. There is, however, only one document that can be regarded as an authentic expression of the Ethiopian point of view. It came at the end of the negotiations when Salt's arguments had made their impact. Nevertheless, Welde Sillasē's letter in Gi'iz to George III was composed by the *ras* and his scribes, not by Salt and Pearce, and therefore merits a more careful analysis.

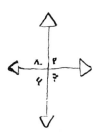

Having first thanked George III for what he had so generously given to him (with *no* mention of his own sovereign), Welde Sillasē explained that Salt did not go to the King because 'there is no king orthodox in the faith', a state of affairs which had made it necessary for Welde Sillasē to turn against Ras Gugsa who had proclaimed an unorthodox person King. He returned to the presents pointing out that there were gifts for the church as well as others of a secular nature by

which he might gain the victory over his enemies. He stressed that he was surrounded by pagans (*aremī*, which here obviously includes Muslims) on all sides,
including the coast, and thanked George III for the opportunities of communication provided by the presence of British ships in the Red Sea. After this he
explained his faith in the two births of Christ and accused his opponents of
trying to make him abandon this faith, though it was in accordance with the
Scriptures, in favour of the doctrine of three births. This was 'the important
matter'. The letter ended with a request—the only one—that George III
arrange for the travel of the new *abun* to Tigrē.[92]

One of the most striking features of this document is the absence of any reference to trade. After all, Welde Sillasē had in his letter of 1805 *supposedly* expressed his hope that British ships would trade directly with him, and in Salt's
instructions, and possibly also in the reply of George III, the prospects of trade
were stressed.[93] Further, in spite of the expressed appreciation of an English
ship to facilitate communications, the Muslims on the coast are not singled out
as any greater problem than other 'pagans' surrounding the country. There is
no request that the British occupy Massawa, still less any indication that Welde
Sillasē thought of doing it.

It is quite obvious that Welde Sillasē did not want to disturb the relatively
peaceful coexistence between his people, the coastal tribes and the Turkish
authorities at Massawa. He was aware of the interdependence, and as the
strongest party in the triangle, he saw no reason for fundamental changes.
Occasional disputes did not prevent the flow of trade, whether arms or other
merchandise, in which Welde Sillasē and the other Ethiopian rulers and their
commercial agents were interested. Missions to Egypt to maintain contact with
the Coptic patriarch and bring new bishops to Ethiopia were able to travel.
They, as other travellers, were sometimes subjected to extortion or used for the
purpose of extortion,[94] but the request of Welde Sillasē for assistance with the
journey of a bishop from Egypt is not sufficient to prove that the Ethiopians
really felt that their oldest and institutionally most important foreign contact
was endangered. To the extent that a British occupation of Massawa and the
other islands off the coast was discussed at all, it is, therefore, only natural that
Welde Sillasē would reply along the lines reported by Pearce and Salt, namely,
that it was entirely up to the British themselves.

There does not seem to have been much thought about international boundaries in the Ethiopian state of the early nineteenth century. This is in itself not
very remarkable since the country was surrounded by more or less semi-
dependent tribes or peoples with less political and military organization than
Ethiopia. The frontier of importance was the Red Sea coast, and it is here that

---

92 FO 1/1, fol. 73, Welde Sillasē to George III, n.d., Gi'iz original. The English translation
    (fols 155–6) is almost literal, and barely comprehensible in some passages.
93 ibid., fols 18–19, Valentia [to Canning], 20 Oct. 1808; IO, Home Misc. 456E, George III to
    Gwalu, Dec. 1808: '. . . and lead to the innumerable and immense benefits of a great and
    lasting intercourse (or trade—*lati et perpetui commercii*)'. See also above, pp. 44, 46.
94 Weld Blundell, *Chronicle*, p. 476; [Pearce], *Life*, Vol. II, pp. 54–5. In the second of these
    two cases, Pearce mentions that the *na'ib* demanded 500 thalers 'as a standing or original
    custom on the passage of the patriarch through his dominions'.

Salt's two visits throw some light on the situation before the relative equilibrium was disturbed. Though the effects of Salt's own visits were transient and should not be exaggerated, they reveal the problem which the Ethiopian state would soon have to face as one of the main aspects of its struggle for survival: either tighten the control over the coastal tribes or give them up entirely.

There was no question locally about the sovereignty over Midre Bahir, 'the land on the sea'.[95] This ancient Ethiopian province had for at least one century before Salt's arrival been ruled as one or several sub-provinces of Tigrē.[96] But Midre Bahir included both highlands and lowlands, and the escarpment, about 40–80 kilometres distant from the coastline from Massawa to Arafalī, was not only a topographical boundary. The tribes of the coastal strip were normally more dependent on the *na'ib* of Arkīko than on the chiefs of the plateau. On the main caravan route, for instance, the Taranta pass up to Digsa was looked upon as a kind of boundary.[97] But the effect of this was counter-balanced by the fact that the *na'ib* himself had been for so long a dependent more of the *ras* of Tigrē than of his nominal overlord, the Turkish governor of Hijaz. The former claimed the allegiance of the chiefs of the Asawirṭa and Dana-kil farther south along the coast but did not enforce it. Though Welde Sillasē felt entirely capable of protecting the trade, he could not, as he reportedly told Salt, see much purpose in possessing a barren coast which his people were averse even to visit.[98] That this attitude prevailed as long as it did is one of the factors that endangered the survival of all Ethiopia as an independent state.

At the time of Salt's visits, it was mainly the internal, political struggles with their religious overtones that interested the feudal lords of Ethiopia.[99] Salt minimized this matter as something 'subjoined' to the main topics in Welde Sillasē's letter,[100] but there can be no doubt that the overriding concern of the *ras* of Tigrē was the internal conflict in which the banner flown was that of the purest form of Orthodoxy. In the years following Salt's second visit, Welde Sillasē addressed several letters to him. Nowhere in these is there any reference to agreements about trade, assistance, or foreign affairs of any kind.[101]

Since the first contacts were entirely a European initiative, it is natural that not only the content of the negotiations but also the approach and forms were mainly decided by the European party. That the negotiations took place in Ethiopia gave Salt the advantage of being able to observe the political situation and assess his opponent in the negotiations in relation to his environment, while Welde Sillasē had only Salt's words and personal conduct to go on. It also gave

95   Valentia, *Voyages*, Vol. III, p. 155 and *passim*.
96   Longrigg, *Eritrea*, pp. 76–81.
97   Valentia, *Voyages*, Vol. II, p. 489; Vol. III, pp. 236–7; FO 1/1, fol. 10, Valentia, 13 Sep. 1808.
98   FO 1/1, fol. 91, Salt, 4 Mar. 1811.
99   See above, pp. 34–6.
100   FO 1/1, fol. 186, Salt, 29 Apr. 1810 (*sic*).
101   BM, Add. 19343, fols 1–4, 17. Three of these letters are sealed with Welde Sillasē's seal and there is no reason to suspect that the other two are not genuine. They all contain greetings and some news from Abyssinia about the locust plague and a smallpox epidemic. See also Halls, *Salt*, Vol. I, pp. 305–6, 317–18, 350–3, 381.

Valentia and Salt the opportunity, which they used, of presenting the Ethiopian case to their government in the light best suited to their own personal aims or ambitions. The stress on Welde Sillasē's position as 'the Ras' and 'the Prime Minister' of Ethiopia, although there were half-a-dozen *rases* and the same number of emperors at the time,[102] was due more to wishful thinking and a desire to impress Whitehall than to ignorance of the Ethiopian political scene.

Communication Problems and Their Consequences

Welde Sillasē no doubt had difficulties in placing Valentia and Salt. Valentia's letter of introduction for Salt and his companions was not very enlightening: one of them was called 'head of the police of England', but Salt's own position was not mentioned. Moreover, what did they really want in Ethiopia?[103] When he arrived the second time, Salt carried impressive gifts, which spoke for themselves, but his formal credentials were a letter in Latin directed to Gwalu, the puppet Emperor of Ras Gugsa in Gonder. Salt must have provided a translation as well, but what it contained is uncertain.[104] Welde Sillasē had to struggle with more fundamental questions than the credentials of the envoy, problems caused partly by the intrigues of Europeans against each other. Pearce reported to Salt that a Greek named 'Nus'r Alli' had caused much trouble by telling Welde Sillasē that 'England was a petty state under the rule of the Turks' and that the goods brought in were actually manufactured by the Greeks.[105] There is reason to suspect that Salt was not as successful as he thought in dispelling such misconceptions and informing the *ras* of the position of Great Britain in the world. In the end Welde Sillasē addressed George III as 'King of Kings . . . Leader of the Kings of the peoples of India' with no mention of England or Great Britain.[106]

It is difficult to assess the more immediate problems of communication but they were certainly considerable. Looking back after two years at the negotiations during Salt's first visit, Pearce wrote, '. . . when Mr. Salt was here, the Interpretation went thro: 5 people so that the Ras did not get the proper understanding of any thing whatsoever'.[107] This should not be taken literally. Pearce was apt to exaggerate at times. But the discussions between Salt and Welde Sillasē were most likely interpreted twice, that is with Arabic as the intermediary language. Though Salt and Pearce knew some Arabic, it was not sufficient to carry on the negotiations.[108] None of Salt's own interpreters knew

102   Weld Blundell, *Chronicle*, pp. 470–84.
103   See above, pp. 38, 40.
104   I have not been able to locate any versions of this letter other than the Latin, though Valentia assumed that the King's letter would be written in English with an Arabic translation. A document seen in a church at Cheleqot in 1868 seems to have been a copy of this letter in Ethiopic script. See T. J. Holland and H. M. Hozier, *Record of the Expedition to Abyssinia* (London, 1870), Vol. I, p. 422.
105   Salt, *Voyage*, pp. 360–1; also BM, Add. 19347, fols 5–9, Pearce to Valentia, 28 Feb. 1806.
106   FO 1/1, fol. 73, Welde Sillasē to George III, n.d.
107   BM, Add. 19347, fol. 17, Pearce to Ahmad Chami, 3 Oct. 1807.
108   Valentia, *Voyages*, Vol. III, pp. 62, 209; Vol. II, p. 438.

any Ethiopian language. In the crucial discussions, the commercial agents of the *ras*, either Basha Abdallah or Hajj Hammad or both, were present. They, of course, knew some Arabic, but I have found no indication that Welde Sillasē did. According to the fortunes of the day and the kind of arguments needed in the reports, Salt and Pearce would present the interpreters and in Abdallah's case, the adviser of the *ras* as straightforward and honest, Valentia to the point of recommending their employment as British agents, or 'completely in the interest of' the *na'ib* or the *sharif* of Mecca and therefore not to be trusted, or both unreliable and against the *na'ib* as in Pearce's uninhibited language: 'Bashaw Abdullah is a damned rogue—he has not the least friendship with the Nayib.'[109]

Among the many good reasons for leaving Pearce in Tigrē, there was also the hope that he would learn the language and so be able to exclude Muslim intermediaries in the future. According to Salt, Pearce had been successful. He had 'a complete knowledge' of Tigriñña and knew Amharic well. He therefore acted as Salt's interpreter throughout his second visit.[110] How good Pearce really was is difficult to say. He bragged quite freely of his rapid progress: '. . . I can assure you Sir if I had been that great dunce as not to know both Tigrê and Amharic I shou'd be greatly ashamed, I knew them both two years after you left me . . .'[111] But the way in which he used Ethiopian names in his correspondence reveals serious limitations in his understanding. After two years he still used the female form 'Welette' (daughter) instead of 'Welde' (son) in the name of his own master.[112]

The most serious communication problem in this first attempt to establish European–Ethiopian relations lay, however, in the discrepancy between the professed, vague, but altruistic aim (saving Christian Ethiopia) and the immediate, concrete purpose (money-making) of the party which had taken the initiative. At first Welde Sillasē repeatedly told Salt that he did not understand what he had come for, and several years later Pearce had difficulties explaining why the King of England should send gifts to someone he had never seen.[113] This put Welde Sillasē on his guard and he remained so in spite of cordial personal relations. The idea that Ethiopians met all foreigners with suspicion has been grossly exaggerated, as we shall see later on. Nevertheless, the question of the motives of the Europeans remained a basic problem for the Ethiopian rulers as they started to grapple with the problems of foreign relations in the modern world. Thirty years after Salt's visit, one of Welde Sillasē's successors, Dejjazmach Wibē, gave expression to his exasperation and the determination not to be cheated which must often have moved in the minds of the Ethiopian

109 ibid., Vol. III, pp. 138, 141, 270; Salt, *Voyage*, p. 268; FO 1/1, fols 122–3, Pearce to Salt, 29 Dec. 1809.
110 Salt, *Voyage*, p. 204; FO 1/1, fols 94–5, Salt, 4 Mar. 1811.
111 BM, Add. 19347, fols 67–74, Pearce to Salt, 10 Jun. 1809.
112 ibid., fol. 17, Pearce to Ahmad Chami, 3 Oct. 1807. See also fols 11–14, 67–74, for other examples of errors which would hardly be made by anyone 'perfectly well acquainted' with the language.
113 Valentia, *Voyages*, Vol. III, pp. 56, 62, 138; [Pearce], *Life*, Vol. I, p. 166.

rulers. The colourful words belong to the French–Irish traveller Arnauld d'Abbadie, but the spirit is Ethiopian:

> Take care that you never again tread the soil of my country. The English and you are confined to cursed land and you covet our healthy climate: one collects our plants, another our stones; I do not know what you are looking for, but I do not want it to be in my country that you find it.[114]

114 D'Abbadie, *Douze ans*, p. 531. Wibē was, of course, not as ignorant of the aims and ambitions of his guests as this statement implies. The French vice-consul reported soon after that all travellers carried out their research under Wibē's efficient protection except Lefebvre and the d'Abbadie brothers with whom he was annoyed because they involved themselves in politics. See AECP, Massouah 1, fol. 18, Degoutin to Guizot, 30 Jan. 1842; also below, pp. 83–6.

III

Increasing Pressures and Sporadic Responses

The End of Isolation

For almost twenty years after the second visit of Henry Salt to Ethiopia, there were no important initiatives or developments in Ethio-European relations. Once the French threats of the Napoleonic era had passed and British India was safe, the little interest in the Red Sea and Abyssinia which Valentia and Salt had managed to generate in official circles faded again. What remained was a scholarly and missionary interest which found its main expression in the publication of scripture portions in Gi'iz by the British and Foreign Bible Society.[1] Through Salt, appointed consul general in Egypt in 1815, contact was maintained with Pearce who became the first, somewhat unlikely distributor of the Scriptures in print in Ethiopia.[2] Insignificant as his activity may seem and limited as it certainly was, it nevertheless represents the beginning of the missionary approach which would be so important when the 'scramble into Ethiopia' began in earnest around 1830.

In the following quarter of a century, Ethiopia was flooded by a great number of European travellers and missions of every kind and description. The first to arrive, around New Year 1830, were two missionaries of the Church Missionary Society, Samuel Gobat and Christian Kugler, and a German carpenter named Christian Aichinger who had been recruited by Kugler to accompany them. They were followed by C. W. Isenberg in 1835, and C. H. Blumhardt and J. L. Krapf in 1837.[3] The first of their Roman Catholic colleagues to arrive was Giuseppe Sapeto who travelled together with the d'Abbadie brothers in

---

1 Halls, *Salt*, Vol. I, pp. 321–31. As evidence of the connection it is sufficient to point out that both Valentia and Salt were members of the Bible Society's Abyssinian sub-committee.
2 ibid., Vol. I, pp. 405, 479; [Pearce], *Life*, Vol. II, pp. 128–9, 173–5, 212, 233.
3 C. W. Isenberg and J. L. Krapf, *The Journals of C. W. Isenberg and J. L. Krapf* (London, 1843), p. v; [S. Gobat], *Samuel Gobat, Bishop of Jerusalem, His Life and Work* (London, 1884), pp. 101, 110.

1838.[4] The Lazarist mission in Ethiopia started officially with the arrival late the following year of three additional missionaries with Giustino De Jacobis as the leader.[5]

Simultaneously, interest in the scientific and commercial exploration of Ethiopia increased. The German scholar Eduard Rüppell opened the way in 1832–33. He was followed in 1835–36 by the far less scholarly but interesting young travellers Edmond Combes and Maurice Tamisier who belonged to the Saint Simonian movement in France.[6] The German traveller Baron A. von Katte, in 1836, and two Frenchmen from Egypt, Louis Rémy Aubert-Roche and Jules Dufey, in 1837–38, were primarily interested in commercial prospects. Around 1840 the influx of Europeans, particularly Frenchmen, reached a peak with the arrival of Antoine and Arnauld d'Abbadie in 1838, the scientific missions of Théophile Lefebvre and of P. V. Ferret and J.-G. Galinier in 1839 and 1840 respectively, the return of Combes in 1840 to purchase a port, and the two visits in 1839 and 1842 of the later French consul at Jidda, C. F. X. Rochet d'Héricourt who, like several of the others, hoped to pave the way for French commercial and political influence in the country. At the same time, in 1841, an official British mission under Captain W. C. Harris travelled to Shewa to forestall Rochet d'Héricourt's plans there, and the Belgian consul in Egypt, Édouard Blondeel, extended his exploration of commercial opportunities to northern and western Ethiopia.[7] Unofficial British travellers arriving in the early 1840s included John Bell, Walter Plowden, and Mansfield Parkyns. The first two later came to play important political roles, Plowden as the first British consul in Ethiopia.[8]

Many of the above returned to Europe when they had completed their tasks or exhausted their funds, but others stayed on; the German botanist Wilhelm Schimper, for instance, in Simēn and Tigrē where also Coffin resided, Arnauld d'Abbadie mainly in Gojjam, and John Bell in Begēmdir. The Catholic missionaries also remained though the Protestants were forced to leave, first in 1838 and again in 1843.[9]

The missions or persons mentioned above by no means constitute a complete list. In 1841 the British consul at Alexandria reported that there were more than thirty French travellers in Ethiopia at that time,[10] and the correct figure can hardly have been much lower. The French missions (d'Abbadie, Combes,

---

4 D'Abbadie, *Douze ans*, pp. 1, 5; Lefebvre, *Voyage*, Vol. I, p. 54.

5 Lefebvre, *Voyage*, Vol. I, pp. 107–8. Antoine d'Abbadie was involved in bringing out these missionaries also. See FO 1/3, fols 29–30, d'Abbadie to O'Connell, n.d., probably 5 Jun. 1839; fols 49–50, Palmerston to Campbell, 17 Jun. 1839. See Crummey, *Priests*, pp. 29–61, for further information on the missionaries and their fate.

6 E. Combes and M. Tamisier, *Voyage en Abyssinie, dans le pays des Galla, de Choa et d'Ifat* (Paris, 1838). See above, p. 16, n. 21.

7 A. Duchesne, *Le consul Blondeel en Abyssinie* (Brussels, 1953). Published narratives and reports by the other travellers are listed in the bibliography. As far as I know, Combes has left no published account of his second visit to Ethiopia.

8 M. Parkyns, *Life in Abyssinia* (London, 1853); Plowden, *Travels*. For Bell's arrival, see Ferret and Galinier, *Voyage*, Vol. I, pp. 299, 415–16.

9 Crummey, *Priests*, pp. 45, 54–6.

10 FO 1/3, fols 122–6, Barnett to Backhouse, 19 Sep. 1841.

Lefebvre, Rochet d'Héricourt, and Ferret and Galinier) were getting in the way, not only of the British, but even of each other.[11] On the other hand, the British mission to Shewa in 1841 alone consisted of more than thirty persons.[12]

Whether they were motivated by missionary or scientific interests, by the prospects of commercial opportunities, by a taste for adventure, or by a combination of these factors, whether they were actually commissioned by their governments or not, almost all these Europeans ended up involving themselves in Ethiopian politics and seeking influence at the courts of the Ethiopian rulers. Compared with the preceding 200 years of isolation from Europe,[13] broken only by the occasional traveller once in a generation, this was something completely new. The leaders of the political, ecclesiastical, and commercial establishment in Ethiopia began to understand that the *ferenj* were seriously interested in their country. The very fact that the numbers increased so rapidly indicates that the doors were, in fact, quite open from the beginning. The first stages of European penetration were, it seems, not experienced as a threat in any way, although the ecclesiastical mistrust, which was a heritage from the religious conflicts of the seventeenth century, was not entirely dead.

The rebirth of Egypt under Muhammad Ali, and its expansion into Arabia and particularly the Sudan, caused pressures of a different and much more tangible kind. The 'Turks', as the Ethiopians traditionally called the Muslims beyond their own frontiers, were the only neighbour and potential external enemy with which they reckoned. Though the Turks had caused no serious problems for more than 200 years, their support of Ahmad Grañ's sixteenth-century *jihad* into the Ethiopian highlands and their abortive attempt to occupy northern Ethiopia were not forgotten.[14] Through the conquest of Hijaz by Muhammad Ali, Massawa came under Egyptian rule, and from 1813 onwards the port was periodically governed by an Egyptian.[15] At first this did not make much difference, but a more active policy was introduced along the coast in the 1830s, and still more after 1846, when Massawa and Sawakin were transferred from the *pashalik* of Hijaz to Egypt. The transfer of Sawakin and Massawa was no doubt dictated by the desire of Egypt to co-ordinate its rule in the Sudan with the administration of the coast. For Ethiopia it meant that the same potentially hostile power could exert political and military pressures on both flanks of northern Ethiopia. With the Egyptian conquest of the Sudan in 1820, Egyptian armies and administrators had made their appearance on the western frontiers of Ethiopia. The Ethiopian people had to face an expansive and relatively well-organized neighbour state, something which had not been the case for centuries.[16] Whether Muhammad Ali originally contemplated

---

11 AEMD, Afrique 13, fols 51–60, 'Note sur le voyage de M. Lefebvre en Abyssinie'; d'Abbadie, *Douze ans*, pp. 528–31.
12 Harris, *Highlands*, Vol. I, p. vii.
13 Trimingham, *Islam*, pp. 98–108; Ullendorff, *The Ethiopians*, pp. 11–14, 78–83.
14 As late as the reign of Yohannis IV, the Egyptian aggression was seen in the light of the sixteenth-century struggle. See FO 95/731, no. 143, Yohannis to Victoria, 13 Aug. 1872.
15 Abir, *Ethiopia*, p. 6. See also *idem*, 'The Origins of the Ethiopian–Egyptian Border Problem in the Nineteenth Century', *JAH*, VIII, 3 (1967), pp. 443–61.
16 See Abir, *Ethiopia*, pp. 96–116, 131–2.

the conquest of Ethiopia—there were rumours to that effect in Cairo even before the conquest of the Sudan took place—or not, the geopolitical situation of Ethiopia had been drastically changed. It was almost inevitable that the territorial integrity, possibly the very existence, of the Ethiopian state would sooner or later be challenged.[17]

It would take half a century before the new situation led to an all-out struggle for ascendancy in the region. But on the northern frontiers, and occasionally in the internal politics of Ethiopia, the pressure was felt. The past experience of the Ethiopian people pointed towards an alliance with Christian Europe to meet the threat. The contacts became, as we have seen, increasingly available. The questions are when or how far foreign policy became an Ethiopian priority during the *Zemene Mesafint*, and what role the Europeans played in this respect.

Sebagadis and the Ali/Coffin Mission

About the middle of 1827, William Coffin suddenly appeared in Egypt after seventeen years in Ethiopia. He was on his way to London as the emissary of Dejjazmach Sebagadis Weldu of Tigrē.[18] As 'Ethiopia's first initiative in foreign affairs for many decades',[19] this mission is evidently important. It has been stated that Sebagadis 'needed firearms which could only be obtained with European assistance through Massawa' and that he was also 'interested in foreign skills'.[20] He is even supposed to have asked Britain to 'take the port of Mussowa, and give it to us or keep it', and thus 'for the first time in the modern era an Ethiopian ruler seriously attempted to break the wall of isolation around Ethiopia and create a bridge to Christian Europe'.[21] Interest in firearms and foreign skills was, of course, not a new feature. With regard to these, the important question is what the arms and the artisans were intended for. But the plan of obtaining Massawa through co-operation with Britain was certainly a new departure, something in which Welde Sillasē had shown no interest when it was proposed to him by Salt.[22]

Coffin's relations with Sebagadis are obscure. For many years the latter was

---

17 BM, Add. 19347, pp. 218–22, Salt to Pearce, 29 Jun. 1818; Halls, *Salt*, Vol. II, p. 177, Salt to Mountnorris, 2 Nov. 1820; after his father's death, Valentia had become Earl of Mountnorris. See M. Sabry, *L'empire égyptien sous Mohamed-Ali et la question d'Orient* (Paris, 1930), pp. 66–7, for an authoritative Egyptian historian's conclusion: 'Muhammad Ali, desiring to dominate all the coasts of the Red Sea and all the upper courses of the Nile, already thought of assigning to his African expedition, as its ultimate goal, the occupation of Abyssinia.'

18 FO 78/160, fols 356–7, Barker to Dudley, 1 Dec. 1827; Basel, BV. 31, Gobat to his sister, 14 Dec. 1827; Halls, *Salt*, Vol. II, p. 270. Halls states that Coffin arrived about May, Gobat gives 15 July, and Barker 'some months ago'. Sebagadis was not a *ras*, though Europeans generally gave him this title, probably because it had become well known as the title of Welde Sillasē. His name was, in fact, Suba Gadis, but all Ethiopian historians write Seba Gadis or Sebagadis.

19 Crummey, *Priests*, p. 29.

20 ibid., p. 30.

21 Abir, *Ethiopia*, p. 35.

22 See above, p. 50.

a rebel against Welde Sillasē, in whose service Pearce and Coffin were. After the death of the *ras* and until Pearce fled the country in October 1818, both Pearce and Coffin lived in the domains of the rivals and enemies of Sebagadis.[23] Once Sebagadis had gained control over all Tigrē about 1822, Coffin, of course, depended on him for his continued stay in the country. Coffin had taken part in several campaigns. He had been wounded and by 1823 he had, according to his own story, been captured in action five times. He seems to have gone through much misery and to have adapted himself gradually to the life of an ordinary Ethiopian peasant-soldier, but he wanted to leave the country provided he could take his wife and children with him.[24] Between 1823 and 1827 his fortunes may have improved somewhat, but it seems unlikely that he could have played any role as Sebagadis's adviser or as initiator of the mission to England.[25]

In Egypt Coffin stayed with his old friend Henry Salt and was by him introduced to the CMS missionary Kugler who was then preparing to proceed to Ethiopia together with Gobat. Kugler decided to accompany Coffin to England first, but they were delayed and it was only in July the following year that Coffin approached the Foreign Office on behalf of Sebagadis.[26] He presented two documents: a letter in English, dated Adwa, 24 April 1827, opening with the phrase 'By order of the Ras, Suporguardias To His Bk Majesty George the Fourth' and closing 'By order of Ras Suporguardias William Coffin', and another undated letter in Amharic bearing an illegible seal and, in a crude frame, the words 'Dejj Azmach Suba Gadis Gīyorgīs Silṭan'. In the English document, Sebagadis, if indeed he can be regarded as the author, begins by referring to the visit of Salt sixteen years earlier and the gifts he had brought for the churches of Welde Sillasē. He then mentions four churches of his own and states that he has sent one of his servants with Coffin to re-establish the relationship that had existed before: 'Our Country is afar off but our Religions are the same.' Three requests follow. The first is striking: 'If Your Majesty could send me one hundred of your Light Horsemen for one or two years; as we have plenty of Horses but no good and brave Riders like your Countryman who returns . . . with this letter.' The second is more traditional but very specific: ' . . . a Doctor, Painter, and Carpenter or any other Tradesmen, some paints, Saws, Carpenters Tools, and some lead to finish the churches I have built.' The third is the also striking request, already quoted, that the British take Massawa from the Turks and either hold it or hand it over to Ethiopia, 'as our Country is lost by it, and the Mussulmen on the Red Sea coast'. The document ends with a list of gifts to George IV.[27]

23 [Pearce], *Life, passim*; BM, Add. 19347, fols 151–2, Pearce to Salt, 26 Sep. 1815; fols 276–7, Pearce to Mountnorris, 18 Dec. 1819.
24 Halls, *Salt*, pp. 222–3, Coffin to Salt, 28 May 1823; BM, Add. 19347, fols 276–7, Pearce, 18 Dec. 1819.
25 I have found no evidence to support the view that Sebagadis as ruler of Tigrē 'used wisely the advice of Pearce [certainly not] and Coffin'. Cf. Longrigg, *Eritrea*, p. 81.
26 Halls, *Salt*, pp. 270, 277; CMS, CM/046, Kugler to Bickersteth, 12 Apr. 1828. FO 1/2, fols 4, 8, minutes.
27 FO 1/2, fols 1–2, 6. The English document in the file is reportedly a *copy* of a paper brought

አባትህ፡ክራሽ፡ፍወል፡ዩ፡ሠላቤ፡ፍቀር፡ነብሩ፡እሬጦ፡እንደሑ፡
ከንቱ፡ ያሬ፡ ገፈቀር፡ እኔ፡ እንደ፡ ሕፃት፡ ክርስ ቲ ያን፡ ነዩ ፈ
ገቱህ፡ብሉ፡ክርአያ፡ን፡እቃ፡ይሰደል፡ ነበሬ፡እንደ፡ ለዝዩ
ለ ሬ ፡ ዸዩድል ኝ ፡ ቫ ጴ ቱ፡ክርስ ቲ ያ ፡ ን፡ ስ ፈ ጁ፡ ለ ሁ ሚ፡ እ ርሺ
ኸ ፡ ስ ዩ ድ ል ኝ ፡ ኔ ፡ ነ ፍ ጠ ኛ ፡ ፈ ረ ሸ ፡ የ ሚ ቀ መ ጡ፡ ስ ዩ ድ ኘ ፡ ፅ
ነ ጮ ት ፡ ዩ ራ ቤ ፡ ቤ ቱ ፡ ክ ር ስ ቲ ያ ን ፡ ስ ረ ፡ እ ን ዩ ፡ ሀ ግ ራ ፡ ዴ ው ፡ የ
ሚ ስ ፈ ፡ ለ ፡ ኗ ፡ መ ር ገ ዱ ፡ ቫ ፡ ለ ን ቱ ፡ ይ ፡ በ ሞ ሽ ት ፡ ህ ፡ ጭ ።

ጋ ሽ ፡ ፀ ር ፡ ሽ ት ፡ ፇ ፡ ለ ም ዩ ፡ ከ ኔ ፡ የ ነ በ ፈ ፡ ለ ት
ስ ዩ ጁ ሁ ተ ሁ ፡ ህ ሰ ዩ ፡ ነ ው ፡ የ መ ጡ ፡ ፈ ለ ግ ጡ
እ ቃ ፡ ለ ክ ል ኝ ።

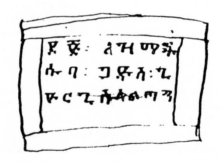

እ ሴ ፡ መ ፀ ፡ እ ክ ጉ ፈ ኗ ዪ ፡ ነ ው
ከ ኮ ፈ ን ፡ ጋ ራ ።

The Amharic letter is brief. It starts without preamble as follows:

Between your father and Ras Welde Sillasē there was friendship. Let us be friends, I with you, in the same way. I am a Christian as you are. Your father sent things for the church. In the same way send to me, for I have built three churches. Send me lead. Send me one hundred cavalrymen, a carpenter, a church builder who will build the way they do in your country.

Then the list of gifts and the framed words follow. Though the name of the addressee seems out of place in what looks most like the drawing of a seal, 'Gīyorgīs Silṭan', called Silṭan Gīyorgīs on the back of the letter, actually stands for King George. At the bottom of the letter there is one more important statement: 'Alī is my envoy with Koffin.'[28]

There are some signs of Tigriñña influence in the language, and the handwriting is very poor. The difference in quality between this document and Welde Sillasē's Gi'iz letter of 1810 is striking. This may be due to the fact that Sebagadis himself had no church or court background and did not worry about using a proper scribe.[29] He knew neither Amharic nor Arabic, and unless he learned to read in his late thirties or forties he was not literate at all.[30]

Coffin certainly did not know sufficient Amharic to have written or dictated the letter. He told the Foreign Office that he believed that the substance of the Amharic letter was the same as that of his English version, and when a translation, with some gaps, of the Amharic had been obtained through the CMS, Coffin was unable to fill in the gaps.[31] The envoy Ali Umar, finally, was the Muslim governor of a district in Agamē.[32] By Kugler's and Gobat's standards he spoke Amharic 'tolerably well' but did not understand Arabic.[33] But since Ali, a Muslim Saho, would hardly have been able to read and write Amharic, the scribe was in all probability a fourth person. A likely candidate in the circumstances was Coffin's brother-in-law Werqē, who lived at Adwa and

---

by Coffin. Almost three years later Mountnorris submitted a second copy of the same document (ibid. fol. 83). The main part of the text closes 'By order of Ras Supergardis signed/ William Coffin'. A list of gifts, which forms part of the text in the other copy, here follows as a kind of P.S. There are some minor discrepancies between the two texts—in the spelling of Ethiopian names, for instance—but the only substantial difference is that a sentence about Abyssinia and England having the same religion is missing in the Valentia copy.

28 ibid., fol. 6.
29 The court at Gonder had played an important role in the maintenance of learning, but it was declining. See Salt, *Voyage*, p. 332; Gobat, *Journal*, pp. 156, 217.
30 [Gobat], *Life*, p. 109; [Pearce], *Life*, Vol. II, p. 145. Gobat was impressed by the personality but certainly not the education of Sebagadis. He wanted to communicate with him but found that Sebagadis 'knew only the Tigré [obviously Tigriñña] and Shoho dialects'.
31 FO 1/2, fols 2, 8–9, minutes and notes on the translation. Professor Lee had found ስንቱ and ለምሽቱህ impossible to translate, and Coffin had nothing to add though these words are as simple as 'for you' and 'for your wife'.
32 Basel, BV. 31, Gobat to his sister, 14 Dec. 1827; [Gobat], *Life*, pp. 104, 108; Rüppell, *Reise*, Vol. I, p. 325.
33 CMS, CM/046, Kugler to Jowett, 30 Oct. 1827; Gobat to Kugler, 17 Apr. 1828; Basel, BV. 31, Gobat to his sister, 14 Dec. 1827.

had been used as a messenger to Egypt by Sebagadis in 1822–23.[34] If Werqē was indeed the scribe, the possibility that he, in collusion with Coffin, went beyond his instructions in the wording of the letter cannot be excluded. Nevertheless the way in which Ali is mentioned as 'the envoy', in fact his whole association with the mission, shows that it was not the invention of these two men. The letter to George IV, moreover, was only one of at least three letters sent by the hands of Ali and Coffin.[35]

The two other messages were one letter in Amharic to the Patriarch Pēṭros VII and another in Arabic to Henry Salt.[36] Both bear the same seal as the letter to George IV. The letter to the Patriarch is, moreover, in the same hand as the letter to the King of England and has the same kind of drawn 'seal' as well, in this case with the words 'Seal of Dejj Azmach Suba Gadis Niguse Alem'. The last two words, 'King of the World', appear also in the real seal which, in the letter to Salt, is legible.[37]

The letter to the Patriarch is a masterpiece of flattery and crushing criticism at the same time. Once Sebagadis has paid his respects to Pēṭros as father and teacher, 'the fifth of the four evangelists, the thirteenth of the apostles, the seventy-third of the disciples', he states that he is entitled to be frank. The problem is Abune Qērilos. Ethiopia has never had a bishop like him: a habitual drunkard and merciless master who has tortured and killed his own servant. He was sent, presumably, to ordain priests and consecrate churches; instead he tries to extort money from people who have travelled great distances to be ordained, and anathematizes because he is not satisfied with the income of his predecessors. Was it deliberately that Pēṭros had selected such a man to be bishop in Ethiopia? Had he sent him because he hated Ethiopia? These are Sebagadis's questions and the answer he wants is a new bishop who can absolve the people and excommunicate Qērilos instead. The Patriarch is invited to mention his price.[38] Sebagadis may well have exaggerated the misconduct and greed of the *abun*.[39] The important point is in any case not the actual

---

34   Rüppell, *Reise*, Vol. II, p. 306; Halls, *Salt*, Vol. II, pp. 222–3, Coffin to Salt, 28 May 1823. Werqē was born in Ethiopia by an Armenian father. See Gobat, *Journal*, p. 57; FO 78/343, fols 253–91, Isenberg to Campbell, n.d.

35   In addition to the two letters described in the following, Ali probably conveyed a letter to Muhammed Ali. See CMS, CM/046, Kugler [to Coates?], 17 Aug. 1829. I have not found this letter, but I suspect that it was related to the demand for a new bishop.

36   BM, Add. 19343, fols 46v.–47r. (one sheet, but folded), Sebagadis to Pēṭros, n.d.; fol. 42, Sebagadis to Salt, 22 Feb. 1827.

37   ibid. Note that Sebagadis's seal is reversed and can only be read with the help of a mirror.

38   ibid., fols 46v.–47r. This important letter never reached its destination but ended up among Salt's other Ethiopian letters in the Aberdeen Papers preserved at the British Museum. At one point it was believed to have been addressed to the King of England. In all probability it has never, except for the first line, been translated until now.

39   Qērilos was certainly a controversial figure. Most sources indicate that the hostility he met was self-inflicted, but many of his actions as well as his ultimate fate are obscure. See Abir, *Ethiopia*, pp. 41–2 and sources quoted; Crummey, *Priests*, p. 26. At the time of the Coffin/Ali mission or just preceding it Qērilos was in Tigrē (Basel, BV. 31, Gobat to Blumhardt, 29 Jan. 1827). Kugler reports that he died in May 1830, but not where (CMS, CM/046, Kugler to Coates, 10 Jul. 1830).

conduct of Qērilos, but the determination of Sebagadis to discredit him completely in a desperate attempt to get another bishop.

Sebagadis begins his letter to Salt by condoling with him on the occasion of the death of his wife. Then he reminds Salt of the days when they had first met and become close friends. Because of this friendship and the assistance he had given to Salt, Sebagadis had asked for some gifts for the churches, and sent gifts himself, but all he had received was a very unsatisfactory painting of the Virgin. He reminds Salt of the gifts he had once brought to Welde Sillasē for his churches, and asks him to show his good heart by sending something with Coffin and Ali on their return. In exchange Sebagadis would send him whatever he wanted from Ethiopia.[40] This was a rather private letter. Salt was not asked as representative of Great Britain in Egypt to do anything to assist Coffin or Ali in their tasks. Thus Sebagadis approached each of the three addressees separately on the problem he wanted each of them to solve for him.

The aims of the 1827 mission, as expressed in the three letters, were very clear and definite: a new bishop (from the Patriarch), paintings of the Virgin Mary and other objects suitable for the embellishment of Sebagadis's new churches (from Salt), lead for roofing and a craftsman or two who could complete the work on the churches in European fashion (from George IV). There is *nothing* about the acquisition of a port or the supplying of firearms. The only request of a military type is the request for 100 cavalrymen, oddly inserted between the lead and the craftsmen. It is highly doubtful that Sebagadis knew anything about this request. If any request in the letters emanates from Coffin himself, it is certainly this one. In 1823, he had written to Salt: 'Had I only got five hundred soldiers of our countrymen, we might take all the country that the Ras formerly governed.'[41] Coffin or his advisers seem to have been aware that the request needed some supporting arguments: '. . . we have plenty of horses but no good and brave Riders like your Countryman [Coffin] . . .'[42]

It is impossible to know exactly when and how the Coffin/Ali mission changed character. By 1827 Coffin was hardly able to express himself in English.[43] The *aide-mémoire* which he presented to the Foreign Office 'By order of Ras Superguardias' had been produced somewhere along the way with the assistance of one or both of his old friends, Salt and Valentia.[44] But the facts are undeniable. The *aide-mémoire* is dated at Adwa about two months after the mission left that place.[45] In Cairo Coffin decided over the protests of Ali to

40 BM, Add. 19343, fol. 42.
41 Halls, *Salt*, pp. 222–3, Coffin, 28 May 1823.
42 See above, p. 59.
43 Salt admits that he was puzzled by Coffin's language in 1823 and had rewritten his letter before sending it on to Valentia. See Halls, *Life*, Vol. II, pp. 222–3; also FO 78/343, fols 284–6, Isenberg on Coffin in his big report to Campbell in 1838.
44 Nowhere in the FO file on Coffin's mission is there a line written by Coffin himself.
45 The Arabic letter to Salt is dated 22 Feb. and the *aide-mémoire* 24 Apr. Coffin and Ali travelled from Massawa to Jidda in March on the same vessel as Rüppell (*Reise*, Vol. I, p. 325).

proceed to England without him.[46] When Kugler was taken into the confidence of Salt and Coffin, the instructions of Sebagadis were still defined as 'firstly to apply . . . for a bishop; secondly to fetch lead for a roof . . . thirdly to take a letter . . . to England'. The first item of this letter was, however, presented as a request that the British government 'fortify Amphila on the seacoast of his district for a place of trade'.[47] Also 'protection by the British' was mentioned alongside with 'soldiers, carpenters, masons, etc.'.[48] In October 1827 Salt died.[49] Most likely it was only when Coffin reached England that Anfilla was replaced by the better-known port of Massawa.

In spite of the support of Mountnorris, Coffin had great difficulties in getting anywhere with the British government. No one seems to have worried much about the fact that he came without Ali or about the discrepancies between his *aide-mémoire* and Sebagadis's letter. But the major issues, the acquisition of a port, the cavalry force, even the artisans, had to be dropped almost without a struggle. Coffin and Mountnorris concentrated their efforts on getting an official reply to Sebagadis's letter, on the presents for the churches and on firearms.[50] All kinds of misunderstandings flourished. At the Foreign Office it was assumed that Coffin was a CMS missionary who desired 'bibles and pictures for his churches', while 'the letter of the Ras rather describes military stores, as the most acceptable presents'.[51] This was precisely the opposite of the truth!

Mountnorris refuted the idea that Coffin was a missionary. He stressed that Sebagadis was certainly not uninterested in the paintings for his churches. They should be sent and they should be exactly like the one Salt had taken to Ethiopia in 1810. The question of who wanted the military stores was passed over in silence. Instead Mountnorris pointed out that there would be no expense in sending Sebagadis 'a few thousand matchlocks which are in store and of no use to us'. Ethiopia needed them badly to counterbalance the growing power of its new neighbour, the Egypt of Muhammad Ali. Moreover, England had reason to be commercially interested in Ethiopia and should be careful not to reject the overtures of Sebagadis.[52] A few months later, Mountnorris added the argu-

46 CMS, CM/046, Kugler to Bickersteth, 12 Apr. 1828; CM/028(a), Gobat and Kugler to Coates, 21 May 1829. According to Rüppell (*Reise*, Vol. I, p. 327), Sebagadis had entrusted the funds of the mission, 2,000 thalers, not to Coffin, but to Ali. What happened to the funds is not clear. The two Ethiopians were in any case left behind without means, 'cheated and robbed', according to an account ([Gobat], *Life*, p. 88) which conceals both Ali's and Kugler's association with Coffin by not mentioning the latter and his mission to England at all.

47 CMS, CM/046, Kugler to Pratt, 8 Oct. 1827; Kugler to Bickersteth, 12 Apr. 1828. Rüppell (*Reise*, Vol. I, p. 340) believed that Sebagadis had accepted a plan of Coffin's to offer the British Anfilla Bay for a commercial and military colony in exchange for 'an auxiliary force of 400 men infantry [not cavalry!] and a considerable amount of arms and ammunition'. But this only means that Rüppell, who never met Sebagadis, accepted as reliable information what came either directly or indirectly from Coffin himself.

48 Basel, BV. 31, Gobat to his sister, 14 Dec. 1827.

49 Halls, *Salt*, Vol. II, p. 277.

50 FO 1/2, fols 15–16, 38–9, Mountnorris to Aberdeen, 27 Oct. 1828 and 19 Nov. 1829.

51 ibid., fol. 36, Aberdeen to Valentia, 26 Sep. 1829.

52 ibid., fols 38–9, Mountnorris, 19 Nov. 1829. Cf. Abir, *Ethiopia*, p. 98.

ment that the Abyssinians would use the firearms to stop the slave trade of the Muslims in the area.[53] In June 1830 the British government granted £250 for lead, pictures, and other articles for the churches and decided to pay Coffin's expenses in England and his return trip.[54] But Coffin did not leave, and the following year Mountnorris raised the question of the arms again. He also proposed that the India Board appoint Coffin their resident in Abyssinia.[55] This proposal was passed over in silence but a shipment of arms from stores in India was now approved.[56] In June 1832 the Bombay government finally announced that it had shipped 1,850 pieces, mainly muskets and carbines, to Mokha where they would be held at the disposal of Coffin.[57]

Mountnorris had pushed for a reply for Sebagadis from the King, but Palmerston thought that this 'would be unsuitable in the present case' and wrote a reply himself with a detailed list of the presents attached.[58] The three pictures of the Virgin with the Child, suspending lamps for the churches, half a dozen swords, one double-barrelled and one single-barrelled gun, various tools and mills are all listed, but no lead for roofing. The 1,850 firearms are mentioned nowhere in the message to Sebagadis. Other documents indicate that they were intended as a gift for the Ethiopian ruler, but nothing could prevent Coffin from introducing them as his own merchandise. Probably he would have to account in goods for the funds received when the mission left Ethiopia, provided he had actually taken them from Ali.[59] Even so these arms represented nothing less than a fortune for Coffin. On his way back to Ethiopia more than five years after his departure, he was accompanied by a surgeon and a 'Professor of Drawing'. In addition to painting in churches, the latter could serve as a secretary for Coffin.[60]

By the time Coffin reached Massawa towards the end of 1832, Sebagadis and Ali Umar were both dead.[61] Ali had returned to Ethiopia three years earlier. We do not know what message he brought from the Patriarch. Probably none at all, since Coffin and Salt had taken charge of Sebagadis's letter to the Patriarch so that it never reached its destination.[62] Because of Salt's death, Ali could bring no answer or gifts from him. But the envoy brought with him Gobat, Kugler, and Aichinger, whom Kugler had found time to recruit during his brief visit to Europe. Though Sebagadis had not asked for missionaries, they

53   FO 1/2, fol. 41, Mountnorris to Aberdeen, 21 Apr. 1830.
54   ibid., fol. 54, memorandum by Aberdeen and Backhouse, 15 Jun. 1830.
55   ibid., fol. 62, Mountnorris to Palmerston, 10 Mar. 1831; fols 80–2, Mountnorris to Astell, 19 Mar. 1831.
56   ibid., fols 85–6, [Backhouse] to Villiers, 27 Jul. 1831.
57   ibid., fol. 151, Bombay Government to East India Board of Directors, 5 Jun. 1832.
58   ibid., fols 91–2, Mountnorris to Palmerston, 26 Sep. 1831; fols 95–6, Backhouse to Mountnorris, 19 Dec. 1831; fols 112–14, Palmerston to Sebagadis, 6 Feb. 1832.
59   See above, p. 64, n. 46.
60   FO 1/2, fols 143–4, Backhouse to Barker, 7 May 1832. In fact, Isenberg mentions him in his 1838 report to Campbell as Coffin's secretary but also states that he died at Adwa in 1833. Nothing more is heard of the doctor.
61   Gobat, Journal, pp. 286–9, 318–19.
62   This is obvious from the fact that it is found together with Salt's other Ethiopian letters in the Aberdeen Papers preserved at the British Museum.

and Ali trusted that they would be well received because of Aichinger's skills and also Kugler's medical knowledge.[63] In this assumption they were correct. Sebagadis seemed very pleased to receive them. Very soon he was discussing church buildings and their decoration with the missionaries, and Aichinger, who became Sebagadis's special favourite, went to work on his churches.[64]

Ali remained in favour with Sebagadis and was soon considered for a new mission to Egypt to bring an *abun*. There had been plans to send Qērilos back to Egypt but he died before this happened. In Tigrē Sebagadis reportedly asked every Christian family to contribute 1 thaler towards the expenses of obtaining a new bishop.[65]

Sebagadis was not the only Ethiopian ruler who tried to solve the question of a new leader for the church in the country, nor was Ali Sebagadis's only agent. When Ali and Coffin arrived in Egypt in 1827, a mission led by a monk from Dembīya named Welde Gīyorgīs was already there.[66] He had been sent by the most powerful chiefs in central Ethiopia, Ras Yimam of Begēmdir, Ras Hayle Maryam of Simēn, and Dejjazmach Maru of Dembīya. Welde Gīyorgīs hoped to be able to recruit an Armenian bishop, reportedly because Qērilos had destroyed all confidence in the Copts. He had given Gobat the opinion, however, that Sebagadis as the enemy of the three chiefs of central Ethiopia was protecting Qērilos. Welde Gīyorgīs failed to find a suitable Armenian candidate. He also learned that Hayle Maryam had died.[67] In this situation he decided to return to Ethiopia but instead of going straight to Gonder, he went to Tigrē, presumably because he had found out the truth about the relations between Sebagadis and Qērilos.[68] By the time Ali and the missionaries reached Ethiopia, Welde Gīyorgīs was on a new mission to the Patriarch together with one of the leading churchmen of Tigrē named Gebre Maryam.[69] It was while this mission was away that Qērilos died and Sebagadis decided to send Ali on a new mission to the Patriarch.

But 1830 was a particularly troubled year in Ethiopia. A coalition had been formed between Hayle Maryam's successor, Dejjazmach Wibē, and Sebagadis against Mariyyē, who had succeeded to the position of *ras* of Begēmdir after his brother Yimam's death in January 1828. But the northern chiefs failed to co-ordinate their actions properly. While Sebagadis, after a campaign in

---

63 CMS, CM/046, Kugler to Pratt, 8 Oct. 1827; CM/028(a), Gobat and Kugler to Coates, 21 May 1829; Basel, BV. 31, Gobat to Blumhardt, 30 Nov. 1829.

64 CMS, CM/028(a), Gobat and Kugler to Coates, 19 Feb. 1830; CM/046, Kugler's journal 25 Feb.–24 Apr. 1830.

65 CMS, CM/046, Kugler to Coates, 10 Jul. and 6 Aug. 1830.

66 This is the 'Girgis' of the missionary reports. See Basel, BV. 31, Gobat to Blumhardt, 22 Aug. 1827; CMS, CM/046, Welde Gīyorgīs to CMS, 1 Oct. 1830.

67 CMS, CM/028(a), Gobat to Bickersteth, 26 Jan 1827; Basel, BV. 31, Gobat to Blumhardt, 29 Jan. 1827. Cf. Crummey, *Priests*, p. 26.

68 CMS, CM/028(a), Gobat to Bickersteth, 21 Feb. 1828. Both Welde Gīyorgīs and Ali lived with the CMS missionaries in Egypt and taught them Amharic and Tigriñña. The missionaries speak of both with great affection, and Ali in particular remained a very loyal friend.

69 Basel, BV. 31, Gobat to his sister, 1 Jan. 1830; BV. 39, Kugler to Büchelen, 7 Aug. 1830.

1829, started to negotiate an agreement with Mariyyē and remained rather inactive in Tigrē, his ally Wibē was defeated in a battle in June 1830.[70] Dissatisfied because Sebagadis had not come personally to his assistance, Wibē changed sides.[71] Together with Mariyyē, he crossed the Tekkezē and defeated Sebagadis at Debre Abbay on 14 February 1831. This was a battle with far-reaching consequences. Mariyyē fell in the battle. Sebagadis was captured, and executed the following day. Wibē of Simēn received Tigrē from Mariyyē's successor, and gradually made himself the ruler of all northern Ethiopia as far as the Red Sea.[72] The mission to Egypt to bring a new *abun* was first postponed, then cancelled. Ethiopia was to wait ten years for a successor to Qērilos.

As far as the substance is concerned, it is difficult indeed to see any difference between the foreign relations of Sebagadis and Welde Sillasē. On the Ethiopian side, the important issue was the question of church leadership. It is impossible to distinguish between the role played by ecclesiastical and political considerations in the initiatives taken, but it seems quite clear that there was a strong desire both at Gonder and in Tigrē to find a new bishop and make a fresh start. The other desiderata were connected with the aspirations of Sebagadis to be at least the equal of Welde Sillasē as a church builder. There is no indication that Sebagadis felt any need for or wanted European assistance in his relations with the governor of Massawa or the *na'ib*. His envoys passed without difficulties. He instructed the *na'ib* as to who should be allowed to pass through and who should not, and advised him not to impose duties on the missionaries.[73] The *na'ib*, on the other hand, seems to have been quite capable of solving his conflicts with the Turkish governor without outside assistance, as the dispute in 1826 over the payment to his soldiers indicates.[74] *If* any of the funds carried by Ali in 1827 were intended for purchasing firearms, Sebagadis obviously counted on Ali's ability to pass them through Massawa.

Coffin, on the other hand, raised the same issues as Valentia and Salt had done after the visits to Welde Sillasē: a 'Christian port' at Anfilla or Massawa to facilitate trade and relations with Europe, and firearms to protect Ethiopia against the Muslim threat. His requests added up to an appeal for help from the British government against a nonexistent Muslim blockade and a threat which was not yet felt by the Ethiopians. What he really wanted was some British action from which he might be able to profit, British soldiers or firearms by which he believed he would be able to create a position of power in Ethiopia. Coffin could not speak for Sebagadis. Ali was the envoy, Coffin really only his companion on the journey. But this was not only a question of formalities. The gulf between the ambitions and aspirations of the Ethiopian prince and his

70 Basel, BV. 31, Gobat to his sister, 24 Jun. 1830; Gobat, *Journal*, pp. 52, 68, 79, 121, 205, 219, 224, 230; Conti Rossini, 'Cronaca', *RRAL*, 5, XXV, pp. 904–8.
71 Gobat, *Journal*, pp. 243–4.
72 CMS, CM/028(a), Gobat to Coates, 24 Feb. 1831; Gobat, *Journal*, pp. 285–9, 298–9, 327; Rüppell, *Reise*, Vol. II, pp. 401–2; Conti Rossini, 'Cronaca', *RRAL*, 5, XXV, pp. 909–10.
73 Basel, BV. 31, Gobat to his sister, 14 Dec. 1827 and 1 Jan. 1830; Gobat to Blumhardt, 30 Nov. 1829 and 18 Feb. 1830; CMS, CM/028(a), Gobat and Kugler to Coates, 19 Feb. 1830.
74 Rüppell, *Reise*, Vol. I, p. 189.

self-appointed European mouthpiece resulted in the presentation of an invented 'Ethiopian foreign policy'.

Wibē: CMS Missionaries and French Businessmen at Adwa

The successor of Sebagadis, Dejjazmach Wibē, came much closer to real involvement. This was due primarily to the increasing frequency of the contacts and the growing insistence among the Europeans concerned that Ethiopia's rulers accept and support their plans and projects. A new feature in the 1830s and 1840s was the penetration beyond Tigrē of representatives for European interests. The presence of Europeans at several centres of political power simultaneously caused new uncertainties since it created the opportunities for actual interference in the internal power struggles.

By receiving all of Tigrē in addition to Simēn and Welqayit which he had 'inherited' from his father, Dejjazmach Wibē controlled a larger territory than Sebagadis had ever done. It took several years, however, before he had crushed the opposition against his rule of the Tigreans in general and the sons of Sebagadis in particular. There is no indication that he took advantage of the departure of Gobat in December 1832 or the visit of Rüppell in 1832–33 to send any messages to Egypt or Europe.

In May 1835, however, he sent an Armenian named Betlehem on a mission to Egypt. Born at Tiflis in Georgia, Betlehem had travelled widely and recently arrived in Ethiopia from Java. He knew some English and Arabic and professed to be interested in ecclesiastical affairs. According to missionaries and other foreigners, the aims of the mission were to bring an *abun* for Ethiopia and to obtain instructions that the arms brought by Coffin and deposited at Massawa should be released so that Wibē could get hold of them.[75] Betlehem's mission was unsuccessful. Muhammad Ali reportedly refused to receive him, the British consul general, Colonel P. Campbell, to have anything to do with the import of arms to Ethiopia since they would only increase the bloodshed there, and the Patriarch to do anything about a new bishop unless he received 6,000 thalers for the appointment. Betlehem's mission was probably less official than he pretended. He is reported to have said that he lost the letters he carried from Wibē on the way.[76] In fact, there is no proof that he ever had any.

This does not mean, of course, that there is any reason to doubt Wibē's interest in solving the ecclesiastical question or his desire to get hold of Coffin's arms. The bringing of a bishop would strengthen his reputation as the new champion of Christianity. As for the arms, their mere availability so close by

---

75 Basel, BV. 77, Isenberg to Blumhardt, 30 May 1835; CMS, CM/035, Isenberg to Coates, 13 Jun. 1835; Rüppell, *Reise*, Vol. II, p. 291; Combes and Tamisier, *Voyage*, Vol. I, pp. 196–7, 251–2. Combes and Tamisier made the acquaintance of Betlehem immediately on their arrival at Adwa in May 1835 and were present in Wibē's camp when Betlehem left on his mission.

76 CMS, CM/035, Isenberg to Coates, 11 Jul. 1836. In view of the liberties taken by so many 'envoys' of Ethiopian rulers in this period, I feel that the uncertainties are too great to permit any conclusions.

and the risk that they would fall into the hands of Kasa (Kasayē) Sebagadis or any of his other rivals were sufficient reason for Wibē to try to lay his hands on them. But he had other means of doing so than diplomatic initiatives, namely, pressure on Coffin and his associates or an outright attack on Arkīko.[77] Moreover, there is no indication that he felt any need for these arms to defend himself against Egyptian attacks. It was the internal conflicts that dominated the political scene: the struggle for control over Tigrē and an eventual campaign by Wibē against Ras Ali of Begēmdir.[78]

Nevertheless, the Egyptian activities on the western frontier of Ethiopia were causing increasing unrest. In 1830 the governor of Sinnar reported that he would have to raid Qadarif, Qallabat, and Atish in order to increase his revenues. Malcontents and 'tax-evaders' crossed into Ethiopia and were pursued by the Egyptian forces. In particular the Egyptians were determined to catch the notorious Mek Nimr, who had killed Muhammad Ali's son Ismail in 1822 and found refuge with many of his people in the north-western borderlands of Ethiopia, where he gathered other malcontents for counter-raids into Egyptian-occupied areas.[79] Wibē must have felt this pressure too. Nimr operated against the Egyptians from Welqayit, and towards the end of 1835 some of Wibē's own troops were engaged against Egyptian forces who were raiding Welqayit in retaliation.[80] But it was farther south, in the commercially important Qallabat area along the route to Gonder itself, that the Egyptian expansion was felt to be most dangerous. Here the task of fending off the Egyptians fell on Dejjazmach Kinfu Haylu of Dembīya. On this sector matters came to a head in 1836–37. Ahmad Ghashim, the *kashif* of Qadarif and Rashid, had problems over establishing his authority on the frontier. After an initial setback, Kinfu mobilized a considerable force and met Ahmad at Wad Kaltabu, where he won a celebrated victory in April or May 1837. This caused some consternation, and the governor general of the Sudan, Ali Khurshid Pasha, requested and received reinforcements from Cairo. Egyptian forces advanced at least as far as Metemma, which was at that time regarded as Kinfu's territory, but the operation was then cancelled.[81]

It has always been assumed that the Egyptian withdrawal in 1838 was the result of British and/or French diplomatic intervention on Ethiopia's behalf.[82] The British consul general certainly reported that he had made representations to Muhammad Ali and had received assurances that Egypt had no plans of

77 Basel, BV. 77, Isenberg to Blumhardt, 26 Sep. 1836. See also Combes and Tamisier, *Voyage*, Vol. I, pp. 231–2.

78 Combes and Tamisier, *Voyage*, Vol. I, p. 252; A. von Katte, *Reise in Abyssinien* (Stuttgart and Tübingen, 1838), pp. 79, 85.

79 See Richard Hill, *Egypt in the Sudan 1820–1881* (London, 1959), pp. 15–17, 40; Abir, *Ethiopia*, pp. 97, 99–100.

80 See Abir, *Ethiopia*, p. 101.

81 FO 78/320, fols 105–14, Campbell to Palmerston, 2 Oct. 1837, with enclosures; Richard Hill, *On the Frontiers of Islam* (Oxford, 1970), pp. 15–21; BN, Ethiop. Abb. 279, fols 19, 43; Conti Rossini, 'Cronaca', *RRAL*, 5, XXV, p. 913. Cf. Abir, *Ethiopia*, pp. 102–3.

82 In addition to sources cited in note 81, also d'Abbadie, *Douze ans*, pp. 553–4.

conquering Abyssinia.[83] But the tone of the reply was quite different from that of 1833, when Muhammad Ali reportedly assured Campbell 'in the most explicit and unequivocal manner, that he had not any intention whatever of interfering directly or indirectly with Abyssinia although that country was in the Terdjihat [list of the Pashas of the Ottoman Empire] as bestowed on Ibrahim Pasha'. Even if he should have had any such intentions, moreover, he maintained that he would at once have abandoned them at the suggestion of the British government.[84] In October 1837, on the other hand, Muhammad Ali—by accusing the Ethiopians of having invaded his territory and having attacked in a treacherous manner—implied that he was justified in punishing them. In fact, he expressed his intention of doing so before withdrawing.[85] Two months later, however, Campbell reported that the viceroy had told him that he wanted peace with the Ethiopians and that 'he would be satisfied with a very slight Atonement and Apology on their part'.[86]

Campbell tried to extract this 'concession' by writing to Coffin and asking him to use his 'official character in Abyssinia' to obtain it from the Ethiopians under threat 'that any intemperance of conduct or any want of moderation on their part would be very unfavourably regarded by the Government of Her Majesty, and might deprive Abyssinia of the strong and efficient support which the kindness of our Government has ever so warmly and so disinterestedly afforded her'. Coffin was instructed to inform Campbell 'without loss of time' of the steps taken and their results.[87] This sounds more like putting pressure on the Ethiopians than on the Egyptians. There is no mention of any reply to this letter. It *may* well be true that the British representations played some role in averting an Egyptian attack. It is just as possible that Muhammad Ali was impressed by Kinfu's threat that he would put 60,000 men into the field if necessary, or that he wanted peace in order to capture more Ethiopian trade through the Sudan, and therefore agreed to peace proposals made by the Ethiopians themselves. In January 1839 the Belgian consul general in Egypt, Édouard Blondeel, who otherwise stressed Muhammad Ali's intention one day to incorporate Abyssinia in his dominions, reported that the viceroy had sent an envoy there with 'words of peace and alliance'.[88] What the correspondence *clearly* shows is that Campbell did not in 1837 act on the basis of Ethiopian appeals for British assistance.

83 FO 1/3, fols 7–22, Campbell to Palmerston, 3 Oct. and 23 Oct. 1837, with enclosures; AECP, Égypte 6, fols 140–1, de Lesseps to Molé, 7 Oct. 1837.
84 FO 1/3, fol. 5, Campbell to Palmerston, 20 Oct. 1833.
85 ibid., fols 19–20, Artin to Boghos, 2 Oct. 1837. Probably the inaccurate information relayed by de Lesseps (AECP, Égypte 6, fols 140–1, to Molé, 7 Oct. 1837) that Shaykh (*sic*) Kinfu was the chief of Muslim tribes hostile to the Christian tribes of Ethiopia was intended to mislead the Europeans in Cairo.
86 FO 1/3, fols 23–4, Campbell to Palmerston, 14 Dec. 1837.
87 ibid., fols 25–6, Campbell to Coffin, 8 Dec. 1837 (copy). It is remarkable how conveniently Campbell invented an 'official character' for Coffin when needed. Palmerston minuted on Campbell's letter 14 Dec. 1837, 'Who is that official and under whom does he act?'
88 AE(Brussels), 2024/II, Blondeel to Theux, 16 Jan. 1839; Hill, *Frontiers*, p. 169. See Abir, *Ethiopia*, p. 106, for an overall assessment of Muhammad Ali's aims with the build-up in the Sudan, 1833–37.

In 1838, however, the rulers of Ethiopia *appear* to have become more aware of the danger and started to think of allies. This is rather strange in the wake of Kinfu's victory, unless, of course, the apprehensions of the British consul general that Egypt would step up its activities were somehow transmitted to the minds of the Ethiopian rulers. Two initiatives to gain European support against Egypt are reported from 1838: Wibē's discussions with the CMS missionaries in January and the appeals from Gonder in May which were brought to Europe by Antoine d'Abbadie.

In mid-February C. Blumhardt reported that the missionaries had been informed on 11 January that Wibē had decided to send an embassy and ask the King of England to protect Abyssinia against the attacks of Egypt. A few days later Wibē had told them that one of them should accompany the embassy. But according to Blumhardt they had decided not to get involved in political matters. They had told Wibē that they could not comply with his request, and the plan had been dropped.[89] On 9 March, less than three weeks after Blumhardt had written this letter, the missionaries and their German friends at Adwa, including Schimper and an officer named Kielmaier, were ordered to leave the country.[90] Nevertheless, it has never been suggested that this eventual refusal to co-operate in the question of an embassy played any role in the expulsion. In his long official report to Campbell about the circumstances surrounding the expulsion, Isenberg, in fact, tells an entirely different story on this question of co-operation. According to Isenberg, a monk named Welde Mīka'ēl, who had 'always professed friendship with the "white people", and was in high respect with Oobieh' had approached him on 13 January about Wibē's desire 'to contract friendship with the English Government, in order that the latter should prevent the Egyptians from entering Abessinia'. Isenberg had, after consulting his friends, promised to assist in this endeavour. Two days later they were called to Wibē and agreed to write a letter along these lines to be sent together with Wibē's own message. Soon after Wibē called them again and requested that one of them join his messengers to England, 'a request which Mr. Blumhardt complied with'![91]

This contradiction shows that the missionaries were of different minds on what course to steer, Blumhardt eager to stress their simple-minded devotion to their religious task, Isenberg anxious to demonstrate that he had done everything possible to please Wibē at a time when the whole existence of the mission was at stake. But Isenberg's report indicates a deeper involvement than a mere willingness to be of service to Wibē. That he should try to take advantage of the opportunity to improve the position of the mission vis-à-vis its powerful local opponents, the leading ecclesiastic, Aleqa Kīdane Maryam, and the chief of the customs, Basha Zeynu,[92] is only natural. Of more significance is the fact

89 Basel, BV. 144, Blumhardt to Blumhardt, 20 Feb. 1838.
90 CMS, CM/013, Blumhardt to Blumhardt, 26 Apr. 1838; CM/035, Isenberg to Coates, 26 Apr. 1838.
91 FO 78/343, fols 253–91, Isenberg to Campbell, n.d., but after the arrival of the missionaries in Egypt. The quoted section of the report is fols 275–6.
92 Zeynu was the son of Basha Abdallah. See above, p. 41.

that he could not see Kĭdane Maryam as a suitable envoy, though the embassy was to include also the above-mentioned Welde Mĭka'ĕl and the old friend of the mission Aleqa Habte Sillasĕ, and still more that he pointed out to Wibĕ the 'impropriety' of applying to Aubert and Dufey 'to undertake the same message to their Government in France'. This showed, in Isenberg's words, 'how little Abessinian Princes understand of Politicks'. Wibĕ replied that it did not matter and postponed the issue. A few weeks later when Wibĕ had returned from an expedition to Agamĕ, Isenberg inquired about the sending of the embassy but was warned not to raise the question with Wibĕ. [93]

In all probability Isenberg was perfectly right in saying that Wibĕ did not understand politics, if to do so meant to realize that Britain v. France, Protestantism v. Catholicism, was the only framework within which he could as much as send a letter to a European colleague. Wibĕ may have felt more puzzled than offended by Isenberg's criticism. What harm could there be in asking both France and England to intervene with Muhammad Ali and, besides, *had* he asked France to do this?

Wibĕ was involved with individual foreigners, not with European governments or mission boards. What he saw was an increasing number of European immigrants, people with obscure aims and sometimes irrational behaviour, at least in Wibĕ's eyes. Most of them came from Egypt and entered through Massawa with letters of recommendation from Muhammad Ali.[94] This naturally caused some suspicion that they might be Egyptian spies though many at the same time warned against the growth of Muslim influence. In Ethiopia they cared little about permits to travel or escorts. They bypassed customs posts when possible and refused to open their baggage or pay duties.[95] They got into trouble with Wibĕ's sub-governors and, if we are to believe their own accounts, some used the same kind of language wandering barefoot in the Ethiopian highlands as Valentia had used with the *na'ib* from his ship in the Red Sea. In difficulty because their interpreter had accidentally shot a person, Combes and Tamisier declared 'that by virtue of our being white men, we do not recognize the authority of anyone'. They were no doubt the type of people who would exaggerate their own bravado, but it is significant that they advised other Europeans to show themselves not only energetic but even brutal in their dealings with the Ethiopians because even the great people 'have always been better disposed towards us when we have maltreated them than when we seemed to comply with their fancies'.[96] When asked to pay 100 thalers to Dejjazmach Haylu Tewelde Medhin of Hamasĕn for passing through, Baron von Katte resorted to what he calls cunning:

Know . . . I am an Englishman, at Massawa there is an English warship, my departure is known, and if there is no news from me within a few days, soldiers will be sent out to

93 FO 78/343, fols 276–7, Isenberg to Campbell, n.d.
94 Combes and Tamisier, *Voyage*, Vol. I, pp. 87–9; Katte, *Reise*, p. 3; AEMD, Afrique 13, fols 252–3, Aubert to de Lesseps, Oct. 1839.
95 Combes and Tamisier, *Voyage*, Vol. I, pp. 164, 267, 288; FO 78/343, fols 262, 272, 275, Isenberg to Campbell, n.d.
96 Combes and Tamisier, *Voyage*, Vol. I, p. 182; Vol. II, pp. 71–2, 341.

look for me. If it becomes known how I have been treated, everything here will be devastated and the population dragged off into slavery.[97]

Not that the Europeans always got away with it. Haylu had about two months earlier been cheated into receiving Dr J. Wolff from the London Society for Promoting Christianity Amongst the Jews as the new *abun* and had given him presents in this capacity. Now the German baron was robbed and received only part of his belongings back. He complained to Wibē but decided to drop the matter although Wibē interfered to clear it up.[98]

Combes and Tamisier as well as Baron von Katte were themselves fore-runners of the flock of adventurers, speculators, men of 'ardent and daring visions', whom they saw turning towards Ethiopia to unite it with the rest of the world.[99] The first two with clearly commercial backing were Aubert and Dufey, agents of the French firm Étienne Rolland et Cie at Alexandria.[100] They had acquired some official backing and financial assistance from the French consul general, Ferdinand de Lesseps, by undertaking to pay the blood price for an Ethiopian who had reportedly been killed at Halay not long before by a Frenchman named Adrien Depron.[101] According to Aubert's own account, he and Dufey arrived at Massawa in June 1837 but soon discovered that no Ethiopian had been killed or injured. He reported, however, that they were themselves plundered and maltreated by Kasa Sebagadis of Agamē before reaching the interior where they finally concluded some commercial agreements at Adwa in January 1838. Dufey then proceeded to Debre Tabor and Ankober while Aubert left for Egypt and France.[102] There is reason to suspect that Aubert was less than honest both about the results of the investigation and about Dufey's and his own experiences with Kasa. At any rate, the two seem to have paid 100 thalers in compensation to the relatives from Halay and 300 thalers to Kasa in order that he should certify that no one had been killed.[103] For this purpose and for expenses of their own they drew on the governor of Massawa, presumably without being authorized to do so, and the successor of de Lesseps found that there was 'such confusion in this whole affair that I think I ought to wait for instructions'.[104]

The most interesting aspect of the final activities of Aubert and Dufey at Adwa is that they coincided exactly in time with the Isenberg–Wibē discussions

97 Katte, *Reise*, p. 34.
98 ibid., pp. 29–30, 35–6, 81, 86–7; FO 78/343, fol. 259, Isenberg to Campbell, n.d. For Dr Wolff as *abun*, see also CMS, CM/035, Isenberg to Coates, 11 Jul. 1836.
99 Katte, *Reise*, p. 135; Combes and Tamisier, *Voyage*, Vol. I, p. 23.
100 L. R. Aubert, 'Communication faite à la Société de géographie . . .', *BSG*, 2, XIII (1840), pp. 280–90; AE(Brussels), 2024/II, Blondeel to Theux, 16 Jan. 1839.
101 AECC, Alexandrie 27, fols 81–93, de Lesseps to Molé, 4 Apr. 1837, with enclosures; fols 95–6, de Lesseps to Aubert and Dufey, 2 Apr. 1837.
102 Aubert, 'Communication', *BSG*, 2, XIII, pp. 283–5. See also Malécot, 'Voyageurs', *RFHO*, LVIII, pp. 147–8.
103 AECP, Égypte 6, fol. 155, Kasa to de Lesseps, 1253 Hijra (1837/38); BN, NAF 21301, fols 40–1; FO 78/343, fol. 265, Isenberg to Campbell, n.d. Depron and his companion Hue (?) are two of the most obscure of the French travellers to Ethiopia. Neither Aubert nor Malécot mentions their names. According to Isenberg they were Saint Simonians.
104 AECC, Alexandrie 28, fols 25–8, Cochelet to Molé, 22 Jul. 1838.

and were by Isenberg believed to have resulted in an application to the French government for support against Muhammad Ali. This was not the case at all. Though Aubert makes as much as possible of 'the treaty of commerce' which he had concluded with the chief merchants of Abyssinia, who had all (!) been gathered in Wibē's camp, and stresses that the signing took place 'under the eyes and by the order of Wibē', it is clear that this was a private trade agreement, and not a treaty of friendship between two states.[105] The two Frenchmen obviously wanted to sell arms and ammunition,[106] and in all probability they and not Wibē took the initiative. It is possible, even likely, that they presented their cause in a different light to the missionaries and everyone other than those directly involved in the projected trade transactions. This would explain Isenberg's mistake. He was, moreover, probably prejudiced against Aubert and Dufey because they had, in his opinion, been politically imprudent and personally licentious when they visited Adwa in September 1837.[107] The very possibility of an agreement between Wibē and these men as representatives of France would naturally give rise to apprehensions, and a desire to counteract their influence, among the missionaries and their German friends,[108] and in this situation any one of them may have started off some talk about British goodwill and possible intervention, which led eventually to Wibē's proposal. In any case, Wibē cannot have been very serious about asking help from Britain, since he dropped the matter so quickly.[109]

In fact, Wibē was under strong pressure, particularly by the majority of the clergy, led by Aleqa Kīdane Maryam, to expel the missionaries from Adwa. They were becoming too many. They had bought land, and showed every sign of planning to stay and convert the people to a foreign faith.[110] Wibē might

---

105 FO 78/343, fols 276–7, Isenberg to Campbell, n.d.; Aubert, 'Communication', *BSG*, 2, XIII, p. 285. Both Isenberg and Aubert report that their last meeting with Wibē took place just before he left for Agamē, and since Aubert and Dufey parted at Adwa on 17 January (Malécot, 'Voyageurs', *RFHO*, LVIII, p. 148), this leaves only four to six days from the first hint of a mission to Britain and the dropping of the idea.

106 AEMD, Afrique 13, fols 252 3, Aubert to de Lesseps, October 1839; J. Dufey and L. R. Aubert-Roche, 'Abyssinie. Voyage commercial et scientifique', *RO*(Paris), I (1843), pp. 315–25.

107 CMS, CM/035, Isenberg to Coates, 3 Oct. 1837. Later the French consul at Massawa reported (AECP, Massouah 1, fols 75–6) that they had failed to gain Wibē's respect by claiming that they were the son of Louis Philippe (Dufey) and of the prime minister of France (Aubert).

108 The missionaries were all German, but they and other Germans were identified with England. See A. von Katte's claim, p. 72 above. See also d'Abbadie, *Douze ans*, p. 551.

109 Abir (*Ethiopia*, p. 104) suggests that Wibē had rethought the whole matter, and decided to call off the embassy because an Egyptian attack on Ali might be to his benefit. To me this interpretation seems a bit far-fetched. If Wibē really expected an Egyptian attack on Gonder to be successful, he must also have seen that his own territory would be as open to further attack as the heartlands of Ali's domains. See FO 78/343, fol. 277, Isenberg to Campbell, n.d. In addition, the possibility could not be excluded that Ali and his Muslim advisers would try to come to terms with the Egyptians at Wibē's expense.

110 See, *inter alia*, CMS, CM/013, Blumhardt to Coates, 18 May and 22 Jul. 1837; Blumhardt to Blumhardt, 26 Apr. 1838; CMS, CM/035, Isenberg to Coates, 3 Oct. 1837; also Crummey, *Priests*, p. 43.

laugh at the accusation that they were building a stronghold for their king and an underground passage to the coast to bring up arms and British soldiers.[111] But it was a fact that some had refused to have their goods examined. They were less generous with gifts than their apparent wealth required, and they were trying to establish privileges which Basha Zeynu was most unwilling to grant.[112] It was therefore not unreasonable to suspect that they were planning to bring in arms. After all, Kielmaier, who arrived in May 1837, was an officer looking for employment.[113] Early the same year, Coffin and the na'ib had arranged for 200–300 of the former's muskets to reach Kasa. People like Aubert and Dufey spread rumours about Egyptian agents and intrigues, but Wibē reportedly responded by telling them that the na'ib had written to him about rumours on the coast that France, Britain, and Germany planned to invade Abyssinia.[114] The professed mission of Aubert and Dufey may itself have been the cause of this particular rumour,[115] but the fact remains that Wibē had every reason to be suspicious, even if only a fraction of the views and pronouncements of people like Combes, Tamisier, and von Katte had reached his ears. Isenberg, moreover, was so blinded by his own feeling of superiority that he did not see the writing on the wall, even at his last interview with Wibē on 25 February. He believed that Wibē was serious when he asked Zeynu if the missionaries were not lords and they themselves slaves, and listened, apparently with approval, to a racist exposition on the Ham-Japheth theme.[116]

The final crisis for the CMS mission was caused by the unexpected arrival at Adwa on 1 March of two additional foreigners, Arnauld d'Abbadie and Giuseppe Sapeto. Isenberg immediately took it upon himself to act as their protector by preventing Zeynu's agent from searching their luggage, which was in any case minimal, since Antoine d'Abbadie had remained behind at Massawa with most of the goods. Habte Sillasē and Prince Tekle Gīyorgīs, who had been a friend of the missionaries ever since Gobat's first arrival, asked why the Europeans were constantly increasing at Adwa, and what the new white people had come for. Tekle Gīyorgīs obviously found that he could no longer protect the missionaries, and, in Wibē's name, demanded a full explanation. The missionaries replied that they had nothing to do with the coming of the new people. Isenberg, however, took the opportunity to add that he was sorry about Wibē's suspicion and the increasingly bad behaviour of the Abyssinians towards

---

111 FO 78/343, fol. 262, Isenberg to Campbell, n.d.; J. L. Krapf, *Travels, Researches and Missionary Labours during an Eighteen Years' Residence in Eastern Africa* (London, 1860), p. 19; Parkyns, *Life*, Vol. I, pp. 150–1. The concept of underground passages is firmly established in Ethiopian folklore and literature.

112 FO 78/343, fols 262, 272, 274–5, Isenberg to Campbell, n.d.; d'Abbadie, *Douze ans*, pp. 17, 551; CMS, CM/035, Isenberg to Coates, 3 Oct. 1837.

113 FO 78/343, fols 285–6, Isenberg to Campbell, n.d.

114 AEMD, Afrique 13, fols 252–3, Aubert to de Lesseps, October 1839. It is quite obvious that the Egyptians must have had agents in Ethiopia at this time. For another reference to Zeynu himself as one, see Conti Rossini, 'Vicende', *RRAL*, 5, XXV, pp. 448–9.

115 FO 78/343, fol. 265, Isenberg to Campbell, n.d., where the mission of the two Frenchmen is connected with the consuls of France, Britain, and Austria.

116 ibid., fol. 277, Isenberg to Campbell, n.d.

foreigners, and, by his own admission, rounded off his comments with a threat, ' . . . expressing my apprehension that their folly in believing every tale that was spread about ourselves in particular, and the English and Franks in general, would be attended with the worst consequences'.[117] This would seem to be sufficient explanation for Wibē's decision to act against the European community at Adwa.

It is just possible that the situation was made still worse by the arrival of Campbell's letter to Coffin, asking him to put pressure on the Ethiopians to apologize to the Egyptians for the battle of Wad Kaltabu. The original of this letter was sent care of the governor of Massawa, and a copy by courtesy of some European travellers, in fact the d'Abbadie brothers.[118] Coffin's presence at Adwa after their arrival is not mentioned, but the possibility that someone got hold of either the original or the copy, and leaked the contents to Wibē, cannot be excluded.[119] The mere fact that Coffin was addressed 'British Agent, Abyssinia' may have caused suspicion and displeasure. There is also the possibility that Coffin met Wibē in Agamē, and conveyed Campbell's message to him. Be that as it may, the six Europeans at Adwa, three missionaries and three other Germans, were all ordered to leave the country forthwith, and all except Schimper left on 12 March 1838.[120] Orthodox ecclesiastical opposition against the mission work was the most important factor behind the expulsion, but there were also signs of a more general xenophobia.[121]

It was the first warning that Europeans were to settle in Ethiopia only under the conditions laid down by the Ethiopians for them. Wibē had shown before that he had nothing against Europeans but also that he did not want to be entertained with endless descriptions of the greatness of European peoples.[122] The events between 11 January and 12 March show how little the Tigrean ruler cared for closer contacts with Europe, if the establishing of these contacts was judged detrimental to other, more immediate interests, such as the consolidation of his rule in Tigrē.

Antoine d'Abbadie's Mission

The arrival of Sapeto and the d'Abbadie brothers actually provided Wibē with the opportunity to take up the idea of an embassy again but he did not. Instead

117 ibid., fol. 278; CMS, CM/013, Blumhardt to Blumhardt, 26 Apr. 1838. See also d'Abbadie, *Douze ans*, pp. 13–16; Giuseppe Sapeto, *Viaggio e missione cattolica fra i Mensa e gli Habab* (Rome, 1857), pp. 105–6.
118 FO 1/3, fols 23–4, Campbell to Palmerston, 14 Dec. 1837. See above, p. 70.
119 Aubert reported (AEMD, Afrique 13, fols 252–3, to de Lesseps, October 1839) that all his and Dufey's mail at about this time was intercepted.
120 CMS, CM/013, Blumhardt to Blumhardt, 26 Apr. 1838.
121 There is no foundation in the first reports of the missionaries for the widespread accusations that Sapeto and the d'Abbadie brothers caused the expulsion of the Protestants by intriguing against them. As we have seen, it was their mere arrival that provoked or at least greatly contributed to the final crisis. That is all the CMS missionaries said, but this was in Europe understood or interpreted as Popish intrigue to eliminate competition, and later it appears, for instance, in Krapf, *Travels*, p. 19. See also Crummey, *Priests*, pp. 45–6, where the intrigue story is called a 'fabrication'.
122 Katte, *Reise*, p. 83.

he allowed Arnauld to fetch his brother and the luggage from Massawa and proceed to Gonder for the exploration and research which the two brothers said they had come to Ethiopia to undertake. They reached Gonder on 28 May, heard about Kinfu's exploits from the Ethiopian side and found that everyone was talking about the revenge which Muhammad Ali was preparing.[123] Since the Egyptian pressure on the western frontier had all but disappeared by May 1838, there is reason to suspect that Antoine and Arnauld either exaggerated or themselves generated the apprehensions. Within a few weeks Antoine had left Gonder on a mission to Paris and London, ostensibly to bring more scientific equipment and to ask for support against the Egyptians.[124] Antoine had other long-term goals as well. He was as interested in the establishment of a Catholic mission in Ethiopia as the Lazarist priest Sapeto, who had quickly come to terms with Aleqa Kidane Maryam at Adwa and even induced some of the clergy there to approach the Pope with some kind of declaration of submission.[125] He also brought two Ethiopians with him to Europe, and one of these, a monk named Welde Kiros, told the Pope that the ičhegē and the liqawint (learned men) of Ethiopia wanted the Pope to be their 'friend and father'. At the same time, the Ethiopian asked for support and education for himself.[126] D'Abbadie's early notes about commercial affairs and his activities in Paris indicate that he entertained certain consular or diplomatic career aspirations.[127] But it is his mission on behalf of the court at Gonder that interests most as a possible expression of Ethiopian foreign policy.

The mission undertaken by Antoine d'Abbadie in 1838 would seem to be the most important of the diplomatic contacts of this period. Even Gobat speaks of people at Gonder who desired British interference to help Ethiopia with its problems,[128] but the d'Abbadie mission is a much more tangible affair. Antoine d'Abbadie did not claim to come as the envoy of one or another regional ruler in Ethiopia, nor was his mission directed towards one only of the

---

123 BN, Ethiop. Abb. 279, fols 19, 25, 29, 32, 33, 38, 43; d'Abbadie, *Douze ans*, pp. 41–4. See Malécot, 'Voyageurs', *RFHO*, LVIII, pp. 151–2, for a brief introduction to the d'Abbadie family.

124 D'Abbadie, *Douze ans*, pp. 43, 45, 523, 553–4. Abir (*Ethiopia*, p. 105) has observed both that the request for assistance was strange since 'by May the crisis was apparently over' and that Antoine d'Abbadie possibly himself 'pressed the idea of calling upon the Powers in order to enhance his own importance . . .' Nevertheless, he accepts that it was the Emperor and nobility at Gonder who wrote the letters and dispatched d'Abbadie.

125 CML, 'Lettres manuscrites de Mgr. De Jacobis', Vol. II, no. 423, Sapeto to Étienne, 10 Dec. 1839; FO 1/3, fols 29–30, Antoine d'Abbadie to O'Connell, n.d. In 1868, when Antoine d'Abbadie wrote about his journey to and from Ethiopia in 1838, he stressed his desire to found a Catholic mission and mentioned that he brought letters from Sapeto to Gregory XVI, but he said nothing about the mandate or letters from the court at Gonder. See Antoine d'Abbadie, 'Abyssinia and King Theodore', *The Catholic World*, VII (1868), p. 275. See also Sapeto, *Viaggio*, p. 106; Coulbeaux, *Histoire*, Vol. II, p. 403; Crummey, *Priests*, p. 59.

126 AECP, Massouah 1, fols 22–74, 'Rapport sur quelques voyages en Abyssinie', 16 Mar. 1842 (the section on d'Abbadie begins on fol. 56); BN, Ethiop. Abb. 272, fol. 17r., Welde Kiros to Gregorius XVI, n.d., two drafts.

127 BN, Ethiop. Abb. 279, fols 16, 21, 39; see also below, pp. 81–2.

128 Gobat, *Journal*, pp. 208, 256.

major powers in Europe. The letters which he carried to Victoria and Louis Philippe were written by or on behalf of the Emperor Sahle Dingil and Ras Ali, in fact, the whole political and ecclesiastical establishment of the country.[129]

Though it was possible to travel from Ethiopia to England in two to three months, d'Abbadie did not approach the British government until May 1839 and the French government probably only in July.[130] By then he had already arranged to return 'with three other missionaries, a botanist and a draftsman', and his main concern in London was to obtain the intervention of the British government with Muhammad Ali so that he would be able to return with an order to the governor of Massawa that he should 'pass through the territory of his vassal the nayb *without paying fee or duty, or giving any present'*. He also asked that a 'British Red Sea cruiser' be ordered to Massawa at the right moment 'to awe the *nayb'*. Finally, he requested that an answer be sent to the letter from 'the King & princes of Abyssinia'.[131]

This letter was delivered to Palmerston on 18 May 1839 in the form of an English translation. It is in d'Abbadie's handwriting and bears the endorsement 'translated & written on the 18th May 1839—by A. Thomson d'Abbadie'. Its odd composition and particularly its unconventional opening reveal something about its genesis:

> These words of sorrow and toil go from the king Sahla Döngöl, the Atshegay Mahatzanta Mikael master of Mount Libanos, the Ras Ali, his chiefs and conquerors the dadj azmatsh Oubi and the dadj azmatsh Könfou to Victoria queen who commands the English, the Indians and the islands of the Ocean.

It closes with the statement that Aleqa Isṭīfanos and Aleqa Ṣedalu 'composed this letter', a type of information never otherwise provided in Ethiopian royal correspondence of the nineteenth century. The text itself states that the letter was written as a result of the arrival of the d'Abbadie brothers who 'told us to send you our tribulation'. Antoine has added a footnote to this phrase explaining that 'the rulers of Abyssinia wished to send a single soldier to England with a verbal message according to the custom of Ethiopia', but that they were told that it would be better to send a letter. The letter then describes the Egyptian attacks—churches burnt down, people massacred or carried away into slavery—and the new situation on the frontier, with Sinnar and Metemma, 'which belonged to our king', occupied by the 'Turks'. The British queen is asked to write and tell Muhammad Ali to recall the Egyptian forces. Some foreign influence on the text itself is revealed in the refutation of Muhammad Ali's declaration that no Egyptian troops had entered Ethiopian territory.[132] Of

129 FO 95/690, no. 140, Sahle Dingil and others to Victoria, n.d.; AEMD, Afrique 13, fols 7–8, d'Abbadie to Soult, 8 Jul. 1839.
130 FO 1/3, fol. 32, O'Connell to Palmerston, 8 Jun. 1839; fol. 41, Backhouse to d'Abbadie 17 Jun. 1839; AEMD, Afrique 13, fols 7–8, d'Abbadie to Soult, 8 Jul. 1839.
131 FO 1/3, fols 29–30, d'Abbadie to O'Connell, n.d.; fol. 34, d'Abbadie to Palmerston, 8 Jun. 1839.
132 FO 95/690, no. 140, Sahle Dingil and others to Victoria, n.d.

this declaration the court at Gonder could know nothing except through the d'Abbadie brothers.

Nevertheless, the language structure alone of the letter proves that it is a translation of an Ethiopian text of some kind. Unfortunately d'Abbadie seems to have failed to deliver this text though he was asked to do so in writing.[133] On the other hand, the opening sentence seems more appropriate as an introduction to some kind of verbal message delivered by a group of people. This, in fact, agrees with Arnauld's statement that a council took place at which it was decided by the King, the *içhegē* and the noblemen to make the appeal, though Arnauld goes on to say that it was delivered as two letters 'in the name of the nation'.[134] As we have seen, Antoine explained to the British government that he had preferred to have the message in writing rather than be accompanied by an envoy, and presumably Isṭīfanos and Ṣedalu were instructed to commit it to paper.[135] The problem with this reconstruction is that Antoine himself contradicted it in an entry for 28 June in the diary of his first journey. On that date he noted that he had heard fresh news about an Egyptian advance from Metemma towards Gonder. He continued:

> In a long discussion which I have had this evening with the *içhegē*, I have told him that I had caused a letter to be written for an intervention by the captain of the English ship but that in my opinion it would lead to nothing. I spoke of the semi-official démarche of Mr. Bowring and *I urged* the eminent priest to send a person of high rank in agreement with Ras Ali. He rejected this but *finally (enfin)* agreed to write two letters, one for the king of France and another for the king of England. In reply to my question (*sur ma demande*) he also told me that an envoy from one court or the other would be well received here, but that a resident consul would be regarded with disfavour because he would cause the religion of the country to be changed.[136]

Here it is Antoine who tries to persuade the *içhegē* in private to send an envoy on his own and Ras Ali's behalf. The *içhegē* turns him down but finally agrees to write the two letters which Antoine wants instead. The importance of European protection, the issues of envoys, consuls, and missionaries are all part of the long discussion. Whether the *içhegē* ever informed anyone else is at least highly doubtful. The letters purport to have been written by or on behalf of five of Ethiopia's leading men. Of these neither Wibē nor Ali (nor his powerful mother Menen) were at Gonder during Antoine's short stay there; nor, in all probability,

---

133 FO 1/3, fol. 41, Backhouse to d'Abbadie, 17 Jun. 1839. This request bears the same date as Victoria's reply to Sahle Dingil and as two letters to Campbell of which d'Abbadie was to be the bearer. Most likely d'Abbadie got these documents without handing over the requested original from Ethiopia. It has at least been impossible to locate at the Public Record Office or the Royal Archives at Windsor Castle.

134 D'Abbadie, *Douze ans*, p. 45.

135 Aleqa Isṭīfanos was an important clergyman and one of Gobat's best friends at Gonder in 1830. He reportedly asked the missionary if he thought the British were willing to assist Ethiopia and particularly the King or the royal family in their misery, and was reprimanded by the *içhegē* for trusting a foreigner so readily. See Gobat, *Journal*, pp. 100, 114–15, 200–1, 208.

136 BN, Ethiop. Abb. 279, fol. 43v. (my emphasis).

was Kinfu. If the latter was around, moreover, he is not likely to have joined in any appeal for assistance from Europeans.[137] This leaves us with Sahle Dingil, the twice deposed and restored puppet Emperor, who may or may not have known.[138] It also leaves us with the question as to whether the *içhegē* agreed to write the letters in the names of the absent chiefs, provided it was kept secret, or never saw and approved the actual texts at all. Not only the original to Queen Victoria but also the one to Louis Philippe have been impossible to trace.[139] The Amharic text has nevertheless been preserved in two almost identical versions in one of Antoine's notebooks. There they are inserted *after* the letter from Welde Kīros to the Pope, which was clearly drafted after the company had reached Rome.[140] Whether the two versions are copied from the original letters penned by Isṭīfanos and Ṣedalu or from drafts made by Antoine and his Ethiopian companions after their arrival in Rome is impossible to determine. In either case, however, it is possible to say with certainty that the letters were produced under the eyes of Antoine. The spelling ወ·ከጦራአ for Victoria, for instance, cannot be arrived at by an Ethiopian having heard the name. Throughout later correspondence, she appears as ቢ·ከቶርያ, ብከቶርያ or even ዪ·ቅጦርያ, but never ወ at the beginning or አ at the end.[141]

While the d'Abbadie element is everywhere conspicuous, there is certainly very little of Ethiopian initiative or even co-operation in the appeal of the court of Gonder to the European sovereigns. Antoine d'Abbadie did not have the mandate from the rulers of Ethiopia which he pretended to have. Ras Ali, not Sahle Dingil, was the head of whatever central government Ethiopia had, and d'Abbadie knew this. Wibe was presumably added because he was the best known of the Ethiopian rulers, Kinfu because the defence of the western boundary was primarily his responsibility. By this course of action, d'Abbadie created the impression that he had been made the envoy of all Ethiopia on a national issue of some urgency. It was a false impression. The political leaders of Ethiopia did not experience the Egyptian problem as an urgent national issue in

---

137   D'Abbadie, *Douze ans*, pp. 44–5, 159, 181, 193, 196.

138   ibid., p. 221. The Catholic author Tekle Haymanot (Conti Rossini, 'Vicende', *RRAL*, 5, XXV, p. 449) mentions a relative of the Emperor, Tekle Sillasē, as the initiator of the appeal to the French king with only the Emperor and the *içhegē* as signatories and no hint about a letter to Queen Victoria.

139   Unfortunately I have not been able to find out in what form Sahle Dingil's letter was presented to the French government. There is not a copy of a translation even in any of the files of the Ministère des Affaires Étrangères. The original would naturally have been presented to Louis Philippe personally, but I was informed by the Comte de Paris in March 1972 that there was no trace of it in the family archives and by the archivist of the Archives Nationales who has catalogued the Fonds d'Orléans (not yet open to scholars) in May 1973 that there were no Amharic letters among the preserved papers.

140   BN, Ethiop. Abb. 272, fols 17–19. This is not the notebook containing diary entries for Antoine's first journey to Ethiopia, but a later one. In these texts, the opening phrase lists only Sahle Dingil, Mahṣentu, and Ali as the writers, with Wibē and Kinfu mentioned as Ali's main vassals.

141   The only other instance of a ወ at the beginning which I know of is in the Amharic version of the Anglo-Ethiopian treaty of 1841, which was produced under Krapf's supervision, and even there the name ends with a ይ : ዊከቶርይ.

1838. They had little reason to do so. D'Abbadie's mission originated in the desire of the European to interfere, not in the desire of the Ethiopian for assistance. Once he had received the commission, such as it was, d'Abbadie himself seems to have forgotten the Egyptian threat and concentrated on how to use the letters to his own advantage. Consul Blondeel reported, for instance, that d'Abbadie had told him when he passed through Egypt in January 1839 that he carried a letter from Wibē (*sic*) for the King of France and 'à son refus' for the Queen of England but that he would address it to the King of Belgium instead if Blondeel could assure him that it would be fully appreciated.[142] Of course, Blondeel may have been indulging in wishful thinking. In view of all the other evidence, it seems quite possible, however, that Antoine d'Abbadie felt completely free to write to whoever he liked in the name of the Ethiopian nation. The mission was *his*, to be used as *he* wished.

D'Abbadie had reason to feel satisfied with the outcome of his visit to London. By mid-June instructions had been issued that any cruiser of the East India Company present in the Red Sea should appear off Massawa at the right moment. In separate letters which d'Abbadie himself carried, Campbell was instructed to approach Muhammad Ali, as soon as d'Abbadie arrived, for an order to the *na'ib* that d'Abbadie and his companions be provided 'every aid and assistance', and to use his good offices 'on the first fitting opportunity, with a view to bring about a cessation of hostilities on the part of the Pasha against the Abyssinians'.[143] Thus the representations would not get in the way of the request for special privileges. Besides some noncommittal phrases about the pleasure it would afford the Queen to use her good offices, the reply to the Ethiopian letter centred on

... the Benefits that must result to Your Highness and to Your Dominions and Subjects, from an extension of that commerce which already exists between them and Her Majesty's European and Asiatic Subjects, through the visits of British and Indian Vessels to the coasts adjacent to Abyssinia ...

and the confident hopes of the Queen

... that Your Highness will afford all possible protection and encouragement to British Subjects and Commerce in Abyssinia, and that you will thereby afford to Her Majesty the most convincing and satisfactory proof of the sincerity of Your Friendship towards Great Britain.[144]

In Paris the following month d'Abbadie played on French nationalistic feelings and was more outspoken about his own ambitions. He deplored the growth of British influence and trade in the Red Sea and suggested that France

---

142 AE(Brussels), 2024/II, Blondeel to Theux, 25 Jan. 1839 and 26 Jan. 1840.
143 FO 1/3, fol. 39, Campbell to Backhouse, 14 Jun. 1839; fols 47–50, Palmerston to Campbell 17 Jun. 1839, 'Separate', and, same date, no. 18
144 ibid., fols 43–5, Palmerston to Sahle Dingil, 17 Jun. 1839. This letter to 'The King of Abyssinia' refers to 'the letter which Your Highness and Your Princes addressed to Her Majesty' and is obviously directed to Sahle Dingil, not to Wibē, as Malécot ('Voyageurs', *RFHO*, LVIII, p. 154) states.

should offer its protection to the countries there in order to prevent England from taking over other places in the same manner as she had occupied Aden. In particular he proposed that France should appoint a well-paid political agent at Massawa and accredit him with the Ethiopian princes. His task should be to establish an independent, friendly state in the hinterland and prevent foreign powers, Great Britain and Russia, from intruding. Now the letter from the Emperor and the great men of Ethiopia was used as an argument to convince the French government of the great desire of these people to get out of their isolation and profit from the good offices and advice of France. In conversations with Kasa Sebagadis in August 1838, d'Abbadie had noticed how interested this chief was in foreign policy, and the two Abyssinians who had accompanied d'Abbadie to Europe were introduced as persons with influential positions at home. The presentation of these 'facts' and the qualifications which d'Abbadie proposed that the agent should have led naturally to the suggestion that he might be willing to accept the position, which he declared that he was.[145] D'Abbadie soon found it necessary to add the profit argument to the political ones and came out with 200,000 thalers' or more than 1,000,000 francs' worth of goods and gold with the annual October caravan to Massawa alone.[146] Asked what princes should receive gifts, d'Abbadie proposed presents for all the more important political leaders, including two mountain guns for Kasa Sebagadis which he said he had already promised him. This was obviously intended to balance the Coffin muskets of which an instalment was delivered in August 1838 in d'Abbadie's own presence.[147]

The Courting of Wibē by Combes and Lefebvre

In the end d'Abbadie lost the commission as French political agent to Edmond Combes and was sent off with a reply to Sahle Dingil only.[148] Combes had allied himself with important French business and shipping circles and claimed that he had already established his influence in Ethiopia. He spoke of the imminent rebirth of Abyssinia and the assistance in this process its rulers had repeatedly applied for from European governments. The example of Algeria showed that France was the right country to meet Ethiopia's needs. Commerce would open the door for civilization and a new colony would soon be established through peaceful conquest.[149] A Compagnie Française et Royale

145   AEMD, Afrique 13, fols 7–8, d'Abbadie to Soult, 8 Jul. 1839.
146   ibid., fols 9–10, d'Abbadie to Désaugiers, 14 Jul. 1839. Even in the best of years, this was an exaggeration. Cf. Pankhurst, *Economic History*, pp. 361–3.
147   AEMD, Afrique 13, fols 11–12, d'Abbadie to Désages, 16 Jul. 1839; fols 7–8, d'Abbadie to Soult, 8 Jul. 1839.
148   ibid., fol. 13, Soult to Cochelet, 17 Aug. 1839; fols 70–3, memorandum, 6 Aug. 1840; AECP, Massouah 1, fols 22–74, 'Rapport', 16 Mar. 1842, contains on fol. 59 the text of Louis Philippe's letter, dated 18 Aug. 1839. Both Sahle Dingil and Ali are here addressed as 'King of Kings'.
149   AEMD, Afrique 61, fol. 10, Combes to Désaugiers, 1 Aug. 1839; fols 11–14, Combes to Molé, n.d.; Afrique 13, fol. 150, Combes to Soult, 9 Jul. 1839. See Pankhurst, 'Saint Simonians', *Proceedings*, pp. 192–218, and Malécot, 'Voyageurs', *RFHO*, LVIII, pp. 165–73, for detailed accounts of the Combes enterprise of 1839–41.

d'Abyssinie was formed for the purpose of purchasing and occupying Zeyla or some other port and establishing a trading emporium there. The company received 6,000 muskets and various other small arms as the staple of its first cargo and in exchange agreed to cede the territory it acquired to the French government for the price paid. The intention was to take along a military force to garrison the new acquisition and protect the colony of workers who were also expected to sail in the first ship, but the French government refused to commit itself to that extent. The company was, however, declared to be under official French protection.[150] Combes was provided with letters and gifts from the French government to Kasayē, Wibē, Ali, and Sahle Sillasē, and it must have been clear to all involved that he would both act as and be regarded as an agent of the French government. At Cairo in December he claimed that he had been offered a consulship at Massawa and had been instructed to buy Zeyla or Anfilla. He demanded that the Egyptian government provide him with free transport and arrange for exemption from all duties.[151] Nevertheless, he seems to have been left without any clear instructions, and when he began to mess up the whole business, the Ministry of Foreign Affairs disavowed him.[152]

After some half-hearted attempts to find out whether Zeyla or Tajura could be acquired or not, Combes turned to his second task. By mid-April 1840 he was at Massawa on his way to Wibē to sign a commercial treaty with him. He confidently declared that this could be done quickly and that, thanks to his position, the treaty would take effect immediately.[153] This unwarranted optimism was rudely shattered in Wibē's camp at May Ṭalo in Simēn. Combes handed over the letter he carried from the French government and a portrait of Louis Philippe, having left most of the other presents at Massawa. But this was probably as far as he got with his business. His credentials were challenged, and on 20 May the tension exploded. That day the d'Abbadie brothers had also arrived, and according to Arnauld a violent quarrel broke out when Combes denied that he used snuff, which Wibē maintained that all Europeans did. Wibē then accused the Europeans, 'these Copts who believe they are [great] men', of being liars and intriguers, expressed regret that he had allowed them to enter Ethiopia to 'abuse our ignorance and capture our good will' and threatened Arnauld with the loss of his tongue and both hand and foot. The three Frenchmen decided they had better leave for the coast at once, and although Combes

150 AEMD, Afrique 13, fols 156–8, Baba and Balguères to Soult, 25 Oct. 1839, and minutes on how to respond to this letter; fol. 162, Combes to Soult, 9 Nov. 1839; fols 163–4, Baba and Balguères to Soult, 10 Nov. 1839; fol. 171, Soult to Baba and Balguères, 6 Dec. 1839.
151 ibid., fols 172–4, Combes to Cochelet, 17 Dec. 1839. See also AECP, Massouah 1, fols 22–74, 'Rapport', 16 Mar. 1842. The section of this report dealing with the mission of Combes is fols 23–43.
152 AEMD, Afrique 13, fols 189–90, minutes on Combes to Thiers, 22 Apr. 1840: 'La Direction ne savait pas qu'il fut chargé de cette affaire [Zeyla] . . . Elle avait . . . insisté pour qu'il ne fut donné aucun caractère officiel à M. Combes . . . Quelles instructions verbales a-t-il donc reçu pour exprimer avec tant d'aplomb toutes ces rêveries.' See also fols 51–60, 'Note sur le voyage de M. Lefebvre en Abyssinie' [9 Jun. 1840], and fols 70–3, memorandum, 6 Aug. 1840.
153 ibid., fols 191–2, Combes to Cochelet, 20 Apr. 1840; fols 189–90, Combes to Thiers, 22 Apr. 1840.

did not admit that he left in disfavour, he certainly did not carry any treaty with him.[154] Again Wibē had taken swift action against some Europeans at the very moment when he was supposed to seek co-operation. Nevertheless, Wibē was not, whatever he may otherwise have been accused of, a hot-tempered man. He no doubt felt he had valid reasons for sending these men away.[155]

Intrigue there certainly was, for Combes and Antoine d'Abbadie later in completely different contexts accused a third party of having turned Wibē against them. By referring to 'some French travellers, since deceased', Antoine pointed straight to Lefebvre's first two companions, Petit and Dillon.[156] But Wibē was obviously more concerned about the involvement of the d'Abbadie brothers in Ethiopian politics than about the intrigues of Frenchmen against each other, and Arnauld was his main target.

Arnauld d'Abbadie had spent one and a half years in the Ṭana region, mainly at the court and in the camp of Dejjazmach Goshu of Gojjam. During this time Goshu had barely escaped an all-out confrontation with Ras Ali by entering into a family alliance with the *ras* through the marriage of his son Birru with Ali's sister. Dejjazmach Kinfu had died, and Ali had decided to deprive his young sons of their lands and give them to Birru. Birru and Goshu were left to enforce Ali's decision themselves which they did through the battle of Qwinzila or Dengel Ber on 4 October 1839. This was bound to cause ill-feeling between the leaders of the Christian opposition against Ali in the Ṭana region and at least temporarily upset Wibē's plans to increase his own influence as the leader of a united front against Ras Ali there.[157] Arnauld was Goshu's and Birru's man and had participated in the battle of Qwinzila. He was not, however, an ordinary soldier like Pearce and Coffin. He was a man of extra-ordinary pretensions who enjoyed a somewhat dubious fame and did not, at least later, hesitate to call himself a *ras*.[158] When he passed through Wibē's camp on his way to meet Antoine at Massawa, there was reserve on both sides. Wibē did not even mention Qwinzila or Dejjazmach Goshu.[159] On his return

---

154 ibid., fols 227–32, Combes to Guizot, 1 Sep. 1841; BN, Ethiop. Abb. 265, fols 19, 25; d'Abbadie, *Douze ans*, pp. 526–31.

155 See also CML, De Jacobis, 'Giornale Abissino', Vol. II, pp. 149–54, for an early account of this event.

156 AEMD, Afrique 13, fols 227–32, Combes to Guizot, 1 Sep. 1841; FO 401/1, pp. 84–6, Antoine d'Abbadie to Palmerston, 5 Aug. 1850. For Lefebvre—and further evidence of intrigue—see below, pp. 85–9.

157 D'Abbadie, *Douze ans*, pp. 387–90, 401, 406–11, 431–44; Conti Rossini, 'Cronaca', *RRAL* 5, XXV, p. 914.

158 D'Abbadie, *Douze ans*, pp. 456–7; AECP, Massouah 1, fols 6–7, Degoutin to Guizot, 8 Sep. 1841. BN, Ethiop. Abb. 254 and 256 contain a number of mostly undated letters from Ethiopians to 'Ras Mīka'ēl' (Arnauld's second given name was Michel) and a few drafts of his own letters using the same designation, but it is impossible to establish if he used the title from the very beginning. J. Tubiana ('Deux fragments inédits du tome second de *Douze ans dans la Haute-Ethiopie* d'Arnauld d'Abbadie', *RO*(Warsaw), XXV, 2 (1961), pp. 27–85) has found one instance (p. 49) where Arnauld quoted Goshu as having used it in 1842, but otherwise it does not seem to appear in Arnauld's French manuscripts.

159 D'Abbadie, *Douze ans*, pp. 516, 554; AECP, Massouah 1, pp. 6–7, Degoutin to Guizot, 8 Sep. 1841; *EHB*, 1841, pp. 12–13, news from Krapf reported by Isenberg.

1. Ancient architectural stele at Aksum

2. The monastery of Debre Bīzēn in Eritrea

3. Massawa

4. Salt plain in the Danakil desert

5. The palace grounds of the imperial city of Gonder

6. Crumbling castles in Gonder

7. The castle of Fasîledes

8. King Têwodros

9. Abune Selama

10. The Meqdela massif with the Islamgē saddle and the peak of Sillasē to the right

11. One of Tēwodros's mortars on its way to Meqdela in 1867–68

12. At rest on Meqdela (Islamgē saddle) a century later

13. Meqdela from the north

14. Bridge over the Mereb, *c.* 1890

15. Amba Alagē, the southern limit of the Italian penetration in 1895

16. Yohannis IV   17. Minīlik II

18. The Adwa battlefield

1 Balgada Araya

2 The seal mostly used by Dejjazmach Wibē

3 The seal of Wibē's 1845 'protectorate request'

4 Nigus Tēwodros

5 Dejjazmach Nigusē

6 Aṣē Tekle Gīyorgīs

7–8 Seals of Yohannis IV

9 Early seal of Minīlik

10–12 Seals of Minīlik II

19. Nineteenth-century Ethiopian seals

Heinemann Educational Books Ltd

Academic & General Publishers

48 Charles Street London W1X 8AH
Telephone 01-493 9103

have pleasure in sending you this copy of

THE SURVIVAL OF ETHIOPIAN INDEPENDENCE

Sven Rubenson

price

£15.00 Net B Cased
£4.50 Net B Paper
(Africa Only)

publication date

18 October, 1976

for the favour of a review

with Antoine, Arnauld was questioned about his plans and by his own admission turned down an offer to enter Wibē's service with a haughty 'I have a better master'. Later Arnauld changed his mind but was not immediately accepted by Wibē.[160]

Antoine's activities were also suspicious. When he left for Europe in 1838, he had visited Kasa Sebagadis and had witnessed the arrival of a consignment of Coffin's arms to this vassal of Wibē's. He had even promised additional arms himself.[161] Soon after Wibē decided that he had had enough of Kasa's repeated rebellions, captured him, and imprisoned him in Simēn.[162] These contacts of Antoine with Kasa were one reason for displeasure. But it is clear from Arnauld's narrative that Wibē's main concern was what Antoine had done in Europe. Arnauld writes that Wibē wanted to monopolize contacts with Europe for himself and that they should probably have told Wibē that Antoine had stopped the Egyptian aggression but that he carried no messages to any other princes.[163]

This would of course have been untrue since he carried the letters from Palmerston and Louis Philippe to Sahle Dingil. Later Antoine told Palmerston that he had asked Wibē to forward the letters to Sahle Dingil but that Wibē had refused.[164] This was most certainly untrue since Wibē would hardly have missed the opportunity to get hold of the letters even if he did not intend to forward them. It is true, however, that Antoine never delivered Palmerston's letter. When the British resident at Aden, Captain Stafford Haines, later prevented him from entering Ethiopia through Berbera or Tajura, Antoine gave the British resident at Aden the letter to deliver as best he could. In the end it was destroyed three years later in Gojjam because the British traveller Charles Beke thought that it might be dangerous to carry it.[165] The d'Abbadie brothers were by then back in central Ethiopia, no worse off because they had no letter from the Queen to deliver. When one recalls that the original letters to England and France were allegedly written in Wibē's own name, among others, this end to Palmerston's reply has a kind of logic in it.

Even if Wibē wanted foreign contacts, he could afford to brush aside the d'Abbadie brothers and Combes. Whether Combes's position as an official representative of the French government was questioned or not, this can hardly have played any major role for Wibē. If Combes had a ship on its way with firearms or other goods he wanted, Wibē could buy without any treaty. In fact, he sent one of his commercial agents to Massawa when 'Ankober' arrived, but almost no business was contracted because the goods had reportedly

160 BN, Ethiop. Abb. 256, fol. 510, Arnauld d'Abbadie to Sahle Sillasē, n.d.; fol. 511, Arnauld to Wibē, n.d. The first of these letters was written in the first months of 1841, the second probably towards the end of the year.
161 AEMD, Afrique 13, fols 7–8, d'Abbadie to Soult, 8 Jul. 1839.
162 D'Abbadie, *Douze ans*, pp. 188, 554; Lefebvre, *Voyage*, Vol. I, pp. 81–2; AEMD, Afrique 13, fols 40–8, Lefebvre to Thiers, 3 Jun. 1840; Parkyns, *Life*, pp. 118–20.
163 D'Abbadie, *Douze ans*, pp. 553, 555.
164 FO 401/1, pp. 84–6, Antoine d'Abbadie to Palmerston, 5 Aug. 1850.
165 FO 1/3, fols 103–6, Haines to the Secret Committee, 9 Dec. 1840; FO 401/2, pp. 194–6, Beke to Russell, 22 Jul. 1865.

been selected without regard to Ethiopian needs or preferences.[166] The main reason may well have been that Wibē expected to receive some arms from France for nothing through Lefebvre who had gone to France for this very purpose about half a year before Combes arrived.

Lefebvre had come to Ethiopia with two companions in May 1839 and first settled at Adwa with Sapeto and Schimper.[167] They were equipped for scientific research, and when Lefebvre was questioned by Wibē at their first meeting, he told him that he had come to see him and to inform himself of the customs of his people. 'What good can that do you? Is the soil of your country unfertile? Have you then no longer any friends since you come to risk your life like this in a foreign land?' Such was Wibē's response as reported by Lefebvre.[168] The newcomers received permission to stay, but neither Wibē nor his advisers were as simple-minded as they seemed to be. The next time they met, Wibē is reported to have said that he wanted to test the science of Lefebvre's medical companions. Others cautioned against the increase of foreigners, who under the pretext of studying might well be spying for Muhammad Ali.[169]

At a third meeting in September 1839, the question of arms and trade came up. As Lefebvre reports it, Wibē wanted to know if, by declaring himself the friend of the French king, he would receive muskets from France as he had done from England through Coffin. Lefebvre said yes but hinted at the commercial advantages which would be expected in exchange. A few days later Wibē reportedly asked Lefebvre if he was willing to return to France with a letter to the French king offering friendship and a commercial treaty. Lefebvre took the opportunity to ask for Anfilla for a French trading centre. Wibē allegedly agreed to this and promised to occupy Anfilla and hand it over to France. A letter embodying this agreement was drawn up by Habte Sillasē, translated into French by Sapeto and 'for more authenticity' signed by De Jacobis and his two companions who had recently arrived. When Lefebvre was about to leave, Wibē allegedly decided to send two Ethiopian envoys also. Lefebvre agreed since this would make the mission more official. He even added two more Ethiopians, including Gobat's former servant and pupil Gebre Maryam as secretary of the embassy.[170] This account by Lefebvre clearly implies that Wibē took the initiative to get arms straight from Europe and agreed not only to cede Anfilla to France, but to occupy it militarily beforehand in order to establish his right to do so. This is the alleged Sebagadis proposal in reverse.

According to Sapeto, he and not Lefebvre played the main role on the Euro-

166 AEMD, Afrique 13, fols. 227–32, Combes to Guizot, 1 Sep. 1841; Ferret and Galinier, *Voyage* Vol. II, pp. 440–1.
167 Lefebvre, *Voyage*, Vol. I, pp. 53–4, 72. For a brief account of his activities and particularly his poor relations with most of the other French travellers and the French vice-consul at Massawa, see Malécot, 'Voyageurs', *RFHO*, LVIII, pp. 157–65.
168 Lefebvre, *Voyage*, Vol. I, p. 69. The following year the staff officers Ferret and Galinier (*Voyage*, Vol. I, p. 420) gave as their reasons that they wanted to acquaint themselves with their brothers in Jesus Christ and look for medicinal herbs.
169 Lefebvre, *Voyage*, Vol. I, p. 85.
170 ibid., Vol. I, pp. 100–9, 139. See also AEMD, Afrique 13, fols 40–8, Lefebvre to Thiers, 3 Jun. 1840.

pean side: *he* was the recipient of Wibē's proposal; *he* concluded the treaty of friendship with Wibē's ministers; it was in *his* hands that the signed or sealed treaty was placed on 6 December 1839. Probably he was, in fact, the main negotiator even if Lefebvre makes him appear as the adviser and interpreter. Of more interest is Sapeto's statement that the agreement had cost him one and a half months of hard work and embarrassment. This implies some difficult bargaining which Lefebvre has passed over in silence. Sapeto's objective was, of course, to secure permission and protection for the Catholic mission, and this he believed that the treaty safeguarded 'in perpetuity', provided the French government accepted it. As for Wibē's objectives, Sapeto makes no mention of arms. What the prince wanted according to him was the protection of France and some artisans. In exchange for this, he had promised to cede the 'island' of Anfilla, divert all the trade from Massawa to the new French establishment there, and protect Frenchmen who settled in Abyssinia.[171]

When Lefebvre arrived in Paris, he found his government less enthusiastic about the project than he had apparently expected. This caused him and his supporters to exaggerate not only the commercial value of Anfilla but also Wibē's engagements: 'King' Wibē had proposed to furnish soldiers to guard the new colony; he was sufficiently powerful 'to maintain us in possession of Anfilla'. In addition, Lefebvre made it sound almost as if he had only reluctantly taken time off from his scientific research to accompany the envoys and act as their interpreter.[172]

This was, of course, not the case at all. When the marine officer Lefebvre planned his expedition in 1838, it was precisely with a commercial and political establishment on the Red Sea coast in mind. The British arms sent to Sebagadis, alleged British plans for an establishment in Annesley Bay just south of Massawa, the risk that Great Britain would gain a second colony, wealthier and more powerful than India—when it was instead the duty of France to carry industry, commerce, and civilization into Africa as she had started to do in Algeria—all figured in Lefebvre's presentation of his project.[173] Lefebvre was by no means the only person advocating the commercial exploitation of Ethiopia along

171 CML, 'Lettres manuscrites de Mgr. De Jacobis', Vol. II, no. 423, Sapeto to Étienne, 10 Dec. 1839; AECP, Massouah 2, fols 205–17, memorandum by Sapeto, 24 Jan. 1858; Sapeto, *Viaggio*, p. 108. But see also G. Sapeto, *Etiopia. Notizie raccolte dal Prof. Giuseppe Sapeto* (Rome, n.d.), pp. 288–9. Cf. Lefebvre, *Voyage*, Vol. I, pp. 84–6, 90, 103–5, for Sapeto's role and the alleged ease with which everything was settled. De Jacobis ('Lettres manuscrites', Vol. II, no. 162, to Étienne, 6 Dec. 1839) indirectly supports Sapeto's report that the negotiations took time, and he commends both Lefebvre and Sapeto for their zeal.

172 AEMD, Afrique 13, fols 51–60, 'Note sur le voyage de M. Lefebvre en Abyssinie'; fol. 50, Gouin to Thiers, 9 Jun. 1840; fols 62–4, Roussin to Thiers, 24 Jun. 1840; fols 68–9, Lefebvre to Thiers, 30 Jul. 1840. See also Lefebvre, *Voyage*, Vol. I, pp. 147, 151–7. There were both general and more specific reasons for French hesitation. The isolation in which the French government found itself on the question of Muhammad Ali's relations with his suzerain in Istanbul dictated prudence. Arnauld d'Abbadie, with whom Lefebvre had quarrelled when they were about to start their first journey into Ethiopia in 1837 (Malécot, 'Voyageurs', *RFHO*, LVIII, p. 152), had written that Anfilla was valueless and besides under Egyptian, not Tigrean jurisdiction (AEMD, Afrique 13, fols 70–3, memorandum, 6 Aug. 1840).

173 AEMD, Afrique 13, fols 21–5, Lefebvre to Louis Philippe, 27 May 1838.

these lines. It was precisely in January 1839, when Lefebvre passed through Egypt on his way to Massawa (and Antoine d'Abbadie on his way back to France), that the Belgian consul general in Egypt, Édouard Blondeel, began to urge his government to join in the race for the wealth of Ethiopia. He was involved with Rolland et Cie, who had sent out Dufey and Aubert, and advocated a French/Belgian or Belgian establishment precisely at Anfilla to capture the trade of Ethiopia, Kordofan, and Darfur and evade both 'the rapacity of the *na'ib* . . . and the customs of Massawa'.[174]

That the inspiration came from Lefebvre therefore seems quite obvious. This is also how De Jacobis, who wrote several letters to support the project, presented it to his superiors.[175] That the Ethiopian prince in this case agreed to the embassy and hoped to gain some arms or artisans through it is at least highly probable. The question is whether he knew anything about the offers he was supposed to be making. Lefebvre was, as already indicated, concerned about doubts as to the authenticity of his mission. He reports that the prime minister, Adolphe Thiers, at a meeting on 12 May 1840 'demanded to see the letter written by Wibē to the king of the French'. Unfortunately he does not say what he showed.[176] The only text to be found in the archives of the Ministère des Affaires Étrangères is a strange document in French. In it, 'King' Wibē, in addition to his own districts, claims that he is the master of all the commercial routes of Abyssinia and exercises influence over the island of Meroe and the Galla peoples. This sounds rather dubious. He then 'requests the alliance of France offering as payment for the friendship which he wants to conclude a bay on the Red Sea and the monopoly of the trade of the rich territory which he rules'. This is all that can be regarded even as a report of the content of the treaty. Then Lefebvre takes over and explains that Wibē wants to have arms and ammunition from a powerful country other than England, and to destroy the influence of the Arabs and Muslim Ethiopians by taking the trade away from them.[177] Why this document should speak of 'a bay on the Red Sea', when Sapeto has the island (*sic*) of Anfilla, and De Jacobis Anfilla and a large portion of the coast, is a mystery, particularly in view of the fact that Lefebvre, in order to get funds, showed the French consul in Egypt Wibē's letter, which then reportedly defined the territory ceded as the Bay of Anfilla.[178]

174   AE(Brussels), 2024/II, Blondeel to Theux, 16 Jan. and 25 Jan. 1839. Duchesne has reported the Belgian archival materials in great detail in *Le consul Blondeel en Abyssinie*, and in many cases in the following I have found it satisfactory to refer to the documents as quoted by him. Unfortunately Duchesne's lack of knowledge of the Ethiopian scene has prevented him from any criticism of Blondeel's rather fantastic reporting.

175   CML, 'Lettres manuscrites', Vol. II, no. 162, to Étienne, 6 (or 7) Dec. 1839; no. 163, to Guarini (?), 8 Dec. 1839; De Jacobis, 'Giornale Abissino', Vol. I, pp. 1–3.

176   Lefebvre, *Voyage*, Vol. I, p. 148.

177   AEMD, Afrique 13, fol. 61. This document looks like an appendix to the memorandum (fols 51–60) on Lefebvre's mission drawn up in the Ministry of Agriculture and Commerce on the basis of Lefebvre's first communications after his arrival and presented to Thiers on 9 Jun. 1840.

178   AECP, Égypte 9, fols 332–3, Cochelet to Soult, 13 Mar. 1840; CML, 'Lettres manuscrites', Vol. II, no. 161, De Jacobis, 4 Dec. 1839; no. 423, Sapeto, 10 Dec. 1839. What the Amharic original contained, if it existed at all, remains an open question. Nevertheless the

Lefebvre used the presence of the Ethiopian 'ambassadors' to inflate the importance of his mission and bring pressure to bear on the Quai d'Orsay, but they were by no means prominent men and had no independent role to play as envoys for Wibē. One, probably two, were actually Lefebvre's personal servants.[179] None of them appears elsewhere in the history of the period except as the servant or confidant of foreigners.

Lefebvre finally received 14,000 francs to buy presents with and, in addition, one howitzer, twelve muskets and twelve pistols but, it seems, no written reply for Wibē to the treaty proposal he had allegedly made.[180] Undaunted, Lefebvre wrote from Massawa that Wibē would place troops at his disposal so that he could take possession of Anfilla in the name of France.[181] But no sooner had Lefebvre reached Wibē's camp at May Ṭalo, than he became completely silent about Anfilla and the trade monopoly. Later the word at Massawa was merely that Wibē had promised not to interfere if the French purchased Anfilla from its owner.[182] The Ethiopian prince presumably had views which did not agree with Lefebvre's grand schemes. The attempt of Combes to reap where Lefebvre had sown must have puzzled Wibē, particularly if he could not recognize the promises he had allegedly made to Lefebvre. And if Combes was an impostor in spite of the letter he carried from the French king, who was Lefebvre who came without one? The French vice-consul, A. Degoutin, had asked Blondeel to transmit a letter from Combes to Wibē and plead with the prince on Combes's behalf, but the Belgian consul refused on the grounds that it was too dangerous. The country was full of rumours about 'invasions, conquests, establishments'. What reply could he give if Wibē asked him, 'But if these French agents do not want to take my country, what then is it that they want?'[183]

In Tigrē and at Wibē's court this fundamental question could no longer be suppressed. The situation was not improved when three of the Ethiopians who had accompanied Lefebvre to Paris turned against him, allegedly accusing him of ambitious plans and of having kept back some of the royal presents, at the same time as they complained about the indifference with which they had been treated in Paris and recalled the missing letter from Louis Philippe. Only Gebre Maryam supported Lefebvre, and when he then started to compare his people with the Europeans and said that 'the princes of Abyssinia were nothing but beggars; that his country was inhabited only by savages incapable of any-

existence of a 'treaty' with very definite commitments by Wibē has not been questioned. See Carlo Giglio, *Etiopia–Mar Rosso* (Rome, 1958), Vol. I, pp. 48, 86; Malécot, 'Voyageurs', *RFHO*, LVIII, pp. 159–60.

179 AEMD, Afrique 13, fols 68–9, Lefebvre to Thiers, 30 Jul. 1840; AECP, Massouah 1, fols 22–74, 'Rapport', 16 Mar. 1842, incorporating report by Degoutin, 1 Mar. 1841, on fols 54–5; AEMD, Afrique 13, fol. 92, minute on Cunin-Gridaine to Guizot, 19 Aug. 1842.

180 AEMD, Afrique 13, fols 70–3, memorandum, 6 Aug. 1840; Lefebvre, *Voyage*, Vol. I, p. 158.

181 AEMD, Afrique 13, fols 76–7, Lefebvre to Cunin-Gridaine, 1 Feb. 1841.

182 IO, Secret Letters from Aden 26, pp. 169–78, Christopher to Haines, 7 Mar. 1842.

183 AE(Brussels), 2024/II, Blondeel to Degoutin, 29 Apr. 1841.

thing but brigandage and idleness . . .' and that everything in Ethiopia in-
dicated 'the profound fall of man', Wibē had once more had enough. Gebre
Maryam was exiled, Lefebvre told that he could not travel in Simēn.[184]
Nevertheless, there was no panic about the presence of foreigners. Lefebvre
was allowed to remain in Tigrē, where he and a young artillery officer named
Schaffner were expected to produce gunpowder for Wibē.[185]

The Wibē–Ali Conflict of 1842: Orthodoxy or Islam, Tigrē or Yejju

The main preoccupation of Wibē in 1840–41 was not relations with European
powers and the future of the coast, but the power struggle within the Ethiopian
state. The circumstances for challenging Ras Ali had become more favourable
than ever before. The rapprochement between Ali and Menen on one hand and
Goshu and Birru on the other which had found its expression in the family
alliance and the disinheriting of Kinfu's sons turned out to be short-lived. In all
probability Ali had never intended Birru to reap the fruits of the defeat of
Kinfu's sons.[186] By mid-1840 Ali had deprived Birru of his new governorship and given it to his own mother Menen. She had married a son of Aṣē
Tekle Gīyorgīs and so her triumphal entry into Gonder also meant that in
August 1840 Sahle Dingil was deposed once more, now in favour of her husband
Yohannis III.[187] This development had given Ali direct control over districts which he had only ruled indirectly before, but it had also prepared the way
for an alliance between Wibē and Birru aimed at the overthrow of Ali.

In order to be successful in this undertaking Wibē needed to unite as much as
possible of the Christian population behind his banner. One way to do this was
to fan the rumours that Ali was secretly a Muslim. This seems to have been
going on much of the time all over the country.[188] Another more positive
action was to satisfy the desire of the people for a new bishop which Ali had

---

184   Lefebvre, *Voyage*, Vol. I, pp. 228–38, quote on p. 236. That Gebre Maryam was here
expressing Lefebvre's own views is indicated by the latter's final assessment of the prospects
of the Ethiopians: God had written on the foreheads of some peoples, 'You will go no
further!' (Vol. III, p. 237). The accusations against Lefebvre for having withheld some of
the presents were not groundless. He had deposited some at the consulate at Massawa and
was obviously prepared to use them only if and when he could acquire Anfilla for them.
See AEMD, Afrique 13, fols 93–4, Cunin-Gridaine to Guizot, 21 Sep. 1842. This also
implies that he did not have the firm offer from Wibē which he had pretended to have in
Paris.
185   Lefebvre, *Voyage*, Vol. I, p. 261; FO 1/3, fols 161–2, Barnett to Aberdeen, 21 Nov. 1841.
186   D'Abbadie, *Douze ans*, pp. 406–7, 486–7.
187   Conti Rossini, 'Cronaca', *RRAL*, 5, XXV, p. 915; d'Abbadie, *Douze ans*, p. 535.
188   D'Abbadie, *Douze ans*, pp. 402–3; Ferret and Galinier, *Voyage*, Vol. I, p. 481; Vol. II, pp.
79–80; Duchesne, *Blondeel*, pp. 137, 140; John G. Bell, 'Extract from a Journal of Travels
in Abyssinia, in the Years 1840–41–42', *Miscellanea Aegyptiaca* (1842), p. 14; Conti Rossini,
'Vicende', *RRAL*, 5, XXV, p. 450. The most specific reports that Ali actually intended to
declare himself or had declared himself a Muslim came from Shewa. Rochet d'Héricourt
reported (Oct. 1839) that Sahle Sillasē told him that Ali's brother had arrived to inform
him on Ali's behalf that he had decided to take this step (*Voyage*, pp. 148, 186). Harris
reported it (Jan. 1842) as an accomplished fact (Abir, *Ethiopia*, p. 115).

failed to do. By early 1841 Wibē had prepared the ground at Cairo and collected the necessary funds. He appointed an impressive embassy under the leadership of Habte Sillasē, now *līqe kahinat* of Tigrē, Abba Gebre Mīka'ēl, and Ri'ise Debr Weldu to go to Egypt and bring an *abun*. De Jacobis was also associated with the embassy, mainly in the hope that his presence would guarantee safe travel and proper reception in Egypt.[189] If he had hoped to influence the appointment in any way, his expectations were frustrated. The new bishop, Abune Selama, had received part of his education from the CMS missionaries in Cairo. Later his attitude towards the Protestant missionaries in Ethiopia varied, but he remained throughout an implacable enemy of the Catholic missionaries and particularly De Jacobis.

That Wibē was eager to use all possible channels to secure a bishop is evident from the reappearance once more of William Coffin as a diplomatic emissary. After the downfall of Kasa at the end of 1838 or in early 1839, Coffin had finally realized that the Sebagadis era was over and had accepted a small governorship from Wibē in exchange, it seems, for part of what still remained of the arms supply he had once brought from India.[190] In June 1841 he arrived at Aden on his way to London with a letter and some presents for Queen Victoria. His mission was 'to solicit British friendship and advice for the Chief [Wibē] is suspicious as to the intentions of the numerous French who have arrived in his territory'.[191] This time Coffin was dissuaded from proceeding beyond Cairo, but with the assistance of someone more proficient in the English language than himself, he enlarged upon the dangers to British influence of the many French travellers who were attempting to settle and introduce factories in Tigrē. He even stated that Wibē would like to know if the British government was pleased 'that he should encourage such foreigners'. Coffin had, of course, told him that French enterprise 'would not be agreeable to England who has always been the protector and ally of Abyssinia', and so Wibē had decided to express his desire that England 'should continue her friendship and protection to enable him to prevent the settlement of any other persons than Englishmen' in his country and

189 See Conti Rossini, 'Vicende', *RRAL*, 5, XXV, pp. 450–7; CMS, CM/045(a), Kruse to Coates, 1 Jul. and 15 Aug. 1840; BN, Ethiop. Abb. 267, fol. 134; Enrico Cerulli, *Etiopi in Palestina* (Rome, 1954–57), Vol. II, pp. 196–7. Ferret and Galinier (*Voyage*, Vol. I, pp. 481–3) state that they met with De Jacobis at Aksum (or Adwa) on 10 Jan. 1841 and that he had recently by general consent been selected to guide the embassy to Egypt. Lefebvre, however, who met De Jacobis soon after, only reported that the bishop was on his way to France to seek funds to build a church (AEMD, Afrique 13, fols 76–7, Lefebvre to Cunin-Gridaine, 1 Feb. 1841). *Later* Lefebvre (*Voyage*, Vol. I, pp. 206–7) claimed that he heard about De Jacobis's role when he arrived at Massawa on 1 Jan. 1841 and found it extraordinary. This should probably be seen in the light of De Jacobis's own report (CML, 'Lettres manuscrites', Vol. II, no. 166, 28 Feb. 1840) that Wibē had asked Lefebvre to push for a new bishop when he passed through Egypt on his way to Europe but that De Jacobis had persuaded the prince to drop the idea in favour of considering a Catholic bishop for Ethiopia instead. See also Crummey, *Priests*, pp. 66, 86, for De Jacobis's own accounts of his involvement.
190 Lefebvre, *Voyage*, Vol. I, pp. 133–4; d'Abbadie, *Douze ans*, p. 554; AECP, Massouah 1, p. 109, Degoutin to Guizot, 10 Dec. 1843.
191 FO 1/3, fol. 135, Haines to the Secretary of the Bombay government, 22 Jun. 1841.

send 'some person in shape of Embassador or Consular Mission' with Coffin on his return.[192]

Although the possibility cannot be excluded that Coffin had discussed some of these matters with Wibē and received verbal instructions for his mission, the Englishman gives himself away in this report. So far Wibē had actually shown little preference for one European nationality over another. Within approximately six months before Coffin left, the Frenchmen Ferret, Galinier, and Rouget, the Englishman Bell, and the Belgian Blondeel with his Italian companion Contarini had all been received and permitted to stay in the country, though not without some hesitation. Wibē reportedly told Blondeel that he was the last one he would receive, and Blondeel, who had practically no presents himself, implied that Wibē's growing dislike of foreigners was due to exaggerated promises given and not kept by men like Lefebvre.[193] According to the French consul, Lefebvre's offers had included one of Louis Philippe's daughters but this should probably be taken as an indication of the level of reporting and slandering rather than anything else.[194] Europeans were dealt with as individual *ferenj*, and generosity, prudence and usefulness to Wibē, as well as ability to keep out of trouble, for instance with the clergy, decided their fate. The idea of expelling all Frenchmen in favour of a colony of Englishmen was certainly as foreign to Wibē's thinking as it was, or rather became, natural to Coffin's as soon as he had started to talk with British officials at Aden.[195]

Wibē's real concern is clearly stated in the Amharic letter to Victoria. First he expressed a desire to hear from the British government, and the references to British relations with Welde Sillasē and Sebagadis as well as the presents sent indicate the kind of response he would like. Here the comparison of French activity with British silence for so many years implies criticism. The purpose of Wibē's letter, however, was to ask the British government to facilitate the task of his ecclesiastical mission to Cairo, which would, it was feared, run into difficulties with the Egyptian authorities. Although the French assured him that *they* had the power, Wibē turned to the British because, as he expressed it: 'We say that the English are strong. They were feared as far as Massawa in [the days of] Ras Welde Sillasē. So show your strength; God knows that we are all Christian'.[196]

192   ibid., fol. 165, Coffin to Backhouse, 19 Nov. 1841; see also fols 122–6, Barnett to Backhouse, 19 Sep. 1841; fol. 128, Coffin to Backhouse, 20 Sep. 1841; fols 139–41, Canning to Coffin, 30 Sep. 1841. To Degoutin (AEMD, Afrique 13, fol. 18, Degoutin to Guizot, 30 Jan. 1842) the purpose of Coffin's mission was to offer Anfilla to Great Britain, and he even pretended to know that Queen Victoria had turned down the offer. Blondeel reported (AE(Brussels), 2024/II, to Lebeau, 17 Mar. 1841) that Coffin had ruined Lefebvre's credit with Wibē.

193   Ferret and Galinier, *Voyage*, Vol. I, pp. 415–17; Duchesne, *Blondeel*, pp. 128–9; AEMD, Afrique 13, fols 227–32, Combes to Guizot, 1 Sep. 1841. There was also an Italian named Valieri with Wibē at this time. See Ferret and Galinier, *Voyage*, Vol. II, pp. 40, 461.

194   AECP, Massouah 1, fols 75–6, Degoutin to Guizot, 18 Mar. 1842.

195   Coffin arrived at Aden just after the Harris mission to Shewa had sailed for Tajura (15 May 1841) to forestall the French at Sahle Sillasē's court. See below, pp. 150–4.

196   FO 1/3, fol. 147, Wibē to Victoria, n.d. The calligraphy and orthography of this document are generally poor but do not provide any good clues as to the writer. It is stamped with a

The British government decided to ignore Coffin's mission and Wibē's letter, at least until the outcome of Harris's embassy to Shewa would be known.[197] As for the appointment of the new *abun*, no intervention was apparently necessary. By the end of May, within a month after the arrival of the mission, Abba Selama was consecrated, and in mid-November he arrived safely at Adwa.[198] Wibē had already made his plans, and Selama was hardly given the opportunity to consider any other course than to support his ambitions to become the *ras* of all Abyssinia. On 12 December 1841 Wibē left Adwa with his Tigrean forces. Selama accompanied him on the campaign to Gonder and Debre Tabor.[199]

After some hesitation Birru Goshu joined forces with Wibē at Maryam Wiha south-east of Gonder, and together they marched on Debre Tabor.[200] Ali seemed both unprepared and unwilling to fight and when the battle took place on 7 February 1842, it was a very confused event. Ali's army was first defeated, and he fled to safety in Wadla. Later in the day, one of Ali's relatives and vassals, Birru Alīgaz, ruler of Yejju and Wadla, managed to rally some of the Gallas and capture Wibē and his entourage. Birru Goshu saw what was happening and escaped to Gojjam. It took several days before Ali was found and could return to his capital. With the assistance of Selama, Wibē quickly and unexpectedly negotiated his own release and the restoration of all his lands.[201] Even the Ethiopian chronicler, accustomed as he was to the sudden changes in the unceasing conflicts, was bewildered by the outcome of the encounter at Debre

round lion seal with the legend in Amharic *Dejjazmach Wibē, ye-Dejja mach* [*sic*] *Hayle lij*, not *Dadj Azmatsh Oobē* and *Dadj Azmatsh Hailē* (*Maryam?*), as the translator Isenberg assumed. I have found no reasons to doubt its authenticity. At any rate, Coffin was not responsible for producing it, which is obvious from the trouble Kruse had to make a translation in Cairo. See CMS, CM/045(a), Kruse to Coates, 15 Sep. 1841.

197 FO 1/3, fols 154–5, Ellenborough to Aberdeen, 23 Oct. 1841.

198 *CMR*, pp. 181–2, Kruse, 20 May and 17 Jun. 1841; Ferret and Galinier, *Voyage*, Vol. II, pp. 67–71; Lefebvre, *Voyage*, Vol. I, pp. 291, 296–7, 311.

199 AECP, Massouah 1, Degoutin to Guizot, 24 Dec. 1841. Cf. Conti Rossini, 'Vicende', *RRAL*, 5, XXV, pp. 461–2, where the Catholic author Abba Tekle Haymanot places the responsibility for the campaign on Selama. This must be part of the anti-Selama bias of this work since the outbreak of the war had long been expected all over Ethiopia.

200 Ferret and Galinier, *Voyage*, Vol. II, pp. 458–60; AE(Brussels), 2024/II, Blondeel to Lebeau, 2 Feb. 1842.

201 Conti Rossini, 'Nuovi documenti', *RANL*, 8, II, p. 381; *idem*, 'Vicende', *RRAL*, 5, XXV, pp. 463–4; AE(Brussels), 2024/II, Blondeel to Lebeau, 20 Jun. 1842; Ferret and Galinier, *Voyage*, Vol. II, pp. 461–72. There is no disagreement between the Ethiopian sources and the narratives of Ferret and Galinier or Blondeel with regard to the above-mentioned basic facts. Of the many European travellers, including Krapf, Lefebvre, Parkyns, and Plowden, who have published narratives about these events, Ferret and Galinier were closest to the place at the time. They seem, however, to have placed the battle about two weeks too late, around 22 February. Blondeel has 6 February and Tekle Haymanot, in 'Vicende', 1 Yekatīt (= 7 Feb.). The latter date is also provided by Antoine d'Abbadie (BN, Ethiop. Abb. 265, fol. 105). In several of the European accounts, Wibē is reported to have paid a ransom, the figures varying from 2,000 thalers in the account of Ferret and Galinier to 40,000 in Lefebvre's (*Voyage*, Vol. I, p. 362).

Tabor:

> And all the world was astonished at the generosity of Ras Ali. What happened at Debre Tabor was marvellous and amazing; however, the Lord rules all nations.[202]

The battle of Debre Tabor is significant not because it produced any important changes, as the battle of Debre Abbay had done in 1831, but because of what it reveals about the political situation at the time. Wibē's primary goal was clearly defined: to defeat and depose Ras Ali and take his position. Whether he aspired to the rank of *niguse negest* as well is more uncertain.[203] Abune Selama obviously wanted to establish himself at Gonder as the supreme ecclesiastical authority over all Ethiopians. This forged the alliance between the two. Although the Tigrean chiefs were far from loyal to Wibē, they were divided against each other, and Wibē had nothing to fear from them as long as his campaign was successful.[204] Ali was in a much more difficult position. Birru Goshu openly defied him; Menen had problems pacifying parts of her new fief; Farīs and Birru Alīgaz of Lasta and Yejju respectively were uncommitted; and only the year before the battle of Debre Tabor, Ali had been checked by his own Muslim Galla vassals when he tried to march through Wello to attack Sahle Sillasē.[205]

On the other hand, Wibē's attempt to make his campaign a crusade against Islam failed badly. Selama's reported excommunication of Ali and Menen seems to have had little effect except probably on Yohannis, the nominal Emperor, who escaped from Gonder to join Wibē.[206] The two most prestigious Christian princes outside Simēn and Tigrē, Sahle Sillasē of Shewa and Dejjazmach Goshu of Gojjam, Birru's father, refrained from participation in spite of their own recent conflicts with Ali. There were, moreover, unquestionably Christian chiefs who fought on Ali's side. Wibē's own half brother, Dejjazmach Merso, who had recently governed Tembēn as his vassal,[207] was one of them. Another was Dejjazmach Birru Alīgaz who decided the outcome of the battle in Ali's favour. In fact, Ali's Muslim vassals from Wello seem to have shown far less interest in this struggle than Merso and Birru Alīgaz. The province of Dawint with which Birru was rewarded after the battle was quite

202   Conti Rossini, 'Nouvi documenti', *RANL*, 8, II, p. 381.
203   Ferret and Galinier, *Voyage*, Vol. I, p. 480; Vol. II, p. 78; Lefebvre, *Voyage*, Vol. I, pp. 233–4, 292–3. See above, p. 35, for the view of Arnauld d'Abbadie that both Ali and Birru Goshu harboured imperial aspirations in some form or another. The evidence is, however, not convincing for any one of the three princes.
204   Lefebvre, *Voyage*, Vol. I, pp. 317–19; Vol. II, pp. 6, 45.
205   Conti Rossini, 'Nuovi documenti', *RANL*, 8, II, p. 380; Bell, 'Extract', *Misc. Aegyptiaca*, 1842, pp. 14, 19; Isenberg and Krapf, *Journals*, pp. 324, 328, 335. Blondeel (Duchesne, p. 136) seems to have come quite close to the truth when he wrote in 1841 that only the jealousy between his vassals explained the little power Ali had.
206   Lefebvre, *Voyage*, Vol. I, pp. 319, 357–8; Conti Rossini, 'Nuovi documenti', *RANL*, 8, II, p. 381; Bell, 'Extract', *Misc. Aegyptiaca*, 1842, p. 25; Ferret and Galinier, *Voyage*, Vol. II, p. 248.
207   Lefebvre, *Voyage*, Vol. I, pp. 186–7.

logically taken, without prior consultation, from the leading Muslim chief, Ali's cousin Imam Līben Amedē of Werre Hīmenu.[208]

To regard the confrontation between Wibē and Ali primarily as a struggle between Christianity and Islam is therefore an oversimplification, to say the least. The uniting bond in Ali's camp was not Islam but the desire to preserve the Yejju dynasty in power in central Ethiopia. Birru Alīgaz, as well as Merso through his mother, belonged to this Yejju family of rulers. For Merso personally, the war meant a possibility to oust Wibē and succeed to his father's lands. After the victory over Wibē, Merso also received Simēn and Tigrē and went there to take possession. But then Ali released Wibē, and when it turned out that the latter was not able to retake Simēn, Ali went personally to his assistance. Merso was defeated and fled, first to the sanctuaries of Waldibba and then to the Içhegē Bēt in Gonder.[209] Ali then offered him Lasta if he could take it from Birru's brother, Farīs Alīgaz, who had been Ali's most serious rival in Begēmdir ever since Ali became ras in 1831.[210] No sooner had Merso succeeded in doing this than Ali turned against him again and imprisoned him. As for Birru Alīgaz, he was before the end of the year 'insidiously captured' by Ali, stripped of all his lands, and together with his brother handed over to Wibē as a state prisoner. As soon as it suited Wibē, however, he let them go. Merso was also released again and invested with Gojjam where he had to fight Birru Goshu on Ali's behalf.[211]

This goes on and on during the *Zemene Mesafint*. If there was a pattern at all, it was that of a feudal warfare in which the ties between overlord and vassals functioned only when the larger unit was threatened. Once the immediate threat had passed, as it did at Debre Tabor, the tensions and struggles within the unit surfaced again. It was on this level, *within* the sub-kingdom of Begēmdir, that the tension between Muslim and Christian played a role, but there is no evidence that Ali's unscrupulous treatment of his Christian vassals was really based on religious preference. The explanation is rather that they were felt to be more dangerous to his own position than his Muslim vassals and therefore had to be kept at loggerheads with each other.

Before the battle of Debre Tabor, Ali is reported to have asked Abune Selama to mediate and declared that he wanted the bishop to rebaptize him if he doubted that he was a Christian; after the battle he is said to have taken an oath

---

208 Isenberg and Krapf, *Journals*, pp. 343, 348. Ferret and Galinier (*Voyage*, Vol. II, p. 469) state that it was Birru's brother Farīs who received Dawint, while Birru received some other areas. The source material emanating from Wello is very scarce. Krapf, travelling through the province about one month after the battle, was given a friendly reception twice by Imam Līben. Some of the Imam's forces had taken part in the battle, but there seems to have been little talk about the war with Wibē. Though Krapf repeatedly refers to the fanaticism of the Muslim Wello, his own experiences at the court of Līben, 'the Representative of the Mahomedan power in Abyssinia . . . the Muhamedo, as they significantly call him', belie these statements (*Journals*, pp. 342, 347).

209 Conti Rossini, 'Nuovi documenti', *RANL*, 8, II, p. 381; Ferret and Galinier, *Voyage*, Vol. II, pp. 472–4.

210 Conti Rossini, 'Cronaca', *RRAL*, 5, XXV, pp. 911–12.

211 Conti Rossini, 'Nuovi documenti', *RANL*, 8, II, pp. 381–2; Lefebvre, *Voyage*, Vol. II, pp. 130–1.

that no ox had ever been killed in his camp except in the name of the Father and the Son and the Holy Ghost.[212] Stories of this kind express the concern of the ordinary Ethiopian for ritual purity. In these respects, Ali had no doubt shown indifference and tolerance towards Muslim practices.[213] Even the fact that he used a Muslim name is not without some significance. But it is difficult to believe that he ever declared himself to be a Muslim or even seriously considered doing so.[214] Both Ali and his advisers knew that he depended for his position at least as much on the loyalty of his Christian subjects as on that of his Muslim supporters. About Ali's personal inclinations we know still less. Even the chronicler who in one connection did not shrink from comparing Ali with Ahmad Grañ sums up the discussion of Ali's faith with a resigned: 'The Lord only knows!'[215]

But Ali's personal stand and the delicate balance between Christian and Muslim influences in Begēmdir and Wello are only one dimension of Ethiopia's problem with Islam at this time. Although the Egyptian pressure on Ethiopia's western boundary had decreased temporarily in 1838,[216] Egyptian and Arab infiltration did not cease, and the hazy Ottoman claims to suzerainty over Habesha were becoming even more explicit. Muhammad Ali's desire to create an entirely independent Egyptian state led to war with the Sultan in 1839. When Egypt was militarily successful, several of the European Powers, led by Great Britain, intervened in favour of the Sultan and imposed a settlement in which Muhammad Ali had to give up almost all his Asian territories, including the Hijaz, for the limited gain of a hereditary viceroyalty over Egypt.[217]

In October 1840, while the war was still going on, Ali Rida Pasha in Bagdad informed the British agent there 'of his nomination by the Porte to the Government of Arabia, *and its usual accompaniment Abyssinia*, and of his determination to dispatch his Lieutenant to Jeddah as quickly as possible . . .'[218] The Pasha of Hijaz was one step ahead and had already sent an important agent named Muhammad al-Basrawi to visit the courts of Wibē and Ali. Arnauld d'Abbadie met and talked with him at Massawa in August 1840 and again at Jidda about a year later.[219] On the second occasion the governor, Uthman Pasha, reportedly talked with Arnauld about the Ottoman claims to sovereignty over Ethiopia, and Muhammad seems to have been very open about the aims of his mission to Ras Ali. He told Arnauld that he was instructed to convey presents to Ali, try to win him for Islam, and in the name of the Sultan promise him

212 Ferret and Galinier, *Voyage*, Vol. II, pp. 463, 470.
213 During Lent 1841 Bell ('Extract' *Misc. Aegyptiaca*, 1842, p. 14) made the remark that Goshu fasted but Ali did not and was therefore regarded as a Muslim.
214 This is the view of Ferret and Galinier (*Voyage*, Vol. II, p. 80), who seem to have looked much more objectively at the Ethiopian political scene than most of the other European travellers. That Rochet and Harris (see above, p. 90, n. 188, and Abir, *Ethiopia*, p. 115) had another view may be the result of the fact that news and rumours about Ali passed through Muslim Wello on their way to Shewa.
215 Conti Rossini, 'Nuovi documenti', *RANL*, 8, II, pp. 382, 389.
216 See above, pp. 69–70, 77.
217 See P. M. Holt, *Egypt and the Fertile Crescent 1516–1922*, pp. 186–7.
218 FO 1/3, fols 61–4, Taylor to the Secret Committee, 10 Oct. 1840 (my emphasis).
219 D'Abbadie, *Douze ans*, p. 558; Vatican, Carte d'Abbadie, Box 16, pp. 9–10.

money, cannon, and soldiers so that he would be able to subdue all northern Abyssinia as far as the coast and force the people to adopt Islam.[220]

As we have already seen, this kind of programme was pretty unrealistic in view of the actual political situation in Ethiopia, and no one knows, of course, if it was actually as drastic as reported by Arnauld d'Abbadie. On the other hand, Muhammad al-Basrawi was far from the only emissary of Ethiopia's Muslim neighbours. Even if Muhammad Ali was himself preoccupied with other matters, and about to lose control of Sawakin and Massawa, he, or at least his governor in the Sudan, Ahmad abu Widan, certainly kept an eye on developments in Ethiopia through Muslim merchants and other agents. In fact, Ahmad Pasha had a kind of permanent representative with Ras Ali from about 1840, Shaykh Ali ibn Muhammad.[221] One of his tasks may well have been to try to interest Ali in Muslim faith and law. But rumours and reports spoke not only of Ali's conversion, but also of appeals for assistance and an alliance between him and the Egyptians.[222]

In two letters written in June 1844, to Muhammad Ali and Ahmad abu Widan's successor Ahmad Manikli respectively, Ali spoke of their friendship using the traditional phraseology: 'your soldiers are my soldiers, and my soldiers are your soldiers' and 'your enemy is my enemy, and my enemy is your enemy'.[223] Since Ali pointed out that his friendship with Ahmad abu Widan had lasted for four years, it seems clear that he dated it from the arrival of Ali ibn Muhammad. But whether these contacts had developed into any kind of alliance before the battle of Debre Tabor is an entirely different matter.

Consul Blondeel, who visited Ali in June 1841, and spent the remainder of that year with Goshu and Birru in Gojjam, reported both that Ali had sent an emissary to Muhammad Ali to ask for help, offering the prospect of a Muslim Abyssinia in reward, and that the Egyptian viceroy had sent a sympathetic reply couched in the above-mentioned phraseology. Nevertheless, he also reported, half a year later from Gonder, that there was no foundation for the rumours about Ali's Muslim faith, and from Khartoum, after his arrival there, that his friend Goshu, the very champion of Christianity in the Tana region, had begged him to dissuade Ahmad Pasha from replying to Ali's offers of an alliance and to accept his own instead![224] These statements, like so many others by the Belgian consul, should not be taken too seriously. What really mattered to him was to have his government believe that he was told in confidence, wherever he came, about the secret plans of the Ethiopian rulers, that he was their adviser

---

220 Vatican, Carte d'Abbadie, Box 16, pp. 9–10.
221 ENA, Bahr Barra, Carton 19, no. 43, Ali to Muhammad Ali, 7 Jun. 1844.
222 See Abir, *Ethiopia*, pp. 113–15.
223 ENA, Bahr Barra, Carton 19, no. 43, Ali to Muhammad Ali, 7 Jun. 1844; no. 44, Ali to Ahmad Manikli, 7 Jun. 1844. The quotations are from the second letter. Ali also uses the most profuse Muslim greetings at the head of his letters, presumably to give the impression that he was a true follower of the Prophet.
224 AE(Brussels), 2024/II, Blondeel to Lebeau, 23 Jul. 1841, 15–25 Jan. and 20 Jun. 1842. Among the Ethiopian princes, Goshu was the favourite of both Blondeel and, in a more sincere way, Arnauld d'Abbadie.

and received offers of treaties, alliances, and cessions of territory:

> Now . . . I find myself almost by force the intimate counsellor of Itēgē Menen and the
> *içhegē*, as I was at Debre Tabor, at Dembeça, at Dīma, at Gudera, the counsellor of
> the *ras*, of Goshu, of Birru, and the prisoner-king; and the result of our secret con-
> ferences is . . .[225]

Of greater significance is the fact that Ras Ali in his letter to Muhammad Ali
of 7 June 1844 told the Egyptian viceroy of the battle of Debre Tabor as if he
had not sent any information during the more than two years that had passed
since the event. Besides, the whole purpose of the letter, as well as of the one to
Ahmad Manikli of the same date, was to inquire what had become of some
presents which Ali had been informed that he would receive. These gifts were
quite normal: gilded saddles, coffee pots, cups, cushions, velvet, and other
precious cloth, and they seem to have been held up at Khartoum because of the
death of Abu Widan in October 1843. In view of all the requests for, and gifts of,
firearms reported by Europeans, it is interesting to note that there is no hint of
any arms among the presents or of any disappointment that the Egyptians had
not assisted Ali in the civil war.[226]

It is true that Egyptian forces operated in the Ethiopian borderlands in
1840–42. But they had other, more tangible aims than lending support to Ras
Ali in his struggle with Wibē and Birru. In the north, Ahmad abu Widan was
determined to subdue the Beja tribes of the lower Gash and, as a result of his
campaign in 1840, Kasala was founded and subsequently developed into the
chief military and administrative centre of the eastern Sudan. Secondly, Ahmad
had the problem of Sudanese chiefs who followed Mek Nimr's example and
escaped from Egyptian rule and taxation to the Ethiopian marches where
Ahmad went to hunt them down. Thirdly, he was precisely in 1840–41 engaged
in extensive raiding for slaves along the frontier as far south as Kurmuk.[227]

As governor of Dembīya, Ali's own mother Menen ruled the border provinces
from Armaçhiho in the north to Agewmidir in the south, that is, most of the
affected districts. In this situation it is highly unlikely that Menen invited
Egyptian troops into her territories. On the contrary, she complained bitterly to
Ahmad Manikli about the inroads and slave raids of his *kashif* and asked him to
return 700 of her enslaved subjects. She proposed co-operation to bring peace
to the frontier districts after the disorder of the last year or years of Ahmad abu
Widan's rule, but nowhere did she hint at any desire, past or future, for Egyptian
assistance in the conflicts between her son Ali and his rivals.[228] That the
Catholic missionary Luigi Montuori, for instance, reported otherwise was probably due to the desire of the Catholic missionaries to have Wibē turn to them

225 ibid., Blondeel to Lebeau, 15–25 Jan. 1842; Duchesne, *Blondeel*, pp. 137, 153, 162, 168–71.
226 ENA, Bahr Barra, Carton 19, nos 43 and 44.
227 See Holt, *Modern History*, pp. 55–8; Hill, *The Sudan*, pp. 70–2.
228 ENA, Bahr Barra, Carton 19, no. 56, Menen to Ahmad Manikli, n.d. This letter cannot be
    dated very precisely but it was most certainly written either in June 1844 when Ali's
    letters were written or soon after. Shaykh Ali ibn Muhammad, who was at Menen's court
    in Gonder in June 1844 (Tubiana, 'Deux fragments', *RO*(Warsaw), XXV, 2, p. 48), is not
    mentioned in her letter as in Ali's letters of that month.

and to France for assistance.[229] In spite of the disorder in Ethiopia, and the tension between Muslims and Christians in some parts, the Ethio-Egyptian problem was basically a question of border conflict and further Egyptian annexations, not one of interference in the internal affairs of the country. It was the representatives of European powers who excelled in soliciting requests for aid and trying to strike bargains for ports, territories, or overall commercial control of the country.

Blondeel's Projects

On the Ethiopian scene no one played the game of proto-imperialism with more gusto and fewer scruples than Consul Blondeel. He even suggested to his government before going to Ethiopia that he would try to get 200–300 men through an alliance with Wibē so that he could destroy the tribes on the coast and partition their territory.[230] At Massawa the picture was different. Blondeel reported that he had received an offer from the real owners to buy Anfilla with its hinterland as far as the salt plains for 2,000 thalers; unfortunately he could not accept it, for the time being at least, since he did not have the money or the power to challenge Lefebvre, though the offer itself proved, as he noted, that Wibē had sold or tried to sell to France what did not belong to him.[231]

Finding the situation in the north complicated and possibly dangerous, Blondeel refused to involve himself in any negotiations with Wibē.[232] Once he had reached central Ethiopia, however, nothing in the way of political change, of alliances and concessions seems to have been too fanciful or far-fetched for the Belgian consul. In Gojjam he encouraged Dejjazmach Goshu, who had great difficulties defending his province against his own son, to mention what he needed to gain control over all Ethiopia, and allegedly received the reply: 'With one hundred Belgians there is nothing that I could not do, [but together] with the assistance of the whites I would need 100,000 thalers and 7,000 muskets . . .'[233] *If* this conversation took place and was serious, the 100 Belgians were most

---

229 AECP, Massouah 1, fols 138–40, Degoutin to Guizot, 5 May 1845. See also below, pp. 109–111.
230 AE(Brussels), 2024/II, Blondeel to Theux, 25 Apr. 1840, Liedts to Lebeau, 14 Aug. 1840. The Belgian government presumably found this too risky. Blondeel should be instructed to refrain from using force.
231 Duchesne, *Blondeel*, pp. 110, 118–21.
232 AE(Brussels), 2024/II, Blondeel to Degoutin, 29 Apr. 1841. If he did so in spite of the views expressed in this letter, no record has been preserved. See Duchesne, *Blondeel*, pp. 128–9.
233 AE(Brussels), 2024/II, Blondeel to Lebeau, 20 Sep. 1841. The quote is from the part of the dispatch which was written in cipher. In the original there is a *mais* in clear text between the two clauses in cipher. Duchesne (*Blondeel*, p. 150) seems to have used another transcription than the one attached to the original dispatch and quotes 'but without the assistance'. To me the rendering 'but with' in the sense 'but in addition to' is just as plausible. At any rate it is ridiculous to believe that Goshu or any other Ethiopian chief would regard 100 European soldiers on one hand and 7,000 muskets and 100,000 thalers on the other as equivalent alternatives.

likely what Blondeel thought he could contribute, and the money and muskets what Goshu would like to have.

Goshu was advised to put his requests in writing to the 'emperor' of Belgium. The letter, copied into Blondeel's dispatch of 20 September 1841, contained three points: if he received some arms and money, Goshu would soon put an end to the civil wars; Belgium would have to chase the Turks from Massawa since this could only be done by a sea power; if a consul came, he would be received and protected as a friend. Blondeel added that he had not wanted to reveal any of his own ideas and therefore neither mentioned the alternative to chasing the Turks from Massawa 'nor requested that which Goshu should give in return' in case Leopold I agreed to an alliance.[234] In his own mind, however, the consul had fixed his price; he deplored the fact that he was unable to enter into binding agreements, for it would have been easy for him to obtain *the cession of all Tigrē* from Goshu for 100,000 thalers and 7,000 muskets. But his inventive brain was occupied with many possibilities: to buy Anfilla for between 1,000 and 5,000 thalers; to buy Agamē from Wibē (no price tag); to buy all Tigrē from Ali, who detested Wibē and who had never had as much as 1,000 thalers at his disposal (and would therefore presumably sell cheaper than Goshu); to provide assistance for Gwangwil Sebagadis, the governor of Agamē, who would gladly cede his province if he could only get revenge on his mortal enemy Wibē; etc.[235] It is interesting to note that Blondeel recorded *one* unprovoked request from Goshu: a few Belgian artisans, or the opportunity for some people from his court to go to Belgium and receive instruction there. Blondeel proposed Catholic missionaries instead, and Goshu obliged with a letter asking for them.[236]

A few days later, Goshu was defeated by his son Birru. Blondeel visited the victor, who allegedly confided 'his most secret and most important affairs' to the consul. It should surprise no one that these included a treaty with Belgium! Blondeel could report that 'the treaty concluded with Goshu', and communicated in the dispatch of 20 September, had been renewed 'in still clearer terms' with Birru. It would have been easy for him, moreover, to conclude another one like it with Ali, 'but he is a child and would not know how to keep quiet . . .' The only tangible proof of the negotiations with Birru, however, is a letter from 'the *nigus* of Gojjam, Dejjazmach Birru' to the *Propaganda Fide*, requesting some-

---

234 AE(Brussels), 2024/II, Blondeel to Lebeau, 20 Sep. 1841. It is impossible to state with certainty whether Goshu's 'letter' is a very free translation of an Amharic document or possibly a dictated message or speech. No Amharic documents exist among the Blondeel papers. The former consul stated many years later that he had lost documents in a shipwreck in 1857 (FO 401/2, pp. 836–8, Blondeel to Scarlett, 12 Oct. 1867), but it seems unlikely that he should have kept original letters to his sovereign for fifteen years.

235 AE(Brussels), 2024/II, Blondeel to Lebeau, 24 Sep. 1841.

236 ibid. This letter, too, is copied into Blondeel's dispatch. A copy in Italian is found in APF. SRC, Africa Centrale, Etiopia ecc. . . . 4, fol. 251. See also Duchesne, *Blondeel*, pp. 154–6. Arnauld d'Abbadie also tried to interest Goshu in Catholic missionaries, but they were intended primarily for mission work among the Galla south of the Abbay (BN, Ethiop. Abb. 254, fol. 1, Goshu to Gregorius XVI, n.d.). The origin of this letter is revealed in a marginal note on the French translation (fol. 4): 'Lettre inspirée et dictée au Prince par M. Arnauld d'Abbadie'.

one to teach Christianity to the Galla south of the Abbay.[237] Just in case the young *ras* might 'grow up', Blondeel had Ali's mother ask him to place before the king of the Belgians a convention stipulating the cession of Agamē and Antalo against 15,000 thalers and 3,000 muskets, payable within six months after Belgium had taken possession of the ceded territories. Blondeel found this 'offensive and defensive treaty' acceptable but felt he could not take charge of it, for who could tell the outcome of the battles to be fought? More than once the consul stressed that he was keeping all doors open, making it possible for Belgium to choose its allies, acting as if a colony was to be established without compromising his government or himself: '. . . I have always confined myself to giving the advice to claim the alliance with or the protection of my King without ever promising anything.'[238]

This is indeed a fitting summary of the Blondeel approach by one who should know what he was talking about. The Belgian consul was by no means exceptional in this respect. But there is another aspect in which he seems to have outdone his colleagues: though he listed desiderata to his own government, he seems to have been almost as reluctant to define his requests to the Ethiopian chiefs as to promise them anything. No wonder his negotiations were all abortive, his 'treaties' and 'conventions' barely drafted, never signed! To Blondeel it did not seem to matter. In his general report, and later, he cited the desire of the Ethiopian chiefs for protection as an indication that Abyssinia would be easy to conquer (*sic*) and easy to rule; all of it or as much as Belgium might want as its protectorate. To him, the purchase of Anfilla and the diversion from Massawa of the trade were only the first step towards the creation of a vast Belgian colony, a market of 20 million (!) people exclusively for Belgium. Too busy building castles in the air, Blondeel had failed even to visit Anfilla.[239]

One can only speculate about the impression made by a man like Blondeel in Begēmdir and Gojjam. Dejjazmach Goshu must have found it amusing, to say the least, if Blondeel actually called him king and alternated between the titles emperor and *dejjazmach* for King Leopold.[240] Goshu knew the difference all too well. A grandson of the famous Ras Haylu of Gojjam and himself the leading nobleman of the province, he had probably for many years desired the rank of *ras*, before he finally obtained it from Emperor Sahle Dingil in 1848.[241] That the Gojjamē prince had a French *ras*, Arnauld d'Abbadie, among his own

237 AE(Brussels), 2024/II, Blondeel to Lebeau, 22 Nov. 1841, 15–25 Jan. 1842; APF.SRC, Africa Centrale, Etiopia ecc. . . . 4, fol. 254. Crummey (*Priests*, pp. 73–4) mistakenly quotes this letter as coming from Goshu.

238 AE(Brussels), 2024/II, Blondeel to Lebeau, 2 Feb. and 15–25 Jan. 1842.

239 Duchesne, *Blondeel*, pp. 181–7, 199. It is indeed difficult to understand the enthusiasm of Duchesne for Blondeel's projects, '. . . quel sens des réalités!' (ibid., p. 4); or of C. J. Jaenen ('Blondeel, The Belgian Attempt to Colonize Ethiopia', *African Affairs*, LV (1956), pp. 214–18) for Blondeel's 'outstanding service' as one of Belgium's 'most remarkable diplomatic agents', particularly as he writes: 'His most outstanding undertaking was probably the negotiation of alliances with Ethiopian chieftains which would afford Belgium a colony in East Africa.' The above survey demonstrates that no alliances had been *concluded*, least of all any that would automatically provide Belgium with a colony.

240 Duchesne, *Blondeel*, pp. 142–3.

241 Conti Rossini, 'Nuovi documenti', *RANL*, 8, II, p. 395.

retainers can hardly have increased his respect for the envoy of a Belgian *dejjazmach*. And *if* Blondeel even hinted at buying all or part of Tigrē from Goshu or from Ali and Menen, it is most unlikely that they took the proposals seriously.

Nevertheless, Blondeel represented something that had come to stay and influence the history of Ethiopia for a century. In the extension of his crude proposals, there would be many European attempts to gain a foothold in Ethiopia by interfering when internal tension and conflict mounted. In the meantime, more travellers would gather increasingly important political inform-ation and establish contacts on all levels. After the invasion of the early forties, there was no question of keeping European observers away from the Gonder area until it had lost its political importance. But for some years more the main pressure of the Europeans would concentrate on Tigrē and the northern border-lands, and it was also there that the Egyptian expansion would pose the greatest threat to the survival of Ethiopia.

Increasing Conflict in the North

When Wibē departed for Begēmdir in 1841, Tigrē had been left in the hands of his less than loyal vassals. The most important of these was Balgada Araya Sillasē Dimṣu representing the claims of the house of Welde Sillasē. At the news of Wibē's defeat, he came forward as the champion of Tigrean autonomy.[242] Lefebvre immediately prepared to renew his political activities. On 17 February 1842 he dispatched a glowing report of commercial opportunities and offered to occupy Anfilla the moment he received instructions to do so.[243] A few days later he was off to visit Araya Sillasē and ask him to take possession of the port in the name of the French king. Consul Degoutin was far from certain that Araya would agree to the donation and added that the ruler or owner of Anfilla, Aliah Aydu, had besides made her submission to the Sultan.[244] A few months later Araya had consolidated his position. Lefebvre's appetite increased. He pretended to be a man of great political importance at Araya's court and to have received the important province of Hamasēn instead of Anfilla. Degoutin reported that the French explorer was about to raise the French flag over this new colony when he was instructed from Paris to cease all political activity and concentrate on his scientific work.[245]

As might be expected, Coffin was also present, allegedly engaged in an attempt to outdo Lefebvre and get hold of Hamasēn for the British.[246] But

242 Lefebvre, *Voyage*, Vol. I, pp. 320, 352–3; Vol. II, pp. 1–9, 31–40; Isenberg and Krapf, *Journals*, p. 501.
243 AEMD, Afrique 13, fols 86–91, Lefebvre to Cunin-Gridaine, 17 Feb. 1842.
244 AECP, Massouah 1, fols 75–6, Degoutin to Guizot, 18 Mar. 1842. See also IO, Secret Letters from Aden 26, pp. 170–1, Christopher to Haines, 7 Mar. 1842; Lefebvre, *Voyage*, Vol. I, pp. 317–20, 339, 352–3.
245 AECP, Massouah 1, fol. 77, Guizot to Degoutin, 4 Jun. 1842; fols 79, 86–7, Degoutin to Guizot, 16 Aug. 1842 and 20 Apr. 1843. See also Lefebvre, *Voyage*, Vol. II, pp. 39–40, 49–59.
246 BN, NAF 22430, fol. 221, De Jacobis to Antoine d'Abbadie, 1 Aug. 1842. Cf. IO, Secret Letters from Aden 26, pp. 365–72, Christopher to Sanders, 2 Oct. 1842. Coffin had returned from his journey to Egypt by early May. See Isenberg and Krapf, *Journals*, p. 528.

there is really no evidence that Araya contemplated giving away his territory to foreigners. He wrote to the French consul to announce that he was now the ruler of Tigrē and that he desired friendly relations with foreign powers, but in the letter, penned and most likely drafted by Schimper, there is no hint about grants of or requests for territory in any form.[247]

Rather than risk a meeting with Wibē after having so deliberately courted Araya, Lefebvre decided to escape to Shewa via Lasta. If we are to believe his own account, he gave Araya a parting lesson in political opportunism:

> Moreover, remain a friend of the Europeans, not in the way Wibē is, in order to receive muskets and a few curiosities, but loyally because with their support you will no doubt one day govern all Abyssinia . . . Beware of showing suspicion towards foreigners, inspired by the fear that they may want to invade your land, not because this is un-likely, but because you cannot prevent it if it is decided. Today when it is known that your country is healthy and fertile and when it is not unknown that it is the key to the interior of Africa, a European nation must some day, probably soon, occupy Abyssinia. Make use of the opportunity for yourself; be friendly with the conquerors who will make you great as soon as they see in you a loyal and useful instrument. Bear in mind, moreover, that your country will only know how to rise from its anarchy through the protection of a more enlightened people.[248]

Assuming that Lefebvre was even half as outspoken as this speech indicates— and nothing in his conduct otherwise shows much prudence—the alternatives for the future, accommodation or resistance, were placed before at least this Ethiopian chief as early as the 1840s.

After a fairly short visit to Shewa, Lefebvre passed through Begēmdir and Tigrē as quickly as possible and left Ethiopia in August 1843.[249] Ferret and Galinier had left one year earlier.[250] Isenberg and Krapf made an attempt to return to northern Ethiopia in April 1843, but in spite of Wibē's initial per-mission the opposition was too strong.[251] Coffin was once more in disfavour because of his reluctance to give up 400 remaining muskets to Wibē and, naturally, because of his contacts with Araya Sillasē. He did not dare to return to Tigrē but stayed at Massawa.[252] De Jacobis and Schimper, who had

247 BN, Ethiop. 184, fol. 64, Araya Sillasē to Degoutin, 20 Jul. 1842. This is the original of Araya's letter, stamped with a lion seal bearing the name of 'Bal Gada Araya'. The letter is in French, and beside the seal it is signed 'Pour lui Schimper'. No translation is men-tioned, and it is unlikely that any Amharic version has existed. There is no reason, however, to doubt that it was written on Araya's instructions. When Degoutin forwarded a copy to Paris, he omitted the date and the subscription with Schimper's name. In the extract published by Lejean (Théodore II, p. 253) Schimper's name, but not the date, is also omitted.

248 Lefebvre, Voyage, Vol. II, pp. 100–1. Cf. above, pp. 89–90, Gebre Maryam expressing some of these views in a cruder manner in front of Wibē.

249 Lefebvre, Voyage, Vol. II, p. 341. Three members of his mission died in Ethiopia; one left before Lefebvre but died on his way to Europe.

250 Ferret and Galinier, Voyage, Vol. II, p. 531.

251 AECP, Massouah 1, fols 86–7, Degoutin to Guizot, 20 Apr. 1843; Krapf, Travels, pp. 108–10.

252 AECP, Massouah 1, fol. 110, Degoutin to Guizot, 10 Dec. 1843. Marston (Britain's Imperial Role, p. 174) states that he was 'expelled in disgrace by Ras Oubie for failing to get an

joined the Catholic church, gladly took over Coffin's former fief of Intiçho with the intention of making it a small self-governing Catholic colony.[253] De Jacobis became for a few years the central figure in Wibē's contacts with Europe. His ultimate goal was a Catholic Ethiopia; his immediate concern was to establish a firm foothold for the mission in Tigrē; his means to secure the good will of Wibē and other powerful personalities were generous gifts, including the arms and ammunition (originally eighty-three pieces of various models and 5,000 cartridges) which had never been handed over by Combes, and an unassuming approach, so different from the overbearing and unbending attitude of Isenberg.[254]

For Wibē and the commercial community at Adwa, good relations with some foreigners were not unimportant. In exchange for hospitality and the protection of Europeans in Tigrē, the Ethiopian merchants and other travellers would expect some assistance, for instance from the French consul, in dealing with the Turkish or Egyptian administration at Massawa. There was also the myth that France had saved Ethiopia once from an Egyptian invasion. Though he regarded it as 'something very remarkable' that the Ethiopians, particularly in Tigrē, should have come to the conclusion that they had been saved by French intervention, De Jacobis welcomed the error as 'an act of Providence'.[255] He would soon be given the opportunity to prove the eventual interest of France in the welfare of Wibē and his subjects in connection with the first serious conflict over Massawa in the nineteenth century.

In July 1843, troops belonging to Na'ib Yahya of Arkīko, allegedly supported by a few Turkish soldiers from Massawa,[256] invaded Hamasēn, burnt a village, kidnapped children to be sold as slaves, and made off with some cattle. The highlanders retaliated by raiding the flocks of the *na'ib*.[257] Mutual small-

---

answer to his letter' (see above, p. 92), but Wibē was certainly more concerned about the muskets and the, most likely correct, rumours that Coffin had offered them to Araya Sillasē but withheld them from himself.

253 CML, De Jacobis, 'Giornale Abissino', Vol. II, pp. 175–9, 199–202; AECP, Massouah 1, fols 96–8, De Jacobis to unknown, 4 Oct. 1843 (extract); fol. 121, Degoutin to Guizot, 20 Jul. 1844; AEMD, Afrique 13, fols 319–24, Schimper to Guizot, 15 Oct. 1844.

254 AECP, Massouah 1, fols 83–84, De Jacobis to unknown, 10 Feb. 1843; fol. 104, Soult to Guizot, 20 Oct. 1843; fol. 106, Guizot to De Jacobis, 26 Oct. 1843; fols 117–18, Degoutin to Guizot, 25 Apr. 1844; CML, 'Lettres manuscrites', Vol. II, no. 181, 1 Sep. 1841; Lefebvre, *Voyage*, Vol. II, pp. 325–7. See also Malécot, 'Voyageurs', *RFHO*, LVIII, pp. 178–9; Crummey, *Priests*, pp. 45, 56.

255 AECP, Massouah 1, fols 94–5, memoir by De Jacobis addressed to the consuls of France in the Levant and to the *Supérieur général* of the Lazarists in Paris, Spring 1844: '. . . par une dispensation de la Providence, s'est accrédité en Abyssinie . . . que la France y soit déjà et unanimement regardée comme la Sauvegarde de l'Independance Ethiopienne . . . chose bien remarquable.'

256 As a result of the settlement between Muhammad Ali and the Sultan in 1840, Massawa reverted nominally to the Ottoman governor of Hijaz, but de facto control seems to have been exercised by the *na'ib*. See Abir, *Ethiopia*, p. 119.

257 AECP, Massouah 1, fols 96–101, extracts of letters from De Jacobis, 4 Oct. 1843, and Schimper, 24 Sep. 1843, annexed to the former's memoir, Spring 1844.

scale raiding was no unusual activity, and kidnapping was, according to the French consul, 'always a good deed in the eyes of the Muslims of this country'.[258] But the raid of July 1843 was led by Muhammad Yahya, the son of the *na'ib*, personally and was probably on a larger scale than usual. At all events, Wibē seems to have decided to take advantage of the incident to settle a few scores with the *na'ib* and the Turkish governor at Massawa. In an ultimatum to the *na'ib*, reported by the French consul, he demanded that Coffin be handed over with all that remained of the arms provided so long ago as a gift for his predecessor; in addition, 3,000 head of cattle should be restored and about 600 thalers returned to Christian merchants who had been forced to pay too high dues. The *na'ib* replied that as an official of the Ottoman government he had no authority over Europeans, and Coffin that the *na'ib* refused to allow him to import the arms into Abyssinia.[259] Degoutin was worried. He estimated that Wibē could bring down 10,000 men to pillage the coast, while the *na'ib* could not raise more than 3,000 at the most and only 300 with muskets. It would, however, be difficult or impossible for Wibē to maintain himself for any length of time in the lowlands.[260]

In December it was reported that Wibē had crossed the boundaries of the *na'ib*'s lands,[261] but instead of attacking Arkīko and Massawa, he relied on the effects of a trade boycott and continued negotiations. The caravans were stopped at Adwa. It was even reported that trade had been diverted towards the Sudan and Tajura.[262] These were powerful arguments, and by March the *na'ib* had collected a large tribute, which reportedly included one month's salary from all his troops, and sent it to Wibē. Reinforcements were expected from Jidda for a counter-attack, but the governor there, Uthman Pasha, also gave orders that the rates should be modified and the abuses which made it so difficult for the Abyssinian merchants to trade through Massawa should be removed.[263] Whether conditions had actually worsened in 1842–43 is difficult to establish. Many European observers commented on the high customs rates and the additional dues that were extorted from the merchants. Ferret and Galinier who passed through Massawa on their way to France in August 1842 stated that the duties charged by the Turks from the Ethiopians amounted to

258 ibid., fols 123–4, Degoutin to Guizot, 4 Sep. 1844. For a British report on the kidnapping, see IO, Secret Letters from Aden 26, pp. 365–72, Christopher to Sanders, 2 Oct. 1842.
259 AECP, Massouah 1, fol. 109, Degoutin to Guizot, 10 Dec. 1843.
260 ibid., fol. 110, Degoutin to Guizot, 10 Dec. 1843 (second dispatch this date). The figure for the *na'ib*'s forces is probably realistic though it is much lower than the estimate of 10,000 made in 1842 (ibid., fols 19–20, Degoutin to Guizot, 20 Feb. 1842) when the French consul wanted to dissuade his government from occupying Anfilla. Compare also Blondeel's estimate (Duchesne, p. 122) of 500 men in 1841. The most conservative estimate of Wibē's army before the battle of Debre Tabor was 18,000–20,000 (Ferret and Galinier, *Voyage*, Vol. II, p. 461), so it is not impossible that he could attack Arkīko and Massawa with 10,000 men including a few thousand with firearms. Schimper (AECP, Massouah 1, fol. 101, 24 Sep. 1843) threatened with no less than 20,000.
261 AECP, Massouah 1, fol. 112, Degoutin to Guizot, 4 Jan. 1844.
262 ibid., fols 113, 117–18, Degoutin to Guizot, 6 Mar. and 25 Apr. 1844.
263 ibid., fols 113, 115, Degoutin to Guizot, 6 Mar. and 5 Apr. 1844.

plundering.[264] The tribute received and the promises given that conditions would be improved caused Wibē to call off the boycott of Massawa. The bulk of his army was directed towards Bogos to levy tribute there and tie this district closer to Hamasēn and Tigrē to which it had been tributary in the past.[265]

It is difficult to know what Wibē's ultimate intentions were when he threatened to attack Arkīko in 1843. His grievances against the *na'ib* and a general desire for booty go far to explain Wibē's actions, and the compromises he accepted do not point towards any definite plans to conquer or occupy the coast facing Massawa as early as 1843.[266] There are indications, however, that Wibē's withdrawal was conditional and caused, at least in part, by the activities of De Jacobis and Schimper, who both protested on Wibē's behalf against the kidnapping in general and the raid of July 1843 in particular. At first they seem to have thought that the French consul had sufficient influence with the Turkish authorities to remove both the governor of Massawa, Rustum Agha, and Na'ib Yahya and all his descendants from office.[267] Later De Jacobis made a formal announcement in Wibē's name—but not necessarily on his instructions—to the consuls of France in the Levant and the head of the Congrégation de la Mission in Paris. According to this, Wibē hoped that France would look into the difference between the *na'ib* and himself and declared that he would not attack Arkīko and Massawa until he was convinced that France would not intervene and that he, therefore, had to find a solution himself. De Jacobis declared that Wibē could have captured both Arkīko and Massawa in April 1844.[268]

Degoutin was more optimistic about the safety of the island at least, but mainly on the grounds that Wibē would not take the risk of a war with Turkey.[269] Since he was a trader himself, he was nevertheless worried about the conflict. He also feared that the British would take advantage of the situation to buy Massawa from the Turks and reported that a British officer, Lt William Christopher, had made an unsuccessful attempt to get it for 300,000 thalers.[270]

---

264 Ferret and Galinier, *Voyage*, Vol. II, p. 447. These two travellers were not personally involved in any commercial projects and were generally much more moderate in their statements than most of the other Europeans.
265 AECP, Massouah 1, fols 94–5, memoir by De Jacobis, Spring 1844. See also Trimingham, *Islam*, p. 165; Munzinger, *Ostafrikanische Studien*, pp. 199–200.
266 Abir (*Ethiopia*, p. 120) nevertheless maintains that '. . . Wube's impossible demands were only a pretext to conquer the coast or part of it'.
267 AECP, Massouah 1, fols 98–101, Schimper, 24 Sep. 1843 (extract).
268 ibid., fols 94–5, memoir by De Jacobis, Spring 1844; fol. 121, Degoutin to Guizot, 20 Jul. 1844; AEMD, Afrique 13, fols 319–24, Schimper to Guizot, 15 Oct. 1844. A certain Gebre Īyesus, *şehafe ti'izaz* (chancellor) at the court of Wibē, was in contact with De Jacobis at this time (CML, De Jacobis, 'Giornale Abissino', Vol. III, letter inserted 27 Apr. 1844), but there is no evidence that the announcement originated at the court.
269 AECP, Massouah 1, fols 110, 113, Degoutin to Guizot, 10 Dec. 1843 and 6 Mar. 1844.
270 ibid., fol. 114, Degoutin to Guizot, 24 Mar. 1844. An offer of 300,000 thalers to the Turks for Massawa is most improbable, particularly since the British at this time rejected all Turkish claims to sovereignty on the African side of the Red Sea and would not offer that much to a local chief. See FO 78/3185, fols 185–7, Canning to Aberdeen, 1 Aug. 1843; fols 195–200, Cotton and Shepherd to Ripon, 21 Sep. 1843; fols 220–4, Hodson to Aberdeen, 15 May 1844.

Though he appreciated the attempts of Schimper and De Jacobis to increase Catholic and French influence in Tigrē, the consul was openly sceptical about the reported success.[271] Even the news that Coffin's district Intiçho had passed into the hands of Schimper and the mission did not impress him.[272] He had no faith in Wibē and showed no desire to become involved in the conflict on his side.

By early September 1844 hostilities broke out again. The immediate reason was a special case of kidnapping. The nephew of a Christian chief in Hamasēn, Welde Gabir, was kidnapped to Arkiko and in spite of protests sold at Massawa. The chief reacted with a raid into Muslim territories, reportedly killing twenty persons and carrying away 2,000 head of cattle. An immediate attack by Wibē on the coast was expected, and the Turkish governor left to bring reinforcements from Jidda.[273] But Wibē vacillated again. Instead of attacking he opened up negotiations with the na'ib.[274] The Tigrean ruler had a more serious problem to face, one in which his interests and those of the na'ib actually coincided.

The foundation of Kasala and the subjection of the Beni Amir had created a third base for Turco-Egyptian pressure on Ethiopia in addition to Qallabat and Massawa. The tribes or tribal federations inhabiting the northernmost parts of the Ethiopian highlands and the slopes down to the coast north of Massawa— the Bilēn (or Bogos), the two divisions of Marya, the Mensa and the Habab (or Bēt Asgede)—were now liable to hostile incursions from the west. Although their rulers had in the past been vassals of the Ethiopian king, the ties had become increasingly tenuous. The sense of affinity had been further weakened by the process of islamization which over a period of about twenty years from 1820 onwards had turned most of the Marya and Habab into Muslims, though they still used Christian names and kept Sunday as their weekly holiday. By the 1840s the Habab had become subject to the na'ib of Arkiko, but his position as a ruler was far from clear, and the French consul concluded in the true spirit of European colonialism: 'This country, which in fact does not belong to anyone any more than New Zealand belongs to the savages who inhabit it, will become the possession of the first Power that wants it.'[275]

Though Degoutin thought in terms of a European occupation, the first to register her interest was Egypt. The lands of the Marya, Habab, Bilēn, and Mensa were not only valuable in themselves, they also formed a wedge blocking

271 AECP, Massouah 1, fols 117–18, Degoutin to Guizot, 25 Apr. 1844. There are reasons to believe that the relationship between De Jacobis and Wibē was not as close as the letters of the missionary to Europe seem to indicate. In a pathetic letter to Wibē, apparently written late in 1844, the missionary begs for permission to buy a piece of land for a grave at Gwela, since it would not be right that the body of a Christian priest should be eaten by hyenas (CML, De Jacobis, 'Giornale Abissino', Vol. III, Amharic letter—probably returned original—inserted between pp. 485 and 486). Cf. Crummey, Priests, pp. 68, 88.
272 AECP, Massouah 1, fol. 121, Degoutin to Guizot, 20 Jul. 1844; AEMD, Afrique 13, fols 319–24, Schimper to Guizot, 15 Oct. 1844.
273 AECP, Massouah 1, fols 123–4, Degoutin to Guizot, 4 Sep. 1844.
274 ibid., fols 125–6, Degoutin to Guizot, 1 Oct. 1844.
275 ibid., fols 117–18, Degoutin to Guizot, 25 Apr. 1844; Sapeto, Viaggio, p. 159; Trimingham, Islam, pp. 158–68.

Egyptian advance from Kasala to Massawa. The Egyptian administration wanted to regain control over Sawakin and Massawa. An unsuccessful attempt to reach an agreement with the Porte was made in 1843.[276] An extension of the Taka province to include all the hinterland of Massawa would naturally strengthen Egypt's case vis-à-vis the Porte. To Ethiopia the implications could be tremendous. A Massawa incorporated in the Egyptian Sudan was something very different from a Massawa in theory governed and protected by Hijaz but in fact at the mercy of the *na'ib* and, in the last instance, the *ras* of Tigrē.

In November 1844 an Egyptian army of 5,000–6,000 men overran Habab and was reported on the frontiers of Wibē's territories only three or four days' march from Massawa.[277] It is not possible to determine whether Wibē understood the implications of the situation and decided that a demonstration of power in the direction of Kasala was the best strategy or was simply tempted by the prospect of collecting booty from a defenceless population. At any rate, Wibē made no attack on Massawa in 1844. Instead he raided Bogos and the lowland population in the direction of Kasala. Wibē wanted to solve the complicated Arkīko/Massawa issue through negotiations, and in February 1845 he made an attempt with Na'ib Hasan who had received the appointment from Jidda when Yahya died in October.[278] Unsatisfied with Hasan's response, Wibē selected Muhammad ibn Yahya for *na'ib* instead. He informed the governor, Rustum Agha, and asked the French consul to support his request that the appointment be changed. The matter was referred to Uthman Pasha at Jidda, and rumours arose that Rustum in addition to a battalion of troops had received orders to stop the pay (more than 1,000 thalers a month) to Arkīko and send a mission to Wibē to sign a peace and trade agreement which would eliminate the powerful position of the *na'ibs* altogether.[279] The abolition of the institution of *na'ibs* would have been a radical solution to many problems, but their rule had been sanctioned by long usage, and if the proposal reached Wibē, he must have understood that the intention of the Turks was to establish themselves on the mainland.

He turned to the French consul, pushed for a reply about the appointment of Muhammad and stated in general terms that only people who came on friendly business would be allowed to enter the country.[280] Degoutin answered that the matter, as Wibē should know, required action by Uthman Pasha. As far as Rustum was concerned, he had assured the consul of his sincere friendship for Wibē and his hope for an early and favourable reply. Degoutin added as his own opinion that the governor of Massawa would certainly not dare to go against

276 See Holt, *Modern History*, p. 58.
277 AECP, Massouah 1, fols 128, 130–1, Degoutin to Guizot, 16 Nov. 1844 and 20 Feb. 1845.
278 ibid.; Parkyns, *Life*, Vol. II, pp. 344–51; CML, De Jacobis, 'Giornale Abissino', Vol. III, pp. 488–9.
279 AECP, Massouah 1, fols 132–4, Degoutin to Guizot, 15 Apr. 1845.
280 ibid., fol. 135, Wibē to Degoutin, April 1845 (copy of Wibē's letter in Arabic). This may be the letter to which Schimper was referring (ibid., fols 209v.–13, Schimper to Degoutin, 28 May 1845) when he wrote that Wibē had received a very obscure message from the governor and not knowing if it was intended to be friendly or hostile, he answered in the same manner.

Wibē's will, since Wibē would then close the route and not allow anyone to put his foot on shore as long as he lived. He advised Wibē, therefore, to be patient and allow the caravans to pass until the matter was cleared up.[281]

Trade, not politics, was Degoutin's main concern. He reported, without excitement, his correspondence with Wibē and continued with the arrival of a British ship, the departure of an emissary to Wibē to get Coffin reinstated as governor of Inticho, which would mean that the Catholic mission would lose this base, and even rumours that the British intended to offer Wibē an alliance so that they could negotiate with Muhammad Yahya for Arkīko.[282] With De Jacobis and Schimper the case was altogether different. They felt the need for political action to place Wibē under a debt of gratitude towards France and above all prevent the British from gaining influence with him. The 1844 appeal of De Jacobis for moral support and arbitration in the conflict over Arkīko had met with little or no response. Schimper had no more success with a direct request to the French government in October 1844 for a few hundred muskets to be used partly as a gift to Wibē, partly to arm a small contingent under his own command.[283] Something more substantial had to be done. In May 1845, under the immediate threat of losing Inticho to Coffin again, Schimper agreed, or more likely volunteered, to seek French protection or assistance against the Turks. The other side of the coin was that a formal request from Wibē might be regarded in Paris as an application for protectorate status under France and therefore arouse the interest of the French government.

The Schimper/De Jacobis 'Protectorate'

On 21 May Schimper arrived at Gwela and told De Jacobis that Wibē wanted him to obtain 'the protection of the King of France against the Turks'. Together they drafted a letter in Wibē's name, and Schimper returned to have the document sealed by the prince. A week later he was back at Gwela again with the stamped letter. Only then was the French consul informed and asked to come to Halay for consultations on the matter.[284]

The document prepared for the French king had parallel Amharic and French texts and carried a square lion seal with Wibē's name.[285] It had nothing to say about the concrete problems of Arkīko and Massawa for which Wibē had asked Degoutin to help find a solution. Instead it contained the kind of general

281 ibid., fol. 136, Degoutin to Wibē, 28 Apr. 1845.
282 ibid., fol. 137, Degoutin to Guizot, 5 May 1845.
283 AEMD, Afrique 13, fols 319–24, Schimper to Guizot, 15 Oct. 1844.
284 CML, De Jacobis, 'Giornale Abissino', Vol. III, pp. 519–20; AECP, Massouah 1, fols 209v.–13, Schimper to Degoutin, 28 May 1845. No copy of this letter was dispatched to Paris at the time, but it was copied and forwarded with other correspondence in April 1849 from Jidda. The relations between Schimper and De Jacobis on one hand and Degoutin on the other were strained at the time of this initiative. See, in addition to Schimper's letter, CML, 'Lettres manuscrites', Vol. II, no. 224, 4 Mar. 1845, and no. 226, 10 Jul. 1845, both from De Jacobis.
285 AECP, Massouah 1, fol. 141, Wibē to Louis Philippe, 24 May 1845.

phrases about friendship and protection which might be construed into a request for protectorate status:

> I send you a letter that you may be unto me a friend [and] that you may protect Ethiopia and myself, for the Turks prepare on two sides, Sinnar and the Red Sea, to help all the Muslims who live in Ethiopia to destroy the Christians. As for myself, I will lovingly protect all your people who have come or will come to me.[286]

Though Wibē may well have approved and placed his seal under a text worded in this manner, there is some reason to doubt the authenticity of the document actually dispatched to Europe. Soon after Schimper's return, De Jacobis mentioned in a draft letter in his diary the possibility of providing a copy for someone in the mission (Étienne), but what he sent a month later was a sealed duplicate.[287] Secondly, the French translation was not made until 29 June, when the meeting with the consul finally took place,[288] and it seems odd that Schimper and De Jacobis should have delayed this work until the last minute unless they felt that they were justified in making alterations in the text if necessary. At any rate, the impression given that Wibē had sealed a bi-lingual document is misleading. If De Jacobis had come to the conclusion that he had better forward a sealed duplicate through mission headquarters and there was only one document, or if the idea of an official French text occurred late, or if alterations were found desirable, nothing prevented Schimper from manufacturing the very primitive seal used, a seal which appears, *nota bene*, only this one time and is quite different from the seals used by Wibē before and after this occasion.

It is not, however, of primary importance whether the letter was rewritten or not. Even if it was, De Jacobis may well have felt obliged to reproduce the Amharic text faithfully. It had been worded by him in the first place, as he freely admitted,[289] and the reference to the Turks helping the Ethiopian Muslims to destroy the Christians covered Wibē's primary concern with developments at Arkīko and in Semhar, Habab and other border areas. The important issues are whether it was Wibē or the foreigners who really sought 'protection' and what 'protection' was supposed to mean in the context.

The first question is easy to answer. De Jacobis does it himself by stressing that Schimper in particular had laboured 'to *persuade Wibē to request* instead of

---

286   My translation from the Amharic text. The French version is substantially the same though more elaborate and more specific: 'It is therefore right that I claim today from Your Majesty both friendship and powerful protection against my enemies, the Muslims, who prepare themselves (so it seems) for war against the Christians of Ethiopia . . . both in the direction of Sinnar and in the direction of the Red Sea while they seek to create a party for themselves amongst the Muslim population of our country . . .'

287   CML, De Jacobis, 'Giornale Abissino', Vol. III, p. 532; 'Lettres manuscrites', Vol. II, Wibē's letter attached to no. 226, De Jacobis to Étienne, 10 Jul. 1845. The French version is exactly the same as in AECP, Massouah 1, fol. 141, and the variations in the Amharic version are not significant.

288   CML, 'Giornale Abissino', Vol. III, p. 543.

289   CML, 'Lettres manuscrites', Vol. II, no. 226, De Jacobis to Étienne, 10 Jul. 1845.

English protection, that of France, with the aim in the first place of improving the position of the Catholic and Lazarist mission of Abyssinia'.[290] How this was done is indicated by Degoutin who reported that the missionaries had 'inoculated their fears' into Wibē and made him decide 'to demand the Protectorate of France'; they had 'communicated their panic to Prince Wibē'.[291] How genuine this 'panic' was and how successfully it was communicated is an open question. Promises of further gifts may have played an equal role, for De Jacobis turned with great urgency to this matter in early June.[292] It seems absolutely clear, at any rate, that it was not Wibē but Schimper and De Jacobis who sought protection in the first place.

What 'protection' meant to the parties involved is a rather more complicated question. The primary concern of Schimper and De Jacobis for protection against Coffin, Abune Selama and everyone else who might want to expel them or deprive them of property or opportunities already granted was taken care of by Wibē's promise to protect French subjects in his country in the future.[293] In return the French king should befriend him and protect him against Turkish attacks. This is the *quid pro quo* of Wibē's letter, but certainly not the end of the matter as far as Schimper and De Jacobis were concerned. The protection they ultimately wanted was the declaration of a French protectorate over Wibē's territories. This would effectively exclude future British/Protestant influence and could be used against Ethiopian political and ecclesiastical leaders if necessary. Probably aware that Wibē's letter fell short of requesting protectorate status, they emphasized that Wibē's 'demand' was made 'in legal form' and 'in accordance with the Public Law of the Nations'.[294] Schimper admitted that Wibē lacked the 'means of considering in a sufficiently fair and exact manner the importance of his demand and the obligation with which he would find himself burdened in case the Government would want to accept it in the fullest sense possible *(dans le sens d'une éxtension complette)*', but nevertheless expected that the request would, because of its 'legal form', at least guarantee French influence in preference to that of any other nation.[295]

De Jacobis and Schimper seem to have raised the question of implications with Wibē, though how frank they were is impossible to know. After the meeting at Halay, Degoutin expressed regret that De Jacobis had not found it possible to present the whole matter in writing since he would have been able to explain himself better than both the secretary of Wibē (in this case no other than De Jacobis) and Schimper. Verbally, however, the consul had been told that Wibē

290   ibid. (my emphasis).
291   AECP, Massouah 1, fols 138–40, 146–7, Degoutin to Guizot, 1 Jul. and 2 Sep. 1845.
292   CML, De Jacobis, 'Giornale Abissino', Vol. III, pp. 520–6, 533–7.
293   Neither Schimper nor De Jacobis were Frenchmen, of course, but this is only a parallel to the 'German Englishmen' expelled from Adwa in 1838. The important distinction was religion, and the German Schimper had therefore changed from an Englishman to a Frenchman by becoming a Catholic!
294   AECP, Massouah 1, fols 142–3, Schimper to Degoutin, 1 Jun 1845; CML, 'Lettres manuscrites', Vol. II, no. 226, De Jacobis to Étienne, 10 Jul. 1845. See also 'Giornale Abissino', Vol. III, p. 543.
295   AECP, Massouah 1, fols 142–3, Schimper to Degoutin, 1 Jun. 1845.

had asked for the advice of De Jacobis who had explained the case of Tahiti and other protectorates. Wibē's reply had been that

> he would not willingly cede his sovereign rights over Tigrē, Simēn or anything else on the other side of the mountains of Arkīko or Semhar [i.e. beyond the mountain passes leading into the highlands as seen from the coast], but that he would voluntarily abandon the roads of Arkīko and all the trade of the mainland [designating, most likely, Arkīko and its immediate hinterland as opposed to Massawa] to France in exchange for a protection which would consist in preventing the Turks from occupying Abyssinia.[296]

This account of Wibē's standpoint sounds plausible. He knew that the Turks had landed some soldiers at Arkīko though he had ignored it in order to facilitate a peaceful solution.[297] He wanted a change at Arkīko, one which would prevent Turks and Egyptians from occupying the seaboard or using the *na'ibs* to extend their influence farther inland. He had twice refrained from seeking a military solution and had, as we have seen, tried to use the influence of the French consul with the Turkish governor to find a peaceful one.

Wibē was certainly not unaware of the desires of the Europeans to gain a foothold on the coast. Earlier activities (Lefebvre, Combes, Blondeel, Coffin) had been directed mainly towards the acquisition of Anfilla. But the trade was heavily concentrated to Arkīko and Massawa. The years of Egyptian rule had increased Massawa's lead; so had the decrease in political importance of eastern Tigrē after Wibē's takeover. But unless the Porte was willing to sell it, Massawa could be acquired only through outright occupation at the risk of international complications. Neither London nor Paris were prepared for anything of the sort. The subtle way was to gain control over Arkīko, for 'with a voluntary cession of the section of the mainland of the roads of Arkīko all the commerce of the country would flow to this point, and the Turks who are really in possession only of the island of Massawa would find themselves forced to abandon it sooner or later'.[298] Wibē's consent, however, was necessary if interruptions in the flow of trade were to be avoided. This had already been demonstrated. For Wibē, co-operation with a European establishment had its advantages, at least it must have seemed so. Though he could conceivably eliminate the power of the *na'ibs* himself, he could not possibly hope to make the trade bypass the Turks at Massawa without co-operation with some other power engaged in Red Sea trade and politics.

This does not necessarily mean that Wibē had made a firm offer to abandon Arkīko and its immediate hinterland to France, still less that he had promised to add *de facto* occupation to the vague, abstract sovereignty he claimed, simply to

296   ibid., fols 138–40, Degoutin to Guizot, 1 Jul. 1845. In Degoutin's report it appears as if De Jacobis had met Wibē and discussed protectorates with him. The diary of the missionary ('Giornale', Vol. III, pp. 513–43) seems to exclude any meeting after 21 May. The exchange of views must therefore have taken place either through Schimper or at some earlier time.
297   AECP, Massouah 1, fols 209–13, Schimper to Degoutin, 28 May 1845.
298   ibid., fols 138–40, Degoutin to Guizot, 1 Jul. 1845.

be able to make a legal and factual cession of the territory to the French. Probably he had stated that he would not resist French occupation there as he would Ottoman, that he preferred to have the French as neighbours rather than the Turks. Probably the matter had not even been discussed. The fact that it is not mentioned in Wibē's letter and the way in which it emerges in Degoutin's dispatch indicate that it was a second best for Schimper and De Jacobis, thrown in when they felt obliged to admit that Wibē had actually refused to accept protectorate status for what was unquestionably his country. It was not Wibē who was trying to deceive the French government; it was the Europeans on the spot who felt the need to stress Wibē's sovereign rights over Arkīko and Semhar in order to make his cession of them worthwhile for France to accept.

If we assume, moreover, that the exchange of views with Wibē about protectorates took place as reported to Degoutin, it is also evident that all the three Europeans knew positively that Wibē refused to pay for friendship and protection with infringements on the sovereignty of highland Abyssinia as opposed to the coastal strip. They also knew that the Egyptian army in Habab had returned to the Sudan long ago and that 500 Turks at Massawa could not invade the highlands. It was in spite of this that the consul accepted that the missionaries had 'inoculated their fears' into Wibē and made him decide 'to demand the Protectorate of France'.[299] And by the time Degoutin came to the end of his long report the only question was whether the French government would accept 'the protectorate of Abyssinia by France' or not.[300]

The line of conduct of De Jacobis and Schimper has much in common with that of Antoine d'Abbadie in 1838.[301] But it points forward more than backward. Though diplomatic skill would increase on both sides—and the attention to formalities with it—Wibē's 'request for protectorate status' had the main ingredients in common with Minīlik's forty-five years later: the created illusion of urgent need for assistance, the document with the seal which bound the Ethiopian party, and the decision, against better judgement, of the European party to read into the document what was not there.[302]

If Foreign Minister Guizot had been a less moderate and cautious politician than he was, a French protectorate over northern Ethiopia might have been declared in 1845 without further ado. Guizot's immediate reaction, however, was negative: 'Restrain the zeal of these gentlemen [De Jacobis and Schimper].'[303] In connection with the activities of Combes and Lefebvre a few years earlier, he had declared that France was interested only in absolutely peaceful acquisitions. It did not seem likely that Wibē asked for protection if there was no danger of hostilities at all.

---

299 See above, p. 111.
300 AECP, Massouah 1, fols 138–40, 146–7, Degoutin to Guizot, 1 Jul. and 2 Sep. 1845. It is mainly the complete absence of analysis of the French documents that makes the accounts of Douin (*Ismaïl*, III, 1, 235–7) and Giglio (*Etiopia–Mar Rosso*, Vol. I, 1, pp. 48–9) of these negotiations so unsatisfactory.
301 See above, pp. 76–82.
302 See below, pp. 385–9.
303 AECP, Massouah 1, fol. 139, minute on Degoutin to Guizot, 1 Jul. 1845.

Guizot had, moreover, become disgusted with the methods used by the amateur diplomats on the Red Sea coast: Lefebvre's dubious embassy and unauthorized attempts to acquire Anfilla and Combes's attempt to cheat his own government out of 90,000 francs by writing out a purchase contract for Edd for ten times the correct amount—besides having acquired the place from someone who did not own it.[304] Degoutin was instructed to tell Wibē that the French government could intervene diplomatically at Istanbul and Cairo in favour of any Christian country which needed such assistance. But to accept the responsibilities of a protectorate against a territorial concession was a completely different matter, and if this question was raised again by Wibē or in his name, the reply was no. France did not want to acquire any more protectorates. And De Jacobis should be told to stick to his mission work and not meddle with politics.[305] Degoutin exceeded his instructions somewhat by informing Wibē through Schimper that the French government had immediately approached the governments in Istanbul and Cairo and told them 'that every attack on their part and every invasion against the Christians of Abyssinia would be an act contrary to the law of nations and that all the Christian territories of Abyssinia being protected by France, an aggression would be a casus belli'.[306]

In the meantime the governor of Massawa had presumably received orders from Hijaz to appease Wibē, and Muhammad Yahya had been appointed na'ib. When the governor of Massawa, however, failed to receive the expected gratuity for making the appointment, he made an attempt to collect it by force from the population of Arkīko but was defeated and, according to the French consul, released only against a promise that no Turkish soldier would be sent to the mainland again. Then the two branches of the dynasty of na'ibs came to terms with each other and formally declared Arkīko an independent state about New Year 1846. This lasted less than two months. When a new governor arrived at Massawa, he paid all the arrears from Rustum's time, and the old interdependence was restored.[307]

In spite of his earlier advice to Wibē to be patient, the consul believed that Wibē could and should have established his authority at Arkīko as early as July or August. Now the opportunity had passed while he had been waiting for the reply from France. De Jacobis and Schimper, who saw this too, suggested that if France feared complications with the na'ibs, Wibē would gladly cede Bogos instead. This does not seem very likely, and there is no evidence that it had been discussed. At all events, the suggestion shows how anxious they were to get the French government involved. Degoutin commented that he was sure Wibē

304   AEMD, Afrique 13, fols 95–6, Guizot to Cunin-Gridaine, 25 Oct. 1842. For the treaty concluded by Combes on 12 Sep. 1840, see AECP, Massouah 1, fol. 4. See also ibid., fols 34–43, 'Rapport sur quelques voyages en Abyssinie', 16 Mar. 1842, and above, pp. 82–9.

305   AECP, Massouah 1, fol. 148, Guizot to Degoutin, 15 Nov. 1845; Égypte 17, fol. 203, Guizot to Barrot, 14 Nov. 1845.

306   AECP, Massouah 1, fols 213–14, Degoutin to Schimper, 28 Feb. 1846. See also CML, De Jacobis, 'Giornale Abissino', Vol. IV, p. 1.

307   AECP, Massouah 1, fols 149, 151–4, Degoutin to Guizot, 10 Dec. 1845, 2 Jan. and 24 Feb, 1846. See also Munzinger, Ostafrikanische Studien, pp. 165–6.

would be satisfied with the promise of French protection for nothing and would not speak again about territorial concessions unless he was pushed once more by De Jacobis and Schimper! But then De Jacobis received his instructions, and things calmed down for a while.[308]

Egyptian Foothold on the Coast: Wibē's Reaction

The possession of Massawa was no longer as attractive to the Ottoman government as it had been. It was becoming increasingly difficult to maintain the fiction that the rulers of Arkīko were Ottoman vassals, governing Habeshistan for the Porte. They demanded the traditional payments from Massawa but preferred to regard the money as a kind of tribute rather than as pay for their troops.[309] The conflicts had shown that Massawa in the last instance had to depend on Ottoman troops for its protection, and Hijaz had to bear the costs. The compensation in form of higher customs rates for goods *reimported* into the Ottoman empire (12 per cent as against 5 per cent for goods from foreign countries as stipulated in the convention of 1838 between the Porte and several European countries) was largely eliminated by the refusal of the British government to regard merchandise coming from Massawa, or any of the other ports of the Red Sea except Mokha, as exported from Ottoman territory and therefore liable to the higher customs rate when arriving at Jidda.

The Ottoman possession of the port of Massawa as such was not openly challenged, but the idea that any of the territory for which it was an outlet could be regarded as part of the Ottoman empire was rejected. On the Arabian side matters were not quite so simple but with respect to Abyssinia, '. . . the question may at once be satisfactorily disposed of—no authority of any kind, either as to the appointment of Governors or otherwise, is, or has, for a very long time past, been exercised by the Turkish Government . . .'[310] At Massawa the French consul made a distinction between 'the products of the Muslim coast', for which he was prepared to accept 12 per cent, and the products originating in Abyssinia, for which the 5 per cent rate should apply. But there was continuous trouble over the application of the tariffs, including appeals from Paris to Istanbul, and as late as December 1846, Degoutin reported that the Abyssinian caravans of that year had been forced to pay 20 per cent instead of 5 per cent, although they had been assured through the agent himself before leaving Gonder that they would receive fair treatment.[311]

Though there was no doubt a good net profit from the customs house at Massawa in spite of all the embezzlement,[312] these troubles may have contri-

---

308 AECP, Massouah 1, fols 146–7, 155, Degoutin to Guizot, 2 Sep. 1845, 5 Mar. 1846.
309 ibid., fols 138–40, Degoutin to Guizot, 1 Jul. 1845; cf. fols 119–20, Degoutin to Guizot, 15 May 1844.
310 FO 78/3185, fols 185–7, Canning to Aberdeen, 1 Aug. 1843; fols 195–200, Cotton and Shepherd to Ripon, 21 Sep. 1843; fols 220–4, Hodson to Aberdeen, 15 May 1844.
311 AECC, Massouah 1, fols 66–7, Degoutin to Guizot, 18 Nov. 1844; fols 72–3, Guizot to Degoutin, 28 Jun. 1845; fols 76, 80 *bis*–81, Degoutin to Guizot, 19 May, 24 Dec. 1846.
312 ibid., fols 68–9, Degoutin to Guizot, 10 Jan. 1845; AECP, Massouah 1, fols 273–4, Rolland to Tocqueville, 15 Aug. 1849.

buted to the decision of the Sultan to grant Muhammad Ali's request in 1846 to have Sawakin and Massawa placed under Egyptian administration once more.[313] This did not mean, of course, that they ceased to be Ottoman territory or that the claims to suzerainty over Ethiopia were dropped. On the contrary, the British ambassador at Istanbul was told in 1848 'that Massowa and Suakin belonged unquestionably, *as parts of Abyssinia*, to the Ottoman Empire'.[314] The new governor, Ismail Haqqi, arrived at Massawa in March 1847, and a more active policy was again introduced on the coast. The new administration was instructed, or so it said at least, to explore all the coast, which caused Degoutin to ask for instructions on what to do about the dubious French possession of Edd.[315] The crucial issue was as usual Semhar, the mainland just opposite Massawa. Wibē was engaged in a new conflict with Ali, and in his absence the rulers of Arkīko made their choice by raiding the Christian highlands in Muhammad Ali's name.[316]

In 1846–47 the conflicts and political turmoil in central Ethiopia reached a new climax. The unrest was partly due to the intransigence of Abune Selama on doctrinal matters, and in June 1846 he was expelled from Gonder to Tigrē by Menen and Ichegē Mahsentu. The immediate cause of the expulsion was Selama's unwillingness to release Sahle Sillasē and Shewa from an earlier anathema. The result was that Ali, Menen, and the *ichegē* were also cursed with all their followers. In this situation Wibē decided, probably at the instigation of Selama, to release a number of political prisoners, including Birru Alīgaz, who had been entrusted to him by Ali. There is no evidence, however, that he planned any campaign, and when Ali attacked in January 1847, he remained on the defensive in his mountain strongholds of Simēn where he had little to fear. After having pillaged Wegera, Ali made peace with Wibē and turned to his many other problems: Birru and Goshu in Gojjam, Birru Alīgaz in Lasta and the rising new rebel, Kasa Haylu from Qwara, the future Tēwodros.[317]

Compared with 1842, this was a minor crisis for Wibē. Nevertheless it had prevented him from making his power felt on the northern frontier at the crucial moment. In early April he wrote and welcomed Ismail Haqqi to his governorship but pointed out at the same time that he claimed suzerainty over Arkīko. Since he had installed Na'ib Muhammad, he regarded him as his vassal.[318] The problem was that Muhammad had changed sides, and hostilities had broken out between him and Welde Gabir of Hamasēn. Turkish troops, moreover, were already present at Arkīko. Wibē had authorized Schimper to settle any eventual problems, but it turned out that neither his nor Degoutin's word carried any weight with Ismail. The governor refused to receive Wibē's letter

---

313 Douin, *Ismaïl*, III, 1, p. 238; Abir, *Ethiopia*, p. 123.
314 FO 78/3185, fols 267–9, Canning to Palmerston, 27 Sep. 1848 (my emphasis).
315 AECP, Massouah 1, fol. 175, Degoutin to Guizot, 1 Apr. 1847; Abir, *Ethiopia*, p. 131; Hill, *The Sudan*, pp. 83–4.
316 AECP, Massouah 1, fols 172–3, Degoutin to Guizot, 15 Mar. 1847.
317 Conti Rossini, 'Nuovi documenti', *RANL*, 8, II, pp. 385–93; *idem*, 'Vicende', *RRAL*, 5, XXV, pp. 476–81. See also Abir, *Ethiopia*, pp. 127–9; Rubenson, *Tēwodros*, pp. 37–9.
318 AECP, Massouah 1, fols 214–15, Wibē to Ismail, 9 Apr. 1847. This is a French translation of the original which was dated 1 Mīyazya 7339, i.e., 8 Apr. 1847.

because it was in Amharic, and Muhammad Yahya denied that he had ever been appointed by Wibē.[319]

In what the consul regarded as a very offensive reply, Wibē was told that if he had any claims he would have to come and support them with his army. Although Degoutin disliked the tone, he agreed in substance: the contested area belonged legally and in fact to the Sultan.[320] To Wibē he expressed regret that he had not been able to arrange the delimitation of Semhar and Arkīko as Wibē desired but advised against any attempt to use force for the time being. Instead Wibē had better address an appeal straight to Muhammad Ali since the new governor might be ignorant of what exactly he was supposed to take possession of. Degoutin also renewed his promise to protest officially in the name of the French government if the governor of Massawa approached Christian territory, an assurance which cost the consul a reprimand in the next dispatch from Paris.[321] With Schimper, Degoutin was frank: the governor had 'positive orders to occupy the mainland, even by force of arms, if he met with the slightest resistance . . .' And the regular Egyptian forces between Berber and Massawa were no less than 20,000 men. Wibē should have acted earlier. It was now too late.[322] Whether Degoutin's advice played any role any longer is difficult to say. Wibē was at any rate tied down by the presence of Ali's army in Wegera.

In the meantime Ismail destroyed the autonomy of the na'ibs, aided no doubt by the rivalry that existed between Muhammad and Hasan. He ordered one of them to lead an invasion into Hamasēn and take some Egyptian soldiers with him. When the selected chief failed to rally the necessary forces, Ismail used the divisions to get both the na'ibs and the other leaders to Massawa. He then landed forces of his own and burnt Arkīko to the ground on 16 June 1847.[323] The population refused to accept Turkish rule and fled to the hills, even into Christian districts. A fort was built on the site and an Egyptian garrison installed.[324] Muhammad retained nominal authority as na'ib, but the tribute

319   ibid., fols 215–19, Schimper to Ismail, 15 Apr. 1847; fols 219–20, Schimper to Degoutin, 15 Apr. 1847; fols 220–31 (sic), Degoutin to Schimper, 24 Apr. 1847; see also for relations between the na'ib and Welde Gabir, IO, Secret letters from Aden 29, pp. 289–91, Eden [to Johnston], 17 Dec. 1846.
320   AECP, Massouah 1, fol. 176, Degoutin to Guizot, 23 Apr. 1847. Degoutin later found out that the letter which Muhammad had written on Ismail's instructions was, in fact, never sent, but the substance of the message no doubt reached Wibē. See also AECC, Massouah 1, fol. 86, note on copy of Degoutin to Guizot, 27 (sic) Apr. 1847.
321   AECP, Massouah 1, fol. 177, Degoutin to Wibē, 23 Apr. 1847; fol. 181, Guizot to Degoutin, 7 Jul. 1847.
322   ibid., fols 220–31 (sic), Degoutin to Schimper, 24 Apr. 1847.
323   ibid., fols 178–9, Degoutin to Guizot, 20 May and 17 Jun. 1847; IO, Secret Letters from Aden 30, pp. 385–8, Adams to Lowe, 4 Sep. 1848; see also Plowden, Travels, pp. 354–6; Munzinger, Ostafrikanische Studien, p. 166.
324   AECP, Massouah 1, fol. 182, Degoutin to Guizot, 15 Jul. 1847; FO 401/1, pp. 24–5, Plowden to Palmerston, 16 Aug. 1848. Note that FO 401/1 actually consists of two series of documents and that pages 1–25 therefore appear twice. The first short series Preliminary Correspondence respecting the Circumstances which led to the Establishment of a Consulate at Massowah: 1846–47 will be cited FO 401/1 (Preliminary), the second only FO 401/1.

or subsidy, in fact his share of the tax on the trade, was abolished and he was powerless.[325]

The next in turn was Degoutin. He had expected European trade to benefit from the change of administration,[326] but he soon found his own freedom of movement, both literally and commercially, severely restricted. By December 1847 the quarrels over tariffs, trade monopolies, and the freedom for Europeans to come and go as they liked led to a crisis. Degoutin reported that Bishop (later Cardinal) Massaja had been arrested and his own house at Minkullu on the mainland had been set on fire. While he requested Paris to protest at Cairo, he declared that if the governor only met his demands with regard to trade and freedom of movement, he would not bother to complain any more about the robbing and persecution of the native merchants.[327] When Walter Plowden arrived at Massawa as British consul to Abyssinia in August 1848,[328] he found that the elimination of the *na'ib* certainly did not help. On goods from Ethiopia, duties were levied

> according to the arbitrary pleasure of the Governor, amounting in some instances, including irregular fees and presents, to 25 and even 30 per cent on the value. In all questions, as far as I can learn, regarding merchandize, Abyssinia is regarded by the Egyptian Government as a tributary Province.[329]

After Degoutin's reply in April 1847 and the events that followed, Wibē must have understood that the French consul could or would not help him to solve the problems of his northern frontier and the use of Massawa as a port for Ethiopia. Obviously the French king was not as concerned about the safety and welfare of Abyssinia as De Jacobis had so often assured him. Abune Selama's return to Tigrē in 1846 and the unrest caused by Wibē's opponents while he was tied down in Simēn by Ali's army made it increasingly difficult or politically unwise for Wibē to protect the Catholic mission. The presence of one Catholic bishop— Massaja who had arrived in November 1846 to start the work of the Capuchin mission to the Galla—and Montuori's project of placing another Roman Catholic at the head of the Ethiopian church in Sahle Sillasē's and Ali's territories stiffened opposition. Massaja was expelled from Tigrē in November 1847, and the following year Wibē was forced to make the choice between Selama and De Jacobis. Through Schimper, De Jacobis was informed that he had to leave Wibē's territories, and in October he withdrew from Gwela to Minkullu.[330]

325 FO 401/1, pp. 26–7, Plowden to Palmerston, 17 Sep. 1848.
326 AECP, Massouah 1, fols 156–9, Degoutin to Guizot, 24 Dec. 1846.
327 AECC, Massouah 1, fols 82, 90–2, Degoutin to Guizot, 15 Mar., 15 Jul., and 25 Aug. 1847;
     AECP, Massouah 1, fols 186–7, Degoutin to Guizot, 20 Dec. 1847; SOM, Océan Indien,
     10/43, Lefebvre to Montebello, 27 Sep. 1847.
328 FO 401/1, p. 22, Plowden to Palmerston, 15 Aug. 1848.
329 ibid., pp. 29–30, 33–4, Plowden to Palmerston, 29 Oct. and 10 Dec. 1848.
330 AECP, Massouah 1, fols 156–9, 188–9, Degoutin to Guizot, 24 Dec. 1846, 20 Dec. 1847;
     fols 193–4, Degoutin to Bastide, 10 Nov. 1848; CML, De Jacobis, 'Giornale Abissino',
     Vol. IV, pp. 56–7, 81, 83, 94–8; Conti Rossini, 'Vicende', *RRAL*, 5, XXV, pp. 483–7.
     See also Crummey, *Priests*, pp. 70–1.

Wibē undoubtedly felt that the missionary and the French consul had betrayed his cause; so had Na'ib Muhammad. There were no longer any buffers between the governor of Massawa and the ruler of Tigrē. Wibē allegedly demanded that the Egyptians evacuate Arkīko and Minkullu within forty-eight hours, hand over the *na'ib*, and pay 2,000 thalers annually as Wibē's share of the taxes collected on the trade. The governor refused, and a Tigrean army of 2,000–3,000 men, led by Wibē's general Kokebē and two of his sons, descended on Arkīko and Minkullu. The villages were burnt and looted in early January 1849, including the property of the consuls and the Catholic mission. No serious attempts to dislodge the Egyptian garrison from the fort or to cross over to Massawa were made.[331] It was later reported that the governor had paid a ransom of 12,000 thalers.[332] This amount, the same as the *na'ibs* used to receive per year, was approximately one third of the annual net profit of the port at the time.[333] It may be exaggerated, as were no doubt the reported numbers of dead (1,000–1,200), prisoners (700–800), and head of cattle captured (10,000).[334] But the raid was at any rate a serious reminder that Wibē was not prepared to accept the loss of influence and revenue caused by the Egyptian occupation of Arkīko and the elimination of the *na'ib*.

For Ethiopia as for the other parties involved in the struggle over Massawa, which was again transferred from the Egyptian government to the Sublime Porte in 1849,[335] the issue was really not one of sovereignty, but of revenue. It all boiled down to the question of how the profit of the growing trade was to be shared; firstly between Ethiopian, Arab, Indian, and European traders, secondly between the Ethiopian, Egyptian, and Turkish governments. Wibē had no particular desire to govern or administer Massawa as long as the Ethiopian traders were not robbed by a combination of legal and illegal imposts, and he received a fair share of the revenues collected.

For almost a decade Degoutin had manoeuvred between Wibē and the Turkish/Egyptian administration, to which he was accredited, trying to prevent a military clash between the two while building up his own position as consular agent into a locally powerful institution. Neither he nor De Jacobis had received much encouragement from the French government, and they had so far completely failed to create the basis for a French protectorate over northern Ethiopia. It is typical of the atmosphere in which these men worked that Degoutin ascribed the events of January 1849, not to the general failure of his

---

331 AECP, Massouah 1, fols 203–7, Degoutin to Drouyn de Lhuys, 5 Jan., 6 Jan., and 10 Jan. 1849; fols 207 (2nd folio with this number)–208, Schimper to Fresnel, 5 Feb. 1849, with notes by Fresnel; fols 237–44, Arnaud to Bastide, 6 Feb. 1849; CML, De Jacobis, 'Giornale Abissino', Vol. IV, p. 104; FO 401/1, p. 32, Haines to the Chief Secretary to Bombay Government, 28 Jan. 1849. Since Degoutin repeats the figures 2,000 and 3,000 for the Ethiopian force involved at Arkīko, the higher figures of Haines (8,000–12,000) must include troops in the neighbourhood who did not participate in the action.

332 IO, Secret Letters from Aden 30, pp. 457–8, Haines to Malet, 16 Feb. 1849.

333 FO 401/1, pp. 33–4, Plowden to Palmerston, 10 Dec. 1848.

334 AECP, Massouah 1, fols 237–44, Arnaud to Bastide, 6 Feb. 1849. See Conti Rossini, 'Nuovi documenti', *RANL*, 8, II, pp. 397–8, for an Ethiopian note on this expedition.

335 FO 401/1, p. 35, Murray to Palmerston, 18 Mar. 1849.

policy, but to British intrigue. He in fact declared that he had discovered, 'o, horror', that Consul Plowden, Coffin and Lefebvre(!) had planned the Ethiopian attack for three months and directed the looters specifically to the small French/Catholic settlement at Minkullu.[336] The truth about the specific accusations—such were made also by Plowden[337]—is difficult to come by. The real blow was, of course, the very appointment of a British consul to Abyssinia and his arrival at a time when matters were becoming difficult for other reasons.

Plowden and Rolland: Wibē Disillusioned, Ali Indifferent

Walter Plowden had spent more than three years travelling in central Ethiopia before he decided to try his hand as an emissary of Ras Ali to London. He arrived at Massawa in October 1846 and immediately appealed to the Foreign Office for funds to continue his journey with some presents and an envoy, added by Ali 'for the sake of form'. Some months passed before the funds arrived. The mission left Massawa only in April, and Plowden reached London in August 1847. The envoy, a certain Aleqa Desta, remained behind in Cairo, allegedly because he had become so frightened by a shipwreck in the Red Sea that he refused to continue the journey.[338] Obviously Plowden did not regard his presence as essential. Plowden carried no letter from Ali, and the presents had not amounted to much even before the shipwreck. He was rather vague about the purpose of the mission: 'It is not to be supposed that the Ras . . . could have in view any more definite result than a certain interchange of courtesy, and the consequent facilities and protection that would be afforded by him to English travellers.'[339] There was no mention of firearms or assistance in any other form, nor was there any mention of territorial concessions or commercial privileges. Whether it was Ali or Plowden who had initiated this mission is impossible to know with certainty, but everything points to the Englishman rather than the *ras*. That Plowden wanted the Foreign Office to believe that he had only reluctantly accepted to carry the presents does not exclude the possibility that he had initiated the whole affair precisely in order to get his travel to England and back—with some presents—at the expense of the British government.

At first he stressed the desirability of keeping Ethiopia open 'to the man of

336   AECP, Massouah 1, fols 206–7, Degoutin to Drouyn de Lhuys, 10 Jan. 1849; fols 237–44, Arnaud to Bastide, 6 Feb. 1849; fols 246–8, Arnaud to Drouyn de Lhuys, 15 Apr. 1849. Lefebvre had returned to Ethiopia in mid-1847 on a mission to recruit labourers for the island of Bourbon. In this he failed completely, but he stayed on in the country as a farmer and local trader. His relations with Degoutin were certainly very poor in 1848 and this may explain the consul's inclusion of his name. See SOM, Océan Indien, 10/43, Lefebvre to Montebello, 8 Aug. 1847 and following dispatches; also AECP, Massouah 1, fols 191–2, Degoutin to Lamartine, 1 Jul. 1848.

337   FO 401/1, p. 37, Plowden to Palmerston, 28 Jan. 1849; Plowden, *Travels*, pp. 373–4.

338   FO 1/4, fol. 11, Plowden to Palmerston, 15 Oct. 1846; fol. 19, Palmerston to Murray, 10 Dec. 1846; Plowden, *Travels*, pp. 315, 353; FO 401/1, p. 23, Plowden's accounts, 15 Aug. 1848, for the name of the envoy.

339   FO 401/1 (Preliminary), pp. 7–10, 'Memorandum by Mr. Plowden', 12 Aug. 1847.

science or the zealous missionary', but no sooner had he arrived in London than the talk turned to trade opportunities and an eventual treaty.[340] He had met and talked with Lefebvre on his way, and in London it was known that Rochet d'Héricourt was about to go back to Ethiopia, presumably to put a treaty he had signed with Sahle Sillasē three years earlier into effect.[341] Plowden had arrived at an opportune moment when Charles Beke and others were pressing for some action in Ethiopia. A consular agency at Massawa had been proposed as early as November 1846 and Beke's name had been considered and dropped. Within ten days after Plowden's first memorandum explaining his mission, Palmerston had made his decision: 'I will appoint Mr. Plowden Consul at Massowah . . .' A treaty should be drafted for him to sign with the Emperor and the *ras*; no attempt to obtain possession of any territory should be made.[342]

The latter decision referred, no doubt, to Plowden's suggestion that the appointment of a consul at Massawa to protect the Ethiopian merchants would be useful; 'but that the occupation of that island, if possible, by the English would be the most effectual means of establishing a permanent and valuable trade with the whole of the interior of this portion of Africa'. As alternatives, Plowden proposed either a British establishment at Anfilla combined with a treaty with Wibē about diverting the trade to this port, or a bargain with the *na'ib*, 'who is still acknowledged virtually as Sovereign of the mainland', about the purchase of Arkīko.[343] Having dealt at length with the vexed question of sovereignty and of the position of the *na'ib*, he concluded, '. . . it appears to me that this haze of undefined rights or claims, resolves itself on all sides into the simple facts of strength and possession . . .' In Plowden's view, however, the Turkish rights to the island of Massawa could 'scarcely be disputed', an opinion which the Foreign Office was most unwilling to accept. Plowden clearly preferred to be placed on British ground and argued for Anfilla again, but Palmerston maintained, 'all we want is trade, and land is not necessary for trade'.[344] In the end Plowden was made consul for Abyssinia, not for Massawa, thus avoiding an explicit recognition of Turkish sovereignty and making it possible for him to settle wherever he preferred on the coast and maintain that he was on Ethiopian soil.[345]

All this discussion about the coast, further complicated by news of the transfer of Massawa to Egypt and the activities (grossly exaggerated) of the new governor, had obscured the questions of the presents and the treaty. In January 1848

340 FO 1/4, fol. 11, Plowden to Palmerston, 15 Oct. 1846; FO 401/1 (Preliminary), p. 7, Memorandum, 12 Aug. 1847.
341 FO 401/1 (Preliminary), p. 3, Beke to Palmerston, 9 Nov. 1846; p. 6, Murray to Palmerston, 18 Jun. 1847; SOM, Océan Indien, 10/43, Lefebvre to Montebello, 8 Aug. 1847.
342 FO 401/1 (Preliminary), pp. 1–2, Beke to Palmerston, 28 Aug. 1846; pp. 3–5, Stephen to Addington, 27 Nov. 1846, with enclosures and minutes; p. 11, minute, 22 Aug. 1847, on Addington to Plowden, 18 Aug. 1847.
343 ibid., pp. 11–13, 'Memorandum on the Trade of Abyssinia', n.d. (between 18 and 22 Aug. 1847).
344 ibid., pp. 14–16, 'Memorandum', 28 Aug. 1847 (no. 3), with minutes.
345 ibid., p. 22, minutes by Hammond and Palmerston, 19–21 Nov. 1847; FO 401/1, p. 9, Palmerston to Cowley, 13 Jan. 1848.

Plowden received his commission, instructions, a letter for Ras Ali, addressed oddly to 'His Highness the Ras of Tigré', and a draft of the treaty to be concluded with the Emperor without 'any material alterations'. Of the £400 for presents, only £90 were used for firearms, which meant only a few samples for the personal use of the *ras* and some other chiefs.[346]

The changes that had taken place at Massawa and Arkiko in Plowden's absence made it unlikely that he would be able to operate there as a protector of Ethiopian and a promoter of British trade. He immediately paid a visit to Anfilla and suggested an establishment there under an Italian associate of his, provided the British government would promise protection. Recent visits by Lefebvre and Antoine d'Abbadie were mentioned to show the need for action.[347] But Plowden's main concern was to establish as satisfactory relations as possible with Wibe and then proceed on his mission to Gonder and Debre Tabor. Wibe was happy to hear that Plowden would provide better protection of Abyssinian merchants at Massawa. He also declared that he desired good relations with the British.[348] The restoration of Intiçho to Coffin (August 1848) and the expulsion of De Jacobis (October 1848) were indications of Wibe's changing attitude though the accusation that the arrival of the British consul actually caused the expulsion of the Catholic mission is hardly justified.[349] There were other signs of the changing climate too. Rochet had not gone to Shewa but preceded Plowden through Massawa to Gonder in an attempt to secure for the French whatever the British were going to get.[350] On his way back to the coast he visited Wibe in Simēn, and though he reported a friendly reception, he did not receive the usual letter professing friendship and interest in assistance.[351]

After discussions with the leading Christian merchants—Plowden was travelling with Neggadras Kidane Maryam of Gonder—and a first interview with Wibe in January 1849, just before Rochet's visit, Plowden felt he could foretell certain actions: the merchants would probably petition for British protection through Ras Ali; Wibe might claim British protection from Turkish attacks on his territory. The consul hoped that the British government would reply to any appeal from Wibe with a declaration that it did 'not consider the possession of the Island of Massowah to involve any authority over the coast'. If this was done, Wibe could reappoint one of the *na'ibs*, who had fled from Massawa, to govern

---

346 FO 401/1, pp. 1–6, Palmerston to Plowden, 3 Jan. 1848, with enclosures; pp. 10–11, Plowden to Addington, 24 Jan. 1848; p. 83, minutes on Butler to Addington, 20 Jul. 1850. For Plowden's appointment and instructions, see also Marston, *Britain's Imperial Role*, pp. 174–80.

347 FO 401/1, pp. 23, 25, Plowden to Palmerston, 16 Aug. and 17 Aug. 1848; AECP, Massouah 1, fols 246–8, Arnaud to Drouyn de Lhuys, 15 Apr. 1849.

348 FO 401/1, p. 30, Plowden to Palmerston, 29 Aug. 1848; Plowden, *Travels*, pp. 359–60, 377.

349 AECP, Massouah 1, fols 195–9, 246–8, Arnaud to Bastide, 10 Nov. 1848, to Drouyn de Lhuys, 21 Dec. 1848 and 15 Apr. 1849. Degoutin (ibid., fols 193–4) insinuated that the d'Abbadie brothers were behind the expulsion!

350 AEMD, Afrique 61, fols 226–33, instructions by the Ministry of Commerce, January 1847; fols 248–393, narrative by Rochet d'Héricourt. See also Malécot, 'Voyageurs', *RFHO*, LVIII, pp. 305–6.

351 AEMD, Afrique 61, fols 377–80.

the coast for him.[352] Clearly this was a course of action which both suited Wibē and agreed with the earlier British attitude to Ottoman claims as well as, of course, British commercial interests.

In view of this, it is a significant indication of the priorities of the Ethiopian prince that his first explicit request was for 'men who make lime, if possible five, otherwise three'. He clearly intended them to settle in his country for he promised to give land or salary as they preferred.[353] The consul, to whom this letter was addressed, added the information that Wibē wanted them for the building of a church and recommended that an architect, preferably also with experience as a bridge constructor, four masons, and a carpenter be sent.[354]

Plowden's own concern, a formal request for British friendship and protection against Turkish attacks, was expressed in a second letter addressed to 'King Zīqṭorya', which was as close as the scribe could come to the name of the famous queen. Wibē explained that 'in former days' Massawa had been in the hands of his ancestors but that the Turks had taken it 'when all of us fought with each other'. Two years ago the Turks had taken a further step by sending an army and occupying Minkullu and 'the gate of Dehono' (as Arkīko was also called at the time). The tribute which had in the past been paid regularly by the na'ibs had ceased, and therefore Wibē had sent an army and chased the Turks back to Massawa. Since Victoria was a strong Christian king (sic), Wibē now sought friendship 'that an army of Muslims may not come and pillage and take from us our country, and that he whom you also dislike may remain [where he is] and not get hold of land or tribute'.[355] Though inspired by Plowden and written by an Ethiopian who was more permanently associated with him,[356] this letter can safely be regarded as an expression of Wibē's views, correct in its account of past events but rather vague in its request for assistance against the Turks. The request itself is more a statement of certain facts or assumed facts than an appeal for specific assistance: you are a Christian prince so you are my natural ally against the Muslims; you dislike the Turk so you will not want him to gain territory or revenue at my expense; you love the Abyssinian; good.

A comparison with the English translation reveals that the consul wanted a little more. In the Amharic version the opening statements about Massawa clearly refer to the situation before and after the civil wars and Turkish occupa-

---

352 FO 401/1, pp. 37–8, Plowden to Palmerston, 27 Jan. and 28 Jan. 1849; Plowden, *Travels*, pp. 376–82, 390–3. This was Na'ib Muhammad who had been replaced by Hasan again. He had been a close associate of Coffin's and was now, it seems, prepared to hold office under Wibē once more. See AECP, Massouah 1, fols 273–4, Rolland to Tocqueville, 15 Aug. 1849.

353 FO 1/5, fol. 306, Wibē to Plowden, n.d. The letter is written in typical Ethiopian *qum ṣiḥfet* and unsealed.

354 FO 401/1, p. 40, Plowden to Palmerston, 3 Mar. 1849.

355 FO 1/5, fol. 310, Wibē to Victoria, n.d., Amharic original. This letter is written by another hand than Wibē's letter to Plowden. It bears a round lion seal very similar to the one used in 1841 (see above, p. 92). The legend has been changed, however, to *Dejjazmach Wibē* only, but in both Amharic and Arabic.

356 This seems to be a fair conclusion since a letter from Ali to Victoria, written several months later and also forwarded by Plowden, is in the same hand.

tion in the sixteenth century. The translation has '*recently* when we quarrelled amongst ourselves, the Turks took possession of Massawa'. In the phrase where Wibē expresses his desire that the Turks be prevented from expanding their possession, Massawa is mentioned with the addition 'though that even they have no right to'. Plowden obviously wanted London to believe that Wibē claimed Massawa as a *recently* lost possession, but even in its English form Wibē's request was realistically limited to 'insist on their [the Turks] remaining content with the possession of the island of Massowah ... without setting foot on the mainland or interfering with the Naib that I appoint at Arkeeko and the coast'.[357] This would be sufficient, for Plowden of course knew, as Valentia had stated forty years earlier,[358] that Massawa was of no value except as the port of Abyssinia. He therefore recommended decisive diplomatic action:

> I trust that your Lordship will take immediate occasion of this opportunity for deciding the question between the Abyssinians and the Governor of Massowah in favour of the former; which will put us at liberty to choose the favourable harbour for our commerce and intercourse with Abyssinia; should your Lordship so arrange this affair, as that the Turkish Government should lay no claim to anything beyond the island of Massowah, the rest may be safely left to me, and I trust that your Lordship will assist me thus far and promptly, as it may be long before so favourable an opportunity presents itself, or any European obtain the influence I now possess in these countries.[359]

This was as far as Plowden went. He was well aware of the limitations imposed by his instructions and by Wibē's obvious desire to see proof of British goodwill before committing himself to any kind of co-operation. Besides, Plowden's priority was the treaty with Ali, and he had to turn his attention to that matter without further delay. This provided the French agents with their last opportunity to regain the confidence of Wibē and prevent a successful British establishment on the coast. Degoutin's successor as French vice-consul at Massawa, Eugène Rolland, reported that no diplomacy would make Wibē accept that the Turks had any rights on the mainland. On this issue the French stand would have to be as unequivocal as the British had been in the past. If Wibē nevertheless showed signs of favouring the British, Rolland suggested that he be threatened with the Turks or with arms supplies to his rival Araya Sillasē. Whatever the outcome of renewed negotiations, Anfilla or Edd should be occupied as a base for French influence and trade. As Degoutin before him, Rolland deplored the absence of French warships. One only had turned up at Massawa in ten years. Though the Ethiopians loved the French and hated the British, they feared the latter and ran the risk of ending up under their yoke. According to Rolland, France could instead with a little effort become the owner or protector of the whole country and capture a trade amounting to 6,000,000 francs within one or two years[360]

357 FO 1/5, fol. 311, Wibē to Victoria, n.d., English translation (my emphasis).
358 See above, p. 42.
359 FO 1/5, fols 308–9, Plowden to Palmerston, 3 Mar. 1849.
360 AECP, Massouah 1, fols 259–60, Rolland to Drouyn de Lhuys, 22 Jun. 1849; fols 271–2, Rolland to Tocqueville, 14 Jul. 1849.

De Jacobis and Schimper went into action to set up a meeting between Rolland and Wibē, and although he had received no reply from Paris, Rolland left Massawa on 16 September for Wibē's camp at Hawzēn. De Jacobis had ventured to return to Gwela a few days earlier, but was instructed by a delegation from Wibē, including Habte Sillasē and Lefebvre, to leave Tigrē again immediately.[361] Wibē was apparently not prepared for any major concessions to the Catholic mission. Nevertheless, Rolland interpreted a friendly reception as a sign that Wibē felt he needed the French. This in Rolland's view was due mainly to the activities of Plowden who was allegedly intriguing with Abune Selama and Araya Sillasē against Wibē and at the same time instigating Wibē to make an attack on Massawa which would provide the opportunity for Ali to invade Tigrē and the British to occupy the coast.[362] In fact there was no risk of any attack by Ali at this time, occupied as he was with Birru Goshu in Gojjam.[363] The problems between Wibē and Abune Selama hinged largely on Wibē's eventual tolerance towards the Catholic mission, and Wibē had already shown that he would not risk his position in Tigrē for this cause.[364] As for the coast, it was the Turkish/Egyptian activities that bothered Wibē, not the British. He had little reason to prefer French assistance to British in this matter, and there is no evidence that he did.

This emerges quite clearly from an analysis of the three documents which Rolland secured as evidence of the success of his mission: a kind of power of attorney for the French president to negotiate a Turkish withdrawal from the Ethiopian mainland, a treaty between Wibē and Rolland to be ratified by the French government, and a letter to Rolland declaring that Wibē regretted the attack on the house of the French consul at Minkullu. The documents were written in Amharic and French. The French translation and the authenticity of Wibē's seal were certified by Lefebvre and Schimper. Rolland decided to keep the originals of the documents at Massawa and forwarded copies, certified by himself, to Paris.[365] Under these circumstances it is impossible to say with certainty whether these documents are genuine or not. If they are not, it means

361 ibid., fols 280–1, 283–4, Rolland to Tocqueville, 16 Sep. and 6 Nov. 1849; fols 290–1, Rolland to Lahitte, 15 Dec. 1849; CML, De Jacobis, 'Giornale Abissino', Vol. IV, pp. 111, 114–19.

362 AECP, Massouah 1, fols 283–4, Rolland to Tocqueville, 6 Nov. 1849.

363 FO 401/1, p. 69, Plowden to Palmerston, 2 Jan. 1850; Conti Rossini, 'Nuovi documenti', RANL, 8, II, p. 398.

364 De Jacobis accepted the compromise that he would be allowed to reside at Alītēna and did his utmost to support Rolland in Paris. See 'Giornale Abissino', Vol. IV, pp. 119–20, 122, 124; AECP, Massouah 1, fol. 282, De Jacobis to Tocqueville, 12 Oct. 1849; fols 283–4, Rolland to Tocqueville, 6 Nov. 1849.

365 AECP, Massouah 1, fol. 287, Wibē to Louis-Napoléon Bonaparte, 2 Oct. 1849; fol. 288, Treaty between Wibē and Rolland, 2 Oct. 1849; fol. 289, Wibē to Rolland, 2 Oct. 1849. These documents are second copies bearing the note that the first were lost in a shipwreck. On all three Rolland has certified that they were copied on 20 December 1849 from the originals deposited at the consulate. The original of Wibē's letter to Rolland was picked up much later by Consul Lejean (BN, Ethiop. 184, fol. 84) and proves the involvement of Lefebvre and Schimper and the authenticity of Wibē's seal on that document at least. I have not been able to trace the originals of the two more important documents.

that the main result of Rolland's mission was that it gave Wibē the opportunity of confirming that De Jacobis had to accept restrictions on his movements.

There are indications, however, that Wibē did agree in some way or other to the wording of the documents.[366] On the one hand, the very simple language, the unusual opening phrases, the incorrect dating—French texts dated one day earlier than Amharic—and the use of *nigus* as Wibē's title in two of the documents, all point to a foreign author of the Amharic texts. Several French travellers, Lefebvre in particular, called Wibē *king* in their correspondence, but in *no* documents which can be traced beyond doubt to Wibē himself does he style himself so. On the other hand, the treaty text, which was of course the most important and was allegedly made in two copies, has 'Dejjazmach Wibē, the ruler of . . .' in the Amharic text, 'Oubié, roi du . . .' in the French. Of greater importance are the differences in substance.

The Amharic version of the 'power of attorney' defines the areas on the coast which belong to Wibē as Shiho (Saho), Adal, Ṭilṭal and Habab while the French speaks only about terminating the differences concerning the ownership of the Red Sea littoral. In the Amharic, Wibē asks that the Turks withdraw voluntarily 'so that I do not send my army and so that there is no bloodshed' and concludes 'for my mouth is your mouth, what you say is what I say (የኔ ፡ አፍ ፡ ያንተ ፡ አፍ ፡ ነውና ፡ የተናገርኸው ፡ ነገር ፡ እኔ ፡ የተናገርኩት ፡ ነው ።)' which in the French reads:

> We declare that we accept without consultation and in advance all that will be decided by the said French government in this respect [concerning the littoral], and will abide by its decision whether it be favourable or not to us (Nous déclarons accepter d'hors et déjà tout ce qui sera résolu par le dit Gouvernement Français à cet égard, et nous en tenir à sa décision qu'elle nous soit ou non favorable).[367]

This is not just a free translation using legal language. The emphasis on Wibē's prior acceptance of whatever decision the French government might reach shows what Rolland wanted. There is no reason why it could not have been reflected in the Amharic text, unless we assume that it was placed before or read out to Wibē for approval. If one accepts, therefore, the Amharic text as a genuine expression for Wibē's views, it is clear that the Tigrean ruler was quite prepared to have the French president act as his spokesman with Istanbul, but it is also clear that the condition for a peaceful settlement was Turkish withdrawal. Wibē was certainly not giving the French government a *carte blanche*.

The two versions of the treaty reveal the same type of duplicity. In the French text Wibē is supposed to have pledged himself 'to give her [France] the right to create as a protectorate, and to the exclusion of all other nations, permanent establishments at the places on the coast suitable to this nation . . . (à lui donner le droit de former à titre de Protectorat, et à l'exclusion de toutes les autres nations, des établissements permanents sur les points du littoral qui seraient à la

366 A reference by Wibē to an unanswered letter several years later supports the thesis that Wibē wrote to France at this time. See SOM, Océan Indien, 10/43, Lefebvre to Ducos, 19 Aug. 1853.

367 AECP, Massouah 1, fol. 287, Wibē to Louis-Napoléon Bonaparte, 2 Oct. 1849.

convenance de cette puissance . . .)'. According to the Amharic text the French were to guard so that *foreign enemies* (እንግዳ ፡ ጠላት ፡) did not enter, and with Wibē's permission Frenchmen, but no other foreigners, would be allowed to build a house or houses on the coast (ቤት ፡ ይሰራሉ ፡ በባሕ[ር] ፡ ዳር ፡).[368] Here again is the difference between accepting a far-reaching abstract obligation, a European protectorate over the coast with all its implications, and what could reasonably be expected from the ruler of Tigrē.

For Wibē it was a very concrete case. The French had kept quiet when the Turks occupied Arkīko and Minkullu, and Degoutin had as a consequence seen his house at Minkullu destroyed at the beginning of the year. If they could now prevail upon the Turks to evacuate the mainland, Wibē would allow them to build a new house or houses there. For 1,000 muskets and two mountain guns, Wibē even promised that they would not have to share the place with any other foreigners,[369] i.e. Plowden and Coffin. This does not mean that Wibē had shifted his sympathies again and preferred Rolland to Plowden or France to Great Britain, still less that he had authorized the French consul to prevent all other foreigners from entering Ethiopia. For Wibē the emphasis was on *enemy*, not *foreigner*, and he certainly intended to decide for himself who were his enemies—and his friends. In fact, it is not likely that Wibē took the Rolland mission very seriously. By 1849 he had more than ten years' experience of official and semi-official French emissaries. Not one of them had carried through what they had themselves proposed. Lefebvre had undertaken a mission ten years earlier; Schimper and De Jacobis five years earlier. Except for some gifts, both had come to nothing. The same in fact happened again. Rolland's first dispatches were lost, and before any reply reached him, he had quarrelled with the Turkish authorities at Massawa and left for Cairo. The French government reviewed the confused case of Wibē's offers of ports and privileges and decided that the time had not yet come to act. Wibē heard no more of Rolland's initiative, and when Lefebvre tried again to be sent as an emissary four years later, the Tigrean ruler allegedly refused because he had received no reply.[370]

At the time of Rolland's visit, Wibē was still waiting for some response from London. Because of Plowden's stay with Ali to get the commercial treaty signed, it took about a year before Wibē received any replies to his two requests and then they were both negative. 'The Queen,' wrote Palmerston, '. . . would gladly do anything which might be agreeable to you in this respect if the circumstances of the case admitted of her supporting your claims. But the Sultan of Turkey is also a friend of the Queen . . .'[371] Though the British government had maintained some eighteen months earlier that the interference of Muhammad Ali even with Sawakin (!) and Massawa was an encroachment on Abyssinia,[372] Palmerston now thought it inadvisable to meddle. As for workmen,

---

368 ibid., fol. 288, Treaty, 2 Oct. 1849, paragraph 2.
369 ibid., paragraph 3.
370 AEMD, Afrique 61, fols 21–37, memoranda on the treaty and Rolland's departure from Massawa, May 1850; SOM, Océan Indien, 10/43, Lefebvre to Ducos, 19 Aug. 1853.
371 FO 401/1, p. 43, Palmerston to Wibē, 3 Jul. 1849.
372 FO 78/3185, fol. 258 Palmerston to Cowley, 6 Dec. 1847. See also above, p. 121.

Plowden was instructed to 'divert his [Wibē's] thoughts from the notion of obtaining the assistance of English workmen'; possibly the need could be met by Indians.[373] Wibē's reaction was 'characteristic' and, one might add, predictable:

> This letter from Queen Victoria is polite, but the substance in three words is, We wont assist you; you say that you are friendly to us and to our religion; I do not see it yet. You say that you are more powerful than the Mahometan; you do not prove it. It is now many years since I have been in correspondence with several European nations on the faith of promises of assistance in two points that I much wish to gain—one the protection of my merchants, the other the suppression of the Slave Trade at Massowah in concert with Ras Ali and the Franks on the coast. With pleasure should I see Massowah in the hands of the Christians. I have the power perhaps to take it, but could not keep it against ships and cannon. We shall see with time if you English are like all the rest.[374]

Obviously some editing by Plowden cannot be excluded, for instance, on the suppression of the slave trade and Massawa, issues which Plowden might have found it useful to emphasize. On the other hand, Wibē had earlier shown concern about the kidnapping of Christian children for the slave market at Massawa. As far as the possession of Massawa was concerned, Wibē's attitude was reasonable under the circumstances and not much different from that of Ras Welde Sillasē forty years earlier.

Above all, Wibē's statement is an expression of disappointment and disillusionment. For fifteen years the Tigrean ruler had been approached by these Europeans who spoke of common faith and friendly feelings, of the greatness of their countries and the power of their kings, of their desire to assist the Christians against the Muslims and co-operate with the Ethiopian rulers in the development of a trade pattern more profitable to the Ethiopians. They had come of their own accord and made their promises or at least raised hopes. In all this there is a note of resignation. The only matter that seems to have angered Wibē was the fact that he had been refused a few workmen to assist in the building of his church, as if he could not be trusted to provide for them and protect them.[375]

Friendship with Wibē and either improvements at Massawa or the creation of an alternative outlet in its neighbourhood were obvious objectives for anyone who wanted to profit from the trade of Ethiopia in general and its northern provinces in particular. For Consul Plowden, and the Foreign Office, they were nevertheless secondary. Circumstances had led Plowden to form friendships with Ras Ali and the commercial community of the Gonder region. He evidently counted much more with Ali as Wibē's overlord than other European observers did.[376] In Plowden's scheme of operations, therefore, a strong position at

---

373   FO 401/1, pp. 42–3, 46, Palmerston to Plowden, 3 Jul. and 23 Jul. 1849.
374   ibid., p. 64, Plowden to Palmerston, 2 Apr. 1850, no. 8.
375   ibid., p. 64, Plowden to Palmerston, 2 Apr. 1850, no. 9.
376   That Palmerston addressed his letter to 'His Highness the Ras of Tigré', may seem confusing. Even if he was confused himself, the notion behind is that of the 'Prime Minister' of Abyssinia, so deftly introduced by Salt for *Ras* Welde Sillasē *of Tigrē* many years earlier. See above, p. 48.

Gonder was the primary objective. Commercial control there, backed by a treaty obligation for Ali to see to it that no customs duties were charged elsewhere for any goods going to or coming from Gonder, would provide the power to capture control all the way down to the coast. This reasoning is obvious in both his instructions and the terms of the treaty which Plowden brought to Ras Ali for signature.

Firstly, the treaty was to be 'drawn up in the name of the Emperor, or in the joint names of the Emperor and the Ras, and should be signed by both'.[377] Secondly, the only import duty to be paid was 5 per cent on the estimated value of the goods at the market place of Gonder. Once this had been paid to 'His Majesty of Abyssinia', British subjects should be free to dispose of their goods 'at any place or places within the territories of Abyssinia without any license being required . . . and without any prohibition, restraint, or further duty or impost of any kind being imposed upon the buyer'. Export duties there should be none whatsoever.[378] The concepts of most favoured nation and of reciprocity were introduced, but the latter did not include the 5 per cent tariff proposed.[379] Thirdly, an obligation on both parties to 'endeavour to keep open and to secure the avenues of approach betwixt the sea-coast and Abyssinia' was included, as was an obviously not reciprocal clause providing for exclusive British consular jurisdiction in all disputes 'between British subjects or between British subjects and the subjects of His Majesty of Abyssinia, or between British subjects and the subjects of any other Foreign Power'.[380] It is not difficult to see that this proposed agreement could become a very powerful instrument in the hands of an active consul.

During Plowden's long absence from central Ethiopia, Ali had brought his conflict with Wibē to an end. He was also about to come to terms with his ambitious son-in-law Kasa Haylu, the future Tēwodros, who had caused him much trouble for more than two years. Only the perennial problem of Birru Goshu's insurrection in Gojjam remained.[381]

Rochet d'Héricourt's visit to Gonder and Debre Tabor had taken place after the rains of 1848 at the height of Kasa's second rebellion. His attempts to establish equally good relations with both sides were bound to fail, and though he reported a friendly reception by Ali, there are no indications even in his own narrative that he managed to interest the *ras* in any commercial treaty.[382] Plowden wisely bypassed the territory under Kasa's control and arrived safely at Debre Tabor with the gifts from the British government. Ali was delighted with the presents and tried to reward the consul by giving him two villages in exchange.[383]

In the treaty, however, the *ras* showed no interest, and Plowden deferred the

377 FO 401/1, pp. 1–2, Palmerston to Plowden, 3 Jan. 1848.
378 ibid., pp. 2–5, Draft of treaty, articles V–VIII.
379 ibid., articles IV and IX.
380 ibid., articles XIII and XVII.
381 See Rubenson, *Tēwodros*, pp. 37–41; Abir, *Ethiopia*, pp. 127–31.
382 AEMD, Afrique 61, fols 319–20, 329–30, 341–2.
383 Plowden, *Travels*, pp. 396–9, 403–4.

matter in the hope, no doubt, that Bell would be able to help in persuading him later.[384] From Plowden's viewpoint, one of the 'worst traits' in Ali's character was 'an aversion to any serious business, and a supercilious indifference to anything that does not immediately concern himself—consequently, to anything regarding Europe'.[385] It is true that one can detect a certain lack of energy and determination in Ali's handling of state affairs. But the significance of Plowden's statement is that it demonstrates the somewhat absurd attitude of so many European envoys of this period. Because of the economic and political consequences of their activities, their proposals deserved to be taken seriously. Nevertheless it was absurd of them to *expect* Ethiopian rulers to regard documents intended to safeguard the interests of a few foreigners as more serious business than the subduing of a rebellion or the purchase of a new horse, for that matter.

After more than eight months, spent largely following the *ras* on a campaign in Gojjam, Plowden and Bell finally managed to get Ali's signature to the treaty of 2 November 1849.[386] Plowden's graphic description of the ceremony further illustrates how unprepared the Ethiopian ruler still was for the type of foreign contacts which now claimed his attention:

> Accordingly, one morning, I went into his inner tent, and had the Treaty read to him by my scribe. After the Abyssinian manner, he kept talking to his favourite *shoomeree* about a horse that was tied in the tent, and that was nearly treading me underfoot half a dozen times (we all sat on the ground, the Ras inclusive). On his asking me some trifling question, in answer, I begged his attention to what was being read, to which he assented, and yawned exceedingly; however, it was got through, some points having been explained and dwelt upon by me. Whereupon, the Ras said that he saw no harm whatever in the document; on the contrary, that it was excellent, but appeared to him exceedingly useless, inasmuch as he did not suppose, as Abyssinia was then constituted, that one English merchant would or could enter it in ten years.[387]

Whatever discussion took place, if any, left no traces in the signed treaty. The English text agrees with the draft, and the Amharic version, in the hand of Plowden's scribe, is a faithful translation. There is only one mistranslation, the granting of consular jurisdiction in Ethiopia to 'the consul of the king of Abyssinia'. If this is not just a slip of the pen, Plowden and/or his secretary had plainly decided to take no risk, but to make the clause acceptable by confusing the issue, as if Plowden and his successors were to depend on the Ethiopian rulers for their appointment and authority.[388] The only problem Plowden had was

384 FO 401/1, pp. 41–2, Plowden to Palmerston, 3 Mar. 1849; Plowden, *Travels*, p. 408. Bell was paid 100 thalers 'for services with Ras Ali'; see Plowden's accounts, 21 Aug. 1848–4 Apr. 1850 (FO 401/1, p. 82).
385 Plowden, *Travels*, p. 403.
386 ibid., pp. 409–20; FO 401/1, p. 69, Plowden to Palmerston, 2 Jan. 1850.
387 Plowden, *Travels*, p. 420. Some allowance must be made for poetic licence, but the crucial comment by Ali 'that the proposals were excellent, but that probably in ten years one English merchant might trade to Gondar' appears also in Plowden's official report to Palmerston, 2 Apr. 1850 (FO 401/1, p. 61).
388 FO 93/2/1, Treaty of Amity and Commerce between Great Britain and Abyssynia, 2 Nov. 1849; English text printed in *PP. Commons*, 1852, LIV, pp. 1–8.

that he had instructions to obtain the signature of the Emperor along with that of the *ras*, but he decided that his government would have to do without it rather than 'alarming the jealousy of the Ras'.[389] The latter signed as 'Alī Niguse Habisha' (King of Abyssinia). Since 'His Majesty of Abyssinia' (presumably intended to mean the Emperor) of the English text was translated 'Niguse Habesha' throughout the treaty, Ali was in fact the contracting party.[390] Nevertheless, a second seal, allegedly representing the approval of an unidentified Emperor, was placed at the bottom of the document along with Ali's seal. This made the issue sufficiently confused to allow more than one interpretation. Aware of how little impact he had made on Ali with his diplomacy, Plowden recommended that a ratification of the treaty be sent to the *ras* 'to impress him with the reality of the transaction'.[391] This was done, but the first copy was stolen from Plowden, and so it was only on 1 March 1852 that Ali received the ratification.[392]

That Ali did not fully understand the significance of the 1849 treaty is plain. He saw it as an unnecessary attempt to secure protection for British merchants at Gonder: unnecessary because they would not come anyhow, and because he could protect them without a treaty if they did, and if he wanted to. That any Ethiopian merchants would ever take advantage of the clauses which guaranteed freedom of movement and commercial privileges for them in Great Britain was completely beyond his horizons. In his letter of thanks for the presents brought by Plowden, however, he raised the question of protection of Ethiopian merchants at Massawa for which there was no explicit provision in the treaty.[393] This was, of course, completely in line with what Plowden wanted. But Ali also had a request of his own, and it was characteristically remote from the mundane affairs of the treaty.

An Ethiopian Emissary: Jerusalem and Cairo

The Ethiopian pilgrims to the Holy Land and the small religious community living in the convent of Dayr as-Sultan needed protection. Even before Plowden had arrived, Ras Ali had raised this matter with Gobat who had been Anglican bishop of Jerusalem since 1846.[394] About the same time as the treaty was signed, he wrote to Gobat again, and Plowden was asked to support his re-

389　FO 401/1, p. 69, Plowden to Palmerston, 2 Jan. 1850; see also pp. 41–2, Plowden to Palmerston, 3 Mar. 1849.
390　FO 93/2/1.
391　FO 401/1, p. 61, Plowden to Palmerston, 2 Apr. 1850.
392　FO 93/2/1, Receipt, 1 Mar. 1852; FO 401/1, p. 78, Palmerston to Plowden, 15 Jun. 1850; p. 120a, Plowden to Palmerston, 24 Jun. 1851; p. 122, Plowden to Palmerston, 8 Apr. 1852.
393　FO 1/6, fol. 71, Ali to Victoria, n.d. (Nov. 1849). Ali also expressed some concern that his own gifts, of which the most valuable item was four elephants' tusks, were not equal to those of Queen Victoria. Nevertheless he hinted that he would be happy to receive some more, including some cash with which to pay his soldiers. The British government agreed to include 500 thalers, with two rifles, six percussion guns, percussion caps and some more cloth in the next gift, but Plowden declined to forward the money as unnecessary. See FO 401/1, pp. 94, 106–7, Palmerston to Plowden, 19 Oct. 1850 and 18 Mar. 1851.
394　Cerulli, *Etiopi*, II, pp. 193–231; Crummey, *Priests*, p. 115.

quest.[395] But the attempt of Gobat and Consul James Finn to help the Ethiopians gain control over their chapel in Dayr as-Sultan failed, and in 1852 political and ecclesiastical leaders in Ethiopia joined hands in an attempt to reach a better settlement.[396] Ali and Wibē wrote almost identical letters to Queen Victoria pleading for her interference: 'How can I lose my inheritance while you are [my friend] (ምነው ፡ ጸንቶ ፡ ሳለሸ ፡ ርስቴን ፡ መነቀሉ ።)? While everyone sits in peace on his inheritance, I have been uprooted.'[397]

It is interesting to note that the British consul, though present with Ras Ali until the beginning of March 1852 when the last letters must have been written, nevertheless seems to have played no part in this appeal to his sovereign. He makes no mention of the issue in any of his dispatches to London, and it seems unlikely that he should have forwarded the letters to Jerusalem instead of London if they had been entrusted to him. It may well be that Bell offered to forward Ali's first letter to Gobat in 1848 in order to prevent Rochet d'Héricourt from obtaining a commission to ask for French protection for the pilgrims.[398] This does not exclude the possibility that the first initiative came from Ethiopian ecclesiastics,[399] for whom the safety of the pilgrims and the rights of the Ethiopian convent were matters of primary importance. At any rate no consular prompting was necessary or evident. The fate of the 'inheritance' in Jerusalem was not a matter for consuls but for kings and bishops, and there was no need for other emissaries than the priests, monks, and other pious Ethiopians who had been travelling the route to Cairo and Jerusalem for centuries past.[400]

Ali's messenger to Gobat in 1850 was a former *içhegē* named Gebre Maryam, who according to Blondeel had been his closest confidant at Gonder in 1842 and had wanted to accompany the Belgian consul to Cairo to ask for the recall of Abune Selama.[401] This does not necessarily mean that he had Catholic

---

395   FO 401/1, pp. 96, 101–2, Finn to Palmerston, 30 Nov. and 9 Dec. 1850. In fact, Bell wrote to Gobat 28 Dec. 1848 (Spittler-Archiv, XXX/3) that Plowden had received letters for Victoria about this matter in 1848. If so, he had failed to forward them. See AECP, Massouah 1, fols 273–4, Rolland to Tocqueville, 15 Aug. 1849, for a report that Plowden was promising British support in the matter.

396   Cerulli, *Etiopi*, Vol. II, pp. 239–91; FO 401/1, pp. 124A–5, Gobat to Malmesbury, 29 Jun. 1852, with enclosures; p. 126, Bunsen to Malmesbury, 5 Jul. 1852.

397   FO 1/7, fol. 79, Ali to Victoria, n.d.; fol. 80, Wibē to Victoria, n.d. Wibē's letter is sealed with the same seal as he used on his letter to Victoria in 1849. Ali's letter bears a different seal from the one he used in 1849 as well as on the receipt for the ratification in March 1852. The handwriting is *qum şihfet*, and Wibē's letter seems to be copied from Ali's.

398   See above, p. 129.

399   So stated in Bell to Gobat, 28 Dec. 1848.

400   The Foreign Office, however, found the procedure strange. See FO 401/1, p. 124B, minute by Hammond, 7 Jul. 1852.

401   Duchesne, *Blondeel*, pp. 166, 168, 173. Gebre Maryam seems to have been *içhegē* for a short period only, preceded (see above, p. 78) and followed by Mahşentu Mīka'ēl. The two have been confused or mistakenly identified by several authors, but Mahşentu was in Wadla in February 1842 (Conti Rossini, 'Vicende', *RRAL*, 5, XXV, p. 463) when Blondeel was advising Gebre Maryam at Gonder. See Hiruy Welde Sillasē, *Wazēma* (Addis Abeba, 1928/29), p. 113, for the *içhegēs* of this period. Crummey (*Priests*, p. 75) describes Mahşentu as favourable to Catholicism, probably converted. Some of his sources seem to refer to Gebre Maryam.

sympathies, but on his way to Jerusalem he did visit De Jacobis at Minkullu (late November 1849), showed him a letter written in Ali's name, and asked him to support the cause of his mission.[402] In Cairo he contacted or was contacted by Degoutin. This resulted in a letter from the former consul to Blondeel, now chargé d'affaires in Istanbul, stating that Gebre Maryam had arrived with letters from Ras Ali to the King of the Belgians, offering the cession of Agamē, as requested by Blondeel eight years earlier. The reason given for the long delay was Abune Selama's opposition, but now (*sic*) that the bishop had been expelled from Gonder, the business could be concluded.[403] The French consul general, A. Le Moyne, did not take Gebre Maryam's mission very seriously,[404] but Blondeel certainly did. He alerted Brussels, recommended mutually exclusive courses of action—for instance, ratification of the earlier 'treaties' with Goshu along with the acceptance of Ali's 'offer'—and tried to interest a Prussian colleague in a joint colonization of Agamē. But he did not manage to reach Cairo or Jerusalem in time to meet Gebre Maryam.[405] He had to be satisfied with the opportunity of sending some letters with one of Gebre Maryam's fellow-pilgrims, who was still in Jerusalem, occupied with the business of the Ethiopian convent. Blondeel wrote to Ali, Gebre Maryam, and De Jacobis, asking the latter to translate and forward the letters to the two Ethiopians and press for answers. Ali was told to explain his offers clearly, and advised to ask for men and arms, not money.[406]

In spite of the inconsistencies, Blondeel's ultimate objective was clear. Gebre Maryam's role and aims were both contradictory and obscure. He allegedly carried letters to the Belgian king, and offered to go to Istanbul and deliver them to Blondeel. This he did not do, nor did he see to it that the Belgian got them any other way. What Gebre Maryam carried for the King of the Belgians, if anything, therefore remains unknown. Even Blondeel admitted later that it may have been a simple note with no commitments.[407] Nevertheless, Degoutin too, seems to have seen great new opportunities open up, for he promptly bought Edd for 20,000 francs from the Nanto-Bordelaise company which claimed ownership on the basis of Combes's purchase ten years earlier and tried to resell it to the French government for 400,000 under the threat that he would otherwise let the British have it.[408]

Gebre Maryam's contacts with De Jacobis, Degoutin, and Blondeel can, of course, be taken as evidence of anxiety in French/Catholic circles over Plowden's activities. But there is absolutely nothing to show that Ali was apprehensive about the treaty he was signing with Plowden. If Gebre Maryam was, it

402 CML, De Jacobis, 'Giornale Abissino', Vol. IV, pp. 123–4.
403 AE(Brussels), 2024/II, Degoutin to Blondeel, 10 Mar. 1850 (copy certified by Blondeel).
404 AECP, Massouah 1, fol. 304, Le Moyne to Lahitte, 14 Mar. 1850.
405 Duchesne, *Blondeel*, pp. 206–12. See also above, pp. 99–101.
406 Duchesne, *Blondeel*, p. 216, letters to Ali and De Jacobis, dated 6 Feb. 1851; CML, De Jacobis, 'Giornale Abissino', Vol. IV, p. 146; AVA 2/5, Blondeel to Gonzaga, 6 Feb. 1851. I am indebted to Dr Richard Caulk for information about the contents of the AVA.
407 Duchesne, *Blondeel*, p. 213.
408 AECP, Égypte 22, fol. 62, Degoutin to Lahitte, 1 Jul. 1850; fols 58–61, Delaporte to Lahitte, 1 Jul. 1850.

remains to be explained not only why he did not follow up the matter with French authorities in Egypt or Palestine, but also why he informed the British consul general in Syria about the whole matter as soon as he reached Palestine.[409]

In fact, Gebre Maryam's conduct looks very much like an attempt to imitate some of the European envoys in Ethiopia. Had not his mentor, Blondeel himself, travelled from chief to chief in Ethiopia, received hospitality, and demanded escorts by virtue of his position? Had he not made proposals to one chief after the other and in the end committed himself to nothing and to no one? Blondeel's excuse was that he really had no authority to make any commitments. In all probability, Gebre Maryam had still less. His real mission concerned the convent in Jerusalem. The rest was not serious but might provide some protection and financial assistance in a foreign land.

The problem for Ethiopia was that the Europeans were serious, at least about their objectives. Somehow, some day, an Ethiopian would get trapped. At the Belgian consulate in Cairo Blondeel deposited a declaration for Gebre Maryam to sign if he turned up again:

> In the name of the Father, the Son, and the Holy Ghost, I, Gebre Maryam, the *ičhegē* of Ethiopia, declare in the name of His Highness Ras Ali, sovereign ruler of Ethiopia, that I cede to His Majesty the King of the Belgians, Leopold I, and to his descendants with full sovereignty the whole province of Agamē from Addīgrat to the sea.[410]

The same document also laid down that all trade should be directed exclusively through the new Belgian territory. In return Ali would receive a treaty of friendship providing for mutual military assistance. Whether the former *ičhegē* could have been induced to sign this document or not is an open question. By the time Gebre Maryam returned to Cairo on his next mission in June 1852, the Belgian consul general knew that his government was unprepared to take a decision and therefore abstained from bringing up the matter. This settled it. Gebre Maryam showed no sign of having either instructions or any personal desire to negotiate an agreement with Belgium, whatever the terms.[411]

As in 1849–50, Gebre Maryam's mission in 1852 had little or nothing to do with the activities of European consuls in Ethiopia. He was to return to Jerusalem in the hope that Gobat, fortified with Ali's and Wibē's letters to Victoria, would be able to reverse the unfavourable decision about the convent. Of all times, the Coptic Patriarch chose the height of this conflict to send Da'ud, the abbot of the monastery of St Antonios, to Ethiopia to mediate between Abune Selama and his opponents and prevent the sympathies for the Catholic missionaries and their teaching from increasing further.[412] But the Patriarch also

409   Duchesne, *Blondeel*, p. 207. Gebre Maryam could hardly know that the Belgian government at this time looked towards London rather than Paris for guidance.
410   ibid., pp. 213–14.
411   ibid., pp. 214–15, Zizinia to d'Hoffschmidt, 6 Jul. 1852.
412   Cerulli, *Etiopi*, Vol. II, p. 294. See Crummey, *Priests*, pp. 70–9, 90, for the attitudes of leading clerics and of Ali and Wibē towards the mission at this time.

wanted money. Da'ud was instructed to tell Wibē, Ali, and whoever else was concerned in the matter that the court case in Jerusalem had cost the Patriarch considerable sums of money which they now owed him; that, moreover, he spent large sums annually for travel, food, and burials for Ethiopian pilgrims. Amounts were suggested. If the Ethiopians were not prepared to pay all, '. . . see to it that they send us something!'[413]

It was during Da'ud's stay in Ethiopia that Gebre Maryam was sent on his second mission to Jerusalem. Whether he brought anything for the Patriarch is uncertain. By the time he reached Cairo, Pētros VII had died, on 5 April 1852, after forty-three years in office.[414] For the Egyptian viceroy, however, the envoy brought twelve horses as a present from Ras Ali. This had already been reported from Khartoum,[415] and it seems safe to conclude that the Ethiopians were seeking an ally in their struggle to have the judgement concerning the convent changed.[416] The death of the Patriarch provided Gebre Maryam with unexpected opportunities to apply pressures. He sent the letters to Gobat and remained in Cairo.[417] The majority candidate for the vacant office was none other than Da'ud; he had already been elected but Gebre Maryam did his utmost to reverse the decision, accusing him of immorality during his stay in Ethiopia and of having tried to incite the Ethiopian rulers to attack Egypt. Abbas Pasha was impressed by Gebre Maryam's arguments; investigations were started, and it was only two years later that Da'ud was finally consecrated Qērilos IV.[418] By then the political situation in Ethiopia had changed completely: Ras Ali was eliminated and the future Emperor Tēwodros had informed the viceroy that he had no objections to Da'ud's elevation.[419]

The missions of Gebre Maryam in 1850 and 1852 reveal how completely the Europeans had identified Ethiopian foreign contacts with their own initiatives and interests. The British found it surprising that Ali and Wibē had bypassed their consul; the Belgians saw Gebre Maryam's appearances in Cairo primarily as an attempt to follow up Blondeel's colonization schemes; the French, finally, seem to have been almost bewildered at the sight of an Ethiopian envoy who did not ask for their advice. In 1850 Le Moyne spoke disparagingly of Gebre Maryam's 'illusion about the real importance of his mission' which he believed to be the search for Belgian support to overthrow the Emperor.[420] In 1852 he thought that the envoy had come to demand that Egypt return some territory to Ethiopia under the threat that it would otherwise be invaded,[421] while his

413   Cerulli, *Etiopi*, Vol. II, pp. 299–300, Buṭrus (Pēṭros VII) to Da'ud, n.d.
414   M. Chaine, *La Chronologie des temps chrétiens de l'Égypte et de l'Éthiopie* (Paris, 1925), p. 254.
415   Duchesne, *Blondeel*, p. 214.
416   See Aleme Eshete, 'Une Ambassade du Ras Ali en Egypte: 1852', *JES*, IX, 1 (1971), pp. 1–8, for a different interpretation. The mission can obviously have had more than one objective, but it is not likely that a request by Ali for aid against Kasa (Tēwodros) was one of them. See below, p. 139.
417   Gobat forwarded the letters to London on 29 June (FO 401/1, p. 124A).
418   Cerulli, *Etiopi*, Vol. II, pp. 296–7; AECP, Massouah 1, fols 376–7, Delaporte to Le Moyne 18 Jul. 1852.
419   FO 401/1, pp. 172–3, Bruce to Clarendon, 7 Jun. 1854.
420   AECP, Massouah 1, fol. 304, Le Moyne to Lahitte, 14 Mar. 1850.
421   AECP, Égypte 24, fols 135–7, Le Moyne to Turgot, 19 Jul. 1852.

consul in Cairo, P. H. Delaporte, marvelled that this 'Abyssinian vizier' had the audacity to challenge a patriarchal election and bring the matter before the secular authorities. Since Gebre Maryam was not advised to do this by the French, the consul predictably concluded that he was the instrument of an intrigue by the British consul general and the CMS missionaries in Cairo, aimed at increasing British influence in Ethiopia at the expense of French.[422] The head of the Lazarist mission at Alexandria knew better: Gebre Maryam, not Da'ud, was pro-Catholic, and support for his attempts to secure Ethiopian rights in Dayr as-Sultan would benefit the mission in Ethiopia.[423] At one point Delaporte seems to have hoped that the Copts would actually uphold their election of Da'ud since Gebre Maryam would then have Ali break with the Coptic church once and for all and accept De Jacobis as bishop of Ethiopia. French influence would then be without rival in all Ethiopia.[424] This was wishful thinking on several levels. Gebre Maryam was not *iċhegē*, had not been so for many years, and the extent of his influence is doubtful.[425] Ali had been friendly and tolerant, but not committed. In retrospect, even De Jacobis saw that his attitude since 1850 had not been promising.[426] At any rate, Ali could no longer deliver even Begēmdir; *all* Ethiopia had never been within his grasp.

The End of the Zemene Mesafint: *An Ethiopian Affair*

The *Zemene Mesafint* was swiftly approaching its end. In two years of manoeuvring and four major battles—Gur Amba 27 November 1852, Gorgora Bichiñ 12 April 1853, Ayshal 29 June 1853, and Deresgē 9 February 1855—Dejjazmach Kasa of Qwara eliminated those who had represented the political leadership in central and northern Ethiopia for a quarter of a century. Goshu fell at Gur Amba, Birru Alīgaz and other important vassals of Ali's at Gorgora Bichiñ. Ali, Birru Goshu, and Wibē were defeated and effectively removed from the political scene. As King of Kings Tēwodros, the former district governor from the western lowlands prepared himself to make an all-out effort to change the course of Ethiopian history.[427]

In the struggles that brought the *Zemene Mesafint* to an end, foreign contributions, whether individual or collective, are conspicuously absent. It was not that the foreign presence had disappeared. It was simply irrelevant in the decisive confrontation. John Bell lived near Debre Tabor, and was available both as

422 AECP, Massouah 1, fols 376–7, Delaporte to Le Moyne, 18 Jul. 1852.
423 ibid., fols 369–70, 371–5, Le Moyne to Drouyn de Lhuys, 6 Aug. and 10 Sep. 1852.
424 AECP, Égypte 24, fols 159–62, Delaporte to Drouyn de Lhuys, 15 Aug. 1852.
425 Conti Rossini, 'Nuovi documenti', *RANL*, 8, II, pp. 383–409, *passim*. Theodor von Heuglin, who travelled together with Gebre Maryam from Khartoum to Metemma in December 1852 when the latter returned to Ethiopia, spoke of him as a prominent churchman but not as *iċhegē*. See his *Reisen in Nord-Ost-Afrika* (Gotha, 1857), pp. 4, 55.
426 Aleme, 'Une Ambassade', *JES*, IX, 1, p. 8, quoting De Jacobis to Sturchi, 2 Jan. 1854. But see Crummey, *Priests*, p. 72, for the hopes still held by the Catholics at the time.
427 For Kasa's background and rise to power, see Rubenson, *Tēwodros*, pp. 15–45, with sources quoted there.

adviser to Ali and as contact man between him and Plowden. After the battle of Gur Amba, the consul reported that much would depend on the 'continued fidelity or neutrality' of Wibē, but concluded: '. . . at present the position and the power of the Ras will be in nowise endangered'.[428] He continued to place all his hopes for growing British influence in the maintenance of the status quo, with Ali as supreme ruler and Wibē as his albeit troublesome vassal, who had to be courted as well.[429] Even after Kasa had, in April 1853, defeated the army sent against him jointly by Ali and Wibē, Plowden reported that he was 'now negotiating with the Ras for the public proclamation of the Consulate, and the principal points of the Treaty we have concluded with him', but by the end of the year he admitted that the treaty with Ali was 'likely to become a nullity'.[430] There is, however, no indication that Ali asked for or was offered assistance of any kind in the struggle. After Ayshal, Plowden seemed a bit surprised about this, and suggested that he be allowed to spend £100–200 at his own discretion if Ali should send a request for 'money, guns or powder'.[431] The amount suggested shows that it was only a question of token assistance to retain goodwill. It was never used.

For the Catholics in Begēmdir, the choice seemed easy. Ali had protected them, and they feared Kasa's Orthodox zeal.[432] But if Ali expected any meaningful support, he was bound to be disappointed. De Jacobis's colleague, Fr (later Mgr) L. Biancheri, alerted the new French consul at Massawa, who after ten days at his post reported rumours that Kasa's revolt was instigated by Plowden, and financed by the Patriarch in Cairo! That this misleading information was judged in Paris to be very important made no difference in Ethiopia.[433] Ali was already eliminated.

The alternative was now to support Wibē in some way, but in April 1854 Selama prevailed upon him to expel all Catholic missionaries from Tigrē. In exchange, Wibē had, according to the French consul, almost certainly obtained Selama's promise that he would excommunicate Kasa. To suit his own wishes, the consul 'foresaw' that Kasa would defeat Wibē and shut up the bishop in some monastery, whereupon the Catholic mission would become 'more powerful than ever in Ethiopia'.[434] This was a convenient approach which entailed neither support nor prior commitment. But the assumption that Selama would turn against Kasa, who had invited him to Gonder after eight years of exile from the capital, was totally unrealistic. De Jacobis had preceded him in an attempt to save what the mission had gained so far, but Kasa, who saw the need

428 FO 401/1, p. 137, Plowden to Malmesbury, 24 Jan. 1853; also pp. 142–6, Statement of Relations with Abyssinia, submitted 23 Mar. 1853.
429 ibid., pp. 142–6, Statement, 23 Mar. 1853; p. 149, Plowden to Malmesbury, 2 Apr. 1853.
430 ibid., pp. 150, 159, Plowden to Clarendon, 24 May and 21 Dec. 1853; Heuglin, *Nord-Ost-Afrika*, pp. 98, 110, 129.
431 FO 401/1, p. 162, Plowden to Clarendon, 25 Jan. 1854.
432 Crummey, *Priests*, pp. 72, 95. See also G. Massaja, *In Abissinia e fra i Galla* (Florence, 1895), pp. 38–67, for evidence of this missionary's fear of Kasa.
433 AECP, Massouah 1, fols 382–4, Delaye to Drouyn de Lhuys, 15 May 1853; fol. 397, Drouyn de Lhuys to Delaye, 20 Oct. 1853.
434 AECP, Massouah 2, fol. 15, Delaye to Drouyn de Lhuys, 24 Apr. 1854.

for ecclesiastical unity, chose co-operation with Selama instead of tolerance.[435]

In several ways Wibē was in a better position to seek support than Ali or Kasa. When Plowden had failed to recruit the desired craftsmen, the botanist Schimper had been engaged to build Wibē's new church at Deresgē, and in 1852–53 he and a German painter, C. E. Zander, were living there close to the Tigrean prince.[436] In February–March 1853, as his son was preparing to march against Kasa, Wibē was visited by the Austrian consul in Khartoum, K. Reitz, and his secretary Theodor von Heuglin, who had come through Gonder to negotiate trade agreements with Wibē and Ali. From the other direction, Coffin and Lefebvre turned up to see Wibē on some business. The prince was ill and refused to see any of them. Schimper did his best, and sent away the Austrian representatives with some kind of document, but the fact that they were not made to wait until Wibē had recovered indicates that the interest was not very great.[437] After Kasa's victories in April and June, however, Wibē wrote and asked Plowden to import firearms. He was prepared to buy them, but Plowden's influence with the Turkish governor was not sufficient to pass them through Massawa. He therefore appealed to his government: 'it is not reasonable to expect anything for nothing from an Abyssinian Chief; nor can Dejaj Oobeay understand how on the one hand I request, and even obtain his friendship, and on the other refuse him so slight a request'.[438] There is no indication that Plowden succeeded in this effort. Wibē was anyway the best armed of the contestants. With his greater awareness of the realities of Ethiopian politics, Plowden had formed closer ties with Abune Selama, for 'whatever changes of chiefs or dynasties may occur, the Aboona will probably be always highly revered both by the populace and their rulers'.[439] It was not until Selama had established himself at Gonder in June and July 1854 that Plowden began to welcome the possibility that Kasa would grasp supreme power; and it was November before Kasa sent his first courtesy message to the consul.[440]

If Ali and Wibē in the final struggle had little or no advantage from their long connections with Europeans, Kasa had almost no contacts to begin with. With the exception of De Jacobis, the Catholic missionaries preferred to stay out of his reach.[441] In 1848 Kasa had clashed with Rochet d'Héricourt, reportedly over a few guns and pistols which the Frenchman had intended for Ali, but which

435   CML, De Jacobis, 'Giornale Abissino', Vol. V, pp. 1, 3, 20, 38–9, 98; Crummey, *Priests*, pp. 96–7.
436   Heuglin, *Nord-Ost-Afrika*, pp. 69–70, 83–4; Conti Rossini, 'Nuovi documenti', *RANL*, 8, II, pp. 400, 403. For the background and activities of Zander, see Richard Andree, *Abessinien, das Alpenland unter den Tropen und seine Grenzländer* (Leipzig, 1869), pp. 30–1.
437   Heuglin, *Nord-Ost-Afrika*, pp. 55, 79, 84, 88, 94; FO 401/1, p. 149, Plowden to Malmesbury, 2 Apr. 1853.
438   FO 401/1, p. 157, Wibē to Plowden, n.d., Plowden to Clarendon, 20 Oct. 1853. There is no Amharic version with the original correspondence in FO 1/7.
439   ibid., p. 152, Plowden to Russell, 28 Jul. 1853, no. 24.
440   ibid.. pp. 193–228, Report, 9 Jul. 1854, especially p. 215; pp. 231–3, Plowden to Clarendon, 25 Sep. and 6 Nov. 1854.
441   Heuglin (*Nord-Ost-Afrika*, p. 51) makes the point that no foreigners were present in Gonder when he arrived there in January 1853.

Kasa wanted.[442] Five years later, Kasa explained his anti-French attitude to Heuglin and Reitz as the result of a visit by a bragging Frenchman who had said that he would return in a balloon straight from Paris. Kasa, so the story goes, took charge of the Frenchman's arms and other property, but promised to return them when his guest returned in the balloon.[443] But Kasa could also be friendly towards foreigners. In the crucial period immediately following the battle of Gur Amba, he gave a great welcome to Reitz and Heuglin, who had taken the opportunity to join Gebre Maryam on his return to Ethiopia through Khartoum. But instead of sending them back to Khartoum to find arms for the continuation of the war, he spoke about long-term plans for recruiting European craftsmen or sending his own people to Europe for training. He did not even seem to resent that the envoys were on their way to his enemies, but assisted them in their onward journey.[444] They passed through his camp again on their way back to the Sudan, and Heuglin left as late as one week before the great battle at Gorgora Bichiñ on 12 April.[445] Clearly, neither he nor any other European was present or commanded Kasa's army at this time. As for armament, Heuglin described the primitive manufacturing of powder and balls for Kasa's estimated 800–1,000 muskets,[446] which is not many considering Kasa's great interest in modern arms and the fact that he had been governor of the districts bordering the Sudan for many years. Twenty years earlier, Coffin had brought twice that number to Massawa in a single shipment.[447]

Only the question of Egypt and its eventual interference remains. It has been suggested that the principal objective of Gebre Maryam's mission in 1852 was 'the search by Ali for a foreign alliance', directed primarily against Kasa.[448] In fact, it is doubtful that Kasa had declared his rebellion before Gebre Maryam left.[449] Besides, it was Kasa and not Ali who stood alone in the struggle, so there was no reason for Ali to suspect that he would need foreign assistance. But in a general way, at least, Gebre Maryam's mission strengthened friendship between Ali and the viceroy, for on his return he was accompanied by an envoy with presents in return for Ali. And when Reitz and Heuglin continued their journey through Metemma to Gonder, in spite of the news about Gur Amba,

442 AEMD, Afrique 61, fols 319–27.
443 Heuglin, *Nord-Ost-Afrika*, p. 44.
444 ibid., pp. 4, 34, 40–1, 43, 48–9. Lejean (*Théodore II*, p. 135) has a strange story about a treaty concluded by Tēwodros on this occasion, and torn up ten years later. I have found no evidence to support his story, which is clearly incorrect in several respects. Cf. 'Th. v. Heuglin's Reise zu Kaiser Theodoros und der Festung Magdala, Februar bis Mai 1862', *Petermann*, 1867, pp. 421–35.
445 Heuglin, *Nord-Ost-Afrika*, pp. 111–13.
446 ibid., pp. 107–8; cf. Delaye's erroneous opinion (AECP, Massouah 1, fols 387–8, Delaye to Drouyn de Lhuys, 20 Aug. 1853): 'His army . . . is commanded by some Europeans, whose advice is exactly followed.'
447 See above, p. 65.
448 Aleme, 'Une Ambassade', *JES*, IX, 1, p. 1. See above, pp. 131–6, for the primary reason for Gebre Maryam's missions.
449 Conti Rossini, 'Nuovi documenti', *RANL*, 8, II, pp. 401–3. Kasa's rebellion is said to have taken place at the time when Merso sought refuge in the *Ichegē Bēt* at Easter (11 April) 1852.

Gebre Maryam and the Egyptian decided to avoid the territory controlled by Kasa.[450]

In the meantime, the news of Kasa's victory had spread to Khartoum, and a congratulatory mission had reached Kasa, bearing gifts, including some enormous flintlocks from the governor general, Ismail Haqqi.[451] This is sufficient evidence that Kasa's relations with the Egyptians were no worse than Ali's, though he had fought them in person, which Ali had never done. At Dabarki, in 1848, he had suffered the only serious defeat of his early career at their hands. His preoccupation with artillery, and the desire to drill his soldiers, emanated from that encounter.[452] But in spite of the raids and counter-raids over an undefined or poorly defined boundary, Kasa must have had other and more friendly contacts with his neighbours the 'Turks'. He had associated a great deal with Muslims in the border districts, spoke Arabic, and probably tried to drill his troops with the help of some Turkish soldiers.[453] Several of his district governors in the border areas were Muslims, including Takruri *shaykhs*, and a kind of double sovereignty had been established over Qallabat with the important market of Metemma.[454] In early 1853, the appearance of an Egyptian army at Metemma even caused rumours that the 'Turks' were coming *to Kasa's aid* in the war against Ali. The rumours turned out to be false, but the very fact that they were spread indicates that someone thought they might be believed.[455] There is nothing to show that the Egyptians were really asked or prepared to involve themselves on either side. The Ethiopians fought their own battles in 1852–55. No foreign commitment was sufficiently firm or strong to influence the outcome in any perceptible way. A quarter of a century had not been sufficient to produce any champions of European versus Turk, British versus French, Catholics versus Protestants, in a decisive Ethiopian power struggle.

Eritrea Conceived

It was on the northern outskirts of the Ethiopian state, at Massawa and in the Bogos area, that foreign powers increased their influence in the early fifties. Between Wibē and the Turkish governor at Massawa, the tension, the claims, and counterclaims prevailed. In the early months of 1850, Wibē maintained his official demands on the governor for the annual tribute he had in the past received through the *na'ib*. The governor compromised, sent some presents and brought in reinforcements from Jidda. These were used mainly for raids against the Habab, who refused to pay tribute and fought back. The position of the

450 Heuglin, *Nord-Ost-Afrika*, pp. 4, 13, 16, 18, 23, 100.
451 ibid., p. 102.
452 Rubenson, *Tēwodros*, pp. 39–40.
453 [Zeneb], *Tēwodros*, p. 9; Rassam, *British Mission*, I, p. 270; FO 401/1, p. 151, Plowden to Russell, 25 Jul. 1853; pp. 214–15, Plowden, Report, 9 Jul. 1854.
454 Heuglin, *Nord-Ost-Afrika*, pp. 26–9, 118, 125. See also Douin, *Ismaïl*, III, 1, pp. 38–9.
455 Heuglin, *Nord-Ost-Afrika*, p. 100.

Turks remained precarious on the mainland.[456] As late as December 1852, a major attack was expected at Massawa, but it seems as if Wibē was never prepared to take the final step.[457] He may have continued to hope for a peaceful solution in his favour through French or British intervention. When Rolland's successor, L. Delaye, arrived in 1853 after a vacancy of three years at the consulate, he was instructed to inform Wibē that the French government had decided not to ratify the agreements made by Rolland in 1849.[458] The decision was by then three years old.[459] Nevertheless, fearing the consequences of Wibē's disappointment, Delaye decided not to carry out his instructions, and received the approval of his superiors in Paris for this course of action.[460] Though Plowden may have exaggerated his influence over Wibē, there is no reason to doubt the thrust of his advice during these years:

It is owing to the respect of Dejajmatch Oobeay for Her Majesty, and to my representations, that he has scrupulously abstained from any warlike expedition in the neighbourhood of Massowah; otherwise, though he could not effect, perhaps, a permanent conquest, it would be easy for him to coerce the Pasha into accordance with his requests. I have advocated this policy from humanity, to save the border tribes from the consequences of an invasion, unprovoked by them, but from which they are the principal sufferers; their Turkish Governor and soldiers shutting themselves up in their stone fortress or island, on the first alarm.[461]

On the other hand, the British consul consistently maintained that the Turks had no rights whatsoever on the mainland, and was supported in this stand by his government. He would have liked to see the Turks turned out of Massawa altogether, but as a second best he advocated, in vain, the development of Anfilla or some other suitable place into a British rival port.[462] The Turkish administration responded with plans to extend its direct control. An expedition in February 1853 to assert the authority of the Sultan over Anfilla was, for instance, postponed at the last minute only because the local Saho showed too great hostility.[463] In the meantime, the Ethiopians were not only losing revenue and influence over the trade generally: Massawa was at least periodically closed to all arms import. How drastically things had changed since the days of Welde Sillasē is revealed by the fact that a carriage specifically ordered by Plowden for one of the cannon imported by Salt was not allowed to pass.[464]

456 FO 401/1, pp. 73–4, Adams to Haines, 11 Apr. 1850; p. 72, Haines to the Government of Bombay, 18 Apr. 1850; AECP, Massouah 1, fols 330–1, Pasquale to Le Moyne, 11 Sep. 1850.
457 FO 401/1, pp. 135–6, Plowden to Malmesbury, 14 Dec. 1852.
458 See above, pp. 125–7.
459 AEMD, Afrique 63, fol. 34, Lahitte to Aupick, 17 Jun. 1850.
460 AECP, Massouah 1, fols 382–4, Delaye to Drouyn de Lhuys, 15 Jun. 1853; fol. 397, Drouyn de Lhuys to Delaye, 20 Oct. 1853.
461 FO 401/1, p. 185, Plowden to Clarendon, 1 Jul. 1854.
462 Plowden dealt with these matters in a number of his dispatches. See, in particular, FO 401/1, pp. 66, 99, to Palmerston, 4 Apr. and 28 Oct. 1850; pp. 226–7, Report, 9 Jul. 1854.
463 AECP, Massouah 1, fols 332–3, Le Moyne to Lahitte, 31 Dec. 1850; FO 401/1, p. 139, Plowden to Malmesbury, 13 Feb. 1853.
464 FO 401/1, pp. 79, 104, Plowden to Palmerston, 12 May and 15 Dec. 1850.

Finally Plowden had to appeal to London for orders that something as insignificant as eight or ten 'fowling-pieces and rifles' for Wibē personally be let through.[465] When Plowden insisted on the need for an alternative port, he was no doubt moved mainly by the desire to promote a trade from which he himself would benefit directly or indirectly. But this does not, as future developments showed, invalidate his opinion that the want of an alternative port was one of the greatest difficulties which future rulers of Ethiopia would have to overcome.[466]

As if it was not sufficient to tax Ethiopia's export and import, the Turkish administration had begun to covet another source of revenue, the Ṭilṭal salt plains some 70–80 kilometres inland from Anfilla. These were of tremendous importance to the Ethiopians. Not only had they as far back as history goes received most of their supplies of the indispensable commodity from Ṭilṭal, but salt bars were the main currency of the country.[467] An occupation of Ṭilṭal would make it possible for the Turks to interfere with and tax Ethiopian internal trade as well. Fortunately for Ethiopia, the governor of Massawa lacked the military resources necessary for the occupation, but his brazen claim, reportedly in a letter straight to Wibē, that the salt plains were 'the property and territory of his Master the Sultan', indicates the direction matters were taking.[468]

Neither Anfilla nor Ṭilṭal was primarily a territorial issue for the governments involved: Ethiopian, Turkish, or European. No outsider really cared to govern the Saho or the Ṭilṭal.[469] To the west of Massawa, however, the situation was different. Here the thesis that there was no Ottoman territory on the African mainland was not applicable. Instead, the problem was to establish the eastern limits of the Egyptian Sudan. In the 1840s, Wibē had reacted to the Egyptian inroads into what Consul Degoutin had in 1844 defined as no-man's-land by sending his armies on raids as far west as Kunama.[470] The net result, however, of the raids and counter-raids of the decade was that most of the lowland Muslim tribes north and west of Massawa, the Habab and the Beni Amir in particular, had been subjected to Egyptian rule, while the Bogos area had been forcibly incorporated in Wibē's territories. But the situation was both complex and unstable. The payment of tribute did not necessarily carry with it protection against raids from the other side, still less organized government. Some tribes therefore had to pay tribute in both directions, others paid no regular tribute at all but suffered an occasional raid. 'No-man's-land' was shrinking, but there were as yet no attempts to reach mutual agreements about boundaries.[471]

465 ibid., p. 185, Plowden to Clarendon, 1 Jul. 1854.
466 ibid., p. 187, Plowden to Clarendon, 10 Jul. 1854.
467 See M. Abir, 'Salt, Trade and Politics in Ethiopia in the "Zämänä Mäsafint"', *JES*, IV, 2 (1966), pp. 1–10.
468 FO 401/1, p. 184, Plowden to Clarendon, 30 Jun. 1854. See also FO 401/1 (Preliminary), pp. 20–1, Plowden to Stanley, 17 Nov. 1847, enclosure.
469 FO 401/1, pp. 270–2, Plowden to Clarendon, 17 Feb. 1856. For the difficulties encountered by the Turkish governor with the Saho in 1853–54, see Munzinger, *Ostafrikanische Studien*, pp. 167–8.
470 See above, pp. 107–8.
471 Munzinger, *Ostafrikanische Studien*, pp. 199, 292, 296; Trimingham, *Islam*, pp. 160, 162, 165, 168.

A first Egyptian raid into Bogos in 1850 indicated that the governor of Taka had no intention of calling a halt before the plateau. When he returned in a major invasion in January 1854, burnt the main village Mogareh and carried away some 350 women and children and 1,800 head of cattle to Kasala, the strongest reaction came not from Wibē or his governor in Hamasēn but from the Lazarist missionary Giovanni Stella and Consul Plowden.[472] Stella, who had established the mission in Bogos in 1852, seems from the very outset to have thought in terms not only of a Catholic community but of a European protectorate or colony as well. He stressed that the Bogos and Mensa were independent peoples, who by virtue of their independence and their Catholic faith were seeking 'the protection of the French government' against the incursions of the *na'ib* and the governor of Taka. If this were granted, many of the neighbouring tribes, the Beni Amir, Barya, Kunama, would follow.[473] Plowden, on the other hand, reported that the leaders of the Bogos had declared that they owed allegiance and paid tribute to Wibē but that he could not protect them against Egyptian attacks because of the confusion in Ethiopia. Therefore they would like the consul to build a consulate and fly the British flag in their country. Under no circumstances did they want to adopt the Muslim faith and accept Egyptian rule.[474] Plowden's own attempts to obtain the immediate release of the captured people from the governor at Kasala failed, but protests by the British consul general in Cairo led to an investigation and ultimately to the return of the captives and the removal and punishment of the governor by the Egyptian government.[475]

As the Ethiopian crisis neared its climax and Wibē remained tied down in Simēn, Plowden entered more and more fully into the role of protector of the Ethiopians in the northern borderlands. No opportunity to protest against encroachments on Hamasēn, Mensa, or Bogos by the governor of Massawa was missed. Even joint actions between the British and French representatives took place,[476] and Stella appealed to Plowden to interfere on behalf of the Mensa and assist in the unification of the Bogos, for 'they will not listen except to you'.[477] Plowden repeatedly stressed the need for clearly defined boundaries be-

---

472 FO 401/1, p. 169, Plowden to Clarendon, 29 Mar. 1854; p. 170, Plowden to Muhammad Khusraw, 16 Apr. 1854; Douin, *Ismaïl*, III, 1, pp. 49–50. See also Giglio, *Etiopia–Mar Rosso*, Vol. I, p. 64, and Crummey, *Priests*, p. 111, for the foundation of the mission 1852 and Stella's role.

473 AECP, Massouah 1, fols 389–90, Stella to Delaye, 22 Aug. 1853.

474 FO 401/1, pp. 167, 169, Plowden to Clarendon, 15 Mar. and 29 Mar. 1854; p. 171, The inhabitants of Bogos to Plowden, n.d., forwarded 18 Apr. 1854. Plowden (ibid., p. 240, to Clarendon, 9 Jan. 1855) likewise defined Mensa as 'an undoubted portion of the Abyssinian territory'. See also Munzinger, *Ostafrikanische Studien*, pp. 158, 174–5.

475 FO 401/1, p. 171, Plowden to Clarendon, 20 Apr. 1854; p. 173, Bruce to Clarendon, 16 Jun. 1854; p. 174, Clarendon to Bruce, 30 Jun. 1854; p. 177, Bruce to Clarendon, 30 Jul. 1854; pp. 232, 246, Plowden to Clarendon, 3 Nov. 1854 and 1 Mar. 1855.

476 AECP, Massouah 2, fol. 46, Delaye and Plowden to Ibrahim Pasha, 20 Nov. 1854 (a slightly different copy, wrongly dated 10 Dec. 1854, is found in FO 401/1, p. 235); fols 44–5, Delaye to Drouyn de Lhuys, 29 Nov. 1854; FO 401/1, pp. 233–4, Plowden to Clarendon, 28 Nov. 1854.

477 FO 401/1, p. 241, Stella to Plowden, 2 Jan. 1855.

tween Ethiopian and Egyptian territories and saw this as a task to be undertaken by the European governments.[478]

Aware that his own government was not interested in territorial acquisitions, he neither pretended that the Bogos and Mensa were independent peoples, as Stella had done in 1853, nor did he propose any formal protectorate over them. The difference, however, was not fundamental, for the consul saw his actions as provisional, '. . . rather with reference to the future than the present, that these provinces may not be wrested from Abyssinia until such a time as it may please Her Majesty's Government to consider the best means of providing for their permanent security at least from Mussulman arms; conquest here signifying conversion'.[479]

In the meantime, the successful activities of the consul and the work of the Lazarists were turning the eyes of the population increasingly towards the foreigners for protection and guidance. The latter acted in the name of Ethiopian interests, defending Ethiopia's rights in the borderlands. But slowly, almost imperceptibly, the loyalties of the population were shifting. Though the purchase contracts and sham treaties of Lefebvre, Combes, Blondeel, and others may have given some Europeans the idea that they had acquired rights on the Ethiopian Red Sea coast, it was the developments in Bogos and Mensa in the 1850s that created the favourable climate for future colonial undertakings. Bogos in the 1850s foreshadowed Bogos in the 1870s. Here Eritrea was, in fact, conceived.

The Initial Promise of Shewa

While the rulers of Tigrē, and to a somewhat lesser degree Begēmdir, were throughout the period 1830–55 almost continuously confronted with European initiatives of one kind or another, the European assault on Shewa was mainly confined to five years: 1839–43. Nevertheless it was, at first glance, a much more successful operation, resulting in an elaborate treaty of friendship and commerce between Great Britain and Shewa, and a shorter but, from a political angle, more important treaty between France and Shewa.[480] Neither of the two, however,

478   ibid., p. 226, Report, 9 Jul. 1854; pp. 234, 240, Plowden to Clarendon, 28 Nov. 1854 and 9 Jan. 1855, no. 3.
479   ibid., pp. 240, 248, Plowden to Clarendon, 9 Jan. 1855, no. 4, and 4 Mar. 1855.
480   FO 93/94/1, Treaty of Amity and Commerce . . . 16 Nov. 1841 (English text), 18 Nov. 1841 (Amharic text); AED, Traités, Éthiopie, Traité politique et commercial . . . 7 June 1843. The British treaty has been analysed and its Amharic text published in facsimile by E. Ullendorff and C. F. Beckingham, 'The First Anglo-Ethiopian Treaty', *JSS*, IX (1954), pp. 187–99. Both versions of the treaty with France were published, but without date or signatures, by Rochet d'Héricourt himself (*Second voyage*, pp. 375–8). Malécot ('Voyageurs', *RFHO*, LVIII, pp. 297–8) has reproduced this French text without referring to the original. The Amharic texts, finally, of both the British and the French treaties were included in the history which Blattēngēta Hiruy Welde Sillasē was printing at the time of the outbreak of the Ethio-Italian war in 1935. The printing was stopped, and only a few copies of Hiruy's incomplete work exist. I have used Qēs Badima Yalew's copy, which contains 112 printed and 14 manuscript pages. In this work, which I shall cite as Hiruy, *Tarik*, the

was followed up by the development of diplomatic or commercial relations. The Anglo-Ethiopian treaty, though unquestionably genuine, and ratified and published by the British government, never played any role whatsoever. This has always been recognized, and it seems almost as if no one had ever expected that it should count. The Franco-Ethiopian treaty, on the other hand, though neither ratified nor even published by the French government until 1888, was discussed in the 1880s and 1890s as a basis for the establishment of the Obok/Jibuti colony, and for refusing to acknowledge the exclusive rights which Italy claimed by virtue of the Wiçhalē treaty.[481] In the words of one writer, it 'answered the sentiments and interests of the two countries so well that it has in spite of all remained the true charter of French–Ethiopian friendship'.[482]

Whatever their future importance or lack of importance, the two treaties negotiated with Sahle Sillasē by Harris and Rochet d'Héricourt respectively raise some important questions. Was the apparent success due to the superior skill of Harris and Rochet as compared with that of their contemporaries Lefebvre, Combes, Blondeel, et al., or was Sahle Sillasē more aware of the importance of regulating his relations with foreign rulers and their subjects than Wibē, Ali, or Goshu? On the European side, the general cause of the activities leading to the treaties is clear: the British occupation of Aden in 1839, and Muhammad Ali's withdrawal from the Red Sea coasts, triggered an intense French–British rivalry in the whole area, but particularly around Bab al-Mandab. Combes's attempts to acquire Zeyla and Tajura, and British actions to block them, are part of this development; so are the missions of Harris and Rochet d'Héricourt to Shewa.[483] As for the Ethiopian side, it has been suggested that Sahle Sillasē, motivated by a desire to modernize his kingdom and acquire firearms, took important initiatives himself to bring about the missions.[484] But if Sahle Sillasē had a genuine, 'largely strategic' interest in foreign contacts,[485] something which exactly suited British and French plans for the exploitation of Shewan trade, the question remains why he closed the door to all foreigners as soon as he had signed the first two international treaties of modern Ethiopia.

From several points of view, Sahle Sillasē was a more promising ally, or at least trade partner, than any of the other Ethiopian rulers with whom the Europeans were involved in the 1830s and 1840s. His position was questioned by no one in Shewa; his word was the law of the land. Some visitors

---

treaties are printed on pp. 33–4. Only minor, mainly orthographic corrections have been made in the Harris treaty, while the text of the Rochet treaty has been improved linguistically, and includes also the date, place and signing parties. See below, p. 161.

481 A. J. H. de Clercq, *Recueil des Traités de la France (1713–1906)* (Paris, 1861–1919), XV, pp. 340–1; AEMD, Afrique 138, fols 127–8, Étienne to Spuller, 29 Oct. 1889; fols 249–61, Étienne to Ribot, 28 Aug. 1891, with attached memorandum by Lagarde, same date.

482 Coulbeaux, *Histoire*, Vol. II, p. 375, n. 3. See also A. de La Pradelle, *Le Conflit italo-éthiopien* (Paris, 1936), pp. 29–30.

483 Lefebvre, *Voyage*, Vol. II, 'Notice', pp. 75–7; Rochet d'Héricourt, *Voyage*, pp. 362, 367–8.

484 See R. H. Kofi Darkwah, 'The Rise of the Kingdom of Shoa 1813–1889' (unpublished dissertation, London, 1966), pp. 48–55.

485 Pankhurst, *Economic History*, p. 4.

expressed their dislike of his despotism, but all agreed that the Shewans were more prosperous and enjoyed more security than other Ethiopians.[486] Much of the King's income was revenue from the trade between Shewa and the coast.[487] This trade was profitable to the Afar chiefs as well, and thus a common interest united the political leaders and commercial communities of highland and lowland.[488]

Around 1840, the Hawash river served in a general sense as a boundary between Sahle Sillasē's domains and Adal, as the territory of the Afar was called. Along the main caravan route to the coast, effective administration stopped at the border towns and customs posts of Cheno and Fare, some 20–30 kilometres from Ankober.[489] Shewa was thus separated from the coast by a vast area populated by independent nomadic tribes. But the economic interdependence, and Sahle Sillasē's tremendous prestige as a ruler, provided him with considerable influence over the tribal rulers as far off as Tajura on the coast itself.[490] This became evident precisely in connection with the first attempts of the Europeans to establish themselves in Shewa.

Because of the strict control which Sahle Sillasē maintained over all his governors, it was more difficult for a foreigner to enter Shewa than any other part of Ethiopia.[491] Without the explicit order of Sahle Sillasē, a European could neither enter nor leave his kingdom, and it was generally believed that persons with useful skills had little chance of getting permission to leave, once the King knew about their abilities.[492] Nevertheless, several Frenchmen, including Combes, Tamisier, and Dufey, had visited Shewa between 1835 and 1838 and left again, Combes and Tamisier on the grounds that they knew no useful

486 Lefebvre, *Voyage*, Vol. II, p. 191; Vol. III, pp. 217–18; Rochet d'Héricourt, *Voyage*, pp. 284–5; idem, *Second Voyage*, pp. 247–8, 253; Harris, *Highlands*, Vol. II, p. 94; Vol. III, p. 33; Charles Johnston, *Travels in Southern Abyssinia, through the Country of Adal to the Kingdom of Shoa* (London, 1844), Vol. II, pp. 184–9; Douglas C. Graham, *Glimpses of Abyssinia: or, extracts from letters written while on a mission from the Government of India to the King of Abyssinia in the years 1841, 1842, and 1843*, ed. Anna, Lady Erskine (London, 1867), pp. 6–7. See also Abir, *Ethiopia*, pp. 160–1.
487 Rochet d'Héricourt, *Second Voyage*, p. 246; Harris, *Highlands*, Vol. III, p. 306.
488 C. F. X. Rochet d'Héricourt, 'Considérations géographiques et commerciales sur le golfe Arabique, le pays d'Adel et le royaume de Choa', *BSG*, 2, XV (1841), pp. 269–93, in particular p. 276; idem, *Second Voyage*, p. 42; Harris, *Highlands*, Vol. I, p. 64; Vol. II, p. 231.
489 Rochet d'Héricourt, *Voyage*, pp. 125, 127, 259, 264–5; Harris, *Highlands*, Vol. I, pp. 323–4, 330, 334, 341; Vol. II, pp. 228–31; Vol. III, pp. 209, 251–2; Johnston, *Travels*, Vol. I, pp. 480–9. These passages, and a number of others, indicate both the concept and the position of a boundary which could no doubt be defined with more certainty. It did not, however, play the same role in the future struggle with the Egyptians and the Europeans as the north-western frontier areas.
490 FO 1/3, fols 82–6, Krapf to Haines, August 1840; Rochet d'Héricourt, *Voyage*, p. 119; idem, *Second Voyage*, pp. 54, 275; Harris, *Highlands*, Vol. I, p. 411. See also Harris, Vol. II, pp. 228–31, for Sahle Sillasē's reasons for not attempting any conquest of the Afar.
491 Combes and Tamisier, *Voyage*, Vol. II, pp. 318, 324; Isenberg and Krapf, *Journals*, pp. 56, 106–7; Lefebvre, *Voyage*, Vol. II, pp. 187–96; Rochet d'Héricourt, *Second voyage*, pp. 163–6.
492 Harris (*Highlands*, Vol. II, p. 392) maintained that his treaty with Sahle Sillasē would put an end to the obsolete national maxim 'never to permit the stranger who had once entered, to depart from Abyssinia'.

trades,[493] Dufey because he promised to come back very soon.[494] A German named Martin Brezka, who had been working for Rüppell as a hunter, had also been there for some time.[495] There is no indication that Sahle Sillasē had actually invited any of these Europeans, as opposed to merely permitting their entry. Nor was Rochet d'Héricourt invited when he first arrived in 1839.

The first, even indirectly documented, initiative of Sahle Sillasē to bring Europeans to Shewa is his invitation to the CMS missionaries in 1837. He was, of course, well aware of the work of the missionaries in northern Ethiopia. Habte Sillasē was a Shewan and well known to the King, who received a printed copy of the four Gospels from Gobat as early as 1830.[496] Nevertheless, Sahle Sillasē's invitation may not have been entirely spontaneous, since it was Brezka who wrote the letter.[497] Of greater importance for an understanding of the following events is the fact that Sahle Sillasē's requests were quite specific. He reportedly asked for medicines and for a mechanic or, probably, for the church builder Aichinger, whose fame had reached him. Aichinger had left for Europe, and Isenberg sent a theological treatise of 693 quarto pages instead![498] In a second message, Sahle Sillasē asked for 'medicine, a gun, masons, etc. . . .', and when Isenberg and Krapf, after their expulsion by Wibē and a visit to Cairo, reached Shewa in May 1839, the King expected them to prove themselves as 'physicians, architects, artists, etc.'.[499] They were asked if they had written and bound their books themselves, if they had made the gun which they presented to the King, if they understood 'how to prepare sugar and brandy' or 'to stamp dollars'.[500] Though they were neither willing nor able to satisfy Sahle Sillasē's expectations, they were allowed to remain and start their missionary work. The King even provided for them, but showed little interest in their activities.[501]

In the correspondence and early conversations with the missionaries, Sahle Sillasē had thus clearly revealed his motives for inviting them. The King was, according to all the visitors to his court, passionately interested in arts and crafts, in the construction of towns, bridges, and mechanical devices, and in the local production of the types of goods which trickled into Shewa from the coast.[502] But nowhere in the reports of the early conversations is there any

493 Combes and Tamisier, *Voyage*, Vol. II, p. 347–8; Vol. III, 3–4.
494 Dufey and Aubert-Roche, 'Abyssinie', *RO*(Paris), I, p. 321.
495 ibid., p. 325; CMS, CM/013, Blumhardt to Coates, 22 Jul. 1837; *EHB*, 1840, pp. 10–11, Krapf, 9 Jun. 1839; Andree, *Abessinien*, p. 130.
496 Gobat, *Journal*, pp. 82, 151, 195. After the CMS missionaries had been expelled from Adwa in 1838, the invitation went to Sapeto instead, but he was prevented by illness from accepting it. See Crummey, *Priests*, p. 72.
497 Andree, *Abessinien*, p. 130.
498 CMS, CM/013, Blumhardt to Coates, 22 Jul. 1837; CM/035, Isenberg to Coates, 3 Oct. 1837; Andree, *Abessinien*, p. 130.
499 Isenberg and Krapf, *Journals*, pp. 55, 61–2.
500 ibid., pp. 58–9, 64, 83.
501 ibid., pp. 77, 94–5, 161.
502 See, *inter alia*, Combes and Tamisier, *Voyage*, Vol. II, pp. 347–9; Vol. III, pp. 8–9; Dufey and Aubert-Roche, 'Abyssinie', *RO*(Paris), I, pp. 319, 321; Rochet d'Héricourt, *Voyage*,

suggestion about establishing diplomatic or commercial relations, or about the import of firearms on a large scale. In spite of Dufey's visit in June and July the year before, and the striking lecture which he reports that he gave to Sahle Sillasē on the benefits of international trade, including arms on the scale of tens of thousands, the King obviously continued to view foreigners primarily or exclusively as potential employees at his court and as bearers of a few presents, always including a beautiful gun or two, intended as a means of winning his favour.[503] It would take many years before the Ethiopian rulers really accepted that most of their visitors from Western Europe had ambitions other than entering their service.

Rochet and Krapf at the Court of Sahle Sillasē

In some respects Charles François Xavier Rochet from Héricourt was the right man in the right place when he arrived at Sahle Sillasē's court in October 1839. He was a tanner and a professional chemist who had spent several years in Egypt, trying to make a fortune by manufacturing indigo for Muhammad Ali.[504] Besides a few double-barrelled guns and pistols, his luggage included various instruments and a powder mill.[505] He had great plans for crossing the African continent from east to west, but he was travelling without obligations to anyone, and could stop wherever he liked.[506] He seems to have accepted without any regrets that Sahle Sillasē stopped him in Shewa. They discussed the greatness of France, its government and army, its resources and industry, particularly the manufacturing of arms. Rochet was asked to get his powder mill in operation and was soon engaged also in the manufacturing of sugar under the eyes of the King himself. He told Sahle Sillasē that he had found coal at Cheno, and this reportedly led to long talks about mineralogy.[507] Obviously he won the favour of the King. Instead of continuing his journey into the interior of Africa, he decided to return to France and try to establish closer relations between Shewa and his home country. That Rochet did this on his own initiative is evident from his account. The King opposed his decision to leave. Rochet insisted and was instructed, 'at least', to ask the King of France to grant Sahle Sillasē his friendship and to return once more to Shewa.[508]

---

pp. 137, 141, 197–200; Harris, *Highlands*, Vol. II, pp. 62, 388–90; Vol. III, pp. 351–5; Johnston, *Travels*, Vol. II, pp. 275, 417–18.

503 Dufey and Aubert-Roche, 'Abyssinie', *RO*(Paris), I, pp. 319–20. Even the manner in which Dufey left the Shewan court underlined this attitude. He promised to return from Mokha within fifty days with medicine for Sahle Sillasē (ibid., p. 321) and was provided with 300 thalers for the journey (Rochet d'Héricourt, *Voyage*, p. 140). Instead he proceeded to explore the Red Sea trade, and died on his way to Egypt about half a year later. His journals were saved, and reached Aubert-Roche. The article cited here consists almost exclusively of extracts from the journals. See Malécot, 'Voyageurs', *RFHO*, LVIII, p. 150.

504 Malécot, 'Voyageurs', *RFHO*, LVIII, pp. 279–81.

505 Rochet d'Héricourt, *Voyage*, pp. 142–3.

506 *idem*, 'Considérations', *BSG*, 2, XV, p. 269.

507 *idem*, *Voyage*, pp. 137, 141–2, 191, 197–8.

508 ibid., pp. 314–15.

On 3 March 1840 Rochet left for France, and by the end of the year he appeared in Paris with a letter and some presents for Louis Philippe. This letter was allegedly dictated by Sahle Sillasē himself in the presence of Rochet,[509] but unfortunately the Amharic original is unknown if, indeed, it has ever existed. Only a French translation, certified by Lefebvre and dated Alexandria, 27 October 1840, is available in the archives of the Ministère des Affaires Étrangères. It contains a list of the presents, some expressions of friendship and a request that Rochet should be sent back soon with information on what the French king would like to have from Ethiopia. In it Rochet, however, also received an endorsement as Sahle Sillasē's agent in no uncertain terms: '. . . . our word [is] that of Rochet to whom I have confided my thoughts'.[510] Certain discussions on Rochet's return to Shewa imply that he had been asked to make some purchases, but this business was on a very limited scale, for instance, *eight* double-barrelled muskets.[511] We really know nothing with certainty about Sahle Sillasē's aims or expectations at the time when Rochet left.[512]

In much the same way as Aubert, Combes, and Lefebvre before him, Rochet outlined the brilliant commercial and political prospects which awaited France in Ethiopia and especially in Shewa: a market of at least 1,000,000 consumers, exploited by no one, a royal treasury holding at least 30 million francs which the King did not know how to use, and the opportunity of dominating Shewa, through Shewa all Ethiopia, and through Ethiopia Egypt, for in Rochet's opinion nothing would be able to stop an army of Abyssinians and Gallas from successfully invading Egypt. In order to create close relations between France and Shewa, and presumably start off this development, Rochet asked for two small cannon, 150–200 muskets and carbines, some swords and pistols, and other goods, which he could present to Sahle Sillasē as samples of French industry.[513] Rochet seems to have made a favourable impression on the officials of the Ministry of Foreign Affairs in Paris and was given all that he asked for,[514] though it took some persuasion before he was granted the Legion of Honour,

---

509 ibid., p. 317.

510 AEMD, Afrique 13, p. 287, Sahle Sillasē to Louis Philippe, 27 Oct. 1840 (eventual original 2 Mar. 1840).

511 Rochet d'Héricourt, *Second voyage*, pp. 133, 161. Cf. AECP, Massouah 1, fol. 85, Degoutin to Guizot, 15 Apr. 1843.

512 The question of the authenticity of this letter has to my knowledge never been raised and cannot be answered without the original. A comparison between the AEMD copy and Rochet's published version (*Voyage*, pp. 317–18, also published, without reservations, by Malécot, 'Voyageurs', *RFHO*, LVIII, pp. 286–7) shows that Rochet vacillated. He changed the *ras* of the opening phrase 'Ras Saculé Selaré [*sic*], Roi de Choa' but made it 'Negueuste' (kings) instead of *nigus* (king), and he added 'Sahlé-Sallassi, roi de Choa' by way of signature at the bottom. The appearance of Lefebvre as a translator is also a bit strange. He arrived at Alexandria from France on 27 October (Lefebvre, *Voyage*, Vol. I, p. 199), and Rochet obtained the translation, if that is what it is, the same day.

513 AEMD, Afrique 13, fols 279–86, 'Considérations Politiques et commerciales . . . par M. C. F. X. Rochet d'Héricourt', n.d.; fols 293–4, Rochet to Guizot, 8 Jun. 1841. See also Rochet d'Héricourt, *Voyage*, pp. 362–3, 367–8.

514 AEMD, Afrique 13, fol. 298, Soult to Guizot, 17 Jun. 1841; AECP, Massouah 1, fols 70–1, 'Rapport', 16 Mar. 1842.

which he felt he needed in order to keep the confidence and consideration of Sahle Sillasē, particularly in view of the fact that Lefebvre would come with his.[515]

While Rochet was away, the anti-French forces went into action in Shewa. The key person in these activities was Krapf. In his published diary he states only that he was called from Ankober to Angolela on 27 June 1840 and the following day instructed by Sahle Sillasē to translate a letter to the East India Company.[516] In this letter Sahle Sillasē deplored that 'arts and sciences' were not yet developed in his country and asked for assistance in terms of 'guns, cannon, and other things, which are not to be got in my Country'.[517] The letter gives every impression of being genuine, even in the English translation, and it is, moreover, not likely that Krapf in his position would take the risk of trying to deceive the British authorities at Aden and Bombay. But this does not mean that the initiative came from Sahle Sillasē or that Krapf was just a translator.

The CMS missionary had hurried to Shewa one year earlier to prevent the French (and therefore the Catholics) from gaining influence over Sahle Sillasē and through him over the rest of Ethiopia.[518] He had been forced to leave Tigrē after three months and wanted to secure a foothold in southern Ethiopia. He was not interested in military matters or political influence for its own sake. While Rochet went about building up his position, Krapf concentrated on teaching and linguistic work. But he expected assistance. The German officer Kielmaier, who had shared the fate of the missionaries at Adwa in 1838, was on his way from Cairo in company with a young Ethiopian called Samu'ēl Gīyorgīs, the son of Sebagadis's envoy and Gobat's friend, Ali Umar. But on 27 May, Krapf received the news that Kielmaier had died in the Dankali desert, and a few days later Samu'ēl arrived with further information.[519] This seems to have aroused the missionary. He learned that Kielmaier had negotiated with the British agent at Aden, Captain Haines, for supplies of 'materials of war, if he should succeed in executing his military objects in Shoa', and that Haines had forwarded his petition to the government of Bombay. In view of this, he thought he 'might venture to speak in little words with the King about this petition'.[520] This

---

515 AEMD, Afrique 13, fols 301, 304, Rochet to Guizot, 24 Jul. and 29 Sep. 1841.
516 Isenberg and Krapf, *Journals*, pp. 250–1. Krapf maintained (*Travels*, p. 29) that Sahle Sillasē had himself 'conceived the notion of sending letters and presents to the East India Company . . .'
517 FO 78/3185, fols 163v.–4, Sahle Sillasē to the East India Company, n.d., but certainly written 28 Jun. 1840; the English text of this letter has also been published by Ullendorff and Beckingham ('The First Anglo-Ethiopian Treaty', *JSS*, IX, p. 194) from IO, Bombay Secret Proceedings 159, no. 1486 C. The differences are mainly editorial and of no significance. I have not been able to locate the Amharic originals which may have remained in archives in India.
518 Basel, BV. 110, Krapf to Blumhardt, 12 Jan. 1839.
519 Isenberg and Krapf, *Journals*, pp. 247–8. For Samu'ēl's connection with Ali, see [Gobat], *Life*, p. 144. Later in life he sometimes called himself Samu'ēl bin Ali. See FO 401/2, pp. 221–2; also below, p. 169.
520 FO 78/3185, fols 120–2, Krapf to Haines, 22 Jun. 1840. This letter is, in Haines's copy for London, dated 22 July, but this is obviously wrong by one month since it is mentioned in a letter of 1 July (fols 166–73) as written on 22 June.

was the origin of Sahle Sillasē's letter to Bombay. The King reportedly first asked Krapf to write a letter in English for Samu'ēl to take, but then accepted Krapf's suggestion to write personally. He was in no particular hurry, however, and postponed the matter two or three weeks. In the meantime Krapf took the initiative of advising Haines that 'a small quantity of materials of War, and some well qualified military persons who make use of them to the satisfaction of the King' might prevent Rochet from succeeding in his plans, preserve British interests, determine policies in general in Shewa and 'open the channel of discoveries, commerce, and civilization to the centre of Africa . . .'[521]

On Krapf's advice Sahle Sillasē addressed his letter to 'the great English Company in India'. A covering letter was written to Haines, and both were translated into English by Krapf.[522] The missionary regretted that he could not take the letters himself, and it was agreed that Samu'ēl should return with them. In several letters which he also sent with Samu'ēl, Krapf revealed his anxiety about Rochet's plans.[523]

According to Krapf, Rochet had told Sahle Sillasē that, in order to become the ruler of all Abyssinia, the King should organize his army in the way the French army operated. The necessary arms for this he offered to go and bring from France. But Rochet had also told Krapf that he intended to use the first 1,000 troops he had trained to turn against Sahle Sillasē and make himself the ruler of Ethiopia: 'As there is a British India, so a French Abyssinia . . .' To gain his aims, Rochet was even prepared to unite and use the Galla tribes. With an army of 200,000 Galla, he would unite his French Abyssinia with the French possessions on the Senegal river and make Africa 'the continent in which France may have free hands'.[524]

This sounds almost too fantastic to be true, and it is difficult to resist the feeling that Krapf was overstating his case. On the other hand, if Rochet could suggest in a serious report to the French government that Ethiopian troops might conquer Egypt, there is no reason to think that he could not entertain Krapf with fanciful stories about Senegal. Krapf, moreover, believed that the Galla had commercial contacts with the west coast of Africa.[525]

With the exception of Rochet's alleged 'revolution against a respectable and lawful King',[526] Krapf's suggestions and the reasons given for them were very similar to Rochet's ideas. Sahle Sillasē should be provided with military supplies and personnel to strengthen and modernize the Shewan army so that he could subdue all Abyssinia and put an end to the civil wars. Other reforms would follow as a consequence of the military reforms. Thus England 'might save the Abyssinian people . . . from a total ruin . . .' Secondly, all East and

---

521 ibid.
522 FO 78/3185, fols 163–4, copies of the English texts with a note about the translation.
523 ibid., fols 166–73, Krapf to Haines, 1 Jul. 1840; FO 1/3, fols 53–6, Krapf to Campbell, 3 Jul. 1840; CMS, CM/044, Krapf to Coates, 4 Jul. 1840; Isenberg and Krapf, *Journals*, p. 252.
524 FO 1/3, fols 53–6, Krapf to Campbell, 3 Jul. 1840.
525 FO 78/3185, fols 166–73, Krapf to Haines, 1 Jul. 1840.
526 FO 1/3, fols 53–6, Krapf to Campbell, 3 Jul. 1840.

Central Africa would be opened up to the British: 'The friends of Commerce, of discoveries, of the propagation of civilization will not be disappointed as soon as England has opened the centre of Africa by way of Shoa.' Thirdly, and this is only the other side of the coin: '. . . the revolutionary plans of Mr. Rochet and the French influence in the Eastern Africa can be destroyed in its [sic] root'.[527]

It is difficult to say whether Krapf really anticipated any success for Rochet. He also expressed fear that Sahle Sillasē would very soon discover Rochet's personal ambitions and close Shewa to all foreigners including missionaries.[528] At all events, once Krapf had initiated the matter, he showed great concern that 'this design must have been executed by the English Government in India, before Mr. Rochet arrives from France'.[529] This was why he had advised Sahle Sillasē to write to India rather than England, and in a new letter in August, he told Haines, 'Whoever, Frenchmen or English will come at first [sic], will get the greater influence with the King'.[530] By mid-September Samu'ēl had reached Tajura.[531] Krapf's concern was shared by the British authorities at Aden and Bombay, and in December Palmerston was informed that the Bombay government recommended a British mission to Shewa.[532] In the meantime Haines planned the embassy on a large scale and suggested great generosity with presents not only for Sahle Sillasē but for the Afar rulers along the route as well.[533] Combes and the d'Abbadie brothers were prevented from making their way into the interior through Tajura or any of the other ports in the area. Whether this was entirely due to Haines's machinations or not is uncertain, but he was certainly not helpful.[534]

The Anglo-Ethiopian Treaty

In April 1841 Captain W. C. Harris received his instructions to go to Shewa, undertake as much scientific and commercial exploration as possible, look into the slave trade, and obtain the signature of Sahle Sillasē on a treaty which would

527 FO 78/3185, fols 166–73, Krapf to Haines, 1 Jul. 1840. The same arguments are repeated in the letter to Campbell, 3 Jul. 1840.
528 ibid., fols 120–2, Krapf to Haines, 22 Jun. 1840.
529 ibid., fols 166–73, Krapf to Haines, 1 Jul. 1840; FO 1/3, fols 53–6, Krapf to Campbell, 3 Jul. 1840.
530 FO 1/3, fols 82–6, Krapf to Haines, August 1840.
531 FO 78/3185, fols 160–2, Barker to Haines, n.d. (Sep. 1840).
532 FO 1/3, fols 73–4, Reid to Haines, 15 Oct. 1840; fol. 81, Haines to Willoughby, 28 Oct. 1840; fol. 67, Hobhouse to Palmerston, 14 Dec. 1840.
533 ibid., fols 107–10, Haines to Willoughby, 20 Nov. 1840.
534 AEMD, Afrique 13, fol. 221, Combes and Broquant to Cie française d'Abyssinie, 30 Dec. 1840; fols 15–17, Arnauld d'Abbadie to Cochelet, 27 Dec. 1840, with enclosed copies of correspondence between Antoine d'Abbadie and Haines, 12 Dec. and 19 Dec. 1840; FO 1/3, fols 103–6, Haines to the Secret Committee, 9 Dec. 1840; fol. 118, Haines to Willoughby, 2 Feb. 1841 (extract); BN, Ethiop. Abb. 256, fol. 510, Arnauld d'Abbadie to Sahle Sillasē, n.d. (from Tajura, May 1841). After the unhappy meeting with Wibē (see above, p. 83), Antoine had gone first to Aden and then to Egypt, where he met Rochet and presumably agreed to return in order to look after French interests in Shewa in Rochet's absence. For this, see also FO 1/3, fol. 51, Coates to Palmerston, 1 Dec. 1840.

secure 'a free and unrestricted commercial intercourse' with Shewa.[535] The first experience of the Harris mission was that the good will of the Afar chiefs could not be turned on and off from Aden. Several claimed in various ways that they were 'the key of the road to Hábesh'.[536] In spite of intimidation and lavish presents, three members of the mission were killed in a night attack near Lake Assal about one day's march from the coast, and threats that the embassy would have to turn back or face death were repeated at Kilelu about halfway between the coast and the Hawash.[537] Nevertheless, Harris pressed on, only to find out when he arrived on the frontiers of Shewa in July that he was far from welcome. He suspected that the governor of the borderlands, Welasma Muhammad, and other Shewan officials in charge of trade and customs for the King were intriguing against him. This is far from unlikely since they may have felt that European trade would become a threat to their own sources of income. Harris contributed to their suspicion by refusing to allow the customs officials to touch the considerable amount of goods which his caravan brought. But in view of the eagerness with which Sahle Sillasē normally received foreigners, it is difficult to believe that they could have been held up for two weeks as close to the King's court as Aliyu Amba, except on his own orders.[538] Finally they were permitted to present themselves to the King with their gifts, an unparalleled collection of shawls, scarves, clocks, musical boxes, a Brussels carpet, etc., and finally the cannon and 300 muskets. Harris had insisted on an artillery salute and on riding with his escort into the presence of the King, an incredible breach of etiquette.[539] If it is true that the people believed Harris to be the King of the Egyptians, as Graham wrote a week after the reception,[540] the envoy had certainly done his share in creating that impression.

Sahle Sillasē was impressed with the gifts but hardly delighted with the pretensions of the thirty foreigners he now had on his hands. They represented a third type of European, quite different from both the obliging artisans or agents, a category to which also Rochet belonged, and the missionaries with their sometimes inconvenient but understandable desire to teach and preach. Harris and his companions talked much about arts and sciences, e.g. the use of the loom,[541] but had obviously not come with the intention of carrying out the work themselves. Though they were officers and soldiers and accompanied the King on a campaign against the Galla, they did not fight to the satisfaction of the

535 See Ullendorff and Beckingham, 'Treaty', *JSS*, IX, pp. 195–7, for a detailed account of these instructions.
536 Harris, *Highlands*, Vol. I, p. 49.
537 ibid., pp. 67, 81, 127, 133, 218–21.
538 ibid., pp. 318, 323–34, 365, 371–5, 397. See also Rochet, *Second voyage*, p. 143. If Arnauld d'Abbadie's letter from Tajura (BN, Ethiop. Abb. 256, fol. 510) had reached Sahle Sillasē, it might explain some of the hesitation, for he had done his best to discredit the English 'intriguers'.
539 Harris, *Highlands*, Vol. I, pp. 404–9.
540 Graham, *Glimpses*, p. 8. Also Harris notes that the British were called 'Gyptzis' (*Highlands*, Vol. II, p. 2), i.e. Copts or Egyptians, which was used all over Ethiopia along with *ferenj* for Europeans.
541 Harris, *Highlands*, Vol. II, p. 391.

Shewans but were accused of having 'eaten the royal bread and destroyed none of the enemies of the state'.[542]

What Sahle Sillasē had asked for, or been offered by Krapf when he wrote to India, was arms and artisans. What Harris now asked for in exchange for the arms was a signed agreement that his countrymen would be permitted to enter and leave Shewa at will, and to travel and trade freely throughout the King's domains and beyond, importing their merchandise into Shewa with only 5 per cent duty and exporting whatever they wanted without any duty whatsoever. By mid-November, Harris had with Krapf's assistance persuaded Sahle Sillasē to sign a treaty to this effect.[543] A comparison between the English and Amharic texts of the treaty clearly reveals that the Amharic is a translation of the English.[544] Eleven of fourteen operational clauses were, moreover, aimed precisely at securing the 'free and unrestricted commercial intercourse' of Harris's instructions. In the remaining three (III, IX, and XV), an attempt was made to demonstrate that all rights and obligations were to be mutual, i.e. Shewan subjects would—in case they came to Great Britain—be permitted to move about and trade with the same privileges as British subjects in Shewa.

It is highly doubtful that Sahle Sillasē understood the implications of the signing of an international treaty. One member of the embassy is, in fact, reported to have 'candidly admitted the King did not know the character or purport of the paper he had signed; and had only been made aware of the new responsibilities he had incurred, by a sharply worded expostulatory letter . . . on an occasion subsequently to the signing of the treaty . . .'[545] When Harris mentions the King's 'desire that certain articles agreed upon might be drawn up on parchment, and presented for signature', this can only reflect the European negotiator's desire to present the Ethiopian party as more active and therefore more responsible for the agreement and its observance than actually warranted by the circumstances. Krapf was much more straightforward and spoke of *persuading* Sahle Sillasē 'to subscribe to the terms of a Treaty' and of the 'great perseverance, prudence, and firmness' used by Harris to reach this goal.[546] Krapf may well have done more of the persuading than anyone else, for he had entirely identified the future of the mission in Shewa with the success of the British embassy. He was determined to secure a foothold in Abyssinia, by whatever means possible, and veiled threats may well have been included among his

---

542   ibid., p. 206. The reason given by Harris for not participating was that the Galla were defenceless. See also Graham, *Glimpses*, pp. 24–5.

543   FO 93/94/1, articles IV–VIII, XIII–XIV.

544   This is established beyond doubt by Ullendorff and Beckingham ('Treaty', *JJS*, IX, pp. 187–93) who also examined a separate Amharic text which they regard as a draft version of the final text of the treaty. See also Hiruy, *Tarīk*, p. 34.

545   Johnston, *Travels*, Vol. II, p. 22; also pp. 69–71, where this admittedly critical observer finds the doings of the embassy in Shewa 'curiously analogous' to the account in *Heimskringla* of King Athelstan's embassy to King Harold of Norway: 'Here is a sword, which King Athelstan sends thee, with the request that thou wilt accept it.' He did, and the ambassadors said, 'Now thou hast taken the sword . . . and therefore art thou his subject, as thou hast taken his sword.'

546   Harris, *Highlands*, Vol. II, p. 392; Isenberg and Krapf, *Journals*, p. 263.

arguments. In September, more than two months before the treaty was signed, he wrote to a missionary colleague in Cairo, 'If the King will not, they will teach him, as they taught the Pasha . . .'[547]

There is not the slightest reason to doubt that the treaty was proposed, worded, and pushed through by the European party. But why did Sahle Sillasē allow himself to be persuaded to sign? This is not a question to which a conclusive answer can be found. Perhaps he signed partly in recognition of the arms and other gifts he had received, partly in the belief that by signing he would secure a steady supply of arms, ammunition, and other goods which he wanted. But there were other factors as well.

The signing took place at the height of a serious ecclesiastical crisis in Shewa. Sahle Sillasē had asserted his independence of Gonder in ecclesiastical matters by appointing a *Tewahido* (*Hulet lidet*) to the leading church position in Shewa. As a result he found himself in conflict with both the *ichegē* and Ras Ali, as well as with powerful sections of the clergy in Shewa itself. At the same time the arrival of Abune Selama heralded a new confrontation in the north and possible ecclesiastical changes at Gonder. In this situation, both Sahle Sillasē and the *Tewahido* leaders in Shewa, who seem to have been on better terms with Krapf than the opposing party of *Ye-şegga lij*, probably hoped that friendship with the British would facilitate good relations with Selama, a former pupil of Krapf's colleagues in Cairo. But Sahle Sillasē finally gave in to the pressures. Within a week after the treaty had been signed, the *Tewahido* leaders were replaced. Shewa stayed out of the war between Wibē and Ali, and when Selama after the battle of Debre Tabor tried to reinstate the *Tewahido* party, Sahle Sillasē was as stubborn as he had been towards the *ichegē* before. For Krapf and the British embassy, the identification of their interests with those of Selama became a liability, not an asset.[548]

The great care taken to produce a beautiful diploma, a single sheet of paper, 75 × 32 cm., with English and Amharic texts in parallel columns headed by the British Royal Arms and an Ethiopian representation of the Trinity in colours and followed by seals of red shellac, as well as the solemn ceremonies of the signing as recorded by Harris,[549] indicate that the British envoy wanted to impress Sahle Sillasē with the importance of what he was doing. In this he may well have succeeded up to a point.[550] Nevertheless it is hard to believe that the King of Shewa regarded this agreement as particularly binding or irrevocable. A solemn agreement entered into between Ethiopian princes was called a *kīdan* or a *qal kīdan* (ቃል ፡ ኪዳን ፡). This term has approximately the same religious connotations as 'covenant', and it was the religious sanction of such an

---

547 CMS, CM/044, Krapf to Kruse, 4 Sep. 1841. See Crummey, *Priests*, pp. 51–2, for further information on Krapf's attitude and involvement.

548 See Crummey, *Priests*, pp. 50–3; Abir, *Ethiopia*, pp. 157–9. Selama's first instructions to Sahle Sillasē arrived before Krapf left Shewa in March 1842, but they did not seem to have any *immediate* effect on Sahle Sillasē's attitude towards Krapf (Isenberg and Krapf, *Journals*, pp. 269–74).

549 Harris, *Highlands*, Vol. II, p. 393.

550 Lefebvre (*Voyage*, Vol. II, p. 265) reports that the King was distressed one and a half years later about the treaty he had signed.

agreement, mostly an oath taken in front of a representative of the church, that made it irrevocable.[551] There is no mention of any oath between Sahle Sillasē and Harris, and the translation of 'treaty' with *andinnet* (አንድነት ፡), which means 'concord', 'understanding', implies a less formal or solemn agreement than *kīdan* or the term *wil* (ውል ፡) which is later used for 'treaty' in Ethiopian diplomacy. In form as well as in substance, the 1841 treaty was Harris's and Krapf's creation. Whether or not this European-type agreement would work in an Ethiopian setting, only experience could prove.

Neither Harris nor Krapf can have had any great illusions in this respect. Harris stayed on in Shewa. Members of his embassy were engaged in making drawings and supervising the building of a new palace for the King.[552] Further presents were also required to feed the 'Anglomania' in Shewa.[553] The task of putting the agreement with Sahle Sillasē to a first test fell on Krapf. Two missionary colleagues, J. C. Müller and J. Mühleisen-Arnold, had been waiting for some time to penetrate to Shewa through Tajura. When Krapf heard of their second failure to get through, he decided to go and assist them.[554] He left Shewa in March 1842 and arrived at Massawa about two months later after having been robbed by a Galla chief in Wello, who was at least supposed to be on friendly terms with the King of Shewa.[555] Krapf seems to have received a bad shock and to have placed some of the blame for his misfortune on Sahle Sillasē or at least to have demanded that the King recover and restore his property to him. According to Harris, this had angered Sahle Sillasē, which is not surprising.[556]

Since Müller and Mühleisen had returned to Cairo and Krapf wanted to go to Egypt anyhow to meet his future wife, the attempt to return to Shewa through Tajura was postponed for a few months.[557] Angered by his experiences on the journey to Massawa and confronted once more with the French and Catholic presence in Tigrē,[558] Krapf was in no mood to restrict himself to spiritual weapons. He advocated British control of Abyssinia, 'whatever measures must

---

551 The word used for testament in *Old* and *New Testament* is *kīdan*. A binding marriage is also a *kīdan*. Lefebvre (*Voyage*, Vol. I, p. 314) mentions a *kâlekidane* between Wibē and Selama before the 1842 war against Ali, and Ferret and Galinier (*Voyage*, Vol. II, p. 459) report that the alliance between Wibē and Birru on this occasion was sanctioned by an oath.

552 Harris, *Highlands*, Vol. III, pp. 351–5; Graham, *Glimpses*, p. 31.

553 Graham, *Glimpses*, pp. 11, 40–1.

554 Isenberg and Krapf, *Journals*, pp. 261–4. See also Johnston, *Travels*, Vol. I, pp. 4, 44–6; Vol. II, pp. 9–10, 15, 24, 41, 128, for this traveller's difficulties both at Tajura and on his arrival in Shewa.

555 Isenberg and Krapf, *Journals*, pp. 270–528; *EHB*, IX (1842), pp. 77–83, Krapf, 8 Jun. 1842.

556 See Crummey, *Priests*, p. 55. Both Krapf's diary and the letter published in *EHB* prove the absurdity of the allegation that the Galla chief acted in collusion with Sahle Sillasē. Nevertheless, the accusation was believed and spread. See Johnston, *Travels*, Vol. II, p. 70; Plowden, *Travels*, p. 178. Partly it may have originated in a misunderstanding caused by Krapf's frank expectation (*Journals*, p. 387) that Sahle Sillasē would recover and restore his property to him.

557 Isenberg and Krapf, *Journals*, p. 528; Krapf, *Travels*, p. 106.

558 Isenberg and Krapf, *Journals*, pp. 501, 507, 511, 528.

be applied', and suggested that the new treaty would soon provide a pretext for taking action: '. . . the slightest transgression should be attended by a military demonstration'.[559] In a letter to Basel, Krapf simply took for granted that Abyssinia would soon be British. In his opinion England had to take it to prevent France from connecting Algeria with Egypt and Ethiopia and thereby weakening and destroying the British interests in the Mediterranean, the Red Sea, and the Indian Ocean. Besides the political aspects, there were also, he added, the promising commercial prospects.[560] But Krapf was wrong. The idea of subduing Shewa to enforce the treaty was rejected at Bombay.[561] It might be too costly. The British authorities had never been as impressed with the commercial prospects of the interior as the French. In connection with Coffin's 1841 mission, the India Office had expressed as its opinion,

> . . . that there is no probability that any benefit will result from intercourse, or inter-ference, either with Shoa, or Tigré, which will repay the expense of Missions and Agents, and that, unless the French Government should manifest an intention of interfering with those Countries, it would be better to have nothing to do with either of them.[562]

The British government under Sir Robert Peel and Lord Aberdeen, more-over, was trying to restore the French–British entente which had been so seri-ously affected by the Eastern Question in 1839–40, and this would hopefully ease the rivalry in Abyssinia too. The condition was, of course, that France would agree to stay out. From the horizon of Aden this meant preventing Rochet, who had been on his way since New Year 1842,[563] from landing his arms and returning to Shewa. After the experiences of other French travellers including the d'Abbadie brothers and Combes, the Ministry of Foreign Affairs in Paris hardly expected Rochet to get through Tajura, which was mistakenly believed to have been bought and permanently occupied by the British.[564] When Rochet arrived there about 1 June, he found that this was not the case. Nevertheless he was prevented from landing his goods and was according to his own report finally told that the Sultan of Tajura was acting on orders from Aden.

Rochet dispatched a letter to Sahle Sillasē and returned to Mokha to wait for an answer.[565] In early September he crossed again to find that Sahle Sillasē had replied and had written to the Sultan as well, telling him not to hinder Rochet if he did not want to see his own subjects in Shewa in chains.[566]

559 ADEN, AIA 22, fols 134–143, to Haines, 2 Jun. 1842.
560 Basel, BV. 110, Krapf to Hoffman, 10 Jun. 1842.
561 Crummey, *Priests*, p. 53.
562 FO 1/3, fols 154–5, Ellenborough to Aberdeen, 23 Oct. 1841.
563 Rochet d'Héricourt, *Second voyage*, p. 6.
564 AEMD, Afrique 13, fol. 221, Combes and Broquant to Cie française d'Abyssinie, 30 Dec. 1840; fols 227–32, Combes to Guizot, 1 Sep. 1841; AECP, Massouah 1, fols 71–3, 'Rap-port', 16 Mar. 1842; fols 88–9, Degoutin to Guizot, 28 May 1843.
565 Rochet d'Héricourt, *Second voyage*, pp. 37–44.
566 ibid., pp. 54–6.

While it is not easy to establish whether the chiefs on the coast had earlier been acting on the orders of Haines or Sahle Sillasē or, which is not unlikely, on their own initiative in preventing various Europeans to proceed inland,[567] it now became very clear who was really 'the key of Abyssinia' on this front. In this matter Sahle Sillasē could obviously dictate his will to the coastal chiefs. Rochet left for Shewa, but when Krapf arrived with his colleagues in November, they were informed by the Sultan of Tajura that he had written orders from the King of Shewa not to allow any foreigner except Rochet to advance into the interior.[568] Krapf went to Zeyla in the hope that he would be able to proceed from there. He wrote to Sahle Sillasē, and Harris pleaded with the King on his behalf, but the way to Shewa for Krapf and his colleagues was effectively closed.[569]

It is not surprising that Krapf would later blame Rochet for Sahle Sillasē's refusal to grant him re-entry into Shewa.[570] But as at Adwa five years earlier,[571] the decisive factor seems to have been clerical and possibly popular opposition. Harris reports that meetings took place in the churches of the capital and deputations were sent to the King to implore him not to allow Isenberg or Krapf to come back. Finally the King reportedly called Harris and told him that he would not allow Isenberg and Krapf to return under any circumstances. He cited popular opposition and said that he had sufficient difficulties over doctrinal matters in his kingdom without the additional trouble that these missionaries would cause. Harris admits that he used both threats and promises but that they made no impact on the King.[572]

In fact, Harris's own stay in Shewa was approaching its end. Whether he was actually told to leave or not is fairly unimportant.[573] By 1843 at least, he must have understood that the treaty he had signed was a dead letter and that nothing he could do would make any difference. When he left, the doors were closed behind him. No British subjects or other British-protected Europeans penetrated to Shewa for decades to come.[574] Thirty years later, Minīlik was

---

567 Rochet reported to Krapf in April 1840 that he had been told at Tajura that Sahle Sillasē had ordered the Sultan to close the road. The King denied the truth of this report. See FO 1/3, fols 82–6, Krapf to Haines, August 1840.

568 *MM*, 1843, IV, p. 38, Mühleisen, 3 Dec. 1842; Krapf, *Travels*, p. 107.

569 *MM*, 1843, IV, pp. 45–54, Krapf, 5 Apr. 1843, quoting Harris to Krapf, 1 Mar. 1843. See also Crummey, *Priests*, pp. 54–5, where Krapf's attempt to return is described on the basis of India Office materials, including a translation of Sahle Sillasē's undated order to the Sultan to prevent all but Rochet from entering the country.

570 Krapf, *Travels*, p. 108.

571 See above, pp. 74–6.

572 *MM*, 1843, IV, pp. 45–54, Krapf, 5 Apr. 1843, quoting Harris to Krapf, 1 Mar. 1843.

573 In his published narrative, Harris is completely silent about his departure. Graham had written in August 1842 that Harris had decided to remain in Shewa and that he would therefore take charge of the embassy and conduct it back to India within about six months' time (*Glimpses*, p. 71), but it is doubtful whether Harris was any more popular than the others.

574 Krapf later (*Travels*, p. 31) states rather critically that Harris was satisfied with the nominal success of the mission and did not care about the implementation of the treaty since he did not believe in the possibilities of a profitable trade.

very apologetic about what he clearly believed was an impolitic expulsion of the embassy.[575]

Rochet's Fraud

Krapf had hoped that the embassy, by remaining in Shewa, would be able to restrain anti-British and anti-missionary feelings and thus keep the door open for his return. Sahle Sillasē may well have kept Harris, partly at least, because he wanted to confront him with Rochet.[576] Once this confrontation had taken place, and it is not likely that it was as friendly as Rochet describes it,[577] the British could leave. In mid-February, Rochet received politically more compatible company. Lefebvre once more turned up at the critical moment. On Rochet's recommendation Sahle Sillasē allowed him and his companion Dr A. Petit to cross the border between Wello and Shewa.[578] Rochet had a comparatively strong position. He had brought gifts almost as valuable as Harris's and assumed, not without some justification, that he was trusted and liked where the British had been mistrusted and disliked. The main reason for this was that Rochet travelled without the ostentatious escort and grand airs which caused suspicion against Harris.[579]

Although Rochet had no specific instructions to negotiate a treaty,[580] this was his ambition. For whatever it was worth, Harris had left with a treaty which stipulated considerable commercial advantages for Great Britain. How could Rochet possibly be expected to be satisfied with less? Although he published the text, all he says about the agreement in his narrative is that he obtained a treaty of commerce '. . . to guarantee the advantages, very distant perhaps, which he [Sahle Sillasē] stipulated in favour of our country'.[581] Lefebvre had a little more to say: on 1 May 1843 he had been consulted by Sahle Sillasē on the matter and had advised the King, who regretted having signed the treaty with England, that he should carry out his obligations under that treaty but grant France and every other nation that asked for it the same advantages as he had granted the British; this would be his best protection against encroachments; the King decided to give Rochet a treaty; the following day Rochet called on Lefeb-

575   See below, p. 272; also [O, Abyssinia Original Correspondence 3, pp. 759–61, Minīlik to Goodfellow, 3 Jul. 1870.

576   AECP, Massouah 1, fols 11–12, Degoutin to Guizot, 1 Dec. 1841; *MM*, 1843, IV, pp. 42–5, Krapf, 22 Jan. 1843.

577   Rochet d'Héricourt, *Second voyage*, pp. 140, 161, 284. Harris does not mention the return of Rochet or the financial assistance which Rochet says he gave to the British embassy in order to make it possible for them to leave. A financial transaction no doubt took place. See Malécot, 'Voyageurs', *RFHO*, LVIII, p. 296.

578   Rochet d'Héricourt, *Second voyage*, pp. 163–6; Lefebvre, *Voyage*, Vol. II, pp. 193, 196, 215.

579   Rochet d'Héricourt, *Second voyage*, pp. 123, 141–4, 159–62; Lefebvre, *Voyage*, Vol. II, pp. 193, 263.

580   In a general way Rochet was instructed to obtain concessions for French trade (AECP, Massouah 1, fol. 70, 'Rapport', 16 Mar. 1842), but that was all. I have found no copy of any instructions, and it was clearly stated after his return that he had acted without proper powers in signing a treaty (AEMD, Afrique 13, fols 306–7, Guizot to Hélouis-Jerelle, 8 Apr. 1846).

581   Rochet d'Héricourt, *Second voyage*, p. 275; treaty text on pp. 375–8.

vre to settle the main clauses; Rochet took it to the King who found it satisfactory without any changes. According to Lefebvre, therefore, only the question of recopying it for Sahle Sillasē's signature remained when he and Petit said farewell to Rochet at Ankober, accompanied the King to Angolela, and departed for Gojjam on 11 May.[582] Rochet had decided to return via Tajura and went to Aliyu Amba to prepare his caravan. He returned, however, to say farewell to Sahle Sillasē at Angolela and it would presumably be at this last visit that the treaty was signed.[583] It is in this connection only that Rochet mentions the treaty in his narrative. Moreover, it is in French dated 7 June 1843. By then Lefebvre had already reached Mahdere Maryam.[584]

The text of the treaty indicates what Rochet wanted from Sahle Sillasē and what he was prepared to offer in exchange: most favoured nation status in view of any future privileges granted to others, 3 per cent import duty only (as against 5 per cent in the Anglo-Shewan treaty), and the right for Frenchmen to trade all over Shewa and to buy and sell houses and land there; these clauses were not made reciprocal, but instead Rochet promised that France would protect Shewan subjects on their pilgrimages to Jerusalem and invited Sahle Sillasē to 'hope that in case of war with the Muslims or other foreigners France will regard his enemies as her own'.[585]

The document presented by Rochet to the French government raises many questions. It is a scroll of parchment, 71 cm. long and 15·5–17·5 cm. wide.[586] The Amharic and French texts appear side by side as in the Harris treaty, but there are neither illustrations at the top nor seals below. The Amharic version is plainly an attempt to translate the French text, but the style is so awkward that it is barely comprehensible in some places, for instance, the preamble and article 3. It may well be the product of a foreigner dictating to an Ethiopian what to write. A number of errors in the use of the suffix – ን indicate Tigriñña influence. This points to Lefebvre who had assisted Rochet at Alexandria about three years earlier and to one of his Ethiopian employees from the north.[587]

582 Lefebvre, *Voyage*, Vol. II, pp. 265–9.
583 ibid., p. 266; Rochet d'Héricourt, *Second voyage*, pp. 259, 269–70, 274–5.
584 Lefebvre, *Voyage*, Vol. II, p. 305. I see no reason to accept Malécot's statement ('Voyageurs', *RFHO*, LVIII, p. 298) that the treaty was *signed* before Lefebvre and Petit left Angolela on 11 May. Malécot seems to have consulted only the text published by Rochet himself. The date 7 Jun. 1843 appears both in de Clercq, *Recueil des Traités*, XV, pp. 340–1, and in L. M. Pierre-Alype, *L'Éthiopie et les Convoitises Allemandes* (Paris, 1917), pp. 125–6. On the other hand, it is not impossible that Lefebvre did some editing on 11 May just before he left. The Amharic dating 'Written in Ginbot at Angolela on the day of Yohannis, written in the year 1843' is a very strange mixture of Ethiopian and European. The day of Yohannis could refer to 4, 12, or 27 Ginbot (Rochet, *Second voyage*, p. 398), and 4 Ginbot was 11 May. But the day of Yohannis Afe Werq (Chrysostom), in Rochet's list 12 Ginbot/ 19 May, is more likely. Had it not been for 'the year 1843' instead of 1835 or 7335, one would not have suspected a European mind behind this dating.
585 AED, Traité politique et commercial . . . 7 Jun. 1843, articles 3–6 and 1–2 respectively, French text.
586 The parchment seems to have been damaged by oil and is a little difficult to read in some places. It has also been gnawed by rats along one side.
587 See above, p. 149. Rochet did not, as far as I know, claim to know Amharic which Lefebvre did.

The handwriting is that of a good Ethiopian scribe and produced with an Ethiopian pen, with the exception of the last line, the 'signature' of Sahle Sillasē. This is written in much thinner lettering as if produced with a European steel pen. Some of the letters look a bit awkward, too, and lead one's suspicions towards a European hand. Finally, and most important, the King's name is in the 'signature' preceded by a preposition. Instead of ሣህለ ፡ ሥላሴ ፡ we find በሣህለ ፡ ሥላሴ ፡ (*by* Sahle Sillasē) under the Amharic text and either በ- or ለ-ሣህለ ፡ ሥላሴ ፡ (*to* Sahle Sillasē) under the French text. Whatever the explanation for this, it excludes the possibility that Sahle Sillasē has *signed* the document. No one would prefix a preposition to his signature. *If* the idea was that one of his court officials should sign on his behalf, the construction requires ትእዛז ፡ (order, command) or some such word at the end of the phrase, followed by the signature of the King's *ṣehafe ti'izaz* or secretary. This is missing and the signature that follows is Rochet's own.[588]

In the 1880s and 1890s when the French government referred to the Rochet treaty to protect its commercial interests in Ethiopia, the Ethiopian government professed ignorance of the content of the treaty and asked repeatedly for a copy of the Amharic text.[589] Whether the Ethiopians received a copy or not at that time is uncertain, but in 1935 the Ethiopian minister of foreign affairs, Blattēngēta Hiruy, had a copy. This is not taken from Rochet's publication since it includes the subscription. The verbal similarities with the Amharic original, moreover, prove that it is not a translation from the French version. In addition to some rather unsuccessful attempts to improve the dating, Hiruy's published text has one remarkable feature. It closes, 'ያቶ ፡ ሮሼ ፡ ፌርማ ፡ የሣህለ ፡ ሥላሴ ፡ የሸዋ ፡ ንጉሥ ፡ ማኅተም ፡'—'The signature of Mr. Rochet. The seal of Sahle Sillasē, King of Shewa'.[590] A *seal*, at last, also for this treaty!

The conclusion is inescapable: the Franco-Shewan treaty of 1843 is a fraud. It is only a draft prepared by Rochet and Lefebvre, and dressed up with 'signatures', dates, and 'written in two copies' or 'fait en double', so that it resembles a formal treaty. When Rochet arrived in France about two years after he had left Shewa and finally submitted his 'treaty',[591] the Ministry of Foreign Affairs *did* question the validity of this document. But the reasons for this had *nothing* to do with the question whether Sahle Sillasē had agreed to the clauses of the treaty or not. Instead it was argued, firstly, that it would be difficult to carry out the obligations of article 2 about the protection of Ethiopian pilgrims and, secondly, that Rochet had signed the treaty without the necessary powers. Probably, the writer argued, this fact had not escaped Sahle Sillasē's attention,

588   AED, Traité politique et commercial . . . 7 Jun. 1843.
589   AEMD, Afrique 138, fols 252–61, Lagarde, 'Note pour Monsieur le Sous-Secrétaire d'Etat', 28 Aug. 1891; fols 490–4, Lagarde, 'Question du Harrar et Obok', Note confidentielle, 23 Jul. 1895.
590   Hiruy, *Tarīk*, p. 34. The subscription is included as article 7 of the treaty. The date has been completed to read Ginbot *30* which is as close as one could come to 7 June without changing the month. For the twentieth century but not the nineteenth, it is, in fact, a correct conversion. The Ethiopian year 1836, not the correct 1835, is entered with the European year 1843.
591   Malécot, 'Voyageurs', *RFHO*, LVIII, pp. 298–9.

and this explained why the treaty lacked some of the signs of authenticity of the Anglo-Shewan treaty. In fact, the argument continued, it was not clear whether Sahle Sillasē regarded the document as a formal treaty or a kind of promise to enter into an agreement. Though the French government was unwilling to commit itself as to the validity of the treaty, it was thought advisable to act in such a way that the government would be able to make use of the treaty in the future.[592] In brief, the treaty was regarded as valid and binding for the Ethiopian party who had refused to accept and sign it, but not for the European party whose agent had drafted and proposed it and also pretended that it had been signed.

But there was in this transaction another kind of duplicity, too, which would be repeated in future European treaty-making with Ethiopia. Rochet was aware that he was asking for considerable privileges for French subjects and their commercial activities. He must also have been aware of the opposition of the Muslim trading community represented by men like Welasma Muhammad.[593] In order to reach his goal, Rochet therefore offered not only French protection of Ethiopian pilgrims, as already mentioned, but what amounted to a political and military alliance from which Ethiopia would have everything to gain and nothing to lose. After an assumption that the French and the Ethiopians had the same faith, article 1 in the Amharic version continued:

> If other enemies, be it European or Muslim, should arise against the King of Shewa the King of the French will fight against them [lit. be hostile towards them]. Then the King of Shewa will rejoice.[594]

This is a translation of '. . . the King of Shewa *ventures to hope* that in case of war with the Muslims or other foreigners, France will regard his enemies as her own'.[595] It seems quite clear that Rochet was here—in the Amharic text— offering Sahle Sillasē something which he knew that he could not possibly deliver and preferred not to have explicit in the French text.

As for Sahle Sillasē, even this offer was not sufficient to make him sign, and this is from the Ethiopian point of view the interesting fact. The King might have been guided by a number of different considerations in rejecting the agreement. Sahle Sillasē did not feel threatened by his Muslim neighbours. He may, however, have heard enough about the plans of Rochet from Krapf and about those of the British from Rochet, to decide that the less he had to do with either France or England the better.[596] The arguments which Lefebvre said

592   AEMD, Afrique 13, fols 306–7, Guizot to Hélouis-Jerelle, 8 Apr. 1846.
593   See Rochet, *Second voyage*, p. 140; Harris, *Highlands*, Vol. III, pp. 360–4, for a conflict with the governor of Yifat involving both Rochet and Harris.
594   AED, Traité . . . 7 Jun. 1843. Rochet had from the beginning stressed the importance of not allowing the Shewans to find out that there was any difference between their faith and that of the French (Rochet, *Voyage*, pp. 141, 149–50, 189–90), but it is unlikely that Krapf allowed this ignorance to prevail. The view that Sahle Sillasē by this article acknowledged that Shewa officially accepted the Roman Catholic faith (Coulbeaux, *Histoire*, Vol. II, p. 375) would be absurd even if he had signed the treaty.
595   My emphasis.
596   In his first book Rochet is throughout quite positive towards the 'excellent M. Graphfe' (*Voyage*, p. 319) but later he repeats stories told about Krapf's intrigues against him (*Second voyage*, p. 135). Krapf, on the other hand, accuses Rochet of slandering him (*MM*,

he had used to persuade Sahle Sillasē to sign the treaty with France were certainly not reassuring: to break the treaty with Great Britain would be dangerous for Shewa; the route used by Ahmed Grañ could easily be used by a European army.[597] The idea that he would improve his position by signing one more treaty obviously did not appeal to the King of Shewa. In addition, Sahle Sillasē had lost some of his confidence in Rochet personally. The Frenchman had made the mistake of travelling as a bearer of royal gifts and as a merchant at the same time, and Sahle Sillasē probably suspected that he had been cheated into paying for what were intended as presents.[598]

Finally there was, of course, the fundamental difference in outlook. Sahle Sillasē had no interest in foreign relations as such. He was not isolated commercially and saw no purpose in changing the trade pattern. Like the rulers in the north, he had nothing against individual Europeans. He liked their presents and could use their skills. He was prepared to reward them, too, as individuals. But the idea that the Europeans as a category should acquire a special legal status in his country and have commercial rights and privileges which infringed on his own monopolies, while they would themselves be protected from infringements by kings whom he had never seen, must have perplexed the Shewan king. Neither Harris's pomp nor Rochet's ingenuity sufficed to institute this kind of change. Sahle Sillasē was not more, probably less, aware of the need to regulate his relations with foreign rulers and their subjects than his colleagues in northern Ethiopia.

It was not because of Rochet's success that the Anglo-Shewan treaty became a dead letter. His own treaty never saw the light of day. It is significant that he should write that the advantages of it would probably be 'very distant', and that neither he nor Lefebvre went back to Shewa although they both returned to Ethiopia again.[599] The usual explanation that the treaties were not followed up because the trade prospects were too poor and the caravan routes too insecure is only half of the truth, at the most. It was Sahle Sillasē who closed his frontiers to Europeans, and this he did, not because he was disappointed with the apparent unwillingness of the British and French to follow up the treaties, but because he wanted no follow-up.[600]

1843, IV, pp. 42–5, Krapf, 22 Jan. 1843; *Travels*, p. 108). See also Conti Rossini, 'Vicende', *RRAL*, 5, XXV, p. 468.

597 Lefebvre, *Voyage*, Vol. II, pp. 265–6.

598 AECP, Massouah 1, fol. 85, Degoutin to Guizot, 15 Apr. 1843. According to Rochet himself, he had been instructed to purchase certain articles for the King and Queen. These he delivered separately and received 1,400 thalers for them, which he then lent to the British mission (*Second voyage*, pp. 127–8, 133). The most important of these articles were eight double-barrelled guns for which Rochet had paid about 20 thalers each or altogether 160 thalers (ibid., p. 47). Since Rochet had received 500 thalers when he went to Europe (*Voyage*, p. 319), Sahle Sillasē may well have been surprised at the request for payment, which was by any standards exorbitant. This did not prevent Rochet from trying to get 12,000 francs from the French government for the mission at a later, probably more opportune date (AEMD, Afrique 13, fol. 309, Rochet to Soult, May 1847).

599 See above, pp. 121, 127, 129.

600 Cf. Malécot, 'Voyageurs', *RFHO*, LVIII, p. 299, and Darkwah, 'Shoa', pp. 51–2, 54, where the opposite view is expressed.

The Legacy of Suspicion in Shewa

One more contact was made from the European side during the *Zemene Mesafint*, but it led to nothing. The Lazarist missionary Luigi Montuori visited Shewa in 1846 to interest Sahle Sillasē in the replacement of Abune Selama by a Catholic bishop. Montuori seems to have been convinced that both Sahle Sillasē and Ali were in favour of his plan, but he was not able to convey his enthusiasm to the Vatican. Therefore Ali's and Sahle Sillasē's commitment was never tested.[601] Excommunicated as he was by Selama, Sahle Sillasē may well have expressed some support for the idea, but this does not imply that he was prepared to open up Shewa for the type of political and commercial influence which Harris and Rochet had sought.

Sahle Sillasē died in 1847, but the anti-European sentiment which was created primarily by the Harris mission prevailed in Shewa during the reign of his son Hayle Melekot.[602] An attempt was made to re-establish contact with Great Britain, but the strange outcome strengthens rather than weakens the impression of aloofness and suspicion. In May 1849, an Ethiopian presented himself at the British consulate in Cairo with a brief, unsigned note from the King of Shewa, Beshah Wired, to the Queen of the *ferenj*.[603] That Beshah Wired was used rather than the royal name Hayle Melekot may be due simply to the fact that the King was known to Krapf and other foreigners under the former name. That Queen Victoria should be addressed as Queen of the Europeans is rather more significant. It indicates how little impression the British–French rivalry as such had made or how transitory it must have been. The main point of the letter is to rebuke the Queen for having ignored the death of Sahle Sillasē and to offer her the opportunity of making amends for her negligence by sending Krapf with a gift.[604] A gift of twenty-six elephant tusks and thirty-one rhinoceros horns for the Queen was, according to the envoy, already on its way to Aden. The British consul general, who questioned the envoy and satisfied himself that the letter was genuine, was also told that the King wanted some European artisans who could 'make a crown, and make cannons, and paint pictures, and build palaces'.[605]

It was agreed that the Ethiopian, who was making a pilgrimage to Jerusalem, should return via Cairo for the reply. He does not seem to have turned up again. A reply from London and a box with 300 gold sovereigns (the equivalent of 1,500 thalers) were then forwarded to Aden where they were eventually handed over to Hayle Melekot's commercial agent, Hajj Ibrahim Shehem. Great was the surprise at Aden when the box was returned with a message from the King that he did not want the money which he had tested and found not to be gold. The agent reported that Hayle Melekot was disappointed because he had expected

601   See Crummey, *Priests*, pp. 71–3.
602   FO 401/1, p. 71, Plowden to Palmerston, 3 Jan. 1850.
603   FO 1/5, fol. 302, Beshah Wired (Hayle Melekot) to Victoria, n.d., forwarded from Cairo, 21 May 1849.
604   ibid.
605   FO 401/1, p. 39, Murray to Palmerston, 21 May 1849.

something on the scale of the Harris mission.[606] It is more likely that the King was prevented from accepting the gift by the same anti-European forces that had compelled Krapf and Harris to give up Shewa.[607] Whatever the reason, the incident shows how difficult it was to create confidence and establish anything resembling ordinary diplomatic relations. Twenty-five years after the Harris mission, Minīlik recalled that the British had left under a cloud because of a prophecy that people from faraway would come and destroy Shewa.[608] In this part of Ethiopia the suspicion created by the first influx of Europeans was profound.

Summary

The complexities of the Ethiopian political situation, no less than the great variety of European motives at play, caution against any attempts to generalize attitudes and developments during the quarter of a century which separates the Ali/Coffin mission of 1827 from the end of the *Zemene Mesafint*. Nevertheless the incoherence should not be exaggerated. Behind apparently isolated and sometimes conflicting initiatives and reactions, certain patterns can be detected.

Firstly it must be emphasized that Ethio-European contacts throughout the period originated mainly in European initiatives. It was the Europeans who needed or wanted something from Ethiopia, as from the rest of the world: spheres of influence, strategic bases for their own conflicts, markets for surplus goods, sources of raw materials, mission fields, new homes. The justification for imperialism was fully developed with reference to Egypt and the Red Sea area in the 1830s:

> It seems to be a law of nature that the civilised Nations shall conquer and possess the countries in a state of barbarism, and by such means however unjustifiable it may appear at first sight, extend the blessings of knowledge, industry and commerce among people hitherto sunk in the most gloomy depths of superstitious ignorance.[609]

606 FO 401/1, p. 44, Palmerston to Hayle Melekot, 4 Jul. 1849; p. 59, Palmerston to Murray, 23 Jan. 1850; pp. 94–5, Hobhouse to Palmerston, 31 Oct. 1850, with enclosures; p. 120C, Haines to Bombay government, 22 Mar. 1852; FO 1/7, fols 15–16, 'Jelul bin Saleh Selassi' to Haines, November 1851. I have not been able to locate the original of the 1851 letter from the King of Shewa. The dating and the phraseology preserved in the translation prove beyond doubt that it was written in Arabic and by a Muslim, probably by the agent who carried it. The use of an Arabic seal is not surprising, but the strange designation of the King certainly raises some questions, which cannot, however, be answered with the sources available to me. Almost twenty years later Ibrahim Shehem's son Abu Bakr referred to the rejection of the gold simply as the rejection of European friendship (IO, Abyssinia Original Correspondence 3, pp. 892–7, Abu Bakr to Minīlik, n.d.).
607 IO, Secret Letters from Aden 32, pp. 59–77, Cruttendon to Haines, 7 Apr. 1852.
608 FO 1/20, fol. 215, Minīlik to Victoria, n.d., received 6 Aug. 1867.
609 FO 78/3185, fols 22–49 (quote on fols 31–2), Mackenzie to Johnston, 1 Jun. 1837. This study is not intended as a contribution to the debate about the motives and impelling forces behind the extension of European influence and rule to Africa and Asia. That is essentially a problem of European history. The point is that the historical record, as demonstrated here, proves beyond doubt that European imperialism was well on its way in this area before 1850.

This view did not, however, go unchallenged. The occupation of Aden, for instance, caused an anonymous writer to condemn

> ... the moral and political delinquency of the system we have so long pursued—of taking the previous owner's consent for granted, whenever it suited our views to possess ourselves of a fortress, island, or tract of territory, belonging to any nation not sufficiently civilized to have had representatives at the Congress of Vienna.[610]

By and large the governments in London and Paris were not in favour of territorial acquisitions on the Red Sea coast, much less in the Ethiopian hinterland. Guizot's response to the De Jacobis/Schimper proposal of 1845 and Palmerston's 'trade, not land' instructions to Plowden are but two of many expressions for this negative attitude towards acquisitions *per se*.[611] The 'white man's burden' could be used as an argument, if necessary, but the political leaders of Europe by no means regarded it as a governmental obligation to shoulder it. This was the task of explorers and pioneers, of commercial companies and missionary societies. The dilemma was that the agents of European 'civilization', confident of their superiority, arrogant and haughty as they often were, nevertheless discovered that they were in fact weak and vulnerable. In this situation they turned to warships off the coast, appointments as government agents for themselves, or the general protection of consuls and treaties. Implicit in this procedure was a tendency to intimidate. Ultimately there was the solution of occupation and European rule in one form or other. In the Ethiopian case this outcome was taken for granted at a very early stage, for instance, by Combes, Lefebvre, and Krapf.[612] Still earlier Baron von Katte had suggested that Europe establish order in Abyssinia with a few thousand muskets, a couple of cannon and some capable officers. In his view a European colony in Tigrē would be very easy to establish.[613]

As the above analysis of the contacts between 1827 and 1855 shows, the Europeans in the field tried to bridge the gap between the non-involvement or wait-and-see policies of their governments and their own aims and interests by presenting the latter as the 'requests' and 'offers' of Ethiopian rulers. In other words, European initiatives were disguised as Ethiopian.[614] This applies to several major issues: requests for protection against the Turks or Egyptians (Isenberg and Antoine d'Abbadie 1838, De Jacobis/Schimper 1845), the invitation to occupy Massawa (Coffin 1827), the cessions of Anfilla, Arkīko, the whole

610 *Blackwood's Edinburgh Magazine*, LIII (January–June 1843), p. 485.
611 See above, pp. 113, 121.
612 See above, pp. 82, 103, 157.
613 Katte, *Reise*, pp. 83–4, 146–7.
614 Cf. Marston, *Britain's Imperial Role*, p. 173: '. . . the powers were led into these policies [towards Abyssinia 1840–48] by the tactics of the Abyssinian rulers rather than by their own desires.' This view simply ignores the really active element. Donald Crummey has in his article 'Initiatives and Objectives in Ethio-European Relations, 1827–62', *JAH*, XV, 3 (1974), pp. 434–44, also in my opinion allowed European agents and missionaries to speak for the Ethiopians more than necessary and as a consequence arrived at a more active Ethiopian policy vis-à-vis Europe during the closing decades of the *Zemene Mesafint* than I have.

littoral, Agamē, or all Tigrē (Lefebvre 1839, Blondeel 1841–42, De Jacobis/ Schimper 1845, Rolland 1849) and, obviously, the request for protectorate status implied in some of the communications.

In those cases where original letters from the Ethiopian rulers exist, they seldom support the claims of the Europeans involved; sometimes they clearly contradict them. As for the treaties, the first British agreement signed (Harris/ Sahle Sillasē) led, not to the opening up, but to the closing of Shewa; the second (Plowden/Ali) was signed by the Ethiopian party on the assumption that it would not have any consequences. The French were even less successful: Rochet forged Sahle Sillasē's name in order to enjoy the appearance of success, while Lefebvre/Schimper/Rolland, after ten years and many 'offers', nevertheless omitted spelling out their request for a protectorate over the coast in *the Amharic text* of their 1849 'treaty' with Wibē. As for the major issues of territorial concessions, commitments which might limit the independence or freedom of action of the Ethiopian rulers, or actual influence on the political affairs of the country, the first quarter of a century of pressure and intrigue brought little change.

In the commercial field the impact was not much greater. The trade had started to pick up before the Europeans began to become seriously interested in it in the 1830s, and the prospects were, as we have seen, painted in glowing colours by one traveller after the other. To make it really profitable to Europeans some changes were certainly needed and suggested. The first step was to limit or abolish taxation of the trade by the Turks and Egyptians, and this was where most of the effort was expended. The next step which figured in a number of proposals was to take control of the caravan trade of the main routes inland. This is where the Harris, Rochet, and Plowden treaties with their stipulations of unrestricted freedom of movement and 3 or 5 per cent customs duties, to be paid once only, come in. Just for comparison, one might mention Lefebvre's report in 1842 that Abyssinian merchants normally doubled their capital for every trip from Gonder to Massawa in spite of twelve customs posts and many more difficulties at Massawa than a European merchant would have.[615] Thirdly, as Harris pointed out, trade could be quickly increased 'by teaching the natives to have artificial wants'.[616] Sahle Sillasē deprived Harris of the opportunity to start this educational programme. But the threat remained. At the very close of the *Zemene Mesafint*, Beke suggested that a person (read himself) be offered £5,000 (about 25,000 thalers) annually for ten years to establish a British trading centre on the edge of the Tigrean plateau.[617]

For one item there seemed to be no need to cultivate 'artificial wants'. There was no doubt a genuine interest in firearms among the leading princes and their closest vassals or rivals. No other single item is mentioned more often in the communications to European rulers. Nevertheless the documentation does not support the strong emphasis *on Ethiopian appeals* for arms. In this case, too, the

615 AEMD, Afrique 13, fols 86–91, Lefebvre to Cunin-Gridaine, 17 Feb. 1842.
616 Harris, *Highlands*, Vol. III, p. 334.
617 IO, Secret Letters from Aden 34, pp. 445–55, Beke to Coghlan, 31 Jul. 1855. Consul Plowden received £500 annually when he took up his position (FO 401/1, p. 5, Palmerston to Plowden, 3 Nov. 1848).

initiative was European. Although Salt had demonstrated what could be obtained from Europe, it was not to buy or beg firearms from England that Sebagadis dispatched Coffin in 1827. And when Coffin returned after five years with 1,850 muskets and carbines, it took him more than ten years to dispose of them. Aubert and Dufey were associated with a firm importing arms into Egypt; so was Blondeel. They were simply looking for new markets. Rochet brought a powder mill when he first came to Shewa. Kielmaier had started to make arrangements for having arms forwarded to him in Shewa before Krapf raised the matter with Sahle Sillasē and brought about the Harris mission. Combes, finally, brought a shipment of 6,000 muskets and other small arms and had to send them back to France again.[618] The truth of the matter is that the Europeans were pushing arms on the Ethiopians during most of the period. This is not surprising in view of the interests of the armament industry, but it has been overlooked because so many disguised their activity as compliance with Ethiopian requests.

The Ethiopian response was in fact slow, with the obvious exception that an exchange of gifts was always welcome. In twenty years' time the firearms presented probably added up to 1,000 pieces all told or about half of what Coffin alone had brought. What share the Europeans eventually captured of the increasingly clandestine trade is impossible to know.[619] A reasonably safe guess as to the total number of firearms available in the country towards the end of the period is almost as difficult to make.[620] What is certain, however, is that the advantage of easier access to firearms did not decide the outcome of the major struggles: Sebagadis in 1831 and Wibē in 1855 were both losers: Tēwodros fought his way to the throne in spite of inferiority in terms of fire power. The time when firearms would be decisive had not yet come in Ethiopia.

The only two areas where one can detect basically Ethiopian requests for assistance are the protection of Ethiopian Christians travelling or residing in Muslim lands and the import of technology. The former is evident in the insistence on protection at Massawa, the appeals concerning Dayr as-Sultan and possibly De Jacobis's association with the ecclesiastical mission to Cairo in 1841. The latter is documented in contact after contact, from Sebagadis's request in 1827 for a carpenter who could put a lead roof on a church to Wibē's request in 1849 for some men who could make lime for the construction of his church at Deresgē. Sahle Sillasē was primarily interested in Aichinger and not Isenberg, and in Rochet as a chemist and not as a merchant/politician. In this respect there was continuity from Welde Sillasē's requests for carpenters, smiths, a doctor, and someone 'who understood raising water'.[621] There was also continuity in that most requests for craftsmen went unheeded. Except for improved techniques in

618   See above, pp. 63–5, 73–4, 82–6, 103–4, 148, 150–1.
619   They were certainly involved, and Plowden defended himself against attacks (FO 401/1, p. 105, Plowden to Palmerston, 16 Mar. 1851), probably based on an incident reported by Rochet (AECP, Massouah 1, fol. 353, 13 Aug. 1851). The difficult task of studying the arms trade in the Red Sea remains to be undertaken.
620   See Pankhurst, *Economic History*, pp. 581–2; *idem*, 'Firearms in Ethiopian History, 1800–1935', *Ethiopia Observer*, VI, 2 (1962), pp. 135–80.
621   See above, pp. 41, 59, 66, 123, 131–2, 147–8.

the production of gunpowder, there was little emphasis on war materials. Greek and Armenian gunsmiths seem to have satisfied the needs in that field.[622]

On the whole, the disappointment and disillusionment was mutual. It is unlikely that the Ethiopian rulers fully understood the implications of the activities of Lefebvre and Blondeel, Harris and Rochet. But some of the steps taken certainly indicate that they were far from naive. With reference to Rochet's and Plowden's activities, Degoutin wrote in 1848: '. . . the black princes, however savage they may seem, are much more cunning than the Europeans, who in the end are always their dupes'.[623] From Wibē's angle it looked a bit different.[624] The truth is that the Ethiopians were rapidly learning.

Prior to 1830 very few Ethiopians had travelled beyond Cairo and Jerusalem. At the courts of Sebagadis and his contemporaries no one knew French or English. Gobat started the practice of bringing young Ethiopians to Europe for training and the Lazarists followed suit. Other Ethiopians travelled as 'ambassadors' with Antoine d'Abbadie, Lefebvre, and others. Some of the most influential ecclesiastical leaders visited Rome with De Jacobis in 1841. Others gained insight through the manifold contacts they had with Europeans in Ethiopia. As a consequence Plowden was reported to have a whole staff of young Ethiopians who had been educated abroad.[625] Some of those who had travelled with and been employed by Europeans later entered the service of Ethiopian rulers and thus brought both linguistic knowledge and inside information about the activities of the Europeans to the Ethiopian courts. Both Ali Umar's son, Samu'ēl Gīyorgīs, and the sons of Coffin's brother-in-law Werqē were already second-generation middlemen. The former had been taught and baptized by the CMS missionaries. He had travelled in Egypt, Syria, and India and accompanied Kielmaier and Beke to Shewa. When Rassam met him in the service of Tēwodros in the 1860s, he judged that he was 'better informed than any of his countrymen, not excepting those who have been educated at Malta and Bombay'. Besides, he had 'a keen intellect, surpassing in that respect every Abyssinian I have met with . . .'[626] Habte Sillasē had a different background, and though he had been close to the CMS missionaries and the Catholics alike, he had never entered the service of any foreigner. His long career as an intermediary and adviser to both sides must nevertheless have made it possible for him to help Wibē draw the line and has eventually earned him the high praise of being 'the prototype of a creative nationalist, open to progressive influence, yet constantly reserving his own autonomy'.[627]

---

622 At one point Wibē was pressed to invite someone to come and manufacture cannon but what it really led to is uncertain. See BN, Ethiop. Abb. 254, fol. 162, Anon. to Wibē, n.d.; 256, fol. 513, Deres to Wibē, n.d. The person referred to in the letter of Wibē's commercial agent Deres was probably the Italian Valieri who reportedly repaired one of the cannon brought by Salt and was forced to participate in the battle of Debre Tabor against his own will. See Ferret and Galinier, *Voyage*, Vol. II, pp. 40, 461.

623 AECP, Massouah 1, fols 191–2, Degoutin to Lamartine, 1 Jul. 1848.

624 See above, p. 128.

625 AECP, Massouah 1, fols 271–2, Rolland to Tocqueville, 14 Jul. 1849.

626 Rassam, *British Mission*, Vol. I, p. 258.

627 Crummey, *Priests*, p. 77.

The attitudes of the minor chiefs and population in general depended on two factors: eventual orders from superior authorities and the conduct of the European travellers themselves. In general the laws of hospitality towards strangers were observed. A missionary like Gobat found friends everywhere and seems to have been offered whatever he wanted, but then his needs were clearly very modest. Other travellers who offered to pay for the provisions they needed seldom met difficulties. But experiences varied. Ferret and Galinier found that the rich or average people were always generous while the poor closed their doors. But then they accepted this as natural since the poor had nothing, even to sell.[628] Baron von Katte found that he had to pay for lodgings in one village and concluded that the missionaries had praised a hospitality that did not exist at all.[629] Away from the main routes and centres, several European travellers introduced themselves or were introduced by their servants as the bishop, or as brothers of the bishop, and were very well provided for.[630] Eventually this kind of deceit was discovered, and the white skin lost some of its usefulness.

Europeans who came on official business of any kind, who made contact with the rulers and travelled with their permission, were normally looked upon as the guests of the rulers. Orders were issued to the district chiefs and village heads to provide pack animals and supplies.[631] Particularly in Shewa, where the system was well organized, this was a guarantee that the foreigner received what he needed. On the other hand nothing could be obtained there even against payment without the King's approval.[632] In other places, it could happen that the chief simply selected a fat ox for the foreigner from the nearest flock without consulting, probably without knowing the owner, as Ferret and Galinier reported about Araya Sillasē at the height of his popularity.[633]

Organized or haphazard, the burdens in the end fell on the peasantry. They were used to them:

> [The governor] . . . can demand from them contributions on fifty pretexts—he is going on a campaign, or returning from one; he has lost a horse, or married a wife; his property has been consumed by fire, or he has lost his all in battle; or the sacred duty of a funeral banquet cannot be fulfilled without their aid.[634]

The Europeans soon discovered resentment against the additional contributions caused by their visits. Lefebvre heard that the British mission was disliked by the people in Shewa because of the increased taxation it caused.[635] Blondeel reported that he found plundered villages and an angry population as he travelled in the footsteps of Lefebvre. He regarded it as below the dignity of any

628   Ferret and Galinier, *Voyage*, Vol. II, pp. 193–5.
629   Katte, *Reise*, p. 43.
630   Dufey and Aubert-Roche, 'Abyssinie', *RO*(Paris), I, p. 318; Lefebvre, *Voyage*, Vol. II, 133, 155; Ferret and Galinier, *Voyage*, Vol. II, 521–4.
631   D'Abbadie, *Douze ans*, pp. 41–2.
632   Harris, *Highlands*, Vol. II, pp. 15–17.
633   Ferret and Galinier, *Voyage*, Vol. II, p. 162.
634   FO 401/1, p. 203, Plowden to Clarendon, 9 Jul. 1854.
635   Lefebvre, *Voyage*, Vol. I, p. 266.

European to accept hospitality under conditions which made 'the poor Abyssin-ian people abhor the Whites'.[636] While benefiting from it himself, Krapf criticized the system too: firstly because the village heads could order sufficient provisions from the peasants to cover the needs of their own households for many days; secondly because the chiefs always expected presents in return. Since the latter were not shared, the people became unfriendly towards the stranger for eating his bread at their expense.[637] On a different level there was the criticism of the nationalists at Sahle Sillasē's court that the foreigners had 'eaten the royal bread and destroyed none of the enemies of the state'.[638]

Twenty-five years of contacts had in many ways made relations easier. Condi-tions for dialogue and co-operation were becoming available. But suspicion and disillusionment were also spreading. Few Europeans cared or were able to see themselves through the eyes of Africans and Asians. One who did was Mun-zinger:

> When we arrive in foreign lands, we will probably be received quite friendly the first time. After the three sacred days of hospitality the host and the guest take a closer look at each other and then one may rest assured that few people who know us will be delighted at our visit.[639]

By 1855 the scrutiny had only begun. The Ethiopians, who saw the Europeans as fellow-Christians and therefore natural allies against the 'Turks', were not hasty in their rejection of the European advances.

The one development which would seriously threaten the survival of Ethiopian independence had taken place on the northern frontier. More concerned with the maintenance of peace than the Ethiopians themselves, the Catholic mission-aries and the consuls had in fact contributed to the establishment of a Turkish/ Egyptian bridgehead on the mainland opposite Massawa. At the same time their activities to protect the local population against attacks, and the relatively greater success of the mission work in the frontier districts, had combined to create favourable conditions for a popular movement which would be neither Muslim and pro-Egyptian nor Orthodox and pro-Ethiopian, but Catholic and pro-European. In comparison with this, the European 'purchases' or 'treaty acquisitions' of minor islands and ports from local sultans were less important, though they helped to establish the view that these people could dispose of their small territories at will and therefore weakened traditional ties with the Ethiopian hinterland.

636   AE(Brussels), 2024/II, Blondeel to Degoutin, 29 Apr. 1841.
637   Isenberg and Krapf, *Journals*, pp. 280–1.
638   See above, pp. 153–4.
639   Munzinger, *Ostafrikanische Studien*, pp. 13–14.

IV

Unification and an Active Foreign Policy

Tēwodros—Unifier, Restorer, Modernizer

The coronation of Dejjazmach Kasa of Qwara as King of Kings Tēwodros in February 1855 signified the end of the *Zemene Mesafint* and the beginning of a new era in Ethiopian history. For the first time in several generations, supreme authority in the Ethiopian state and factual military and political power were united in the same person. In the choice between succeeding Ras Ali as the guardian of a puppet Emperor and usurping the throne for himself, Tēwodros had not hesitated to choose the latter course. By adopting Tēwodros as his throne name, he sought the legitimacy and support of a cherished myth, for this was the name of the eagerly awaited Ethiopian prince who was to put an end to the trials and tribulations of his people and rule the world in righteousness, peace, and prosperity.[1]

Inherent in the demand of the new ruler that he be accepted as the Tēwodros of the prophecies was an apparently strong and genuine commitment to the ideals of the legend: a theocratic state governed in harmony by king and bishop. To a considerable extent Tēwodros drew on the past for inspiration. There was a strong emphasis on *re*unification, *re*storation, *re*construction in much of what he said and did. This does not imply, however, that his policies, seen in the perspective of Ethiopian history, were retrogressive. Behind the struggle to restore royal and episcopal authority and some kind of national unity, there was a growing awareness, not only of the dangers which threatened Ethiopia from the outside, but also of the need for modernization. Tēwodros tried to create a national army and appoint salaried officials. Though he was himself an intensely religious man, he attempted to limit spiritual authority to spiritual matters and drastically reduce the land holdings of the church. He encouraged the use of the national language Amharic at the expense of the church language Gi'iz; he stressed the construction of roads rather than of the churches and palaces of Sebagadis, Wibē, and Sahle Sillasē. Clearly much of this was not a return to the past but an

---

1 See Rubenson, *Tēwodros*, pp. 46–51, with sources cited; also Mathew, *Ethiopia*, p. 206.

attempt to meet the challenges of the future, and there is more than one suggestion in it that Tēwodros was acquainted with the concepts of post-Reforma-
tion European nation-states and absolutism. As might be expected, Tēwodros's
strong personality and his faith in his destiny as the restorer of Ethiopia's greatness also influenced his attitude towards foreigners and the governments they
represented.[2]

In dealing with the Europeans and Egyptians, Tēwodros had certain advantages over his predecessors: firstly, knowledge about Europe and the Europeans
had increased in the country, and secondly, Tēwodros could with greater justification than any of the *mesafint* before him claim to speak for all Ethiopia. This
was initially recognized not only by Consul Plowden but by Mgr De Jacobis as
well.[3] It was also recognized by most of Christian Ethiopia, for Tēwodros had
accomplished a reconciliation between Abune Selama and the *ičhegē* at Gonder
and was solemnly crowned by the bishop after his victory over Wibē in February
1855.[4]

It is important, however, to keep in mind that Tēwodros did not succeed in
unifying Ethiopia. After his coronation he turned south, subdued the Wello
Galla, captured Meqdela which was later to become his state prison, treasury,
and last refuge, and defeated the Shewan army. King Hayle Melekot died before
the decisive battle at Bereket on 19 November 1855, but a second son of Sahle
Sillasē, Hayle Mīka'ēl, accepted the governorship as *mer'idazmach* of Shewa under
Tēwodros and administered the province loyally for three years. Later, however,
Tēwodros was faced with insurrection in Shewa. He crushed an uprising led by
Hayle Mīka'ēl's brother Seyfu in 1859 and campaigned with diminishing success
in 1862, 1864, and 1865 against Ato Bezzabih, to whom he had entrusted the
province in 1858. When Hayle Melekot's young son Minīlik escaped from
Meqdela in June 1865, Shewa was irrevocably lost to Tēwodros, who made no
further attempts to subdue it.[5]

The situation in other provinces was much the same, if not worse. Wello was,
in fact, never pacified, although Tēwodros consumed an extraordinary amount
of his time and energy to accomplish that goal. In Gojjam a member of the old
ruling family named Tedla Gwalu had raised the standard of rebellion already
when Tēwodros was on his first campaign in Shewa, and though often defeated,
he always escaped and could return to the fight. In Tigrē Tēwodros appointed,
among several others, Wibē's old rivals Araya Sillasē Dimṣu and Kasa Sebagadis

---

2 Rubenson, *Tēwodros*, pp. 52–70; Donald Crummey, 'Tēwodros as Reformer and Modernizer', *JAH*, X, 3 (1969), pp. 457–69. The personality and policies of Tēwodros are controversial topics which cannot (with the exception of foreign policies) be dealt with in this
   study. Crummey's article is an excellent analysis of the 'modern' features of Tēwodros's
   policies. Margaret Morgan ('Continuities and Traditions in Ethiopian History. An investigation of the reign of Tēwodros', *Ethiopia Observer*, XII, 4 (1969), pp. 244–69) stresses the basic
   continuity which prevailed in the social and economic system in spite of Tēwodros.
3 For De Jacobis, see Crummey, *Priests*, pp. 95–8.
4 Rubenson, *Tēwodros*, pp. 44–5.
5 ibid., pp. 52–3, 77–8, 80–1. See also Hiruy, *Tarīk*, pp. 38–43, for a good, though somewhat
   biased, account of these events based largely on the chronicles of Gebre Sillasē and Aṣme
   Gīyorgīs.

as his governors. Some were more loyal, others less, but the real danger in the north during the first five years of Tēwodros's reign lay in the two brothers, Nigusē and Tesemma Welde Mīka'ēl, who claimed the political heritage of their uncle Wibē. From Simēn, Agew Nigusē, as he was commonly called because of the Agew origin of his father, led the resistance against the rule of Tēwodros. He found allies and supporters as far south as Dembīya and Wag, and became the focus of initiatives to create a northern, Catholic kingdom entirely independent of Gonder/Debre Tabor. In two major campaigns around New Year 1860 and 1861, Tēwodros weakened and finally eliminated Nigusē and Tesemma. The year or two following his victory over Nigusē mark the climax of Tēwodros's career from the point of view of military control over the country. But the increasingly violent methods he had resorted to failed to quell the spirit of independence and rebellion, and in 1863 and 1864 new rebel leaders emerged: Ṭiso Gobezē in Welqayit and Wagshum Gobezē Gebre Medhin in Lasta.[6]

In the end Tēwodros left Ethiopia as divided as he had found it. When he committed suicide at Meqdela in 1868, moreover, a foreign army stood in the heart of the country. What then was his contribution or that of his contemporaries to the survival of Ethiopian independence? Certainly the obvious answer seems to be: none. That, however, is not true. In his short reign, Tēwodros provided important directions for his successors. Least of all is it true that 'his foreign policy and the conditions which alone made it possible, died with the Emperor Theodore'.[7]

The main foreign policy issues which the new ruler had to face were those inherited from the preceding period: the obtrusive European interest in the country in general and how to deal with it, the French–British competition and its possible consequences, the advantages and disadvantages of allowing Catholic and/or Protestant missionaries to gain adherents, the relations with Egypt, and the crucial question whether the Europeans could be trusted as friends of Ethiopia in an eventual war with the Muslim neighbour. It was in the manner in which he approached these issues that Tēwodros differed from his predecessors. For Tēwodros it was, as we shall see, a question of initiative, of active involvement and sustained effort to reach what he regarded as important national goals: the educational and technological advancement of Ethiopia and the containment and reversal of Egyptian expansion. An active foreign policy was about to replace the sporadic responses of the previous period.

Missionaries and Craftsmen

Basically Tēwodros had a positive attitude towards Europeans. He wanted to associate with them and make systematic use of their knowledge and skills in the formation of his own policies and in the modernization of his kingdom. Initially,

---

6   Rubenson, *Tēwodros*, pp. 67–8, 75–81. See Donald Crummey, 'The Violence of Tēwodros', *JES*, IX, 2 (1971), pp. 107–25, for the latest attempt to describe the interplay between the political and personal causes behind Tēwodros's failure.

7   Mathew, *Ethiopia*, p. 207.

moreover, he was not the proud, overly suspicious, cruel, and vengeful character that so many writers have described. He met John Bell in Ali's camp at Ayshal and found Zander commanding Wibē's artillery at Deresgē, but this did not prevent him from befriending them and giving them positions which implied the greatest trust in their loyalty.[8] It is remarkable, too, that Europeans, almost unanimously, described their first meetings with Tēwodros as very encouraging and successful.[9] Nevertheless all too many ended up as his enemies, some imprisoned for years.

No doubt Tēwodros's failure to maintain satisfactory relations with the Europeans can be explained, in part at least, in terms of his increasingly erratic personality and growing tendency to violence.[10] In order to understand the development of Ethio-European relations in a wider context, it must be more fruitful, however, to look for the signs of basic conflicts of interests and see whether Tēwodros's attitudes and acts were not dictated by an awareness of their existence and the possible threat they constituted to the unity and sovereignty of Ethiopia. It has been suggested that if we need 'a key to all that happened, it is contained in these three words: I mistrust much'.[11] If Tēwodros openly admitted this 'mistrust' to Consul Plowden at the beginning of his reign, was it not because he felt there were justifiable reasons for it?

The first problem Tēwodros had to solve with foreigners was what reply to give to De Jacobis about the future of the Catholic mission. Whether Tēwodros personally believed that religious uniformity was important for political unity is difficult to say. His attitude towards factionalism within the Orthodox church indicates that he did. At any rate Abune Selama claimed spiritual jurisdiction over all Ethiopian Christians, and this excluded the approval of activities by a rival Catholic bishop.[12] The Emperor was almost forced to choose between Selama's support for his programme of national renewal and the advantages which might be gained from a policy of tolerance towards the Catholics. The personal animosity between the two bishops made compromise all but impossible. De Jacobis was ordered to leave Ethiopia through Metemma. At first he refused, and when he finally left in November 1854, he made his way back to

8 Henry A. Stern, *Wanderings among the Falashas in Abyssinia* (London, 1862), pp. 70, 73; Andree, *Abessinien*, p. 31. The case of Bell as *Līqemekwas* Yohannis is well known. Zander was first put in charge of a treasury and arms depot at Gorgora and was later used in many different capacities by Tēwodros. See, in addition to Andree, the missionary correspondence in Spittler-Archiv.

9 See above, p. 139, for Heuglin; FO 401/1, pp. 250–7, Plowden to Clarendon, Report, 25 Jun. 1855; pp. 456–9, Cameron to Russell, 31 Oct. 1862; Stern, *Wanderings*, pp. 56–61; AEMD, Afrique 61, fols 130–3, Lejean to Drouyn de Lhuys, 28 Jan. 1863.

10 Although he has focused his attention on this negative aspect, Crummey in his well-balanced article on the violence of Tēwodros (*JES*, IX, 2) shows how far we have come from Sir E. A. Wallis Budge's 'arrogant and overbearing and cunning megalomaniac half sodden with mead and brandy' (*History*, Vol. II, p. 517) or Alan Moorehead's 'mad dog let loose' (*The Blue Nile* (New York and Evanston), 1962, pp. 205–6).

11 Mathew, *Ethiopia*, p. 186, quoting from Plowden, *Travels*, p. 461.

12 Rubenson, *Tēwodros*, pp. 57–9. For Tēwodros's attitude towards factionalism, see also [Gobat], *Life*, p. 303, and for Selama's claims, dispatches by Plowden throughout 1853 and 1854, FO 401/1, pp. 137, 139, 161–2, 247.

Halay on the northern frontier. The last Catholic missionary in the central provinces, Giusto da Urbino, decided to leave as well.[13]

This outcome seems to have been almost inevitable. Tēwodros was anxious that it should not be misinterpreted. He wrote to the French vice-consul at Massawa that he welcomed European artisans, travellers, and explorers to Ethiopia in exchange for French protection of his subjects abroad but that he would not allow Catholic missionaries in his kingdom, since all his subjects ought to have the same faith.[14] Reporting this letter, Consul Delaye informed his government that he had decided not to send any reply. Instead he had written officially to Plowden to protest to Abune Selama and tell him that the Emperor's letter was completely absurd, since it implied that he would have to expel all the Jews, Greeks, Armenians, Muslims, and Protestants too. Delaye suggested reprisals: letters of excommunication of Selama should be obtained from Patriarch Qērilos and spread in Ethiopia, and Selama's property in Cairo and elsewhere should be confiscated to compensate for the losses of the mission.[15]

It is understandable, perhaps, that Delaye should miss the point of Tēwodros's letter and ask: what about the Protestants, i.e. the British? In March 1855, the CMS missionary of the 1830s and 1840s, J. L. Krapf, passed through Massawa together with a younger missionary named Martin Flad and an early protégé of Lefebvre's, Mahdere Qal Tewelde Medhin, who during twelve years of absence from his country had travelled much and received both Catholic and Protestant education. They were on their way to Gonder to explore the prospects for a new Protestant missionary endeavour.[16] At the same time, Plowden also left for the King's camp, reportedly on a direct invitation from the new ruler.[17] De Jacobis and the French representatives at Massawa concluded, not only that Selama directed Tēwodros's religious policy, which was only to be expected and no doubt true up to a point, but that Plowden was behind it all: Catholicism was being destroyed to make room for Anglicanism, and, obviously, British influence.[18] They decided, therefore, to disbelieve or ignore the King's offer of

---

13 See Crummey, *Priests*, pp. 92–9.

14 BN, Ethiop. 184, fol. 85, Tēwodros to Delaye, 1854/55.

15 AECP, Massouah 2, fols 63–6, Delaye to Walewski, 23 Jul. 1855. A less drastic intervention by Qērilos or Da'ud, as the French continued to call him, had already been requested at Cairo (ibid., fols 61–2 Walewski to Delaye, 9 May 1855).

16 Crummey, *Priests*, pp. 116–17. For Krapf, see above pp. 55, 150–2, 156–8; for Mahdere Qal (Maderakal), AEMD, Afrique 13, fol. 109, Guizot to Étienne, 10 Aug. 1844 (and following letters); Krapf, *Travels*, pp. 445–6; FO 401/1, p. 311, Pullen to Malmesbury, 7 Nov. 1858; pp. 315–16, Miles to Houlton, 12 Jan. 1859; A. Girard, *Souvenirs d'un voyage en Abyssinie* (Cairo, 1873), pp. 193–5. Mahdere Qal's importance lies in his wide contacts and the fact that he was an interpreter for Tēwodros for much of the latter's reign.

17 FO 401/1, p. 247, Plowden to Clarendon, 3 Mar. 1855; p. 244, Baroni to Bruce, 15 Apr. 1855.

18 ibid., p. 258, Plowden to De Jacobis, 27 Jun. 1855; AECP, Massouah 2, fols 63–6, Delaye to Walewski, 23 Jul. 1855; fols 79–90, De Jacobis to Walewski and Napoleon III, 24 Feb. 1856; fols 111–16, Beillard to Walewski, 17 Jul. 1856. Four years later, however, the Sardinian missionary Leone des Avanchers spoke of Tēwodros's attitude and persecution of the Catholics in terms of a general religious policy, with no reference to the fact that Protestant mis-

co-operation in secular matters; in fact, they tried for five years completely to ignore his claims to be the sovereign of Ethiopia.

It was largely coincidence that the Krapf mission arrived so soon after the expulsion of the Catholic missionaries and provided Selama and Tēwodros with the opportunity of clarifying their position towards the rival persuasion. Krapf and Gobat, who was behind the project, had no illusions about any Anglican bishop of Ethiopia or rival clergy. Krapf was to ask for permission for a group of lay missionaries educated at the St Chrischona Institute to form a small settlement, teach their crafts and trades, and preach the Word of God to their pupils and servants.

Passing through Adwa, Krapf and Flad were told by Mirçha Werqē[19] that Tēwodros had said that he would instruct the consuls not to allow any missionaries or teachers to enter Ethiopia. At Debre Tabor, Selama advised them directly and indirectly (through John Bell) not to raise the question of preaching or any other religious activities with the King. The bishop only mentioned at the audience that the foreigners would want to practice their own faith, and this Tēwodros agreed to, provided the bishop himself had no objections. Tēwodros defined his first needs: a gun maker, an architect and a printer (what he wanted was actually a seal engraver). Officially at least, the King was allowed to remain ignorant of the religious nature of Krapf's mission.[20] This does not necessarily mean that he was unaware of the ultimate objectives. On the contrary, with Gobat and Krapf involved, it is difficult to see how he could be.[21] But whether he knew or not, the fact remains that Selama either did not want or dare to raise the question, or was unable or unwilling to secure the permission for a Protestant mission enterprise, even one without any ecclesiastical pretensions. What the King wanted was employees, essentially men of Bell's, Schimper's, and Zander's category, though with somewhat more specialized skills. He was determined not to have missionaries.[22]

Confronted with the missionary spirit and the views of the Chrischona brethren, Tēwodros nevertheless exhibited an open mind. Flad returned in May 1856 with three fellow-missionaries, C. Bender, G. Kienzlen, and J. Mayer. Two more, K. Saalmüller and T. Waldmeier, came in April 1859. Although Tēwodros was disappointed that the first arrivals did not have the qualifications he had asked for, they were allowed to remain, and when they went to work for him, mainly constructing roads and repairing small arms to begin with, he soon discovered that they had more to offer him than their knowledge of rock-

sionaries had then been granted some freedom to work (ASMAI 36/1–1, to Cavour, 2 Apr. 1859).

19 A son of Coffin's brother-in-law Werqē (see above, pp. 61–2), trained in a mission school in Bombay (Krapf, *Travels*, pp. 438–9, 443).

20 Crummey, *Priests*, pp. 117–18, with sources cited; the warning about Tēwodros's attitude received at Adwa in Spittler-Archiv, D 2/1, 'Neue Abyssinische Mission . . .', p. 3.

21 It is impossible to be certain on this point. Crummey seems to believe that the King was misled (*Priests*, p. 119) or 'completely ignorant' ('Reformer and Modernizer', *JAH*, X, pp. 461–2). If so, this was the first, but certainly not the last, major misunderstanding caused by lack of frankness among the Europeans involved with Tēwodros.

22 See also 401/1, p. 244, Baroni to Bruce, 15 Apr. 1855; and below, pp. 180–1.

blasting, carpentry, and metalwork. Long conversations about spiritual matters revealed much common ground. Tēwodros, who was known to be a diligent reader of the Scriptures in Amharic even before he met the Protestant missionaries, shared their emphasis on the authority of the Bible and the importance of studying it. Therefore he was quite prepared to encourage the distribution of the Scriptures, which was one of the main objectives of the missionaries. His programme of national renewal, moreover, had important spiritual and moral overtones, and he found little guidance or co-operation from his own clergy, whom he despised. A first suggestion by the King to reduce the amount of privileged land in the hands of the clergy in order to provide necessary revenue for a national army and administration—an act which the German missionaries could easily approve—led to a serious clash in September 1856.[23] In this situation, the Protestant missionaries 'offered him a theology that was able to encompass both his hostility to the formal structure of Ethiopian Christianity and his deep religious faith'.[24]

In this receptivity and positive interest in Evangelical doctrine, there was, however, no hint of approval for a missionary-directed Protestant church. The policy of Tēwodros and Selama in this respect was absolutely firm. When Henry Stern asked for permission to establish a mission among the non-Christian Felasha in 1860, approval was given on condition that all converts were baptized into the Orthodox church. The same condition was laid down for two Chrischona brethren, W. Staiger and F. Brandeis, who arrived in 1862 to open up a second mission to the Felasha. Flad transferred to Stern's mission but neither he nor the newcomers were allowed any long period of independent mission work.[25] Everything indicates that Tēwodros was prepared, even eager, to receive not only foreign technology but new ideas and impulses from abroad, and this in fields as far apart as military organization and theology. Sometimes he expressed a preference for the Europeans and their civilization in shocking terms: 'Do not believe I am an Abyssinian at heart; no, I am as one of you.'[26] 'No doubt, you have heard of our, the Ethiopian people's, ignorance and blindness.'[27]

Nevertheless, Tēwodros was a nationalist, and it was precisely because he wanted to make his people the peer of any other nation in the world that he invited assistance. Krapf had essentially the same outlook as Lefebvre, but it is not too difficult to imagine what would have happened to him in 1855 if he had tried to make the kind of speech Lefebvre reported that he had made to Araya Sillasē in 1842.[28] It is not impossible that Tēwodros sensed that the presence

23 See Crummey, *Priests*, pp. 120–5; Rubenson, *Tēwodros*, pp. 55–7, 68–70. The road-building, in particular, was noted by Zeneb (*Tēwodros*, p. 41). For the kind of language Tēwodros could use to priests, see Spittler-Archiv, D 3/9, Saalmüller to Schneller, 12 Oct. 1859.
24 Crummey, *Priests*, p. 125.
25 ibid., pp. 128–32, 137.
26 Spittler-Archiv, D 3/5, Kienzlen to Gobat, 4 May 1859.
27 FO 1/26, fol. 210, Tēwodros to Victoria, 29 Jan. 1866. See also Stern, *Wanderings*, p. 149; ASMAI 36/1–1, Leone des Avanchers, to Cavour, 2 Apr. 1859.
28 See above, p. 103; also Spittler-Archiv, D 3/6, Krapf to Spittler, 11 Mar. 1854.

and influence of Europeans entailed a threat to the future independence of Ethiopia. At any rate, he showed that he wanted his foreign employees to cut their ties with Europe and be integrated in the Ethiopian society as much as possible.

Before the Chrischona missionaries had even started their work for the King in 1857, Flad was told when he asked for permission for Bender to make a trip to Europe: 'I am fed up with the coming and going of the Europeans.'[29] Though they had all apparently intended to bring wives from Europe, only Flad did so. The other five married in Ethiopia.[30] Everything indicates that Tēwodros regarded them as his subjects—his 'children', as he often called them—and that he was less at ease with the position of the Felasha missionaries, who received their support from abroad. When the crisis came in 1863–64, and the mission stations were closed, it was not the evangelization of the Felasha that Tēwodros was striking at, but the relative independence of a group of foreigners and their contacts with Great Britain.[31]

There were some ups and downs also in the King's relations with his European workmen: the five Chrischona brethren and a few individual adventurers, including Jaquin, Bourgaud, and Moritz Hall, who, together with Kienzlen, Saalmüller, and Waldmeier, were mainly responsible for the establishment of the cannon foundry at Gefat.[32] Excluding Flad and his colleagues who were forced to join them in 1864, the group never seems to have exceeded ten in number, and was almost certainly much smaller than Tēwodros would have liked.[33] In view of the circumstances, they served Tēwodros well—and loyally—until the bitter end at Meqdela. They drew much criticism from their fellow-Europeans, and were disliked by many Ethiopians whom Tēwodros forced to work under their direction, but the King appreciated their loyalty and rewarded them.[34] There was not one Englishman among them (except Charles Speedy for a short period),[35] and they certainly had no direct share in causing the conflict with Great Britain.

29 Spittler-Archiv, D 3/2, Flad to Krapf, 26 Oct. 1857.
30 For intentions, see *inter alia* Spittler-Archiv, D 3/9, Saalmüller to Schneller, 12 Oct. 1859; D 3/2, Waldmeier to Gobat, 30 Sep. 1860; for outcome, Markham, *Abyssinian Expedition*, pp. 75–6. Tēwodros was allegedly very pleased with the marriages. See Spittler-Archiv, D 3/8, Mayer to Spittler, 25 Oct. 1859; D 3/2, Waldmeier to Gobat, 30 Sep. 1860.
31 Crummey, *Priests*, p. 137.
32 Spittler-Archiv, D 3/9, Saalmüller to Schneller, 12 Oct. 1859 and 13 Jan. 1861; D 3/1, Bender to Gobat, 20 Nov. 1861; D 3/12, Waldmeier to the St Chrischona Committee, 24 Nov. 1862; AECP, Massouah 3, fols 98–9, Gilbert to Thouvenel, 20 Mar. 1861; Waldmeier, *Erlebnisse*, pp. 7–21.
33 FO 401/1, p. 283, Plowden to Clarendon, 12 Nov. 1856; Spittler-Archiv, D 3/5, Kienzlen to Gobat, 4 May 1859; D 3/9, Saalmüller to Schneller, 12 Oct. 1859; Stern, *Wanderings*, p. 228.
34 Spittler-Archiv, D 3/5, Kienzlen to Gobat, 4 May 1859; D 3/2, Flad to Krapf, 3 Oct. 1859; D 3/9, Saalmüller to Schneller, 12 Oct. 1859; D 3/2, Stern to Gobat, 19 Dec. 1860; D 3/9, Saalmüller to Schneller, 13 Jan. 1861; D 3/1, Bender to Gobat, 20 Nov. 1861; D 3/12, Waldmeier to the St Chrischona Committee, 24 Nov. 1862; FO 401/1, p. 327, Plowden to Malmesbury, 1 Mar. 1859.
35 See Waldmeier, *Erlebnisse*, p. 110, for a list; for Speedy, Spittler-Archiv, D 3/1, Bender to Gobat, 20 Nov. 1861.

Tēwodros and Plowden: Sovereignty and Reciprocity

The letter of Tēwodros to Consul Delaye in 1855 demonstrated that he did not regard the expulsion of the Catholic mission as a foreign policy issue, except inasmuch as it expressed his right as a sovereign to decide what foreign subjects and foreign activities to permit in his country. For Tēwodros it was simply a step that had to be taken in the interest of internal peace and stability. It was De Jacobis and his supporters who saw it in terms of Protestantism versus Catholicism, and at least presented it to Paris as the elimination of French influence in favour of British. This view caused them to hope for and expect the rapid downfall of Tēwodros, and to throw all their support behind the King's main rival, Agew Nigusē.[36] Initially this left the field open to Consul Plowden to promote his own or Britain's interests. More important, the presence of an official representative of a European government presented Tēwodros with the opportunity of defining his attitude towards European powers, as opposed to European guests in his country.

As far as Plowden was concerned, the establishment of a Protestant mission in Ethiopia was by no means a priority. On the contrary, it is difficult to find a single statement in his many dispatches, before or after 1855, which supported the activities of missionaries in Ethiopia, whether Catholic or Protestant.[37] There is no evidence that he played any role in the expulsion of De Jacobis, but there is equally no evidence that he had any share in the reappearance of Protestant missionaries. When the new endeavour was planned, Krapf chose to label Plowden 'a Papist', from whom no help could be expected,[38] and at the very moment when Krapf and Flad were about to present their request to Tēwodros, he wrote that he expected the *abun* to promote British interests 'if no missionaries are sent'.[39] After his own first meeting with Tēwodros, about two months later, he defended the King's policy not to permit any missionaries to preach in Ethiopia and concluded:

> Certain I am that it would be far wholesomer for the cause of progress, that neither this [the Roman Catholic] *nor any other Mission* should *at present* set foot in Abysssinia . . .[40]

This stand, whatever the reasoning behind it, exonerates Plowden from the charge of pronounced partisanship. In a respectful and conciliatory letter to

36   AECP, Massouah 2, fols 79–90, De Jacobis to Walewski and Napoleon III, 24 Feb. 1856; fols 104–5, Beillard to Walewski, 30 Jun. 1856. See also below, pp. 189–96.

37   The interference in Bogos at the request of the Catholic Stella (see above, p. 143) was part of Plowden's campaign against Turkish/Egyptian expansion. Later, when it suited his own interests, he turned against Stella too (AECP, Massouah 2, fols 117–20, Beillard to Walewski, 27 Jul. and 1 Sep. 1856).

38   Spittler-Archiv, D 3/6, Krapf to Barth, 2 Apr. 1853. This was incorrect. But, ironically, De Jacobis's supporter Delaye was later discovered to be a Protestant (AECP, Massouah 2, fols 79–90, minute on De Jacobis to Walewski and Napoleon III, 24 Feb. 1856).

39   FO 401/1, pp. 244–5, Plowden to Clarendon, 7 Apr. 1855.

40   ibid., pp. 257–8, Plowden to Clarendon, 27 Jun. 1855 (my emphasis).

De Jacobis, he emphasized that opposition was, moreover, useless: the King did 'not permit himself to be led either by the *abun* or by whoever it might be'.[41] About one year later, he pleaded with De Jacobis to obey the King and evacuate Halay in order to save his Ethiopian converts from persecution:

> [Tēwodros] believes that he has the sovereign right to do what he wants without restriction [*absolument*] in his kingdom, having no treaty or agreement with any European power which can prevent him, and I have no power to change his decisions. Appeal to Mgr De Jacobis to believe that the King is not a child like the chiefs who have preceded him . . . This is not the moment to insist on any mission in Abyssinia.[42]

This is a very strong statement by one who had known both Wibē and Ali for more than a decade, repeatedly visited both of them on official business and negotiated a treaty with the latter. Clearly Tēwodros had impressed the consul as an extraordinary man, a person with a mature mind, keen intelligence, and unyielding determination to safeguard his independence.[43] It is highly unlikely that the consul wanted to waste any of his goodwill on attempts to influence the King's religious policy. He must have sensed at once that he needed all the prestige of his office if he was to reach the political and commercial objectives for which he had come to Gonder.

In spite of his statements to the contrary before leaving Massawa, Plowden does not seem to have had any invitation from Tēwodros.[44] That he nevertheless cancelled an already approved visit to England (his first in seven years) to make the trip to Gonder indicates that he hoped to bring about some major breakthrough in the commercial field, which was his primary concern. The obvious basis for negotiations was the treaty signed with Ali in 1849.[45] Plowden reported a grand and friendly reception but nothing about negotiations until the evening before his planned departure. Bell and Selama acted as intermediaries and may well have prepared the ground. As reported by Plowden, the King sent and asked why the consul had come. Plowden stressed in reply that he had not come 'in any official capacity' and that he only wanted to 'know and report His Majesty's disposition respecting the establishment of a Consulate and friendly relations generally'. The treaty, though in theory legally binding for

41 ibid., p. 258, Plowden to De Jacobis, 27 Jun. 1855; also in Plowden, *Travels*, pp. 473–4, dated 25 Jun. 1855. At the same time Stella was strongly advised not to build a church at Keren (AVA 2/5, Plowden to Stella, 25 Jun. 1855).
42 BN, Ethiop. 184, fol. 62. This is the second or final sheet of the original of a letter from Plowden almost certainly to Baroni and written or received in May 1856. Plowden advised the addressee to read it in the presence of the other missionaries and to give De Jacobis a copy if he wanted it (this suggestion is crossed out—by Plowden or Baroni?)
43 See also FO 401/1, pp. 251–7, Report, 25 Jun. 1855, for Plowden's views of the new ruler: ' . . . of untiring energy, both mental and bodily, his personal and moral daring are boundless . . . Indefatigable in business, he takes little repose night or day; his ideas and language are clear and precise; hesitation is not known to him . . .'
44 Cf. above, p. 176, n. 17, with FO 401/1, p. 255, Report, 25 Jun. 1855.
45 See above, pp. 129–31.

Ali's successors, was referred to with some care: 'I hinted also at what had been arranged with the Ras Ali.' The King's reply was:

> I know nothing of what Ras Ali may have done; I am young and inexperienced in public affairs; I have never heard of a Consulate under the former Kings of Abyssinia, and this matter must be referred to my Council and the principal people of my Court.[46]

The following day several attempts were made, reportedly with the assistance of Selama and Bell, to persuade Tēwodros to agree to a British consulate. Plowden even reported that he 'ventured to hint that the sea-coast and Massowah might possibly be given up to him on his consent'. The bait was rejected:

> I cannot consent to a Consulate, as I find in the history of our institutions no such thing . . . In refusing your request for a Consulate, my only reason is that it appears an innovation, but do not forget my friendship for you, and cause your Queen also to regard me as a friend. After the rains I shall send to Her Majesty an Embassy and letters, and when these wars are finished I will give every favour and protection to Englishmen who may visit my country: do you also visit me and write to me.

Plowden had every reason to be disappointed with the outcome, but he seems to have tried to deceive himself, or at least his government, into believing that he had actually gained half a victory and that the prospects were still bright:

> . . . it will be seen that the King's refusal is hardly a refusal, and that he does not wish to break off all Treaty with us, but rather the contrary, being only startled by the clause about jurisdiction of Consuls . . . I see much to hope for in these conversations. It is well to find a King in Abyssinia proud of his dignity, alive to his responsibility, capable of considering grave matters, and of replying with decision, not lightly giving assent to a thing he does not understand, and yet seeking for our friendship in all ways that he can understand. Nor is it very important to obtain a direct accord until such a time as his power shall be firmly fixed. Whenever he does sign a Treaty, to whatever effect it may be, he will fully appreciate his obligations, and faithfully fulfil them to the extent of his authority . . . It is apparent from the honourable and friendly manner in which I took my leave, and from the King's expressions, that he does not regard his refusal as a matter that should break off our correspondence, or give offence. He has refused rather the form than the substance of our proposals.[47]

In spite of Plowden's obvious attempt to minimize the differences of opinion, the message of King Tēwodros comes through very clearly. The King completely rejected the concept of a resident European consul, i.e. the presence of someone in his kingdom entitled to exempt from his own jurisdiction all foreigners—and their business transactions and conflicts, not only with each other but with his own subjects as well![48] As early as 1838, Antoine d'Abbadie had noticed resistance to the idea of a European consul at Gonder,[49] and by 1855 sufficient

46 FO 401/1, pp. 254–6, Report, 25 Jun. 1855.
47 ibid.
48 FO 93/2/1, Treaty, 2 Nov. 1849, Article XVII. See above, p. 129.
49 BN, Ethiop. Abb. 279, fol. 43v.

Ethiopians had observed consuls in Egypt and elsewhere in the Middle East for Tēwodros to know that they could not easily be ignored once they had been accepted.[50] We can be quite sure that if Tēwodros spoke of his own inexperience and the lack of precedents in the manner reported by Plowden, then he did so mainly to make his negative reply sound more polite. He was sufficiently intelligent to understand the implications of the consular jurisdiction proposed to him, and he certainly rejected the substance as well as the form.

The prospect of seeing the Turks removed from Massawa must, however, have appealed to Tēwodros. From what we know about Sebagadis and Wibē, they would have accepted the offer without hesitation. For Tēwodros the price was too high. Besides, he was confident that he could take Massawa from the Turks himself as soon as he had completed the unification of the country.[51] Plowden shared this view, and it was his plan that England should act as 'the honest broker' on condition that Tēwodros, in addition to the consulate, agreed to appoint a European governor (under the jurisdiction of the consul, of course) at Massawa. This would solve the remaining difficulty of Plowden's project for the exploitation of Ethiopia, 'the want of a sea-port in the hands of either England or Abyssinia'.[52] How specific Plowden had been in uncertain, but the King no doubt understood that Ethiopia would regain *factual* control of her main port only through her own strength and determination.

To begin with, Tēwodros wanted more, and independent, information about international affairs. The Crimean war had broken out the year before. England and France, whose spokesmen had tried for two decades to make the Ethiopians understand that relations with the one excluded relations with the other, had joined hands to support Muslim Turkey against Orthodox Russia. This was hard to understand for a ruler whose ultimate goal in life was the liberation of the Holy Land from Muslim rule.[53] Ever since the appearance of Salt, the Europeans had been declaring that their aim was to protect Christian Ethiopia against Turks and Egyptians. Before trying to chase the Turks away from Massawa or going to war with Egypt, Tēwodros could use some more insight into European politics.

This thinking was, no doubt, behind the abortive attempt by Tēwodros to establish contact with Russia immediately after his coronation.[54] It was also

---

50 See Plowden, *Travels*, p. 461: '. . . if I did not love you personally, I should have sent you away on the first mention of a consulate'. See also Henry Dufton, *Narrative of a Journey through Abyssinia in 1862–3* (London, 1867), pp. 147–8.

51 FO 401/1, p. 254, Report, 25 Jun. 1855.

52 ibid., pp. 254, 256, Report, 25 Jun. 1855; pp. 270–2, Plowden to Clarendon, 17 Feb. 1856; also pp. 264–5, Bruce to Stratford de Redcliffe, 16 Feb. 1856.

53 See Rubenson, *Tēwodros*, pp. 60–1.

54 FO 401/1, pp. 244–5, Plowden to Clarendon, 7 Apr. 1855; Krapf, *Travels*, pp. 443–4. Unfortunately I have not been able to find any information about this mission from Russian sources. The earliest documents on Ethiopia which I have received from the AVPR date from the 1870s. According to Plowden, the messenger used was a Syrian. One person who may well have encouraged Tēwodros's scepticism about both the British and the French, was the Greek merchant Johannes Kotsika of Kasala and Qallabat (see Methodios Fouyas, 'An unpublished document edited and translated into English', *Abba Salama*, I (1970), pp. 15–66).

behind his plans to send embassies to several European powers, including the one to London. Naturally he also wanted to explain his position and policies, for instance on missionary activities, through trusted emissaries of his own. Plowden recommended that the embassy be received in London, but it is doubtful whether he fully understood the significance of 'equal terms' in his own statement: 'He, in fact, only wishes to treat on equal terms . . .'[55] For Tēwodros this was not a question of 'only', not a formality. The basic principle of Ethiopia's relations with European powers was expressed in those words though it would take forty years and the catastrophe of Adwa before the Europeans understood and accepted it, grudgingly and temporarily.

Plowden was invited to remain at Gonder as the guest of the King until the rainy season ended, but then Nigusē's rebellion in Simēn had begun, and travel was unsafe.[56] Tēwodros asked the consul to stay on,[57] and so he did for five years. At first he seems to have believed that he would eventually be able to influence the King to agree to the consulate in some form. The latter pressed for a reply about the arrangements for his own ambassadors to go to England.[58]

It was November 1856 before the consul received a reply from London to his report of June the preceding year. His proceedings were approved; Tēwodros was to be congratulated to his rise to power but advised to abstain from religious persecutions in the future; his ambassadors were welcome, provided he gave a distinct assurance that he renounced all idea of conquest in Egypt or at Massawa.[59] No reference was made to Plowden's suggestion about the future of the port. This destroyed whatever influence Plowden may, with Bell's assistance, have acquired over the preceding eighteen months. The consul reported that he placed a translation of the dispatch in the King's hands.[60] Tēwodros was hardly pleased to be reminded again of the earlier persecution against the Catholics, which had been carried out in full understanding with, if not at the instigation of, Plowden's friend, Abune Selama. The demand that he should renounce all ideas of going to war against the Egyptians or Turks was even more serious, particularly since there was no suggestion that the British government would help solve the problems of Massawa and the coast by diplomatic means.

The governor of Massawa had in the meantime tried to depose Na'ib Muhammad; hostilities had broken out, and Egyptian troops at the governor's disposal had pillaged in Hamasēn. There were also threats against Mensa and

---

55 FO 401/1, pp. 254, 256–7, Report, 25 Jun. 1855.
56 ibid., p. 255, Report, 25 Jun. 1855; p. 263, Plowden to Clarendon, 2 Sep. 1855; Plowden, *Travels*, p. 460.
57 FO 401/1, pp. 269, 272, Plowden to Clarendon, 22 Dec. 1855 and 5 Mar. 1856.
58 ibid., pp. 263, 277, 279–81, Plowden to Clarendon, 2 Sep. and 28 Oct. 1855, 23 Jun., 5 Aug., and 5 Oct. 1856.
59 ibid., pp. 259–60, Clarendon to Plowden, 27 Nov. 1855.
60 ibid., p. 283, Plowden to Clarendon, 12 Nov. 1856; pp. 329–30, Plowden to Malmesbury, 28 May 1859. There is no way of knowing if the translation was correct, but since the dispatch arrived open (most likely the work of 'French' agents), it is quite possible that Tēwodros's spies could report the contents independently of Plowden. See ibid., p. 281, Plowden to Clarendon, 10 Nov. 1856.

Bogos.[61] The British had protested in Cairo and Istanbul.[62] The foreign secretary had, in fact, considered Plowden's proposal 'to transfer the port of Massowah to the Government of Abyssinia' and advised the Sultan 'to enter into an arrangement for the transfer'.[63] But since Plowden had not been informed that his plan was even being considered, he had no positive hints to drop this time.

Aside from the issue of the Roman Catholic mission, the consul found little difficulty in defending Tēwodros against the implied charges of religious persecution:

> First, with regard to the persecution of Mahomedans. Up to this time the King has not forced a single individual of that creed to change his faith . . . I may inform your Lordship that some German Protestant missionaries are now in the country . . . the King allows them to ramble about where they please, and to distribute their books as they like without remark; this I believe is not allowed even in so enlightened a state as Sardinia.[64]

On Egypt, the King's reaction was:

> That he had hitherto given no provocation to Egypt, and that, while he reserved to himself the right to demand hereafter certain territories, gradually wrested from Abyssinia, during the reigns of feeble princes . . . he promised to take no steps of a hostile nature until he should hear our reply.

Tēwodros had decided not to give any written reply. Arms and instructors, artisans and engineers seem to have been discussed again. With nothing to offer him, the consul concluded that Tēwodros would 'probably say that as our friendship offers him no advantage; so he will not seek for it'.[65]

In December 1856 Patriarch Qērilos arrived on a visit to Ethiopia, and in January 1857 there were rumours about an impending attack from the Sudan. This complicated Plowden's position, but he thought it 'would scarcely be a misfortune should a quarrel with a powerful people show the Abyssinians their own weakness, and thus induce them to seek earnestly and more humbly for the friendship and support of their fellow-Christians in Europe . . .'[66] It was as if Tēwodros had read the consul's mind; he had his pride, too. Pressed for a decision, he repeatedly told Plowden that the matters he had come about could wait.

61 IO, Secret Letters from Aden 35, pp. 25–6, 209–11, Baroni to Coghlan, 20 Dec. 1855, 30 Mar. and 6 Apr. 1856; FO 401/1, pp. 270–3, Plowden to Clarendon, 17 Feb. and 22 Apr. 1856; p. 274, Baroni to Bruce, 14 May, 1856; AECP, Massouah 2, fols 99–102, 117–20, Beillard to Walewski, 31 May, 27 Jul., and 1 Sep. 1856. The French agent reported that it was the *na'ib* who threatened Mensa and Bogos, instigated by Plowden.
62 FO 401/1, p. 275, Clarendon to Stratford de Redcliffe, 2 Jul. 1856.
63 ibid., pp. 264–5, Bruce to Stratford de Redcliffe, 16 Feb. 1856; pp. 266, Clarendon to Stratford de Redcliffe, 6 Mar. 1856.
64 ibid., pp. 282–3, Plowden to Clarendon, 11 Nov. 1856. See above, pp. 177–8.
65 FO 401/1, p. 283, Plowden to Clarendon, 12 Nov. 1856.
66 ibid., pp. 286–8, Plowden to Clarendon, 15 Jan. 1857. For the visit of Qērilos, see below, pp. 210–11.

He would first deal with his internal enemies, and find a temporary solution at least to the conflict with Egypt. He would not seek British friendship out of fear. He maintained, moreover, his refusal to hear about any foreign consul in his kingdom.[67] By September Plowden was instructed that while he could give up the clause about judicial powers if necessary, he should remind the King that good faith prevented his repudiation of the 1849 treaty. The consul, however, found it too dangerous 'to refer to this or any other matter connected with a Treaty, until . . . the King shall bring on the *tapis* his idea of an Embassy to England . . .'[68] Plowden was about to give up the whole business; Flad reported that the consul despaired.[69]

When the Patriarch was finally dismissed in November 1857, Tēwodros took the opportunity to send a letter to Queen Victoria. It was friendly, but said very little. The King had not written earlier because he had not yet pacified his country and consolidated his rule. He hoped with God's help to achieve this, and would then send Plowden and some of his own *shimagillē* (advisers) to inform the Queen so that she could share in his joy. They were both Christ's children, and it was for the sake of the love of Christ that he wanted her friendship.[70] There is no commitment regarding Egypt, nor any reference to the consulate or any other treaty obligations.

Plowden noted that Tēwodros had avoided calling him a consul, and maintained that the King would never 'consent to the residence of Consuls here, or to the planting of a flag in any part of his dominions'. He also pointed out that Tēwodros had refused to ask for any material assistance though invited to do so, and this in spite of the fact that he now knew that others were preparing to aid his rival Nigusē. The consul believed that the refusal was due to Tēwodros's concern about his dignity as the King of Ethiopia, and suggested, not without hesitation, that a gift of 200–300 muskets with caps and powder should nevertheless be sent 'as a sign of true and disinterested friendship'.[71] Small amounts of purchased arms and powder of course passed through Massawa for Tēwodros or his governors in the north. Besides Plowden's agent Baroni, Schimper and the Italian missionary Leone des Avanchers were reportedly involved in the import of arms and powder, on this more private and commercial basis.[72] When the

67   FO 401/1, pp. 288–9, 292–3, Plowden to Clarendon, 5 Feb., 2 Apr., and 20 May 1857.
68   ibid., p. 295, Clarendon to Plowden, 3 Mar. 1857; p. 299, Plowden to Clarendon, 7 Sep. 1857. See also Spittler-Archiv, D 3/2, Flad to Krapf, 26 Oct. 1857.
69   FO 401/1, p. 293, Plowden to Clarendon, 20 May 1857; Spittler-Archiv, D 3/2, Flad to Krapf, 26 Oct. 1857.
70   FO 1/10, fol. 161, Tēwodros to Victoria, n.d. (November 1857). This is the Amharic original stamped with the only seal which appears on any of Tēwodros's letters from this date onwards. The English translation follows on fol. 162.
71   FO 401/1, p. 304, Plowden to Clarendon, 25 Nov. 1857; Dufton, *Narrative*, pp. 101–2, 147. For the French contacts with Nigusē, which were no secret at Gonder (FO 401/1, pp. 280–1, Plowden to Clarendon, 5 Oct. 1856; p. 296, Baroni to Coghlan, 18 Sep. 1857), see below, pp. 189–92.
72   AECP, Massouah 2, fols 117–18, 134–5, 155–6, Beillard to Walewski, 27 Jul., 10 Feb., and 5 Aug. 1857; BN, Ethiop. 184, fol. 68, Kasa [Sebagadis] to Baroni, n.d., received 3 Nov. 1856. The note that this letter was from the 'future Tēwodros' is misleading. Even if the transaction took place in early 1856, it is out of the question that Tēwodros or anyone in his

British government agreed to the suggested gift of arms, Plowden recommended that they be kept at Aden until Tēwodros had occupied Tigrē, which shows that the consul did not intend them to play any role in the internal conflicts. In the end, the British government backed out; an ornamented rifle for the King, without ammunition, was all that was sent.[73]

Plowden continued to report that the King was eager to send an embassy to London,[74] but he was quite aware that Tēwodros was not going to accept co-operation on British terms. The consul therefore recommended a policy in two stages: to begin with, the British government should continue to restrain Sa'id Pasha from any eventual attack, in order to give Tēwodros time to pacify the country. But if the King thereafter refused to accept the British proposals, it would

be expedient perhaps that the Viceroy of Egypt should show him the power of discipline and the resources of civilization, thereby compelling him to have recourse to the friendly mediation of allies . . . It is evident that should such a blow be given to his yet infant authority it cannot resist the shock, and Egypt must then possess Abyssinia as the lesser evil.[75]

He also decided that he might as well leave Ethiopia and await future developments in England. Tēwodros was about to receive an embassy from Sa'id Pasha, and did not care whether Plowden stayed or not. Illness prevented the immediate departure of the consul, and he found himself once more charged, in no uncertain terms, with the task of telling Tēwodros on behalf of the British government that his religious policy was objectionable.[76] Plowden, who had so often defended the King's policy, maintained that the rebuke was both inadvisable and futile, but finally complied. In so doing he used pretty harsh words, in the English version of the letter at least.[77] Tēwodros accepted it as a letter from Victoria, the only reply he received to his friendly letter of November 1857, but was unmoved by the accusations that he had persecuted French subjects. All he had done was to refuse to allow De Jacobis to teach in his country.[78]

The King was actually too busy with the impending campaign against Nigusē

---

service should have styled the King 'Dejjazmach Kasa'. For Padre Leone the supplying of some arms was probably the means he chose to be able to cross Tēwodros's territories to Kefa. See also AEMD, Afrique 61, fols 42–3, Leone des Avanchers to Faugère, 4 Sep. 1856.

73 FO 401/1, p. 306, Malmesbury to Plowden, 8 Apr. 1858; p. 318, Plowden to Malmesbury, 15 Nov. 1858; pp. 320–2, correspondence between Foreign Office and War Office, May–July 1859; p. 322, Hammond to Plowden, 31 May 1859; p. 336, Plowden to Malmesbury, 5 Oct. 1859.

74 ibid., pp. 310–11, Plowden to Clarendon, 5 Jun. 1858.

75 ibid., p. 319, Plowden to Malmesbury, 20 Nov. 1858.

76 ibid., pp. 326–8, 335, Plowden to Malmesbury, 1 Feb., 2 Feb., 27 May, and 20 Sep. 1859; pp. 308–9, Malmesbury to Plowden, 25 Jun. 1858.

77 ibid., pp. 329–30, 333, Plowden to Malmesbury, 28 May and 18 Jun. 1859; pp. 353–4, Plowden to Russell, 2 Feb. 1860; p. 354, Plowden to Tēwodros, 25 Oct. 1859.

78 Spittler-Archiv, D 3/9, Saalmüller to Schneller, 12 Oct. 1859 (completed as late as 11 Nov. 1859, if not still later).

to take much notice of Plowden's letter, but the consul thought he knew what his reply would have been:

> ... namely, that he will admit travellers, merchants, and Europeans of all nations into his dominions, but that he will never tolerate any sect or class of men who preach a doctrine contrary to that of his established church, and that he does not acknowledge the right of any other nation or ruler to interfere in his affairs, secular or spiritual.[79]

Plowden may well, because of his own priorities, have exaggerated both the King's willingness to accept merchants and his unwillingness to accept missionaries. It was not preaching but the implications, internal and external, of a second ecclesiastical hierarchy that bothered Tēwodros.[80] The preoccupation in Paris (and therefore London) with the fate of De Jacobis and the Catholic mission has tended to obscure the fact that the stand taken by Tēwodros on that issue was only a manifestation of his determination not to acknowledge the right of any foreign nation to interfere in his affairs, *secular or spiritual*.

This determination was the guiding principle of the Ethiopian ruler in all his dealings with the British consul who tried to represent Europe and lay the groundwork for interference. In five years Plowden did not even manage to be acknowledged as a consul, much less secure any of the judicial and commercial privileges embodied in the 1849 treaty. These matters had to await the day when Tēwodros's own envoys would be able to report on how these things operated in European countries. Instead of gaining influence, Plowden had gradually lost the little good will which his early contacts with Bell and Abune Selama had given him. The unwillingness of the consul to raise the issue of the Catholic mission once more, and the harshness with which he finally addressed the King reflect the strained relations of his last year at Gonder.[81]

It would be wrong to ascribe Plowden's failure to personal shortcomings. He showed far more knowledge and understanding of Ethiopian affairs than most other Europeans who resided in the country in the nineteenth century. He did not underestimate Tēwodros nor misunderstand his aims. The King wanted relations with Europe and Europeans in Ethiopia in order to develop the country, but on his own conditions. Plowden was personally and by his position as British consul committed to a policy of economic exploitation which called for some influence on the decisions of the ruler. The conflict of interests was too great. In January 1860, the Foreign Office finally ordered Plowden to get out of Abyssinia. Before the instructions could reach him, he had left for the coast, only to lose his life in a skirmish with a small band of rebels just outside Gonder.[82] Tēwodros was, quite naturally, affected by the violent death of the consul, which

79 FO 401/1, pp. 353–4, Plowden to Russell, 2 Feb. 1860.
80 See above, pp. 177–8.
81 Flad (Spittler-Archiv, D 3/2, to Krapf, 3 Oct. 1859) stated in plain words that the King had broken off friendly relations with the consul; Zander was instead in great favour.
82 FO 401/1, pp. 337–8, Russell to Plowden, 18 Jan. 1860; p. 358, Colquhoun to Russell, 2 May 1860, with enclosures from Baroni, 30 Mar. 1860, and from Mircha, Mahdere Qal and Muhammad, 18 Feb. 1860; ADEN, AIA 286, Bell to Baroni, 12 Mar. 1860; AECP, Massouah 3, fols 33–5, Nigusē to Thouvenel, 8 Mar. 1860.

was by many regarded as a political assassination, and promised to take revenge on the rebel chief Garred, who was his own nephew.[83] But it was when John Bell died less than one year later in a battle, in which also Garred lost his life, that anti-foreign elements in the population expressed their satisfaction that the support of the Europeans had disappeared.[84] That Bell, 'the King's man', should be regarded as the powerful foreigner, and not the British consul, indicates how completely Tēwodros had maintained his independence of the first resident representative of a foreign government in Ethiopia.

Nigusē and the Catholics: The Prospect of Two Ethiopian States

In 1855 the French representative at Massawa had rejected the plea of Tēwodros for some understanding of his actions towards the Catholic missionaries. This attitude was maintained for five years, and not only prevented all direct communication between Tēwodros and the representatives of France, but caused the latter to involve themselves in the civil war on Nigusē's side.[85] At first there was some hope that the Coptic Patriarch could be persuaded to go to Ethiopia, or at least send a delegation there, to force Abune Selama and Tēwodros to reverse the decisions on the Catholic mission.[86] Qērilos had earlier written to Selama to stop the persecution,[87] and in 1856 he went to Ethiopia. But if he made any attempt to argue the case in front of Tēwodros, it can only have contributed to the disgrace into which he fell immediately after his arrival.[88]

De Jacobis hoped that Tēwodros would not last long, and recommended the French government to invite Aṣe Yohannis, who was reported to be a Catholic, to France, in preparation for his return to the throne.[89] Yohannis had already been promised financial support, but how De Jacobis could count on him as a potential de facto ruler is a mystery.[90] In fact, a new choice was made by mid-1856. Bishop and vice-consul threw their support behind Nigusē Welde Mīka'ēl, the nephew and political heir of Wibē.

83 FO 401/1, p. 362, Playfair to Wood, 12 May 1860; 'Th. von Heuglin's Expedition nach Inner-Afrika', Petermann, 1861, pp. 347–8.
84 Spittler-Archiv, D 3/9, Saalmüller to Schneller, 13 Jan. 1861. According to Stern (Wanderings, p. 128), the battle in question took place on 31 October. It was Stern's statement that 'three thousand rebels, with their leader, Gerat, were . . . mercilessly butchered in cold blood . . .' that later infuriated Tēwodros against the missionary.
85 See above, pp. 176–7.
86 AECP, Massouah 2, fols 79–90, De Jacobis to Walewski and Napoleon III, 24 Feb. 1856; fols 109–10, memorandum on De Jacobis's proposals, July 1856.
87 ibid., fols 109–10, memorandum, July 1856; AVA 1/1, Qērilos to Selama, 2 Oct. 1853 (copy of a translation).
88 See below, pp. 210–11. Qērilos did not arrive in a French ship, as De Jacobis had proposed, but through the Sudan, and the French consul reported his arrival at Gonder as a rumour long after it had taken place. Nevertheless, he also reported that it was a protest against Selama's and Tēwodros's intolerance that caused the King's anger. See AECP, Massouah 2, fols 134–5, 147–8, Beillard to Walewski, 10 Feb. and 7 May 1857.
89 AECP, Massouah 2, fols 79–90, De Jacobis to Walewski and Napoleon III, 24 Feb. 1856.
90 ibid., fol. 22, Yohannis to Napoleon III, 1853/54, in fact July 1854; fols 61–2, Walewski to Delaye, 9 May 1855.

During the rainy season of 1855, Nigusē had scored some victories over Tēwodros's forces in the Gonder region, but he soon returned to build up his strength in Simēn and Tigrē.[91] It was commonly expected that Tēwodros, who returned from Shewa in July 1856, would undertake a campaign to Simēn and Tigrē immediately after the rainy season of that year.[92] In this situation, Nigusē wrote to Napoleon III and asked for assistance:

> Be my father and I will be your son. Now a rebel king has risen against me. Since he has destroyed the Christians, help me according to your knowledge, if possible by *Nehasē* [August], if not, by *Meskerem* [September]. Until then I will wait, moving about here and there. I have made Abune Ya'iqob [De Jacobis] [my] father. Moreover, I will not act against your will.[93]

There is no reason to doubt that this letter was written by an Ethiopian. The quality of the paper and the very poor stamp used do not indicate any direct participation by foreigners. The same can be said about the unrealistic expectation that military assistance of any kind could arrive within two to three months, and the absence of references to 'protection', cession of the coast, and permission for the Catholic missionaries to travel and work in the country.[94]

On the other hand, it was almost certainly the Catholic bishop and the French agent who had once more taken the initiative. After a vacancy of about nine months, Vice-consul Chauvin Beillard arrived at Massawa in May 1856, and in a dispatch where he reported that he had taken charge of the consular archives on 17 May, he also mentioned that Nigusē had been alerted about Plowden's activities.[95] Moreover, the bearer of Nigusē's letter went straight to De Jacobis, who could report only nine days after it had been written that the chief had asked for recognition by Napoleon, and that the vice-consul had undertaken to forward the request, provided that Nigusē promised freedom and protection to the Catholics. This condition had allegedly been ratified both in the letter to Paris (which was incorrect) and in one to De Jacobis himself, and it clearly indicates who was behind the initiative.[96]

In his covering dispatch to Nigusē's letter, the French vice-consul provided important additional information: Nigusē had given the Catholics a refuge, and had offered to declare De Jacobis the *abun* of Abyssinia; he urged the vice-consul

91 FO 401/1, pp. 268, 273, Plowden to Clarendon, 28 Nov. and 15 Dec. 1855, 22 Apr. 1856; Fusella, *Tēwodros*, p. 25; Lejean, *Théodore II*, p. 59.
92 FO 401/1, pp. 277, 279, Plowden to Clarendon, 23 Jun. and 5 Aug. 1856; [Zeneb], *Tēwodros*, p. 27.
93 AECP, Massouah 2, fol. 107, Nigusē to Napoleon III, 9 Jun. 1856 (Amharic original). The French translation (fol. 106) is fairly correct in substance.
94 Cf. above, pp. 109–13, 125–7.
95 AECP, Massouah 2, fols 99–102, 117–18, Beillard to Walewski, 31 May and 27 Jul. 1856; Lejean, *Théodore II*, pp. 88–9.
96 CML, De Jacobis, 'Lettres manuscrites', Vol. II, no. 371, 17 Jun. 1856. In a rather transparent attempt to shield De Jacobis from any eventual criticism for involving himself once more in politics, Beillard stressed (AECP, Massouah 2, fols 104–5, to Walewski, 30 Jun. 1856) that the bishop would have nothing to do with Nigusē's letter, not even translate it. See also Luigi Fusella, 'L'ambasciata francese a Nĕgusē', *RSE*, VII (1948), p. 180.

to fly the French flag in Tigrē, and asked for instructors for his army and advisers for himself.[97] If these offers and requests came from Nigusē at all— and in that case as a verbal message—they can only have been made in response to suggestions and conditions proposed to him. The alternative is that they were invented by the messenger, the bishop, and/or the vice-consul.[98]

The invasion of Simēn and Tigrē by the King did not take place as expected. Preoccupied with other matters, he left the situation there to Kasa Sebagadis and other governors such as Dejjazmach Haylu Tewelde Medhin of Hamasēn, who had also been sent back to his old province after Wibē's fall. Kasa's return to Agamē after fifteen years' absence led to renewed persecutions of the Catholics there.[99] But during the first half of 1857 Nigusē consolidated his power in Tigrē, and even Kasa came to terms with the successful rebel.[100] This was a period of tremendous confusion and the most fantastic rumours in the north: Tēwodros was dead or insane or had been deserted by his whole army; Plowden and the *abun* were actually ruling the country; an Egyptian army accompanied by some Frenchmen, including Ferdinand de Lesseps, had reached Gonder.[101]

Although he had still no reply from Paris, Beillard took the opportunity, no doubt in consultation with De Jacobis, to send Abba Imnetu to Nigusē's camp when the latter arrived in Agamē in May 1857. After a month there, he could report that Nigusē was the master of all Tigrē, and that Kasa served in his army; nevertheless, Nigusē had only 3,000 to 4,000 muskets, which would be far too few if Tēwodros attacked.[102] In August, Nigusē sent a delegation to Massawa to proclaim to the Turkish governor that he was now the ruler of Tigrē, and to ask Beillard what the French government had replied to his request for military assistance. Embarrassed that he had no reply to give, the vice-consul, according to his own account, answered that aid had been sent and

97 AECP, Massouah 2, fols 104–5, Beillard to Walewski, 30 Jun. 1856.
98 I have not been able to identify the messenger or envoy, but everything points to a Catholic and confidant of De Jacobis. A likely choice would have been Abba Imnete Maryam (Imnetu), who had been used several times before to establish contacts of this kind and who played a major role in the negotiations that followed. See CML, De Jacobis, 'Giornale Abissino', Vol. IV, pp. 61, 104, 111, 132; Vol. V, pp. 134, 138; Vol. VI, p. 1. Another possibility is Debtera Kinfu, who was mentioned by Plowden (FO 401/1, pp. 300, 302–3, to Malmesbury, 8 Sep. and 18 Nov. 1857) as a Catholic convert and confidant of De Jacobis for many years, but in the service of Nigusē in 1857.
99 FO 401/1, pp. 277, 280–1, Plowden to Clarendon, 23 Jun. and 5 Oct. 1856; AECP, Massouah 2, fols 129–30, 134–5, 142–5, Beillard to Walewski, 27 Dec. 1856, 10 Feb. and 25 Apr. 1857; CML, De Jacobis, 'Giornale Abissino', Vol. V, pp. 124–5.
100 CML, De Jacobis, 'Giornale Abissino', Vol. V, p. 134; AECP, Massouah 2, fols 151–2, Beillard to Walewski, 13 Jul. 1857.
101 AECP, Massouah 2, fols 127–8, 147–8, 151–2, 157–8, Beillard to Walewski, 16 Nov. 1856, 7 May, 13 Jul., and 10 Sep. 1857; CML, De Jacobis, 'Giornale Abissino', Vol. V, pp. 122, 124, 132; AECP(Brussels), Égypte 2, Zizinia to Vilain, 19 Jan. 1857.
102 AECP, Massouah 2, fols 151–2, Beillard to Walewski, 13 Jul. 1857; CML, De Jacobis, 'Giornale Abissino', Vol. V, p. 134. There seems to have been a very good understanding between the bishop and the vice-consul at this time (Crummey, *Priests*, pp. 100–1), and the choice of envoy also indicates that De Jacobis was involved. I have found no evidence, however, that he actually visited Nigusē himself during the first year of contacts. Cf. FO 401/1, pp. 280–1, Plowden to Clarendon, 5 Oct. 1856.

that Nigusē ought to contact the Egyptian army which now threatened Tēwodros from the Sudan.[103]

Beillard returned the visit in September in company with some Ethiopian Catholic priests and with a small gift of fifteen muskets.[104] He believed, however, that his visit would be of great value to Nigusē as a kind of recognition of the 'new king' by a great European power. The presence of a British consul with Tēwodros would be counterbalanced by the accreditation of a French consul with Nigusē. But Beillard wanted more than Plowden was getting from Tēwodros. He again reported that he was asked to fly the French flag in Tigrē, and gave a long account of a council at which the Ali–Plowden treaty of 1849 was discussed. It was allegedly agreed, firstly, that the treaty was invalid; at least, it had not been signed 'since he [Ali] did not know how to write'; secondly, that Plowden was not a regularly accredited consul anywhere in Ethiopia; thirdly, that whatever the status of the treaty and the consulship of Plowden, it was permissible to take action against his messengers and agents in Tigrē, 'a great blessing for Tigrē . . . and, I may as well say it, a great comfort for the Catholic mission if not for the French agency at Massawa'. Aware that he would probably be criticized in Paris for his participation in these discussions, Beillard reported that he had upheld the official position of his colleague, and added that 'the interference of a foreigner in the affairs of the country displeases no one here'; Plowden was envied and hated only because Tēwodros allowed him to dominate everyone and everything.[105] The third conclusion had immediate consequences. One of Plowden's couriers was arrested at Adwa; eleven dispatches and letters were taken, opened, and sent to Beillard for information and translation. The vice-consul maintained to Paris that he sent everything back without looking at it; but he believed he knew anyhow what the letters contained![106]

Either the spirit in Nigusē's council was very different from what Plowden had met in his dealings with Tēwodros, or Beillard was misled by the Catholic priests who accompanied him and interpreted for him. Tēwodros was reported to have lost everything except Lake Ṭana with 'its island', which three British cannon sufficed to protect temporarily against spears and firearms of poor quality. What Nigusē therefore expected from France was a few cannon, 'to march on Dembīya, and capture the famous island'. Much of Beillard's long report is this kind of nonsense, but he also saw, and reported, some of the actual weaknesses of Nigusē's position: a completely untrained and undisciplined army

---

103   AECP, Massouah 2, fols 153–4, Beillard to Walewski, 5 Aug. 1857. See also Lejean, *Théodore II*, pp. 89–90.

104   FO 401/1, p. 296, Baroni to Coghlan, 18 Sep. 1857; pp. 301–2, Plowden to Clarendon, 15 Nov. 1857; Fusella, 'L'ambasciata', *RSE*, VII, p. 180; Sapeto, *Etiopia*, pp. 324–5.

105   AECP, Massouah 2, fols 172–80, Beillard to Walewski, 19 Oct. 1857.

106   ibid., fol. 187, Beillard to Walewski, 7 Nov. 1857. Plowden was quite naturally enraged that his important dispatches of September 1857 had fallen into the hands of his enemies. He alleged that the culprit was Debtera Kinfu, and that De Jacobis was present when it happened, but this does not necessarily mean that the bishop was behind the action. See above, p. 191, n. 98, with references; also Spittler-Archiv, D 3/2, Flad to Krapf, 26 Oct. 1857.

of no more than 4,000 riflemen and 10,000 spearmen, and no organized government of his territories whatsoever.[107]

The French vice-consul had no cannon to provide, and if he supplied Nigusē
with small arms, it was certainly on a commercial basis, since he had no funds.[108]
He managed, however, to recruit some persons who were supposed to be
able to manufacture cannon, and sent them to Nigusē. Probably they were
capable of doing so in different circumstances, but they seem to have failed
completely in Tigrē.[109] At least one of them, a Frenchman named Joseph
Mackerer, left after a while and went to Gonder to offer his services to Tēwodros
instead.[110] Though he continued to attack and ridicule the opponents of
De Jacobis and Nigusē, the 'triumvirate of the persecution' (Tēwodros, Selama,
Plowden) and 'the poor madman whom five or six Englishmen still call the
Emperor Tēwodros',[111] Beillard was no longer enthusiastic about Nigusē,
whom he accused of irresoluteness, ineptitude, and lack of courage. He blamed
De Jacobis, too, for not teaching the young prince to be more resolute and, if
necessary, severe in his administration, and by mid-1858 there was clear evid-
ence of tension between the bishop and the vice-consul.[112]

The two men had different priorities. Beillard was mainly interested in the
safety of the trade both at Massawa and along the routes from Gonder. He was
eager to see Nigusē destroy Tēwodros because he believed that it would mean the
destruction of Plowden and his agent Baroni.[113] On the other hand, Beillard
was afraid that an occupation of Hamasēn by Nigusē would precipitate an attack
on Massawa or Arkīko either by Nigusē himself or by one of Tēwodros's appointees in the north.[114] He must also have been very concerned about the complete silence with which his many dispatches since May 1856 had been met.[115]
When his superiors in Paris finally decided to respond, in May 1858, Beillard
was informed that there would be no reply to Nigusē's request for assistance, and
warned not to do anything which might entail obligations towards Nigusē in his
struggle against Tēwodros. His reserved attitude, noticeable only in the later
dispatches, was approved.[116]

The main concern of De Jacobis was the safety of his flock in northern
Ethiopia, and permission for himself to continue mission work in Tigrē. He

---

107 AECP, Massouah 2, fol. 187, Beillard to Walewski, 7 Nov. 1857.
108 ibid., fols 153–4, 252–3, 281, Beillard to Walewski, 5 Aug. 1857, 27 May and 21 Sep. 1858.
109 ibid., fols 246–7, Beillard to Walewski, 7 May 1858.
110 Spittler-Archiv, D 3/9, Saalmüller to Schneller, 12 Oct. 1859.
111 AECP, Massouah 2, fols 142–5, 187, 246–7, Beillard to Walewski, 25 Apr. and 7 Nov. 1857,
     7 May 1858.
112 ibid., fols 225–6, 246–7, 252–3, 273–4, Beillard to Walewski, 16 Apr., 7 May, 27 May, and
     16 Aug. 1858; BN, Ethiop. 184, fol. 92, De Jacobis to Beillard, 24 Sep. 1858.
113 AECC, Massouah 1, fols 185–6, 192, Beillard to Walewski, 15 Sep. 1857 and 15 Sep. 1858;
     AECP, Massouah 2, fols 252–3, 272–4, Beillard to Walewski, 27 May and 16 Aug. 1858.
114 AECP, Massouah 2, fols 225–6, Beillard to Walewski, 16 Apr. 1858.
115 In May 1858 he pleaded (ibid., fols 252–3, to Walewski, 27 May 1858) for one word, just
     one, in reply to his dispatches.
116 AECP, Massouah 2, fols 263–5, Walewski to Beillard, 14 May 1858; see also fols 238–45,
     'Note pour le Ministre concernant les affaires d'Abyssinie', 5 May 1858.

therefore preferred to see Nigusē consolidate his position and extend his control to Hamasēn (and possibly Bogos) rather than risk everything in a premature battle with Tēwodros. This difference with regard to immediate objectives was at least one of the factors behind Beillard's accusation that the mission was involved in politics on its own.[117]

Neither De Jacobis nor other spokesmen for the Catholic church were deterred by the lack of enthusiasm for Nigusē demonstrated at Massawa and in Paris. In a long memorandum from Rome, the pioneer of the Lazarists in Ethiopia, Giuseppe Sapeto, argued that Nigusē was a man of peace who was prepared to pay tribute to Tēwodros as a loyal vassal, provided he was granted the same autonomy in Tigrē as his predecessors had enjoyed. Sapeto urged the French government to inform Tēwodros of this, and at the same time to send a mission to Nigusē with a few cannon.[118] De Jacobis wanted a Tigrean mission to Rome and Paris, but Beillard resisted the idea.[119] It was only in September 1858, as Beillard prepared to leave his post, that an understanding seems to have been reached between the bishop and the vice-consul again. On 21 September, Beillard was still uncertain whether he should visit Nigusē before leaving;[120] he had, in fact, refused to do so for almost one year.[121] Three days later, however, De Jacobis wrote and called for his assistance:

> The affair increases and I limit myself to informing you that I have seen the King. He is perfectly in your hands, in my hands, in our hands . . . Yesterday he started out for Hamasēn. He will invite you to be so kind as to visit him in order to assist him by your advice . . .[122]

Ten days later De Jacobis reported that the vice-consul had visited Nigusē in his camp in Hamasēn, and had made him decide to send ambassadors to Napoleon III.[123] It was probably a sudden and successful attack by Nigusē on Dejjazmach Haylu of Hamasēn that paved the way for the meeting. With Hamasēn and Serayē in his hands, Nigusē looked much more impressive from the horizon of Massawa. Unfortunately, there is no report by Beillard about the meeting.[124] De Jacobis's letter to Beillard, however, makes it abundantly clear that the bishop, and no one else, engineered the agreement about the embassy. It

---

117 ibid., fols 273–4, Beillard to Walewski, 16 Aug. 1858.
118 ibid., fols 205–17, 'Exposé historique des missions catholiques des missionaires Lazaristes français en Abyssinie, fait par l'un d'entr'eux pour obtenir de Sa Maj. Imp. une protection bienveillante et efficace', 24 Jan. 1858.
119 ibid., fols 246–7, Beillard to Walewski, 7 May 1858; Lejean, *Théodore II*, p. 92. It was mentioned by De Jacobis to Rome as early as December 1857. See Crummey, *Priests*, pp. 102–3.
120 AECP, Massouah 2, fol. 281, Beillard to Walewski, 21 Sep. 1858.
121 ibid., fols 273–4, Beillard to Walewski, 16 Aug. 1858.
122 BN, Ethiop. 184, fol. 92, De Jacobis to Beillard, 24 Sep. 1858.
123 AECP, Massouah 2, fol. 282, De Jacobis to Walewski, 4 Oct. 1858.
124 Lejean, *Théodore II*, pp. 95–6. Beillard left for Europe on 2 October, and De Jacobis seems to have been informed of the outcome of the meeting by Imnetu. See CML, De Jacobis, 'Giornale Abissino', Vol. V, p. 138.

also seems to indicate that Nigusē was unaware of some of its implications.[125]

The ambassadors selected were Abba Imnetu and a 'cousin' of Nigusē's, Lij Ṭaqayē. A French traveller, Lepère de Lapereuse, was to accompany the two as their secretary and interpreter.[126] It was probably agreed that he should step aside in favour of Sapeto as soon as the delegation reached Rome.[127] The central role of De Jacobis in this diplomatic initiative is further demonstrated by the long memorandum with which the bishop provided the envoys. In this he maintained, firstly, that all the European travellers from Gobat to Plowden (and he lists sixteen whom he knew personally) as well as all the French vice-consuls from Degoutin to Beillard were unanimous in their opinion that the regeneration of Abyssinia could only take place through a rapprochement with Europe; secondly, that the necessity of this had been felt by the Ethiopians throughout their history as well as by recent rulers: Sahle Sillasē, Ali, Wibē, and even Tēwodros. After this long introduction, De Jacobis presented the young victorious prince, 'King Nigusē', who had won the sympathies of the rulers of Shewa, Amhara, and Gojjam and himself added Dembīya and Begēmdir to the provinces which he had inherited from his uncle Wibē. Finally, the bishop outlined the objectives of the embassy which, on his advice, was to visit Rome as well as Paris. The envoys were instructed to express Nigusē's feelings of attachment to and veneration for the Pope and declare his intention to embrace Catholicism as soon as the political situation made this possible without endangering peace in the country; for the time being, he guaranteed the Catholics in his territories the free exercise of their faith and their ministry. In Paris they were to announce the desire of Nigusē to be regarded as an ally of France and his willingness to allow French consuls to fly the French flag in his country. If the French government would inform him of their commercial, political, and strategic objectives in the area, Nigusē, moreover, declared in advance that he would do everything in his power to fulfil their desires. In return the envoys were to ask the French to assist in the struggle against Tēwodros by furnishing arms and, if possible, placing auxiliary troops at Nigusē's disposal.[128]

125 Crummey emphasizes (*Priests*, pp. 101–4) the reluctance with which De Jacobis involved himself in these negotiations. This is no doubt the attitude which emerges from the bishop's correspondence with Europe. See, in addition, Sapeto, *Etiopia*, p. 333. Nevertheless he was actively involved not only in the last stages, and it is unlikely that his priests or other followers would have engaged themselves as they did without approval or encouragement.

126 AECP, Massouah 2, fols 283–6, De Jacobis, 'Mémoire sur l'Ambassade envoyée à Sa Majesté Napoléon III, Empereur des français, par Négoucié, roi d'Abyssinie, le 26 Octobre 1858'. In his letter to Beillard (BN, Ethiop. 184, fol. 92), De Jacobis spoke of the envoys as 'our two priests'. Whether Ṭaqayē qualified as a Catholic priest or replaced one of the two originally selected is not known. He was at any rate almost certainly a Catholic, since Sapeto introduced Imnetu as his father confessor in his account 'Ambasciata mandata nel 1869 [sic] dal governo francese a Negussié . . .', *BSGI*, VI (1871), pp. 22–71. See also Fouyas, 'An unpublished document', *Abba Salama*, I, p. 57.

127 Fusella, 'L'ambasciata', *RSE*, VII, p. 181; Lejean, *Théodore II*, p. 92; APF.SRC, Africa Centrale, Etiopia ecc . . . 6, fol. 246, De Jacobis to Sapeto, 1 Dec. 1858.

128 AECP, Massouah 2, fols 283–6, De Jacobis, 'Mémoire', 26 Oct. 1858; lengthy extract in Sapeto, *Etiopia*, pp. 332–8.

In his own letter to the French emperor, Nigusē allegedly expressed willingness to receive French consuls in his domains, requested assistance in very general terms and explained that he had taken up arms against Tēwodros because this 'fanatic savage' had imposed a new creed on everyone.[129] Both this letter and one to the Pope, speaking favourably about the Catholic faith, were almost certainly written by De Jacobis on Nigusē's behalf.[130] Additional letters from De Jacobis to the Pope and to mission headquarters in Paris to do everything possible to assist the embassy were also dispatched with the embassy on 8 November.[131]

In Rome the envoys delivered their message to the Holy Father and were, on their return from Paris, given a papal letter to Nigusē, which was, however, not delivered to him, probably because De Jacobis did not find it satisfactory from the point of view of his relations with Nigusē.[132] In Paris they were given an audience by Napoleon III, but, judging from the Emperor's reply to Nigusē, little other encouragement.[133] In an attempt to create more interest, Sapeto declared that Nigusē in addition to other concessions was prepared to cede territory on the coast to France, which would make it possible for her to benefit from the immense wealth of the country and prevent British control of the Red Sea. He proposed a treaty with Nigusē establishing a French consul in Abyssinia with all the prerogatives of consuls in the Orient, the cession of Zulla (and possibly Ras Dumara) with an undertaking by Nigusē to divert the caravan trade to the French port, and the landing of 500–600 men to place the consul at Adwa and eventually support Nigusē militarily.[134] There is nothing to indicate that Ṭaqayē and Imnetu had been authorized to offer cessions of territory. But there can be no doubt that Imnetu was informed of the suggestions made by Sapeto in this respect, and reported them to Nigusē on his return to Ethiopia in September 1859.[135]

129   Sapeto, *Etiopia*, pp. 339–40. There is a mention of an autographed letter, presumably from Nigusē, in a Quai d'Orsay memorandum of 15 March 1859 (AECP, Massouah 2, fols 309–10), and a letter from Nigusē is also mentioned in a draft of Napoleon's reply in AED, Protocole C41, Éthiopie, but I have not been able to trace any text of this letter other than the French version in Sapeto's printed notes.
130   Sapeto, *Etiopia*, pp. 340–1, De Jacobis's reported reply to Sapeto when the latter criticized Nigusē's letter for being too vague: '. . . look here, he [Nigusē] told me, when that letter is to be sent, take my seal, write and sign everything as you find best. I have opened my heart; you can therefore be the interpreter of it to the Holy Father.'
131   CML, De Jacobis, 'Giornale Abissino', Vol. V, p. 138; 'Lettres manuscrites', Vol. II, no. 383.
132   Fusella, 'L'ambasciata', *RSE*, VII, pp. 181–2; AECP, Massouah 2, fols 343–6, Gilbert to Walewski, 20 Dec. 1859. Lejean (*Théodore II*, p. 92) states that the letter was withheld but gives no reason other than 'inexplicable intrigues'.
133   AED, Protocole C41, Napoleon III to Nigusē, undated draft
134   AECP, Massouah 2, fols 313–20, Sapeto to Napoleon III, 10 Apr. 1859.
135   ibid., fol. 333, Nigusē to Napoleon III, 1 Nov. 1859, Amharic original; fols 331–2, French translation certified by Gilbert. The dating of this document is extremely confused. The original is dated both in the Gregorian calendar, 1 Hidar (November) 1859 (= 22 Ṭiqimt 1852 E.C.), and in the Ethiopian calendar, 24 Ṭiqimt 1851 (= 2 Nov. 1858). Since only a careless conversion of the Gregorian year to the Ethiopian can explain the mistake with regard to the year, it seems best to assume that the Gregorian date, though

In the meantime Nigusē had been approached by a number of other people who wanted to protect the Catholics, secure political and commercial advantages, or supply arms and mercenaries. In February 1859 the missionary Leone des Avanchers, acting on behalf of the Sardinian government, presented Nigusē with a draft treaty which would guarantee religious freedom for Catholics, European as well as Ethiopian, in Nigusē's territories, and establish reciprocal consular representation and commercial privileges. How far he got in his negotiations is difficult to say. He added and signed 'fait au camp du . . . (made in the camp of . . .)' to the draft, noting that he had 'received the reply from the mouth of the prince that he would be very happy to be able to conclude it with the government'. In a covering letter two days later, he confirmed that Nigusē was prepared to 'sign and fulfil all the conditions of the attached treaty', and added that the prince would not refuse to cede a province in the neighbourhood of the port of Andada (between Zulla and Anfilla) in exchange for 300–400 European soldiers or, still better, a number of rifles and cannon. But Nigusē's own written response was vague. Instead of 'We accept in every particular the above-mentioned proposal and we are prepared to sign the treaty referred to at once . . .', one finds 'I was very happy to hear that what you wanted was that we conclude a friendly alliance and establish a complete commercial convention, but let your deputy come soon and conclude this convention'.[136] There is no mention of the Catholic mission work, still less any hint of a request for military assistance or an offer of territory. What Padre Stella and the Italian trader and would-be consul, Antonio Rizzo, wanted the Sardinian government to interest itself in acquiring was, in fact, nothing less than the important province of Hamasēn.[137]

Other people involved were mainly gunrunners and adventurers who converged on Massawa as the prospects of making money became known. The leaders seem to have been an Irishman, Kirwan Joyce, and an Austrian, Bernard Gerhard. Baroni's first reports in April spoke of a large Catholic organization committed to a holy war against Tēwodros and of expected arms shipments to the tune of 10,000–20,000 rifles. Baroni admitted, however, that he could not vouch for the truth of everything the newcomers were said to have told their

---

written in Amharic, is the real date; 24 Ṭiqimt 1852 is actually 3 Nov. 1859. In the French translation, the dates are 20 October 1859, which is 10 Ṭiqimt and not 9 Ṭiqimt as the document has. For Imnetu's return, see ADEN, A1A 286, Baroni to Coghlan, 24 Sep. 1859. Ṭaqayē had perished after a shipwreck.

136 ASMAI 36/1–1, 'Traité d'amitié et de commerce . . .', 10 Feb. 1859; Nigusē to Victor Emmanuel II, 10 Feb. 1859; Leone des Avanchers to Cavour, 12 Feb. 1859. These documents are printed in *AP.DD*, 1889–90, XV, pp. 8–11. See Roberto Battaglia, *La prima guerra d'Africa* (Torino, 1958), pp. 58–66, for a careful analysis of this first Italian attempt to gain a foothold on the Red Sea coast and in Ethiopia. Battaglia maintains (p. 63) that the missionary was involved in deliberate ambiguity, while Fusella ('L'ambasciata', *RSE*, VII, p. 176) and Giglio (*Etiopia–Mar Rosso*, Vol. I, p. 56) speak of the offer of territory and the request for military assistance as if they were established facts, and Crummey (*Priests*, p. 105) of the treaty as if it had been actually concluded.

137 *AP.DD*, 1889–90, XV, pp. 15–17, Stella to Cavour, 3 Oct. 1859; pp. 17–19, Rizzo to Cavour, 9 Oct. 1859; ADEN, A1A 286, Baroni to Coghlan, 24 Apr. 1859.

friends. Much lower but surer figures were mentioned for the arms and ammunition actually sold and delivered to Nigusē, 450 rifles on one occasion, 700 on another, but there is no reason to doubt that there were promises of more, including cannon, allegedly at 750 thalers a piece or in exchange for a governorship.[138] That Kirwan Joyce represented anything but his own economic interests is highly unlikely.[139] Nevertheless, it is understandable that talk of a Catholic crusade against Tēwodros arose; in fact, De Jacobis had himself, in his memorandum on Nigusē's embassy to Paris, expressed the desire to go to Europe and emulate Peter the Hermit.[140] The rumours and the reports about Europeans who were coming to act as military instructors in Nigusē's army increased the likelihood that Tēwodros would no longer postpone his long-awaited attack. For Nigusē, as the ruler of a predominantly anti-Catholic Tigrē, they can only have been a liability[141]

The outcome of the embassy to Napoleon III was hardly reassuring. Even the noncommittal reply of Napoleon was probably not handed over.[142] Nigusē

138   ADEN, A1A 286, Baroni to Coghlan, 16 Apr., 20 Apr., 24 Apr., 28 Apr., 24 Aug., 5 Dec., and 17 Dec. 1859; FO 401/1, pp. 331–2, Baroni to Plowden, 8 May 1859; IO, Secret Letters from Aden 37, pp. 179–80, Coghlan to Anderson, 1 Jul. 1859. On a summary to Anderson, 3 May 1859 (ibid., pp. 101–7; FO 401/1, pp. 323–5), of Baroni's April letters, someone minuted, 'This is a wild story but it may perhaps be worth sending to F.O.' In view of the quick profits, Baroni may well have done a bit of clandestine trading with Nigusē himself. See FO 1/11, fols 25–6, Joyce to Russell, 6 Feb. 1860.
139   IO, Secret Letters from Aden 37, pp. 261–3, Coghlan to Anderson, 8 Oct. 1859. The Irishman had been an artillerist in India, interpreter in the Crimea, and head of the secret police in Egypt (ibid., pp. 101–7). At Aden he professed anxiety for the cause of Tēwodros, and Coghlan admitted (ibid., pp. 173–4, to Anderson, 21 Jun. 1859) that he was unable to determine to which side Joyce belonged, but a few months later (ADEN, A1A 286, to Anderson, 26 Nov. 1859) he reported that Joyce had smuggled arms through customs in Vice-consul Gilbert's luggage and departed for Nigusē's camp. In 1863 Joyce emerges at the Foreign Office accusing Plowden of immorality and Baroni of having sold the correspondence of the consulate to 'so-called French priests' (which may have been true). His own record was reported from Cairo: a fugitive bankrupt, recently condemned to six months in prison for forcible abduction of a girl under age: 'He is not a lunatic and he is no fool—but a dangerous man.' (FO 1/11, fols 187–90, minutes, 17 May to 18 Jun. 1863; fol. 260, Colquhoun to Hertslet, 13 Jul. 1863). Gerhard later acted as Austria's first consul at Massawa (FO 401/1, pp. 405–6, Baroni to Playfair, 20 Sep. 1861).
140   AECP, Massouah 2, fols 283–6, 'Mémoire', 26 Oct. 1858.
141   On military instructors, see, for instance, IO, Secret Letters from Aden 37, pp. 125–6, Coghlan to Anderson, 6 Jun. 1859; on concern about Catholicism, Stanislas Russel, *Une Mission en Abyssinie et dans la Mer Rouge 23 octobre–7 mai 1860* (Paris 1884), p. 124; ADEN, A1A 286, Baroni to Coghlan, 24 Apr. 1859. Baroni describes an unsuccessful attempt by some Catholic priests to establish themselves at Adwa in April 1859. De Jacobis remained at Halay, his colleagues in Bogos. There is no evidence that the mission was gaining converts or friends except in the border areas of Akkele Guzay, Bogos, and Mensa. See also Crummey, *Priests*, p. 107. The view of Marston (*Britain's Imperial Role*, pp. 246–7) that the deaths of Plowden and Bell played a major part in the decision of Tēwodros to attack is evidently incorrect, if for no other reason than that they were both still alive.
142   AED, Protocole C41, Napoleon III to Nigusē, undated draft. The fact that Nigusē does not mention any letter is almost certain proof that it did not reach him. It was probably withheld by De Jacobis, as was the letter from the Pope. The bishop received only a courtesy reply from Paris (AECP, Massouah 2, fol. 321).

had, moreover, supplied his envoys Ṭaqayē and Imnetu with funds to purchase arms in Europe. This was almost certainly the main purpose of the mission as far as he was concerned. But these arms had been seized at Suez in the very presence of the French consul there. Niguse's first request to the new vice-consul at Massawa, Théodore Gilbert, was to arrange for their release and shipment to Massawa. He never received them, and later accused the vice-consul of having given them away to his own friends and servants.[143] There was obviously no intention of permitting even a friendly Ethiopian ruler to do any arms shopping except through local gunrunners.

On the basis of Imnetu's reports of what had been discussed with the French government, Niguse decided to make his position clear in writing:

> . . . I beg you to watch over the freedom of my country, to bring enlightenment to my country for me, to protect me from the hands of the plundering Tēwodros. In order to bring this about, two things are necessary. Firstly, if you send me your deputy to look into everything as I asked you before, I will protect him in my country as myself. I will have the French flag planted. Secondly, what I want is two gun-batteries with the artillerists [to serve them]. For what you do for me and for what you will be doing for my country by joining the sea[s] by the Suez canal, I will give you Zulla which is called Ras Dumara.[144]

In the French translation of this document, certified by Gilbert, there is much more emphasis on the sinister ambitions of the British in Ethiopia: Tēwodros is a creature bought by the British; for fifteen years Plowden has in vain tried to get permission to fly the British flag at Gonder (which contradicts, of course, the statement about Tēwodros as a mere British tool). Finally, the claim that Niguse was a Catholic is implied in the phrase 'our holy church', which does not appear in the Amharic original.[145] In his covering letter, Gilbert stressed these aspects still further: Plowden had long tried to induce Niguse to abandon the cause of France, but the latter had remained faithful to his adviser, De Jacobis, whom he had by royal decree proclaimed the 'grand Abouna' of Simēn and Tigrē. There is no evidence that this was true. Reporting it, Gilbert advised his government to send some kind of reply expressing gratitude and promises of good will even if they did not intend to help Niguse; otherwise he might accept from Britain what he did not get from France.[146] A mission to make sure that this would not happen was already on its way.

143 BN, Ethiop. 184, fol. 86, Niguse [to Gilbert], 2 Nov. 1859; AEMD, Afrique 61, fol. 50, Niguse to Napoleon III, 22 Aug. 1860.
144 AECP, Massouah 2, fol. 333, Niguse to Napoleon III, 1 Nov. 1859, Amharic original. Zulla was not called Ras Dumara. The phrase 'Ras Dumara yemībal Zullan' indicates that Imnetu and Niguse had misunderstood the French request for *one* of these places.
145 ibid., fols 331–2. These differences indicate that the Amharic letter was not produced by Imnetu, Gilbert, or De Jacobis at Massawa. The earlier date of the translation (see above, p. 196, n. 135), on the other hand, may mean that there was prior agreement between these three on what the letter was to say, and that Gilbert did not bother to change date or wording, either because he did not know of the changes or because he thought his own version was better.
146 AECP, Massouah 2, fols 325–30, Gilbert to Walewski, 18 Nov. 1859.

Count Stanislas Russel was sent out under the auspices of the Ministry of Algeria and the Colonies.[147] It was made very clear in his instruction that the mission was exploratory and that he should carefully avoid everything which 'in any degree whatsoever' might bind his government. He was even expected to maintain that his voyage was completely unofficial and to inform the consular agents of his objective only 'in case of absolute necessity'. The objective was to explore the African coast of the Red Sea and collect exact information about the political, maritime, and commercial advantages of various places from Massawa to the Gulf of Tajura with a view to a French establishment and relations with Abyssinia, in particular the recruitment there of labourers for the French colony of Réunion. The only reference to Nigusē included in the instructions was that he had, with De Jacobis as his intermediary, claimed the 'protectorate of France'.[148]

At Massawa, where he arrived on 11 December, Russel found De Jacobis and Imnetu waiting. A messenger was sent to Nigusē's camp at Hawzēn to announce the arrival of the mission, while Russel proceeded to explore Desē and Zulla. The courier returned on 28 December, and the following day Russel left Zulla, accompanied by Sapeto, Imnetu, and a European escort of ten officers and marines. De Jacobis was supposed to join the group from Halay.[149] Instead, the embassy became his guests there for more than one month. Russel had arrived too late. Tēwodros had finally attacked.

On 1 January 1860, when rumours at Halay spoke of an imminent battle on the Tekkezē and a retreat by Tēwodros, the King was already at Hawzēn.[150] Nigusē's support immediately crumbled; his troops deserted him in such numbers that he had to leave large supplies of firearms behind as he retreated, first northwards as far as Serayē, and then west- and southwards in order eventually to find refuge in Simēn.[151] Tēwodros did not go beyond Adwa himself, but district governors and other chiefs declared for him, including some in the immediate neighbourhood of Halay. In the early days of February, the mission station was surrounded, and Russel, who had insisted some weeks earlier that

---

147   There are three published accounts (already cited) of the mission by persons involved in it or close to it: Stanislas Russel, *Une Mission*, Giuseppe Sapeto, 'Ambasciata', *BSGI*, VI, pp. 22–71 (also in *Etiopia*, pp. 346–63), and Abba Tekle Haymanot, the latter published by Fusella, 'L'ambasciata', *RSE*, VII, pp. 176–91. See Malécot, 'Voyageurs', *RFHO*, LVIII, pp. 313–21, for other French activities in the Red Sea in 1858–59 and for the differences of opinion between the ministries involved.

148   SOM, Océan Indien, 19/104, Chasseloup-Laubat to Russel, 13 Oct. 1859; printed with significant omissions in Russel, *Une Mission*, pp. 263–6. The absurdity of trying to keep the mission secret is demonstrated by the fact that Baroni could inform Aden (ADEN, A1A 286, to Coghlan, 7 Oct. 1859) that a mission was expected before Russel had even received his instructions.

149   Russel, *Une Mission*, pp. 11–44, *passim*, and pp. 268–70 (letter from Russel to Chasseloup-Laubat, 28 Dec. 1859); Sapeto, 'Ambasciata', *BSGI*, VI, pp. 23–4.

150   Russel, *Une Mission*, pp. 72, 97, 99, 108, 271; ADEN, A1A 286, Baroni to Coghlan, 20 Jan. 1860, with a copy of Bell to Baroni from Hawzēn, 1 Jan. 1860.

151   Zeneb (*Tēwodros*, p. 47), Welde Maryam (*Tēwodros*, pp. 23–4), and the anonymous chronicler (Fusella, *Tēwodros*, p. 25) convey the impression that Nigusē's soldiers were poor and his retreat a stampede. See also AECP, Massouah 3, fols 15–16, Gilbert to Walewski, 5 Feb. 1860; FO 401/1, pp. 354–5, Plowden to Russell, 3 Feb. 1860; Lejean, *Théodore II*, pp. 96–7.

Nigusē send him an escort under a *dejjazmach* to show him the honour due to an ambassador of France,[152] was about to be taken by force to Tēwodros instead. To save the situation, De Jacobis promised to be the guarantor for the members of the embassy. The surveillance was relaxed, and during the night between 7 and 8 February Russel made his secret escape, leaving De Jacobis to face the consequences.[153]

Russel's instructions not to pose as an official representative of France were very clear. The fact that he was the bearer of some gifts to the 'King of Tigrē', a pistol, a revolver, a double-barrelled rifle, and some other items worth 2,000 francs altogether, nevertheless implies that he was supposed to meet Nigusē,[154] and he did not hesitate to make the attempt, or so it seems at least. When he failed and took the gifts back to Massawa, he put the blame on Nigusē, who first sent no escort and then deliberately prevented the meeting by withdrawing when they were within two days' distance of each other.[155] But Russel made a virtue of necessity and decided to regard his mission as a great success. In the process he implied that his trip into the country had actually been unnecessary, since Nigusē had taken the precaution of sending 'his proxy, Abba Imnetu, with fully prepared treaties and his seal' to meet him at Massawa as early as October.[156] But this was hindsight.

It was only after a crucial exchange of messages between Halay and Nigusē's camp at Addī Mengontī in Serayē in mid-January that Russel started to mention negotiations with Imnetu in his notes, and only at the end of that month that he reported them to his government. By then he had obtained Nigusē's seal on, and himself signed, the convention about labourers for Réunion, as well as concluded 'another more important' and absolutely secret negotiation, known only to De Jacobis, who had acted as an interpreter.[157] This implies, of course, that Sapeto was kept out, which is verified by the latter's statement that it was after the return of the embassy to Massawa that 'Russel, who had realized the impossibility of approaching Nigusē, stipulated a treaty of friendship with his representative Imnetu, by which the *ras* conceded many commercial advantages to France and at the same time ceded to her the bay of Zulla' in exchange for 'assistance in men, arms and ammunition'.[158]

152 Russel, *Une Mission*, pp. 49, 111; Fusella, 'L'ambasciata', *RSE*, VII, p. 185.
153 AECP, Massouah 3, fols 17–21, Gilbert to Walewski, 28 Feb. 1860; fols 22–3, Russel to Gilbert, 12 Feb. 1860; SOM, 19/104, Russel to Chasseloup-Laubat, 15 Feb. 1860, printed in *Une Mission*, pp. 277–83, with some significant changes; ADEN, A1A 286, Baroni to Coghlan, 15 Feb. 1860; *Annales*, XXVI (1861), pp. 62–75, Delmonte to Guarini, 14 Feb. 1860; Fusella, 'L'ambasciata', *RSE*, VII, pp. 186–91. The long and detailed account of Russel's diary or memoirs (*Une Mission*, pp. 140–75) is contradicted by the other sources, including his own letters (pp. 268–93), and marred by his all too evident attempts to cover up the somewhat dishonourable circumstances of his flight, but the details of this side of the embassy must be omitted here.
154 SOM, 19/104, Ministry of Algiers and the Colonies memorandum, 27 Oct. 1859.
155 Russel, *Une Mission*, pp. 124–6, 141, 148, 271–4.
156 ibid., pp. 147, 158.
157 ibid., pp. 110–20, 274–8.
158 Sapeto, *Etiopia*, p. 361. Sapeto has his dates wrong, but also in 'Ambasciata' (*BSGI*, VI, p. 68) he speaks of the concluding of the treaty in the context of the return to Massawa.

A third picture, which is difficult to reconcile completely with either Russel or Sapeto, emerges when one looks at the documents which Russel carried off to France. Firstly, there is a power of attorney for Imnetu to negotiate and conclude agreements with the ambassador of Napoleon, dated Hawzēn the 30th of Meskerem 1851 (should be 1852), with a French translation dated 30 September 1851 (1859); secondly, a treaty providing for the cession of the bay of Zulla and the islands of Desē and Wida and requesting French protection of the coast as far as Zeyla, dated on board the *Yemen* at Zulla the 20th of Tahsas 1852, correctly rendered as 29 December 1859 in the French translation; thirdly, a convention about the recruitment of labourers, a French consulate in Ethiopia and protection of French subjects and Catholics, dated Halay on the 1st of Tir 1852, incorrectly rendered 8 January 1860 in the French translation instead of 9 January.[159] If correct (except for the minor errors in converting Ethiopian dates to Gregorian or vice versa), these dates imply not only that Russel had completed all the negotiations before he began to mention them in his notes and correspondence, but that he and Imnetu had, in fact, signed the most important of the agreements on board the *Yemen* before they started out for Nigusē's camp at Hawzēn. This seems highly improbable, since the only interpreter available then was Sapeto, who, according to Russel, was kept out of these negotiations and, in fact, himself reported that the treaty was concluded much later at a different place.[160] All six documents, moreover, give the impression of having been written, or at least signed, at the same time. At the bottom of both the Amharic and the French versions, including the power of attorney, Imnetu has written in identically the same handwriting, which differs slightly from his more careful calligraphy in the texts: 'I am Abba Imnete Maryam from Abba Gerīma.'

In view of this, it seems most probable that both of the treaties, and possibly the power of attorney as well, were drawn up, in their final form at least, and signed at Halay in mid-January with De Jacobis rather than Sapeto as the confidant of both sides. Why they should have decided to antedate the treaties can only be a matter for speculation. Possibly Russel wanted an earlier date on the political one in view of a possible British action to acquire Zulla or the islands from the local chiefs, possibly because he thought the document would carry more weight if it were dated while Nigusē was still in full control of his

159   SOM, 19/104, 'Pouvoirs d'abba Emneto', 'Contrat de cession et de protectorat', 'Contrat relatif aux travailleurs-libres', numbered 1, 2, and 3. These documents have not been published, nor have they, to my knowledge, been cited in the literature. Malécot, who used the SOM archives extensively for his study, writes ('Voyageurs', *RFHO*, LVIII, p. 321) on the basis of a letter from Russel dated 'on board the *Yemen*, 8 January 1860' (the day after Russel had arrived at Halay) that Imnetu at a meeting at Halay 'finally' signed 'a triple convention': (1) the cession of Desē and Adulis; (2) the protectorate over the whole coast; (3) the authorization to recruit workers for Réunion.

160   There are a number of indications that relations between Russel and Sapeto were strained during the crucial period, and that Russel did not keep Sapeto informed of what he was doing. See, for instance, Russel, *Une Mission*, pp. 111–12, 126, and Sapeto, 'Ambasciata', *BSGI*, VI, pp. 61–5. Sapeto, in fact, favoured an agreement between Nigusē and Sardinia instead of France, as indicated by Lejean (*Théodore II*, pp. 94–5).

kingdom.[161] At any rate, it seems to be more difficult to find a plausible explanation of why Russel should introduce De Jacobis as the interpreter if the treaty had been already concluded before they met at Halay.

Whatever the circumstances of the immediate negotiations, there is no indication that Niguse was personally involved in them. Prompted by De Jacobis and the French vice-consul at Massawa, he had asked for military assistance in 1856 on the basis that he was actually fighting to keep the enemy of the Catholics and of France out of his domains. Urged on by hopes of assistance and by offers of compensation made in his name but quite likely without his prior knowledge, he had after three or four years of negotiations specified his request for military assistance: two batteries with service; and the compensation: permission for a representative of France to reside in his country and the cession of Zulla and, possibly, Ras Dumara.[162] When he sent Abba Imnetu back to Massawa in November 1859 with the letter containing this offer, he allowed him to keep the new royal seal, engraved 'King of Ethiopia' in Amharic and French, presumably so that Imnetu would be able to seal any eventual document embodying the agreement.[163] As already indicated, the 'power of attorney' authorizing Imnetu 'to add and deduct from the matters at his [own] pleasure' was in all probability not given to him by Niguse but was worded and sealed together with the treaties at Halay in January.[164] Nevertheless, Niguse *did* empower Imnetu to seal an agreement on his behalf.[165] The confidence which this implied was misplaced. Imnetu either did not care or was unable to look after the interests of his master.

Firstly, neither of the two treaties contains *mutual* obligations. Niguse's offer of Zulla was immediately interpreted by Russel as a gratuitous cession.[166] In Article One of the treaty this is accentuated by the addition of *libre* (free) in front of *cession* in the French text and *befeqade* (by my will) in the Amharic. Articles Two to Four contain Niguse's request for protection of the coast as far as Zeyla and his pledges to protect French establishments there and not to accept the protection of any other nation without Napoleon's approval. There was no basis for these clauses in Niguse's letter, and in this case it is not likely that Imnetu was fully aware of their significance. The Amharic text of Article Two simply

---

161 Russel, *Une Mission*, p. 119.

162 See above, pp. 190, 199.

163 This seal appears on at least ten preserved documents from February 1859 to August 1860, some of which must have come from Niguse himself. Both friends and enemies made a great fuss about the seal and the power bestowed on Imnetu by virtue of his carrying it. See, *inter alia*, Russel, *Une Mission*, pp. 54, 158, 276; Sapeto, *Etiopia*, p. 346; ADEN, A1A 286, Coghlan to Anderson, 13 Feb. 1860.

164 I find it hard to believe Russel's statement (*Une Mission*, p. 158) that Imnetu had been dispatched to Massawa in October with 'treaties completely prepared'. Certainly the documents brought to France were not just sealed drafts from Hawzen. Both style and content contradict any such conclusion. For the dubious involvement of the Catholics, see also Conti Rossini, 'Vicende', *RRAL*, 5, XXV, pp. 528–9.

165 See for this also SOM, 19/104, Niguse to Napoleon III, 13 Jul. 1860.

166 Russel, *Une Mission*, pp. 18, 269. Note that Russel speaks of a choice between Zulla and Ras Dumara in the first instance (which agrees with Gilbert's translation of Niguse's letter in AECP, Massouah 2, fol. 332) but both places in the second.

asks Napoleon to protect the coast and islands (*yebs-inna dessēt*) since Nigusē has no ships, while the French text states in very specific terms, '. . . I therefore request *and concede* to him [Napoleon] the protectorate over the territories (*le protectorat des pays*) of my kingdom which extend on the littoral of the Red Sea and as far as Zeyla . . .' Instead of including the compensation in terms of specific military assistance requested by Nigusē, Imnetu agreed to the following Article Five:

> My giving this is in order that you and your successors, the kings of France, shall protect [me] against enemies who come from the sea and from my country, and preserve my kingdom for my grandchildren.

In the French version this was further watered down:

> From my side, and in exchange and [as the] sole condition of this free cession which I make to Emperor Napoleon III, I ask of him only the recognition of the legitimacy of my power and of my rights and that my kingdom shall remain in perpetuity within my family and my legitimate offspring.[167]

Here the military assistance has disappeared completely, replaced by the recognition of Nigusē's legitimacy as a ruler. Nor is it mentioned in the second treaty, where Nigusē's request that a French delegate be sent to his country, 'as I sent before', is converted into an undertaking to grant the inviolability of a *gedam* (Ethiopian monastic asylum) to a French consulate, to protect the lives and property of all persons with a French passport and to permit the Catholics to live wherever they liked.[168]

Secondly, Nigusē was denied even the opportunity of seeing his copy of the document he had sealed, and thus the possibility of using it as evidence that he had received international recognition. In spite of the complete absence of specific French obligations, Russel placed a cautious *vu* (seen) above his signature on all the documents, as if to indicate that he was only *informed* of these 'Ethiopian proposals'. More important, he decided that he had better leave no evidence behind that he had even negotiated with the ruler of Simēn and Tigrē. Dispatching the treaties to Paris at the beginning of March, he assured his government that if they did not approve of the documents, then they were legally void, and continued, '. . . no trace remains of them; I have not left copies of them in Abyssinia . . . thence, it follows that these documents can await the time and pleasure of His Majesty without becoming invalid'. [169]

There is no way of knowing how much Imnetu ever reported to Nigusē about the treaties. At any rate, it was the military assistance which was uppermost in

167 SOM, 19/104, 'Contrat de cession et de protectorat' (my emphasis).
168 SOM, 19/104, 'Contrat relatif aux travailleurs-libres'.
169 AEMD, Afrique 63, fols 96–103, Russel to Chasseloup-Laubat, 29 Feb. 1860. Cf. Russel, *Une Mission*, pp. 283–91, where Russel's two letters, 29 Feb. and 2 Mar., from Aden, were printed including (under 2 Mar.) the last part of the above quotation but omitting the passage about the option of regarding the documents as invalid and the precaution of not leaving any copies for the other contracting party!

the mind of the Tigrean ruler. What he had expected in December 1859 was a French artillery force, not an ambassador with a pistol, a revolver, and a double-barrelled rifle, asking for an escort. If he had not become aware of the true state of affairs earlier, his eyes must have been opened by a message from Russel about 15 January, in which the envoy, according to his own account, declared that he had not come to participate in any war, but solely to bring Nigusē the compliments of the French emperor and look into the political state of affairs in Abyssinia. It was in this situation that Nigusē called off the planned meeting with Russel, told him to return to the coast, and withdrew to the western lowlands to escape capture by Tēwodros's forces. The King followed him across the Tekkezē, but diverted his attention to the political situation in Dembīya and to revenging the death of Plowden.[170]

When a messenger from Massawa sought out Nigusē again in early March, he was in Simēn, and his most pressing concern was to inform the French government of the circumstances of Plowden's death. He freely admitted that the attacker, Lij Garred, was in his service, but stressed that no one should be blamed for the killing; Plowden had died as a soldier at the hand of soldiers, and not as the representative of England.[171]

In early May Nigusē returned to Tigrē, and further contacts were made between him and Gilbert. But Gilbert felt that the situation was too uncertain for him to visit Nigusē, and the latter was becoming increasingly suspicious and disappointed with the vice-consul. Gilbert's direct involvement with the population in Akkele Guzay and Agamē and his gifts to chiefs there, as well as his contacts with Tēwodros, must have contributed to Nigusē's feeling that he had been abandoned.[172] In July and August the Tigrean ruler accused the vice-consul, in two letters sent straight to Paris, of having seized sixty-four rifles bought by Ṭaqayē and Imnetu in Europe and having eventually distributed them among his own friends and servants, at the same time as he assisted importers of arms for Tēwodros. In case the French emperor still wanted to open a consulate in

---

170 Russel, *Une Mission*, pp. 111, 124–5; Sapeto, 'Ambasciata', *BSGI*, VI, pp. 60–1; Fusella, 'L'ambasciata', *RSE*, VII, p. 185; *idem*, *Tēwodros*, p. 25; ADEN, A1A 286, Bell to Baroni, 28 Jan. 1860; Schimper to Baroni, 19 Feb. 1860; Stern, *Wanderings*, pp. 51, 54; Spittler-Archiv, D 3/9, Saalmüller to Schneller, 13 Jan. 1861.

171 AECP, Massouah 3, fols 33–5, Nigusē to Thouvenel, 8 Mar. 1860, in the French translation dated 30 February (for 30 Yekatīt). A second letter from Nigusē to Thouvenel and one to Gilbert, also dated 30 February, were reported to Paris at the same time (fols 31–2, Gilbert to Thouvenel, 1 Apr. 1860). In the letter to Gilbert (fol. 36, only French translation), Nigusē allegedly expressed the hope that Thouvenel would make Napoleon decide to take possession of the ceded territory without delay. In both he explained why he had retreated and remained on the defensive. Since the Amharic version of the letter to Thouvenel (removed from the Quai d'Orsay files but preserved among Thouvenel's papers in AN.AP 255) was almost certainly produced at Massawa—the handwriting is rather peculiar and the date is 12 Megabīt (=20 Mar. but still 30 Feb. in the French version!)—it seems safest not to place any confidence in the contents of either of those two letters.

172 AECP, Massouah 3, fols 24–5, 38–40, 49–52, 56–7, 73–8, 85–90, Gilbert to Thouvenel, 26 Mar., 20 May, 30 Jul., 2 Aug., 20 Oct. 1860 and 10 Jan. 1861, with enclosures; fol. 53, Bell to Gilbert, 13 Jun. 1860; BN, Ethiop. 184, fols 94–5, De Jacobis to Gilbert, 10 Apr. and 18 Apr. 1860.

Tigrē, Nigusē made it clear that Gilbert was not acceptable for the post. He affirmed, however, that Imnetu had been authorized to conclude the treaty, and expressed the hope that the French assistance would arrive by the end of the rainy season. Relations with the missionaries remained cordial.[173]

It was the end of October before the first of Nigusē's two letters was even translated in Paris.[174] Gilbert was not informed about its arrival but was told that the whole affair of Russel's mission was the object of a serious investigation. In the meantime, he was authorized to keep Nigusē favourably inclined by visiting him, if he came to the district bordering on Massawa. He was warned, however, not to compromise the French government in any way in the internal Ethiopian power struggle.[175] No meeting took place. Time had run out for the advocates of a Franco-Tigrean alliance. De Jacobis, who had played the leading role, albeit behind the scenes in most of the attempts, died on 31 July 1860 on his way back from the coast to Halay.[176] In January 1861 Tēwodros arrived in Tigrē 'like lightning, having marched day and night from Shewa in 17 days'. Nigusē and Tesemma were taken by surprise, captured, and executed.[177]

This ended twenty years of intrigues aimed at acquiring a French rival port to Massawa, capturing control of the trade of Abyssinia and ultimately establishing a formal protectorate over the northern part of the country. Like his predecessors before him, Russel had gone far beyond any written instructions given to him; like them, he had not hesitated to turn Ethiopian requests into obligations, and relatively minor offers into far-reaching concessions. As a result, the treaties he carried home to France were potentially very important documents. If implemented in accordance with the French text, they would have created a French 'Eritrea' thirty years before the Italian, and, with the unification and modernization policies in Ethiopia only in their infancy, this might well have led to the partition of Ethiopia into a northern Tigrean-Amhara and a southern Amhara-Galla state. That there was no attempt to implement the treaties has been attributed to the disagreements and rivalries over foreign and colonial policy in the French government and, above all, to French concern over British reactions.[178]

The failure of the 'French' initiatives from the d'Abbadie brothers and Lefebvre to De Jacobis and Russel was, however, essentially a failure to cope

---

173   AEMD, Afrique 61, fols 47–53, Nigusē to Napoleon III, 13 Jul. and 22 Aug. 1860; APF. SRC, Africa Centrale, Etiopia ecc . . . 6, f. 627, Nigusē to Delmonte, 28 Sep. 1860. I have not been able to establish how the letters to Paris were forwarded, but they certainly bypassed the consulate at Massawa. Both were translated in Paris by Antoine d'Abbadie.

174   BN, Ethiop. Abb. 254, fol. 160, Berthemy to Antoine d'Abbadie, 26 Oct. 1860.

175   AECP, Massouah 3, fols 79–80, Thouvenel to Gilbert, 26 Oct. 1860.

176   Annales, XXVI, pp. 118–26, Delmonte to Étienne, 3 Aug. 1860.

177   Fusella, Tēwodros, p. 26; AECP, Massouah 3, fols 94–6, Gilbert to Thouvenel, 30 Jan. and 1 Feb. 1861. The chronicler's statement reflects the impression in Tigrē but is not literally true. For Tēwodros's whereabouts in the second half of 1860, see Spittler-Archiv, D 3/9, Saalmüller to Schneller, 13 Jan. 1861; D 3/1, Bender to his family, 15 Jan. 1861.

178   Malécot, 'Voyageurs', RFHO, LVIII, p. 321.

with the basic reality that the Ethiopians '(like us) want an eye for an eye and twenty shillings for one pound', as General Gordon put it in a different context twenty years later.[179] Even when confronted merely by a Catholic priest acting for a rebel governor and a weak ruler like Nigusē, Russel resorted to duplicity. The question whether the Russel treaties were legally binding for Ethiopia (or even for Nigusē) is purely academic.[180] In the Amharic text of the clause about the cession of Zulla, it is clearly assumed that some additional act, a *mutual* ratification, was expected to take place.[181] Unless the military assistance was forthcoming, moreover, there was certainly no *agreement* in the real sense of the word.

Finally, whatever obligations Nigusē had accepted died with him. It was his French/Catholic advisers who had literally elevated the rebel to 'King of Ethiopia', and the French government knew better than to attempt to use the Russel treaties even as a starting point in their later relations with Tēwodros. In fact, the treaties were regarded as so dubious and so dangerous that Gilbert was instructed, two days after the news about Nigusē's death had reached Paris, to preserve 'the treaty signed by Nigusē' as an 'absolute secret' and 'never to allow it to be suspected' that he had known about its existence. The British government was told on the one hand that Russel's mission had had nothing more in view than a coaling station, on the other that the question of the sovereignty of Tigrē was a very complicated issue on which the French and British consuls had opposing views.[182] The transition towards a more realistic policy had, in fact, begun immediately after Tēwodros's first attack on Nigusē. Russel's widely rumoured but totally unrealistic plan to visit Tēwodros and arrange for the partition of Ethiopia into two states was dropped. Five years after his coronation, Tēwodros was recognized as the supreme ruler of Ethiopia, including the north, also by the representatives of France and of the Catholic mission.[183]

179 George Birkbeck Hill, ed., *Colonel Gordon in Central Africa 1874–1879* (London, 1899), p. 408.
180 French writers seem to have more or less taken for granted that the treaty ceding Zulla and Desē was binding for Ethiopia; thus G. Charmes in the preface to Russel, *Une Mission*, p. xxvii, and Malécot, 'Voyageurs', *RFHO*, LVIII, p. 321. The Italian view is that the legal validity of the treaty need not even be considered: thus Giglio, *Etiopia–Mar Rosso*, Vol. I, p. 52: 'It is superfluous to point out that the cession of Zulla was void of all legal value, since Nigusē had no power to make it.' Annotating Sapeto's *Etiopia* (p. 361) in the 1880s, the Comando del Corpo di Stato Maggiore indicated the reason for this: 'This treaty had no validity because Nigusē had no rights over the Bay of Zulla and because no cession of territory was valid if it was not made by the King. At that time, Nigusē was nothing but a rebel . . .'
181 SOM, 19/104, 'Contrat de cession . . .', Article One: 'ይህንን ፡ ውል ፡ በምንወስንበት ፡ ጊዜ ፡ . . . (when we conclude this agreement . . .)'.
182 AECP, Massouah 3, fols 103–6, Thouvenel to Gilbert, 29 Mar. 1861; FO 401/1, p. 357, Cowley to Russell, 19 Apr. 1860. But see also Lejean, *Théodore II*, p. 248, and an attempt to benefit from the 'treaty', documented in AEMD, Afrique 63, fols 371–2, 383–5.
183 ADEN, A1A 286, Baroni to Coghlan, 1 Jan. 1860; Russel, *Une Mission*, pp. 102, 275; AECP, Massouah 3, fol. 53, Bell to Gilbert, 13 Jun. 1860, in reply to an apparently acceptable letter to Tēwodros written as early as 27 Feb. 1860; see also CML, De Jacobis, 'Lettres', Vol. II, nos 414 and 415, and *Annales*, XXVI, pp. 86–92, Delmonte to Sturchi, 20 Mar. 1860.

Tēwodros and the Turks: War or Peace?

From the very beginning of Tēwodros's reign it was widely believed and reported that he would launch a major attack on Egypt at the earliest possible moment. A severely anti-Muslim internal policy and plans to divert the waters of the Nile in order to ruin Egypt were reported by Plowden as early as April 1855. After his first visit to the King, Plowden spoke about designs on Massawa and the Egyptian frontier by the new ruler, adding that he did not 'hesitate to dream of the conquest of Egypt, and a triumphant march to the Holy Sepulchre'.[184] These expectations were no doubt born and nourished by the Tēwodros myth and were strong enough to contribute to a mutiny in the King's army while he was on his first campaign to Shewa in 1855–56.[185] But Tēwodros was not then on his way to Jerusalem, and there are no indications that he ever allowed dreams of this kind to divert his attention from more immediate and pressing issues. As far as Egypt was concerned, he had inherited an undefined and disturbed boundary.

Tēwodros was himself a man of the western frontier. He had spent much of his youth and early manhood there, sufficient to be disparagingly called—by those closer to the centres of power—a *qwelleñña*, a *ye-fiyyel ireñña* (a lowlander, a goat-herd).[186] Like his father Haylu of Qwara and his half-brothers Kinfu and Gebru before him, he had competed with representatives of the Egyptian government for the control over tribes, trade, and tribute on the frontier. As governor of Qwara and later Menen's successor in Dembīya, he had borne the responsibility for the defence of the border districts, and it was at the hands of the 'Turks', at Dabarki in 1848, that he had suffered the only major defeat of the brilliant military career that had brought him to the throne of Ethiopia.[187] As for Massawa, Tēwodros was certainly aware of the need to prevent any increase of Turkish–Egyptian power there or among the coastal tribes. Otherwise Plowden was on hand to advise him on the matter, even to induce him to trade some concessions to England in exchange for the port.[188] In view of Tēwodros's personal background as well as his singular commitment to the restoration of what he understood to be the Ethiopia of his forefathers, it was therefore not unreasonable to expect an early outbreak of hostilities. The unsettled situation certainly provided opportunities for aggressive action from either side:

> In this direction, no de jure boundary delimits the respective possessions of Egypt and Ethiopia; between the two states there extends a contested zone where the de facto boundary moves as either of these countries show aggressive dispositions. This zone

184   FO 401/1, pp. 244–5, Plowden to Clarendon, 7 Apr. 1855; pp. 251–7, Report, 25 Jun. 1855.
185   [Zeneb], *Tēwodros*, p. 25; for the Tēwodros myth, see Rubenson, *Tēwodros*, pp. 49–51, 57, 60.
186   Rubenson, *Tēwodros*, pp. 29, 32–3.
187   ibid., pp. 39–40; see also above, pp. 69, 140.
188   See above, pp. 182–3.

forms, at the foot of the highlands of Abyssinia, a vast semicircle which extends from Qallabat near the Atbara to the neighbourhood of Massawa on the Red Sea.[189]

Within this contested zone, into which Egyptian forces and influence had penetrated during the decades immediately preceding Tēwodros's reign, some tribes or districts acknowledged, in various ways, their dependence on both Ethiopia and Egypt. In order to safeguard, as much as possible, its position as a trading centre, Metemma, for instance, paid tribute to both sides,[190] while the situation at the other end of the disputed strip was described as follows by the Swiss scholar and explorer Werner Munzinger:

> The Abyssinians have no need to conquer a country which nature has given to them without further ado. Thus the inhabitants of Semhar live under a double dependence, that of Abyssinia for grazing, of Massawa for trade, of both for security. They therefore pay tribute to both and when people say that Semhar belongs to the Turks, they are telling only half the truth.[191]

In the areas in between, Mek Nimr's son Umar, mostly referred to simply as Wad Nimr, governed a frontier district for Tēwodros and continued his father's 'private' war against the Sudanese authorities.[192] Farther north the struggle for control over the Kunama, Barya, Marya, Bogos, Habab, and Mensa continued between the Egyptian governor of Taka on one hand and the Ethiopian governors of Adiyabo and of Hamasēn on the other. During the first years of Tēwodros's reign, his governors in the north, Mirrach Welde Sillasē and [Welde] Sadiq Mirrach (Walad Marrag) of Adiyabo and Dejjazmach Haylu of Hamasēn, seem to have succeeded in pushing back the Egyptian positions somewhat. The governor of Taka abandoned his advanced position at Kufit among the Barya in 1857, and in 1859 most of the tribes between Massawa and Kasala were paying tribute to Ethiopia only.[193]

There is no evidence that these, relatively speaking, minor changes in Ethiopia's favour were the results of any overall policy of aggression against Egypt.[194] Changes in the Sudan effected by Muhammad Sa'id Pasha, who had become viceroy of Egypt the year before Tēwodros's coronation, reduced the Egyptian pressures on the frontiers. In order to keep down the costs of administration, garrisons were reduced or withdrawn from outlying posts. Thus Kufit was evacuated for financial reasons, not because of Ethiopian attacks.[195] It was only to be expected that Tēwodros's governors in the border districts

---

189 Douin, *Ismaïl*, III, 1, pp. 37–8, summing up the situation in the last years of the viceroyship of Muhammad Sa'id (1854–63).

190 ibid., pp. 38–9; Theodor von Heuglin, *Reise nach Abessinien, den Gala-Ländern, Ost-Sudán und Chartum in den Jahren 1861 and 1862* (Jena, 1868), pp. 406–8; AEMD, Afrique 61, fols 91–4, Lejean to Thouvenel, 29 Jan. 1862.

191 Munzinger, *Ostafrikanische Studien*, p. 137.

192 Samuel W. Baker, *The Nile Tributaries of Abyssinia* (London, 1867), pp. 138–41.

193 Douin, *Ismaïl*, III, 1, pp. 40–52; Munzinger, *Ostafrikanische Studien*, p. 199.

194 Cf. Douin's opinion, *Ismaïl*, III, 1, p. 52.

195 Hill, *The Sudan*, pp. 89–90, 94–5, 103.

would take advantage of whatever opportunities they found to move their positions forward.

Aware of the problems and anxious to avoid hostilities, Plowden had tried a form of appeasement—the abortive 'offer' of Massawa—as well as repeated warnings that peace with Egypt was a condition for British friendship.[196] He had alerted his colleague in Egypt, who added his advice to Plowden's own. Tēwodros's reply, forwarded by Plowden, was that he had left his governors 'with orders to protect my territories simply' and that he would not 'depart from those usages that become all sovereigns', presumably a reference to the principle that a declaration of war was to precede any hostilities.[197] A few months later he repeated that 'he had hitherto given no provocation to Egypt', but that he reserved his rights to demand, at some future date, the retrocession of territories earlier lost to Ethiopia. Plowden assumed that these included 'the Arab country on his northern frontier as far as the village of Sennaar, also Massowah, and the high lands of Mogos [Bogos], Mensa, Halhal, the Hababs, etc., all of which tribes still speak the Abyssinian language . . .'[198] Though Plowden's overall assessment of the situation was no doubt correct, he seems to have been something of an alarmist (as has so often been the case with Europeans in Ethiopia). There is more than a hint of irritation in Tēwodros's replies as reported by the consul. Tēwodros was feeling his way but was certainly not prepared to have Plowden or the British government dictate his attitude towards Egypt.

When the Coptic Patriarch arrived in Ethiopia in December 1856 with a letter from Sa'id Pasha, a different channel of communication was opened.[199] Qērilos was well known to Tēwodros, who had actually supported his elevation to the position of Patriarch only two or three years earlier.[200] It was also through Qērilos that Tēwodros had made his first contacts with Egyptian authorities after his accession to the Ethiopian throne.[201] The visit of the Patriarch was no doubt intended not only to solve certain ecclesiastical problems, but also to improve the relations between Egypt and Ethiopia.[202]

Qērilos was given a royal reception but soon aroused the suspicion and wrath of Tēwodros by some of his requests and by taking the initiative, together with Selama, of drafting a reply in the King's name to Sa'id Pasha. Tēwodros's chronicler simply states that it was a request for 'many things and many

---

196   See above, pp. 182–5.
197   FO 401/1, p. 272, Plowden to Clarendon, 5 Mar. 1856; pp. 273–4, Bruce to Clarendon, 20 Jun. 1856.
198   ibid., p. 283, Plowden to Clarendon, 12 Nov. 1856. See also above, p. 185.
199   ENA, Bahr Barra, Carton 19, no. 71, Tēwodros to Muhammad Sa'id, 13 Nov. 1857.
200   See above, p. 135.
201   BM, Add. 51304, Anon. to Tēwodros, May (?) 1855. This letter in Arabic to Tēwodros, found among the Gordon Papers, looks like an original but could, of course, be a sealed copy. It is dated 1271 Hijra, possibly 8 Ramadan. The seal is not legible, but the contents clearly indicate that it is a reply by an Egyptian official, possibly a governor of the Sudan, to a letter from Tēwodros announcing his accession.
202   Flad, *Zwölf Jahre*, pp. 19–20; Stern, *Wanderings*, pp. 78–9; Lejean, *Théodore II*, p. 84; Douin, *Ismaïl*, III, 1, p. 57.

workers'.²⁰³ Although Tēwodros had the letter read publicly to justify his temporary arrest of the two prelates, there is some uncertainty as to what it really contained. Plowden reported that the letter asked the viceroy 'to send all the Coptic soldiers in his service, three Turkish officers to discipline the Abyssinian troops, regimental bands, pioneers, sappers, engineers, bakers, doctors and medicines, cannons and muskets', all in exchange for forty mules for Sa'id Pasha's artillery. Qērilos and Selama denied that their letter requested troops, and Flad believed that the request was simply for Sa'id to release some Copts who had been forcibly enrolled as soldiers in the Egyptian army and that the people to come to Ethiopia were 'thirty workmen from Egypt' to replace the British and Germans in the country. Whether there was any indication in the letter that the released soldiers were to serve in Ethiopia or not, Tēwodros was clearly disgusted with the interest of the Patriarch in military matters (allegedly including a review of the King's army). He also saw the request to replace the Europeans as an attempt to isolate him and make him dependent on Egypt. At the same time, he declared that he would hold his own against Pasha, Patriarch and the Queen of England too, if Britain happened to be behind Egypt.²⁰⁴

News of Sa'id Pasha's visit to the Sudan, which coincided with the Patriarch's to Ethiopia, and rumours that the viceroy intended to attack Ethiopia contributed to Tēwodros's harsh treatment of Qērilos and Selama.²⁰⁵ Though they were released from confinement after a few days, it took almost a whole year (until November 1857) before the Patriarch was finally permitted to return to Egypt. By then it had become obvious that Sa'id Pasha had no immediate aggressive plans against Ethiopia. As his own envoys to accompany Qērilos to Cairo, Tēwodros appointed a trusted priest, Aleqa Gebre Iyesus, and one of his officers. They took with them a gift of seven horses and some traditional Ethiopian arms—and a letter to Sa'id Pasha in which Tēwodros expressed his appreciation for the visit of the Patriarch as well as the hope that their friendship would continue and increase.²⁰⁶ How this was to be achieved was left to the envoy and Qērilos to explain. It is quite obvious, however, that cannon and rifles were discussed as evidence of friendship rather than a military or technical mission.²⁰⁷

203 [Zeneb], *Tēwodros*, p. 29.
204 FO 401/1, pp. 286–8, Plowden to Clarendon, 15 Jan. 1857; J. M. Flad, *Notes from the Journal of F. [sic] M. Flad, one of Bishop Gobat's Pilgrim Missionaries in Abyssinia* (London, 1860), pp. 47–50. Crummey ('Reformer and Modernizer', *JAH*, X, 3, p. 463) gives precedence to Flad's account. Plowden's is at any rate exaggerated.
205 FO 401/1, pp. 286–9, Plowden to Clarendon, 15 Jan., 17 Jan., and 5 Feb. 1857; p. 290, Bruce to Clarendon, 29 Apr. 1857; Hill, *The Sudan*, p. 94. Besides, '. . . there were certainly other things', as Flad (*Notes*, p. 48) wrote, including differences of opinion between the two prelates.
206 ENA, Bahr Barra, Carton 19, no. 71, Tēwodros to Muhammad Sa'id, 13 Nov. 1857. Besides the Amharic original of this letter, there is a slightly embellished Arabic version, also sealed but dated 24 Nov. 1857. See also [Zeneb], *Tēwodros*, p. 31; Spittler-Archiv, D 3/2, Flad to Krapf, 26 Oct. 1857, with a postscript written 'on the Nile'; Flad, *Notes*, pp. 75–7.
207 FO 401/1, p. 303, Plowden to Clarendon, 22 Nov. 1857.

As was customary, the envoys paid a visit to Jerusalem before returning,[208] but when they finally arrived in Ethiopia again, in February 1859, they were accompanied by an Egyptian envoy, Abd al-Rahman, who brought truly royal gifts: four heavy cannon, 100 double-barrelled guns, five tents and numerous boxes with silk cloth and other presents.[209] This can hardly have failed to convince Tēwodros that Sa'id Pasha was eager to prove himself a friendly neighbour. In 1859, with unceasing rebellions in Wello, Seyfe Sillasē's uprising in Shewa, and the growing urgency to do something about the situation in Tigrē, this must have been a welcome realization for Tēwodros.[210]

Unfortunately the unsettled conditions of the frontier continued to cause friction and incidents, particularly in the Qallabat area. An unsuccessful attack on Metemma in early 1860 by a band of marauders identified as Tigreans cannot in itself have been regarded as a very serious incident.[211] But in May the same year Umar Wad Nimr reportedly made a successful inroad into the territories of the *Shukriya* beyond Qadarif, and claimed, in the name of Tēwodros, 'the taxes of all Upper Nubia'.[212] This may well have been a private initiative by Wad Nimr. The thrust of the invasion was after all directed towards his own homeland, which had been lost by his father to the Egyptians. At any rate, when the governor Hasan Bey Salama protested to Tēwodros, the King not only denied with indignation that he had ever given any orders to tax Egyptian subjects but also promised to order Wad Nimr to return everything he had taken. Though he maintained that he had territorial claims on Egypt, Tēwodros also pointed out that he was negotiating with Sa'id Pasha to find a peaceful solution.[213] Messengers from Wad Nimr appeared before the King during the rainy season of 1860, but unfortunately there is no record of their business.[214]

In a letter to Sa'id Pasha himself one year later, Tēwodros countered some complaints by the Egyptian ruler about Umar Nimr and another Sudanese chief named Abu Rawash, who had likewise crossed the frontier into Ethiopia, presumably to avoid the heavy Turkish taxation. According to Tēwodros, Umar had also complained about inroads into his province inside Ethiopia. But instead of threatening to retaliate, Tēwodros suggested that Sa'id send someone concerned with these matters so that they could be properly investigated, the looted

208 ibid., pp. 309–10, Finn to Malmesbury, 21 Jun. 1858.
209 [Zeneb], *Tēwodros*, pp. 39–40; ENA, Bahr Barra, Carton 19, no. 110, Tēwodros to Hasan, 27 May 1860; Spittler-Archiv, D 3/9, Saalmüller to Schneller, 12 Oct. 1859; FO 401/1, p. 327, Plowden to Malmesbury, 2 Feb. 1859.
210 [Zeneb], *Tēwodros*, pp. 40–7. Plowden's dispatches of 1859 and early 1860 (FO 401/1, pp. 327–55, *passim*) tell the same story of unrest and war.
211 Stern, *Wanderings*, pp. 36–7; Guillaume Lejean, 'Voyage en Abyssinie', *TM*, 1865, II, p. 230.
212 Lejean, *Théodore II*, p. 120.
213 ENA, Bahr Barra, Carton 19, no. 110, Tēwodros to Hasan, 27 May 1860. In May 1860 Tēwodros married Dejjazmach Wibē's daughter at Debre Tabor. He released her father and was reportedly working on a peaceful solution to the Tigrean problem in order to avoid the necessity of a second campaign against Nigusē. See Stern, *Wanderings*, pp. 111–12, 122; Spittler-Archiv, D 3/2, Flad to Gobat, 30 Aug. 1860; D 3/9, Saalmüller to Schneller, 13 Jan. 1861.
214 Stern, *Wanderings*, p. 150.

property returned, and the guilty on both sides punished. He even refrained from the otherwise almost routine remarks about the territories in dispute having belonged to his forefathers as rulers of Ethiopia. Finally, he promised to write again with Abd al-Rahman, who had been detained in order to witness the successful pacification of the country but was expected to leave after the rainy season.[215] As late as the middle of 1861, Ethio-Egyptian relations at the top level thus remained friendly, or at least non-belligerent, in spite of border incidents and continuous reports and rumours about mutual plans and preparations for war. If Sa'id Pasha had shown restraint, so had Tēwodros. Sa'id seems, however, to have sent no reply to Tēwodros's letter of May 1861, and so by the end of 1861 the period of restraint and dialogue came to an end.[216]

The deterioration of Ethio-Egyptian relations and the crisis of 1862–63 are usually attributed to Tēwodros's hatred of everything Muslim and his desire to win fame as a conqueror. More specifically, it was because of his receiving and supporting the *Nimrab*, 'inveterate bandits', and other fugitive outlaws from the Sudan, and because of his threats and provocations that Sa'id Pasha was forced to appoint Musa Hamdi Pasha as governor to restore order in the Sudan and protect it against an Ethiopian invasion. It was finally an allegedly 'insolent', 'hysterically violent' letter from the King that made Musa act around New Year 1863.[217]

Unfortunately the precise date and nature of this letter seem to be as difficult to establish as the boundary between Egyptian and Ethiopian territories. Musa Hamdi was appointed before Sa'id left for Europe in April 1862 and was given increased powers and additional troops, allegedly because Tēwodros was about to embark on the conquest of Sinnar.[218] Rumours of this kind were certainly rife in Cairo during the first half of 1862; Dr Beke added the age-old threat that Tēwodros planned to turn the waters of the Nile away from Egypt.[219] On the other hand, it was rumoured in Ethiopia as early as November 1861 that Sa'id Pasha was on his way to attack the country with 40,000 men.[220]

Henry Dufton, who passed through Khartoum in July 1862 on his way from Egypt to Ethiopia, and his more famous countryman, Sir Samuel Baker, who arrived there from the Ethiopian frontier in June and left for Albert Nyanza on

215 ENA, Bahr Barra, Carton 19, no. 111, Tēwodros to Sa'id, 21 May 1861. This corresponds to the Arabic date 11 Al-kadda, but it is possible also to read Zul-kadda with no specified date. For Abd al-Rahman's rather unhappy stay in Ethiopia, his departure, and suicide in Berber on his way home, see Spittler-Archiv, D 3/9, Saalmüller to Schneller, 13 Jan. 1861; FO 401/1, pp. 456–9, Cameron to Russell, 31 Oct. 1862; Flad, *Zwölf Jahre*, Vol. I, p. 20; Rassam, *British Mission*, Vol. I, p. 193.

216 An undated draft or copy of a letter found in Bahr Barra, Carton 19 (no. 5) is more likely the message to which Tēwodros responded on 21 May 1861. In spite of his extensive use of the Egyptian archives, Douin gives the impression (*Ismaïl*, III, 1, pp. 57–64) that there were no direct contacts between Sa'id and Tēwodros after the 'fiasco' of the Qērilos mission in 1857.

217 Douin, *Ismaïl*, III, 1, pp. 37, 52, 59–64; Hill, *The Sudan*, pp. 107, 109.

218 Douin, *Ismaïl*, III, 1, pp. 59–60.

219 AECP(Brussels), Égypte 3, Zizinia to Rogier, 19 Jun. 1862; FO 401/1, pp. 419–20, Beke to Russell, 14 Jun. 1862.

220 Spittler-Archiv, D 3/1, Bender to Gobat, 20 Nov. 1861.

18 December, spoke of the letter in terms of the past. Dufton was even of the opinion that it was 'the letter sent by Theodore to Said Pasha' which caused the dispatch of 'Musa Pasha with 10,000 men into the Soudan'. Baker was informed of the content of the letter by Musa Pasha, who reportedly declared that 'he was preparing an expedition in reply . . .', 'that the king was mad, and that were it not for the protection given to Abyssinia by the English, the Egyptians would have eaten it up long ago . . .'[221] Nevertheless, in spite of a fairly regular correspondence, Musa seems to have reported the letter to Cairo only at the end of December 1862.[222]

On his arrival in the Sudan, Musa found no signs of any Ethiopian invasion. Both Baker and Theodor von Heuglin, moreover, could inform him that Tēwodros and his army had been nowhere near the Egyptian frontier during the first half of 1862.[223] Nor did the imperial army turn up after the rainy season. Nevertheless, Tēwodros did have some plans to visit the frontier after the rains, for around May 1862 Shaykh Jumma of Metemma (Qallabat) received a letter from the King with instructions to secure grain and honey for his army.[224] The background to this was no doubt the attempt by Shaykh Ahmad (or Hammad) Wad Mira to depose Jumma and take his place. Ahmad had spent a few years in an Egyptian prison for an earlier attempt to seize the lucrative post by violent means. According to Baker, who passed through Metemma in April, Ahmad had on his release declared himself the subject of Egypt and received Egyptian troops for an attack on Metemma; though he defeated Jumma in January 1862, this did not secure him the position as shaykh of the Takruri; Jumma appealed to Tēwodros, who reportedly summoned the two rivals, confirmed Jumma in his position, and detained Ahmad in Dembīya. According to the French vice-consul Guillaume Lejean, who passed through on his way to Tēwodros six months later, it was Ahmad who in vain appealed to Tēwodros.[225] Be that as it may, the significant point is that the conflict was referred *to Tēwodros*. Negotiators from Qallabat were present in Tēwodros's camp in southern Wello in April.[226] It seems quite clear, therefore, that the shaykhs of Metemma, while distributing a share of their income in both directions, nevertheless maintained their old allegiance to the Ethiopian ruler. Jumma in fact told Baker in no uncertain terms that 'this was Abyssinia, and the firman of the Viceroy of Egypt was a bad introduction, as the Egyptians forced them to pay

221   Dufton, *Narrative*, pp. 24, 185 (for date, p. 2); Baker, *Nile Tributaries*, pp. 559–60 (for dates, pp. 561, 574).

222   In addition to Baker's account, Douin (*Ismaïl*, III, 1, p. 64) cites Musa Hamdi's dispatch to Cairo, 27 Dec. 1862, but his record of the main points of the letter is an almost literal translation of Baker's. He also follows Baker in characterizing the letter as 'insolent' and the King as 'mad'. Hill (*The Sudan*, p. 109) has 'hysterically violent' for the letter but retains Musa's description to Baker of Tēwodros as 'mad'. The possibility that Tēwodros wrote two provocative letters cannot, of course, be excluded. Neither of them is found, however, with the other Ethiopian letters in Bahr Barra, Carton 19.

223   Baker, *Nile Tributaries*, pp. 279–518, *passim*; Heuglin, *Abessinien*, pp. 253–419, *passim*.

224   Guillaume Lejean, 'Gallabat et Gadabhi', *Nouvelles Annales*, 6, X, 1 (1864), p. 19.

225   Baker, *Nile Tributaries*, pp. 507–9; Lejean, 'Gallabat', *Nouvelles Annales*, 6, X, 1, p. 18. Cf. Douin, *Ismaïl*, III, 1, p. 39; ENA, Bahr Barra, Carton 19, no. 5, 3rd entry.

226   Heuglin, *Abessinien*, p. 372.

tribute at the point of the bayonet, although they had no right to enter this country'.[227]

It was not Tēwodros who began to disturb the status quo in 1862. He was engaged in a ruthless campaign in Wello and northern Shewa.[228] The problems and the fears of the frontier were brought to him. The Qallabat delegation was not the only one. Shaykh Muhammad Be'id came at the same time from as far off as the Beni Amir of the Barka valley, presumably to declare his loyalty to the King and seek his support against the Egyptians.[229] In fact, the troubles along the frontier of which the Egyptians complained were of their own making. Due mainly to oppressive taxation, several other tribal leaders had followed the early example of Mek Nimr and led their people across the frontier into Ethiopian territory. Shaykh Ahmad abu Sin of the Rufa'a of the Dabarki area, for instance, had settled, reportedly with 10,000–15,000 men, at Dunkur in the middle of Qwara. On the Atbara north of Metemma, the Abu Rawash mentioned in Tēwodros's letter of May 1861 had allegedly taken 9,000–10,000 men with him out of Sudanese territory. In the eyes of the Egyptian authorities, these people were deserters and criminals who should be hunted down and forced to return.[230] Tēwodros and his governors, on the other hand, regarded them as 'political refugees' and allowed them to settle in the sparsely-populated frontier districts, but even if they had wanted to they had little power to prevent them from going back and forth across the undefined boundary. Gradually the claim of the Egyptian authorities to the people as Turkish subjects influenced the views of where this boundary was to be drawn. This becomes immediately apparent if one compares maps of the area compiled in the 1840s with, for instance, Heuglin's map of 1867.

Though the early maps obviously contain many errors and differ considerably with regard to the location of a number of places, they agree roughly on an Egyptian boundary running from the Mereb (Gash) somewhere between Kasala and Teseney, south-south-west through the confluence of the Tekkeze (Setit) and the Atbara at old Sufi to a point just west of Rashid, and then southwards towards Famaka on the Blue Nile. The map of Muhammad Ali's Austrian mining expert, Jos. Russegger, indicates a second boundary between Abyssinia on one hand, and on the other hand the Beja, 'in part tributary to Abyssinia', and other 'tribes of Ethiopian pastoralists' north of the Tekkezē and along the Atbara. This second boundary cuts the Atbara north of Metemma and joins, at a point south-west of the town, what is from there on a common Egyptian–Ethiopian boundary.[231] The Weiland–Kiepert map of 1846, however, pro-

227 Baker, *Nile Tributaries*, p. 507.
228 Heuglin, *Abessinien*, pp. 340, 362; 'Reise der Herren Th. v. Heuglin, Dr. Steudner und H. Schubert im östlichen Theile des Hochlandes von Abessinien, Februar bis Mai 1862', *Petermann*, 1862, pp. 424–7; Spittler-Archiv, D 3/12, Waldmeier [to Schlienz], 14 May 1862.
229 Heuglin, *Abessinien*, p. 371. See Douin, *Ismaïl*, III, 1, p. 63, for the fate of Muhammad after his return.
230 Douin, *Ismaïl*, III, 1, p. 62; Lejean, *Théodore II*, pp. 228–9; Hill, *The Sudan*, p. 109.
231 Jos. Russegger, *Karte von Ost Sudan umfassend die Länder Kordofan, Nuba, Sennar . . . Abessinien und den Galla Ländern* (Stuttgart, 1843).

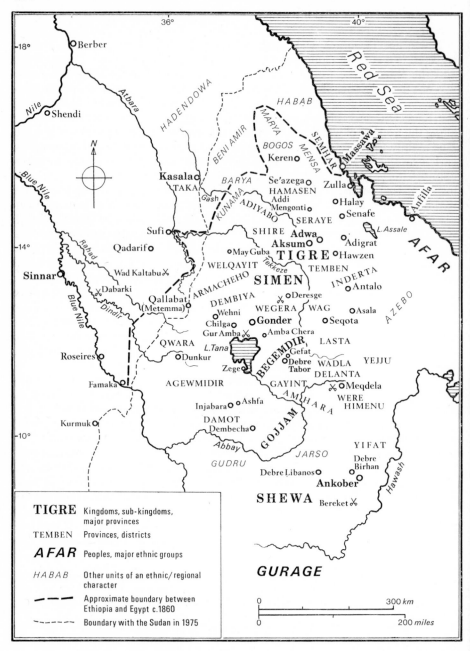

MAP 3 *Ethiopia under Tēwodros*

vides a strip of 'no-man's-land' between Egyptian and Ethiopian territory including, *inter alia*, the Ginjar,[232] whose relationship to the Abyssinians may or may not have been that of a subject people.[233] What these maps, however, establish beyond doubt is that the Takruri of the Metemma area *were still regarded*—by Europeans who collected most of their new information from the Egyptian side—as Ethiopian subjects, while farther north the Dubaina on the west side and Shanqilla tribes on the east side of the Atbara were supposed to inhabit a kind of buffer zone only vaguely dependent of Ethiopia.[234] To Mansfield Parkyns, who arrived on the Atbara opposite Sufi after a visit to Mek Nimr at May Guba, the matter was clearer. There at least, crossing the river meant crossing over from Ethiopian to Turkish territory.[235]

On Heuglin's map twenty years later, Metemma/Qallabat and Bazēn (Kunama) are shown as independent territories, and where Ethiopia and Egypt meet between these two units, the boundary is drawn 100–150 kilometres east of the Atbara, thus including a vast province called Gezirat al-Luban or simply 'Mek Nimr' in the Egyptian possessions. Both Qallabat and Bazēn, moreover, jut out into Egyptian territory so conspicuously that the map itself seems to call for a rectification of the boundary through the incorporation of these two units as well.[236] The only basis for the inclusion of Mek Nimr's province, however, was that he and his followers had migrated from the Sudan forty years earlier. Nimr's son Umar regarded himself as a governor or vassal of Tēwodros, and resisted Turkish rule as stubbornly as his father.[237] Baker, who travelled in the area for nine months in 1861–62 (while Heuglin never visited it) reported about the raids and counter-raids that took place, but he was in no doubt about where the *de facto* boundary was:

> The country on the opposite or eastern bank of the Atbara is contested ground; in reality it forms the western frontier of Abyssinia, of which the Atbara river is the boundary . . . Sofi being upon the frontier, the laws are merely nominal . . . Should any man commit a crime in Abyssinia, he takes refuge over the border; thus, criminals of the blackest character are at large.[238]

232 C. F. Weiland and H. Kiepert, *Die Nilländer oder Aegypten Nubien und Habesh gezeichnet von C. F. Weiland 1840 berichtigt von H. Kiepert 1846* (Weimar, 1846).

233 The activities of Tēwodros and his Ginjar-Shanqilla companion Idris in the area in the 1840s ([Zeneb], *Tēwodros*, pp. 8–9) indicate a positive answer.

234 For earlier information on the situation in this area, see James Bruce, *Travels to Discover the Source of the Nile* (Edinburgh, 1790), Vol. IV, pp. 316–41. Bruce made no attempt to draw a western boundary for Ethiopia on his map (Vol. V). Note, however, that the map of Michael Russell in *Nubia and Abyssinia* (Edinburgh, 1833) has Welqayit on both sides of the Atbara, and the Ginjar included with Qwara inside the Ethiopian border.

235 Parkyns, *Life*, Vol. II, pp. 391–6. Some of the confusion was no doubt due to the habit of the travellers of speaking of the last village or town in the highlands where Tigriñña or Amharic was spoken as the last *Abyssinian* village or the frontier town (ibid., p. 344).

236 Th. von Heuglin, *Karte von Aethiopien (H'abeš, Takah & Ost-Senar)* . . . (Jena, 1867).

237 Baker, *Nile Tributaries*, pp. 140–1, 277–80, 444.

238 ibid., pp. 138, 181. There is much circumstantial evidence of this as well; see pp. 214, 247, 278–9. Lejean, in 1861, also found that Sufi was the border town in this area; he drew the boundary through Algaden and Sufi to Fazughli (AEMD, Afrique 61, fols 91–4, to Thouvenel, 29 Jan. 1862).

This worked both ways, of course, as Baker also admitted:

> Altogether, the society in this district was not *crême de la crême*, as Mek Nimmur's territory was an asylum for all the blackguards of the adjoining countries, who were attracted by the excitement and lawlessness of continual border warfare.[239]

By 1862, after a reprisal raid which took the Egyptians all the way to the stronghold of the *Nimrab* at May Guba, 100 kilometres east of the Atbara, Umar was also prepared for a peaceful solution. He attempted to use Baker as his negotiator, promising not to cross the Atbara again if he would be left in peace east of the river. This offer was repeatedly rejected out of hand by Musa Pasha.[240]

Under these circumstances, it is hardly remarkable that Tēwodros should have decided that his presence on the frontier was called for. Many of the tribes along the border clearly looked to Ethiopia for liberation from Egyptian oppression. Even Dr Beke, who was notoriously anti-Tēwodros and advised the British government repeatedly to have nothing to do with him, admitted that it was 'generally understood there [at Khartoum] that the natives would prefer the Abyssinian to the Turco-Egyptian rule'.[241] The King's letter to Jumma proves no more than that Tēwodros believed that a show of force on the frontier would consolidate this favourable situation, but it is not unlikely that his 'insolent' letter to Musa Hamdi, allegedly claiming as Ethiopia's boundary the Nile from Khartoum to Shendi and then straight across to the Atbara, was intended as a threat that he would in the last resort invade and occupy the territory. The most interesting point in the letter, as reported by Musa, is the mention of Shendi and, just before, the observation that Wad Nimr and [Welde] Ṣadiq Mirrach were vassals of Ethiopia and not Egypt.[242] This seems to imply that Tēwodros, after the Egyptian raid on May Guba and Musa's refusal to accept Wad Nimr's offer of the Atbara as a *de facto* boundary, was prepared to back the aspirations of the *Nimrab* to return to the Nile as Ethiopian rather than Turkish vassals. If this is correct, the unrelenting attitude of the Egyptian authorities towards the descendants of Mek Nimr and his followers played a major role in causing Tēwodros to increase and specify his territorial claims in the west. It does not prove, however, that the King planned an immediate conquest at the head of his own army, even if the rumours by the time they reached the French press were framed as an Ethiopian declaration of war.[243]

In the end, Tēwodros neither invaded the Sudan nor even paid his intended visit to Qallabat. Since the King was at the zenith of his power in 1861–62, in terms of both political and military control, the reason for his restraint is not

239   Baker, *Nile Tributaries*, p. 451.
240   ibid., pp. 444, 459, 559.
241   FO 401/1, pp. 435–6, Beke to Layard, 2 Sep. 1862; see also Lejean, *Théodore II*, p. 119; Dufton, *Narrative*, p. 24. For Beke's attitude towards Tēwodros, see FO 401/1, pp. 338–41 (26 Dec. 1859), 374–5 (7 Feb. 1861), 433–4 (22 Aug. 1862).
242   Douin, *Ismaïl*, III, 1, p. 64.
243   AEMD, Afrique 61, fols 135–6, cutting from *Le Monde*, 15 Mar. 1863, citing *La Patrie*.

likely to be found in any concern about internal security.[244] He had at his immediate disposal a large and experienced, but increasingly restless army, estimated at 40,000–50,000 fighting men and twice that number of camp-followers. This number did not include the troops of Tigrē and Lasta, which could also be mobilized, particularly for anything presented as a national cause. Many believed that the King could at this time rally 100,000–150,000 armed men if necessary.[245] An incursion into the Sudan was therefore not beyond Tēwodros's military resources, and the advantages of a campaign against an external enemy might well have outweighed the risks involved. But the western frontier was only part of the 'Turkish' problem that faced Ethiopia in 1862.

The elimination of Nigusē had brought Tēwodros face to face with Turkish expansion on the Red Sea coast. As long as the French hoped that they could obtain control over the littoral through their transactions with Nigusē, they maintained that the whole coast belonged to Ethiopia, however vague the suzerainty over some of the coastal chiefs might be.[246] Faced with the failure of this plan and with British attempts from Aden to obtain a foothold in the neighbourhood of Massawa through agreement with some local chief, the French decided to seek another ally. Consul Gilbert conveniently discovered that the Turkish governor of Massawa would like to occupy Desē and was instructed not to oppose this; if necessary in view of an imminent British action, he should actively encourage the governor to press the Turkish claims.[247]

One year later the Turks had taken possession of the island of Desē and the ports of Zulla and Edd. There were indications that the governor of Massawa planned further annexations. Plowden's successor, Captain C. D. Cameron, felt that there might be advantages to Great Britain in the Turkish occupation but could not help pointing out that Ethiopia's main supplies of the rock salt used as internal currency and the sulphur used for powder production were in the danger zone. The consul met emissaries sent by the governor of Tigrē to find out exactly what was going on along the coast, and believed it to be 'a matter of certainty' that Tēwodros would sooner or later overrun 'the Turkish possessions on the Coast'. He nevertheless seems to have hoped that he could prevent this 'if the pretensions of the Turks were placed within proper bounds'.[248] When he learned that Tēwodros had been informed, he urged his government to warn Istanbul:

244 Spittler-Archiv, D 3/1, Bender to Gobat, 20 Nov. 1861; FO 401/1, Cameron to Russell, 22 Jul. 1862.
245 Heuglin, *Abessinien*, pp. 356–8; Dufton, *Narrative*, p. 181; Lejean, 'Voyage', *TM*, 1867, I, p. 354; FO 401/2, pp. 70–3, Ayrton to Russell, 19 Sep. 1864. Heuglin's companion Steudner (*Petermann*, 1862, p. 425) has the lowest figure for the King's own army at this time: 30,000 soldiers.
246 AECP, Massouah 3, fols 47–8, Gilbert to Thouvenel, 30 Jun. 1860.
247 ibid., fols 81–2, Gilbert to Thouvenel, 10 Dec. 1860; fols 103–6, Thouvenel to Gilbert. 29 Mar. 1861; also AECC, Massouah 2, fols 21a–f, Thouvenel to Lejean, May 1862.
248 FO 401/1, p. 407, Baroni to Russell, 14 Dec. 1861: pp. 410–11, Cameron to Russell, 20 Mar. 1862; 'Heuglin's Expedition', *Petermann*, 1862, pp. 22–3.

. . . the Turks must be kept back, particularly as they calculate on a certain approval on our part of their proceedings, and will assuredly bring themselves into collision with Theodore, if they encroach *so rapidly* on the interior as they have been lately doing.[249]

Later he found that Tēwodros had instructed the governor of Hamasēn to collect tribute as usual but avoid all provocation. Only if he was attacked should he call for troops from Tigrē and resist.[250] At his first interview with the King on 7 October, Cameron learned, however, that his apprehensions were justified. Tēwodros spoke with anger about the Turks who 'were encroaching on him on every side'; they had, as he expressed it, planted seven flags on the sea-coast and were advancing 'from the Egyptian quarter'.[251]

Besides the two border problems, there was a third matter in which Tēwodros felt that he and his people were wronged by the 'Turks'. Ever since the appeal of Ali and Wibē in 1852, the convent in Jerusalem and the Ethiopian pilgrims there had enjoyed a semi-official British protection.[252] Consul Finn had not failed to take credit for this in communications to Tēwodros,[253] but he had been far from successful in his attempts to get formal and legal recognition of the property rights of the Ethiopians.[254] In 1862 relations between the Copts and Ethiopians deteriorated; they quarrelled over the keys to the church they used in common, and, in Finn's words, '. . . the Copts have lately taken to beating them [the Abyssinians] more than formerly, both men and women . . .' The Turkish authorities sided with the Copts, and Finn's attempts to assist the Ethiopians were met by the old claim that all Abyssinians were Ottoman subjects. By stressing the ecclesiastical authority of the Patriarch of Alexandria, a Turkish subject, over Copts and Abyssinians alike, the claim received an additional interesting dimension, but the main arguments remained 'the political principle that the Sublime Porte will never recognize the Abyssinians as a people independent of their dominion' and the fact that 'ancient Firmans or other documents issued on their behalf used to pass through the hands of the Civil Governor of Jeddah'. Finn reported that he drew some parallels: the Patriarch and the Pope, Jidda and Calais, Abyssinia and Algiers, but avoided bringing up the otherwise appropriate argument that the Sultan also claimed to be 'King of India'. The Turkish pasha was unimpressed. Russell minuted: 'They [the Abyssinians] are an independent State. But we need not protect Abyssinians more than Algerines.'[255]

Though Tēwodros had most probably heard about the events in Jerusalem before, Cameron did not exactly calm his fears by handing over an account in

249   FO 401/1, p. 437, Cameron to Hammond, 27 May 1862 (my emphasis).
250   ibid., p. 439, Cameron to Russell, 22 Jul. 1862.
251   ibid., pp. 456–9, Cameron to Russell, 31 Oct. 1862. See also Lejean, *Théodore II*, p. 75, and for Turkish claims and apprehensions, letters from Pertew Effendi to Jidda and Istanbul, 1861 and 1862, in SP.HNA, Carton 1503/2.
252   See above, pp. 131–6; FO 401/1, p. 415, FO memorandum, 23 May 1862.
253   FO 401/1, pp. 309–10, Finn to Malmesbury, 21 Jun. 1858.
254   ibid., pp. 325–6, Finn to Malmesbury, 27 May 1859.
255   ibid., pp. 409–10, Finn to Bulwer, 11 Mar. 1862; pp. 413–14, Finn to Russell, 7 May 1862, with minutes; p. 426, Finn to Bulwer, 3 Jun. 1862.

Arabic of the outrages and the fruitless attempts of Consul Finn to assist the Ethiopians.[256] In order to understand the importance of this matter to Tēwodros, it is necessary to recall that the traditional, pious Ethiopian has always had a tremendous attachment and veneration for the Holy Land. The very idea that Jerusalem was in the hands of unbelievers was offensive, almost incomprehensible to Tēwodros.[257] His own attachment to the cause of liberating Jerusalem is clearly expressed in one of the appellations he used in the ceremonial bragging called *fukkera: Ye-Habesha bal, ye-Īyerusalēm ičhoñña* (the husband of Abyssinia, the betrothed of Jerusalem).[258] The prospect of losing even the symbolic presence, the 'inheritance' of Ethiopia in the Holy Land, must have been at least as serious to Tēwodros as encroachments on the frontiers of the country.

At the end of the rainy season 1862, Tēwodros faced a crucial decision. Whether the events in the Sudan, on the Red Sea coast and in Jerusalem were really connected or not, to Tēwodros they all represented different aspects of Turkish oppression and aggression against Ethiopia. It is hardly surprising that he felt aggrieved and was prepared to hit back on one front or another. But there was an additional concern. What would France and England do if he accepted the challenge and went to war with the Turks? Could he count on arms and ammunition, on the active support of one or the other on the coast, or at least their approval and moral support? Or would they side with the Turks as they had done in the Crimean war? The new British consul to Ethiopia arrived as if summoned precisely to clarify this point. According to Cameron's report, Tēwodros began by simply telling the consul that he intended to go and fight the Turks and would send ambassadors to the European courts to explain and justify his action. In further interviews he asked if the British were willing to sell arms to him and if they would prevent Turkish or French interference on the coast in case he marched against Egypt. Without replying to these questions, Cameron took the first possible opportunity to tell the King that England could not arrange for the safe conduct of his ambassador through Egypt if there was war or even 'skirmishes on the frontier'. Tēwodros then repeated that he would fight in defence of his country and faith; '*but he made this important addition, that he would not make or bring on war until he had made an appeal to all Christendom*'.[259] In order to further deter Tēwodros, Cameron on the one hand informed him that the Porte would be warned not to do anything that would cause offence and showed him a letter he had himself written to the British consul in Khartoum asking the latter to do his utmost to preserve peace. On the other hand, the King was also informed that the French were about to establish a settlement at Tajura to be used as 'a base of operations against Abyssinia', that Sa'id Pasha had gone

---

256 ibid., pp. 456–9, Cameron to Russell, 31 Oct. 1862. On 14 May 1862, Flad wrote to Gobat that Debtera Gebre Īyesus, possibly Tēwodros's envoy of 1857, was about to leave for Jerusalem (Spittler-Archiv, XXX/8).
257 Stern, *Wanderings*, p. 56; Waldmeier, *Erlebnisse*, pp. 17–18; Lejean, 'Voyage', *TM*, 1865, II, pp. 271–2; Dufton, *Narrative*, p. 117.
258 See Rubenson, *Tēwodros*, pp. 60–1.
259 FO 401/1, pp. 456–9, Cameron to Russell, 31 Oct. 1862 (my emphasis).

to France and that the Sultan was in Egypt. 'This various intelligence', observed Cameron, 'seems to have pressed heavily on His Majesty.'[260]

Cameron had thus made the decision still more difficult for Tēwodros by implying that there was some understanding between France and Turkey— 'Your Majesty has many enemies besides the Turks and Egyptians . . .'[261]— and by suggesting that England would restrain Turkey if only Ethiopia kept the peace. The King decided to write immediately to several of the rulers in Europe. To Victoria and Napoleon III, at least, he pointed out that he intended to fight for his lost provinces, but made only the most general appeal that his Christian colleagues ought to come to his assistance.[262] Cameron and a Frenchman, Auguste Bardel, who had arrived with Cameron, were asked to take the respective letters and return with the answers, which was expected to take about six months.[263]

In the meantime, the blow fell. Undeterred by anyone, Musa Pasha undertook an 'inspection tour of the frontiers' in February/March 1863 at the head of 8,000 men. The tour included the invasion of Qwara and the burning-down of Dunkur (early February), the looting of Metemma and a reconnaissance as far as Wehnī (about 12–17 February), the incorporation of Gedhabi through the submission of its *shaykh*, and a new, futile attempt to catch Umar Nimr far inside Ethiopian territory (late February). Nevertheless it fell short of Musa's declared intention 'to create a wilderness with a depth of seven marches to prevent all incursions by the Abyssinians into Sudanese territory'.[264] This would have depopulated vast areas and brought the frontier to the shores of Lake Ṭana. But the consequences were bad enough. Tēwodros lost both vassals and potential allies in the Sudan. Egyptian administration was strengthened along the frontier, and Ethiopian domination over Metemma was temporarily weakened.[265]

That Tēwodros held his hand, refrained from retaliation even in the face of

---

260   ibid.
261   FO 401/1, pp. 460–1, Cameron to Tēwodros, 22 Oct. 1862.
262   FO 95/721, no. 126, Tēwodros to Victoria, 29 Oct. 1862; AEMD, Afrique 61, fol. 105, Tēwodros to Napoleon III, 29 Oct. 1862. The date 20 October stands for 20 Ṭiqimt, i.e. 29 Oct. The letter to Victoria is written in both Amharic and English, the one to Napoleon III in French only, but both are sealed. The latter is in the handwriting of Mahdere Qal. In Amharic the appeal reads, 'እናንተም ፡ ተገፋልኝ ፡ ክርስቲያኑን ፡ እስላም ፡ አጠቃህ ፡ ሲለኝ ።'—a somewhat obscure sentence which can be translated 'You too, allow yourself to be oppressed with me [i.e. share my sufferings] when the Muslims try to oppress me, the Christian.' It has been rendered simply, 'See how the Ilam [*sic*] oppress the Christian.'
263   FO 401/1, pp. 461–3, Cameron to the political resident, Aden, 2 Nov. 1862; p. 465, Cameron to Russell, 1 Nov. 1862.
264   Douin, *Ismaïl*, III, 1, pp. 64–7. This account is based entirely on Musa's own dispatches in ENA. See also Lejean, 'Gallabat', *Nouvelles Annales*, 6, X, 1, p. 19. Cameron travelled through the northern parts of the area affected in May 1863, and reported (FO 401/2, p. 16, to Russell, 15 Aug. 1863) that Musa had taken a force of 14,000 men to Metemma, 'avowedly with the object of tempting King Theodore to open an attack'.
265   Lejean, 'Gallabat', *Nouvelles Annales*, 6, X, 1, pp. 23–4, 26. But see also FO 401/2, pp. 283–5, Rassam to Merewether, 27 Nov. 1865; Blanc, *Narrative*, p. 114; Rassam, *British Mission*, Vol. I, pp. 164, 169.

Musa's provocation, indicates how seriously the King took the conditions laid down by Cameron, and how strictly he was prepared to keep his promise not to engage even in 'skirmishes on the frontier'. Consul Lejean believed that the King refrained from counter-attacking because of fear of Musa's two cannon, and wrote, disparagingly, that he stayed on the shores of Lake Ṭana, in order to eat 'fresh fish, in view of Lent'.[266]

Ethiopia and Europe: Shattered Expectations

During the 1850s Tēwodros had repeatedly shown that he preferred, as far as possible, to deal with his two foreign policy issues as separate matters. He wanted to establish contacts with European powers for what they could contribute to the development of Ethiopia, not in order to find allies against his powerful neighbour, whom he hoped to be able to deal with through direct negotiations or by military means, if necessary. It was the British government and Consul Plowden who had insisted that he keep peace with Egypt. Plowden was all for secure boundaries and Ethiopian sovereignty over Massawa, but he wanted Tēwodros to be indebted to England for these benefits, so that he would become more susceptible to British influence.[267] The French had tried to gain a more direct control on the coast through Nigusē, and had on at least one occasion posed as the allies of Egypt, a policy which was abruptly reversed on the fall of Nigusē.[268]

In this situation the remarkable consistency of Tēwodros's policy asserted itself. The French consul at Massawa was informed that the King wanted to cultivate friendly relations with France no less than with any other European power. Frenchmen were welcome to visit and reside in Ethiopia. Foreign as well as Ethiopian Catholics were promised freedom of religious practice and protection on condition that they did not interfere in politics and did not demand that he should accept that the faith of Rome was superior to the faith of his fathers.[269] Though the deaths of Plowden and Bell in 1860 had removed his primary contacts and advisers on the matter, Tēwodros pushed on with his project of an embassy to England. Immediately after the defeat of Nigusē, he called Baroni to come to Adwa and take charge of the ambassadors, who were to bring Queen Victoria the news of his victory.[270] Baroni asked for instructions at once and even wrote to Aden for paper and wax for Tēwodros, but it was June before he received permission to go to Adwa, and in September he was still pleading for some guidance on what to do about the embassy, which was expected to leave at the end of the following month. In the meantime he appeased Tēwodros with

266 Lejean, 'Gallabat', *Nouvelles Annales*, 6, X, 1, p. 20.
267 See above, pp. 141, 182–7.
268 See above, pp. 191–2, 207.
269 AECP, Massouah 3, fol. 53, Bell to Gilbert, 13 Jun. 1860; fols 111–12, Tēwodros to Gilbert, n.d. (most likely April 1861).
270 FO 1/11, fol. 226, Tēwodros to Baroni, n.d. (middle of January 1861). See Stern, *Wanderings*, pp. 149, 228–9, for discussions about the embassy in 1860 and Bell's expectation that he would be a member of the group to go to London.

a consignment of gunpowder and assurances of British friendship.[271] On 9 February 1862, Cameron arrived at Massawa with no other instructions on the matter than to find out the purpose of the King's embassy. It was June before he reached Gonder, and October before he joined Tēwodros in his camp.[272]

In the meantime Gilbert had rejected the King's 'simple letter' and pressed for a more formal guarantee authorizing the Catholic missionaries to reside wherever they liked.[273] A few additional European adventurers had arrived but failed to live up to their promises or Tēwodros's expectations, and both the missionary craftsmen and the workers among the Felasha felt that their relations with the King and, in the case of the artisans, with the people were deteriorating. Though others were more moderate, Flad spoke of a general, hidden hatred of the King towards Europeans showing up more and more.[274] Discoveries about the kind of recognition Nigusē had gained through his contacts with Europe caused Tēwodros to wonder why all his approaches were ignored or met by criticism on the issue of religious freedom.[275] Cameron's arrival in this atmosphere was bound to be crucial.

The British consul reported an excellent reception. Tēwodros was happy with the friendly letter from Lord Russell and the engraved rifle and pistols which were handed over as a token of Queen Victoria's gratitude for what he had done in connection with Plowden's death. But difficulties soon arose. Cameron began to speak about reviving the 1849 treaty and disappointed Tēwodros by not being prepared to take charge of the ambassadors and arrange for their safe journey through Massawa and Egypt; in fact, excluding the possibility of an embassy unless Tēwodros refrained from all hostilities on the western frontier. At one point he was reportedly dismissed without as much as a farewell audience.[276] In part this may have been due to the intrigues of a French adventurer, Auguste Bardel, who had joined Cameron on his trip into the country in the hope of finding a market for arms.[277] According to the account of the Frenchman, 'Providence wanted to use the arms of the British against themselves'; so he had been given the opportunity to manage the consul's affairs when the latter fell ill. To outsiders he was known as Cameron's secretary, though this was later denied by the consul. At any rate, Bardel bragged to the French government that he

271 FO 401/1, pp. 381, 383, 394, 396, Baroni to Russell, 23 Jan. and 15 Feb. 1861, Murray to Baroni, 11 Apr. 1861, Baroni to Russell, 25 Jun. and 8 Sep. 1861; ADEN, A1A 319, Baroni to Playfair, 9 Apr. and 14 Nov. 1861; BN, Ethiop. 184, fol. 65, Baroni to Tēwodros, 5 Nov. 1861.

272 FO 401/1, pp. 396–7, Murray to Cameron, 16 Nov. 1861; pp. 410, 439, 456–9, Cameron to Russell, 9 Feb., 22 Jul. and 31 Oct. 1862.

273 AECP, Massouah 3, fols 127–8, Gilbert to Thouvenel, 25 Jun. 1861.

274 Spittler-Archiv, D 3/9, Saalmüller to Schneller, 13 Jan. 1861; D 3/1, Bender to Gobat, 20 Nov. 1861; D 3/2, Flad to Gobat, 3–4 Dec. 1861; D 3/11, Schimper to Gobat, 6 Feb. 1862; XXX/8, Flad to Gobat, 14 May 1862; 'Heuglin's Reise', *Petermann*, 1867, p. 430; Waldmeier, *Erlebnisse*, pp. 9–15.

275 Lejean, 'Voyage', *TM*, 1867, I, p. 374; *idem*, *Théodore II*, pp. 109–10.

276 FO 401/1, pp. 456–61, Cameron to Russell, 31 Oct. 1862, Cameron to Tēwodros, 22 Oct. 1862. See also above, pp. 182–7. For a detailed Ethiopian description of the reception, see Fusella, *Tēwodros*, pp. 27–30.

277 Guillaume Lejean, 'Notes d'un voyage en Abyssinie', *TM*, 1864, I, p. 78.

had intrigued against Cameron, bribed chiefs and priests, and thus deprived the consul of all influence.[278] All the foreigners in Ethiopia, including his own countrymen, seem to have agreed that he was a scoundrel.[279] He was certainly a most unreliable person,[280] but this was something Tēwodros could hardly have known in October 1862. The King decided to use both Cameron and Bardel as his couriers.

Letters were prepared for Victoria and Napoleon III. Tēwodros introduced himself, the man whom God had raised up 'out of the dust' to save Ethiopia, and his achievements and determination to reclaim the territories lost to the Turks. The specific request in both letters concerned his planned embassies. As far as London was concerned, he could see only one problem: 'And now that the Turks are there on the coast to prevent me from sending my envoy with friendly gifts together with Consul Cameron, write to me at what place someone will meet him. May Consul Cameron bring the answer.' Napoleon was asked whether the envoys would be well received or not, the reply to be sent by the hand of Bardel.[281] When Cameron and Bardel were leaving, letters were being prepared for Holland, Russia, and some of the German states as well. The planned embassies would no doubt have been charged with specific tasks such as purchasing arms and recruiting skilled personnel for service in Ethiopia. But the wording of the letters shows that Tēwodros was initially groping for recognition and reassurance. He wanted his Christian colleagues in Europe to understand his situation. Afraid that he would be regarded as the aggressor, he wanted, as Cameron put it, 'to justify his conduct'.[282]

It is not difficult to find explanations for Tēwodros's feelings of insecurity. England and France, in particular, seemed to be on the friendliest terms with Turkey and Egypt. Europeans in great numbers were involved in the modernization and development of Egypt. They seemed to travel freely and in safety, and the Egyptian ruler himself was received in European capitals. At the same time the presence and obvious power and influence of the Europeans on the Red Sea coast, in Cairo and Jerusalem, had not prevented annexations at the expense of Ethiopia or injustice towards Ethiopians. Tēwodros's political horizon was still limited, his main categories religious: 'That a Christian nation like the English

278 AEMD, Afrique 61, fols 211–21, '2me Rapport', 10 Mar. 1863; FO 1/17, fols 423–6, report by Flad, 10 Jul. 1866; Waldmeier, *Erlebnisse*, p. 25; FO 1/26, fols 247–53, Cameron to Stanley, 28 Sep. 1868.
279 AEMD, Afrique 61, fols 106–27, 'Abyssinie. Première partie. Travail de M. le Dr Lagarde', n.d. (mid-1865); Stern, *Captive Missionary*, pp. 80, 84; Flad, *Zwölf Jahre*, Vol. I, pp. 70–3, 88; Vol. II, p. 15; Waldmeier, *Erlebnisse*, pp. 60–1. But see also his own version of their relations in *The Standard*, 29 Sep. 1868.
280 See above, p. 20. One cannot help wondering how Bardel's report could be filed away without a question-mark, when he has Tēwodros asking De Jacobis to crown him *after the death of Niguse* (January 1861), though Tēwodros had been crowned since 1855, and De Jacobis, moreover, died before Niguse.
281 FO 95/721, no. 126, Tēwodros to Victoria, 29 Oct. 1862; AEMD, Afrique 61, fol. 105, Tēwodros to Napoleon III, 29 Oct. 1862. See above, p. 222, n. 262.
282 FO 401/1, pp. 456–9, 464–5, Cameron to Russell, 31 Oct. and 1 Nov. 1862. The purchasing of arms was mentioned, as was the recruitment of an engineer for road-building and some medical doctors (pp. 461–3, Cameron to the political resident, Aden, 2 Nov. 1862).

should tolerate idolatry in India, and uphold the power of Mohammedanism in Egypt and Turkey, he could not understand . . .'[283] The more essential was it to find out if he could obtain the moral support of his Christian 'cousins'. This was why he promised the British consul to postpone all hostilities against the Turks.

Two months after the departure of Cameron and Bardel, Guillaume Lejean arrived in Ethiopia as the vice-consul of France charged with the tasks of negotiating a commercial treaty with Tēwodros on the lines of the Plowden–Ali treaty of 1849, protecting Catholic missionaries in Ethiopia and exploring the market for French merchandise.[284] The gifts he brought were far from impressive, and his task of convincing the King that French policy had changed was far from easy. Nevertheless, he reported an excellent reception. Tēwodros brushed aside the embarrassment over the presents with a generous '. . . the friendship of France is worth more than all the gifts in the world'. He listened attentively to the exposition of traditional French policy in the East: the protection of the Christians there. Then he raised his own favourite theme of obtaining European instructors for his people and spoke of the envoys, already selected, whom he planned to send to France and England as soon as assurances arrived from the two powers that they could guarantee the safe travel of his people through Egypt, hopefully by July. Lejean, according to his own report, assured Tēwodros that the Egyptians could not block the embassies, since no war had been declared between the two countries.[285]

The French government found Lejean's dispatch encouraging and assured him that the Egyptian ruler would be approached about the safe transit through Egypt of the Ethiopian ambassadors.[286] In fact, they were far more concerned that Bardel's appearance in Paris, where it was believed in March 1863 that an Ethio-Egyptian war had actually been declared and had already broken out, might lead the Egyptians to suspect that France in any way sympathized with Tēwodros's plans. In the reply which Bardel received to take back to Tēwodros (and which was copied to Cairo), there were least of all any commitments to support Ethiopia.[287] How the French government could be optimistic about future relations with Ethiopia in these circumstances is a mystery.

Meanwhile, in Ethiopia, Lejean had already clashed with Tēwodros. This

283 Stern, *Wanderings*, p. 56.

284 AECC, Massouah 2, fols 4–25, instructions for Lejean, 25 Apr.–7 May 1862 (3 documents); AEMD, Afrique 61, fols 102–3, Lejean to Faugère, 9 Apr. 1862; AED, Protocole C41, undated draft of Drouyn de Lhuys to Tēwodros; Lejean, *Théodore II*, pp. 138–9.

285 AEMD, Afrique 61, fols 130–3, Lejean to Drouyn de Lhuys, 28 Jan. 1863. Lejean's account is glowing, but see Dufton, *Narrative*, p. 108, and Waldmeier, *Erlebnisse*, pp. 27–8, for indications that the King was annoyed with some of the 'nonsensical things' presented to him and expressed some doubt about the sincerity of the French change of attitude. Waldmeier interpreted at the meeting. For envoys, see Lejean, 'Voyage', *TM*, 1867, I, p. 371.

286 AECP, Massouah 3, fols 132–3, Drouyn de Lhuys to Lejean, 27 Mar. 1863.

287 AEMD, Afrique 61, fols 400–1, Drouyn de Lhuys to Tastu, 27 Mar. 1863; fols 398–9, Drouyn de Lhuys to Tēwodros, 24 Mar. 1863; also fols 394–5, minutes.

clash was in a sense the beginning of the end and therefore as important as the better-known conflict with Cameron. In both cases the real causes have been obscured.[288] After the first talks in late January, Lejean was given the option between proceeding to Massawa and residing in Ethiopia. He chose the latter, although he must have known that Tēwodros did not recognize any special consular privileges and himself wrote '. . . that Abyssinia is one vast state prison for all travellers; but it is fair to add that the extreme kindness of the Sovereign greatly alleviates the inconveniences of this situation'.[289] In view of what happened later, it is worth noting that what Lejean found objectionable here was really Tēwodros's policy of controlling the entry and exit of foreigners. Within the country those who were not employees of the King were allowed to move about quite freely, though not without some supervision and protection. This applied to Lejean himself even after his clashes with Tēwodros. In 1862 and 1863 Tēwodros was moreover very liberal with visas: for example, entry or re-entry for T. von Heuglin and H. Steudner, J. Baptist, Cameron and his staff, the hunters K. Schiller and T. Essler, the missionaries F. Brandeis and W. Staiger, Dufton, Lejean and Lagarde, Stern and H. Rosenthal; and exit for Captain Charles Speedy, the missionary C. Bronkhorst, and Bishop Massaja, in addition to most of the above, in fact to all who applied to leave before November 1863. The case of the missionary C. Haussmann at Metemma is particularly revealing. In mid-1863, he received a letter from Tēwodros permitting him to enter and leave Ethiopia at will, without being bothered by any customs officers.[290]

On 10 February 1863 Lejean decided that he wanted to accompany Tēwodros on a campaign against Tedla Gwalu in Gojjam. It was about three weeks later, on 2 March, that the consul asked for permission to leave for Massawa. This was refused out-of-hand, perhaps on grounds of Lejean's personal safety, but also because Tēwodros had decided—and Lejean initially, it seems, accepted—that he would stay in Ethiopia until Bardel returned. Lejean insisted repeatedly, first through messengers and finally at an afternoon audience, that he should be allowed to depart. Instead he was arrested, and released the following day only on condition that he would not try to leave without permission.[291]

Though there was talk about Tēwodros having been scared or annoyed by

288   Malécot ('Voyageurs', *RFHO*, LVIII, p. 325), for instance, explains Lejean's arrest entirely as the result of Tēwodros's vicious mood after the resistance of the Gojjamites and Lejean's insufficient knowledge of prevailing court etiquette and the King's character.

289   AEMD, Afrique 61, fols 130–3, Lejean to Drouyn de Lhuys, 28 Jan. 1863; Dufton, *Narrative*, pp. 100–1.

290   Waldmeier, *Erlebnisse*, p. 35, where the Amharic original of this letter is reproduced. Stern was reportedly (ibid., p. 39) given the same kind of passport. Information on the travel and the entry and exit of the other persons mentioned is found scattered in their own writings, in the diplomatic correspondence and in such sources as *Erlebnisse* and Flad's *Zwölf Jahre*.

291   AEMD, Afrique 61, fols 137–8, Lejean to Anon., 8 Mar. 1863; Lejean, 'Notes', *TM*, 1864, I, pp. 78–80; *idem*, *Théodore II*, pp. 142, 151; Waldmeier, *Erlebnisse*, pp. 28–30; Dufton, *Narrative*, p. 187.

Lejean's touching the hilt of his sword or even wearing it in the King's presence,[292] it is more likely that he lost his temper and seized the consul because the latter persisted in arguing with him. In his first account of the arrest, Lejean gave two reasons: the frustration of Tēwodros because of the setbacks in Gojjam and the 'absurd suspicion' that the consul was in collusion with the Egyptians. In his earliest and most detailed *published* narrative, Lejean omitted the 'absurd suspicion' but added that the King had just learnt that the Egyptians 'had occupied his province of Gallabat'; further that he was intoxicated and that he wanted to hold the consul as a hostage because he feared that Napoleon III would ignore the letter he had sent with Bardel.[293]

The talk about Tēwodros's setbacks in Gojjam was obviously an attempt to divert attention from the real issues, and the same most probably applies to the hint about intoxication.[294] None of the other Europeans in the camp—and there were several—got into trouble at the time, though it should have been a great deal easier for Tēwodros to find a reason or a pretext for venting his anger on them in connection with the campaign. The events on the frontier were much more serious, and the news of Musa Pasha's looting of Metemma (about 12–17 February) and the appearance of Egyptian soldiers at Wehnī would in all probability have reached Tēwodros just a day or two before the arrest of Lejean. It may have been coincidence that Lejean requested his leave just then, but it would have been hard for Tēwodros to believe. Had not Lejean been present in Khartoum while Musa prepared his attack? Had he not arrived in Ethiopia through Metemma only two months before the Egyptian army? He had spoken in general terms about his country as the protector of the Christians in the Orient, but there is no indication that he warned Tēwodros of the impending attack. That Tēwodros *did* suspect Lejean of collusion of some kind is attested by the fact that the *na'ib* of Arkīko, Muhammad Abd al-Rahim, who was otherwise reputed to be Tēwodros's loyal vassal and ally on the coast and who was also with the King in Gojjam, was arrested at the same time as Lejean. He was released one month later and was compensated by additional grants of land when he returned to the coast, where he changed his residence from Arkīko to Aylet, reportedly because he wanted to get away from the day-to-day contact with the Turks.[295] In view of the French support for Nigusē and Cameron's warnings or hints about a French–Egyptian alliance directed against Ethiopia,[296] Tēwodros's suspicions were natural rather than absurd. After all, Lejean had come with the intention of establishing a full-fledged consulate in Ethiopia with guaranteed immunity under a French flag and jurisdiction over French citizens

---

292   AEMD, Afrique 61, fol. 117, 'Abyssinie' by Lagarde; FO 401/2, pp. 4–5, 15, Cameron to Russell, 1 Jul. and 2 Oct. 1863.
293   AEMD, Afrique 61, fols 137–8, Lejean to Anon., 8 Mar. 1863; Lejean, 'Notes', *TM*, 1864, 1, pp. 78–9.
294   This attempt at diversion was noted by Waldmeier at the time (*Erlebnisse*, p. 30).
295   AEMD, Afrique 61, fols. 396–7, Lejean to Drouyn de Lhuys, 21 Mar. 1863; Lejean, *Théodore II*, pp. 145, 246; *idem*, 'Voyage', *TM*, 1867, I, p. 388; FO 401/2, pp. 82–3, Rassam to Merewether, 4 Nov. 1864.
296   See above, pp. 221–2.

and protégés. He seems, moreover, to have entertained the illusion that Bogos, Hamasēn, and Tigrē(!) were already French possessions, and no sooner had he got into difficulties than he suggested to Paris the occupation by force of Tigrē, which he promised would be easier to carry out than any of the French conquests made in Senegal. He also maintained that access to the coast would be no problem, since the *na'ib* would cede with pleasure the small zone necessary.[297] Though he may have been prudent in his discussions with Tēwodros, it is more than likely that Lejean had revealed some of these ideas to the Europeans at Gefat and that they had reached the King's ears in some form or another.[298]

At any rate, Tēwodros wanted to know what he could expect from France in the future and had sent Bardel to find out. It was when Lejean dissociated himself from Bardel, began to cast suspicion on his countryman's character, and argued back to the King that the latter 'accepted no more instruction' but lost his patience and arrested him.[299] A new attempt at the end of May brought the following angry response:

> If he [Napoleon III] has sent you in the interest of friendship and love, I have told you in front of Mr. Kienzlen and my children [the Europeans working for Tēwodros] to remain quietly until the man I sent [Bardel] returns to me. If you have come to quarrel and fight, tell me. I will hear you.[300]

That Lejean, in order to get away, engaged in the defamation of Bardel was particularly annoying to Tēwodros. The King was, in fact, becoming disillusioned with the intrigue and slandering among the Europeans at his court, and both spoke and wrote ironically about their superiority:

> From the time I was born until I became a man I heard the reports; over and over again I was told that, by the power of God, there are in Europe, in the countries of the foreigners, those whose governments do not fall, who lack nothing in terms of law and order, in whom there is no deceit, and, by the power of God, I was very happy. If you tell me now that that man [Bardel] is a liar, that he is a deceiver, by what sign am I to believe that he is really a deceiver [and] a liar?[301]

297 AEMD, Afrique 61, fols 137–8, Lejean to Anon., 8 Mar. 1863; fols 396–7, Lejean to Drouyn de Lhuys, 21 Mar. 1863.
298 ibid., fols 118–19, 'Abyssinie' by Lagarde.
299 AECC, Massouah 2, fols 37–8, testimonial by Kienzlen and Saalmüller, 10 Jun. 1863, about Lejean's arrest, requested and forwarded by Lejean himself (ibid., fol. 35). Waldmeier was also present in the group interpreting for the King and Lejean (*Erlebnisse*, p. 29).
300 BN, Ethiop. Abb. 254, fol. 313, Tēwodros to Lejean, n.d., Amharic copy in Antoine d'Abbadie's hand; AECC, Massouah 2, fols 35–6, Lejean to Drouyn de Lhuys, 6 Jun. 1863, with enclosed copies of Lejean to Tēwodros, 27 Jun. 1863, and Tēwodros to Lejean, n.d., in translation. This translation is correct in substance, but in his published account ('Voyage', *TM*, 1865, II, p. 270), Lejean presented a different version, in which Tēwodros accused him of conspiring with the *shifta* (rebels).
301 BN, Ethiop. 184, fol. 77 *bis*, Tēwodros to Lejean, n.d., Amharic original. There is no copy, translation, or reference to this document in Lejean's correspondence with the Ministry of Foreign Affairs. It is impossible to date exactly, but would seem to belong either to the crisis of 2 March or to the exchange of letters in May–June (AEMD, Afrique 61, fols 121–2). Lejean carefully avoided this issue, but Lagarde reported that he was shown a letter from

As far as Tēwodros was concerned, Bardel would supply the answer by either returning or staying away. By September 1863 Bardel appeared in Gonder with a letter from the French government. His return, of course, pleased the King, but the letter was found unsatisfactory in several respects. Tēwodros decided to settle his score with France and its official representative as publicly as possible. Not only Lejean, Lagarde, and Cameron, but also the Felasha missionaries and the artisans from Gefat were called to Gonder. There, on 28 September, the translated letter was read out to a group including at least Bardel, Zander, Waldmeier, Kienzlen, Flad, Stern, Haussmann, and Cameron.[302]

Besides wishing Ethiopia peace and progress, the French government's letter made two points. Firstly, the French emperor was the protector of the Catholic missionaries all over the world, and nothing would please him more than hearing that they were treated with the respect due to them, particularly as all governments worthy of being called civilized had adopted the principle of religious freedom. Secondly, Tēwodros would be ill-advised to start a war against powerful neighbours without properly considering his own resources. As for the embassy, the commitment was vague: the French emperor would always be pleased to establish friendly contacts with Ethiopia in the interests of trade.[303] Adding insult to injury, Napoleon III had not replied personally but had instructed his minister, his *ashkar* (servant), to write instead. Bardel did not improve the situation with his description of the indifferent reception he had received in Paris. Bardel knew how dangerous it might be to reveal this, but seems to have reversed a previous determination to conceal it.[304]

Tēwodros rejected the French reply as disrespectful on four counts: his emissary had not been properly received; Napoleon III had not answered the letter personally; he had not affixed his seal to the reply; and the French foreign minister had in Napoleon's presence told Bardel that Tēwodros was 'a mere brigand'.[305] Moreover, and this was the most weighty argument, the reply

---

Lejean to Tēwodros in June 1863 and asked whether he also thought that Europeans were good, generous, and intelligent when they could write as Lejean had done, denouncing Bardel as a thief and a man without faith. See also Waldmeier, *Erlebnisse*, p. 36, and for an opinion about the relations between the Europeans in general, Rassam, *British Mission*, Vol. I, p. 261, and FO 401/2, pp. 702–3, 'Note of Conversation with M. Lejean . . .', 24 Aug. 1867.

302   Although he was not present in the inner circle all the time, the account of these events by Lagarde (AEMD, Afrique 61, fols 122–4) is the most detailed, but also Cameron (FO 401/2, pp. 4–5, Cameron to Russell, 2 Oct. 1863) and Haussmann (in Flad, *Zwölf Jahre*, Vol. I, pp. 54–6) provide detailed accounts written very soon after the events. For Lejean's version one must go to 'Voyage' (*TM*, 1865, II, pp. 271–2) and *Théodore II* (pp. 159–60), since his dispatch about these events seems to have disappeared. Stern's account (*Captive Missionary*, pp. 38–43) contains interesting but doubtful detail, while Waldmeier's version (*Erlebnisse* pp. 39–40) is brief and matter-of-fact.

303   AEMD, Afrique 61, fols 398–9, Drouyn de Lhuys to Tēwodros, 24 Mar. 1863.

304   ibid., fol. 124, 'Abyssinie' by Lagarde; fols 409–10, Bardel to Faugère, 7 Aug. 1863.

305   FO 401/2, pp. 4–5, Cameron to Russell, 2 Oct. 1863. In Stern's account (*Captive Missionary*, p. 42), Napoleon was told that Tēwodros cut off the hands and feet of his enemies; but then Stern believed—and correctly so—that the whole interview with the French emperor was invented. See AECC, Massouah 2, fols 52–3, Drouyn de Lhuys to Lejean, 18 Jan. 1864.

was really no answer to Tēwodros's letter at all.[306] The King reportedly threw the letter on the ground and stamped on it to show his anger and defiance. He refused to see Lejean, though he extracted a public declaration from the consul that France recognized him and him only as the legitimate ruler of Ethiopia. He also demanded that Lejean prove his accusations against Bardel, but received the reply that this could not be done with materials available in Ethiopia.[307] According to Waldmeier, Tēwodros's response was brief but final: 'I have liars enough in my country, let M. Lejean depart from here.' [308] The consul did not wait to be told twice, and Lagarde decided to leave with him.[309]

Lejean's later assertions that he was suspected by virtue of his position only, but never personally disliked by the King, were clearly dictated by his desire to exonerate himself from personal blame for the failure of his mission.[310] Tēwodros's own letters prove that he resented Lejean's attacks on Bardel and his stubborn refusal to accept the King's word as final. Nevertheless, it is difficult to see how better personal relations could have saved the situation. The response of the French government was too negative to be acceptable to Tēwodros, who was, moreover, offended because Lejean had approached him with samples of cloth, as if he was a shopkeeper. If the French policy of protecting the Christians in the Middle East, of which Lejean had spoken, simply meant for Ethiopia the protection of Catholic priests and bishops forced upon the country, it was not what Tēwodros was looking for: '. . . he had wanted Christian friendship, as from one king to another. It had been refused—and M. Lejean might return to his master.' [311] The French consul preferred to make Tēwodros's words seem applicable to all Europeans:

> I know . . . the tactics of the European governments when they want to seize a country in the Orient. First they send missionaries, then consuls to support the missionaries, then battalions to sustain the consuls. I am not a rajah from Hindustan to be made a fool of like that: I prefer to engage the battalions at once.[312]

Though the words are almost certainly not authentic, Tēwodros's experiences with the French justified the allegation of the missionary–consul relationship. His decision to expel the consul and thereby break off relations with France was born primarily out of his determination not to be dictated to by any European power. In that sense, the meeting at Gonder represents a shift of emphasis away from the problem of relations with Egypt and Turkey to that of relations with Europe. Could a non-European expect to be accepted as an equal by European

306 Haussman (Flad, *Zwölf Jahre*, Vol. I, pp. 55–6) also lists the objections as four, including this instead of the remark about Tēwodros's background or character.
307 AEMD, Afrique 61, fols 123–4, 'Abyssinie' by Lagarde; Stern, *Captive Missionary*, pp. 42–3.
308 [Theophil Waldmeier], *The Autobiography of Theophilus Waldmeier* (London, 1886), p. 81.
309 AEMD, Afrique 61, fol. 125, 'Abyssinie' by Lagarde.
310 Lejean, 'Voyage', *TM*, 1865, II, p. 271.
311 FO 401/2, pp. 4–6, Cameron to Russell, 2 Oct. and 5 Oct. 1863; Waldmeier, *Erlebnisse*, p. 40; Rassam, *British Mission*, Vol. II, pp. 60–1.
312 Lejean, *Théodore II*, p. 160.

rulers? Tēwodros was still, with increasing impatience, awaiting the reply of the most important member of that circle, Queen Victoria.

Consul Cameron must have felt that his day of reckoning was approaching. Instead of going to London with the royal letter, he had sent it off to Aden and gone off to visit Bogos, Kasala, and Metemma. This trip seems to have been undertaken partly to re-establish British influence in Bogos by seeking justice for the looted Christians there, partly to check the new wave of tax- and tribute-collecting from both Kasala and Massawa, prompted in part at least by Musa Pasha's visit to Taka in March–April 1863, and partly to explore commercial opportunities, especially cotton production. Cameron warned the na'ib of Arkīko and the governor of Massawa not to collect tribute from Ethiopian sub¬ jects. The implied accusation was not lost on the Porte. In its complaint to London it was, however, careful to mention Habab only, while the real problems were farther inland. Cameron felt obliged to report his findings to Tēwodros, but the dilemma in which he had placed himself by obtaining the King's promise not to engage in any border warfare for the time being made him do so 'putting the best colour I can on facts which it is impossible for me to ignore'. This may have contributed to Tēwodros's suspicion with regard to Cameron's activities, for he was of course continuously informed by his own men, too.[313]

In June 1863 Cameron returned to Ethiopia and settled down with the missionaries at Jenda, and soon afterwards Tēwodros arrived there after his victory over Tedla Gwalu at Injabara. He was visibly displeased and disappointed that the consul had failed to bring a reply to his letter, and suspicious about Cameron's motives for visiting the Sudan as well. But he accepted, for the time being, Cameron's assurances that the reply would soon arrive, and remained on friendly terms with the missionaries, though Stern in particular seems to have felt uneasy about the future, probably because he knew that he was disliked and, as a British subject, identified closer with Cameron than the others did.[314]

The consul was sufficiently troubled on the eve of the Gonder council to advise the missionaries to be prudent and express their opinion on the desirability of religious freedom only if pressed to do so by the King. Nevertheless, Lejean himself gave Flad and the Swiss (German) missionaries credit for having supported him on this issue.[315] Stern is not mentioned; besides the consul's

---

313   FO 401/1, pp. 477, 497–9, 501–2, Cameron to Russell, 1 Jan., 31 Mar., and 18 May 1863; pp. 503–4, Cameron to Colquhoun, 20 May 1863; p. 510, Aali to Bulwer, 16 Sep. 1863; SP.HNA, Carton 236/1, Cameron to the *wekil* of the *na'ib*, 20 Mar. 1863; to Pertew Effendi, governor of Massawa, 31 Mar. 1863; FO 1/26, fols 247–53, Cameron to Stanley, 28 Sep. 1868; Blanc, *Captivity*, p. 33. It is understandable that Cameron in this final report defends himself against accusations of meddling in political matters and stresses the commercial aspects of the trip.

314   FO 401/2, pp. 15–16, Cameron to Russell, 1 Jul. and 15 Aug. 1863; pp. 172–7, Rev. Stern to Mrs Stern, April 1865; FO 1/26, fols 250–1, Cameron, 28 Sep. 1868; Flad, *Zwölf Jahre*, Vol. I, pp. 52–3; Waldmeier, *Erlebnisse*, pp. 34–7; Welde Maryam, *Tēwodros*, pp. 30–1.

315   FO 401/2, pp. 5–6, Cameron to Flad, 20 Sep. 1863; Lejean, *Théodore II*, p. 160. In his final report to the Foreign Office (FO 1/26, fol. 251), Cameron passed over his warning without mention and stressed everyone's determination to 'speak up for toleration'.

warning, he may have been influenced to keep silence by his close friendship with Abune Selama, who remained as hostile as ever to ecclesiastical establishments other than his own.

Nevertheless it was on Stern's head that the next blow fell, only two weeks after the expulsion of Lejean. Stern had received the King's permission to leave for Massawa, but unfortunately he did not use it when Lejean left. Tēwodros was annoyed when Stern unexpectedly appeared to take his leave. There were language problems which led to his being arrested in the royal camp, brutally beaten, and chained. Two of his Ethiopian companions were beaten to death. Both the circumstances of the intended farewell interview and Tēwodros's personal dislike of Stern certainly contributed to the harshness of the treatment. The search which followed of all Stern's papers at Gonder indicates, however, that there was more behind the arrest.[316] What Tēwodros was really looking for is difficult to say with certainty. According to Flad, who was ordered to participate in the search with several others, the King believed that Stern carried a letter from Abune Selama to the viceroy of Egypt which might prove the existence of an alleged conspiracy between the bishop, Cameron, and Stern to have parts of Ethiopia transferred to Egypt.[317]

There was also talk about a deal by which Selama had allegedly sold church lands in Ethiopia to the consul and the missionary. What was found at a second search one month later, and often assumed, at least, to have been the aim of the search in the first place, were offensive statements about the King in a copy of *Wanderings among the Falashas in Abyssinia*, for example, that Tēwodros was the son of a poor *koso*-vendor and that rebels had been 'mercilessly butchered in cold blood'. Objectionable material written by Stern's fellow-missionary H. Rosenthal and by Mrs Flad were also found. The former had produced a narrative with 'My first meeting with the wild beast' as a chapter heading and, presumably confusing *teskar* (commemoration of a deceased) with *sekkere* (to booze, to get drunk), alleged that the King had invited Acting Consul Baroni to come to Abyssinia so that they could get drunk together; Tēwodros had in fact wanted Baroni to come to commemorate the anniversary of Plowden's death. According to Stern, Rosenthal had also, in a letter to his brother, expressed the opinion that Ethiopia would be better off under Egyptian rule than under its own kings. All was translated into Amharic by Samu'ēl Gīyorgīs and Birru Pēṭros. At a public trial, to which all the Europeans were again called, Stern and Rosenthal were accused of having reviled the King, and though the British consul himself was obliged to pronounce a verdict of 'Guilty', no final sentence fell.[318]

---

316 FO 401/2, pp. 11–12, Haussmann to Petherick, 4 Jan. 1864; pp. 63, 172–7, Rev. Stern to Mrs Stern, 12 Apr. 1864 and Apr. 1865; Stern, *Captive Missionary*, pp. 44–53; Flad, *Zwölf Jahre*, Vol. I, pp. 57–9; Waldmeier, *Erlebnisse*, pp. 41–2.

317 Flad, *Zwölf Jahre*, Vol. I, p. 71; also Stern, *Captive Missionary*, p. 72.

318 Since Haussmann left Ethiopia within a week after the end of these events, his accounts (FO 401/2, pp. 11–12, to Petherick, 4 Jan. 1864, and Flad, *Zwölf Jahre*, Vol. I, pp. 61–70) are the earliest and possibly the most trustworthy. Stern's accounts (FO 401/2, pp. 172–7, to his wife, April 1865, and *Captive Missionary*, pp. 76–103, 146–8) contain more detail but also a number of contradictions, especially the latter very emotional narrative. For the offensive materials quoted and the translators, see Stern, *Wanderings*, pp. 63, 129; Flad,

Throughout the five to six weeks (13 October–20 November) during which Stern was the main target of Tēwodros's anger and frustration, the question of what reply Queen Victoria would send, if any, was never far below the surface. Stern was not suffering for his missionary activities at all, and only partly for his personal conduct and objectionable writings. To a considerable degree he was substituting for Consul Cameron and the British nation. It is not insignificant that Bardel and Samu'ēl Gīyorgīs appear repeatedly in the accounts as the main tools of the search and to a very great extent as instigators of the troubles. Bardel had started his career in Ethiopia by falling out with Cameron. Rightly or wrongly he blamed other Europeans for having played a role in creating the conflict between Lejean and himself, and though that conflict was not the main reason for Lejean's expulsion, it certainly had not helped French interests. Bardel allegedly informed Tēwodros that he had visited London before returning to Ethiopia and had been told by an employee of the Foreign Office that the British government would never answer his letter because 'The English are the friends of the Turks but not the friends of the Christian king of Abyssinia'. According to Flad, Tēwodros later accused Bardel of having caused the enmity between him and his 'friends', as he called the Jenda/Darna group, including Cameron, and of having tried the same with his 'children', the Gefat group of foreigners. Bardel is even said to have admitted this himself when he came to share the prison of Cameron and Stern.[319]

Samu'ēl Gīyorgīs was at this time one of the royal secretaries and had been sent with Cameron to the coast the year before as *baldereba*, a combination of guide, interpreter, provisioner, and spy. Cameron had dispatched him from Bogos to Massawa to wait for the reply from London that never came. Samu'ēl resented the treatment he had received, and probably suspected that the consul got rid of him because he did not want him to observe what he was doing and saying in the Sudan.[320] Samu'ēl was by now an old hand at political intrigue, Ethiopian as well as foreign, and allegedly very close to the King. It is not likely that he would hesitate to intercept and read the letters of Europeans if he suspected that they contained treasonable material. Flad admitted later that he and Cameron had tried to bribe Samu'ēl to be helpful after the arrest of Stern, and that he had taken the money but recommended the search of the missionary's papers. Though Samu'ēl obviously disliked Stern, as so many others did, it is more doubtful that he was generally speaking as hostile to foreigners, and Englishmen in particular, as Stern represented him.[321]

Zwölf Jahre, Vol. I, pp. 67, 72; Waldmeier, *Erlebnisse*, pp. 42–5, the latter revealing some information suppressed by the others.

319 Flad, *Zwölf Jahre*, Vol. I, pp. 71–2; FO 401/2, pp. 341–4, Flad to Clarendon, n.d., received 10 Jul. 1866; FO 1/26, fol. 251, Cameron to Stanley, 28 Sep. 1868. See also above, pp. 224–5.

320 FO 401/1, pp. 466–8, 501–2, Cameron to Russell, 18 Nov. 1862 and 18 May 1863.

321 FO 401/2, p. 291, Flad to Rassam, 21 Aug. 1865; FO 1/26, fol. 252, Cameron to Stanley, 28 Sep. 1868; Stern, *Captive Missionary*, pp. 48, 80, 188, 190. For Samu'ēl's earlier career, see above, p. 169. Rassam (*British Mission*, Vol. I, pp. 249–50, 258–64) speaks well of Samu'ēl, and lays much of the blame for the difficulties on a former servant of Baroni's and Cameron's, named Ingida Werq, instead.

At Jenda, in July or August, Cameron had reportedly offered Tēwodros his head if the reply from London did not arrive within two months.[322] By October, the time was up; almost a year had passed since Tēwodros had written his urgent message. The King's irritation was visible and mounting. Cameron, for instance, offered to make him a gift of some machinery and was asked for the reply to his letter. Promised again that it would arrive in due time, Tēwodros reportedly answered, 'I hope it will not contain such friendship as was offered by France'. When Cameron pleaded, in the name of long-standing British–Ethiopian friendship, for the release of Stern, Tēwodros refused to see him and sent the curt reply, 'Where are the proofs of that friendship?'[323] Though not himself arrested and maltreated, the consul was meant to feel the King's disfavour and his own powerlessness. And Cameron must certainly have been wondering, too, where the expected reply from the Queen was.

On 22 November 1863, two days after the trial of Stern, one of Cameron's staff, Kerans, arrived from Massawa *with the first response* to Cameron's dispatch of 31 October the year before:

> . . . I have to state to you that it is not desirable for Her Majesty's Agents to meddle in the affairs of Abyssinia, and you would have done better if you had returned to your post at Massowah when the King told you to do so. This it will be right that you should do at once, and you will remain at Massowah until further orders.[324]

There was not even a mention of the fact that the dispatch had contained a letter from the King. Cameron's warnings from Bogos that Tēwodros might 'either allow his grievances to accumulate, in order to lay them before Europe hereafter, or at once take violent measures to compel the Turks to a certain amount of decency in their transactions on his frontier' resulted in no more than a reminder of his position as a mere consul and of the earlier order to return to and remain at Massawa.[325] A third letter acknowledging the consul's dispatches from the Sudan repeated the disapproval of his 'proceedings in Abyssinia' and instructed him to 'abstain from all interference in the internal affairs of that country' and, again, remain at Massawa. This was a most unfair censure. Whatever Cameron may have done in excess of his original instructions, it was *not* interfering in the internal affairs of Ethiopia, and though the prediction that he would 'get himself and his Government into trouble' was already being fulfilled, it was not due primarily to any 'reckless conduct' on Cameron's part but to the reckless indifference of the Foreign Office with regard to Tēwodros's letter to Victoria and the projected embassy. On dispatch after dispatch, the only minute reads: 'No notice'. Six months after the Foreign Office had *received* the King's letter and his promise through the consul that he would refrain from all hostilities against the Egyptians and the Turks to allow time for consul-

322 [Waldmeier], *Autobiography*, pp. 80–1.
323 FO 1/26, fol. 252, Cameron to Stanley, 28 Sep. 1868; FO 401/2, pp. 11–12, Haussmann to Petherick, 4 Jan. 1864.
324 Flad, *Zwölf Jahre*, Vol. I, p. 69; FO 401/1, pp. 479–80, Russell to Cameron, 22 Apr. 1863.
325 FO 401/1, pp. 497–9, Cameron to Russell, 31 Mar. 1863; p. 501, Murray to Cameron, 13 Aug. 1863.

tations, there was not a word, even for the consul, on the issues raised.[326] That this was a deliberate decision is evident from a minute of the following year: 'No notice beyond this [the order for Cameron to go to Massawa] was to be taken of his Despatches'.[327]

Cameron had no choice but to ask Tēwodros for permission to leave. His request was refused, but no other action was taken against him for the time being. Presumably he was able to convince Tēwodros that there was still a possibility of a friendly reply from London. A further five or six weeks of suspense followed. There were widespread rumours that Egyptian armies were again approaching the frontiers.[328] One of the strangest expeditions of the period actually left Cairo in early October for the Ethiopian frontier. Ostensibly its leader, Count Raoul du Bisson, had come to found a cotton-growing colony in the Sudan, but he carried 400 rifles and four cannon in his baggage and 'revealed' to Ismail Pasha, viceroy of Egypt since the beginning of the year, that he was a French 'general' and had been sent out to create a military establishment and threaten Tēwodros with revenge for his arrest of Lejean. Ismail, who wanted to launch a new attack on Ethiopia without causing too strong European opposition, welcomed the opportunity for an operation in which France would find itself involved from the beginning. But du Bisson was not sure whether he wanted to found his colony on Sudanese or Ethiopian soil, and whether, if he went to war with Ethiopia, he wanted to do so in the name of France or Egypt. Ismail withdrew his support and the whole project miscarried at Kufit in May the following year.[329]

The timing is not unimportant. Consul Petherick reported from Khartoum *on 23 November* that du Bisson had arrived there with Musa Pasha and that 'the destination of the General is to be Abyssinia, but whether by way of Massowah, Taka, or Gallabat, and eventually to what part or to what purpose, has not yet fully transpired . . . Rumours are also afloat of preparations for another attempt on Abyssinia by the Egyptian Government . . .' This would be known at Gonder about one month later. One of Cameron's servants actually testifies that it was just when 'a report came that the Turks were about to invade Abyssinia from Matoomha' that the consul renewed his request.[330] Distressing news from Jerusalem aggravated the situation. Not satisfied with the chapel, the Copts and Armenians had bribed the Turkish authorities and succeeded in having the Ethiopians expelled from their convent as well. Finn's successor as consul had

---

326 ibid., pp. 456–76, minutes by various; pp. 486–8, Appendix, 11 Jun. 1863, to Memorandum by Hertslet; p. 508, minutes by Murray, 28 Aug. 1863; pp. 508–9, Russell to Cameron, 8 Sep. 1863. It is not possible to ascertain whether Cameron received all three or only one of the dispatches but it makes little difference.

327 FO 1/14, fols 105–6. This minute was omitted even from the Confidential Prints. See also Henry M. Stanley, *Coomassie and Magdala* (London, 1874), p. 280.

328 FO 401/2, pp. 11–12, Haussmann to Petherick, 4 Jan. 1864.

329 Douin, *Ismaïl*, III, 1, pp. 74–96. This is a comprehensive account based on the Egyptian and French sources. But see also FO 401/1, pp. 516–17, Colquhoun to Bulwer, 8 Nov. 1863; FO 401/2, pp. 2–3, Colquhoun to Russell, 11 Jan. 1864.

330 FO 401/2, pp. 2–3, Colquhoun to Russell, 11 Jan. 1864; pp. 64–5, Statement of Wadeer, 14 Jul. 1864; pp. 84–6, Rassam to Merewether, 2 Dec. 1864.

no orders to assist them, and by late September they were preparing to abandon Jerusalem altogether. Gobat had advised Tēwodros by letter to write to Queen Victoria—as if he had not already done so! Flad commented that the withdrawal of protection in itself was sufficient to convince the King that Britain was no longer a friendly nation.[331]

To request leave in these unfavourable circumstances and in spite of the King's earlier reply that the consul would not be allowed to leave until the answer from Queen Victoria had arrived was, in spite of instructions, a serious blunder, aggravated by a four-day deadline for the King's reply. To Tēwodros this was the ultimate evidence that there would be no answer to his letter, that the British had in fact sided with the Turks.[332] On 3 January 1864, deeply offended and angered, the King chained the consul, his European staff, and the four remaining Felasha missionaries. Flad recalled Tēwodros's explanation, that he had chained Captain Cameron because he had received no answer from the Queen; Stern and Rosenthal because they had abused him; and the others because he had found that all white people were wicked.[333] In London two years later, the missionary bluntly told the Foreign Office, 'If Mr. Kerans would have brought a letter for the King, whether good or bad—neither the Consul nor his subjects would have been imprisoned and deprived of all their property.'[334]

The King evidently recognized degrees of wickedness, however, for the missionaries (except Stern and Rosenthal) and two Germans who were only loosely associated with Cameron were freed after a month and directed to join in the work of the Gefat colony. The others, eight in number after Bardel had been obliged to join those he had intrigued against, remained in chains, and were in November taken to Meqdela.[335]

This outcome of his attempts to establish closer ties with Europe was a terrible blow to Tēwodros. He had given the Europeans who came to Ethiopia a friendly reception and, in return, he had counted on technical assistance, particularly in the field of armaments, and hoped for diplomatic support, possibly an alliance, in view of his conflict with Turkey and Egypt. The lack of response from Britain meant that there would be no embassy to Europe, no acceptance of Ethiopia into the community of the Christian nations of the world. He did not know whether to blame the British government or its consul. He was clearly disgusted (as his

331 Spittler-Archiv, XXX/22, Gobat to Tēwodros, 13 Jun. 1863; FO 401/1, p. 513, Moore to Bulwer, 28 Sep. 1863; FO 401/2, pp. 391–2, Flad to Murray, 21 Sep. 1866; Flad, *Zwölf Jahre*, Vol. I, p. 80. Whether an insulting and threatening letter to the King from Lejean at Massawa arrived before or just after the arrest of Cameron is impossible to know. See, in addition to Flad's account, Stern, *Captive Missionary*, pp. 135–6; FO 401/2, p. 29, Haussmann to Petherick, 14 Feb. 1864; Waldmeier, *Erlebnisse*, pp. 40–1.

332 Stern, *Captive Missionary*, p. 123.

333 Flad, *Zwölf Jahre*, Vol. I, pp. 75–6; FO 401/2, p. 29, Haussmann to Petherick, 14 Feb. 1864.

334 FO 401/2, pp. 341–4, Flad to Clarendon, n.d., received 10 Jul. 1866.

335 Flad, *Zwölf Jahre*, Vol. I, pp. 80–2; FO 401/2, p. 63, Rev. Stern to Mrs Stern, 12 Apr. 1864; pp. 126–8, Flad to Rassam and Schimper to Rassam, 26 Jan. 1865. The reasons given for Bardel's arrest are contradictory. He had made a trip to Kasala, presumably on the King's behalf, and it was on his return in early February that he was arrested (ibid., pp. 241–2, Bardel to Bardel, 12 Jul. 1865; Stern, *Captive Missionary*, pp. 136–7, 141).

letters to Lejean showed) with the intrigue and lack of goodwill among the Europeans in general and with what he regarded as ineptitude and downright foolishness in the representatives of the leading European powers and he did not mind saying it publicly:

> Really I do not know what is the matter with my cousins Napoleon and Victoria that they send me such creatures: the Frenchman is a wicked fellow [*buda*, lit. sorcerer] and the Englishman an ass.[336]

At the same time there are indications that he had probably begun to see the lack of response in racial terms: Is it because I am black and poor that I am despised?[337]

Tēwodros's accusations against Cameron were not limited to the simple fact that no reply to his letter had arrived. The consul was also associated with the 'abuse' of Stern and Selama, who had been dragged into this matter as well. But, in particular, the King was offended by the way in which Cameron had handled the business of that letter:

> When the consul named Cameron told me that he was the Queen's servant, and I awarded him the marks of distinction of my country and gave him provisions for the journey, sending him off to make me a friend of the Queen, he came back having stayed some time with the Turks. As for my letter, he told me he had not received any reply for me. I said to myself, 'What have I done that they should hate me and treat me with animosity?' and, by the power of God, I kept silent.[338]

The consul had in other words gone off to eat and drink with the enemies of the King instead of undertaking the task entrusted to him.[339] This could not be undone. The only possible way of repairing the damage was to get a reply from London and hope that it would be satisfactory to the King. And so Cameron relayed his brief but clear message: 'No release until civil answer to King's letter arrives.'[340]

When Lord Russell, the foreign secretary, was informed in early March about

336 Lejean, 'Voyage', *TM*, 1865, II, p. 271. Whether this is an authentic statement by Tēwodros or not is impossible to know. It may have been put into his mouth by Cameron or Lejean, but it clearly illustrates the derisive and abusive tone noted also by Flad (*Zwölf Jahre*, Vol. I, p. 71). For earlier intrigue, see Spittler-Archiv, D 3/1, Bender to Gobat, 20 Nov. 1861.
337 Flad, *Zwölf Jahre*, Vol. I, p. 75.
338 IO, Eur. F 103, no folio no., Tēwodros to Rassam, 5 Jul. [1865], Amharic original; also fols 43–4, Tēwodros to Rassam, 14 Mar. 1866; translations printed in Rassam, *British Mission*, Vol. I, pp. 93–4, Vol. II, pp. 33–4. Under the influence, no doubt, of the way in which Europeans later told the story, the anonymous chronicler asserted that Cameron had brought back a reply to Tēwodros and that he was arrested and maltreated only because he had not handed over Tēwodros's letter to the Queen in person (Fusella, *Tēwodros*, pp. 30–1).
339 FO 1/26, fol. 252, Cameron to Stanley, 28 Sep. 1868; FO 401/2, pp. 172–7, Rev. Stern to Mrs Stern, April 1865.
340 FO 401/2, pp. 18–19, pencil note signed C.D.C. to Speedy, 14 Feb. 1863, enclosed in Merewether to Colquhoun, 21 Apr. 1864, and Colquhoun to Russell, 28 Apr. 1864.

the events of November and warned that Cameron would not be permitted to leave Ethiopia until the King received an answer to his letter, he responded with a demand and a threat. There was still no concern about the reason for the detention. Only the news that the consul was actually *chained* and the terse no-release message caused a query: 'Is there any letter of the King of Abyssinia unanswered? R.' It was quickly returned 'without comment' from the India Office, where it had been awaiting somebody's attention for more than a year, and the long journey to Meqdela began. Not that anyone foresaw a military expedition:

> Force is of course out of the question, and the condition imposed by the King of Abyssinia of our receiving an Embassy from him has already been objected to, and could scarcely be countenanced, seeing that we should have to pay the whole of their expenses.
> I believe the best chance will be to send a letter of the Queen in very general terms, desiring friendship, and a letter from me saying we can hold no intercourse with the King, nor deliver the Queen's letter, unless he liberates Consul Cameron, Mr. Stern, and any other British subjects he has in custody . . . We must avoid promising any assistance against the Turks.[341]

Neither side, it seems, grasped the full significance of what had happened: the expulsion of one consul and the imprisonment of another had no doubt dashed the expectations of the Europeans that there was some cheap and easy way to gain influence over Ethiopia, but there was still no awareness of the price that would have to be paid to extricate the pioneers of that influence. For Tēwodros and other Ethiopians who had begun to look to Europe in earnest for recognition, support, and co-operation, the frustration must have been profound. The fruit of their expectations was a handful of European prisoners and semi-prisoners. As for Ethiopia's situation vis-à-vis Turkey and Egypt, Tēwodros must have sensed, without access to Foreign Office minutes, that he had been mistaken when he thought that European powers could be moved to support him in any way. But he was yet to learn that the Queen of England would wage war against him to have her subjects released.

Tēwodros and Britain: The Defiance of the Defeated

By 1865 Tēwodros was a defeated man in the sense that he could no longer hope —realistically—to succeed with either his unification of Ethiopia or his foreign policy. His conviction that he was a man of destiny had been so strong, his initial successes so great and his ambitions so boundless that he seems, however, to have been incapable of facing the harsh reality. His tendency to resort to violence in the face of opposition of whatever nature had already gained the upper hand. As his frustration and isolation grew, so did his defiance. The chances of finding a solution to the issue of the chained consul which would save

341 ibid, p. 12, Russell to Colquhoun, 9 Mar. 1864; pp. 20–1, 25, minutes by Russell and Murray, 18–19 May 1864.

face for both sides were slim indeed. Tēwodros was given the initial satisfaction that Queen Victoria finally sent a friendly reply to his letter. The British government hoped that this would solve the conflict so that relations with Ethiopia could be closed. Tēwodros, on the contrary, hoped that the letter signified an open door, closer ties, a move from words to deeds.

There was some awareness in London, too, that Tēwodros could not be bullied into compliance. Russell dropped his idea of a menacing letter. Even the first letter from the Queen, in which the Ethiopian embassy to London was discouraged, albeit on the grounds that it was really unnecessary to expose the envoys to the difficulties and dangers of the long journey, was recalled from Cairo. Tēwodros was, after all, not ignorant of the state of communications, and would understand that this was a pretext. The substitute letter contained a promise that an embassy would be well received if Tēwodros should still desire to send it after having permitted Cameron and the other imprisoned Europeans to leave. The letter was, moreover, sealed with the large signet and signed by Victoria, but not countersigned, to avoid every possibility of misunderstanding. In Cairo an Arabic translation was obtained, and letters from the Patriarch to Tēwodros and Abune Selama were added to support the mission, which was entrusted to Hormuzd Rassam, a Christian Iraqi on the staff at Aden.[342]

In July 1864 Rassam arrived at Massawa and wrote to Tēwodros that he would be happy to proceed to the court himself if the King so desired. Otherwise he hoped that Tēwodros would send down Cameron and a trusted person to take back the Queen's letter. As for the intended embassy, if Tēwodros would send the envoys, Rassam promised to arrange for their travel to England, where the Queen would be very pleased to receive them. Finally, he longed to have the pleasure of reading the 'pleasing and most gracious contents' of the King's answer.[343]

The letter reached Tēwodros by 19 August, but he seems to have been in no mood to reply at all. Since the Queen had taken two years to answer his letter, he may have thought it only proper that her messenger should wait too.[344] A second letter from Rassam sent through Na'ib Muhammad in October 1864 brought no response either. It was only Rassam's third letter in March 1865 that was answered, and not exactly in a 'pleasing and gracious' manner.[345]

The favourable moment for Tēwodros to establish fruitful relations with Europe and prevent further Egyptian advances had passed. It was not only a question of overcoming resentment and suspicion fed by further news or rumours about European designs on northern Ethiopia, in which the names of

342   ibid., pp. 48, 112–13, Victoria to Tēwodros, 26 May 1864, first and second versions; p. 53, Reade to Russell, 2 Jul. and 3 Jul. 1864; pp. 55–7, memorandum by Ayrton, 4 Jul. 1864; p. 46, Murray to Merivale, 11 Jun. 1864; pp. 49–50, instructions to be given to Mr. Hormuzd Rassam; pp. 108–10, memorandum by Coghlan, 8–10 Feb. 1865.
343   ibid., pp. 69–70, Rassam to Tēwodros, 24 Jul. 1864.
344   ibid., pp. 81–2, Rassam to Merewether, 12 Oct. 1864; pp. 98–9, Rassam to Layard, 28 Dec. 1864; p. 125, Welde Maryam Fenta, 22 Feb. 1865; pp. 132–3, Rev. Stern to Mrs Stern, 17 Jan. 1865, published in Pall Mall Gazette, 1 Apr. 1865.
345   FO 401/2, pp. 83, 143, Rassam to Tēwodros, 17 Oct. 1864 and 29 Mar. 1865; IO, Eur. F 103, Tēwodros to Rassam, 5 Jul. [1865].

du Bisson, his earlier associate Count de Moynier, as well as Stella and the acting French vice-consul at Massawa, Werner Munzinger, were all mentioned.[346] The power and authority of Tēwodros had reached their peak in 1861–63.[347] But the increasing ruthlessness with which the King had conducted his campaigns had led to disaffection. Lacking the financial means to feed his army, he had permitted his soldiers to pillage even peaceful areas; his rule and taxation had become arbitrary, and he had made enemies among the clergy by reducing the church lands. After a short and superficial *rapprochement* with Abune Selama at the time of Bardel's return, Tēwodros broke completely with the bishop. At about the same time in 1864, his soldiers began to desert in large numbers.[348]

The first of a new group of rebel chiefs arose in Welqayit in mid-1863. Ṭiso Gobezē, as he was called, not only threatened communications with the coast through Simēn but also Tēwodros's hold over Wegera, Dembīya, and the old capital itself. Enraged at the support given to the rebel by people at Gonder, the King pillaged and burnt the town before, in effect, giving it up to Ṭiso Gobezē. In Lasta the opposition flocked to the banner of Wagshum Gobezē Gebre Medhin, who had seen his father executed by Tēwodros, but nevertheless served the King a few years before heading his own uprising. By early 1865 it was foreseen that one of these two chiefs would seize upon Tigrē.[349] Equally serious was the development in the south, where Tēwodros's governor Bezzabih had declared himself king of an independent Shewa in 1864, the Wello were stirring once more, and Tedla Gwalu was recovering from his defeat at Injabara. The King's attempt to recapture Shewa around New Year 1865 failed.[350] Half a year later, on 30 June, Prince Minīlik escaped from Meqdela and ten years as a semi-prisoner.[351] After that Tēwodros did not even try to regain Shewa. Though he still had some loyal governors on the frontiers, notably Haylu Tewelde Medhin and [Welde] Ṣadiq Mirrach in the north, the King and

346 FO 401/2, pp. 84–6, Rassam to Merewether, 2 Dec. 1864; pp. 86–7, Welde Maryam Fenta, 24 Nov. 1864; pp. 126–7, Flad to Rassam, 26 Jan. 1865; Stern, *Captive Missionary*, p. 190; Douin, *Ismaïl*, III, 1, pp. 96–7.

347 This does not negate Crummey's observations ('Reformer and Modernizer', *JAH*, X, 3, pp. 467–8; 'Violence', *JES*, IX, 2, pp. 119–20), with which I agree, that the personality and the leadership of Tēwodros had begun to deteriorate as early as 1859–60.

348 FO 401/2, pp. 64–5, Wadeer, 14 Jul. 1864; pp. 81–2, Rassam to Merewether, 12 Oct. 1864; pp. 86–7, Welde Maryam Fenta, 24 Nov. 1864; Lejean, 'Voyage', *TM*, 1865, II, pp. 259–62; Flad, *Zwölf Jahre*, Vol. I, pp. 70, 82; Stern, *Captive Missionary*, pp. 145–68. Without giving any exact date, the chronicler (Welde Maryam, *Tēwodros*, pp. 24–5) states that it was after the birth of Tēwodros's son Alemayehu, born 1861, that the King began to disregard established order, oppress the poor, and reject the advice of the bishop. See also Crummey, 'Violence', *JES*, IX, 2, p. 123.

349 FO 401/2, pp. 81–2, 156–8, Rassam to Merewether, 12 Oct. 1864 and 12 May 1865; Lejean, 'Voyage', *TM*, 1867, I, pp. 366–7; Stern, *Wanderings*, p. 57; idem, *Captive Missionary*, pp. 179–80; Carlo Conti Rossini, ed., 'Epistolario del Debterà Aseggachègn di Uadlà', *RRAL*, 6, I (1925), pp. 450–1, 10 Oct. 1864; [Zeneb], *Tēwodros*, pp. 32–4; BN, Ethiop. 259, fol. 5.

350 FO 401/2, pp. 100–1, Rassam to Badger, 20 Jan. 1865; pp. 142–3, 156–8, Rassam to Merewether, 10 Apr. and 12 May 1865; Stern, *Captive Missionary*, pp. 201, 216.

351 FO 401/2, pp. 218–20, Rassam to Merewether, 15 Aug. 1865; Welde Maryam, *Tēwodros*, p. 32 (with wrong year, also in French translation, p. 39); Gebre Sillasē, *Minīlik*, p. 55.

his army were by mid-1865 completely encircled by powerful rebel chiefs.[352] Only Begēmdir and the north-western parts of Wello remained under his direct control. Flad wrote from Debre Tabor on 30 March 1865, 'The whole country is in a most disturbed condition, rebels rising everywhere', and Cameron stated from Meqdela a week later, '. . . the country is on the eve of dissolution'.[353]

What made Tēwodros respond to Rassam's third letter is difficult to say. Such factors as the tone of the letter and the messenger employed, a brother (in fact more probably a cousin) of Samu'ēl, named Ibrahim, may have played some role; probably the King simply felt that Rassam had waited long enough, and sent Ibrahim to Massawa to contact him. It is possible, too, that Minīlik's escape had made Tēwodros realize the desirability of solving the problem without further delay. At any rate, Ibrahim arrived at Meqdela on 4 July, was immediately called to the King and hurried off the following day with the reply that Rassam should come as quickly as possible via Metemma. To show that the offence was by no means settled, Tēwodros, besides stating his grievances against the consul and the other captives, deliberately omitted to seal his letter.[354]

The invitation reached Rassam after he had almost given up hope and was contemplating sending the Queen's letter by a messenger, particularly as Cameron had written, 'For God's sake don't think of coming up here, with or without a safe conduct. You will only get chains for your pains . . . If . . . the letter in your hands had been sent, with a polite ultimatum accompanying it, it might have got us out, or brought matters to a crisis, either one way or the other.'[355] When Rassam's pessimistic reports, implicitly recommending a tougher language and eventually military action, reached London in June and July, they merged with a rising wave of demands in Parliament and mission circles for information and decisive action to get the prisoners released.

The attempts of Lord Russell and his staff at the Foreign Office to cover up the neglect with regard to Tēwodros's letter to the Queen had failed. In June 1864 the foreign secretary could still write to his own top man in Egypt, '*In so far as imperfect accounts* can be relied on, there *seems* to be *some reason to suppose* that King Theodore *may* have imprisoned Captain Cameron because he had not received a letter from the Queen, which Captain Cameron *had led him* to expect . . .'[356] When a brother-in-law of Cameron addressed an appeal for

---

352 FO 401/2, pp. 156–8, 218–20, Rassam to Merewether, 12 May and 15 Aug. 1865; Conti Rossini, 'Epistolario', *RRAL*, 6, I, pp. 451–5, n.d. (late 1865 or early 1866).

353 FO 401/2, pp. 159–60, Flad to Rassam, 30 Mar. 1865; pp. 162–3, Cameron to Rassam, 6 Apr. 1865; see also pp. 186–7, Rassam to Merewether, 23 Jun. 1865; pp. 249–50, Statement of Lemma Haylu, 20 Sep. 1865; Flad, *Zwölf Jahre*, Vol. I, p. 86.

354 FO 401/2, pp. 142–3, Rassam to Merewether, 10 Apr. 1865; pp. 218–24, Rassam to Merewether, 15 Aug. 1865, with enclosures, Tēwodros to Rassam, Samu'ēl and Matta to Muhammad Abd al-Rahim, and Samu'ēl to Abdallah, all dated 5 Jul. 1865; statements of Ibrahim and other messengers, 14 Aug. 1865; p. 235, Cameron to Rassam, 14 Jul. 1865; IO, Eur. F 103, Tēwodros to Rassam, 5 Jul. [1865].

355 FO 401/2, pp. 162–3, Cameron to Rassam, 6 Apr. 1865; p. 163, Flad to Rassam, 25 Mar. 1865 (wrongly dated 25 *May* in the print); pp. 153–5, 186–7, Rassam to Merewether, 12 May and 23 Jun. 1865.

356 ibid., pp. 47–8, Russell to Colquhoun, 16 Jun. 1864 (my emphasis).

aid to Queen Victoria in January 1865, mentioning Tēwodros's letter and the long delay before any notice was taken of it,[357] Russell still felt sufficiently confident to lie brazenly:

> The King of Abyssinia wished to be invited to come to this country, and to be assisted against the French; and, as these requests could not be complied with, he imprisoned the Consul and the missionaries.[358]

In May 1865, however, the House of Lords requested copies of the relevant documents including Tēwodros's letter, and the following month the first instalment of *Papers relating to the Imprisonment of British Subjects in Abyssinia* was released.[359]

The news that Tēwodros had finally responded, including information that Cameron had been unchained, came just in time to prevent an alternative mission to Tēwodros with a harsh but simple demand that the British captives be released.[360] From Meqdela and London alike, Rassam was urged to proceed to the court of Tēwodros as fast as possible.[361] With his two companions Dr H. Blanc and Lieutenant W. F. Prideaux, he left Massawa on 15 October, 1865 and reached Metemma on 21 November. As soon as he received the news that Rassam had arrived there, Tēwodros sent an escort to conduct the envoy to the royal camp. The mission proceeded on 28 December; the escort and local chiefs provided for all its needs during the month it took to reach the camp at Ashfa in Damot, where it was given a grand reception.[362]

Tēwodros was visibly pleased with Rassam's arrival and with the Queen's letter. He lost no time before informing the envoy that he wanted to have the quarrel settled. For a second audience the following day, he had already prepared a reply for Queen Victoria, wherein he allegedly reported 'his forgiveness to the European prisoners' and his handing them over 'to take out of Abyssinia'. Rassam was very pleased with the letter and felt sure the Queen and the British

---

357 ibid., pp. 101–2, Desborough to Victoria, 31 Jan. 1865.
358 G. E. Buckle, ed., *The Letters of Queen Victoria, Second Series* (London, 1926–28), Vol. I, pp. 249–50, Russell to Victoria, 5 Feb. 1865. By this time the failure to reply and the secrecy about the contents of the royal letter had already given rise to fantastic reports in the newspapers that Tēwodros had asked for Queen Victoria's hand in marriage. Though refuted in the *Bombay Gazette* as early as 3 January 1865, the argument was used in the heated debate about the expedition almost three years later (Richard Pankhurst, 'Popular Opposition in Britain to British Intervention against Emperor Tewodros of Ethiopia (1867–1868)', *Ethiopia Observer*, XVI, 3 (1973), pp. 141–203).
359 FO 401/2, pp. 148–9, Address of the House of Lords for Papers, 23 May 1865.
360 ibid., pp. 187–9, Russell to Stanton and to Palgrave, 21 Jul. 1865; p. 192, Memorandum to be presented to King Theodore, 21 Jul. 1865; pp. 213–14, Russell to Stanton, 9 Sep. 1865. The information that Cameron had been unchained was later found out to have been a fabrication by the messengers (ibid., p. 250, Rassam to Layard, 29 Sep. 1865).
361 ibid., pp. 235–6, Cameron to Rassam, 14 Jul. and 16 Jul. 1865; pp. 289–90, Flad to Rassam, 1 Aug. 1865; p. 226, Russell to Stanton, 19 Sep. 1865; p. 254, Murray to Merewether, 26 Oct. 1865.
362 ibid., pp. 258–60, Merewether to Layard, 19 Oct. 1865, with enclosures; pp. 283–5, 299–300, 308–10, Rassam to Merewether, 27 Nov., 27 Dec. 1865 and 1–11 Jan. 1866; Rassam, *British Mission*, Vol. I, pp. 181–248.

public would share his feelings.[363] It is true that the English translation, made by Rassam and his own interpreters, contained the statement:

> Had the illustrious Hormuzd Rassam, whom Your Majesty has mentioned to us in your Letter, not been sent to us about the matter of Cameron and others, but the lowest of your servants, he would have been received graciously by us. We now send with Hormuzd Rassam Cameron and all the other Europeans about whom Your Majesty has written. Your Majesty can learn from those who fear the Lord the ill-treatment and abuse which we have received at the hands of the above-mentioned Europeans, and the Copt who called himself Metropolitan, the Aboona Salama.

But in the Amharic original, the King only promised to release Cameron:

> When you tell me that you have sent Hormuzd Rassam concerning the matter of Cameron, would I say no even if it were the slave of your slave, let alone yourself, that wrote to me? All right, I am sending [him] to you (ishī, sedijeliwo allehu). But what those others did to me in company with the Egyptian who came and claimed to be a bishop, you can find out by asking someone who fears God.[364]

Though the English translation was also sealed, the responsibility for the discrepancies between the two versions must be placed on Rassam, who actually bragged that Tēwodros had '. . . said he wanted to show the world how he trusted me, by signing a letter the contents of which he did not know, relying on me for its accuracy'. At his own request, Rassam was furnished with a sealed Amharic text as well.[365] In neither version, however, is there any mention of forgiveness of the offenders, conditional or otherwise. It is impossible to establish what was stated verbally about the release of the prisoners and the possible conditions of a pardon, but there is no reason to believe that Tēwodros made any commitment beyond the text of the letter, for Rassam persisted in citing the letter and nothing else as evidence that the King had 'forgiven the prisoners and virtually made them over'.[366]

Publishing their narratives two or three years later, Rassam maintained that

---

363 FO 401/2, pp. 320–5, Merewether to Clarendon, 12 May 1866. Most of this dispatch consists of a letter from Rassam written largely in the form of a journal from 28 January to 4 February, and a more summary account of events from 5 February to 21 March. See also Rassam, British Mission, Vol. I, pp. 248–55, 264–8; Fusella, Tēwodros, pp. 32–3.

364 FO 1/26, fol. 210, Tēwodros to Victoria, 29 Jan. 1866, Amharic original; fols 212–13, English version.

365 Rassam, British Mission, Vol. I, p. 268. None of the resident Europeans who knew Amharic were present in the camp (Blanc, Captivity, p. 129); also Mirčha Werqē, Mahdere Qal, and the other Ethiopians who knew English and French seem to have been absent. If Samu'ēl had acquired any knowledge of English during his youth, there is no indication that he had retained it (British Mission, Vol. I, p. 261). But he knew Arabic well; Tēwodros could also use this language, and it was Rassam's mother-tongue, so there was no need for misunderstandings. Since Rassam had three Ethiopian interpreters, Omar Ali, Welde Gebri'ēl, and Desta (ibid., Vol. I, pp. 187, 207, 272), he could check translations from Amharic to Arabic. The step from Arabic to English was entirely within Rassam's own ability, but could only be checked imperfectly, if at all, by Tēwodros.

366 Rassam, British Mission, Vol. II, p. 27, entry dated 9 Mar. 1866.

it was 'certain, that at the end of January, 1866, Theodore had no thought of detaining' the mission, while Blanc asserted that the King had never intended to dispatch his 'humble, apologizing letter' to Victoria.[367] The latter is wrong, of course, for Rassam was given the letter and was allowed to correspond with the coast. The truth lies somewhere between these two extremes. Rassam's own accounts, as well as Tēwodros's letters to the envoy, reveal beyond doubt that the King had by no means forgiven the Europeans—'. . . insolent people, who outraged God and the one whom he had made ruler, and I do not know, nor understand, whether these people are Jews or heathens, who do not know God . . .'—and also that he intended Rassam to play an important role in settling the question of their guilt.[368]

Tēwodros even seems to have hesitated whether he should release the prisoners at once or negotiate terms with the British envoy first, and almost three weeks passed before he actually sent one of his officials to unchain the Meqdela captives and bring them to Rassam at Qoraṭa. This action implied, of course, that Rassam would be allowed to take them with him out of the country, and Tēwodros even wrote that he intended this to take place *betolo*, i.e. quickly or soon.[369] At the same time, it forced the King to raise the question of how the renewed friendship between his country and England was supposed to contribute to the enlightenment and development of his people. It is only natural that he preferred Rassam to translate the declared friendship into concrete offers. The King had received the British envoy as no foreigner had been received before him; within less than two months he had supplied Rassam with 10,000 thalers (£2,000) towards the expenses of his embassy and presented him with gifts amounting to an estimated additional 15,000 thalers.[370] He had sent for the prisoners and made arrangements for handing back their property and compensating them for what had been lost.[371] Clearly, the ball was now in Rassam's court.

Even if the British were unwilling or unable to ally themselves with Ethiopia against the Turks, they still had much to offer. In his letter to the Queen, already, Tēwodros had dropped the kind of hint this proud and at the same time humble man was apt to make: 'You must have heard of our, the Ethiopian people's, ignorance and blindness.'[372] And he did not fail to remind Rassam: 'May

367 ibid., Vol. II, p. 67; Blanc, *Captivity*, p. 130.
368 FO 401/2, pp. 320–5, Merewether to Clarendon, 12 May 1866; Rassam, *British Mission*, Vol. I, pp. 227, 252, 267, 297–303; IO, Eur. F 103. The latter is the collection of Rassam's private papers. It includes most of the Amharic and Arabic originals of Tēwodros's letters to the envoy. English translations of these, fairly correct in substance, are found in FO 401/2, pp. 460–70, and *British Mission*, Vols I and II, *passim*. See, in particular, Tēwodros's letters of 9 Dec. and 12 Dec. 1865, and 25 Feb., 6 Mar., and 14 Mar. 1866 (IO, Eur. F 103, fols 32–3, 37, 40, 43–5).
369 IO, Eur. F 103, fol. 35, Tēwodros to Rassam, n.d., but 17 or 18 Feb. 1866.
370 FO 401/2, pp. 320–5, Merewether to Clarendon, 12 May 1866; pp. 341–4, Flad to Stanley, n.d., received 10 Jul. 1866; Rassam, *British Mission*, Vol. I, pp. 305–6; Vol. II, pp. 45–6.
371 IO, Eur. F 103, fol. 37, Tēwodros to Rassam, 25 Feb. 1866; Rassam, *British Mission*, Vol. II, pp. 12–13.
372 FO 1/26, fol. 210.

God preserve my friendship and my love in your hearts [and] may he cause you to open my blind eyes for me.' Rassam, somehow, failed to take note of the signals, and replied, '. . . I am ready to leave Abyssinia for England as soon as I shall obtain your leave, which I hope you will grant me before long . . .' [373] Tēwodros was obliged to tell the envoy in two different letters that he had things to discuss with him when the prisoners arrived from Meqdela.[374] Informed verbally that the King wanted to try the released prisoners in the presence of the envoy, the latter took it upon himself to persuade Tēwodros to drop the idea. The King agreed to a procedure by which Rassam would question the former captives and obtain their admission whether or not they were guilty of having abused him. The 'trial' was held on 15 March, three days after the Meqdela prisoners had arrived and, as expected, the accused admitted that they had done wrong. Rassam had been told that Tēwodros would expect some kind of compensation, a *fiqir kasa*. The King himself wrote, once again, that he desired the knowledge which could be brought from Europe and which would open his eyes. And this time he backed up his request by quoting Victoria's letter:

> I have sent to you my trusted servant and friend, Mr. Hormuzd Rassam . . . Consult with him about all that you want from us. *He will do it for you.*[375]

This was a translation, or rather a mistranslation, of the Queen's words:

> And so, not doubting that you will receive Our servant Rassam in a favourable manner, and give credit to all that he shall say to you on Our part, as well as *comply with the requests which he is instructed to make to you,* We recommend you . . .[376]

Rassam and his companions Blanc and Prideaux all insinuated that this extraordinary mistranslation was intentional, possibly made on Tēwodros's explicit instructions, possibly the result of a later alteration of the Amharic text. But

373   IO, Eur. F. 103, fol. 39, Tēwodros to Rassam, 2 Mar. 1866; fol. 64, Rassam to Tēwodros, 4 Mar. 1866.

374   ibid., fols 40–1, Tēwodros to Rassam, 6 Mar. and 9 Mar. 1866. In his attempts to free himself from all blame in the failure of his mission, Rassam asserted that Tēwodros's tone changed completely on 6 March and that this was due to the news that Dr Beke had arrived at Massawa on a private mission to obtain the release of the missionaries in particular (Rassam, *British Mission*, Vol. II, pp. 21–5, also 42–3, 46, 64). There is really no evidence that Beke's mission in any way contributed to the failure of Rassam's. To the extent that Tēwodros's attitude may have been changing, it was more probably due to information having reached him that the British government really wanted to have as little as possible to do with Ethiopia. See FO 401/2, pp. 800–4, Beke to Stanley, 9 Oct. 1867, with a letter to the editor of the *Morning Herald*, 7 Oct. 1867, and FO 1/29, fols 150–1, Beke to Clarendon, 30 Apr. 1869.

375   IO, Eur. F 103, fol. 45, Tēwodros to Rassam, 14 Mar. 1866, Amharic original (my emphasis); Rassam, *British Mission*, Vol. II, pp. 26–7, 31–6; FO 401/2, pp. 320–5, Merewether to Clarendon, 12 May 1866; Blanc, *Captivity*, pp. 144–7.

376   Rassam, *British Mission*, Vol. II, pp. 38–9 (my emphasis). For versions of Victoria's letter preserved in Ethiopian tradition, see Welde Maryam, *Tēwodros*, p. 29, and Fusella, *Tēwodros*, p. 33.

none of them provided evidence for their allegations, and it seems highly unlikely that Rassam should have been unable to find out the truth either from his own interpreters or from Samu'ēl who made the translation from Arabic to Amharic under his own or Prideaux's supervision.[377] Though Samu'ēl was the King's employee at the time, he later entered the service of the envoy, shared the latter's secrets, and could have clarified this crucial point even after the death of Tēwodros.[378]

Though Flad and Waldmeier informed Rassam that *fiqir kasa* meant something more substantial than verbal promises of lasting friendship, Rassam decided to ignore both the *fiqir kasa* issue and, though not prepared to inform the King of the mistranslation, also, as far as possible, the request for artisans and tools implied in Tēwodros's letter. If the King had originally intended, as some of his first letters to Rassam indicated, to permit the envoy to depart with the released prisoners and trust that the mission would nevertheless inaugurate a period of positive friendship, he now began to talk of keeping Rassam in Ethiopia until some material evidence of the friendship arrived.[379]

After the 'trial' of 15 March, Tēwodros declared that he had forgiven the offenders. Rassam and the Gefat artisans were called to Zegē for the announced consultation, and on 26 March the King sounded out the artisans as well as a large assembly of chiefs about Rassam's departure. The envoy insisted on leaving with the released prisoners, and all reportedly advised the King to dismiss him. This was also, according to Rassam, what Tēwodros decided to do.[380] But the King was very disappointed that Rassam had not raised the question of the new artisans and instruments, and Waldmeier, who probably knew Tēwodros best of all the foreigners, was of the opinion that the King had not allowed himself to be persuaded.[381] This, at any rate, turned out to be the case.

For two more weeks, messages passed between the envoy and the King, who seems to have been vacillating about what to do. A new request that the former prisoners should come to the royal camp before leaving was opposed by Rassam lest the very sight of them would kindle the King's wrath. Tēwodros then agreed, or more probably pretended to agree, that they could leave straight for Metemma, while the members of the mission only were to come for a farewell inter-

377 Rassam, *British Mission*, Vol. II, pp. 32, 36–7; Blanc, *Captivity*, pp. 129–30; Markham, *Abyssinian Expedition*, p. 99. Note that Rassam makes Prideaux, the King's Amharic scribe Ingida (who seems to have known no Arabic), Samu'ēl, and one of his own Abyssinian interpreters (of whom all three most probably knew Arabic) responsible for the translation, while Blanc states that the translation was made by Rassam into Arabic and by Samu'ēl into Amharic. Prideaux also passes over his own participation and that of the mission's interpreter in silence, and implies that *three* of the King's employees committed the grave mistakes in the translation. Unfortunately the intermediary Arabic translation, if made in writing, and the copy of the Amharic text which one must assume that Rassam made for himself are not to be found among the Rassam papers at India Office.

378 Rassam, *British Mission*, Vol. I, pp. 263–4.

379 ibid., Vol. II, pp. 35, 40–1, 44; see also Waldmeier, *Erlebnisse*, pp. 51–2; Flad, *Zwölf Jahre*, Vol. I, pp. 87–8.

380 IO, Eur. F 103, fols 46–7, Tēwodros to Rassam, 18 Mar. and 23 Mar. 1866; Rassam, *British Mission*, Vol. II, pp. 42, 52–5, 58–65.

381 Blanc, *Captivity*, pp. 148–51; Waldmeier, *Erlebnisse*, p. 52.

view.[382] When they arrived at Zegē again on 13 April, they were immediately arrested. The other group were also arrested and brought to the King's camp, where they were once more subjected to questioning about their earlier offences and their attempt to leave the country without being properly reconciled with the King. While Tēwodros declared that he wanted the former friendship re-established on all sides, he also returned to the question of the *kasa*:

> ... I require it from you, Mr. Rassam, because you are the Balderaba given to me by the Queen of England. She says in her letter everything I wish, Mr. Rassam will do for you. What my Kasa is, I will tell you afterwards. I don't want gold or silver; I want people who will open my eyes, because I am blind.[383]

According to Blanc, Rassam was also reminded that he had already promised to write for an instructor, and was asked whether he had kept his promise.[384]

Tēwodros had finally made up his mind. Not only Rassam, but also the former prisoners and detainees were to remain in Ethiopia, while Flad alone went to England to bring the *fiqir kasa*, the material evidence that the British friendship was sincere. To the Queen, Tēwodros wrote simply that he was following her advice to consult with Rassam 'about all that you want from us', and closed with the hope that God would reward her with light in heaven for opening the eyes of the blind Ethiopians.[385] To Rassam he specified the items he wanted: 'a cannon-maker, a gunsmith, an iron caster, a sapper, an artillerist ... with their implements ... Write this and send for me, by the power of God.'[386] When he arrived in London, Flad further specified Tēwodros's requests as two gunsmiths, an artillery officer, one or two boat-builders, a cart-wright and an iron-founder, with necessary tools, furnaces and instruments; he added that a small blast steam-engine for the foundry, a turning-bench, a powder-mill, machinery for the manufacture of gun-caps, etc. would also be

382 IO, Eur. F 103, fols 48–52, Tēwodros to Rassam, 30 Mar., 2 Apr., 7 Apr., 9 Apr., and 10 Apr. 1866; Rassam, *British Mission*, Vol. II, pp. 66–81; Blanc, *Captivity*, p. 151.

383 FO 1/17, fols 415–22, Flad to Clarendon, n.d., received 10 Jul. 1866. This report, also in 401/2, pp. 336–41, is the best account of the events of 13–17 April 1866. Waldmeier (*Erlebnisse*, pp. 53–4), Stern (*Captive Missionary*, pp. 267, 270, 278–82) and Blanc (*Captivity*, pp. 153–62) all mention the question of the *kasa*, while Rassam himself, in an account of almost twenty pages (*British Mission*, Vol. II, pp. 82–99), manages to avoid it completely. Though Flad called Tēwodros a 'cruel, inhuman, tyrannical, barbarous, cunning, crafty and sly Despot' in his report (fol. 421—some of the invective was crossed out before printing), he did not insinuate that the mistranslation of the Queen's letter was deliberate (fol. 419).

384 FO 401/2, pp. 367–8, Blanc to Merewether, 26 May 1866. See Rassam, *British Mission*, Vol. II, p. 40, for the promise.

385 FO 95/725, no. 226, Tēwodros to Victoria, 17 Apr. 1866, Amharic original and English translation. Although Rassam states (*British Mission*, Vol. II, pp. 99–100) that Samu'ēl translated the letter *word for word*—obviously from Amharic to Arabic—the envoy has carefully avoided the reference to the Queen's 'promise' in his English version, where the quoted phrase runs: 'upon the extension of our friendship'. See also the draft of the translation, IO, Eur. F 103, fol. 5.

386 IO, Eur. F 103, fol. 53, Tēwodros to Rassam, n.d. (17 Apr. 1866); Rassam, *British Mission*, Vol. II, pp. 101–2.

welcome.[387] It is evident that Tēwodros at this time hoped to be able to recover his position of military strength by producing war materials, especially artillery, on a scale previously unknown to the country. And he was impatient. Before Flad had reached the coast, Rassam was asked to write to Bombay for artisans who knew how to cast cannon, as well as for instruments and books about artillery practice. Though offered 10,000 thalers (£2,000) or even double the amount, Rassam replied that the recruiting would have to be sanctioned from London, but he wrote to Aden for books and fuses for shells.[388]

The political resident at Aden, W. L. Merewether, on leave in England, was entrusted with the task of selecting workmen and presents. Under the not entirely correct impression that the King had committed a clear 'breach of the promises he made in February', Merewether agreed that Tēwodros's 'treatment of Mr. Rassam, and the officers with him, was undoubtedly most unjustifiable, and such as, under ordinary circumstances, would call for severe measures being adopted'. Nevertheless he recommended that the British government should attempt to win Tēwodros's confidence by dealing 'frankly and most liberally' with him. This entailed the recruitment of a technical team of eight persons in all, under an enterprising, well-educated engineer, to serve in Ethiopia for three years, or longer if they so desired, at the expense of Tēwodros but with their salaries guaranteed by the British government, and all the machinery and other equipment they needed. Since Tēwodros would most certainly pay the salaries once the group had arrived in Ethiopia, the total cost would amount to about £3,500 (less, in fact, than Tēwodros was prepared to offer to Rassam). In addition, an artillery instructor should be sent from Aden. The King should, moreover, be told that the long-projected Ethiopian embassy to England was welcome, and that its members could travel with Rassam on his return. Above all, there should be no bargaining in the sense that the new team would enter the country only on condition that the other Europeans had been allowed to leave first. Merewether's well-considered advice was: '. . . fairly and frankly trust the King; show him that his word is fully believed in; lead him to see that the stories which have been told him are false; that nothing but friendly feelings exist towards him . . .' In a sense it was a gamble, but the fact that as well-informed a person as Colonel Merewether, who had every opportunity of questioning Flad and had read all Rassam's dispatches, was confident that it would succeed indicates that Tēwodros was not in 1866 seriously believed to be demented, in spite of the fact that Rassam had pronounced him 'crazy for the last two years', and called him an 'ass' and a 'madcap' in documents not intended for the King's eyes. Less diplomatic persons, like Captain Speedy, had reportedly called the King an ass to his face. But there was one indispensable condition for success: Egypt had to be restrained from any expeditions against Ethiopia.[389]

387 FO 401/2, p. 351, list by Flad, 17 Jul. 1866.
388 ibid., pp. 365–7, Rassam to Merewether, 28 May 1866.
389 ibid., pp. 373–7, memorandum by Merewether, 16 Aug. 1866. For pronouncements on Tēwodros's state of mind, see ibid., pp. 86, 153–5, Rassam to Merewether, 2 Dec. 1864, 12 May 1865; also Rassam, British Mission, Vol. I, p. 253: 'occasionally demented'.

Once more reports and rumours about Egyptian designs on Ethiopia were destined to interfere and cause the failure of the last attempt to establish some kind of Ethio-British friendship and co-operation. In late 1864 Khedive Ismail had begun to put pressure on the Porte to place Massawa and Sawakin once more, and permanently, under Egyptian jurisdiction. He wanted Sawakin as an outlet for Sudanese trade and a point of departure for railway lines to Berber and Kasala, and Massawa as a base for further acquisitions of territory on the northern frontiers of Ethiopia, with a view to extending the province of Taka eastwards across Bogos to the coast, eventually with a railway there also. Using his commitment to stamp out the slave trade as an argument, Ismail enlisted the diplomatic support of Great Britain.[390] In his correspondence with the Porte, he was more frank, promising to extend Ottoman rule to uncivilized tribes in Africa beyond the existing limits of the empire, in other words to the Habesha.[391] Nevertheless, Ismail seems in mid-1865 to have been anxious to avoid clashes with Ethiopia, and though the firman conferring the two ports on Ismail was dated mid-May 1865, and Sawakin was taken over in August, Massawa remained under its old administration until 30 April 1866, when the new governor Hasan Rifat arrived, backed up by a battalion of Egyptian troops under Ismail Sadiq Pasha.[392]

Now a period of feverish activity followed. Within a matter of weeks, Hasan Rifat had located thirty-nine tribes, mainly coastal, 'dependent on Massawa', of which twenty-five paid a total tribute of little more than 5,000 thalers annually, while fourteen had not been subjected to taxation at all. But the real prizes were farther inland, and the territory which could be claimed as having belonged to the Ottoman empire in the days of Sultan Selim (sixteenth century) 'was very elastic'! One saltmine alone, controlled by a Christian chief, reportedly yielded 100,000–150,000 thalers annually, and the annual tribute to be paid by Dejjazmach Haylu of Hamasēn (and Bogos) allegedly amounted to 62,000 thalers.[393]

It was more or less taken for granted that Egypt could easily annex provinces like Akkele Guzay and Bogos, where the work of the Catholic missionaries had weakened the loyalties towards Ethiopia and created an informal protectorate status vis-à-vis France or Britain or both.[394] Lejean's successor at Massawa, Vice-consul Munzinger, warned his government that if it wanted Bogos it would have to act without delay. He clearly realized how tempting it would be for Egypt to occupy in particular Bogos, which 'would become the flower of the whole Egyptian Sudan if it were administered well'.[395] In order to minimize

390   SP.BAGM, Misir Iradeleri 787, Ismail to Fuad, 26 Dec. 1864; Douin, Ismaïl, III, 1, pp. 269–73, 285–8; see also FO 401/2, pp. 538–9, Beke to Stanley, 13 Jun. 1867.
391   SP.BAGM, Misir Iradeleri, 791, encl. 3, Ismail to Fuad, 4 Apr. 1865.
392   ENA, Registre 537, Maia Sanieh, Ismail to Jafar Sadiq, 29 Jun. 1865; Douin, Ismaïl, III, 1, pp. 275–81; AECP, Massouah 3, fol. 194, Munzinger to Drouyn de Lhuys, 4 May 1866.
393   Douin, Ismaïl, III, 1, pp. 283–4, 333, 336; AECP, Massouah 3, fols 198–205, Munzinger to Drouyn de Lhuys, 5 Nov. 1866.
394   AECP, Massouah 3, fol. 155, memorandum by Lejean, 1 Apr. 1865; see also above, pp. 143–4.
395   AECP, Massouah 3, fols 168–77, 184–90, Munzinger to Drouyn de Lhuys, 15 Oct. and 23 Dec. 1865.

the risk of European interference, Hasan Rifat made the remarkable and revealing request that his government 'take urgent measures in view of making France and England officially recognize that this Christian region depends on Abyssinia alone and that they have no right whatsoever to intervene in its affairs'.[396] Border raids, of which there were many, would provide Egypt with its necessary pretext to interfere where gifts and stipends to chiefs did not lead to the voluntary acceptance of Egyptian rule. The prevailing insurrection in Ethiopia facilitated infiltration. While the two most important governors on the frontier, Haylu of Hamasēn and Welde Ṣadiq of Adiyabo, were loyal to Tēwodros, there was the new, powerful rebel of the north, Wagshum Gobezē, and his lieutenants, for instance Gebre Medhin of Akkele Guzay, with whom it was much easier to make contacts. Gobezē, who had returned to Tigrē by June 1866 after some months' absence, would naturally want to rid himself of all chiefs who remained loyal to the King, and in October Hasan Rifat even alleged that Gobezē had asked to have his territory placed under Egyptian sovereignty.[397]

Though it is impossible to know exactly what information reached Tēwodros and when, it is certain that loyal governors and spies reported the Egyptian activities and plans to the best of their knowledge, and did not fail to mention the *ferenj* also. For almost two months after the Egyptian landing at Massawa, however, there seems to have been no suspicion in Tēwodros's mind that Britain might in any way be supporting or approving the Egyptian activities. All the detained Europeans reported that they were treated with consideration, even generosity.[398] This situation changed suddenly on 25 June 1866, after the arrival of a Greek or Armenian priest who had come from Jerusalem. The King called the Europeans and accused Rassam of having kept the Egyptian railway plans secret because the railway to Kasala was being built to carry British, French, and Turkish troops intended for an invasion of Ethiopia. He also stated that he had evidence in a letter from Jerusalem that the British had never been sincere in their professions of friendship, but had all along planned to send troops to avenge the insulting treatment of their consul as soon as Rassam had left with the former captives.[399] The allegations were unfounded, inasmuch as the British government by any means wanted to avoid a costly military engagement in Ethiopia, but they were certainly not absurd or unreasonable. On his arrival in England, Flad reported that Egyptian troops were said to be 'collecting on the borders, to make a descent upon Bogos, a district belonging to the King of Abyssinia', and Merewether expressed the fear that Tēwodros would 'at once conclude that the Egyptian move was in accord with the views of Her Majesty's

396 Douin, *Ismaïl*, III, 1, p. 338.
397 ibid., pp. 285, 332–40; AECP, Massouah 3, fols 180–3, 198–205, Munzinger to Drouyn de Lhuys, 12 Nov. 1865, 5 Nov. 1866.
398 FO 401/2, p. 363, Cameron to Hammond, 24 May 1866; pp. 364–5, Rassam to Clarendon, 27 May 1866; pp. 367–8, Blanc to Merewether, 26 May 1866; Rassam, *British Mission*, Vol. II, pp. 123–4, 130–4, 139.
399 FO 401/2, pp. 388, 428–9, Rassam to Merewether, 26 Jun. and 17 Sep. 1866; Rassam, *British Mission*, Vol. II, pp. 140–5; Blanc, *Captivity*, pp. 170–1; Waldmeier, *Erlebnisse*, p. 55; IO, Eur. F 103, fol. 22, Tēwodros to Rassam, 5 Jan. 1867.

Government'. All the British government felt it could ask, in case the report was correct, was that Ismail '*defer* his hostilities'.[400]

Once more, intrigue amongst the Europeans seems to have aggravated the situation, with Bardel allegedly feeding the flames of Tēwodros's suspicions with reports which he received from the Catholic missionary C. Delmonte at Massawa. Rassam and his companions as well as the earlier Meqdela prisoners, except Mackerer and McKilvie, were arrested and sent off to the mountain prison. All the others had to remain and work under surveillance at Gefat, mainly on the manufacture of artillery.[401]

At the Foreign Office, Merewether's generous plan of sending the artisans requested by the King into the country without demanding the other British subjects in exchange at the border had been described as 'the height of madness'; and when the news that Rassam and the others had been put in chains on Meqdela reached London, the plan was changed. Flad was sent in advance with the reply from the Queen. Merewether was to follow with the artisans and machinery, but only as far as Massawa, where the exchange was to take place in case Tēwodros agreed to release the prisoners and send them down to the coast first. Victoria's letter was sternly worded, and there was some ambiguity with regard to the artisans. The Queen wrote that skilled workmen had been recruited before the news of Rassam's imprisonment reached her, but failed to mention more than the requested tools and implements as dispatched to Massawa.[402]

Flad regarded this omission as fatal to the success of his mission, but the condition that the prisoners had to be released and sent down to the coast before even the machinery would be forwarded may have been just as serious. Not able to travel through Tigrē because of the rebellion there, Flad forwarded a copy of the Queen's letter by messenger on 30 October.[403] It reached Tēwodros at Debre Tabor by mid-December. He had just returned from an expedition to Gonder to catch a rebel force there. Its chief had escaped capture and Tēwodros had completely destroyed the town, including almost all its churches, about forty in all. Their sacred vessels, manuscripts and other treasures were all brought with the priests, monks, and *debteras* to Debre Tabor, which was proclaimed the new capital. This wanton destruction of the old capital caused Tēwodros to be further detested by his people, and bears witness to the deteriorating state of the King's mind. Even Waldmeier, who was regarded as the King's favourite and who otherwise often defended Tēwodros against personal attacks, noted in connection with the events after Flad's departure that the King's nobler qualities

---

400 FO 401/2, p. 348, Flad to Stanley, 14 Jul. 1866; pp. 352–3, Merewether to Stanley, 18 Jul. 1866; p. 353, Murray to Stanton, 19 Jul. 1866 (my emphasis).

401 ibid., pp. 391–4, Flad to Murray, 21 Sep. 1866, with enclosure from Mrs Flad dated 7 Jul. 1866; pp. 482–8, Merewether to Stanley, 28 Feb. 1867, quoting Mrs Flad and Staiger; Waldmeier, *Erlebnisse*, pp. 56–7; see also note 399. Both in his dispatches and in *British Mission* Rassam put much of the blame on Beke's mission, but he also spoke of 'fools and mischief-makers' in general.

402 FO 401/2, pp. 377–8, minute by Egerton, 15 Aug. 1866; pp. 398–9, Merewether to Murray, 1 Oct. 1866; pp. 400–1, Victoria to Tēwodros, 4 Oct. 1866; p. 402, Stanley to Flad, 8 Oct. 1866; pp. 408–9, Merewether to Hammond, 27 Oct. 1866.

403 ibid., pp. 433–4, Flad to Hertslet, 5 Nov. 1866.

were increasingly 'overshadowed and suppressed by his cruelty, arrogance, intemperance and other vices'.[404]

Tēwodros's reaction to Victoria's letter was somewhat ambiguous. On the one hand, he forwarded the copy of the Queen's letter to Rassam to get his advice on what to reply, and when messengers arrived from Flad on 5 January 1867 with the news that the craftsmen and their tools and machinery had actually arrived at Massawa, he decided, without awaiting Rassam's reply, to get both the goods and the workers to come into the country via Metemma. He informed Rassam accordingly, and the latter agreed to support his request, determined, however, to countermand his recommendation through a secret messenger.[405] Mrs Flad seems to have genuinely feared that the King's request would be granted, and pleaded with her husband to return alone:

> And I tell you, yea even I entreat you, don't trust, don't trust, don't trust! Even though showing his distrust so openly, he believes that he will coax in more Englishmen. For God's sake keep your hands clean. Don't give any advice, for it will terminate bad . . . I beg you, I entreat you before the face of God, keep your hands out of the matter. The King's intention is to play a very bad trick. He said to Mr. Waldmeier, 'Call me a woman, if I shall not get them in with all the articles . . .'[406]

On the other hand, Tēwodros made statements to the Europeans at Gefat which seemed to indicate that he neither believed that the goods and people would be sent to him, nor even cared what would happen:

> His friendship with England has reached its end. He neither wants now machinery nor workmen; everything you [Flad] will bring for him is indifferent to him—war or peace. So he is reported to have said, only he wants you to come soon. His messengers for you will leave this to-morrow . . . the whole affair has come to a decided termination.[407]

Waldmeier used still stronger words to describe the King's mood:

> The British should throw all that they have in vain brought to Massawa for him into the sea; he wanted nothing of it; he would also not release the prisoners if they did

404 Waldmeier, *Erlebnisse*, pp. 56–60; Flad, *Zwölf Jahre*, Vol. II, pp. 10–12; FO 401/2, pp. 445–9, 482–8, Merewether to Stanley, 15 Jan. and 28 Feb. 1867; Rassam, *British Mission*, Vol. II, pp. 230–1; Blanc, *Captivity*, pp. 312–15; Conti Rossini, 'Epistolario', *RRAL*, 6, I, pp. 457–60, 15 Apr. 1867.

405 IO, Eur. F 103, fol. 6, Rassam to Stanley, 7 Jan. 1867; fols 20–2, Tēwodros to Rassam, two undated letters written late December 1866 or early January 1867, and a third one written 5 Jan. 1867; FO 401/2, pp. 458–60, Rassam to Stanley, 10 Jan. 1867; pp. 482–8, Merewether to Stanley, 28 Feb. 1867; p. 512, Tēwodros to Flad (not Merewether as superscribed), 7 (?) Jan. 1867. In his narrative (*British Mission*, Vol. II, pp. 234–8), Rassam has confused the order of Tēwodros's letters, while Blanc (*Captivity*, pp. 225–8) has them correct.

406 FO 401/2, pp. 482–8, Merewether to Stanley, 28 Feb. 1867, quoting Mrs Flad, 14 Jan. 1867.

407 ibid., quoting Staiger, 13 Jan. 1867. The Europeans used their own messenger, who reached the coast much quicker than the King's (Flad, *Zwölf Jahre*, Vol. II, p. 13; FO 401/2, pp. 510–12).

not do for him what he desired, and in case the British wanted to begin war, he would rather cut all the Europeans into a thousand pieces than hand them over.[408]

Under these circumstances it seems highly improbable that even an immediate compliance with Tēwodros's request could have led to a peaceful solution of the conflict. On the basis of letters straight from Meqdela, Merewether had already come to the conclusion 'that the last chance of effecting the object of releasing the captives by conciliatory measures has failed'. Intelligence of Tēwodros's dwindling power contributed to Merewether's decision 'to assume a more decided tone with the Emperor'. Rassam was undoubtedly correct when he wrote of Tēwodros, 'Abyssinia is wearied of him'. And Merewether concluded, '. . . unless he can manage to make some brilliant stroke worthy of his earlier career, his rule will come to an end within the next few months'. Merewether therefore recommended a strongly-worded letter to Tēwodros from the Foreign Office and a proclamation to the chiefs and people that they would be punished if they in any way caused injury to the captives but richly rewarded for any assistance or protection given to them. He even expressed the hope that 'the release of the captives could be brought about by means of the successful rebels'. At the same time, however, he advised his government to prepare an expeditionary force of some 6,000 men for shipment from India to Massawa and action in Ethiopia by October if necessary. He also began to explore possible routes for the expedition. An earlier suggestion that Egyptian troops might be used was labelled 'a grave mistake', since it would 'at once turn from us the rebels, who would otherwise be our greatest assistance. For however much the Emperor Theodorus is hated, the Moslem is hated ten times worse . . .' The employment of Egyptian troops 'would be suicide'.[409]

Though there were modifications, above all with regard to the size of the expeditionary force, it was this dispatch by Merewether that became the basis for the planning of the British expedition to Meqdela, for which preparations began as soon as the letter had reached London. The artisans were recalled to England and a letter addressed to Tēwodros on 16 April that the presents would go the same way if the prisoners were not released and on their way to Massawa within three months of the dispatch of the letter from the coast.[410]

In the meantime, Flad returned alone to Debre Tabor to find that conditions had deteriorated still further. In late January a plan to escape by five of the Europeans at Gefat (Staiger, Brandeis, Essler, Schiller, and Mackerer) had been betrayed to the King by Bardel, and they had since then been chained at Debre Tabor. A few days before Flad's arrival and first meeting with the King in Dembīya on 26 April, and possibly as a result of some message which he had sent in advance, the original Gefat colony, 'the King's children', had also been

408 Waldmeier, *Erlebnisse*, p. 59.
409 FO 401/2, pp. 455–8, 482–8, 524–7, Merewether to Stanley, 15 Feb., 28 Feb., and 1 May 1867.
410 ibid., pp. 473–8, Coghlan to Stanley, 20 Mar. 1867, with enclosure; pp. 505–8, Murray to Lugard and to Merivale, 20 Apr. 1867; Stanley to Merewether, 20 Apr. 1867, and to Tēwodros, 16 Apr. 1867; pp. 539–42, memorandum by Durand, 10 Jun. 1867.

arrested and forced to leave their homes for Debre Tabor. They continued to keep the cannon foundry going and were spared the chains; otherwise they were no less prisoners than the other Europeans. Flad's reception was cold but not hostile. Tēwodros was told that only the immediate release of all the European prisoners could regain British friendship for him, but that the machinery and the workmen were still at Massawa and could be brought up in exchange for the captives. Otherwise war was inevitable, and Flad even added that France and Egypt might join in the attack, both Minīlik and Wagshum Gobezē having made contacts with the French. The King seemed indifferent, resigned to the failure of his foreign policy:

> I asked from them a sign of friendship, which was refused to me. If they wish to come and fight let them come . . . I don't fear. I don't trust in power; I trust in God, who says, if you have faith as a mustard grain, you can remove mountains . . . Not only at the time of Captain Cameron, when they gave me no answer to my letter . . . I found out they were not my sincere friends; but I saw it even at the time of Plowden and Bell . . . I leave it to the Lord, and he shall decide between us when we are fighting in the battlefield.[411]

Tēwodros's treatment of the artisans was no doubt partly due to anti-European sentiment, but it was at the same time part of the bigger problem of his declining power and his consequent distrust of almost everyone, including both his old friends and supporters, such as his god-father, Kentība Haylu, and the commander of Meqdela, Ras Kīdane Maryam, and recent appointees, such as the governor of Gayint appointed only one year before, Dejjazmach Tesemma Ingida. They were all arrested. As the King's last major province, Begēmdir, became increasingly hostile to him, he reportedly chained all the nobility there and relied for advice and support on men he had recently raised from the lowest ranks. But the rank and file of his army were also disillusioned, and desertions continued, followed by horrible reprisals. The peasantry did their utmost to hide their grain and keep out of the reach of Tēwodros's army. By May–June they were even fighting back against the soldiers. As a result, famine and epidemic diseases aggravated the situation for those who remained with the King at Debre Tabor. Estimates of the King's army at this time varied from 4,000–5,000 to 10,000. In June, Blanc even put the figure as low as 1,000, and he added, 'The camp and Magdala constitute his kingdom—ruffians and executioners his army.' But, as Blanc put it, 'His name alone is worth 10,000 men . . .' There was, no doubt, an element of wishful thinking in all this, but it is a fact that the King had the greatest difficulties keeping the road between Debre Tabor and Meqdela open, though the first was his capital and the second his main fortress, and the distance between them is only one week's journey on foot. At the same time, Tēwodros's main rivals, Wagshum Gobezē and Minīlik, were

---

411 ibid., fols 510–12, Merewether to Stanley, 30 Mar. 1867; pp. 576–80, Blanc to Merewether, 30 Apr. 1867, fols 643–7, Merewether to Stanley, 11 Jul. 1867, quoting Flad, 3 May 1867; Flad, *Zwölf Jahre*, Vol. II, pp. 15–17, 21–3, 37–40; Waldmeier, *Erlebnisse*, pp. 60–3; Blanc, *Captivity*, pp. 319–27; Fusella, *Tēwodros*, pp. 36–8.

increasing their power and had no problems communicating with the outside world or with the people inside the fortress. Both chiefs were reportedly contemplating an attack on Meqdela, Minīlik in May, Gobezē in June.[412]

When the Foreign Office ultimatum of 16 April 1867 reached Tēwodros on 13 June, he sent the messenger back without any reply.[413] The King had made his final choice, and it was defiance. Except for excursions to collect provisions for his remaining soldiers and labourers, he spent the rainy season at Debre Tabor and the gun-foundry at Gefat, compelling his European workmen and their assistants to cast ever bigger mortars. But when October came, he burnt Debre Tabor, which he had named the new capital of Ethiopia less than a year before. He took with him all the new guns and mortars, including one weighing eight tons, and blasted a road to Meqdela, both literally and figuratively, for the remnants of his once invincible army, estimated during the march as anything between 3,000 and 8,000. Problems of provisioning for the army and the formidable task of dragging the heavy mortars through the ravines of Jidda and Beshilo slowed down the progress. Constructing the road through the Jidda valley took six weeks, Beshilo four weeks. With his European artisans, the King selected the best slopes for the road. Day and night his people toiled, and he often joined them, working with his own hands, removing boulders and levelling the ground. What was normally a week's journey took almost six months. And when Tēwodros arrived at Meqdela on one of the last days of March 1868, the *amba* with the adjoining peaks of Sillasē and Fala was all that remained of his kingdom.[414]

Reluctantly the British government, on hearing that Tēwodros had disregarded the ultimatum, made the final decision in mid-August 1867 to mount a military expedition to release the captives. The undertaking was delegated to the Bombay government and the command was entrusted to the commander-in-chief of the Bombay army, Sir Robert Napier. The required strength of the army was raised from Merewether's suggested 6,000 to 12,000 (4,000 British and 8,000 Indian troops) with at least an equal number of camp-followers. Later the numbers increased further to 14,700 fighting men and about 27,000 camp followers engaged with the transport train and other auxiliary functions, in other words an invading army of some 42,000 men. British officers were sent out to scour the Middle East from Persia to the Mediterranean and as far west as

---

412   FO 401/2, pp. 523–7, 544, 643–7, Merewether to Stanley, 29 Apr., 1 May, 17 May, and 11 Jul. 1867, quoting Rassam, Blanc, and Cameron; pp. 545–51, memorandum by Blanc, 30 Mar. 1867; pp. 576–80, 648–50, 658–62, Blanc to Merewether, 30 Apr., 10 Jun., and 18 Jun. 1867; pp. 715–16, 780–4, Abbot to Stanley, 23 Aug. and 6 Sep. 1867, quoting Rassam and others; Flad, *Zwölf Jahre*, Vol. II, pp. 18–21, 40–3; Waldmeier, *Erlebnisse*, pp. 63–7; Rassam, *British Mission*, Vol. II, pp. 168, 238–41, 250; Conti Rossini, 'Epistolario', *RRAL*, 6, I, pp. 460–2, 21 Sep. 1867; pp. 465–70, Nov./Dec. [1868]; Welde Maryam, *Tēwodros*, pp. 33–42, Fusella, *Tēwodros*, p. 40.
413   FO 401/2, pp. 656–8, Merewether to Stanley, 26 Jul. 1867.
414   Waldmeier, *Erlebnisse*, pp. 66–74, 79–81; Flad, *Zwölf Jahre*, Vol. II, pp. 43–63; Blanc, *Captivity*, pp. 337–44; Holland and Hozier, *Expedition*, Vol. I, pp. 312, 372–3, 401; Markham, *Abyssinian Expedition*, pp. 292–8; Welde Maryam, *Tēwodros*, pp. 46–7.

Spain for mules and other beasts of burden for the transport train. For a week or two, beginning 22 August, the purchasing of mules seems to have been a major preoccupation of both the Foreign Office and the War Office. And the result was impressive: 17,943 mules and ponies, 2,538 horses, 1,759 donkeys, 8,075 bullocks, 5,735 camels, and even 44 elephants were landed at Zulla (Mulkutto) together with enormous stores of supplies.[415]

It was estimated that the expedition would cost £4 million at the most. The British Parliament voted £2 million for expenses during 1867, and the Bombay authorities were authorized to furnish Napier with what he required. When all was over, the Abyssinian war turned out to have cost almost £9 million (about 36 million thalers). In the 1860s this was a sufficiently large amount for the British tax-payers to call for an investigation by a select parliamentary commit-tee.[416] What this amount meant in terms of Ethiopian revenues at the time is very difficult to establish. According to Rassam, the revenues of Begēmdir, including the duties on the trade that passed from Gonder through Çhilga and Metemma, but excluding the tribute in cattle and sheep, under normal circum-stances amounted to 450,000 thalers annually. This is one of the highest, prob-ably the highest, estimate of revenues from any comparable unit by any observer in the nineteenth century. If we nevertheless accept it as correct and typical for the level of taxation in the whole of Ethiopia at the time, Tēwodros might at the height of his power have been able to collect at best some 2–3 million thalers in cash and kind annually, in other words less than one-tenth of what the campaign of eight months cost the British.[417]

Although the use of Egyptian troops for the campaign had been ruled out, some kind of agreement and co-operation with Egypt was called for. The early reconnaissance activities of Merewether and Munzinger had caused some un-easiness in Cairo: if the British landed an army for a campaign against Tēwodros,

---

415 FO 401/2, pp. 672–4, Northcote to Fitzgerald, 16 Aug. 1867, and Stanley to Merewether, 19 Aug. 1867. This volume (pp. 679–933) provides an ample record of the instructions and information exchanged between all authorities involved in the preparation of the campaign up to the end of 1867. Much of it is repeated in the official record by Holland and Hozier, from which the above figures for the strength of the force have been extracted (*Expedition*, Vol. I, pp. 58, 153–8, 166–7, 229–36; Vol. II, p. 157). Markham (*Abyssinian Expedition*, pp. 204–5) provides the, often quoted, figures from the order of embarkation from Indian ports: 16,189 fighting men and 15,873 camp-followers and transport train, or 32,000 men in all, with the footnote that 26,214 followers were actually landed, thus 42,000 instead of 32,000. A still higher figure, 62,000, is sometimes cited (for instance, Mathew, *Ethiopia*, p. 196), but this 'Total number of persons of all classes and professions (sent to Abyssinia for the purpose of the Expedition) . . .' included the naval staff engaged in the transport operations to Zulla (*Expedition*, Vol. I, p. 236). The literature about the expedition is considerable, the latest contribution being Frederick Myatt, *The March to Magdala* (London, 1970), but Markham's work, which contains some criticism of the way the campaign was planned and conducted, clearly remains one of the best.

416 *PP. Commons*, 1868–69, VI, pp. 1–263; 1870, V, pp. 1–738; 1880, XLI, p. 417.

417 Rassam, *British Mission*, Vol. II, p. 16. Unfortunately a thorough analysis of the many incongruous reports about revenues in nineteenth-century Ethiopia still remains to be undertaken. See Pankhurst, *Economic History*, pp. 504–44, for further references to nine-teenth- and early twentieth-century revenues.

would they evacuate the country again, even the port they would have to develop to mount the expedition? To ensure as far as possible that the British
would accept that they were crossing Egyptian territory wherever they landed,
Khedive Ismail sent an officer to distribute Egyptian flags and grant monthly
salaries to the local chiefs along the coast from Massawa to Bab al-Mandab. In
both London and Cairo it was originally taken for granted that Massawa would
be used, but the requests to Cairo and Istanbul for permission to pass British
troops through Egyptian territory were not specific and certainly implied recognition of Ottoman sovereignty over more than the island. The requests contained assurances that Britain had 'no designs of conquest', and permission was
granted along with promises of co-operation in terms of transport and other
facilities.[418]

On the spot, however, Merewether tried hard to have it both ways. He decided
to land the British army at a point near Zulla (Mulkutto) rather than at Massawa, and he tried to keep visible contacts with the Egyptian officials to a min-
imum, in order to demonstrate an Egyptian neutrality in which that country
was far from interested. This policy was not entirely successful. Ismail assigned
four additional battalions to Massawa, and sent Abd al-Qadir Pasha to follow
up the presents and flags with Egyptian officials and small troop detachments for
Anfilla, Edd, Beylul, and Raheita. Egyptian positions along the Ethiopian
frontier were strengthened, and contacts were made with Ethiopian chiefs to
bring them into the Egyptian camp.[419]

Doubting the sincerity of the British assurances that no conquests were intended, Ismail also made a last-minute attempt to prevent the expedition from
taking place by writing to Tēwodros to release the prisoners immediately in
order to save Ethiopia from the fate that had befallen countries as vast and
remote as India and China. He also stressed that an intimate friendship existed
between Egypt and Britain, and warned that he would be obliged to break off
friendly relations with Ethiopia unless Tēwodros complied with his request.
There was, however, no explicit threat that Egyptian troops would attack
alongside the British. The sending of a mission was cleared with the British
government, but the text of the letter was only communicated after it had been
dispatched to Ethiopia.[420]

418 ENA, Soudan, Carton 3/7, undated memorandum on the occupation of the Red Sea
     coast; Abyssinie, Casier 20/9/1, Ismail to Chérif, 31 Aug. 1867. Douin, *Ismaïl*, III, 1,
     pp. 347–52; FO 401/2, pp. 673–4, Stanley to Reade, 19 Aug. 1867; p. 679, Stanley to
     Barron, 22 Aug. 1867; p. 692, Reade to Stanley, 2 Sep. 1867; p. 704, Larking to Hammond,
     3 Sep. 1867, with enclosure; pp. 720–1, Barron to Stanley, 3 Sep. 1867; pp. 755–6, Raghib
     to Reade, 9 Sep. 1867; pp. 821–2, Barron to Stanley, 4 Oct. 1867, with enclosures.
419 FO 401/2, pp. 818, 862, Reade to Stanley, 16 Oct. and 25 Oct. 1867; p. 931, Merewether
     to Bombay government, 23 Nov. 1867; AECP, Massouah 3, fols 214–18, Munzinger to
     Moustier, 15 Nov. 1867; Douin, *Ismaïl*, III, 1, pp. 356–7, 361–7; Holland and Hozier,
     Expedition, Vol. I, pp. 288–9, 309–12.
420 ENA, Registre 24, Abdin, p. 124, Ismail to Tēwodros, 22 Oct. 1867; FO 401/2, p. 798,
     Reade to Stanley, 7 Oct. 1867; p. 806, Stanley to Reade, 10 Oct. 1867; pp. 862–4, Reade
     to Stanley, 25 Oct. 1867, with the English text of Ismail's letter to Tēwodros. In the text of
     the letter as published by Douin (*Ismaïl*, III, 1, pp. 358–60), the reference to India and

A similar policy to the one adopted towards Egypt was initially followed also with the regard to the Ethiopian provinces in rebellion against Tēwodros or simply cut off from the small area still under the King's rule. No formal alliances were requested or formed, but a benevolent neutrality was sought through the means of a proclamation issued by Napier on 26 October, five days before the first troops disembarked at Zulla:

> To the Governors, the Chiefs, the Religious Orders, and the People of Abyssinia . . . bear in mind, People of Abyssinia, that the Queen of England has no unfriendly feelings towards you; and no design against your country or your liberty . . . All supplies required for my soldiers shall be paid for. No peaceable inhabitant shall be molested. The sole object for which the British Force has been sent to Abyssinia is the liberation of Her Majesty's subjects. There is no intention to occupy permanently any portion of the Abyssinian territory, or to interfere with the government of the country.[421]

The British policy of proclaiming Tēwodros alone the enemy and dealing liberally with the population paid off. As soon as the reconnoitring party arrived at Massawa on 1 October, Haylu of Hamasēn sent a messenger to find out what was going on. He had finally given up his loyalty to Tēwodros and joined hands with Kasa Mirča of Inderta and Tembēn, who had declared himself the independent ruler of all Tigrē a few months earlier. Also Kasa wrote to say that he was a friend of the British but would like to know what they had come for. His messenger Mirča Werqē reportedly told the British that Kasa wished them success in their operations against Tēwodros, but wanted them to leave the country afterwards as quickly as possible, promising not to assist the Egyptian enemies of Ethiopia and leaving no consul behind. Mirča remained with the British as a liaison and interpreter. The explanations given by Merewether were found satisfactory, and Kasa offered his assistance. So did lesser chiefs and spokesmen of the population along the planned route into the highlands. By the time Merewether had established himself at Senafē, even Wagshum Gobezē, whose desire to see Tēwodros destroyed was greater than Kasa's, had sent him a letter. To secure the full co-operation of Kasa was of the greatest importance, since about half of the roughly 650-kilometre-long march to Meqdela (actually 420 kilometres as the crow flies) was through territory controlled by him. A delegation (Major A. J. Grant and Munzinger) was therefore sent to Adwa, and a meeting between the prince and Napier was arranged for. It took place near Hawzēn on 25–26 February. Kasa was more preoccupied with local insurrection and a possible attack on Tigrē by Gobezē than by the fate of Tēwodros, and attempted to enlist British support against the former. Napier reportedly refused

---

China is omitted. For a reported reply by Tēwodros, see p. 376. The mutual suspicion or concern between the Egyptian and British governments persisted (FO 401/2, p. 921, Stanton to Stanley, 1 Dec. 1867; p. 938, Stanley to Stanton, 3 Jan. 1868).

421 Holland and Hozier, *Expedition*, Vol. I, pp. 35–6, 328, 330–1; also FO 401/2, pp. 741–3; Stanley to Northcote, 19 Sep. 1867. Munzinger reported (AECP, Massouah 3, fols 214–18, to Moustier, 15 Nov. 1867) that the Catholic mission had kindly printed 400 copies of the proclamation.

to give any guarantees, but promised that he would do his best to persuade Gobezē to keep the peace. In return for this and a promise that he would be rewarded after the campaign was over, Kasa undertook to provide security for the convoys and telegraph lines and to deliver 15,000 kilograms of grain per week to each of the British camps at Addīgrat and Antalo.[422]

The promises of provisions were liberally fulfilled. Antalo alone was provided with some 50,000 kilograms of grain and flour during the first week of March, and the average over a month was around 4,500 kilograms per day. Since daily rations of flour and rice varied from about one-third to two-thirds of a kilogram, this actually provided staple food for 6,500–13,000 men. Cattle were always brought to market, sufficient for rations of up to 1 kilogram of beef per day when other rations had to be reduced. Even in Delanta, where the population had been forced to feed Tēwodros's army for a whole month only weeks before, some 80,000 kilograms of grain and flour were made available to the foreign army during the last few days before the attack on Meqdela. The co-operation of the Ethiopian population in solving the transport problems was just as important, due to exceptionally high losses of imported animals in the early stages of the campaign. In fact, the forwarding of commissariat stores in the highlands from the end of January was largely based on local resources, as admitted in an official report by the senior commissariat officer with the advanced force:

> Through the agency of this [the native] carriage alone were we enabled to forward ample supplies as far as Atsala . . .

There was clearly some truth in the colourful description of the power of 'the dollar' in Ethiopia:

> . . . it causes water to flow from solid rocks; it brings forth food in abundance for 20,000 men and 60,000 animals; it makes the plains to overflow with goats and bleating kids; it causes the inhabitants to pull down their houses, and give their rafters to the Commisariat Department that the food which they had brought for the soldiers should also be cooked![423]

Aided in this manner, two brigades (about 4,000 men) of the British–Indian army reached Wadla by the end of March. Using the road completed by Tēwodros only six weeks earlier, they had no problem crossing the ravine of Jidda (1,000 metres below the level of the plateau) and the Delanta plain. On 9 April they stood at the edge of that plain, with Tēwodros's camp on the Islamgē saddle between the peaks of Fala and Sillasē and Amba Meqdela itself clearly visible across the Beshilo valley. Either side was able to attack within a

422   Holland and Hozier, *Expedition*, Vol. I, pp. 286, 303, 308–11, 317, 320, 330–1, 372–3, 391–6; Markham, *Abyssinian Expedition*, pp. 164–6, 223–7, 262–4, 274, 301–3; AECP, Massouah 3, fols 221–7, Munzinger to Moustier, 29 Feb. 1868.
423   Holland and Hozier, *Expedition*, Vol. I, pp. 334, 338–9, 379–80, 437 (table of supplies at Antalo); Vol. II, pp. 3, 95, 172, 180–4 (first quotation), 309–10; Markham, *Abyssinian Expedition*, pp. 210, 258–61, 279–80, 304–5, 309–10; Stanley, *Magdala* pp. 385 (second quotation), 392–5, 398–9.

matter of a few hours. Napier had taken the precaution of arranging with Wagshum Gobezē's uncle and deputy in the area, Dejjazmach Meshesha, and with Queen Mestewat of the Galla population there, to cut off Tēwodros's line of retreat towards the east or north.[424]

A strange race had reached its end. Tēwodros had started from Debre Tabor ten days before the first British troops landed at Zulla on 21 October 1867, and it was with those ten days only that he had beaten them to Meqdela. The distance covered by Napier was almost three times as great as that covered by Tēwodros. The fact that the British general was crossing unknown and supposedly hostile country had, moreover, dictated a cautious advance. In fact, however, it was Tēwodros who had travelled through enemy territory; his soldiers had marched under the threat of attacks from Gobezē's numerically superior forces, and had been obliged to defend themselves against a hostile peasantry. Tēwodros's problems of provisioning for his army and transporting his artillery had also been much greater than Napier's. Most important of all, Tēwodros could not trust even the four thousand soldiers who still followed him. Given the opportunity, they might abandon his cause as so many had already done. Immobilized in a sense also by his own artillery, the former *shifta* leader, once known for his swift and daring attacks, made no attempt to stop the foreign army. Nowhere along their route had the British–Indian army been attacked; not one of the many difficult and dangerous passes had been defended even by a single Ethiopian soldier. Tēwodros was well aware of this failure. After reaching Meqdela, he told Rassam that he would have acted differently if he had been attacked a few years earlier, but 'As it is, I have lost all Abyssinia but this rock . . .' A few days later Waldmeier reported a similar conversation in which Tēwodros referred to the disloyalty of his troops.[425]

The peaceful character of the British march to Meqdela is amply illustrated by what the official record called 'an incident which might have been attended with serious consequences'. As Meshesha was leaving the British camp after a friendly visit to Napier on 2 April, part of his escort was mistaken for enemy cavalry. A British picket fired and killed one man. Thus 'the first blood was drawn in the Abyssinian campaign'.[426]

What Tēwodros planned to do at Meqdela, if he planned at all, is difficult to know. By the beginning of December, he seems to have heard something about the coming of the British army. He was reportedly 'in a fearful rage' for several days, and increased his surveillance of the Europeans in his camp, hinting darkly that there were people around who wanted to steal donkeys![427] It is, in fact, inconceivable that no spy or messenger should have reached him by then with the news, and most probably also with a copy of Napier's proclamation or the

424 Holland and Hozier, *Expedition*, Vol. II, pp. 21–3, 28–31, 440, 446; Markham, *Abyssinian Expedition*, pp. 304, 310–12.
425 Rassam, *British Mission*, Vol. II, pp. 251–70, 304–5 (quoted), 308; Waldmeier, *Erlebnisse*, p. 293. See also above, p. 256, note 414.
426 Holland and Hozier, *Expedition*, Vol. II, p. 28; Markham, *Abyssinian Expedition*, pp. 306–7.
427 Holland and Hozier, *Expedition*, Vol. I, p. 372; Flad, *Zwölf Jahre*, Vol. II, pp. 53, 56; Rassam, *British Expedition*, Vol. II, p. 254.

letter which the commander-in-chief had directed to the King personally and also distributed widely. Whether he received any of the four copies of Lord Stanley's last ultimatum dated 9 September is more uncertain.[428]

In early February when he began to speak to the Europeans in his camp about the advancing British troops, Tēwodros had apparently resigned himself to the fact that his power and authority were being challenged by an invading army. This, however, did not mean that he was prepared to accept the advice of any-one to let the Europeans go, and thus avert the attack. On the contrary, he allegedly expressed great satisfaction with the turn events had taken:

> I long for the day on which I shall have the pleasure to see a disciplined European army. I am like Simeon who would rejoice, having the Saviour in his arms; but he was old and died, and I am old too, but I hope God will spare me to see them. I am no more proud of my soldiers. We are nothing in comparison to a disciplined army, where thousands of men act on the command of one man.

That he would be called upon either to fight this superior army or surrender did not seem to bother Tēwodros. With characteristic fatalism, he reportedly told Flad:

> If He who is above does not kill me, none will kill me, and if He says, you must die, no one can save me.[429]

It is difficult to escape the conclusion that Tēwodros was in some sense losing touch with reality. As he approached Meqdela, he contacted Rassam again, and a series of friendly but meaningless messages were exchanged, culminating in a letter through which the envoy was informed that he would receive a hundred sheep and fifty cows and that he would be freed from his chains but remain a prisoner 'until we see the intention of your masters (*yegētochihin hunēta istinay dires*)'. Two messages after his arrival at Meqdela indicate how Tēwodros's mind vacillated. On 27 March he declared that he was 'desirous of nothing but peace; and I pray God that your brothers are coming with a good intention'. Two days later he explained:

> The reason I have ill-treated you was because I wanted the people of your country to come to me. I am glad they are coming. Whether they beat me or I beat them, I shall always be your friend.

Within hours of this message, and after a friendly conversation with Rassam, his mood changed and he allegedly told his chiefs:

> Mr. Rassam has made fools of you and of me . . . Did either you or your forefathers ever hear of a friend sending for troops to slaughter his friend's valiant men, ravish

428 FO 401/2, p. 738, Stanley to Tēwodros, 9 Sep. 1867; p. 737, Hammond to Melvill, 18 Sep. 1867; Holland and Hozier, *Expedition*, Vol. I, pp. 34–5, 330–1; Rassam, *British Mission*, Vol. II, p. 265; Blanc, *Captivity*, pp. 352, 381.

429 Rassam, *British Mission*, Vol. II, pp. 266–7 (quoting a letter from Flad dated 11 Feb. 1868); also Flad, *Zwölf Jahre*, Vol. II, pp. 58–9; Waldmeier, *Erlebnisse*, pp. 78–9, 95; Blanc, *Captivity*, pp. 350–2, 355–7. Note that Plowden reported expressions of this kind of fatalism as early as 1855 (FO 401/1, pp. 250–7).

their wives, and reduce his people to bondage? . . . Tell me, however, if you are prepared to fight Rassam's brothers, who are coming against you with guns that dazzle the sight, and muskets that shoot and stab simultaneously? [430]

So irrational and unpredictable, however, was the King's behaviour that he then ridiculed those of his poor chiefs who declared their willingness to fight, telling them that they were ignorant fools and no match for British soldiers. Whatever hopes he may have had that Rassam or Napier would suggest a peaceful solution, which he could accept without losing face, disappeared when he heard about and finally saw that the British army made preparations to cross the Beshilo. During the last days before the attack, he busied himself with arrangements for his defence, and on the morning of 10 April, which was Good Friday, he took up positions with his artillery on Fala and Sillasē, and brought down the garrison of the fortress to his camp on Islamgē to help meet the attack. That morning he refused to receive a letter which had arrived from Napier, though he informed himself of its contents through Samu'ēl. It was a simple demand that the Europeans be sent to the British camp. Even if it had contained a promise that this would avert the attack, it is unlikely that it would have made any difference. [431]

To Waldmeier, who was close to the King throughout the crucial day, Tēwodros said that he wanted no reconciliation. He spoke with regret about the fact that the British had been so slow to act: instead of attacking him soon after he had chained Cameron, they had waited until his power had gone. Waldmeier observed that Tēwodros was very tense and that his behaviour showed a mixture of timidity, pride, and anger. Attempts by his close and faithful follower Ras Ingida to encourage him failed. Nevertheless, when he saw British troops climbing up the slopes from Beshilo, the King reportedly fired his troops with the traditional ceremonial braggadocio, stressing the opportunity for booty and the unbelievable arrogance of the British: they had sent the servant of a woman, a nobody, against the elected and anointed King of Ethiopia, the son of David and of Solomon. Then he went to supervise the loading of his cannon at Fala. He was still undecided, and it reportedly took some prodding by Fītawrarī Gebriyyē and other chiefs before he agreed, 'Good, go down, God help you and forgive you your sins'. [432]

A small plain, called Arogē, halfway between Beshilo and Meqdela, has given its name to the only battle of this strange war. It was about four o'clock in the

430 IO, Eur. F 103, fol. 106, Tēwodros to Rassam, n.d., received 18 Mar. 1868; Rassam, *British Mission*, Vol. II, pp. 254–94 (quoted materials on pp. 273, 282, 287, and 294); also Blanc, *Captivity*, pp. 358–9, 366–72, Stern, *Captive Missionary*, pp. 368–72.

431 Rassam, *British Mission*, Vol. II, pp. 294, 307–17; Flad, *Zwölf Jahre*, Vol. II, pp. 62–4; Blanc, *Captivity*, pp. 372–91. Though Tēwodros would no doubt have fought under all circumstances, it should be noted that Flad in a letter dated 30 Apr. 1868 (*MT*, 1868, pp. 62–3, accused 'some European workmen' of having told the King that his honour demanded that he fight the British.

432 Waldmeier, *Erlebnisse*, pp. 91–6; cf. Markham, *Abyssinian Expedition*, p. 324; Fusella, *Tēwodros*, pp. 42–3.

afternoon of Good Friday when the King opened fire with his guns on Fala. It started with a mishap. By oversight, the first gun to be fired, one of his largest, named Tēwodros, had been loaded twice and burst with a terrific blast. For about two hours, the King kept up the fire with some twelve pieces. According to Waldmeier, around 200 shots were fired, but the confusion was dreadful:

> . . . one of the artillerists had no ball, the second had run out of powder, the third had lost his slowmatch, the fourth had in the rush pushed down the ball first into the bore and then the powder and was now unable to get the shot out again.[433]

An exaggerated description probably, but the fact remains that Tēwodros's guns, served by inexperienced Ethiopians, caused no casualties in the ranks of the advancing British and Indian soldiers. The whole barrage seems, in fact, to have passed over their heads because of the difference in altitude and too powerful charges. When the firing had begun, Gebriyyē led the Ethiopian attack down the slopes. It was hardly expected that afternoon, but Napier's first brigade was quickly organized to meet it. When the Ethiopians came within comfortable range of the British rifle fire (this was the first time in history that the Snider rifle was used), they were simply mown down. As they retired, rockets from the British artillery caused further casualties among them, and towards the end of the battle, shells and rockets began to land with deadly effect also among Tēwodros's people on Fala. Some 18,000 rounds of rifle and 300 of artillery ammunition had been fired before darkness fell. Of the 3,700 British and Indian troops who had crossed the Beshilo, less than 2,000 actually took part in the action. The estimates of the Ethiopians ranged from 4,000 to 7,000, with 3,000 to 4,000 of these supplied with firearms: double-barrelled percussion guns and, mainly, inferior matchlocks. The Ethiopian casualties were 700–800 killed and 1,200–1,500 wounded, 'most of them severely', according to Markham. The British had twenty wounded, 'two mortally, nine severely, and nine slightly'. Better than any detailed description of the battle, these figures illustrate both the enormous disparity in terms of arms and tactics and the courage and perseverance of the Ethiopian warriors in the face of certain defeat. Due to lack of training and experience, and possibly deliberate sabotage by Waldmeier and Saalmüller as well, Tēwodros's artillery had turned out to be worthless, as the King himself noted in his message to Napier the day after the battle. This was in itself a hard lesson. Moreover, the ill-considered attack had halved his army and almost eliminated the advantage of the strong defensive position which Meqdela had offered him.[434]

Tēwodros understood that further resistance would only mean more blood-

---

433   Waldmeier, *Erlebnisse*, pp. 95–6. Markham (*Abyssinian Expedition*, p. 320) states that the first shot was fired at 4.42 p.m., but he is probably wrong by one hour. Cf. Holland and Hozier, *Expedition*, Vol. II, p. 37—battle from four o'clock until seven—and Stanley, *Magdala*, pp. 413–14, 423, implying that the cannonade started soon after 3.30 and ended by 5.30 p.m.

434   Waldmeier, *Erlebnisse*, pp. 95–8; Holland and Hozier, *Expedition*, Vol. II, pp. 35–8, 42 (Tēwodros's 'letter' to Napier the day after the battle), 57 (statement by Welde Gabir after the fall of Meqdela), 308, 441–2 (Napier's dispatch to Northcote, 14 Apr. 1868), 463; Markham, *Abyssinian Expedition*, pp. 316–23; A. F. Shepherd, *The Campaign in Abyssinia*

shed. The only demand that had reached him was for the release of the prisoners, and his mind turned quite naturally to the question of what terms he might obtain in exchange for surrendering them all safe and sound, rather than trying to flee with them, or killing them before fleeing as some alleged that he considered doing. The events of the following three days prove beyond doubt that he did not contemplate that he might be asked for anything more. True, he had fought the British army, because as a king he believed he was obliged to fight in order not to be regarded as a cowardly ruler, but now he admitted defeat and wanted reconciliation. At daybreak the morning after the battle, Prideaux, Flad, and the King's son-in-law, Dejjazmach Alemē Gwalu, left for Napier's camp as a joint delegation from Tēwodros and Rassam. They soon discovered, as might have been expected, that peace was no longer obtainable for the asking. Napier demanded that the King submit to the Queen of England (in other words, surrender his person to the commander-in-chief) and deliver all the Europeans safely in the British camp the same day in exchange for honourable treatment for himself and the members of his family. Waldmeier, who with Flad translated the letter to the King, paraphrased 'submit' and added 'or very early tomorrow morning' to weaken the impact. But Tēwodros accepted no ambiguities. Flad was convinced that the King understood what was expected of him, and reported that he had asked in mockery if the British intended to give him honourable treatment as a prisoner, or assist him to recover his country from the rebels. In the strange and confused document which Tēwodros sent as his reply, the answer to the demand for his personal surrender was: 'A warrior who has dandled strong men in his arms like infants will never suffer himself to be dandled in the arms of others.' More important, the whole letter, which was directed as much to the Ethiopian people and posterity as to the British general, indicated that the writer had reached the end of his dream, his struggle—and his endurance. He did not even use his royal titles: king of kings, elect of God— or the glorious throne-name under which he had striven so hard to change Ethiopia; he wrote simply as 'Kasa, whose trust is in Christ'.[435]

(Bombay, 1868), pp. 237–41. The view that at least Waldmeier and possibly also Saalmüller and other Europeans were engaged in weighing out the first charges for each of the guns on Fala seems to be based mainly on the statement of the servant and constant follower of the King, Welde Gabir, who also indicated that they had perhaps intentionally made the charges too strong. All Waldmeier has to say on the matter is that Ethiopian artillerists were ordered to load the guns, that he intended to warn Tēwodros that the first gun to be discharged had been loaded twice but was prevented by the confusion from doing so. Napier stated in his dispatch that the Europeans denied having served the guns, and Blanc (*Captivity*, p. 393) that the Ethiopian gunners were supervised by Ingida Werq, the son of a Bengal Jew, and by an Egyptian. For a description of the battle by an Ethiopian eyewitness *or* someone listening to an eyewitness, see Fusella, *Tēwodros*, pp. 42–3. This source supports Welde Gabir's statement, but dependence on it cannot be excluded.

435 Waldmeier, *Erlebnisse*, pp. 98–104; Flad, *Zwölf Jahre*, Vol. II, pp. 65–8; Holland and Hozier, *Expedition*, Vol. II, pp. 39–46 ('Tēwodros's letter on p. 42), 442, 447; Rassam, *British Mission*, Vol. II, pp. 318–21. The King's letter is published in all these books and several others. Unfortunately, the original is not to be found in the government archives, and all my attempts to locate it have so far failed. The possibility that the translation is inaccurate cannot be excluded, but both the substance and the expressions appear to be quite genuine.

Under the circumstances, mentally distracted and deranged as Tēwodros was, at least temporarily, this was as close to an abdication and a last will as he could come. Nevertheless, the clear hint that Tēwodros would commit suicide rather than surrender seems to have been lost on both Flad and the other Europeans involved. When Flad and Prideaux had left for the British camp again, Tēwodros suddenly stood up, started praying, bowed three times to the ground, crossed himself and put the muzzle of his pistol to his mouth. Some of his men jumped at him, and, as they jerked the pistol from him, the trigger was pulled and the bullet almost grazed his ear. For the Europeans, who were still completely at the King's mercy, this was a critical moment. But it was as if the abortive suicide attempt and the clamour of some of his remaining faithful followers for the immediate execution of the Europeans, as revenge in advance for their own inescapable deaths, had calmed Tēwodros. He decided instead to release Rassam, Blanc, and the first group of captives, including Cameron and Stern, and so at about nine o'clock on Saturday evening (11 April), escorted by Alemē, Samu'ēl, Waldmeier, and some of the other artisans, the persons on whose behalf the campaign had been launched were all safe in the British camp.[436]

The fact that he had been rescued from his attempted suicide made a deep impression on Tēwodros, restoring his hope and faith in some kind of future. Writing again as King of Kings Tēwodros, he addressed a second letter to Napier early on Easter morning to explain this. He also wrote that he had sent Rassam in the evening to relieve the general's anxiety, and would send down the remaining Europeans as requested, 'even to my best friend, Waldmeier'. Besides, as it was Easter day, he hoped Napier would accept a gift of cows and sheep for his troops. The letter concluded, 'But now that we are friends, you must not leave me without artisans, as I am a lover of the mechanical arts'. A last appeal from the defeated for a share in the technological know-how of the Europeans! This letter was brought to the camp by Bender and the King's chief secretary, Aleqa Ingida, and translated by Samu'ēl and Rassam. Napier was careful to make no written reply, but on Rassam's direct question whether he would accept the cattle or not, he said he would, and this was the message taken to the anxiously waiting Tēwodros by Samu'ēl and Alemē, escorted once again by the European artisans who went back to bring their families and remaining friends. Tēwodros was sorry to see them go, but delighted that his peace offering had been accepted. The geographer of the expedition, Clements R. Markham, was able to appreciate his generosity: 'Not a hostage, not a child, not a box was kept back. It was the act of a king, an act without cunning or treachery, how slight soever, to mar its fulness.' This, unfortunately, could not be said about the British side. Towards evening Tēwodros learned that the gift, 1,000 cows and 500 sheep, had been stopped outside the British camp, and thus understood that he

---

436   Waldmeier, *Erlebnisse*, pp. 104–7; Rassam, *British Mission*, Vol. II, pp. 321–5; Flad, *Zwölf Jahre*, Vol. II, pp. 69–70; Holland and Hozier, *Expedition*, Vol. II, pp. 442–3. It is possible, of course, that the Europeans realized how close to suicide Tēwodros was but that they decided to ignore it, since there was, in fact, not much they could do about it. As early as 1863 both Lejean (AEMD, Afrique 61, fol. 138) and Dufton (*Narrative*, p. 297) formed the opinion that Tēwodros would 'blow out his brains' rather than surrender.

had been deceived. By then all the Europeans and their dependants (except Bardel, who was reportedly too ill to be moved) had reached safety.[437]

Early the following morning (13 April), Tēwodros reportedly dissolved his army and made a half-hearted attempt to escape through the 'back door' of Meqdela (the Kaffir Ber, facing south-east), but too few of his remaining followers were willing to attempt the breakthrough of the Galla encirclement, and so he returned to Meqdela. In the meantime, some chiefs had gone to the British camp, reported his disappearance and offered to surrender with what remained of army and garrison. Napier immediately offered the Galla 50,000 thalers for the King's capture, and accelerated his preparations for occupying the *amba*. As the British and Indian troops, about 3,500 men, began to appear in strength on Fala and Sillasē, the Ethiopians there surrendered at once. A belated attempt by Tēwodros to drag some of the guns from Islamgē inside the defences of the *amba* itself had to be abandoned. Deserted in his last hours by all but a dozen or so of his most faithful followers, and seeking death, Tēwodros rode up and down in front of the British, challenging anyone to come forward and fight him. Finally he withdrew and awaited the end inside the second of the two gates of the Kokit Ber entrance. After two to three hours of heavy shelling and deadly rifle

---

437 Holland and Hozier, *Expedition*, Vol. II, pp. 44–9 (Tēwodros's letter on p. 44), 443–4; Rassam, *British Mission*, Vol. II, pp. 325–30; Waldmeier, *Erlebnisse*, pp. 108–10, 113; Flad, *Zwölf Jahre*, Vol. II, p. 71; Markham, *Abyssinian Expedition*, pp. 333–42; Blanc, *Captivity*, pp. 405–6. The lists of the released persons differ (59 to 67), depending on the inclusion or not of non-Ethiopian servants, and some confusion as to whether Bell's and Parkyn's children in particular were to be regarded as foreigners. Of greater importance is the issue of the peace-offering of cattle. The anonymous chronicler, who presents a rather confused account of the negotiations and the release of the foreigners (Fusella, *Tēwodros*, pp. 44–8), states—as does Waldmeier—that Napier said he would refuse to accept the cattle and sheep *until* all the foreigners had arrived in his camp, which implies that this was the only condition. Napier reported, in his dispatch of 14 Apr. 1868 (*Expedition*, Vol. II, p. 443), that Rassam and others 'acquired the impression' that the 'offering of a few cows' had been accepted by him. In the heated controversy that followed after the campaign was over, Rassam maintained that Napier had replied, 'I accept them', or words to that effect (FO 1/27A, Rassam's report, 1 Sep. 1868, paragraph 348; FO 1/29, fol. 87, Rassam to Argyll, 27 Mar. 1869). Besides quoting Merewether that he had simply nodded, and absentmindedly at that (!), Napier argued that he had originally believed that *a few cows* were of no importance; it was only when the cattle arrived and when he heard that it was a question of 1,000 cows and 500 sheep that he understood the importance of the gift and that its acceptance would be regarded as a pledge of friendship (FO 1/29, fols 83–6, Napier to Argyll, 11 Feb. 1869). Markham (p. 338, n. 1), however, pointed out that there were two versions of the sentence about the gift of cattle, the official 'Today is Easter: be pleased to let me send a few cows to you', and 'This being the Easter festival, I hope I may send 1,000 cows and 500 sheep, as a breakfast for the troops'. If this second version is the correct translation (see also Flad's report, *Expedition*, Vol. II, p. 46), the conclusion is almost inevitable that it was suppressed because Napier did not want it to be known that the magnitude of the offer had been stated to him in writing from the outset. Unfortunately, I have been as unable to find the original of this second letter from Tēwodros as that of the first. It is therefore impossible to establish to what extent Tēwodros was *deliberately* deceived, and whose the main responsibility was. That he *was* deceived is, however, irrefutable. In Ethiopia a tradition arose and has been preserved in the family chronicle of Tēwodros (manuscript which belonged to the late Dejjazmach Kasa Meshesha, pp. 168–9) that the gift was rejected because the cattle had been robbed from the poor.

fire, Meqdela was stormed. It was four in the afternoon; the assault took fifteen minutes, and cost the British army ten wounded. Most of Tēwodros's last followers fell at his side. With capture only minutes away, Tēwodros carried out his declared intention to fall into the hands of God, rather than man.[438]

Whether the pistol with which Tēwodros shot himself was the one he had received from Queen Victoria or not is immaterial. That he died by his own hand is not, for this last act of defiance contributed in some twisted way to the legend of his invincibility. To Napier, it was a matter of national honour, more important even than the release of the captives, to force Tēwodros, the jailer of a British consul and a special envoy, to surrender his own person.[439] When Tēwodros preferred self-inflicted death to captivity, he deprived the British of this ultimate satisfaction and laid the foundation for his own resurrection as a symbol of the defiant independence of the Ethiopian.

For four days only, the Union Jack waved over Meqdela. The stronghold was offered to Wagshum Gobezē through his deputy Meshesha but he declined the offer most probably because Napier was intent on destroying the guns first. So, the treasury thoroughly looted and political prisoners and jailers dismissed, the buildings were set on fire and the simple fortifications as well as the guns destroyed. On 18 April the march back to the coast began. Two months later, the last member of the expedition sailed from Mulkutto. Schimper and Zander preferred to remain in Ethiopia, but eight British citizens and fourteen other Europeans with their dependants took the opportunity to leave.[440] Some had suffered much, and all had experienced privation, moments of acute anxiety, and captivity in some form or another. Nevertheless, it is a remarkable fact that, except for Kienzlen, who died from illness in 1865, no European, after Bell, had lost his life in the service—or in the prisons—of the King. His own subjects had suffered far more from Tēwodros's unpredictable conduct, violence and cruelty: 'The people of my country . . . had provoked me to anger against them. Out of what I have done of evil towards them, may God bring good.'[441]

---

438 Holland and Hozier, *Expedition*, Vol. II, pp. 51–60, 444–6, 467; Markham, *Abyssinian Expedition*, pp. 342–53, 362; Rassam, *British Mission*, Vol. II, pp. 330–4; Waldmeier, *Erlebnisse*, pp. 112–14; Flad, *Zwölf Jahre*, p. 72; Blanc, *Captivity*, pp. 407–8; Fusella, *Tēwodros*, pp. 48–9; Welde Maryam, *Tēwodros*, pp. 57–62. The official estimate of the Ethiopians disarmed on Fala and Sillasē was 8,000–10,000, but this figure is most certainly inflated; the greater number were on Sillasē, and Waldmeier, who took care of the disarming there, estimated that the soldiers numbered about 2,000.

439 Holland and Hozier, *Expedition*, Vol. II, p. 444. But cf. FO 401/2, pp. 741–3, Stanley to Northcote, 19 Sep. 1867, indicating that Napier was by no means obliged to press for the surrender of the King: '. . . *if the King should fall into his hands* by the fate of war, unstained or not by the blood of the prisoners . . . Napier should continue to hold the King in custody . . . until Her Majesty's pleasure can be ascertained . . .' (my emphasis). The original (IO, Abyssinia Original Correspondence 1, pp. 931–52), signed by Stanley and marked 'secret', does not differ from the printed version. See also FO 401/2, pp. 672–3, Northcote to the Governor of Bombay, 16 Aug. 1867.

440 Holland and Hozier, *Expedition*, Vol. II, pp. 75–8, 113; Shepherd, *Campaign*, p. 272; Markham, *Abyssinian Expedition*, pp. 359, 363–8, 372, 383–4, 387–8; Rassam, *British Mission*, Vol. II, pp. 339, 343–6.

441 Holland and Hozier, *Expedition*, Vol. II, p. 42. For Kienzlen, see Waldmeier, *Erlebnisse*, p. 55.

The Significance of Tēwodros and Meqdela

In the context of Ethiopia's nineteenth-century survival as an independent state, the reign of Tēwodros was crucial in many respects. Firstly, Tēwodros perceived as did none of his predecessors among the *mesafint* that the political anarchy, moral laxity, and technological backwardness of his people threatened national survival. The reforms he announced, the policies he tried to implement, the very single-mindedness and perseverance with which he tackled the problems, indicate that he aimed at nothing less than a national revival combined with the transformation of his country into a modern state. About this, there was little doubt during the early years of his reign. Thus, while agreeing, in the spirit of the times, 'that the occupation of Abyssinia by a civilized nation . . . would be the speediest and the most effectual means for uniting this fine country with Europe', Consul Plowden admitted that he did not believe it necessary 'that Abyssinia should be conquered in order to [insure] its civilisation, and the development of its resources'.[442]

The British consul agreed, however, with almost all other observers that Tēwodros was a last chance for Ethiopia: '. . . if he does not succeed in effecting an improvement, no native of the country ever will'. It was the King's person that stood between Ethiopia and 'hopeless anarchy' and 'foreign conquest'. Beke predicted that Tēwodros would never found a dynasty and that 'the time must come—most probably even before his death—when the fabric hastily raised by him . . . will fall to the ground'. Then Ethiopia would return to what it had been in the 1840s, and the mistake of the British government in recognizing a supreme ruler over all Ethiopia could be corrected: '. . . the true policy [i.e. real interest] of England clearly is to recognize each [provincial governor] within his own dominions'.[443] That Ethiopia would either come under European tutelage or suffer conquest by Egypt was almost a foregone conclusion. To Dufton in 1867, it was a matter for doubt whether the Ethiopians would 'be able to maintain even their existence as a nation'. In fact, he believed that it would be only a matter of time before the Ethiopians would have destroyed themselves, 'unless the foreigner come first and rule their country for them'. In his view, Tēwodros was 'the first and only patriot Abyssinia ever saw, and assuredly, will be the last'.[444]

Munzinger, too, saw no future for a united Ethiopia:

> The English expedition to Abyssinia has returned home, and the country has resumed its old appearance except that there is one great man less and many rebels more . . . [Tēwodros] was the only representative and defender of a unique and Christian Abyssinia, the only person in Abyssinia who acted to put ideas into practice; with all

442 FO 401/1, pp. 355–6, Plowden to Russell, 5 Feb. 1860.
443 ibid., pp. 277, 282–3, Plowden to Clarendon, 23 Jun. and 11 Nov. 1856; pp. 433–4, Beke to Layard, 22 Aug. 1862; FO 401/2, pp. 652–6, Beke to Stanley, 12 Aug. 1867.
444 Dufton, *Narrative*, pp. 116, 145, 291. But note also Lejean's view (*Théodore II*, pp. 229–30) that an Egyptian/Turkish invasion would be followed by a religious and patriotic reaction.

his crimes, he accustomed the people [lit. country] to having a fatherland and a king . . .[445]

There was, of course, some justification for painting a gloomy picture of Ethiopia's future. The success of Tēwodros's attempts to unify Ethiopia and secure the financial basis for a national army and some kind of central administration had been both limited and transient, or so it seemed at the time. The reasons he himself gave in the 'letter' to Napier of 11 April 1868 are as close to the truth as any:

My countrymen have turned their backs on me and have hated me, because I imposed tribute on them, and sought to bring them under military discipline.[446]

The idea that anarchy would necessarily follow and increase was nevertheless wrong. Though the fall of Meqdela meant the release of several potentially powerful rivals, for instance Balgada Araya, Wagshum Teferi, Ali Farīs, and Birru Goshu, and some of these did challenge Gobezē and Kasa, the latter managed to consolidate their power locally without too much bloodshed, and then they settled the question of who was to rule northern and central Ethiopia through one brief campaign in June–July 1871.[447]

The successful Kasa was crowned King of Kings Yohannis in January 1872, and though Minīlik remained for seventeen years an uncomfortably powerful rival and vassal, the two managed to avoid any full-scale armed conflict. This was no doubt due to the fact that Yohannis was less committed to a unified state, and more willing to compromise than Tēwodros had been. Nevertheless there was no return to the feudal structure of the *Zemene Mesafint*. Gobezē, Kasa, and Minīlik all aimed at supreme control of the whole Ethiopian state, in a way that Ali, Wibē, and Sahle Sillasē had not done. There is no sign that any of them even considered a return to the practice of puppet emperors at Gonder. On the contrary, Minīlik had begun to style himself King of Kings of Ethiopia even before the death of Tēwodros,[448] and within a few months after the fall of Meqdela

445   AECP, Massouah 3, fols 231–6, Munzinger to Moustier, 23 Aug. 1868.

446   Holland and Hozier, *Expedition*, Vol. II, p. 42.

447   For a list of the liberated chiefs, see Holland and Hozier, *Expedition*, Vol. II, p. 81; for the internal struggles after Tēwodros's death, *inter alia*, FO 1/28, fol. 29, Kasa to Napier, 10 Aug. 1869; fol. 197, Kasa to Victoria, 28 Jul. 1871; FO 95/728, no. 192, Tekle Gīyorgīs to Victoria and Napier, n.d. (before July 1869); AEMD, Afrique 62, fol. 110, Tekle Gīyorgīs to Napoleon III, 7 Jul. 1870; also Munzinger's dispatches from 23 Aug. 1868 to 27 Mar. 1870 in AECP, Massouah 3, fols 231–96, *passim*, and Hassen's, 12 Jun. and 30 Jul. 1871, in AECP, Égypte 49, fols 439–40, and 50, fols 65–8; Douin, *Ismaïl*, III, 2, pp. 287–98, 324–7, with sources cited; BN, Ethiop. 259, fols 6–11.

448   FO 1/20, fol. 215, Minīlik to Victoria, n.d., received 6 Aug. 1867. Because the translator chose to write 'Negoos Menelek' instead of *niguse negest* in the English translation (fols 217–18; FO 401/2, p. 642), and historians have not bothered about the Amharic original, this early and absolutely unique evidence of Minīlik's aspirations to the imperial throne has remained unknown. The Amharic original is a beautiful document, 62 × 27 cm., with representations of the Trinity and the symbols of the four evangelists as well as of Minīlik and Victoria at the top. That the lion in the seal wears no crown is not significant—Aṣē

Gobezē had himself proclaimed Aṣē Tekle Gīyorgīs, King of Kings of Ethiopia.[449]

Until he had defeated Tekle Gīyorgīs, Kasa contented himself with the title *ri'ise mekwanint* (head of the great men), which had been used in the early 1850s by Ali and Wibē, but there can be no doubt that he, too, had set his eyes on the imperial throne from the outset. In fact, he allegedly tried to persuade Napier to acknowledge him as king of kings and supreme ruler of the whole country. In a letter to Napoleon III, in August 1868, he claimed descent not only from the the Tigrean *rases*, Mīka'ēl Sihul and Welde Sillasē, but also from the seventeenth- and eighteenth-century emperors at Gonder, Fasīledes and Bekkafa.[450] A reported conversation between him and the Catholic missionary Delmonte, also in 1868, moreover indicates that he was at least as committed to an indivisible Ethiopia as the other two: 'If I were certain to become king of Abyssinia, I would decide the question [whether to permit Catholic mission work or not] at once; but I rule only Tigrē, or one-third of the Ethiopian kingdom.' [451] It is difficult to imagine any Ethiopian prince making this kind of statement in the first half of the nineteenth century. Above all, however, Kasa's aspirations are revealed by his determined and ultimately successful efforts to bring in a successor to Abune Selama.[452] That he postponed his coronation until he had defeated and deposed Tekle Gīyorgīs does not mean that he ever recognized the latter as his overlord, or contemplated bargaining with the advantage he had acquired in the person of the bishop. The succinct description of the situation by an Ethiopian chronicler runs:

> Tekle Gīyorgīs said to him, 'Since I am the King, send me the bishop [and] keep your country Tigrē.' He said, 'I will not give him [to you].' So they became enemies.[453]

Tēwodros was hardly the kind of person who allowed himself to be easily influenced by others.[454] On the other hand, he did not govern in secret. There

Tekle Gīyorgīs's seal featured an uncrowned lion, while both the seals used by Dejjazmach Kasa before his coronation featured crowned lions—but the words Niguse Negest Minīlik on the seal and the drawing, as well as in the text, certainly are. Merewether missed the point, and wrote in his covering letter (FO 401/2, pp. 641–2, to Stanley, 20 Jul. 1867) that Minīlik would probably aspire to be emperor 'on the death of Theodorus'.

449 IO, Abyssinia Original Correspondence 3, p. 281, Tekle Gīyorgīs to Victoria, n.d. (April 1869 or earlier); AECP, Massouah 3, fols 231–6, Munzinger to Moustier, 23 Aug. 1868; Dimothéos, *Deux ans de séjour en Abyssinie ou vie morale, politique et religieuse des Abyssiniens* (Jerusalem, 1871), Vol. I, pp. 96–7; BN, Ethiop. 259, fol. 6. The exact circumstances of Gobezē's proclamation are difficult to establish, but he seems to have received the support of the clergy of Gonder for his action.

450 Holland and Hozier, *Expedition*, Vol. II, pp. 320 (letter to Napier, 26 Nov. 1867), 415; AED, Protocole C41, Kasa to Napoleon III, 8 Aug. 1868. For Wibē and Ali, see above, p. 132, n. 397.

451 AEMD, Afrique 62, fols 90–3, Delmonte to Étienne, 15 Dec. 1868.

452 See Douin, *Khédive Ismaïl*, III, 2, pp. 298–305, with sources cited.

453 BN, Ethiop. 259, fol. 15v. See also IO, Abyssinia Original Correspondence 3, pp. 495–6, Kirkham to Argyll, 1 Aug. 1869.

454 See Rassam, *British Mission*, Vol. I, p. 259, for a very telling comment by Samu'ēl Gīyorgīs.

is no lack in contemporary accounts of references to public meetings and trials, to councils and occasionally a nation-wide assembly of chiefs or governors.[455] Whether Tēwodros called these primarily to seek advice, educate his people, or simply make his own will known, the fact remains that he put the issues to his people, often in dramatic ways, and there is much evidence to show that he impressed and influenced those who came close to him, not only by his iron will, but by his breadth of vision and by the remarkable amount of knowledge he had acquired.[456] Of the three who succeeded him on the throne, Gobezē and Kasa had been commanders under him; Minīlik had grown up as something between an adopted son and a state prisoner, and was married to one of the King's daughters.[457] In the end they all became his enemies, but this does not exclude the fact that he had helped shape their political goals, internal as well as external. To Munzinger, consular representative of both Britain and France at Massawa, and the keenest political observer of the Ethiopian scene at the time of Tēwodros's death, it was clear that Tēwodros had revived the concept and memories of *one* Ethiopian state in such a manner that they would not easily fade again. In fact, Munzinger deplored this, because the successors were 'going to adopt the programme without having his [Tēwodros's] abilities'.[458]

Nowhere is the influence of Tēwodros on his successors more evident than in their attitude towards foreign powers. Though Minīlik had been informed by his elders about the unhappy conclusion of the Harris mission to Shewa, and was clearly embarrassed about it, he took the initiative in writing to Queen Victoria to announce his accession to the throne and ask that friendly relations be established between their two countries, in spite of the wrong (*ṭifat, bedel*) committed by his grandfather. The style and content of this letter show no direct European influence, and Minīlik's insistence on an immediate answer by the hand of his own Ethiopian messenger indicates whose pupil he was. The messenger was, in fact, dissuaded from proceeding to Europe, but Lord Stanley's reply on behalf of the Queen was both swift and friendly, implying official recognition of Minīlik's position as the ruler of Shewa.[459]

Minīlik followed up this diplomatic success with a letter to Napier, declaring that he would have liked to assist in the campaign against Tēwodros but was unfortunately too far off.[460] In fact, Minīlik had been warned not to inter-

---

455 [Zeneb], *Tēwodros*, pp. 28, 30; Welde Maryam, *Tēwodros*, pp. 26–7; Flad, *Notes*, p. 50; *idem, Zwölf Jahre*, Vol. I, pp. 60, 65–8, 89–90; Heuglin, *Abessinien*, p. 130; Rassam, *British Mission*, Vol. II, pp. 58–9, 92, 167.

456 See above, pp. 172–3, 177–84; also Rubenson, *Tēwodros*, pp. 30–1, 51–2. For the impressions of a relative latecomer on the scene, see Blanc, *Captivity*, pp. 337–9, 344, 376–8.

457 See above, p. 241; also BN, Ethiop. 259, fol. 15; Hiruy, *Tarīk*, pp. 40, 42; Markham, *Abyssinian Expedition*, pp. 86–7.

458 AECP, Massouah 3, fol. 238–43, Munzinger to La Valette, 14 Jan. 1869.

459 FO 1/20, fols 215–18, Minīlik to Victoria, n.d.; FO 401/2, pp. 641–2, Minīlik to Merewether, n.d., and Merewether to Stanley, 20 Jul. 1867; p. 673, Stanley to Minīlik, 19 Aug. 1867; p. 839, Merewether to Stanley, 28 Sep. 1867. For the Harris mission, see above, pp. 152–8.

460 Holland and Hozier, *Expedition*, Vol. II, p. 451.

vene on Tēwodros's side, and might well have preferred not to get involved at all, just in case the British were defeated or decided, in spite of their declarations, to attempt an occupation of the country. Later Minīlik seems to have felt that he had missed an opportunity to strengthen his friendly relations with Britain; but this did not prevent him from writing to Victoria for the means (*mesberiya*—guns or explosives) to break through the rebuilt fortifications of Meqdela.[461] He also applied to the governor of Aden for permission to establish a vice-consulate or agency there.[462] Both Minīlik's request and the British reaction indicate how decisive the events of Tēwodros's reign were. Napier summed up the British dilemma:

> The British Government are resolved not to retain any consular officer in Africa for the purpose of maintaining communication with the Rulers of Abyssinia, and have some grounds in past events for thus removing every possible official channel through which we might be involved in complications with that country, but it would appear unnecessarily cautious and highly inhospitable to refuse the permission solicited by a Prince who has evinced his desire to aid British subjects as far as lay in his power . . . Imprisoned as Abyssinia is, in Egyptian Territory, to refuse the permission asked for would deny the Prince any means of communication with the civilised world and deprive him and his people of the benefit they might derive from intercourse with our Political officer and the Settlement of Aden. No doubt the other Princes will ask for the same indulgence which might be allowed for the same reasons—indeed for still stronger ones, as the assistance of the other Princes was substantial.[463]

Aware of how dearly they had paid for the attempt of their consuls to 'plant the British flag in Abyssinia', and so anxious to avoid similar cases in the future that they were actually closing down even their consulate at Massawa,[464] the British government decided that Ethiopian representation at Aden was an acceptable alternative, and granted Minīlik's request.[465] Thus modern Ethiopia's first official agency abroad—albeit at Aden, and with a Frenchman, César Tian, as the first resident agent—was a direct consequence of the stubborn insistence of Tēwodros that Ethiopia had the right to foreign relations and a foreign policy of her own. Requested to direct future correspondence to the political resident at Aden rather than to London, Minīlik made no objections. After all, his main objectives were to obtain access to a market, where he could

461 FO 95/728, no. 191, Minīlik to Victoria, 4 Mar. 1869. This letter was carried by a second emissary of Minīlik's, Abba Merzē, who was also instructed to await the answer. See IO, Abyssinia Original Correspondence 3, p. 575, Russell to Argyll, 15 Dec. 1869; IO, Eur. F 103, fol. 16, Minīlik to Rassam, 25 Mar. 1870. Abba Merzē (or Meerza), father of Ingida Werq, was a converted Bengal Jew who had been in Ethiopia for almost thirty years, and had served Tēwodros before Minīlik. See IO, Abyssinia Original Correspondence 3, p. 894, note in margin; Markham, *Abyssinian Expedition*, p. 371.
462 FO 1/29, fol. 253, Goodfellow to Merivale, 18 Nov. 1869.
463 ibid., fols 265–6, Napier to Hammond, 1 Jan. 1870; see also fols 250–1, minutes, 14 Dec. 1869.
464 ibid., fols 237–58, *passim*, letters from Goodfellow to Bombay government and India Office, minutes and exchanges between IO and FO, 8 Jul. 1869–17 Dec. 1869.
465 ibid., fols 267–8, Hammond to Merivale, 6 Jan. 1870; IO, Abyssinia Original Correspondence 3, p. 629, Merivale to Russell, 7 Jan. 1870.

buy arms and other goods, and the support of the Aden authorities against the attempts of Sultan Abu Bakr of Zeyla to block the passage of people and goods. Massaja, who had returned to Ethiopia and Shewa at the invitation of Minīlik and who wanted to bring in further missionaries through Zeyla, assisted Minīlik in demanding that the routes be kept open.[466]

Of the three contenders for supreme power after the death of Tēwodros, Wagshum Gobezē (Tekle Gīyorgīs) was, from the viewpoint of foreign relations, in the least favourable position. Napier left neither missionaries nor craftsmen nor, apparently, any of Tēwodros's small foreign-educated staff behind in central Ethiopia. There seems, moreover, to have been some disagreement or misunderstanding between Gobezē and the British commander before the expedition returned to the coast. The *wagshum* did not come when called by Napier to his camp after the fall of Meqdela. Some British believed that he did not care to identify too closely with the foreigners. He may also have been concerned about the close friendship declared between the British and Kasa.[467] In his first letter to Queen Victoria in late 1868 or early 1869, Tekle Gīyorgīs implied that Napier had left in such a hurry that it had become impossible to arrange the interview. More important, he complained that he had never received a pair of field-glasses sent as a gift, because Napier had not bothered to recover them from a thief, and that the British had left without liberating his deputy Meshesha, captured by Ali Farīs, whom the British themselves had liberated at Meqdela.[468] Tekle Gīyorgīs felt that the British favoured Kasa of Tigrē over himself, and when he planned to depose the Tigrean prince in 1869, he wrote to justify his action.[469]

Later Tekle Gīyorgīs took the opportunity offered to him by a Catholic missionary and approached the French government for the moral support he felt he needed. He offered to open up his country for French merchants and a consul, but there was no mention of missionaries. On a trip to visit his converts in the Ṭana region in 1870, Flad turned back from Metemma, reporting that the country was closed to Europeans arriving from the west. But Flad may have been unwelcome as an 'Englishman', not a missionary. Since the Catholics had

466 FO 95/728, no. 193, Clarendon to Minīlik, 30 Nov. 1869; IO, Abyssinia Original Correspondence 3, pp. 587–9, Hammond to Merivale, 21 Dec. 1869; pp. 759–61, Minīlik to Goodfellow, 3 Jul. 1870; pp. 873–4, Tremenheere to Merivale, 5 Sep. 1871; pp. 875–6, Minīlik to Tremenheere, 6 May 1871; pp. 877–8, Massaja to Tremenheere, n.d. (with preceding letter); pp. 885–7, Tremenheere to Merivale, 4 Oct. 1871; pp. 889–91, Massaja to Tremenheere, 21 May 1871; pp. 892–7, Abu Bakr to Minīlik, n.d., translation dated 15 May 1871. For Massaja's return, see APF.SRC, Africa Centrale, Etiopia ecc. . . . 7, fol. 1080, Minīlik to Massaja, n.d., probably June 1867.

467 IO, Abyssinia Original Correspondence 3, pp. 515–26, Napier to Duff, 29 Oct. 1869; Holland and Hozier, *Expedition*, Vol. II, pp. 95, 452; Markham, *Abyssinian Expedition*, pp. 383–4; Shepherd, *Campaign*, p. 349; Dimothéos, *Deux ans*, Vol. I, p. 97; BN, Ethiop. 259, fol. 5.

468 IO, Abyssinia Original Correspondence 3, p. 281, Tekle Gīyorgīs to Victoria, n.d.; pp. 277–8, English translation by Munzinger, 1 Apr. 1869.

469 FO 95/728, no. 192, Tekle Gīyorgīs to Victoria and Napier, n.d., received 29 Sep. 1869; IO, Abyssinia Original Correspondence 3, pp. 767–8, Tekle Gīyorgīs to Rassam, January [1870]. These letters were translated by Flad only after their arrival in Europe.

sought out Tekle Gīyorgīs because of trouble with Kasa, this looked like an overture to a replay of the late 1850s. Whether French/Catholic support of one Ethiopian ruler against another would have been more successful with Tekle Gīyorgīs than with Nigusē is impossible to say. The King's letter was written a week before the outbreak of the Franco-Prussian war, and was finally forwarded to a French head of state one year later, exactly three days after Kasa's unexpected but decisive victory over Tekle Gīyorgīs had ended the reign of the last Ethiopian emperor to rule from Gonder.[470]

It was Emperor Yohannis, rather than Minīlik or Tekle Gīyorgīs, who was given the main responsibility for charting Ethiopia's foreign policies after Tēwodros—and for determining her attitude towards foreigners and their skills. He inherited the insecure borders with Egypt in the north and north-west, and the theoretical ambiguities and practical problems of the disputed Red Sea littoral. He also had to face the acute dilemma, posed by the Catholic mission in Akkele Guzay and Bogos, of how to maintain friendship with the Christian countries of Europe and keep the doors open to desirable influences, without permitting the growth of a religious community hostile to the national church and weakened in its loyalties to the Ethiopian state.

The attempts of Kasa/Tēwodros to cope with these problems through an active foreign policy had failed. His diplomatic initiatives had brought him only trouble. The guns and mortars which he had more or less forced the Europeans in the country to manufacture had in the final test turned out to be useless and the road worse than useless, only hastening his own destruction. There was certainly not much in this to induce Kasa/Yohannis to desire contacts with Europe or to maintain a European presence in his country. As for Napier and the British government, they desired nothing more than to shake the dust of Ethiopia off their feet:

> Her Majesty's Government have no concern with what might befal [sic] Abyssinia from the removal of King Theodore from the country . . . it will in no way concern them what may be the future that awaits Abyssinia; what Ruler may hold power in the country; what civil wars or commotion may arise in it. On grounds of humanity Her Majesty's Government would desire the country to be well governed, and the people to be contented and prosperous; but they do not consider it incumbent on them to set up or to support any form of government or any particular Ruler under which it shall be carried out, in a country in which they have really no British interests to promote.[471]

Kasa received his reward of six howitzers, six mortars and 850 muskets and rifles with ammunition, for the assistance he had provided, but his request for two or

---

470 AEMD, Afrique 62, fol. 110, Tekle Gīyorgīs to Napoleon III, 7 Jul. 1870; fol. 109, Étienne to 'le Chef du pouvoir Exécutive', 14 Jul. 1871; *MT*, 1871, p. 4 in May appendix, Flad, 22 Feb. 1871. For Kasa's victory see BN, Ethiop. 259, fols 10–11, and Douin, *Ismaïl*, III, 2, pp. 324–6.

471 FO 401/2, pp. 741–3, Stanley to Northcote, 19 Sep. 1867. There were, of course, many advocates for a permanent occupation of some kind (ibid., p. 662, Blanc, p. 771, Mansfield, etc.), but the official stand taken was maintained.

three British officers on loan for three months to train his people in the use of the guns was not granted.[472]

If Kasa, in this situation, had made Ethiopia turn in on herself, close the doors and attempt to isolate herself once more, this would only have been natural, particularly in view of the prevalent picture of Kasa/Yohannis as 'the monk and soldier', weak in everything but 'his fanatical hatred of Muslims . . . and aversion from Roman Catholics', representing 'the old, aristocratic and religious Ethiopia', and therefore by definition a reactionary or at least a conservative.[473] Members of the British expedition seem, in fact, to have been almost unanimous in disseminating a very low opinion of Kasa:

> The weak-minded Kasa went about with a sort of crown on his head, which was always coming down over his eyes, and gazed with stupid wonder at the rocket practice of the Naval Brigade. He is evidently a tool of the more powerful chiefs, whom accident has pitchforked into supreme power, and who may or may not be allowed to retain it; but in any case little good can be expected from so poor a creature.[474]

As the representative (vice-consul and acting consul) at Massawa of both France and Britain, before as well as immediately after the Meqdela expedition, and as a political adviser to Napier during the campaign, Munzinger had every reason and much opportunity to assess the personality and position of Kasa. There were nuances in the consul's pronouncements, but the over-all impression is clearly negative: Kasa was suspicious towards foreigners, unpopular among his own people in spite of his noble birth, inferior as a ruler to both Minīlik and Gobezē. Whatever real power he held in 1868 had come to him as the result of lucky circumstances. So trapped had Munzinger become in these views that he could only explain Kasa's success over Tekle Gīyorgīs in July 1871 as a victory 'by sheer accident'.[475]

In fact, Kasa's actions as far as they can be documented show not only a sound sense of priorities but also an approach to foreign contacts and to what they might contribute which strongly resembles the policies adopted by Tēwodros in his early years. Kasa's first step was to send a mission to Cairo (May 1868) to acquire a new bishop, and when the expulsion or curtailment of the Catholic mission was reported to be a condition for this, he decided against the mission in the same manner as Tēwodros had done.[476] On the other hand Kasa was

472 Holland and Hozier, *Expedition*, Vol. II, pp. 94–6.
473 Margery Perham, *The Government of Ethiopia* (London, n.d. [1947]), p. 52; Mathew, *Ethiopia*, pp. 208–9. The personality of Yohannis is little known. Note, for instance, that the two authors cited here, though both British and writing at the same time, state diametrically opposed views: '. . . he was not the man to take advice' (Perham) and 'He was accessible to advice . . .' (Mathew).
474 Markham, *Abyssinian Expedition*, p. 381; see also p. 227 for Grant's earlier description, and Gerhard Rohlfs, *Meine Mission nach Abessinien* (Leipzig, 1883) p. 224. Without telling us that he participated in the expedition himself, Rohlfs blames its members for having created the picture of Kasa as 'a savage, a perfidious person'.
475 AECP, Massouah 3, fols 221–7, 231–52, Munzinger's dispatches, 29 Feb., 23 Aug. 1868, 14 Jan. and 29 Jan. 1869; Douin, *Ismaïl*, III, 2, p. 330, dispatch to Cairo, 25 Aug. 1871.
476 Douin, *Ismaïl*, III, 2, pp. 298–301. The Patriarch's reply to Kasa, 20 Nov. 1868 (ENA, Abyssinie, Casier 20/9/1) stressed only that Kasa was supposed to adhere strictly to the

quite as prepared as Tēwodros before him to employ whatever foreign craftsmen happened to turn up at his court: a French mechanic called René, a Hungarian gunsmith called André, and the Italian builder Giacomo Naretti.[477] When Napier refused to leave behind any British advisers or instructors, Kasa was nevertheless fortunate enough to recruit a military adviser in J. C. Kirkham, who had seen service in China under Gordon, probably as a sergeant, and accompanied the Napier expedition as a sutler. The British government disapproved of Kirkham's return to Ethiopia in no uncertain terms: they had 'no views to communicate to him regarding Abyssinia', and could not take 'cognizance of his proceedings in that country'. Undaunted, Kirkham wrote back that this was entirely to his satisfaction: 'for now I shall have a wide field to work in and use my own judgement in forming an Abyssinian government'. His main task was to try to acquire further arms for Kasa, including a rocket battery, and to recruit some troops and artillery instructors from India, for which Kasa was reportedly quite prepared to pay. In the meantime he was put to work drilling troops, in much the same way as Bell had been employed fifteen years earlier, but, it seems, with a little more success. Kasa also used Kirkham to supervise construction work, such as a fort at Adwa and a water-tank at Aksum.[478]

With some justification Munzinger regarded himself as the protector of all European interests in northern Ethiopia, especially the Catholic mission, and as the obvious channel for Ethiopian contacts with Europe. In addition, he was personally known to Kasa, and there are no indications that personal relations between the two were strained in 1868.[479] It is therefore significant that he was bypassed when Kasa wrote to Napoleon III in August 1868, asking for recognition and friendship. The phrasing of this letter, addressed to 'Luyis Napulyo Bonepart, French king', shows that there was no foreign advice behind the wording.[480] It was forwarded—without translation—through René and

---

faith of Alexandria but an explicit demand for the expulsion of the Catholic missionaries was reportedly forwarded in a letter from the chief envoy, Gebre Igzī'abihēr, which reached Adwa in late September 1868 (Girard, *Souvenirs*, pp. 144–5; AECP, Égypte 44, fols 314–15, Delmonte to Munzinger, 27 Oct. 1868). Thus Munzinger was probably correct when he stated to Paris, 29 Jan. 1869 (AECP, Massouah 3, fols 244–52) that the expulsion of the Catholic missionaries was a condition for the appointment of a new metropolitan. Money was important too; Aleqa Birru allegedly took 20,000 thalers for the Patriarch and Ismail when he left on a second, successful mission in February 1869 (AECP, Massouah 3, fols 261–2, Munzinger to La Valette, 4 Apr. 1869).

477 Girard, *Souvenirs*, pp. 31, 240, 271–2; E. A. de Cosson, *The Cradle of the Blue Nile* (London, 1877), Vol. I, p. 114; Douin, *Ismaïl*, III, 1, p. 408. Two of the craftsmen-missionaries who had worked for Tēwodros, namely Mayer and Bender, were also at Adwa in 1869–70 but planned to establish their new mission work in Shewa (*MT*, 1870, pp. 7, 55–6).

478 AECP, Massouah 3, fols 228–30, 244–52, Munzinger, 23 Aug. 1868 and 29 Jan. 1869; IO, Abyssinia Original Correspondence 3, pp. 3–4, Merivale to Hammond, 7 Jan. 1869; pp. 23–8, Hammond to Merivale, 29 Jan. 1869, with enclosures; pp. 29–30, Merivale to Kirkham, 5 Feb. 1869; pp. 411–13, Kirkham to Argyll, 2 Jun. 1869; pp. 433–7, Kirkham to Stanton, 13 Jun. 1869; pp. 531–6, Kirkham to Napier, 10 Aug. 1869; pp. 527–30, Kasa to Napier, 10 Aug. 1869.

479 See, for instance, BN, Ethiop. 300, fol. 3, Kasa to Munzinger, 26 Jul. [1868]; also Munzinger's dispatches, cited above.

480 AED, Protocole C41, Kasa to Napoleon III, 8 Aug. 1868.

the French traveller A. Girard, because, as Kasa reportedly told the latter, 'Your consul serves two masters and he has only one heart'.[481]

The reply of Napoleon III, which reached Kasa only one and a half years later, was hardly reassuring. There was an implied criticism for having bypassed the Emperor's loyal agent at Massawa, and exhortations to promote the triumph of true religion by protecting the Catholic missionaries.[482] In the meantime, Kasa's relations with the Catholic community had deteriorated badly. This seems to have been due partly to pressures for religious conformity in connection with Kasa's attempts to obtain a new bishop, partly to the unfortunate refusal (in March 1869) of some Catholic villages in Akkele Guzay to pay taxes on the grounds that they—as Catholics—were French and not Ethiopian subjects.[483] Kasa was no doubt also aware of the involvement of missionaries and of Munzinger himself in the appeals of Ethiopian Catholics and some of Kasa's governors or potential rivals to Napoleon III to befriend and protect them.[484]

In the case of Kasa's governor of Hamasēn, Akkele Guzay, and Bogos, Dejjazmach Welde Mīka'ēl Selomon, Munzinger clearly encouraged him to write, and recommended the French government to respond with an invitation for an emissary to come to Paris. The consul believed, 'since the supreme power in Abyssinia is continually changing hands', that France should take the opportunity of securing the friendship of this border chief when it was offered. Welde Mīka'ēl admitted that he governed his districts under Kasa, but a desire to become more independent and secure is implied in the whole initiative.[485] Munzinger was in fact playing a bold game at this time, manoeuvring against Stella in order to lay his hands on the latter's agricultural establishment at Shotel at the same time as he continued the ex-missionary's efforts to detach Bogos from Ethiopia and change it into a European colony or 'protectorate'. Munzinger almost lost his life in an assassination attempt instigated by Stella and his brother-in-law, De Jacobis's former political go-between, Abba Imnetu. Welde Mīka'ēl lost his governorship when Kasa found out about his contacts with France, like his predecessor Dejjazmach Haylu when Kasa had heard of his contacts with Egypt two years earlier.[486]

481 AEMD, Afrique 62, fol. 77, Girard to La Valette, 22 Dec. 1868; Girard, *Souvenirs*, pp. 32, 82–3. For Munzinger's reaction, see AECP, Massouah 3, fols 244–52, to La Valette, 29 Jan. 1869.

482 AED, Protocole C41, Napoleon III to Kasa, 31 Jul. 1869; AECC, Massouah 2, Munzinger to La Tour d'Auvergne-Lauraguais, 23 Jan. 1870.

483 AECP, Massouah 3, fols 271–2, Munzinger to La Valette, 1 Jun. 1869; fols 291–6, Munzinger to Daru, 27 Mar. 1870; FO 95/731, no. 143, Yohannis to Victoria, 13 Aug. 1872.

484 AEMD, Afrique 62, fol. 79, Catholics of Agamē to Napoleon III, n.d.; fol. 81, Aragawī Sebagadis to Napoleon III, n.d., Amharic originals translated in 1868 by Antoine d'Abbadie (fol. 78); AECP, Massouah 3, fols 258–60, Munzinger to La Valette, 4 Apr. 1869, with enclosed translation of Tekle Haymanot, Gebre Maryam, and Fissiha Ṣiyon to Napoleon III, n.d.; AED, Protocole C41, Yohannis [III] to Napoleon III, 11 Jun. 1869.

485 AECP, Massouah 3, fol. 280, Welde Mīka'ēl to Napoleon III, 22 Aug. 1869, Amharic original; fols 278–9, Munzinger to La Tour d'Auvergne-Lauraguais, 31 Aug. 1869.

486 ibid., fol. 285, Munzinger to Tricou, 10 Oct. 1869; fols 287–90, Munzinger to Daru, 18 Feb. 1870; fols 297–9, Munzinger to Daru, 27 Mar. 1870; *MT*, 1870, pp. 62–3, Englund, 12 Apr.

Kasa took the assassination attempt very seriously, and this probably saved the consul from all but a gentle hint that Kasa knew of his collusion with Welde Mīka'ēl.[487] But with regard to the Catholic mission work, Kasa was firm: experience showed, firstly, that to become a Catholic meant to become a French protégé; secondly, that wherever the missionaries were admitted, they created political problems. In his reply to Napoleon III, written while Munzinger was present in the camp, Kasa had one request to make: prevent the Catholics from saying, 'The Church is ours, the priests are ours'. Kasa promised to regard it as a precious gift if Napoleon saved him from these priests— እነዚህን ፡ ካህናት ፡ ቢከለክሉልኝ ፡ ስለ ፡ ብዙ ፡ ገንዘብ ፡ እቆጥረዉ ፡ አለሁ ፡—not because he regarded the Catholic faith as wrong, but because Ethiopia had always received her teachers from Alexandria, and he feared that the continued activities of the missionaries would probably create hostility between the French emperor and himself. This was clearly Kasa's primary concern. Merchants and explorers, however, were welcome, and with Munzinger the prince reportedly raised the questions of creating a disciplined military corps, building roads and introducing flour mills, primarily to be able to cut down on the number of women accompanying the army on campaigns.[488]

That Kasa did not expect Munzinger to comply with his request is evident both from the fact that he took action against the mission within less than three months after Munzinger's visit,[489] and from a letter he addressed to Queen Victoria the same day as he wrote to the French emperor. The occasion for writing to London was a final letter of appreciation accompanied by a gift of field-glasses, which the Foreign Office had sent to Kasa, Tekle Gīyorgīs, and Minīlik alike, thanking them for their assistance to Napier.[490] Kasa took no notice of the advice that he should direct any eventual future correspondence to the political resident at Aden. And the substance of his letter was very different from that of his letter to Napoleon III. Kasa wanted to buy Snider rifles, rocket tubes, and light cannon, and to employ some artillerists to train his people. There is no indication of when this letter was received in London, and no trace of any

or 13 May 1870; Douin, *Ismaïl*, III, 1, pp. 375–6; III, 2, pp. 307, 310–14; Giglio, *Etiopia–Mar Rosso*, Vol. I, pp. 66–7. Stella died a few weeks after the assassination attempt. Imnetu was convicted in an Ethiopian court and handed over to Munzinger, who was later accused of having permitted him to die of starvation, imprisoned at the consulate.

487   BN, Ethiop. 300, fol. 2, Kasa to Munzinger, 17 Nov. [1869]. Five additional letters from Kasa to Munzinger in January and February 1870 (fols 4–8) show that Kasa was anxious both to find and convict the guilty and to maintain the independence of his court in the face of criticism by the consul.

488   AEMD, Afrique 62, fol. 105, Kasa to Napoleon III, 10 Mar. 1870; AECP, Massouah 3, fols 291–6, Munzinger to Daru, 27 Mar. 1870. See also Girard, *Souvenirs*, pp. 136–8, for an interview between Girard and Kasa on 1 Oct. 1868, at which the latter reportedly said, 'They [the missionaries] always involve themselves in the political affairs of my country, and I will no longer hear of them.'

489   AECP, Massouah 3, fols 303–9, Munzinger to Gramont, 2 Aug. 1870, with extracts from letters by Duflot.

490   FO 95/728, nos 193–5, Clarendon to Minīlik, Tekle Gīyorgīs, and Kasa, respectively, 30 Nov. 1869.

translation or reply.[491] But Kasa's self-confidence was increasing, and in August 1870 he simply informed the British government that he had appointed Messrs Henry S. King and Company his representative (wekīl) in London, and that he would soon be sending envoys to London with presents for the Queen. The embassy, dispatched a week or two later, consisted of Aleqa Birru Welde Gīyorgīs, here called ri'ise memakirt (head of the counsellors) but better known as līqe kahinat (head of the clergy), and Mircha Werqē, who was given the credit for having established friendship with Napier, and was now probably Kasa's most important adviser on foreign affairs. Again there was a request for technical assistance: people to teach manufacturing skills (ye-ṭibeb neger sira), particularly all kinds of ironwork.[492]

On instructions from the Foreign Office, the British consul general at Alexandria, Edward Stanton, prevented the embassy from proceeding to London. The immediate concern at the Foreign Office was financial: could the envoys pay their own expenses? But although they declared that they would do so, Stanton was instructed to forward the presents only, explaining that he was 'not authorised to send the envoys themselves'. The Ethiopians, however, considered it 'incompatible with Prince Kassai's dignity to give them [the presents] up'.[493]

It was only after three months of arguing and after having alerted Ethiopia's representative in London, King and Co., that the envoys gave in and handed over the letter and presents for the Queen. Since Stanton apparently found it incompatible with the dignity of Queen Victoria to tell the envoys that there would be no hospitality offered even after their arrival in London, the pretext given to the envoys was that the British government was too busy to receive them. Stanton estimated the value of the gifts to be £1,500, and recommended that articles of at least the same value be sent in exchange, indicating that the priorities of the Ethiopian prince were 'a battery of Mountain guns and some war Rockets'. He also noted that the envoys had hoped to recruit artisans and

---

491 FO 1/28, fol. 55, Kasa to Victoria, 10 Mar. 1870. The annotation states simply, 'Thanks for letter and Presents'.

492 ibid. fol. 65, Kasa to Clarendon, 16 Aug. 1870; fol. 60, Kasa to Granville, 24 Aug. 1870; FO 95/729, no. 170, Kasa to Victoria, 25 Aug. 1870. Kasa introduced the first envoy as Ri'ise Memakirt Gīyorgīs, but it is possible to identify him with none other than Aleqa Birru, later so famous. His initials ኣ ፡ ብ ፡ ኊ ፡ ኅ ፡ and seal appear with Gīyorgīs and Werqē Mircha on a letter addressed from the envoys to Granville (see below, p. 281, n. 494). See also AECP, Égypte 52, fols 187–9, for the appearance of an Aleqa Welde Gīyorgīs as Yohannis's envoy at Massawa in September 1872. Aleqa Birru was influential at Kasa's court from 1868 (Girard, Souvenirs, pp. 132–3, 137–8, 203), headed the embassy that brought the new Coptic bishop, Aṭinatēwos, in July 1869 (AECP, Massouah 3, fols 261–2, 275–7), and was instrumental in recruiting a group of French artisans and adventurers, headed by Godineau, while in Egypt in late 1870 (AEMD, Afrique 62, fols 334–449). This enterprise miscarried, allegedly because Birru allowed himself to be bought by the Egyptians.

493 FO 1/28, fol. 69, Stanton to Granville, 20 Oct. 1870; fol. 72, Granville to Stanton, 21 Oct. 1870; fol. 75, Stanton to Granville, 23 Oct. 1870; fol. 88, Granville to Stanton, 3 Nov. 1870; fol. 90, Stanton to Granville, 7 Nov. 1870.

mining engineers in England. The envoys stressed that they had already waited long enough, and expected a reply within a month.[494]

The Foreign Office found themselves in a dilemma. To reply would be a favour to Kasa, who had deliberately disobeyed the advice given to the Ethiopian princes to communicate only through Aden. On the other hand: 'The difficulties which arose out of the question of answering King Theodore's letters are well known.'[495] Birru returned to Ethiopia but Mircha stayed on, and in May he noted to Stanton that he had read in *The Times* that the foreign secretary, Lord Granville, had told Parliament that the British government had not refused to receive the embassy but had some difficulties providing for the journey. Though discouraged, Mircha expressed the hope that he and his fellow ambassador might be allowed to come to London as originally planned, '. . . to obtain and take back with us from so great and prosperous a country as England some ideas which might be usefully applied towards improving the industry, commerce and prosperity of Abyssinia'; but if that was beyond the resources of the British government, he requested an early and definite reply.[496] With the Treasury wanting to sell the presents intended for the Queen to purchase return gifts, the Foreign Office concerned with 'the policy of impartiality', etc., the matter dragged on and on. By August 1871 Mircha had also returned to Massawa. But there was some concern, too. A reminder from Kasa's consular representative, Henry S. King, in January 1872 caused the following note: 'These savage Princes are, I have no doubt, as punctilious as other people. Theodore certainly was. It is a strong measure to leave a letter unnoticed for several months.'[497]

The letter had in fact been left unanswered for well over a year. But Kasa was a more patient man than Tēwodros, and, moreover, quite confident that his services to Napier would not be easily forgotten. It was in this spirit that he wrote again to Queen Victoria in April 1871 to complain about an arrogant and threatening letter he had received from Munzinger.[498]

Aware of the British lack of interest in Ethiopia and of the unlikelihood that France—fresh from her defeat in the Franco-Prussian war—would be in a position to concern herself with matters in Africa for some time, the former European

494 ibid., fols 103–4, King to Hammond, 12 Dec. 1870; fols 109–11, Stanton to Granville, 13 Jan. 1871; fol. 186, Birru Welde Gīyorgīs and Mircha to Granville, 14 Jan. 1871.
495 ibid., fols 116–22, 133–7, memoranda and minutes, 4 Feb.–10 Mar. 1871.
496 ibid., fols 157–61, Mircha to Stanton, 11 May 1871. For an unofficial warning by Flad not to expect anything from Europe, see *MT*, 1871, pp. 35–6, Englund, 17 Feb. 1871.
497 ibid., fols 166–7, Lowe to Hammond, 5 Jun. 1871; fols 168–81, memoranda and minutes, 6 Jun.–7 Oct. 1871; fols 212–13, King to Enfield, 4 Jan. 1872; fols 214–16, minutes, 6 Jan.–9 Jan. 1872. For Mircha's return, AECP, Égypte 50, fols 146–7, Hassen to Montmorand, 25 Aug. 1871.
498 FO 1/29, fols 271–2, Kasa to Victoria, 21 Apr. 1871; also fol. 307, Kasa to Russell, 20 Apr. 1871. Only English translations of these letters are found in the files. They were sent via Aden—the recommended channel—and reached London only in June 1872, probably because Munzinger managed to lay his hands on them. See J. de Coursac, *Le Règne de Yohannès depuis son Avènement jusqu'à ses Victoires de 1875 sur l'Armée égyptienne* (Romans, 1926), p. 93, for a reported case of interference by Munzinger in 1872.

'double consul' had decided to change sides. In April 1871 Munzinger took over as Egyptian governor of Massawa.[499] Before doing so, he went out of his way to offend Kasa by sending him the following message:

> You have expelled the Catholic priests who lived at Halay . . . know that your kingdom shall be destroyed and that you yourself shall perish as Tēwodros has perished . . . However much France is weakened just now, it is not to the extent of making it impossible for her to come and punish you. And as for me, since I knew how to lead and guide the British into Abyssinia, I shall know how to lead and guide the French against you . . . The aim of this letter is to make known to you the fate which awaits you.[500]

In the British intervention of 1867–68, seen from the Ethiopian side, Munzinger had certainly been a key figure. Since Kasa could not know how empty the boast was, he was both offended and disturbed. He saw Munzinger's message as 'in fact . . . a declaration of war', and wrote that he counted on Queen Victoria, 'next to Christ', to help him out of the difficulties with his enemies. Munzinger's real aim must have been to undermine Kasa's position internally, and Kasa indeed complained to Victoria that the news of Munzinger's threat had been spread in the country.[501] Both Munzinger and the Catholics were placing their hopes in a victory for Tekle Gīyorgīs. On 11 July, just outside the gates of Adwa, Kasa put an end to these hopes, effectively assisted, no doubt, by Kirkham and the small contingent who had been drilled to use the few guns and muskets left behind by the British.[502]

Although Kasa must have felt some disappointment over the long delay of his embassy in Egypt and the lack of response to his letters, none of this is noticeable in the letter by which he informed Victoria of his victory over Tekle Gīyorgīs. His sense of gratitude is as unmistakable as his satisfaction and self-confidence. For the first time he styled himself 'King of Kings' (though still not Yohannis but Kasa); with the exception of Minīlik, not one of his enemies had escaped him: 'By the power of God, I have taken the whole kingdom of Ethiopia into my hands.' Looking towards the future, Kasa had one request only: '. . . as I and you have befriended each other, I beg you to make me friends with all the kings of Europe. I want friendship with all, so that the Christian faith may be strengthened.'[503] Implied in the request was probably an invitation to the British

499   Douin, *Ismaïl*, III, 2, pp. 321–2.

500   AECP, Massouah 3, fols 328v.–9, Munzinger to Kasa, 3 Mar. 1871. It is understandable that Munzinger did not copy this letter to Paris himself. Yohannis showed it to Munzinger's successor as vice-consul, Ernest de Sarzec, when the latter paid his first visit to the Emperor in December 1872. For the activities of Sarzec in Ethiopia, see also de Coursac, *Yohannès*, *passim*.

501   See above, p. 281, n. 498. According to Sarzec (de Coursac, *Yohannès*, pp. 90–1), Schimper tried to interest Yohannis in having a German consul at Massawa and using the good offices of Emperor Wilhelm I to improve relations with France again.

502   See above, p. 270, n. 447; also de Cosson, *Blue Nile*, Vol. I, pp. 148–9.

503   FO 1/28, fol. 197, Kasa to Victoria, 28 Jul. 1871, Amharic original. The locally-produced translation (fol. 198) is in very poor English. Two days earlier Kasa had written and announced his victory to Russell (ibid., fol. 206) and to Napier (H. D. Napier, ed., *Letters of Field-Marshal Lord Napier of Magdala*, London, n.d., p. 21). In these two letters, he still styled himself 'king of Ṣiyon of Ethiopia'.

government to use their good offices with France. On the other hand, a first attempt by Kasa to establish direct relations with the new and powerful German Empire was also made through Schimper and Mayer at this point, and a letter was, in fact, dispatched to Moscow as well.[504]

Kasa's announcement of his victory over Tekle Gīyorgīs reached London in September 1871, but made little difference at the Foreign Office.[505] It was seven months later—and more than two years after Kasa had first written to Victoria—that letters and return gifts were finally prepared and dispatched. Neither the Queen nor Granville had anything to say about Kasa's consular representative, Henry S. King, in London, about Munzinger's activities at Massawa, or about artisans, instructors, or arms purchases—and there were only a few ornamental rifles and pistols among the presents. The political resident at Aden was, moreover, instructed to inform Kasa 'in courteous terms' that the British government would neither accept nor give any presents in the future.[506]

By the time Prideaux reached Massawa with the letters and presents (June 1872), five months had already passed since Kasa had been solemnly crowned King of Kings Yohannis in the cathedral of Aksum. The Emperor was absent from Adwa, consolidating his power on the southern frontiers of Tigrē, and Munzinger was about to precipitate the Ethio-Egyptian war by carrying out a secret occupation of Bogos.[507] Kasa's letter of April 1871 had just reached London and produced the following comment at the Foreign Office: 'Perhaps the fewer communications we have with the Prince the better, but it would hardly do to take no notice of his letter.'[508]

This record of Yohannis's foreign contacts during the three years before his coronation amply demonstrates that Yohannis, like Tēwodros before him, was eager to cultivate friendly relations with European powers and with their subjects; like Tēwodros, too, he made an exception for the Catholic missionaries, because he found that their teaching created loyalties towards and hopes for assistance from authorities outside the Ethiopian state. If anything, Yohannis was more active in his foreign policy than Tēwodros had been, and both he and Minīlik continued in the same way throughout the 1870s and 1880s.[509]

The contacts also demonstrate that the opening of the Suez Canal was not, as is often assumed, accompanied by a European scramble for the Red Sea littoral

504 De Coursac, *Yohannès*, p. 91, Kasa to Wilhelm I, 26 Jul. 1871; AECP, Égypte 50, fol. 293, Hassen to Montmorand, 23 Oct. 1871. Unfortunately it has been impossible to locate the early Ethiopian documents in the German archives. The dossier I Afrika 1, *Die Beziehungen zu Abessinien März 1858–Nov. 1872*, was listed at the DZA after World War II, but could not be found in 1971. See also below, p. 298.

505 FO 1/28, fols 195–6, minutes, 30 Sep. 1871.

506 FO 95/731, no. 135, Victoria to Kasa, 22 Mar. 1872; no. 136, Granville to Kasa, 30 Mar. 1872; FO 1/28, fols 244–6, Hammond to Duff, 29 Apr. 1872; fol. 297, Tremenheere to Yohannis, 12 Jun. 1872; for a list of the presents, fol. 231. Minutes with the drafts in FO 95/731 show that these were prepared as early as March the previous year.

507 FO 1/28, fols 305–12, Prideaux to Tremenheere, 28 Jun. 1872; Douin, *Ismaïl*, III, 2, pp. 333–42.

508 FO 1/29, fol. 276, minute, 4 Jul. 1872.

509 See Zewde Gabre-Sellassie, 'Process of Re-unification' and Caulk, 'Foreign Policy of Menelik II'.

and for a dominating influence in Ethiopia. On the contrary, the years around 1869 were characterized by a withdrawal from Ethiopia after three decades of almost continuous pressure. In the words of one Foreign Office memorandum, 'so far as the F.O. was concerned, it had long been a foregone conclusion that no advantage, but the contrary, had resulted from the Establishment of a Consulship at that place [Massawa] . . . and that, politically, I thought we might not unreasonably say that the Appointment had involved us in complications which it was most desirable for the future to avoid'.[510] The Meqdela expedition itself was essentially not an intervention but a withdrawal. Whenever Meqdela is viewed as anything other than a relief operation and a punitive action against Tēwodros, undertaken largely to satisfy pressures elsewhere, the whole perspective becomes distorted. The conflict arose because Tēwodros was unwilling to let the Europeans off, demanding that they stand by Ethiopia and participate in her development as they had promised, and as they were doing in Egypt. It was probably fortunate for Ethiopia, from the point of view of her survival as an independent nation, that the Europeans withdrew and allowed Egypt to make the first all-out attack. For Tēwodros and Yohannis and their small staff of missionary-educated 'foreign secretaries', however, it seemed like a betrayal.

The Meqdela expedition was supposed to have taught the Ethiopians in general and Tēwodros in particular a lesson: to respect the representatives of European power, whatever the grievances against them or their governments. In fact, the most tangible impact of Meqdela lies on the other side. The constant references to what had happened because of the failure to answer Tēwodros's letter demonstrate that the British government had learned *its* lesson. In the end it took Tēwodros very seriously, and after his fall it was extremely reluctant to have anything more to do with Ethiopia. But the shift from European to Ethiopian initiative which characterized Tēwodros's reign continued. Ethiopia had accepted the challenge of foreign relations originally imposed upon her, and refused to be ignored.

The facilities for dialogue between Ethiopia and Europe had improved further as compared with the pre-1855 period. Samu'ēl, Mahdere Qal, Mircha Werqē, Birru Pētros, and others had travelled widely; among them they knew English, French, and Italian. They were used by Tēwodros as secretaries, translators, and interpreters, and they were almost all involved in Kasa's contacts with Europeans as well.[511]

The diplomatic gains of Kasa/Yohannis were not spectacular, and tend to be overlooked. But a recognized consulate at Aden and a semi-official one in London, even the audacity to address European sovereigns or dispatch an embassy to Britain without prior consultation and approval, indicate what direction Ethiopia was taking. It was clearly not back to eighteenth-century isolation, nor to a situation in which the Ethiopians would merely react to the initiatives of others.

510   FO 1/26, no pagination, memorandum by Murray, 4 Aug. 1868.
511   See above, pp. 169, 176, 222 n. 262, 233–4, 259, 279–80. Additional people in this category at Kasa's court included Aleqa Birru and Lij Haylu (Girard, *Souvenirs*, pp. 107, 132–3).

The European withdrawal was underlined by two events of crucial importance to the future of Ethiopia, both of which played into the hands of Egypt. Firstly, in connection with the preparations for the Meqdela expedition, Britain recognized as valid, *de facto* at least, the Turkish claims to sovereignty over the Red Sea littoral, something she had carefully avoided doing in the past;[512] and secondly, Werner Munzinger, the scholar, explorer, businessman, and 'double consul' at Massawa decided that it lay in his interest as a private empire-builder to enter Egyptian service.[513] A Swiss himself, he appointed an Austrian friend and client, Franz Hassen, as acting vice-consul for France, and allegedly tried to pass him off before Yohannis as a consul for Germany as well.[514] Though a new French vice-consul, E. de Sarzec, was appointed the following year, Munzinger completely dominated the scene for several years, combining his knowledge of Ethiopia and all the prestige of his European past with the means placed at his disposal by Khedive Ismail. Nevertheless, his attempts to divide and defeat Ethiopia failed to such a degree that one is bound to ask if he laboured under some fundamental misunderstanding or misinterpretation of the Ethiopian situation. In fact, this was almost certainly the case, and the phenomenon was not limited to Munzinger.

From the viewpoint of Ethiopian history, Meqdela, as such, represents no more than an incident. A foreign army marched peacefully through the Ethiopian countryside to a mountain prison in the interior, fought a battle of two or three hours almost without casualties, released a number of prisoners and left again. At the same time, a ruler who, for reasons that had nothing to do with the campaign, was already a king 'without land and almost without people'[515] ended his life by committing suicide. This, in brief, is the story of Meqdela. But this was certainly not the way most participants in the British expedition or their backers wanted to view the events.

During the planning stages of the campaign, much had been said in the British press about the dangerous and hazardous character of the undertaking.[516] The size of the expeditionary force had been increased more than once; some £9 million had been spent; and honours and promotions were expected and awarded. Not many were able to take the detached view of Markham that Rassam, Blanc, and Prideaux 'were the only officers in the campaign who had been exposed to any real danger . . .'[517] Napier's official report about the events at Meqdela was loaded with superlatives stressing the 'formidable' character of the position of Meqdela, the 'gigantic natural bastion' of Fala, which 'exceeded anything which we could possibly have anticipated', the 'distressing

512   Cf. above, p. 258, with pp. 121, 141, 185.
513   See below, p. 292.
514   AECP, Massouah 3, fols 311–28, Sarzec to Rémusat, 17 Jan. 1873; de Coursac, *Yohannès*, pp. 94–5.
515   Flad, *Zwölf Jahre*, Vol. II, p. 61; also Markham, *Abyssinian Expedition*, p. 292: 'From this date [10 Oct. 1867] the reign of King Theodore may be considered to have come to an end . . .'
516   Markham, *Abyssinian Expedition*, p. 1; Holland and Hozier, *Expedition*, Vol. I, p. 59; see also Pankhurst, 'Popular Opposition', *Ethiopia Observer*, XVI, 3, pp. 141–203.
517   Markham, *Abyssinian Expedition*, p. 336.

heat' and 'daily storms', the absolute dependence on 'all the Infantry' and 'every Cavalry soldier' available, the admirable spirit and services of the officers and men, 'of which it is impossible for me to write in too high terms', the 'determination and order' and 'the gallant resistance' of the Ethiopians, etc.[518] His secretary Captain H. M. Hozier set the tone for his own book about the campaign with the somewhat polemical statement: 'The difficulties would have been more apparent, had their reduction been less skilful. The danger and possibility of disaster would have been more manifest had they been less carefully guarded against.' 'Never', in his opinion, 'were operations carried out in a country so unfavourable to war . . .'[519] To Henry M. Stanley, the most famous of all Africa journalists and a participant in the expedition, no words seemed too strong:

> . . . the fame of it [the victory] sounded with loud reverberations . . . Princes and potentates, scattered far apace, heard the noise of it and trembled; a peaceful epoch, they saw, had not vitiated England's strength; and *this last, this best, this greatest of victories*, seemingly made so little of, established her prestige on a firmer basis than ever . . . and thus the Modern Crusade became numbered with past events, to be remembered of all men in all lands, among the most wonderfully successful campaigns ever conducted in history.[520]

So the myth of Meqdela was born. The Tēwodros of Plowden's early reports was resurrected to take the place of Markham's 'exhausted hunted lion wearily seeking his lair, to die there unconquered and at bay'.[521] Meqdela became a great British victory over the very unifier of the Ethiopian state and his invincible army. The strength of this myth is apparent from the fact that it has been expounded by British historians ever since: '. . . on Good Friday, the 10th of April 1868, when the British guns blew Theodore's army to pieces, Abyssinian pride received a wound from which even the victory over the Italians at Adwē has not enabled it to recover'. Yohannis, again, is supposed to have seen '. . . the host of the invincible Theodore fade away into nothing before the European weapons of the British'.[522] Some who have avoided this exaggeration of the military aspect of the campaign have stressed, instead, the political achievements of the British, their ability to divide the Ethiopians: 'Those who had revolted or merely chafed under the yoke now saw their chance, and the English were lavish with their promises. The Tigrean viceroys were the first to offer Napier passive assistance in return for a promise to leave their land speedily.'[523]

518 Holland and Hozier, *Expedition*, Vol. II, pp. 453–62. See also Buckle, *Letters*, Vol. I, pp. 530–2, Disraeli to Victoria, 4 Jun. 1868.
519 Henry M. Hozier, *The British Expedition to Abyssinia* (London, 1869), pp. v–vi, 97. Cf. Myatt, *Magdala*, p. 185.
520 Stanley, *Magdala*, pp. 493, 505.
521 Markham, *Abyssinian Expedition*, p. 206.
522 Budge, *History*, Vol. II, p. 549; G. F-H. Berkeley, *The Campaign of Adowa and the Rise of Menelik* (2nd edn, London, 1935), p. xv. See also Moorehead, *Blue Nile*, p. 274: 'Ethiopia, with her defences breached, her lesson learned and her people abandoned to their natural anarchy, slipped quietly out of the news.'
523 Mathew, *Ethiopia*, p. 197.

It is true, of course, that the promises of arms and of a speedy military withdrawal were important; but the revolts were open and of long standing, and the assistance provided by Kasa was far from passive. Moreover, precisely the promise of withdrawal and the assistance prove how wrong it is to speak of the British expedition as a conquest or occupation of Ethiopia, or even a war against the country.

As the special conditions which alone could explain the easy victory of the British—with two dead in action—were played down and forgotten, the ease with which Ethiopia had been 'invaded and conquered', in spite of topography and climate, was remembered. If, moreover, the great unifier had fallen so easily, what would his disunited successors in general and 'so poor a creature' as Yohannis in particular be able to do in the face of a new invasion? Out of the distorted interpretations was born a wrong opinion about Ethiopia in political circles in Europe and Egypt. Unless one takes into account a serious underestimation of Ethiopia's basic unity and military potential, it becomes very difficult to explain why the expeditions of the following decades were so incredibly insufficient.

V

Trials of Strength with Egypt and Italy

The Bogos Crisis

By 1870 the rulers and people of Ethiopia had experienced more than sixty years of uninterrupted European presence in their country. In most cases the Europeans had been welcomed because they were Christian and because of the knowledge and technical skills they brought with them. From Welde Sillasē to Wibē and from Sahle Sillasē to Tēwodros, however, the Ethiopian rulers had maintained their right to determine the kind of assistance they wanted, the kind of conduct they would tolerate, and the limits, physical or otherwise, within which the *ferenj* were supposed to move and operate. Meddling in politics, implied intimidation, or sheer arrogance almost invariably led to temporary arrests or expulsion. Tēwodros in particular made it abundantly clear that he would tolerate no centres of foreign authority in Ethiopia, whether consulates or Catholic mission stations. He refused to ratify earlier treaties and concluded no new ones. There was little to show in terms of European influence for the efforts of six decades, or for the £9 million spent on the Meqdela expedition.[1]

It was only in the northern frontier districts, Bogos in particular, that European influence had secured a footing through the combined efforts of the Catholic mission, the consuls at Massawa, and a few European settlers. The process had started during the last years of the *Zemene Mesafint*, and had continued through the reign of Tēwodros, when Cameron and Lejean spoke of Bogos in terms of a British and French 'protectorate' respectively. That the Bogos in fact benefited from interventions by Europeans at Kasala and Cairo is well attested.[2]

A development somewhat similar to the one in Bogos was about to begin in

1 See above, pp. 46–50, 72–6, 83–5, 89–90, 162–3, 168–71, 175–89, 223–39.
2 See above, pp. 143–4, 171; also FO 401/1, pp. 497–9, Cameron to Russell, 31 Mar. 1863; Lejean, *Théodore II*, pp. 235–41; AEMD, Afrique 61, fols 428–9, Lejean to Drouyn de Lhuys, 7 Jan. 1864; AECP, Massouah 3, fols 141–3, Lejean to Drouyn de Lhuys, 11 May 1864, with enclosed letter from four Bogos chiefs thanking Napoleon III for the intervention.

Barya and Kunama (Bazēn) with the arrival there of Swedish missionaries in 1866. They found that these tribes were tributary to Ethiopia, and it was actually in company with an Ethiopian tax-collector and people from Kunama, Barya, and even Beni Amir that they made their first trip to Adiyabo to obtain the permission of Welde Ṣadiq Mirrach to establish their mission work. They noted, however, that the Barya were Muslim and 'tributary to both Abyssinia and the Turks', and that they longed for Europeans to 'come and liberate them from their oppressors; for they are constantly exposed to plundering by the Turks in particular, whom they hate most, and [they] believe that the help must come from Europe'.[3] This expectation was expressed in requests from villages all around: 'Come to us and stay with us a few days until the Turks go home again; we ask for nothing more, come, come.' On one occasion, some Kunama villages, fearing attacks by the Algaden, a neighbouring tribe under Turkish rule, reportedly told the missionary P. E. Kjellberg: 'You need only sit here with us, and when they hear that we have a *ferenj* amongst us, they will not come.'[4]

Caught between these hopes and the demands of the Egyptian officials at Kufit and Kasala that they act as tax-collectors for Egypt, the missionaries could not win. They reported that they were trying to maintain a neutral position, simply advising the villages to pay their taxes to whatever government they recognized as their own, and mediating whenever possible on their behalf both at Adiyabo and Kufit. When the Egyptians finally invaded Kunama in December 1869, the missionaries could do nothing to prevent the invasion; they were forced to give up their work and return to Massawa.[5]

By advising the Swedish missionaries to go to Barya and Kunama, and by supporting them there, Munzinger may have hoped to increase the European, in other words his own, sphere of influence by extending the buffer zone between Egypt and Ethiopia west of Bogos.[6] But time was running out, and he had too little support. Britain wanted no more of Ethiopia, France was about to be defeated by Prussia, and Sweden was no colonial power. It was Egyptian, not

3 *MT*, 1866, pp. 65–8, Carlsson, 11 Jun. 1866; also 1867, pp. 10–11, Carlsson, 5 Sep. 1866; pp. 11–13, Kjellberg, September 1866; pp. 13–14, Lange, 1 Nov. 1866. See also IO, Abyssinia Original Correspondence 3, pp. 381–7, Munzinger to Russell, 5 Jun. 1869.
4 *MT*, 1868, pp. 26–7, Kjellberg, 2 Dec. 1867; also pp. 18–19, Englund, [2 Dec. 1867]; pp. 68–9, Lager, 31 Jan. 1868. Munzinger, who claimed that he was the first European to visit Kunama and Barya, in December 1860, reported the same attitude on the part of the population. See Keller-Zschokke, *Munzinger*, pp. 20–2.
5 *MT*, 1867, pp. 76–7, 90–3, Carlsson, 13 Jul. and 16 Sep. 1867; 1868, pp. 18–19, Englund, [2 Dec. 1867]; pp. 75–6, Kjellberg, 15 May 1868; pp. 78–9, Englund, 20 Jun. 1868; p. 92, Kjellberg, 18 Aug. 1868; 1869, pp. 43–5, Lundholm, 10 Feb. 1869; 1870, pp. 44–6, Englund, 11 Jan. and 4 Mar. 1870. Though the missionaries on the spot attributed their departure to the disappointment and hostility of the local people whom they had been unable to protect, new missionaries who arrived at Kasala a few months later to reinforce the group were told that the governor of Taka had ordered the expulsion of the Europeans (*MT*, 1870, pp. 66–7, Ahlborg, 8 Jul. 1870). That the Egyptian government did not want the missionaries in Kunama was confirmed later (*MT*, 1871, pp. 83–4, Hedenström, 10 Sep. 1871), and the two explanations do not, of course, exclude each other.
6 *MT*, 1866, pp. 65–8, Carlsson, 11 Jun. 1866, and other missionary letters cited above.

European, imperialism that was to make the first serious attempt to destroy Ethiopia's independence.

Emperor Yohannis was given little time to prepare for the trial of strength with Egypt. In the years between 1868 and 1872, his attention was focused mainly on the struggle for the imperial crown. He needed peace and he needed good relations with Egypt in order to obtain a new bishop for Ethiopia—and for his own coronation. Egyptian reports that he was actually seeking military support against Tekle Gīyorgīs also circulated, but they were probably based more on wishful thinking among Egyptian officials than on reality,[7] and his alleged reply to Munzinger in 1869 that he preferred 'the invasion of the Turks to that of the French missionaries' should not be taken literally.[8] Yohannis was fully aware that Egypt's activities on the Red Sea coast and elsewhere presented a serious threat, and that the defence of Ethiopian territory would fall mainly on him. He replaced Tēwodros's governor of Hamasēn, Dejjazmach Haylu, with Welde Mīka'ēl because he suspected that Haylu was susceptible to Egyptian influence,[9] and called the governor of Adiyabo to Adwa for consultations about the situation on his section of the border.[10]

Khedive Ismail had no doubt hoped to benefit even more from the British expedition and the fall of Tēwodros than he actually did. The Qallabat sector of the frontier had been fairly quiet after Musa's campaign in 1863, but the plans for a strong garrison at Kufit in 1865 and the activities along the Red Sea coast after Egypt had again taken over Massawa were unmistakable signs of a resurgence of the expansionist policies of Muhammad Ali's reign.[11]

No one saw this more clearly than Munzinger, and in 1868–69 he was just as concerned about the threat to Ethiopia as the future Emperor Yohannis. In a report in January 1869 to the French government, he stated his views and fears:

> The Egyptian policy may modify itself or cease its activity, but it never changes. A Catholic Abyssinia, with a disciplined administration and army, a friend of the European powers, is a danger for Egypt. Therefore she must either take Abyssinia and islamize it or retain it in anarchy and misery.[12]

As evidence of a policy of subversion, Munzinger reported that the Egyptian governor had contacted chiefs in Hamasēn and Mensa in order to make himself their 'protector of today and master of tomorrow'. Munzinger was, however, even more worried about Egyptian activities farther west, and denounced a planned telegraph line from Kasala via Kufit to Massawa as nothing but a stratagem to create a pretext for annexing Bogos with its capital Keren:

7   Douin, *Ismaïl*, III, 2, pp. 308–10.
8   AECP, Massouah 3, fols 275–7, Munzinger to La Tour d'Auvergne-Lauraguais, 8 Aug. 1869.
9   See Douin, *Ismaïl*, III, 1, pp. 375–6, 407–8, for Haylu's contacts with the Egyptians in late 1867 and Kasa's action against him, probably in July the following year; also BN, Ethiop. 300, fol. 3, Kasa to Munzinger, 26 Jul. 1868.
10   *MT*, 1869, p. 11, Kjellberg, 24 Oct. 1868.
11   See above, pp. 222, 250–1, 258; for Kufit, Douin, *Ismaïl*, III, 1, p. 219.
12   AECP, Massouah 3, Munzinger to La Valette, 29 Jan. 1869.

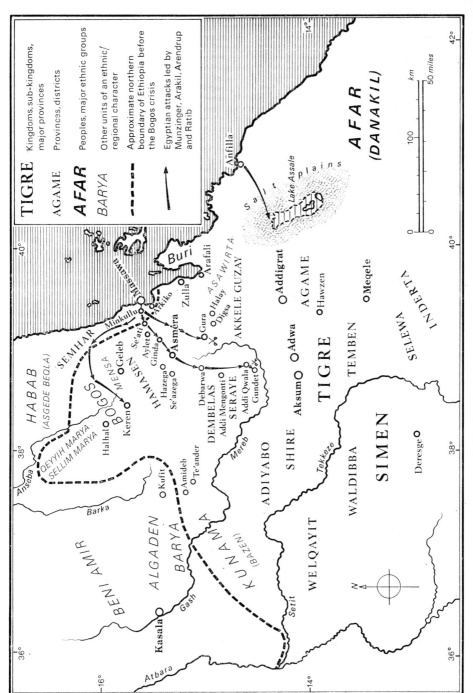

MAP 4   The Egyptian attacks in the north

Besides, the Egyptians, having abandoned Massawa as [a base] too exposed to observation, are building forts at Kufit . . . and collecting troops and provisions there. Are they doing this in order to better subdue the country which they already possess, that of the Barya and Barka? No . . . But the government knows that an excellent camel track leads from Kufit to Adiyabo, the key to Tigrē, and it counts upon the Abyssinians themselves, by their raids, to provide the occasion for going [in] and punishing them at home. Moreover, Kufit is very close to Keren, the main centre on the route from Taka to Massawa.[13]

In December 1869 Munzinger's prediction that the Egyptians would invade Kunama came true.[14] Throughout 1870 the governor of Massawa continued to strengthen his ties with mainland chiefs, Muslim as well as Christian.[15] As for the much-coveted and strategically-placed Bogos, Munzinger was himself destined to carry out the occupation plans he had imputed to the khedive. If Bogos is the key area in the Ethio-Egyptian conflict, Munzinger is the key person. His decision to enter Egyptian service is in fact the first determining factor in the creation of Eritrea. Instead of protecting European interests against Egypt and Ethiopia, and occasionally Ethiopian interests against Egypt, Munzinger became the instrument of the Egyptian expansion. Instead of the tacit consent which Ismail had tried to obtain from the French government in exchange for promises to allow the Catholic mission work to continue,[16] he was given the opportunity to act through the person who, more than anyone else, represented European influence in the area.

Munzinger received his appointment as governor of Massawa on 23 April 1871. One month later he was ready with his proposal to Cairo to annex Bogos, Halhal, and Marya, districts which allegedly belonged to Ethiopia only because of their fear of being pillaged; if they wanted to pass under Egyptian rule, should they not be encouraged? Munzinger believed he could also offer Ismail the population of Hamasēn, who would be only too happy to be allowed to come and live as Egyptian subjects in Habab and Barka; the case would be almost the same with Akkele Guzay. The best opportunity to act would be if Tekle Gīyorgīs attacked Kasa. Then Egypt should at once take advantage of the situation to straighten out her border and get hold of at least 'Bogos and its dependencies', which, according to Munzinger, were of enormous value for the consolidation of Egyptian rule in Taka.[17] Here we see Munzinger simply

13　ibid. Similar arguments for the occupation of Bogos had been expounded by Munzinger in 1865 (AECP, Massouah 3, fols 184–90, Munzinger to Drouyn de Lhuys, 23 Dec. 1865); see also above, p. 250.

14　See above, p. 289.

15　Douin, Ismaïl, III, 2, pp. 317–18. The Christian chief mentioned was Mekonnin, the son of the deposed and imprisoned Welde Mīka'ēl, who had taken up arms against Kasa (Yohannis), but was reportedly defeated by May 1871 (AECP, Égypte 49, fols 437–8, Montmorand to Favre, 15 Jul. 1871).

16　AECP, Égypte 45, fols 212–15, Poujade to La Valette, 17 Mar. 1869; Égypte 46, fols 335–8, Tricou to La Tour d'Auvergne-Lauraguais, 15 Oct. 1869.

17　Douin, Ismaïl, III, 2, pp. 321–4, quoting a memorandum by Munzinger, dated 25 May 1871. Munzinger spoke quite openly to the Swedish missionaries about the 'intention of the

advocating what he had so roundly denounced Ismail for planning two years earlier.

The ideal opportunity, however, was lost when Kasa so unexpectedly and decisively defeated Tekle Gīyorgīs in July 1871.[18] An immediate consequence of Kasa's victory was a new crisis for the Catholic mission. In Tekle Gīyorgīs's camp, a letter from the head of the Catholic mission, Mgr J. M. Touvier, was found and brought to Kasa's attention. Aleqa Birru called it 'a very bad letter', and Vice-consul Ernest de Sarzec, to whom Yohannis showed the letter when the consul first visited Adwa in December 1872, reported that the bishop had urged Tekle Gīyorgīs to go and attack Kasa, promising that he would receive support in the war.[19]

Kasa ordered the missionaries out of Akkele Guzay and Bogos, and the Ethiopian Catholics suffered severe persecution. In this situation Touvier agreed with Munzinger that the Catholic population should formally ask for the protection of Egypt, in other words, that of Munzinger himself. This was reportedly done by a representative of Akkele Guzay in the name of his countrymen. It goes without saying that Munzinger was delighted to accept this task on behalf of the Egyptian government. Though he stressed that he had been reluctant to join in the request, Touvier begged the French government not to prevent the expansion of Egypt, but instead to use its influence to persuade the khedive to accept the offer of new subjects.[20]

Hassen was not convinced that the Catholics would fare better under Egyptian rule. At any rate he tried to persuade the French government to send a military expedition to depose Kasa and occupy the country instead. It would in his opinion be an inexpensive and easy undertaking; 1,500–2,000 men would be sufficient to overthrow Kasa, and chiefs in rebellion in the border provinces, such as Kasa Golja 'Abba Kaisi', would raise the men, if only France would arm them.[21] The French government, however, was anxious not to get involved in any adventures, though it was quite prepared 'to provoke the direct intervention of the Egyptians with Prince Kasa in favour of the missionaries'.[22]

Turks to occupy Abyssinia and restore peace' unless either Kasa or Gobezē managed to get the upper hand and restore order (*MT*, 1871, p. 60, Lundahl, 20 Jun. 1871).

18 See above, p. 270.

19 AECP, Égypte 50, fol. 333, Birru to Hassen, 20 Oct. 1871; Massouah 3, fols 311–28, Sarzec to Rémusat, 17 Jan. 1873; FO 95/731, nos 143 and 144, Yohannis to Victoria and to Granville, 13 Aug. 1872; also a letter to the editor of *Homeward Mail*, June 1872, written by Kirkham on Yohannis's behalf (AEMD, Afrique 62, fols 113–14). Touvier denied that the contents of his letter compromised the mission, but both Hassen and Montmorand (AECP, Égypte 50, fols 330–4) seem to have been convinced that the missionary had committed 'a grave imprudence'. Touvier had, in fact, acted as an intermediary also when Tekle Gīyorgīs wrote to Napoleon in July 1870 (see above, p. 274). For the Catholic mission throughout Yohannis's reign, see Aleme Eshete, *La Mission Catholique*.

20 AECP, Égypte 50, fols 144–5, Touvier to Montmorand, 24 Aug. 1871; fols 146–8, Hassen to Montmorand, 25 Aug. 1871; fol. 100, Montmorand to Rémusat, 29 Aug. 1871.

21 ibid., fols 186, 244–7, Hassen to Montmorand, 10 Sep. and 3 Oct. 1871.

22 AECP, Massouah 3, fol. 310, Gramont to Munzinger, 28 Jun. 1871; Égypte 50, fol. 329, Rémusat to Montmorand, 9 Dec. 1871; ENA, Abyssinie, Casier 20/9/1, Montmorand to Ismail, 19–21 Oct. 1871.

Although both Munzinger and Hassen probably exaggerated in their reports, there was no doubt a lot of intrigue, insurrection, and pillaging going on in Hamasēn and the other frontier districts both before and after Kasa's victory over Tekle Gīyorgīs. Members of the ruling families of Ṣe'azega (Dejjazmach Haylu) and Hazega (Dejjazmach, later Ras, Welde Mīka'ēl) competed for power and tribute with each other, with Kasa Golja, and with governors sent from Adwa. Some of these chiefs were in contact with Munzinger and Hassen, who believed they could be used against Kasa.[23] The French consul general in Egypt was less confident of this.[24] Besides, the Egyptians also had their problems in the area, with Na'ib Muhammad Abd al-Rahim reportedly maintaining dubious contacts with Christian chiefs, looting, and collecting taxes without handing them over to the Egyptian government.[25] The ground was in other words well prepared for foreign intervention. Basically, it was Ethiopia on one side, and Egypt and Europe, represented by Munzinger and the Catholic mission, on the other.

The options presented by Munzinger to Ismail were either to use force against Kasa or to remain indifferent and see France intervene to uphold religious freedom. Since Munzinger cannot seriously have expected French intervention in 1871, the purpose of the second alternative must have been to push Ismail into accepting the first. To make sure that the khedive would not dismiss the opportunity out of hand, Munzinger suggested that 1,000 French troops would be sufficient to destroy Kasa: 'And, in that case, our position will be much more difficult than at the time of the British, whose aims were much more modest. Therefore, it seems to me that it should be most important to prevent this complication at the outset.'[26] The British had wanted only the captives and, if the opportunity presented itself, the person of Tēwodros, who had not been able to face his main rivals for some three years, and for this they had landed 42,000 men.[27] Now Hassen and Munzinger were talking of 1,000–2,000 men to punish the victorious Kasa, force upon Ethiopia a faith which was felt to be alien, and establish some kind of permanent influence. More ambitious aims and a fraction of the means; this is where the story of European/Egyptian arrogance and fatal underestimation of Ethiopia really begins.

Encouraged to intervene on behalf of the Catholic mission, but aware that the use of military force against Kasa would not necessarily be approved in Europe,

---

23 In addition to Douin, *Ismaïl*, III, 2, pp. 321–3, 327, 335, see additional dispatches from Hassen to Montmorand, 12 Jun. 1871–1 Feb. 1872, in AECP, Égypte 49–50, *passim*; also *MT*, 1871, pp. 43–4, 59, 76–7, Lager, 21 Mar., 25 May and 3 Aug. 1871. Samu'ēl Gīyorgīs, who believed he had been treated unfairly by Kasa (IO, Abyssinia Original Correspondence 3, fols 768–70, Samu'ēl to Rassam, n.d., but 1870), and Aleqa Birru were also involved in these intrigues.

24 AECP, Égypte 50, fols 238–43, Montmorand to Rémusat, 6 Nov. 1871.

25 ENA, Soudan, Carton 3/7, Ahmad Mumtaz to Ismail, 15 Apr. 1871. Strictly speaking, this letter is addressed to the *mihradar* (keeper of the seal or chief secretary) of the khedive. Unless the name of this official is mentioned in the documents, I will be citing them as addressed to Ismail.

26 Douin, *Ismaïl*, III, 2, p. 329, Munzinger's dispatch, 25 Aug. 1871.

27 See above, p. 256.

Ismail took the opportunity to send a 'friendly' letter with some presents in reply to Kasa's announcement of his victory over Tekle Gīyorgīs. In fact, the letter was patronizing in the extreme, and the threats were thinly veiled: many of the Great Powers belonged to the Catholic faith; the fate of Tēwodros was there to be considered, and the writer would feel obliged to assist Catholic refugees if the situation did not improve.[28] Once more the Munzinger hint was thrown into Kasa's face, that he might well have to share the fate of Tēwodros.[29]

What Kasa, who had been crowned Emperor Yohannis in January 1872, replied to Ismail's letter does not seem to have been preserved, nor is it possible to establish with certainty whether the reply played any role in Ismail's decision to go from words to deeds. On 3 March the khedive called Munzinger to Cairo in order to consult 'verbally' with him about certain 'rather delicate' questions.[30] One of these was most certainly the occupation of Bogos, for three weeks later Munzinger received his order to annex this province or population group. The remarkable and awkward wording of this order indicates how delicate the issue was judged to be:

> Having informed us verbally that the inhabitants of the tribe of Bogos are presenting you with requests wherein they solicit their annexation by [*rattachement à*] the government . . . we have no objection to acceding to their desire [to live] under the dependency of the government. We transmit to you this order for you to comply with it.[31]

While Munzinger was in Cairo, a report arrived from the governor of Taka that his Ethiopian colleague at Adiyabo had raided two Bazēn villages and received tribute from others. In view of the circumstances—Munzinger's determination to annex Bogos and his summons to Cairo—it is unlikely that this report played any role in the decision on Bogos. It did, however, prompt Ismail to write a new letter to Yohannis, offering the King the choice between arresting and punishing the governor of Adiyabo himself, or admitting that the latter was not under his authority, in which case Ismail would send his troops to do it.[32] Since Yohannis regarded not only Adiyabo but also Bazēn (Kunama) and

28 Douin, *Ismaïl*, III, 2, pp. 331–3, quoting Ismail to Kasa, 26 Nov. 1871, from ENA, Registre 1942, Ordres supérieurs, p. 39.

29 See above, p. 282.

30 Douin, *Ismaïl*, III, 2, p. 337. Ismail's emissary was reported to be on his way back to Egypt on 26 Feb. 1872 (AECP, Égypte 51, fols 194–5, Hassen to Montmorand), not 26 Mar. as Douin (p. 337, note 2) states. It is just possible therefore that he had reached Cairo before Ismail wrote to Munzinger on 3 Mar. 1872.

31 ENA, Registre 1939, Ordres supérieurs, p. 29, Ismail to Munzinger, 25 Mar. 1872; Douin *Ismaïl*, III, 2, p. 338. According to Franz Hassen (AAPA, IB 9, Abessinien 1, to Ramsaner(?), 8 Jul. 1872), Birru Welde Gīyorgīs had now become a traitor and advised Ismail to act since the governor of Hamasēn, Dejjazmach Gebru, was with Yohannis in southern Tigrē.

32 ENA, Abyssinie, Casier 20/9/1 (and Registre 1942, Ordres supérieurs, p. 68), Ismail to Yohannis, 3 Apr. 1872; Douin, *Ismaïl*, III, 2, pp. 337–9. Douin is slightly ambivalent on the importance of the report from Kasala. On the one hand, he writes that 'a border incident provided him [Ismail] with the pretext he sought for extending his territory at the expense of Ethiopia'; on the other hand, that Ismail 'judged that the action of the Abyssinians called for a prompt retort' and decided to occupy 'the region of the Bogos without further delay'.

Barya as Ethiopian territory, he could not but feel that this was a new interference in the internal affairs of his country by the ruler of Egypt.[33]

On his return to Massawa, Munzinger prepared for the occupation of Bogos. Suddenly it seemed less certain that the population actually wanted to become Egyptian subjects. Munzinger reported a preliminary meeting with a representative for the Qeyyih Marya and the Bilēn,[34] and a planned interview with their chiefs. He felt quite confident that they would ask for Egyptian protection, and hoped (!) that the Bogos would follow their example. He urged the khedive to send him reinforcements of 800 men at once for the occupation of the region and the building of a fort at Keren. Munzinger was sufficiently aware of what he was doing to warn his master that they had to expect an Ethiopian counter-attack.[35]

Munzinger's attempts to win over the chiefs of the region continued through May and June, according to his own report with almost complete success. Having received the reinforcements, he then left Massawa on 27 June, made a detour through Habab (Ad Temaryam) north of Mensa, and arrived on 4 July at Keren without having met any resistance.[36] He must either have been very secretive about the purpose of his expedition or have asked his European friends not to reveal anything. Prideaux, who arrived at Massawa with a letter and presents from Victoria for Yohannis only a few days before Munzinger's departure, could only report that the governor had left for the interior with about 1,000 men and that the rumours spoke of Bogos as their destination; the Swedish missionaries volunteered no information whatsoever about the campaign.[37]

Munzinger declared that he would have liked to proceed immediately with the occupation of Hamasēn, 'the key of Abyssinia' as he called it, but he felt that he could not do so without either orders from Cairo or the pretext of an

33 See below, p. 297.
34 The use of 'Bilēn' for a tribe outside Bogos is confusing. Cf. Douin, Ismaïl, III, 2, p. 343. It is basically a linguistic term, normally used when referring to the Agew-speaking population of Bogos. Sometimes 'the Bogos' is used as a synonym for 'the Bilēn', but it usually has a more geographical connotation. The two main tribes of the Bilēn are the Bēt Teqwē and the Bēt Gebre Terkē. It is possible that Munzinger is here using 'Bilēn' for the northern and mainly Muslim Bēt Teqwē, reserving 'Bogos' for the southern, largely Christian Bēt Gebre Terkē, who lived in and around Keren, the main centre of the whole area, including the neighbouring districts of the Marya, Qeyyih (red), and Ṣellim (black), the Mensa, and other minor ethnic groups. See Trimingham, Islam, pp. 153–68, for the tribal configuration of north-central Eritrea.
35 ENA, Soudan et Afrique Orientale, Casier 120/73/5, Munzinger to Ismail, 26 Apr. 1872; Registre 1859, Maia Sanieh, p. 90, Munzinger to Maia, 23 May 1872. Cf. Douin, Ismaïl, III, 2, p. 340.
36 ENA, Soudan, Carton 3/7, Munzinger to Ismail, 22 Jun. and 14 Jul. 1872; Douin, Ismaïl, III, 2, pp. 341–3.
37 FO 1/27B, fols 58–9, Napier to Granville, 3 Oct. 1872, with extracts from a letter by Prideaux; MT, 1872, p. 81, where the editor of the paper comments for the second time on the fact that the missionaries have had nothing to say about the expedition, though letters written as late as October had arrived. Napier's letter is actually one of thirty-five documents issued as a Confidential Paper but this is bound with the Original Correspondence in FO 1/27B. No separate copy is found in the FO 401 series but there is one catalogued as FO 881/2263.

Ethiopian counter-attack. He reported, however, that he had promised some 'emissaries' from the province that he would seize it later.[38] On the western sector of the frontier, the Egyptian garrison at Kufit was pushed southwards to Amideb on the very boundary of Kunama, or Bazēn.[39]

Yohannis was hardly prepared to deal with the Egyptian aggression in 1872. Although he had been crowned at Aksum in January, the rulers of Begēmdir, Gojjam, and Shewa had not yet declared their allegiance. Besides, Yohannis had problems with some of his Tigrean governors and was actually engaged in suppressing a revolt among the Azebo Galla in south-eastern Tigrē when the news about the occupation of Bogos reached him. He immediately returned to Adwa and posted his army along the *de facto* borders of Adiyabo, Dembelas, Serayē, and Hamasēn.[40] Then he turned to diplomacy.

Yohannis's first step was to send a strongly-worded letter to Ismail, protesting that the Egyptian ruler had no call to write the kind of letter he had dispatched in April. Barya and Bazēn had always been dependencies of Ethiopia, and no incursion into Taka had taken place; the governor residing at Adiyabo was the appointee of the Ethiopian king; he had acted on orders when he made the punitive raid, and would certainly not be handed over to any foreign government for punishment. And Yohannis continued:

> . . . as I understand, Monsinger Bey [Munzinger] has, by order of Your Highness, collected an army and has entered the countries of Moujess [Bogos], Halhal and Khamassin [Hamasēn], which are situated between the Abyssinian and Egyptian territories; Khamassin is the original Capital of Abyssinia . . . from these countries my Kingdom extends as far as the coasts of the Red Sea, we hope that the countries on the coast which have been taken from us may be restored . . . If Your Highness desires to argue respecting the territories in question, you can enquire of the Europeans residing there, and moreover if you wish the friendship between us to be durable, Your Highness must not listen to the sayings of mischievous persons, and that you must also give orders for the withdrawal of your troops, but on the other hand if Your Highness has a design to seize the above-mentioned places, let me know . . .[41]

Two weeks later, Yohannis had prepared the most extensive diplomatic action undertaken by any modern ruler of Ethiopia so far. Yohannis's earlier emissaries had not managed to get beyond Cairo, and this time the Emperor chose Kirkham, who now styled himself general, as his special envoy. Yohannis furnished him with letters dated 13 August 1872 to Queen Victoria, the president of France, and the emperors of Austria, Germany, and Russia. The Amharic

38 ENA, Soudan, Carton 3/7, Munzinger to Ismail, 14 Jul. 1872.
39 Douin, *Ismaïl*, III, 2, p. 339.
40 ibid., pp. 344–5; ENA, Registre 1859, Maia Sanieh, p. 90, Munzinger to Maia, 23 May 1872; FO 95/731, no. 143, Yohannis to Victoria, 13 Aug. 1872; AECP, Égypte 51, fols 408–13, Sarzec to Rémusat, 19 Jul. 1872; BN, Ethiop. 259, fol. 18.
41 ENA, Abyssinie, Casier 20/9/1, Yohannis to Ismail, [31 Jul. 1872]. I quote from an English translation of the letter, probably carried to Cairo by Kirkham. French versions with the date 25 Abib 1288 (which should be 25 Abib 1289, which corresponds to 31 Jul. 1872) are found in FO 78/2229 and AAPA, IB 9, Abessinien 1. Neither Douin (it seems), who quotes from FO 78/2229 (*Ismaïl*, III, 2, pp. 346–8), nor I have found the original of this letter.

originals are all in the same handwriting and sealed with the Emperor's new seal, bearing the legend 'King of Kings Yohannis, King of Zion of Ethiopia'. There is no indication that Kirkham or any other European participated in the drafting of these letters. Though he had been away from Europe more than thirty-five years, it is not likely that Dr Schimper, for instance, would have addressed the Austrian emperor as Ferdinand, twenty-four years after the latter had been succeeded by Franz Josef.[42]

In the opening sentences, Yohannis referred to earlier contacts: he thanked Victoria for the recent exchange of gifts; informed Wilhelm I and Alexander II that he had written before, but had received no reply, probably because the Turks seized the letters; and apologized to Thiers and Franz Josef for not having written earlier, while referring at the same time to the long-standing friendship between Ethiopia and their respective countries. He then went on to relate how he had gone to put down a rebellion among the Azebo, and how he had found on his return to Adwa that 'the Turks, Ismail Pasha's men [had] seized his country'. Finally, he accused Ismail of wanting to make him a Muslim and all his subjects slaves, and expressed his hope and trust that his good Christian colleagues in Europe would not want this to happen. In the letter to Franz Josef, he added that 'Ethiopia has become like an island, and is surrounded by Ismail Pasha and the Turks', thus anticipating the 'island concept' of Minīlik's famous circular of 1891. Yohannis evidently felt that he did not need to make any specific requests for support; he stressed that he wanted his European colleagues to know the matter, and left it at that in all the letters, except the one to Victoria.[43]

Probably because he felt that the British government owed him more than the others did, Yohannis was more specific in his letter to Victoria both about Munzinger's invasion of Ethiopia's border districts and about a solution to the conflict. He also explained that he had instructed the governor of the area to punish some Kunama villages for having, among other crimes, killed a British subject, Thomas Powell, with his family and company. This had caused Ismail to write him an unacceptable letter. Yohannis pointed out that he had hoped that the British would help him to recover lands lost to the Muslims long ago. Now that the Egyptians wanted to rule all Ethiopia, Yohannis asked for the Queen's advice, and in particular for 'a good man' who would look into the aggression for him. Apprehensive that the British might be prejudiced against him because of his conflict with the Catholic missionaries, the Emperor also took time to explain his stand on that matter: he was baptized in the name of the Trinity, believed in the gospel of Christ, and received the necessary guidance and instruction for his people from Alexandria; therefore he had told the missionaries to go and teach the many pagan who were still to be found in the world; because of this they had written to Wagshum Gobezē (Tekle Gīyorgīs)

---

42   FO 95/731, no. 143; AEMD, Afrique 62, fol. 115; HHS, PA VIII/78; AAPA, IB 9, Abessinien 1; AVPR, F. Politarchiv D. 2000, fol. 13. All the Amharic originals except the one to the president of France have been located. An original was, however, dispatched to Paris; see FO 1/27B, fol. 60, Lyons to Granville, 15 Nov. 1872.
43   ibid.; for Minīlik's circular, see below, p. 393.

to attack him, and thus caused bloodshed in Ethiopia; they had built churches without his permission, and told the people to come to them and be free from taxation; when the Emperor nevertheless sent a chief to collect the tax, the people refused to pay, and by accident some were shot. Yohannis was quite aware of the root of his troubles: 'It is Munzinger Bey who does all this to me in order to destroy my name.' The English translation of this letter is very unsatisfactory, hardly more than a paraphrase. Most of the accusations against the Catholics are omitted, as is the pointing out of Munzinger as the main culprit; according to Yohannis, the former consul had even bragged (*fekkereliñ*), saying, 'I will guide the Turks; I will come and I will have [them] kill you.'[44]

In a letter to Earl Granville, Yohannis summarized what he had written to the Queen. In addition, he brought up the question of his consul in London, Mr Henry S. King, whom the British government had refused to recognize. Granville was informed that Yohannis had sent a sealed power of attorney to King and that he expected Granville to receive the representative and take note of his requests.[45]

Reports about the invasion of Abyssinia reached European capitals in early August. Initially London, Paris, and Berlin showed some concern, but it was not difficult for Ismail to put across his version of the conflict through the European consuls in Cairo. He admitted that he had sent three battalions to the frontier with Ethiopia but was vague about 'the exact point or points where the inroad of the Abyssinians' had taken place: '. . . it had occurred at three places between Kassala and Massowah, but not in the Bogos district'.[46] What had happened in Bogos was an entirely different matter: the subduing of a rebellious population in an area which had long been Egyptian territory. So cleverly was this 'new thesis' developed and propagated that the British consul general Edward Stanton could write:

> Mr. Kirkham's story . . . appears at present rather to confirm the version of the matter given by the Khedive, as I imagine the Bogos can hardly now be considered strictly as Abyssinian territory, many years having elapsed since its first occupation by Egyptian troops, since which date, as far as I am aware, the district has enjoyed a sort of semi-independence . . . but as the frontier between the two countries has not been strictly

44 FO 95/731, no. 143, Amharic original, 8 Neḥasē 1864 (13 Aug. 1872), and English translation, 10 Aug. 1872. In addition to the copy of the translation in this file, there is an identical one in FO 1/27B, fols 8–12. On both it is stated that the letter was 'translated by the King's interpreter to General J. C. Kirkham, by order of Yourness [*sic*], King of Kings of Ethiopia, at Adwa, on the tenth day of August, 1872', and on the latter Kirkham has signed his name. The paper used and the handwriting prove that the copies were produced in England. The earlier date of the translation may be due to the fact that it was made from a draft. It is more difficult to explain from where Kirkham got the idea that the King's name should be pronounced and written 'Yourness', but he was quite convinced that he was correct (see, for instance, AAPA, IB 9, Abessinien 1, Bernstorff to Bismarck, 22–3 Oct. 1872).

45 FO 95/731, no. 144, Yohannis to Granville, 13 Aug. 1872.

46 FO 1/27B, fol. 56, Stanton to Granville, 10 Aug., 12 Aug., and 24 Aug. 1872; AECP, Égypte 52, fols 64–6, 169–72, Roustan to Rémusat, 27 Aug. and 9 Sep. 1872; AAPA, IB 9, Abessinien 1, Brüning to Bismarck, 13 Aug. 1872; Krause to Bismarck, 14 Aug. 1872; ENA, Registre 25, Abdin, p. 72, [Ismail] to Riad, 24 Aug. 1872.

defined, the renewed occupation of this territory by Egyptian troops may not im-
probably give rise to serious complications between Egypt and Abyssinia.

Stanton declared that he was unable to state 'whether or no the Egyptian
Government is justified in the occupation of Bogos'.[47] On the other hand, he
further confused the issue by accepting Ismail's statement that he had never
claimed the Mereb river as his frontier, though his claim that the Bazēn
(Kunama) were Egyptian subjects actually meant that he demanded territory
even beyond the Mereb.[48]

Kirkham passed through Alexandria at the end of September and arrived in
London on 10 October. The former steward, soldier, hotel-keeper, and sutler
was a somewhat unlikely ambassador, and in view of General Gordon's testimonial, 'I should be averse to recommend him in any way',[49] it is probably
not surprising that the Foreign Office at first wanted to ignore him. Nevertheless, Kirkham insisted on being listened to, and his written statement to Earl
Granville showed considerable grasp of the issues involved. He was probably the
one who was guilty of suppressing most of the accusations against the Catholic
missionaries so that they did not appear in the translations of Yohannis's letters
to Victoria and Granville.

On the other hand, Kirkham rightly stressed that the attack on Bogos, where
Munzinger 'had a large estate', was the immediate cause of the conflict. In
particular, however, he emphasized the need for Ethiopia to have access to the
sea. After the transfer of Massawa to Egypt in 1866—Kirkham wrote 1858, i.e.
the Ethiopian year, which indicates that he was actually relaying a message
from Yohannis also here—the duties on Ethiopian imports and exports through
that port had allegedly been raised to 36 per cent and all import of arms and
ammunition had been prevented. Then Ismail had occupied Anfilla, to which
the Egyptians or Turks had no historical right, 'with the further intention . . .
of taking the large salt plains adjoining, which are absolutely essential to the inhabitants of Abyssinia'. In this situation Yohannis asked, in the words of
Kirkham,

> for the moral assistance, by way of remonstrance of the Western Powers, and especially
> of England, against this aggression, and more particularly *to have the right of road secured
> to the sea for export and import at Amphila Bay* as Abyssinian territory.

As for the boundary farther west (Bogos and Kunama), the King was prepared

> to leave such boundary to the decision of an Arbitrator to be nominated by England
> either solely or in conjunction with the other great Powers.[50]

47 FO 1/27B, fol. 57, Stanton to Granville, 21 Sep., 29 Sep., and 5 Oct. 1872; Douin (*Ismaïl*,
    III, 2, p. 354) admits that this was *une thèse nouvelle*, born between 14 and 24 Aug. 1872.
48 See above, p. 295.
49 IO, Abyssinia Original Correspondence 3, pp. 27–8.
50 FO 1/27B, fol. 59, Kirkham to Granville, 31 Oct. 1872, enclosed 'Statement' (my emphasis).
    Kirkham had raised the issues of Anfilla and the salt plains as soon as he reached Egypt
    (ibid., fol. 57, Stanton to Granville, 21 Sep. 1872).

That the arms embargo was quite strict is plain from the fact that in 1873 sporting guns were included and the British consul general in Egypt, Colonel Stanton, had to intervene to secure an exception for European tourists: they should be allowed to carry two sporting-guns each into Ethiopia. A gift of five rifles and six pairs of pistols from the French president was seized the same year and only delivered to Yohannis on the eve of the battle of Gundet in November 1875.[51] The customs duties and other dues were certainly high and rising. In 1869, the India Office had complained and was assured that action would be taken, and in 1872 Stanton admitted—in an otherwise pro-Egyptian dispatch— that it was 'highly probable' that Ethiopian imports and exports were 'subjected to exorbitant dues'.[52] As for the saltmines, their importance for Ethiopia was clearly recognized:

> To monopolize the trade which is carried out in all these regions, it would be sufficient to seize these mines; for Abyssinia could belong to whoever the salt belonged to, if not territorily, at least with regard to its products and its trade (. . . *car l'Abyssinie pourrait appartenir à qui appartiendra le sel, sinon par son territoire, du moins par ses produits et par son commerce*).[53]

The importance of the saltmines was based not only on the indispensability of the commodity but, even more, on the fact that salt was the main currency used in the internal trade of the country. That Egypt coveted the mines is also well attested; in fact, a new proposal by Munzinger to annex the salt plains, which would produce 'a very nice revenue (*un assez beau revenu*)', is dated precisely the same day as Kirkham's statement to Lord Granville about the matter.[54]

Turning to the khedive for explanations, the British government supported the Ethiopian viewpoint by declaring 'that any question of boundary might be properly referred to a third Party'.[55] Ismail rejected the proposed arbitration out of hand. He based his arguments on the assumption that the dispute was caused entirely by the Abyssinian 'invasion' into some still undefined 'portion of the Province of Taka'. He declared that 'he was bound to demand reparation for injury' and that he intended to occupy Hamasēn as a guarantee that he would obtain it. That he had already annexed Bogos in retaliation was conveniently ignored. To the French consul general, Ismail declared that he would not be deterred from his plans by any obstacle whatsoever.[56]

Consul General Stanton again played into the hands of the Egyptians by

51 Douin, *Ismaïl*, III, 2, p. 415; AECP, Égypte 54, fols 91–249, *passim*, various documents on seizure; Massouah 4, fols 39–48, Sarzec to Decazes, 24 Dec. 1875; fol. 49, Yohannis to Mac Mahon, 6 Dec. 1875; also FO 1/27B, fol. 107, Kirkham to Granville, 4 Jun. 1873; FO 1/28, fol. 341, Yohannis to Schneider, 29 Oct. 1873; de Cosson, *Blue Nile*, Vol. I, p. 218; Vol. II, pp. 57–8.

52 FO 1/29, fol. 232, FO to IO, 30 Oct. 1869; FO 1/27B, fol. 63, Stanton to Granville, 5 Dec. 1872.

53 AEMD, Afrique 62, fols 41–8, memorandum by G. d'Orgeval, 16 Dec. 1867.

54 Douin, *Ismaïl*, III, 2, pp. 317, 361–2; see also above, pp. 142, 219, 250.

55 FO 1/27B, fols 59–60, Granville to Stanton, 7 Nov. 1872.

56 ibid., fols 61–2, Stanton to Granville, 28 Nov. and 30 Nov. 1872, with enclosed memorandum by Sherif Pasha; AECP, Égypte 52, fols 456–9, Roustan to Rémusat, 8 Dec. 1872.

minimizing the annexation of Bogos in favour of a long refutation of Kirkham's 'complaint . . . of an aggression of Abyssinian territory by the occupation of Amphilla, by Egyptian troops'. In fact, the Egyptian occupation of Anfilla had been precipitated five years earlier by the landing of the Meqdela expedition, and Kirkham's complaint was really directed against the exploitation of Ethiopian trade and the arms embargo rather than the occupation as such. What he was asking for was 'the moral assistance' of the British government 'to have the right of road secured to the sea . . .' The urgent need for this was recognized by Stanton who suggested that the solution would be 'to place Abyssinian traders under British protection'—in other words: if not Egyptian, then British control.[57] In the meantime Ismail continued to build up Egyptian military strength in the area. It seemed all too likely that Vice-consul Sarzec's early prediction would come true: 'This occupation of the Bogos is certainly only the prelude to more serious events.'[58] To prevent these from taking place, the British government expressed its disappointment with Ismail's attitude and recommended, in strong terms, that the khedive accept arbitration 'on the part of neutral Powers, as there is good reason to suppose the King of Abyssinia is, on his part prepared to do [this]'. Evidently Stanton found the language too strong; he asked for and received permission to withhold the communication of the dispatch on the grounds that Munzinger had been called to Cairo to explain the situation.[59]

Besides military force, money played an important role in the annexation of Bogos. Taxes were cancelled to gain favour with new subjects, and Munzinger requested and received funds for 'secret expenses, for one should not economize in such matters', as Ismail wrote. On the other hand, the lack of military resistance led Munzinger to believe that he did not need the troops he had received: 'With the battalion of negroes alone, I not only feel capable of protecting the Bogos, Marya and Bazēn, but I would be at Adwa, if I were allowed.' In fact, he was preparing the way and looking for a pretext to invade Hamasēn, at the same time as he tried to persuade Yohannis through Hassen to cede Bogos to him *personally* in return for the withdrawal of the Egyptian troops (and for the person of Kasa Golja). It is unclear whether Munzinger saw himself as the *sovereign* ruler of Bogos but it is not improbable; at any rate Yohannis did not agree.[60]

Ismail and Munzinger quite naturally sought Ethiopian allies against Yohannis wherever possible, but their efforts were not particularly successful. Kasa Golja and some other minor chiefs were actually fugitives—and Egyptian

57 FO 1/27B, fol. 63, Stanton to Granville, 5 Dec. 1872. For the occupation of Anfilla, see above, p. 258, for Kirkham's request, p. 300.
58 FO 1/27B, fol. 63, Stanton to Granville, 5 Dec. 1872; AECP, Égypte 51, Sarzec to Rémusat, 19 Jul. 1872; Douin, *Ismaïl*, III, 2, pp. 352–3, 356.
59 FO 1/27B, fol. 64, Granville to Stanton, 18 Dec. 1872; fols 65–6, Stanton to Granville, 30 Dec. 1872, and Granville to Stanton, 3 Jan. 1873.
60 Douin, *Ismaïl*, III, 2, pp. 343, 353–60; ENA, Registre 1859, Maia Sanieh, p. 110, Munzinger to Maia, 27 Jul. 1872. This document in which Munzinger requests money, is not cited by Douin; otherwise his presentation is very detailed and based on Sarzec's dispatches in AECP as well as the Egyptian archives. See also de Cosson, *Blue Nile*, Vol. I, p. 84. For Munzinger's eventual aspirations, see Keller-Zschokke, *Munzinger*, p. 61; Rohlfs, *Mission*, pp. 50–2.

pensioners; Tekle Gīyorgīs, who reportedly contacted Munzinger, was an Ethiopian state prisoner, and the position of others in terms of territory and authority is difficult to establish. Though the Afar along the Red Sea coast south of Massawa were supposed to have been Egyptian (or Ottoman) subjects since 1862 at least, Munzinger discovered that he needed to take a battalion with him to places like Beylul, Aseb, and Raheita to subdue the rulers there before attacking the sultan of Awsa in order to open up communications 'with the Wello Galla, our natural allies'.[61]

The crucial factor in any full-scale conflict between Ethiopia and Egypt would be the attitudes of Minīlik in Shewa and the heir or heirs of Tekle Gīyorgīs at Gonder. At the time of the Bogos crisis and for some years to come, Minīlik in no way regarded himself as a vassal of Yohannis. He styled himself king of kings and continued his own foreign contacts mainly, it seems, to keep his European colleagues aware of the fact that he claimed to be the legitimate ruler of Ethiopia in spite of the coronation of Yohannis.[62] He did not, however, attack his Tigrean rival in any way or even mention him. In November 1872, Sultan Abu Bakr at Zeyla forwarded a letter or message from Minīlik, allegedly containing a declaration of submission, which is very unlikely, and a request for scientific books, which is more probable. Yohannis, again, is not mentioned, and there is not the slightest hint in Ismail's reply of any submission or any understanding about common action against Yohannis.[63]

With regard to the immediate heir of Tekle Gīyorgīs on the western frontier, Ras Welde Sillasē, better known as Werennā, the position is more confused. Though Yohannis had not crossed the Tekkezē and received recognition as emperor at Gonder, it was *in his name* that Werennā demanded the annual tribute from Shaykh Jumma of Qallabat. At the same time he is reported to have claimed in a letter to Ismail that he was himself 'the king of Abyssinia after Tēwodros'. Probably he did, but an element of wishful thinking on the Egyptian side cannot be excluded. The Egyptian government tried a policy of preventing Jumma from paying and of placating Werennā with gifts, but they failed. Jumma paid, and Ismail decided on a military occupation of another semi-autonomous but historically Ethiopian territory.[64] Shaykh Jumma was

61　Douin, *Ismaïl*, III, 2, pp. 357, 361–2; ENA, Registre 1864, Maia Sanieh, p. 24, nos 6 and 7, Munzinger to Maia, 14 Oct. 1872; Soudan et Afrique Orientale, Casier 120/73/1, memorandum by the chief of staff, General Loring, 30 Nov. 1872; Soudan, Carton 3/7, Munzinger to Ismail, 12 Dec. 1872. See also above, pp. 219, 250.

62　FO 95/731, no. 140, Minīlik to Victoria, 31 May 1872; FO 407/11, pp. 7–8, Brinken to Salisbury, 26 Aug. 1879, referring to a letter from Minīlik to Wilhelm, which is no longer available (see above, p. 283, n. 504); ASMAI 36/1–3, Minīlik to Victor Emmanuel II, 20 Jun. 1872 (mistakenly dated 20 Jan. 1872 by Giglio, *Etiopia–Mar Rosso*, Vol. I, pp. 61–2, 78, n. 63). To make sure that Queen Victoria would really get his message, Minīlik had his letter translated both into French (by Massaja) and German (by J. Mayer). In the German version, dated 21 Jun. 1872, Mayer, however, missed the point by translating *niguse negest ze-Ītyopya*, 'king of kings of Shewa in Ethiopia'.

63　ENA, Bahr Barra, Carton 19, no. 130, Abu Bakr to Ismail, 27 Nov. 1872; Douin, *Ismaïl*, III, 2, pp. 363–4. It has not been possible to locate the letter from Minīlik himself in the archives. For further contacts between Minīlik and Ismail, see below pp. 368–76.

64　ENA, Registre 1859, Maia Sanieh, Adam to Maia, 28 Jul. 1872; Douin, *Ismaïl*, III, 2, pp. 364–5, 401–2; see above, pp. 214–15.

arrested and sent off to jail in Cairo. By May 1873 the annexation of Metemma was an accomplished fact. To the south an invasion of Qwara was reported and in the north an Egyptian garrison was established at Amideb. This was still only on the frontier between Barya and Bazēn, but infiltration among the Kunama was stepped up in the hope that they would gradually accept Egyptian rule and thus justify the Egyptian stand that the whole conflict was due to an 'Ethiopian invasion' into an 'Egyptian Bazēn'.[65]

In the meantime, Kirkham had completed his mission in Europe, visiting Paris and Vienna on his way back to Ethiopia.[66] The tangible results of his mission were not impressive. St Petersburg declared that it was not concerned since no Russian interests were involved; the Czar was not expected to bother about the letter of Yohannis.[67] In Berlin, Bismarck told the Kaiser that any interference in the border dispute might damage the considerable commercial interests of Germany in Egypt; it was not advisable therefore to answer the letter.[68] Vienna turned to Berlin for guidance and was told that Bismarck advised against any action in favour of Abyssinia. This attitude was, by and large, maintained by all.[69] The French government naturally took more interest in the matter and was, moreover, fed by pro-Ethiopian dispatches from Sarzec at Massawa and, though less pronounced, its consul general in Egypt.[70] Nevertheless, Paris was quite prepared to leave the initiative to London and when the French president wrote to Yohannis in December, he completely avoided the issue, simply congratulating Yohannis on his accession to the throne and urging him, as always, to receive and protect all foreigners including French missionaries. The letter was stopped at Massawa, only to be replaced by a similar one in June 1873.[71] A few boxes of small arms sent as a present were seized by the Egyptian authorities, sent to Cairo and returned only in December 1873.[72]

Only Queen Victoria and Lord Granville entrusted Kirkham with a reply to Yohannis. They declared that they had been troubled by the Ethiopian 'apprehensions in regard to the proceedings of Ismail Pasha' but had received 'the most positive assurances' from Cairo that the khedive had 'never contemplated any acquisition or invasion' of Ethiopian territory. Granville added a summary of Ismail's account of the conflict as caused by the attack of 'some marauders on the Abyssinian side'. Both expressed their trust that all the apprehension would

65   ENA, Registre 1864, Maia Sanieh, p. 44, Ala ad-Din to Maia, 1 Nov. 1872; p. 47, Ismail Aiyub to Maia, 27 Nov. 1872; Douin, *Ismaïl*, III, 2, pp. 365–6, 401–4, 412–13; de Cosson, *Blue Nile*, Vol. II, pp. 165–7.
66   FO 1/27B, fol. 63, Kirkham to Granville, 12 Dec. 1872.
67   AAPA, IB 9, Abessinien 1, Alvensleben to Bismarck, 25 Oct. 1872.
68   ibid., Bismarck to Wilhelm II, n.d. Dispatches from London, 22–23 Oct. 1872, and Paris, 26 Oct. 1872, claiming little or no interest in Kirkham's mission in these capitals probably influenced Bismarck's stand.
69   Douin, *Ismaïl*, III, 2, pp. 386, 393–4.
70   AECP, Massouah 3, fols 311–90; Égypte 51 and 52, *passim*.
71   AECP, Égypte 52, fols 402–4, Rémusat to Roustan, 16 Nov. 1872; AEMD, Afrique 62, fol. 135, Thiers to Yohannis, 28 Dec. 1872; fol. 186, Mac Mahon to Yohannis, 10 Jun. 1873.
72   AECP, Égypte 54, fols 91–2, 101–2, Pellissier to Broglie, 4 Sep. and 5 Sep. 1873; fols 245–9, Cazaux to Decazes, 4 Dec. 1873.

have passed by the time their letters reached the King. Of mediation or arbitration in any form, there was not a word.[73]

In the first months of 1873 Yohannis had crossed the Tekkezē, received the submission of Wereñña, and consolidated his power in the Gonder region.[74] It was April 1873 before Kirkham was able to deliver the letters to the King at Amba Chera. Mahdere Qal and Mircha went to work immediately on the translations together with Kirkham. At first Yohannis was quite pleased, but it soon emerged that the British government seemed to have accepted Ismail's declarations that he had neither seized nor intended to seize any Ethiopian territory. Yohannis decided to take the opportunity of sending a new letter at once with the British traveller E. A. de Cosson who had come to visit Ethiopia when Kirkham returned.[75]

In three letters, one written in English by Kirkham but bearing the Emperor's seal, the other two in Amharic, Yohannis once more placed his case before the British government.[76] Firstly, he stated emphatically that Ismail had lied to the British government when he denied having seized any Ethiopian territory; there was 'not one truthful statement' in his reply. To prove this, Yohannis listed the following districts allegedly occupied since the death of Tēwodros:

Qeyyih Barya [Marya], Sellīm Barya [Marya], Boges, Te'ander [locality in Kunama], Hibub, Mensa, Aylet, Asgedē Beqla, Zulla, Tora, Somhalī, Amfīlla. All the country below the escarpment is the land of Hamasēn [belongs to Hamasēn], but he has finished it off and seized everything.

Secondly, the Shanqilla country, i.e. Kunama, was Ethiopian; it was sufficient to refer to the British subject Powell who had come to Adwa and received an escort to go and punish those guilty of having killed his brother there. Ismail's grievance about an Ethiopian chief having raided some Shanqilla was misplaced, not only because these Shanqilla were Ethiopian subjects but also because the raid was a punishment for an attack on a religious community in Waldibba. The Egyptians, moreover, continued their aggressions and had now also occupied Metemma and sent Shaykh Jumma off to jail in Cairo. Thirdly, Yohannis renewed his plea that the British government send someone to look into the causes of the conflict, 'if I am the aggressor [or] if he is the aggressor'.

73 FO 1/27B, fols 64–5, Victoria to Yohannis and Granville to Yohannis, 18 Dec. 1872; also in FO 95/731.
74 BN, Ethiop. 259, fol. 19; FO 1/27B, fol. 42, Kirkham to Granville, 18 Mar. 1873.
75 De Cosson, *Blue Nile*, Vol. I, p. 303; Vol. II, pp. 21–3, 33, 39–42, 109.
76 FO 1/27B, fols 46–8, Kirkham (for Yohannis) to Granville, 13 May 1873; FO 95/732, no. 150, Yohannis to Granville, 15 May 1873; no. 151, Yohannis to Victoria, 4 Jun. 1873. De Cosson had demanded that Yohannis include in his letters a solemn promise to abolish the slave trade in Ethiopia, but Yohannis hesitated and it was only in Kirkham's letter and probably without the King's knowledge that the commitment was included. The author of Cosson brought the first two letters to London (de Cosson, *Blue Nile*, Vol. II, pp. 110, 113–16, 140–2; FO 1/27B, fols 67–8, de Cosson to Granville, 30 Jul. 1873). The letter to the Queen was probably carried by his brother who had stayed behind. At any rate it arrived much later (FO 1/27B, fols 94–5, 111–12, de Cosson to Granville, 16 Dec. 1873 and 20 Jan. 1874).

Finally he asked that he be given a port to communicate and trade through, either Zulla or Anfilla which had earlier belonged to Ethiopia.[77]

Kirkham's letter added a few more names: the Egyptians had erected a saw-mill at 'Subargumé' on the road up to Asmera and were cutting down the forests inside Ethiopian territory; plundering parties had entered Qwara and reached Wehnī, halfway between Metemma and Gonder; Danakil had been invaded, etc. He did not feel that Yohannis was really asking very much:

> All that His Majesty desires, is that the frontier which was recognized at the time of the Magdala campaign should be preserved. Lord Napier of Magdala and General Merewether are both acquainted with the frontier then recognized by Egypt, and if Ismael Pacha will respect that frontier . . . all dispute is at an end. If not the King of Ethiopia begs her Majesty's government, or the British government and any of the other European powers to arbitrate on this case, and determine what are the true frontiers. His Majesty trusts that His Highness the Viceroy will be as willing to abide by their decision as he is, and he hopes that Her Majesty's government will bring all its influence to bear to bring about an amicable settlement of this dispute; thus avoiding a long and bloody war which would otherwise be inevitably forced upon His Majesty for the protection of his country and subjects, which are daily being taken from him.

Convinced that 'Annesley bay and the province of Amphilla belonged to Abyssinia' at the time of the Magdala expedition, Kirkham in particular appealed to the British government to settle the question of an outlet to the sea.[78]

This second attempt to gain British support was even less successful than the first. Stanton had blunted the forceful language intended by Granville for the khedive at the end of 1872. British action at the Porte had been less than success-ful. Munzinger's reports, sometimes minimizing the whole conflict or holding out the prospect of a peaceful agreement with Yohannis on the local level, sometimes concentrating on the atrocities of new Ethiopian attacks, seem to have gained credence with the British representatives in Cairo first and then with the Foreign Office itself.[79] What the former finally achieved was per-mission for Yohannis's envoy to return to Ethiopia after having been detained in Egypt for a whole year. He left without any written reply to the King's letter of July 1872.[80] On the one hand this meant that Ismail's 'ultimatum' never reached Yohannis; on the other hand the failure to reply and the reason given for this were in themselves an offence, and were undoubtedly meant to be so, in

77   FO 95/732, no. 150, Yohannis to Granville, 15 May 1873 (Amharic version with names spelled as in the original). It is not possible to establish with certainty what raids, clashes or punitive expeditions Yohannis and Ismail respectively referred to in their letters. Yohannis may in this letter actually be referring to a raid and counter-raid which took place towards the end of 1872 or even later. See Douin, *Ismaïl*, III, 2, pp. 395–9.
78   FO 1/27B, fols 46–8, Kirkham to Granville, 13 May 1873.
79   FO 78/2229 (no folio numbers in this and some other FO 78 volumes cited in the following), Stanton to Granville, 27 Dec. 1872; FO 78/2283, Stanton to Granville, 10 Jan., 7 Feb., and 2 Mar. 1873, Vivian to Granville, 22 Aug. 1873; for the action at Istanbul and Ismail's diplo-matic manoeuvring generally, see Douin, *Ismaïl*, III, 2, pp. 378–94, 398.
80   FO 78/2283, Vivian to Granville, 22 Aug. and 2 Sep. 1873.

spite of the ostensibly 'friendly' proposals made verbally.[81] With the letters from Yohannis and Kirkham in their hands, the British government expressed satisfaction with the improved feeling of the khedive towards Abyssinia and asked their representative to stress once more their 'lively interest in the well-being, peace, and independence of Abyssinia' which would oblige them 'to remonstrate against any action on the part of Egypt'.[82]

Yohannis was told in Lord Granville's reply to his and Kirkham's letters that it was impossible for the British government 'authoritatively to pronounce' what part of the disputed territory belonged to Ethiopia or how 'well or ill founded' claims advanced by Ismail were. Likewise it was not possible to interfere in the matter of Ethiopia's access to the sea. The government did not 'feel themselves in a position to point out to the rulers who hold possession of the land separating your [Yohannis's] Territories from the Sea coast, the propriety or expediency of making the concession which you desire to obtain'. They could only tell Ismail of their interest in the welfare of Ethiopia. Besides, they had lately received assurances of the friendly disposition of the khedive towards Yohannis and hoped matters could be arranged in 'a friendly spirit'. Yohannis was bound to understand that this closed the case as far as Britain was concerned. In case he might think of new appeals to other European powers, a warning was added about 'having recourse to foreign intervention which may involve you in embarrassments more serious than those from which you seek to escape'.[83] This warning was really unnecessary. While Lord Granville's letter was on its way, Sarzec had visited Yohannis (December 1873) with a message from the French president which did not even mention the conflict. Yohannis reportedly told Sarzec that he and his council were shocked at the indifference of the Christian powers.[84]

Granville's letter, sent by the hand of Reverend Flad, reached Yohannis while he was on a campaign in Gojjam subduing Ras Adal (the later Nigus Tekle Haymanot). Flad reported on his return to Cairo in June 1874 that 'the King refused the friendly offers made to him by the Khedive' and would only come to terms after 'all the territory formerly belonging to Abyssinia had been restored to him including the Sea Port of Amphilia'. According to Kirkham, however, the King was still willing to settle the boundary question by arbitration. Yohannis limited himself to thanking Stanton for forwarding the letter and helping his envoy in Cairo, and to the telling remark: 'I sent my messenger to Ismaïl Pasha and he kept him for one year and sent him to me back without any answer.'[85] In London the stand had hardened: 'The King of Abyssinia

81 Douin, *Ismaïl*, III, 2, pp. 379–81, 418. One of Ismail's excuses in August 1872 for having sent troops to the frontier was that he had received no reply to his letter of April that year (ibid., p. 350).

82 FO 78/2284, Granville to Vivian, 7 Oct. 1873.

83 FO 95/732, no. 152, Granville to Yohannis, 3 Oct. 1873, 'Seen by The Queen and Mr. Gladstone'.

84 AECP, Égypte 55, fols 286–319, Sarzec to Decazes, 20 Apr. 1874.

85 BN, Ethiop. 259, fol. 19; FO 78/2342, fols 170–3, Stanton to Derby, 17 Jun. 1874; fols 176–7, Yohannis to Stanton, 6 Apr. 1874; fol. 182, Kirkham to Stanton, n.d. On the eve of the

seems likely again to embitter the good relations . . .'—'The less we have to do with these Abyssinian Egyptian disputes and intrigues the better'—'Keep absolutely clear of them in future'.[86] The last words were those of the Earl of Derby, earlier Lord Stanley, who had been obliged to deal with Tēwodros from 1866 to 1868. He meant just what he said: Stanton was not even allowed to forward a letter from Kirkham to the khedive but instructed to send it back to the writer.[87]

That Ismail and Munzinger refused to regard the conflict as a boundary dispute and wanted no arbitration did not prevent them from continuing to argue about all the contested districts and localities. In October 1873 Munzinger refuted the whole list presented by Yohannis and Kirkham in their May letters: both the Marya tribes had been added to Egypt in 1825–27 so there was 'not the slightest pretext' for any Ethiopian claim; the Egyptian rights to Bogos were 'by no means so clear' but the inhabitants had begged him 'two years ago to take them under his protection' and he had been almost forced to take possession of the country; Aylet 'was never Abyssinian but always belonged to Massowah'; Zulla and Anfilla 'have been in Turkish Possession for 250 years. Abyssinia never had any right to them and the claim is preposterous.'[88] In order to establish the truth, it would in some cases have been sufficient to look into Munzinger's own *Ostafrikanische Studien*, published less than ten years earlier, and the German translator of Yohannis's letter had even obliged with page references.[89] The truth was not necessarily simple. It is sufficient to recall Munzinger's 1864 description of Semhar, the coastal district just north of Massawa:

> In international law the territory belongs to the Turks; but the Abyssinians have by no means given up the land (*Grund und Boden*) up to the sea because of this . . . Semhar is thus legally and factually much more Abyssinian than people usually think . . . The Abyssinians need not conquer a country which nature has simply given to them. Thus the inhabitants of Semhar live in a double dependence, on Ethiopia for the sake of their pastures, on Massawa for their market; on both for the sake of security. Therefore they pay tribute to both and when one says, that Semhar belongs to the Turks, then one tells only half of the truth.[90]

1875–76 war, Flad claimed that Yohannis had demanded Massawa, Zulla, Anfilla as well as Bogos, Bazēn, Metemma, etc. (ENA, Abyssinie, Casier 20/9/1, Flad to Fleming, 24 Aug. 1875), but this account is throughout very biased in favour of Egypt.

86 FO 78/2342, fols 174–5, FO memorandum, 27 Jun. 1874, with minutes. Unless one accepts Douin's view (*Ismaïl*, III, 2, p. 418) that the release of Yohannis's envoy with an offensive verbal message to Yohannis constituted a *détente*, it is difficult to see that relations had ever improved after the occupation of Bogos in 1872.

87 FO 78/2403, Derby to Stanton, 26 Feb. 1875.

88 FO 78/2284, 'Memorandum of information obtained from Munzinger Bey . . .', transmitted by Vivian to Granville, 18 Oct. 1873; cf. above, pp. 305–6.

89 FO 95/732, no. 150 (German translation). For the relative validity of the historical claims of the two parties, see references to the conflict zones earlier in this book, for instance, pp. 102–9, 116–24, 140–4, 208–23, 250–1.

90 Munzinger, *Ostafrikanische Studien*, pp. 137–8.

From Qwara and Qallabat in the west to the Danakil coast and hinterland in the east all the traditional borderlands of Ethiopia had already been occupied or were threatened by the Egyptian expansion. As the weaker party, Yohannis asked for arbitration.

The pleas of Yohannis for arbitration of the Bogos conflict were the first major and specific request of Ethiopia for international co-operation in the solution of her border problems. These problems were inherent in her very transition from a traditional, feudal state structure with its rather vague concepts of frontiers into a modern territorial state with clearly defined and theoretically inviolable boundaries. It was a transition largely forced upon Ethiopia by the arrival of the Europeans, but it was the activities of Egypt that made it a matter of urgency to find a solution.

It is difficult to believe that Britain lacked the influence necessary to compel Ismail to accept arbitration, alone or together with France, unless the Egyptian ruler was determined at all costs to keep the boundaries open in order to be able to use border incidents as pretexts for never-ceasing new annexations. It is equally difficult to believe that there was not sufficient knowledge of the frontier areas between Egypt and Ethiopia to make an arbitration or mediation attempt meaningful. After all, the Bogos crisis erupted only five years after the well-planned Meqdela expedition had taken place. The truth of the matter is, of course, that British commercial interests, no less than German (or French or Austrian), demanded that nothing be done which could *seriously* upset Khedive Ismail. Both diplomatic representatives in Egypt and European members of Ismail's administration propagated the Egyptian views on the conflict.

Essentially it was Ethiopian interests against a combination of Egyptian and European, for the Ethiopians had already refused to accept European tutelage while Egypt had thrown her doors wide open to European capital, largely on its own conditions. In this situation, Yohannis's diplomatic initiatives, aided by the lone Kirkham, could only delay the all-out attack. Nevertheless, the fact that the British government was alerted, and felt sufficient gratitude towards Yohannis personally for his assistance in 1867–68 to ask questions in Cairo, bought valuable time for Ethiopia which Yohannis used to consolidate his power in central Ethiopia, returning to Tigrē only at the beginning of the rainy season of 1875. The consolidation seems to have included also an agreement of some kind between Yohannis and Minīlik by which the latter acknowledged Yohannis as his suzerain and paid a nominal tribute. There were even reports that a formal 'peace treaty' between the two had been signed on 16 May 1875.[91]

Ismail's expansive drive had for some time been directed towards the lake

91 AECP, Massouah 4, fols 12–16, Sarzec to Decazes, 14 Aug. 1875; *MT*, 1875, pp. 123–4, Lager, 15 Aug. 1875; BN, Ethiop. 259, fols 19–20. Sarzec reported that Yohannis had asked him to notify the French government officially about the agreement. Ethiopian sources have little or nothing to say about the relations between the two princes at this time. Only Hiruy (*Tarīk*, p. 46) states that Yohannis was on his way to Shewa and had reached Zebīṭ when he heard that the Turks were attacking and returned to Tigrē: 'To Nigus Minīlik it was a great joy.'

region of Central Africa and the Somali coast of the Gulf of Aden. He had, in fact, run into more difficulties—with Britain and Turkey—over the acquisition of Berbera and Zeyla than he may have expected. By mid-1875, however, the problems had been ironed out, at considerable expense which Ismail hoped to recover many times over through exploitation of the hinterland, in the first instance Harer.[92] The turn had come to Ethiopia; or was it Yohannis who felt sufficiently secure to take the initiative?

Greater Egypt

There is no simple answer to the question of what caused the outbreak of the war of 1875–76. The territorial component, highlighted by the Egyptian annexation of Bogos, was important. Yohannis had repeatedly stated that he would not agree to the loss of Bogos, and the unrest and incidents along the frontiers indicate that local governors were unwilling to accept the new situation in many places. Nevertheless the King had asked for arbitration and must have understood that he would probably have to pay with the cession of both Bogos and other districts for peace on the frontiers and access to the sea in some form or other. Munzinger's successor as governor of Massawa, Arakil Bey, believed in 1875, as Munzinger had done in 1872, that Yohannis was prepared to give up territory: Bogos, Mensa, and even Ginda which the Egyptians wanted but had not yet occupied.[93] Three years of undisturbed *de facto* possession in the case of Bogos itself had, of course, strengthened Egypt's claim.

The heavy taxation of Ethiopian trade and the arms embargo were from Ethiopia's viewpoint equally if not more serious obstacles to peace. But the deterioration of the trade, the loss of revenue and the costs of maintaining over-sized garrisons caused serious financial difficulties for the Egyptian authorities as well. For Egypt, no less than Ethiopia, the conflict had lasted long enough.[94] The question was: a political settlement or war?

Of Yohannis's plans when he returned to Tigrē in 1875, we know little or nothing.[95] Neither Munzinger earlier in the year nor Arakil in September believed Yohannis would actually take the offensive, at least in the near future.[96] There is very little, moreover, in the King's attitude before, during, or after the war that indicates any desire to settle the differences by military means.

The plans and policies of Khedive Ismail are incomparably better known; the fact that he took the initiative to invade Ethiopian territory in 1875 is undeniable. He claimed, however, that he was taking preventive action only,[97]

92 See Douin, *Ismaïl*, III, 3A, pp. 547–602, for a detailed account of the negotiations over Berbera and Zeyla; also AECP, Égypte 56, fols 302–3, Pellissier to Decazes, 12 Jul. 1875, for a French opinion about the economic importance of Zeyla to Egypt.

93 Douin, *Ismaïl*, III, 3A, p. 358; 3B, p. 715.

94 ENA, Soudan et Afrique Orientale, Casier 120/73/3, Arakil to Khairi, 2 Sep. 1875.

95 No documentary evidence is available, and the chronicles begin their accounts with the landing of new Egyptian troops at Massawa.

96 Douin, *Ismaïl*, III, 3B, pp. 700, 739.

97 See below, p. 314.

and because of the outcome his ultimate plans with regard to Ethiopia remain very much within the field of conjecture. Though his personality and his reign are highly controversial in many respects, there seems to be no controversy about the great ambitions and considerable achievements of the khedive in the field of empire building:

> In three years, from 1874 to 1876, the viceroy founded his great African empire which was to extend the limits of Egypt as far as the equatorial lakes, the shores of the Indian Ocean, the frontiers of the black kingdoms of Chad. A gigantic task, which better than all others, perhaps, attests to the qualities of this great sovereign . . . One phrase could sum up the colonial work of the Khedive; he wanted to make the Nile an Egyptian river, annex to his country all the geographical area of its basin . . . A grandiose conception, showing the stamp of the genius.[98]

At the same time, however, Sir Stephen Cave's opinion in his report 1876 on the imminent financial collapse of Ismail's government has been maintained: 'The Khedive has engaged to some extent in these enterprises [the occupation of Darfur and the expedition to the equatorial lakes] for the sake of the suppression of the Slave Trade, and the Abyssinian war was almost forced upon him.' The ambivalence of those who wanted to represent peace and imperialism at the same time is well illustrated by the American chief of staff of the Gura campaign, General W. W. Loring, who called the war 'an unfortunate event', in which Ismail 'was suddenly involved', but also wrote: 'As Egypt then stood, she had her iron hand on three sides . . . Egypt being the most enlightened commercial nation in north-east Africa, and the Abyssinians being given up to war, turmoil, and the "slave-trade", it was right that Egypt should thus hold the more barbarous nation in check'.[99]

If it was Ismail's ultimate ambition to rule from the Mediterranean to the equatorial lakes and from Chad to the Indian Ocean—and to control all the headwaters of the Nile—it goes without saying that Ethiopia would have to be included in his empire in some form or other. In that case the real issue was not the borderlands but the existence of Ethiopia as an independent state. This was

---

98 Douin, *Ismaïl*, III, 1, Preface, p. ix. See also M. Sabry, *L'empire égyptien sous Ismaïl et l'ingérence anglo-française* (Paris, 1933), pp. 379–81, for a similar interpretation with hints that Egypt, moreover, was carrying out a historical mission as the homeland of Islam and Christianity (the Coptic Church) in Africa.

99 *PP. Commons*, 1876, LXXXIII, pp. 99–118, *Report by Mr. Cave* . . .; W. W. Loring, *A Confederate Soldier in Egypt* (New York, 1884), pp. 173–4, 290. M. Sabry opens a confused defence of Ismail's attack on Ethiopia (*L'empire égyptien sous Ismaïl*, pp. 461–9) by quoting Cave's statement. He goes on to say that, had it not been for England, Muhammad Ali would have conquered Abyssinia (cf. above, pp. 57–8, 69–70); that England and France prevented an Egyptian intervention in Abyssinia as long as the financial and military situation in Egypt was good but then through their official neutrality and secret intrigues favoured a war which might hasten the financial debacle. The point on official neutrality is well taken but the author fails to prove any intrigues in this matter and when he enrolls Kirkham ('very likely') in the British intelligence he is inventing a story. Nevertheless he concludes: 'Thus it is well established that the Abyssinian war had as its main cause, not the territorial ambitions of the Khedive and the intrigues of Munzinger and Arakil Bey, but rather the ambitions of King John and the Anglo-French intrigues.'

what Yohannis really feared,[100] and was bound to try to prevent even at the cost of a full-scale war. In terms of ultimate objectives, it would then be more correct to say that the war was forced upon Yohannis. What Cave, using a more limited perspective, must have meant, however, was that Yohannis had forced the war on Ismail by unbearable provocations or unwillingness to come to terms about trade and security along the frontiers. The circumstances and pronouncements surrounding the outbreak of the war should provide an answer to the question of the immediate, if not the ultimate causes of the war.

Before he left Amba Chera, probably in the early months of 1875, Yohannis received a letter from Ismail. This must have surprised him to no end: firstly, because he had been told by his own envoy one year earlier that Ismail was determined not to write unless Yohannis first sent a polite and friendly letter;[101] secondly, because the letter was written in a friendly tone, ignoring their differences and probably promising that the King's requests for technical assistance in the development of his country would be met. In fact, the letter, addressed to the 'Sultan of Abyssinia', was not intended for Yohannis but for Minīlik who had approached the khedive the year before for 'trustworthy persons having a profound knowledge of arts and crafts'.[102] The bearer of the letter, Na'ib Muhammad Abd al-Rahim, reported on his return to Massawa in May that Yohannis had expressed great satisfaction with the reply he had finally received to his letter written one and a half years earlier, and had declared that his only desire was to come to an understanding with the khedive; he wanted a peace treaty and would raise no claims to the contested territories. Arakil Bey, governor of Massawa since late 1873, relayed this information to Cairo convinced, it seems, that Yohannis did not suspect the real truth. Although Na'ib Muhammad reportedly informed him of the understanding reached between Yohannis and Minīlik, Arakil expressed doubts about the matter and interpreted Yohannis's peaceful attitude as the result of unrest and rebellions against his rule in central Ethiopia.[103]

Whether Yohannis actually accepted the letter as addressed to himself or had his suspicions aroused is a different matter. In the first case he might have concluded either that Ismail now wanted a peaceful solution to their problems or was insincere. But Yohannis may very well have kept a straight face and written a reply even if he suspected that the message was actually intended for his rival. In that case, the letter, however innocuous its wording, would have reminded him of the unpleasant fact that his rival had certain valuable opportunities denied to himself. The only sure and significant result of this odd case of mismanaged diplomacy was that the Egyptian authorities at the end of May 1875 were convinced that Yohannis was prepared to give up territory in order to

100 See above, p. 298.
101 See above, p. 306.
102 Douin, *Ismaïl*, III, 3B, pp. 713, 717–18. Unfortunately, Douin cites only the correspondence between Munzinger and Ismail and Arakil's report to Barrot about these letters, and I have been unable to locate the originals.
103 ENA, Soudan et Afrique Orientale, Casier 120/73/3, Arakil to Barrot, 29 May 1875. Arakil in this dispatch mentions an enclosed letter from Yohannis to Ismail but I have been unable to locate it.

facilitate a peaceful solution to the conflict.[104] Yohannis for his part, whatever he thought of the letter, had little reason to believe that the Egyptians wanted to come to terms.

While Muhammad Abd al-Rahim made his trip to Amba Chera, Arakil followed up Munzinger's earlier proposal to gain control of the salt plains some 80 kilometres inland from Anfilla Bay and just below the escarpment of eastern Tigrē.[105] Though in Arakil's opinion already Egyptian subjects, the Danakil tribesmen there 'did not always have an absolutely correct attitude vis-à-vis the governmental authorities' (in other words they had refused to submit to Egyptian rule); Arakil hoped 'to inculcate healthier notions in them'.[106] To that end, he marched inland from Anfilla with 150, or probably 250, soldiers and two cannon, toured the area for almost three months and determined the localities where forts should be built and permanent garrisons established 'to maintain the order' and effectively control 'the only practicable road' used by the Abyssinian salt caravans. He discovered that 'the Danakil today still believe themselves [to be] outside the scope of the [Egyptian] government'. He understood that military force would be necessary, but was determined to change the old order by which the saltmines had been 'exploited with impunity by the Danakil and the Abyssinians without the slightest tax having been paid for this exploitation'. He made a detailed calculation of the prospective income and arrived at 80,000 thalers annually which would pay for garrisons amounting to 470 men with six cannon and still leave a net profit of 50,000. Finally, Arakil suggested that the occupation of the salt plains would cause several tribes who were not yet subjects of Egypt to seek her protection. In particular, he mentioned the Adal of Awsa and the Azebo Galla. It was, in his opinion, 'a concern of the first order not to give up either the tribes of the highlands or the Galla'.[107]

Arakil's expedition and its aims were no secret to Yohannis. He turned his back on the remaining problems of central Ethiopia and marched north along the edge of the escarpment, making a show of force among the Raya (Zobel) and Azebo Galla, and the Danakil of the area. Along the way, he dismissed his chiefs, no doubt instructing them to guard against further Egyptian advances from whatever side they might come. On the other hand, the fact that the King dissolved his army seems to indicate that he had no intention of invading territory held by the Egyptians.[108]

Towards the end of July the governors of Hamasēn and Serayē returned to their home provinces with their contingents. The King himself was expected to

---

104 Douin accepts this without any reservations whatsoever and concludes his account of the strange affair (*Ismaïl*, III, 3B, pp. 713–15): '. . . one can only admire the ability of the Cairo chancellery to edit messages which could be dispatched indifferently to Yohannis or his rival without causing any negative consequences'.

105 See above, p. 301.

106 ENA, Soudan et Afrique Orientale, Casier 120/73/3, Arakil to Barrot, 12 Feb. 1875.

107 ibid., Arakil to Barrot, 27 May 1875; AECP, Massouah 4, fols 8–9, 12–16, Sarzec to Decazes, 2 Mar. and 14 Aug. 1875. In the second of these reports Sarzec gives the number of Arakil's troups as 250.

108 BN, Ethiop. 259, fol. 20; AECP, Massouah 4, fols 19–20, Sarzec to Decazes, 14 Sep. 1875; *Petermann*, 1877, pp. 157–8, notes by an Austrian, Camill Russ, who was in Adwa at the time.

arrive at Adwa within a month.[109] Munzinger was in Egypt to make final plans for the occupation of Awsa and contacts with Minīlik,[110] but his deputy Ala ad-Din Bey informed Cairo, and Ismail decided to publicize the return of the governors as a hostile act. Ala ad-Din's dispatches were made known to the representatives of the European powers with comments clearly intended to create the false impression that Yohannis was about to attack Massawa. McKillop Pasha and Gamali Pasha were dispatched to Massawa with re-inforcements, and the British representative commented, 'It is to be hoped that he may arrive in time to avert the disaster of the sack of Massowah by the Abyssinians'. No one, of course, could criticize Ismail for wanting to defend Massawa; the war was about to be 'forced upon him'.[111]

On his return to Massawa, Munzinger at first (13 August) confirmed Arakil's alarming reports about large Ethiopian armies near the frontier and an im-minent invasion,[112] but he soon discovered that there was no real threat of any Ethiopian attack and cabled that the reinforcements were not needed. Ismail replied (27 August) that these troops had already cost him considerable expendi-ture and would not be recalled. Munzinger was to deploy the new battalions along the frontier where they would serve best to prevent an Ethiopian attack. Only if he was convinced that there would be no Ethiopian attack in the north should he proceed to Tajura for his own expedition to Awsa.[113]

Arakil was more militant and certainly did not hide it in his dispatches to Cairo in early September. He admitted on the one hand that an attack by the Ethiopians was highly unlikely. On the other hand he felt that Egypt should no longer tolerate the 'hostile demonstrations' of the Ethiopians, in particular the *order* of Yohannis to occupy two passes into the highlands 'sixteen hours' dis-tance from Massawa and about ten hours' distance from Egyptian territory' and his appointment of Kirkham as governor 'not only of Ginda . . . but of Zulla, Anfilla and the great salt plain of Assale as well'. Though the Egyptian claim to Ginda could be contested, this was not in Arakil's opinion the case with the other places. From the military as well as the administrative viewpoint, the best solution would be to rectify the boundaries by occupying Hamasēn. Some weeks later it was 'at least Hamasēn and all of Tigrē'. By his troop collections, the appointment of Kirkham (made more than one year earlier), etc., Yohannis had in Arakil's opinion provided a *casus belli* many times over.[114]

109 Douin, *Ismaïl*, III, 3B, pp. 724–5, citing two telegrams from Ala ad-Din, dated 25 (or 26) and 30 (or 31) July 1875.
110 ibid., III, 3B, pp. 720–4.
111 ENA, Registre 2, Ordres supérieurs, p. 27, Ismail to Munzinger, 12 Aug. 1875; p. 93, Ismail to Arakil, 12 Aug. 1875; FO 78/2404, Cookson to Derby, 11 Aug. 1875 (also in print FO 881/3058, p. 1); AECP, Égypte 56, fols 323–5, Pellissier to Decazes, 15 Aug. 1875; AAPA, IB 9, Abessinien 1, French copies of both of Ala ad-Din's dispatches.
112 Douin, *Ismaïl*, III, 3B, pp. 727–9.
113 ENA, Registre 2, Ordres supérieurs, p. 100, Ismail to Munzinger, 27 Aug. 1875; p. 98, Ismail to Ala ad-Din, 27 Aug. 1875; also Soudan Correspondance Gordon, Casier 118/71/4, second dispatch to Munzinger, same date.
114 ENA, Soudan et Afrique Orientale, Casier 120/73/3, Arakil to Khairi, 2 Sep., 4 Sep., and 23 Sep. 1875; Douin, *Ismaïl*, III, 3B, pp. 738–41; AECP, Égypte 56, fols 326–8, 336–9, Pellissier to Decazes, 22 Sep. and 3 Oct. 1875; *MT*, 1874, pp. 139, Lager, 17 Sep. 1874.

There can be no doubt that Arakil wanted action. That is probably the reason why it did not seem to occur to him that the landing of more than two battalions of Egyptian troops in one week (21–24 August) and their encampment only five to six hours from the frontier, might be regarded as a threat by Yohannis. The normal strength of the three garrisons on Ethiopia's northern frontier (Massawa, Keren, Amideb) was approximately 2,500 regulars. It had been more than doubled and the new troops were well supplied with Remingtons and artillery.[115]

If Munzinger at this point was against an outright attack on the northern frontier, his influence was no longer predominant.[116] Though he had informed Cairo that he intended to wait for news from Ethiopia until the end of the month, the governor general was instructed by Ismail *on 15 September* to depart for Tajura immediately.[117] Two days later the khedive drafted a whole series of orders. The circumstances and the timing indicate that Ismail was not responding to any momentary provocations by introducing a 'new plan' or 'a complete reversal of the policy of conciliation followed until then with regard to Abyssinia'.[118] Instead he was launching his grand attempt to gain control over all territory between the Nile and the Indian Ocean. The invasion of northern Ethiopia was part of this project.

The orders issued *on 17 and 18 September 1875* included instructions to Gordon Pasha to open a route from Albert Nyanza and Victoria to the mouth of the Juba River on the Indian Ocean; to McKillop Pasha to sail for the Juba, establish a permanent military colony there, explore the coast and the river, and advance some detachments into the hinterland; to Radwan Pasha and Abd al-Razik Bey to accompany McKillop and facilitate his mission; to Gamali Pasha to maintain peace and order at Berbera; to Arendrup Bey to proceed to Massawa with additional troops, invade and occupy Hamasēn, and chase away Kirkham from Ginda; and to Arakil Bey and Ala ad-Din Bey to assist Arendrup's mission.[119] The same day, Ismail wrote a friendly and flattering letter to Minīlik accusing Yohannis of evil intentions and planned aggression. He also dispatched an

115 Douin, *Ismaïl*, III, 3B, pp. 729–30, 737–8. The figures of Sarzec (AECP, Massouah 4, fols 17–18, to Decazes, 1 Sep. 1875) amount to 4,250 new troops, but are probably inflated.

116 Keller-Zschokke, who had access to private correspondence, maintained (*Munzinger*, pp. 61–3) that Munzinger did not want to attack Yohannis and that his relations with Arakil and other Egyptian officials had deteriorated.

117 Douin, *Ismaïl*, III, 3B, pp. 745–6.

118 ibid. To arrive at this conclusion, Douin must have overlooked the timing of the instructions. General Loring (*Confederate Soldier*, pp. 290, 301) saw all the expeditions as part of one plan, in which the direct attack on Ethiopia was the main objective while the other actions were undertaken 'to distract the enemy'.

119 French copies of the most important of these orders, dated 17 September and bearing Ismail's signature, are found in ENA, Soudan Correspondance Gordon, Casier 118/71/4, and Soudan et Afrique Orientale, Casier 120/73/2 (McKillop), 73/3 (Arakil), and 73/4 (Arendrup). They are all entered in Arabic in Registre 10, Ordres supérieurs, pp. 3–4, under the date 17 Shaban 1292 (= 18 Sep. 1875). The dispatches to Gordon and McKillop are published *in extenso* in M. F. Shukry, ed., *Equatoria under Egyptian Rule* (Cairo, 1953), pp. 296–302; long extracts of all the important ones are found in Douin, *Ismaïl*, III, 3A and 3B, *passim*.

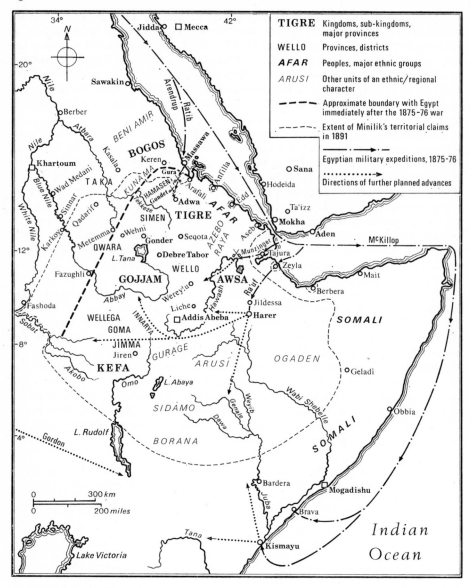

MAP 5   *The threat of encirclement and Minīlik's definition of Ethiopian territory in 1891*

earlier promised gift of 500 rifles with ammunition and instructed the governor at Zeyla to forward Minīlik's envoy Boghos to Shewa with all speed and without even bothering to inspect any of his goods.[120]

The missions entrusted to Gordon and McKillop were not directed against Ethiopia, and it is not likely that they would have affected this country for quite some time even if they had succeeded. As things turned out, Gordon found it impossible to undertake the march to the coast, and McKillop had to be re-called from Kismayu and Brava when the British government decided to uphold the claims of the sultan of Zanzibar to the Benadir coast.[121]

It is the timing of the orders that reveals a connection with the designs on Ethiopia. Gordon had proposed the securing of an outlet to the Indian Ocean for his province of Equatoria in January 1875 and had suggested that his former chief of staff, Colonel Charles Chaillé-Long, be assigned to establish the foothold on the coast. Chaillé-Long, on holiday in France, was advised by General Charles Stone, Ismail's chief of staff and a fellow-American, *on 18 July* to return *by 15 September*.[122] This indicates that planning had started by mid-July with mid-September as some kind of target date. But it was also *on 16 July* that Muhammad Ra'uf Pasha received his orders to leave for Zeyla and prepare for the conquest of Harer, and *on 27 July* that Ismail confirmed Munzinger's instructions to proceed to Tajura and Awsa and that he wrote his first letter promising arms to Minīlik.[123]

Ra'uf was instructed to keep his mission strictly secret as long as possible, then to pretend that it was planned purely in the interest of scientific exploration (the sources of the Sobat river). Once in Harer, he should maintain, however, that he had occupied the town at the request of the population. He left Zeyla *on 18 or 19 September* with an army which was later reported to have totalled 1,200 men, and entered Harer on 11 October. Only the Galla, between Jildessa and Harer, resisted the invasion. But Ismail had no intention of stopping at Harer. Once Ra'uf had secured the important trade centre, the khedive wanted him to proceed with the annexation of districts on the frontiers of Shewa, where coal deposits had been reported, and to send expeditions across southern Ethiopia to the sources of the Blue Nile and the Juba, to tie up eventually with Egyptian outposts at Fazughli and Kismayu respectively. If Minīlik should protest, Ra'uf was authorized to promise riches and marble halls 'in order to succeed in taking possession of the region where the coal exists'.[124] While the Egyptian annexation of Harer was already an additional serious step towards the control and exploitation of the Ethiopian market, it is quite obvious that a successful execution of Ra'uf's instructions would have meant the complete territorial encirclement of Ethiopia by Egypt as well.

120 ENA, Registre 10, Ordres supérieurs, p. 4, Ismail to Minīlik, 18 Sep. 1875; p. 6, Ismail to Ra'uf, 19 Sep. 1875; Registre 2, Ordres supérieurs, p. 92, Ismail to Minīlik, 26 Jul. 1875.
121 Douin, *Ismaïl*, III, 3B, pp. 629–97; Shukry, *Equatoria*, pp. 63–93.
122 Shukry, *Equatoria*, pp. 72–5.
123 Douin, *Ismaïl*, III, 3A, p. 602; 3B, pp. 721–3.
124 ibid., III, 3A, pp. 602–7; 612–27; III, 3B, p. 668; ENA, Soudan, Carton 3/3, Ra'uf to Ismail, 18 Oct. 1875; Registre s.n., Maia Sanieh, p. 32, Ismail to Ra'uf, 11 Nov. 1875; FO 881/3058, pp. 8–9, Nubar to Stanton, 8 Nov. 1875, for the size of Ra'uf's army.

Munzinger's mission had two main purposes. He was to push inland from Tajura, as Ra'uf from Zeyla, annex Awsa and then move on to secure the caravan routes to Wello and Shewa. Munzinger's second task was to contact Minīlik and persuade him to attack Yohannis 'without delay' (10 August); to take all necessary steps 'to push Minīlik, the king of Shewa, to attack Kasa [Yohannis]' and use all his efforts 'to cause a dispute between the two so that they engage in battle' (20 August).[125] If Munzinger succeeded in this, it would mean that *both* Yohannis *and* Minīlik would be removed from the areas which Ismail intended to seize. The connection with *both* Arendrup's *and* Ra'uf's instructions seems too obvious to deny.

Munzinger took his time over the preparations, and it was 27 October when he started out from Tajura. As Ra'uf, he commanded a small army: about 400 men with a few cannon and rocket tubes. Though Ismail had long maintained that the Afar (Danakil) were his subjects, Munzinger was aware that neither of the two most important chiefs, Muhammad Loheyta and Muhammad Anfarī, had in fact agreed to Egyptian rule. Now the former feigned submission and guided Munzinger to Awsa. There the Egyptians suffered a surprise attack in the early morning of 14 November. In spite of their superior arms they were quickly decimated; Munzinger and most of his officers were killed. One week later the remnants of the army, about 150 men, reached Tajura. They reported that their enemies had lost 5,000–6,000 men—undoubtedly a gross exaggeration.[126] Whatever their losses, however, the victory of the Afar was decisive.

The Battles of Gundet and Gura

The care with which Ismail worded his instructions to the Danish colonel, Arendrup, shows that he regarded the straightforward attack on Ethiopia in the north as the politically most sensitive of the four missions. With Benadir, Harer, and Awsa it was sufficient in Ismail's opinion to keep the matter secret while the occupation took place. These areas already belonged to him. Gordon was told, for instance, that he would 'be always on our territory' when he marched from Lake Victoria to the Indian Ocean, and McKillop that his task was not to take possession 'because Juba already belongs to us'; he was only to *affirm* Egypt's rights.[127] Presented with a *fait accompli*, no one was supposed to protest. There was always the argument that the population had actually invited their new masters. This argument had been used against Ethiopia too, but would anyone believe it when Egypt invaded such predominantly Christian provinces as Hamasēn and Serayē? Still less was it possible after the diplomatic activity of Yohannis in 1872–73 to maintain that this territory was a 'no-man's-land' or *de jure* already Egyptian.

Ismail therefore told Arendrup—and gave the British consul general a copy

125   Douin, *Ismaïl*, III, 3B, pp. 721, 726, 731–2, 746.
126   ibid., III, 3B, pp. 792–812.
127   ibid., III, 3B, pp. 639, 641.

of the instructions only ten days later[128]—that Ethiopian troops, allegedly 30,000 men, so close to the Egyptian frontiers damaged Egypt's prestige and economy. He had arrived at the conclusion that Yohannis wanted to force him 'to take the initiative to the hostilities, forgetting no doubt that the one who takes the offensive does not always find himself the aggressor'. Unless Yohannis had withdrawn and changed his attitude (!), Arendrup should invade Hamasēn 'without hesitation', and hold it until the King gave satisfactory guarantees for the safety of the Egyptian frontiers. If the Ethiopians came forward, Arendrup should be able to scatter them with his well-armed troops. In case Yohannis retreated, Arendrup should follow to the boundaries of Hamasēn, or beyond if strategic reasons demanded this. Again, if Arendrup felt that he had more troops than he needed for the occupation of Hamasēn, he should send some to the districts south-east of Massawa (the salt plains) which Yohannis had presumed to claim though they 'belonged' to Egypt.[129] Arakil was instructed to think about the best type of government for Hamasēn, though the decision would depend also on the 'situation of Abyssinia after the retreat or defeat of the King'.[130]

Ostensibly these instructions dealt with nothing more than a provisional annexation of Hamasēn. Ismail's next step was revealed two months later when Arendrup had pushed on through all of Serayē as well and reached the natural and easily defensible frontier of the Mereb. He was promised four additional battalions and told, '. . . your correct tactic is indicated; it is to enter Adwa . . . and make arrangements as if you were going to occupy Adwa in a permanent way'.[131] If the official representatives of European powers were unable or unwilling to see what Ismail was about to do, there were other Europeans (and not the French Catholic missionaries alone) who both saw and approved. Referring to a proposal that Abyssinia be given to Egypt, Reverend Flad suggested that Munzinger would be the most suitable person to govern an (Anglo-) Egyptian protectorate over Ethiopia.[132]

Arendrup landed at Massawa on 26 September and found some 2,500–3,000 troops at his disposal there. The advance from Massawa began on 2 October. Arendrup reached Asmera on 16 October; the capital of Hamasēn, Ṣe'azega, on 18 October. There he was joined by an additional battalion from Keren. Meeting no resistance, Arendrup crossed into Serayē. By 6 November his vanguard had reached its southern boundary, the Mereb, at Gundet. The Ethiopian forces of Hamasēn and Serayē, 3,000 men altogether, had withdrawn across the

---

128   FO 881/3058, pp. 4–8, Cookson to Derby, 27 May 1875, with enclosures. FO 881/3058 is a Confidential Paper entitled *Correspondence respecting the Invasion of Abyssinia by Egyptian Troops.* Most of the original correspondence is found in FO 78/2403 and subsequent volumes. The German consul general knew about the instructions even earlier (GS, Auswärtiges Amt, Restakten, Bunsen to Bülow, 24 Sep. 1875).

129   ENA, Soudan et Afrique Orientale, Casier 120/73/4, Ismail to Arendrup, 17 Sep. 1875.

130   ibid., Casier 120/73/3, Ismail to Arakil, 17 Sep. 1875.

131   ibid., Casier 120/73/4, Ismail to Arendrup, 18 Nov. 1875. In fact, Arendrup was dead when these instructions were issued.

132   ENA, Abyssinie, Casier 20/9/1, Flad to Fleming, 24 Aug. 1875.

Mereb.[133] Arakil made no attempts to explain why the 30,000 Ethiopians threatening Egyptian territory in August and September had turned out to be only 3,000 or even less.[134] Now that the war was on, the propaganda that it was a preventive action was no longer needed.

While the Egyptians thus advanced to within 40–50 kilometres of Adwa, Yohannis and his men showed remarkable restraint. Dejjazmach Gebru of Hamasēn and others, of course, informed Yohannis of the Egyptian activities. But there were many uncertainties. Gebru knew, by mid-October, about the advances from Massawa and Keren and about Munzinger's departure from Massawa 'with 600 Egyptian soldiers for an unknown destination', but also, allegedly and incorrectly, that an army of 6,000 Egyptians had marched on Gonder from Metemma. Aleqa Birru who had betrayed Yohannis already in 1872 and had recently visited Cairo was in Munzinger's company.[135] The latter had instructions, moreover, to spread rumours that the Egyptians had stirred up Minīlik to attack Yohannis in the back.[136] Whether Yohannis believed that or not, he could hardly fail to be uneasy about the activity and whereabouts of 'the angel of Satan (*Ye-Seyṭan melikteñña*)' as he called the man whom he held responsible for the aggression against Ethiopia. His secretary Mahdere Qal did not bother about the distinction between Satan and his instrument and translated 'a man who is the Devel [sic] and the Chef [sic] of it'.[137] As late as September 1875 Yohannis seems to have hoped that the European powers would not permit a major Egyptian aggression against Ethiopia. Vice-consul Sarzec, his only friendly contact with Europe at this time, predicted that the King would only deliver battle as a last way out.[138] In this he turned out to be correct. Sarzec, who was barely keeping ahead of the Egyptians on his journey to Adwa, reported that the governors of Hamasēn and Serayē had 'formal' orders to retreat to Adwa and that he saw both Gebru's soldiers and the population of Hamasēn with their cattle arriving in Serayē on 17 October.[139]

In part the retreat can be explained as deliberate strategy from the Ethiopian side. Yohannis knew from 1867–68 how anxious foreign officers were about

---

133 Douin, *Ismaïl*, III, 3B, pp. 753–68. It is difficult to establish the exact numbers of troops. The above figures are based on Egyptian documents. Sarzec reported that there were 2,500 Egyptians near Massawa and 5,000 at Keren in mid-September and that more were arriving (AECP, Massouah 4, fols 19–25, to Decazes, 14 Sep., 30 Sep., and 6 Oct. 1875).

134 ENA, Soudan et Afrique Orientale, Casier 120/73/3, Arakil to Barrot, 23 Oct. 1875. On 14 September Sarzec (see above note) estimated Gebru's troops, Hamasēn only, at 700–800.

135 AECP, Massouah 4, fols 39–48, Sarzec to Decazes, 24 Dec. 1875. This is a long dispatch written after Sarzec's return from Adwa, but a telegram (fol. 26) dated 16 Oct. 1875 proves that the Egyptian attacks were discussed at this time which is exactly when Sarzec, on his way to Adwa, met Gebru. On Birru, see also ibid., fols 21–3, Sarzec to Decazes, 30 Sep. 1875; BN, Ethiop. 259, fol. 20.

136 Douin, *Ismaïl*, III, 3B, p. 732.

137 FO 78/2632, fol. 100, Yohannis to Victoria, 7 Dec. 1875; fols 95–96a, Mahdere Qal's translation.

138 AECP, Massouah 4, fols 17–18, Sarzec to Decazes, 1 Sep. 1875.

139 ibid., fols 39–48, Sarzec to Decazes, 24 Dec. 1875.

their communications and how they decimated their main force to secure a supply line. On the other hand, there must have been some element of genuine hesitation, for Yohannis did not send out a call to arms until 23 October. At Massawa there were reports that he had shut himself up and was probably ill.[140] The Ethiopian chronicler explained the delay in terms which his readers would understand and approve: 'Aṣē Yohannis heard that the Ismailites had come. For three weeks he prayed to God with great sorrow. And God listened to his prayer.'[141] Three weeks, to the day in fact, had passed between the beginning of the Egyptian advance and Yohannis's mobilization!

After the battle had taken place, Yohannis explained to Victoria what had happened in the following terms:

I had written once and reported [lit. given] to the kings all the evil and aggression he [Ismail] had committed against me. I [then] kept quiet, saying 'Let him do what he likes until they separate us and tell us "You shall not go beyond this and you shall not go beyond this." ' . . . After that [the invasion of Hamasēn] when we asked them why they had come, they said, 'We have not come to seize the country; we have another aim [lit. message].' Then they stood up and invaded Serawē [Serayē]. They marched from Serawē and came; having come closer they camped when there was six hours' distance left to my town [Adwa]. So I said, 'Now they will catch me sitting down.' Since he who does not want to die must kill (ኢላሞት ፡ ባይ ፡ ተጋዳይ ፡ ነውና ፡), I came out and clashed with them . . . Ever since the creation of the world, such aggression as this has not been committed against anyone except me alone.[142]

A translation by the King's interpreter Mahdere Qal of this letter stressed the swiftness of the Egyptian advance and the enormity of the attack: 'I have never seen and heard from the beginning of the world such oppressions unjustice [sic], only I see now happened [sic] to me and to my people, without any fault or reasons.'[143]

Yohannis was clearly annoyed with a letter from Arendrup at Ginda professing peaceful intentions: 'Egypt had no intention to invade Abyssinia or even to conquer Hamasēn . . .', but Yohannis had acted in such a hostile manner that Ismail feared for his possessions; the King was, moreover, such a poor ruler that his own people had complained to Ismail. Yohannis refused to reply. When Na'ib Muhammad Abd al-Rahim returned to request that delegates be sent to negotiate with Arendrup, the King imprisoned him.[144]

On 2 November, the King left Adwa, reportedly at the head of a mere 1,000 men.[145] But his call to arms, strongly supported by Abune Aṭinatēwos, was no doubt couched in terms which the peasants of northern Ethiopia under-

---

140 Douin, Ismaïl, III, 3B, pp. 758, 765.
141 BN, Ethiop. 259, fol. 46; also Chaine, 'Histoire', RS, 21, pp. 182–3.
142 FO 78/2632, fol. 100, Yohannis to Victoria, 7 Dec. 1875 (Amharic original). The letter was sent to Massawa by the hand of Kirkham. He was arrested and the letter was forwarded eighteen months later from Cairo (fol. 93).
143 ibid., fols 95–96a, English version dated 5 Dec. 1875 and signed 'T. Maderakal'.
144 AECP, Massouah 4, fols. 39–48, Sarzec to Decazes, 24 Dec. 1875, relating a conversation with Yohannis at Adwa on 27 Nov. 1875; Douin, Ismaïl, III, 3B, pp. 768–9.
145 AECP, Massouah 4, fol. 41, Sarzec to Decazes, 24 Dec. 1875.

stood: '. . . the children of Ammon and of Moab, the Ismailites rose up against him [Yohannis] in hatred'.[146] In less than two weeks Yohannis reportedly had 50,000 or 70,000 men under his command. These estimates seem much too high; in view of the circumstances 20,000–30,000 would already have been a great achievement.[147] What we do know is that all the important chiefs of northern Ethiopia showed up almost to a man: Ras Araya, governor of Akkele Guzay (and the King's uncle), Ras Barya'u, governor of Tigrē (and Tēwodros's son-in-law), the *dejjazmaches* Gebru and Wēlde Mīka'ēl, the famous Hazega-chief who eventually chose the Egyptian side, the two brothers Basha Gebre Maryam, and Shīaleqa Alula Ingida, the later famous *ras*, and many others. The King's vassals in central Ethiopia, on the other hand, were missing, but that was to be expected in view of the short notice.[148]

During the night of 15/16 November, the Ethiopian army crossed the Mereb and attacked. Arendrup was in the middle of his battle preparations. In a first fierce encounter close to the Mereb in the early morning, the Ethiopians sur-rounded and annihilated about 800 men under the command of Arendrup and Count Zichy. It must have been a perfectly planned and staged surprise attack, since it was allegedly over in less than half an hour (twenty minutes according to Sarzec) with no more than thirty-one killed and fifty-five wounded on the Ethiopian side. A few hours later the Ethiopians had encircled the remainder of the Egyptians, about 1,300 men, in the Gundet or Gudagudē valley. These Egyptians were in a better position to defend themselves. Nevertheless they were also eliminated in an hour or two of heavy fighting in which the Ethiopians reportedly lost 521 dead and 355 wounded. The Ethiopians took some prisoners but not many. Yohannis called upon Majors Dennison and Rushdy guarding the depot at Addī Qwala to surrender. They managed, however, to withdraw leaving all but their small arms behind. But the fear of being pursued was almost more than the 300–400 survivors could bear and many threw away their arms or deserted altogether before reaching Massawa. Within a few days the highlands were evacuated. The Arendrup expedition had miscarried.[149]

146 BN, Ethiop. 259, fol. 46.
147 Sarzec (AECP, Massouah 4, fol. 41) and Russ (*Petermann*, 1877, p. 158) reported 70,000 but may not be independent of each other in regard to this information. Rohlfs (*Meine Mission*, p. 55), who states that he discussed the battle with Yohannis a few years later, suggests 50,000 men. Much of his story is confused or inaccurate. Attacked by Tekle Gīyorgīs in 1871, Yohannis is reported to have had 12,000 men; starting out on his march to Gonder in 1873, about 30,000. With much more time at his disposal, he was supposed to be able to raise 60,000 to 70,000 to face the new Egyptian invasion (see below, p. 327).
148 Douin, *Ismaïl*, III, 3B, p. 770. Arakil's assertion that the Amhara chiefs were absent be-cause none of them wanted to support Yohannis in this war cannot be substantiated and was probably due to wishful thinking.
149 ibid., III, 3B, pp. 776–92. Douin's account is based mainly on the confused reports of Egyptian survivors of the battle, on the official report published in *Moniteur Égyptien*, 3 Dec. 1875, on the book of the American officer of the later Gura campaign, William McE. Dye, *Moslem Egypt and Christian Abyssinia* (New York, 1880), and on Sarzec's long dispatch of 24 Dec. 1875 to his government. The discrepancies of significance for the above summary concern the number of troops involved and the casualties. I have largely followed Sarzec's narrative. Only one week after the battle he met and took care of the fatally wounded Austrian officer Count Zichy (who had been in the front line) and about two weeks later he

Though not literally true, the statements of the Ethiopians about the battle of Gundet embodied a correct assessment of the outcome: 'By the grace of God, I have beaten my enemies. Of all the Egyptians who had invaded my country not a single one has survived; all are dead.'[150] Or, in the words of the chronicler: 'And he killed everyone until the ground was washed with the blood of the Ismailites. He spared nothing, nothing whatsoever (ምንንም ፡ አላስቀረ ፡ ይh ፡ እንኳን ።).'[151] No less important than the elimination of the enemy's troops was the capture of all their arms: about 2,000–2,500 Remingtons or other breechloaders of a quality earlier unknown to the Ethiopian soldier, and fourteen to sixteen cannon and rocket stands with ammunition, etc.[152]

At Addī Qwala, Yohannis and his chiefs consulted about what to do next. No further action was called for to free Serayē and Hamasēn from Egyptian troops. The alternatives were to march on Bogos or Massawa. Yohannis is reported to have contemplated an attack on Massawa but to have dropped it from fear that he might get into trouble with other governments over their nationals.[153] There may have been other equally important considerations, for instance, the whereabouts of Munzinger and the possibility of Minīlik's disloyalty. At any rate the King decided to return to Tigrē with most of his troops, a decision which he carried out immediately (c. 23–24 November).[154]

Back in Adwa, Yohannis addressed an important letter to Victoria which showed that he was, in fact, very concerned about the possible attitude of the European governments to his conflict with Egypt. He was also, and even more so his 'foreign secretary' Mahdere Qal, aware of Ismail's propaganda advantages. After recalling his diplomatic activity in 1872, Yohannis continued,

---

surveyed the battlefield. He therefore had as good opportunities as anyone to reconstruct what had happened. Reporting in absolute numbers, rather than in companies and batteries as Sarzec did, Dye (pp. 136–41) estimated 800–1,000 Egyptians killed, and Russ (*Petermann*, 1877, p. 158) 1,000–1,200, less 80 prisoners of war. Stanton's first report from Cairo (FO 881/3058, p. 9, to Derby, 25 Nov. 1875) mentioned 2,000 dead. Sarzec's figures for the Ethiopian casualties are extremely low but so are Dye's later ones. Russ has no estimates for these. The Egyptian government reported publicly a full day's battle with about 800 Egyptians and 15,000 Ethiopians killed, using the figure for the first encounter as if it covered the whole battle and then grossly exaggerating the length of the battle and the number of Ethiopian casualties. It is highly doubtful that the Ethiopians could even have brought as many as 15,000 into action in the short time and limited space available in the valley.

150 AECP, Massouah 4, fol. 42, Yohannis to Sarzec, 18 Nov. 1875, copied in French in Sarzec to Decazes, 24 Dec. 1875.
151 BN, Ethiop. 259, fols 46–7.
152 *Petermann*, 1877, p. 158; Dye, *Moslem Egypt*, pp. 136–41.
153 Douin, *Ismaïl*, III, 3B, p. 789; Dye, *Moslem Egypt*, p. 146. Two British travellers and commercial adventurers, A. B. and W. Houghton, who had arrived on the eve of the battle of Gundet and were present there and at Addī Qwala, claimed (*PP. Commons*, 1877, LXXXVIII, pp. 333–4, to Derby, 24 May 1876) that they had strongly advised against an attack because it would have hurt many Europeans and Indians. See also FO 78/2500, fols 59–61, Stanton to Derby, 15 Jan. 1876, on the Houghtons.
154 AECP, Massouah 4, fols 43–4, Sarzec to Decazes, 24 Dec. 1875. Sarzec's conversation with Yohannis on 6 December clearly indicates that the King had not yet heard of the death of Munzinger and Birru in Awsa. Cf. Dye, *Moslem Egypt*, p. 147.

'Then, in order to prevent my writing again, he tears to pieces and throws into the sea not only the letters that are sent by me but the letters that come to me from abroad . . . I have no outlet so I cannot write to you. The door is closed to me. But he writes saying that I have committed sins which I have not committed and done what I have not done.' Mahdere Qal added on his own authority, '. . . and also he puts unseemly [sic] in newspapers, which is easy for him'. Once more Yohannis appealed to the British government to look into his conflict with Ismail and 'make us remain in our places. Let me not be less than my fathers, the kings who lived before me; let him not be greater than his fathers who lived before him.' If the British government did not do this, he felt that Ismail would attack again, and then what could he do but defend his country which would mean further bloodshed.[155] The fate of this very letter illustrates Yohannis's communication problem. He again chose Kirkham as his emissary, but although the general was escorting more than 100 released Egyptian prisoners (according to Yohannis, all those who wanted to return) he was himself arrested and died after six months' detention at Massawa. So the letter reached England only in May 1877, and some other letters, which Kirkham surrendered when he was arrested, never seem to have reached their destination at all.[156]

One letter which was forwarded properly was Yohannis's message to Ismail himself. In this the King emphasized that he had shown much patience, refraining from action against 'Satan' Munzinger in 1872 and against Arendrup's troops until they were very close to his capital Adwa. When he finally reacted, however, 'the God of Justice gave them into our hands. In the combat they were unable to last more than one hour.' In conclusion, Yohannis appealed to the khedive to respect the former boundaries, using the argument 'you are not greater than your fathers, and we are not less than our fathers'.[157] Ismail disagreed. His new army was already on its way.

The task of punishing King Yohannis and restoring Egyptian prestige was entrusted to the sirdar (commander-in-chief) of the Egyptian army, Muhammad Ratib Pasha, with General Loring, an American, as chief-of-staff and second in command. All the senior members of the general staff were in fact either Americans, including two colonels, William McE. Dye and Charles W. Field, or Europeans, while the senior commanding officers were Turks. Ismail's son Prince Hasan joined the expedition in late December. Twelve (later increased to sixteen) infantry battalions, one cavalry regiment, four batteries of field and mountain guns and one rocket battery, about 15,000 men, were placed at their disposal, and Ratib was told in his instructions, dated 5 December 1875, that he would immediately receive whatever additional troops he found neces-

155 FO 78/2632, fol. 100, Yohannis to Victoria, 7 Dec. 1875, from the Amharic original, except the comment about the newspapers from Mahdere Qal's translation on fols 95–96a.
156 ibid., fol. 93, Vivian to Derby, 2 May 1877; FO 78/2500, fols 59–61, Stanton to Derby, 15 Jan. 1876; FO 78/2503, fols 141–2, Cookson to Derby, 22 Jul. 1876; ENA, Soudan, Carton 5/1/12, Kirkham to Ahmad Nachat, 18 Dec. 1875; PP. Commons, 1877, LXXXIII, pp. 334–5, Houghton and Houghton to Derby, 26 May 1876; p. 340, Lister to Houghton, 17 Nov. 1876; Douin, Ismaïl, III, 3B, pp. 851–6.
157 ENA, Bahr Barra, Carton 19, no. 137, Yohannis to Ismail, 13 Dec. 1875.

sary. Under no circumstances was he to advance with insufficient forces. Beyond the punishment of Yohannis through the crushing of his army, the aims of the expedition were again rather vague or ambiguous. If Yohannis retreated, Ratib should occupy Adwa and press for negotiations. If the King did not come forward, Ratib should 'hit Adwa with a contribution' and promise to return the following year. No attempts should be spared to excite unrest and rebellion among Yohannis's vassals or to turn the population away from their immediate chiefs.[158]

Ismail continued to display his usual confidence, but he was now aware that his Ethiopian adventure entailed more risks than he had foreseen. No sooner had he dispatched the news about Gundet to Munzinger instructing him not to advance beyond Awsa and to be extra careful in view of possible repercussions, than he received the news about Munzinger's own defeat and death.[159] Ra'uf had problems of his own with rebellious Galla around Harer.[160] For the time being not only Awsa but the headwaters of the Blue Nile and the Juba had to be written off.[161] Whether or not there was any kind of understanding between Yohannis and the Danakil sultans, as assumed later, is impossible to establish.[162] The most serious setback, however, was Gundet. Ismail decided to give priority to the elimination of the spirit of independence and defiance manifested by Yohannis and the Tigreans generally. A potential ally, hopefully, was Minīlik.

The day after he had issued his orders to Ratib, Ismail sent a new letter via Zeyla to Minīlik. He reviewed the events in Awsa, where Minīlik's envoy, Ras (former Aleqa) Birru, had lost his life together with Munzinger, and in the north. He promised that the Danakil would receive punishment in due time since Egypt was not prepared to leave them in a state of rebellion. As for Yohannis, a strong army of 15,000 men which could easily be increased to 20,000 or 25,000 had been sent to Massawa 'to inflict an exemplary punishment on him for the acts which he had committed'. This done, Egypt had no intention, wrote Ismail, of taking possession of Abyssinia and therefore 'in case you should then find yourself at Adwa and establish yourself there, we would be very happy to establish these conditions [for peace] with you, because in our opinion you are more worthy and more fit than others to take possession of this kingdom . . .' Ismail asked for Minīlik's reply as a matter of urgency.[163] The Shewan ruler received the letter in January 1876—and decided to ignore it. Instead the Egyptians received reports that Minīlik had sent envoys and a cavalry force to Yohannis.[164]

There was some concern in European diplomatic circles, mainly for financial

158 Douin, *Ismaïl*, III, 3B, pp. 815–20, 826–8, 832–9.
159 ibid., III, 3B, pp. 802–21.
160 ENA, Registre 10, Ordres supérieurs, p. 32, Ismail to Abu Bakr, 6 Dec. 1875; FO 881/3058, pp. 18–19, 21, Schneider to Salisbury, 3 Dec. and 17 Dec. 1875.
161 FO 78/3188, fol. 385, Stanton to Derby, 5 Dec. 1875.
162 Gabriel Simon, *Voyage en Abyssinie et chez les Galla-Raias. L'Éthiopie, ses mœurs, ses traditions, le Négouss Iohannès, les églises monolithes de Lalibéla* (Paris, 1885), p. 117.
163 Douin, *Ismaïl*, III, 3B, pp. 821–4.
164 ibid., III, 3B, pp. 898, 1047. In the reports, the cavalry force was said to amount to 500–600 men. Afewerq (*Minīlik*, p. 24) maintained that Minīlik had sent 2,000 men.

reasons, about the size of the planned operations; the British in particular, informed as usual at an early stage, were concerned that Ismail's 'financial credit will be seriously impaired by useless and distant wars'. At the very moment when Ismail was requesting British assistance to reorganize his finances, this was an important consideration. But the British government renewed its commitment not to interfere, and with Kirkham detained, Ismail had no problem selling his side of the story: the only purpose of the new expedition was to restore the prestige of his government; after the humiliation inflicted on him, he could not be expected to take the first step towards a peaceful solution and Yohannis refused to do so; the estimated cost of the expedition was only £500,000, but even if it would cost double, the preservation of his African possessions was certainly worth that amount?[165]

Ratib's expedition was not only well planned and well equipped. Maps and other valuable information were systematically supplied by the Roman Catholic missionaries, Duflot in particular. As a result Ratib chose a more easterly route than Arendrup. Every attempt was made to win allies among the Ethiopians. In phrases which call to mind Napier's proclamation in 1867, Ratib stressed that the war was directed against Yohannis personally, 'the oppressor . . . who tyrannizes the human race'. The governors were invited to take the opportunity of negotiating individual agreements with Egypt and restore the political independence which they had enjoyed before Tēwodros unified Abyssinia. The proclamation was allegedly in such poor Amharic that no one could understand it. Nevertheless, disaffection on a large scale was reported from Hamasēn, including overtures from Yohannis's new governor there, Dejjazmach Welde Mīka'ēl.[166] The new Egyptian army advanced cautiously into the interior, erecting fortifications and securing its lines of communication with great care. By the end of January Ratib had reached Gura c. 40 kilometres south-east of Asmera which was as far as he ever got.[167] It was only half as far as Arendrup had penetrated. But, contrary to the original expectations of the Egyptians, Yohannis advanced to meet them at a place which gave them the advantage of having reached the plateau without having moved too far from their base at Massawa.

It is not likely that Yohannis placed much hope in his appeals to London and Cairo after the battle of Gundet. In mid-December he visited Inderta to rally support in his real home area, and probably to explore the attitude of his

165 FO 78/2403, Derby to Stanton, 3 Dec. and 17 Dec. 1875; FO 78/2405, fols 46–8, 93–4, 123–7, Stanton to Derby, 27 Nov., 18 Dec., and 29 Dec. 1875; see also AECP, Égypte 56, fols 482–6, Pellissier to Decazes, 13 Dec. 1875; fols 488–90, Decazes to Pellissier, 16 Dec. 1875. Cave (*PP. Commons*, 1876, LXXXIII, p. 111) estimated the cost at £1 million but this was before the outcome of the battle of Gura was known and the ultimate cost must have been much higher.

166 Douin, *Ismaïl*, III, 3B, pp. 818, n. 1, 839–50, 878–80, 889–95; AECP, Massouah 4, fol. 53, Decazes to Carbonnel, 15 Jan. 1876. On Duflot's contributions, in particular, see Loring, *Confederate Soldier*, pp. 335–6, 379–80. It is also Loring (ibid., pp. 385–6) who provides an amusing account of the attempts of Yohannis and his court to understand Ratib's proclamation.

167 Douin, *Ismaïl*, III, 3B, pp. 860–78.

governors in Wag and Yejju as well. Alerted by Welde Mīka'ēl that the Egyptians were again invading the highlands, he returned to Adwa about 1 February 1876.[168] He summoned Welde Mīka'ēl to his camp at Īyyeha: 'Come by swift marches; do not rest, do not sleep. It is by [the road of] Ṣerēna that he [Ratib or the army] has come.' Instead of obeying orders, Welde Mīka'ēl went over to the enemy. He must have felt that the Egyptians would win and wanted to make sure that he would keep the governorship of Hamasēn. The Egyptians made him a pasha and promised him additional districts as well.[169]

By mid-February Yohannis had collected his forces south of the Mereb and on the nineteenth he crossed the valley to Gundet and Addī Qwala. By and large, the population had obeyed the call to come forward and defend their country and their faith. To the vast majority of the Ethiopians this was a religious war, a battle against the descendants of Hagar, the Ismailites, Moabites, and Edomites, who had come from across the sea to destroy God's people.[170] This time the mobilization also went beyond Tigrē though it is doubtful whether any *sizeable* contingents from outside Tigrē actually turned up.[171] *Before* the Gura campaign, Sarzec and Franz Hassen, who certainly belonged to the best-informed Europeans at the time, told the Egyptians that Yohannis could mobilize 60,000–70,000 men, about one tenth of these with firearms. These numbers presumably included contingents from Begēmdir and Gojjam since the possibility of 30,000 additional troops from Wello and Shewa is mentioned. Kirkham may have wanted to confuse and scare the Egyptian officers by figures varying from 60,000 to 150,000 (with as many as 30,000 with firearms) 'and the rest of the population carrying clubs'.[172] *After* the battle Colonel Dye estimated the Ethiopian fighting force at Gura at 45,000–50,000 men, stressing that it was 'by far the lowest estimate made by anyone who was in a position to judge'. A medical doctor, who had been taken prisoner by the Ethiopians, reported that the camp held about 60,000 combatants of a total of 100,000, but higher, clearly inflated figures were also mentioned.[173]

For a few days in early March Yohannis seemed to hesitate to attack the Egyptians who had more than 11,000 men with forty cannon and ten rocket-

168 ibid., III, 3B, pp. 841–4, 858–9, 876–7.

169 ENA, Bahr Barra, Carton 19, no. 138, Yohannis to Welde Mīka'ēl, 4 Feb. 1876; no. 10, Welde Mīka'ēl to Ratib, Hasan, Loring, and Osman, n.d.; Douin, *Ismaïl*, III, 3B, 889–92; Dye, *Moslem Egypt*, pp. 283–5.

170 'Histoire', *RS*, 21, pp. 183–4.

171 Aleqa Lemlem (BN, Ethiop. 259, fols 20–2) seems to contradict himself when he first stresses how Ras Adal decided to go to the assistance of Yohannis, whatever Ras Welde Sillasē (Wereñña) and others did, and then condemns all except the Tigreans for having stayed at home. The attitude of Yohannis towards his vassals immediately after the war certainly indicates that some were regarded as supporters, others as enemies (Ethiop. 259, pp. 22–3). See also Dye, *Moslem Egypt*, pp. 291–2.

172 Douin, *Ismaïl*, III, 3B, pp. 858–9. Cf. Loring, *Confederate Soldier*, p. 348, with Dye, *Moslem Egypt*, p. 395.

173 Dye, *Moslem Egypt*, pp. 395–6; Loring, *Confederate Soldier*, pp. 410, 438–9. The most exaggerated figure, 250,000 combatants, was produced by the commander-in-chief explaining his defeat (Douin, *Ismaïl*, III, 3B, pp. 940–1).

stands in fortified positions at Gura and Kayakor. Some 5,000 additional troops were on their way to the two forts, and actually arrived at Kayakor during the first day of the battle and the following night. At first Yohannis acted as if he intended to bypass Gura, and the Egyptians began to fear that the Ethiopians might strike at the weaker position Kayakor or even cut the communication lines north of both forts.[174] Probably Yohannis was insufficiently informed about the position on the Egyptian side; probably he wanted to stake everything on a major battle rather than prolong the problems of finding sufficient provisions and water for his large army.

At any rate, on 7 March the Ethiopians moved in between the two forts but so much closer to Kayakor that Ratib felt obliged to march out and engage them in the open field. The Ethiopians advanced in five columns: 1. towards Kayakor; 2. into the gap which still remained between Ratib's right wing (or most advanced position) and the other fort; 3. towards the right wing of the Egyptian army; 4. towards the Egyptian centre; 5. towards the Egyptian left. At 1.30 on 7 March the battle was joined. In spite of the far superior fire power of Egyptian Remingtons, Krupp guns and rocket-stands, the Ethiopians kept on coming, turned the right flank of the Egyptians and forced the latter into a retreat towards Gura which soon developed into a *sauve qui peut*. The Ethiopians pursued the Egyptians until the few survivors escaped to the security within the walls of the fort. Out of seven Egyptian battalions (between 5,000 and 6,000 men), not more than 400–600 men returned safe and sound; 1,300–1,600 wounded managed to save themselves under cover of the darkness. But three to four hours of fighting had cost the Egyptians around 3,500 dead and captured; all the cannon brought into the action were abandoned to the Ethiopians who also captured thousands of rifles. For fear that the Ethiopians would attack him, too, the commander at Kayakor refrained from joining the battle though part of it took place within gunshot of the fort.[175]

For two days after the main battle, i.e. 8 and 9 March, the Ethiopians besieged and attacked the Gura fort. The decimated defenders barely succeeded in keeping off the Ethiopians. But the efforts of the latter to return the artillery fire from the fort with the guns captured from the Egyptians were unsuccessful. The Ethiopians suffered incomparably heavier losses than the Egyptians in these two days, and in the afternoon of 9 March the siege was lifted. In all three days of

---

174 Douin, *Ismaïl*, III, 3B, pp. 902, 909–16, 943–4.
175 ibid., III, 3B, pp. 921–44, 954, 1016; FO 78/2631, fols 86–7, Vivian to Derby, 23 Jan. 1877. Douin's account of the battle is based primarily on the narratives of Dye and Loring. Ratib in his report (ENA, Abdin, Carton 160, to Ismail, 10 Mar. 1875) gave few details of the battle, concentrating on the condemnation of his American staff officers: '. . . I declare that General Loring and his staff are alone responsible for the fate which was in store for us.' The Turkish-American recrimination was mutual. See, for instance, Loring, *Confederate Soldier*, pp. 360, 402–3, 411–12, 418–20. But an unsigned letter (ENA, Soudan et Afrique Orientale, Casier 120/73) dated 15 May from Dye(?) to 'My dear friend'—almost certainly General Stone, the highest-ranking American at headquarters in Cairo—indicates internal criticism in the general staff too: 'Vacillation and incompetency . . . imbecility is perhaps more charitable . . . you must cut off a number of heads. General L.'s doings on field have lost him all confidence . . . and the other poor devil [Ratib?] is a child in battle . . .'

fighting the Ethiopians had reportedly lost 3,500–4,000 dead and about 1,000 wounded, no prisoners of war. Thus the casualties in the three-day battle were quite evenly distributed.[176]

In spite of the failure of the siege, the battle of Gura, though less decisive than that of Gundet, was clearly a major Ethiopian victory. It was not a defeated army that withdrew having captured fifteen to twenty cannon and thousands of first-class rifles.[177] In view of their declared aims with the campaign, Gura meant a terrific setback for the Egyptians. All new instructions were concerned with defence, not attack, and great efforts were made to conceal the truth. Ismail even instructed Ratib to send some messengers who were to report to the khedive in the presence of Europeans that the Ethiopian losses were 35,000 men or more.[178] There were speculations that Yohannis withdrew because of desertions in his army, and assertions that he had sued for peace.[179] It is more likely that difficulties of provisioning for the army called for a withdrawal, and it was an Egyptian officer, Ratib's secretary and *de facto* adjutant general, Muhammad Rifat Bey, who actually initiated the peace negotiations as early as 8 March.[180]

Negotiations in the Aftermath of Gura

Yohannis's first response to Muhammad Rifat's cease-fire proposal was a letter to Hasan Pasha in which the King reviewed the causes of the clashes:

> Your armies have attacked our territory . . . You have come with your armies and have constructed fortifications on our territory . . . *If you desire to open negotiations* with this aim [a cease-fire] *you should send us a delegate or let us know* so that we can send you one on our part.

Ratib replied that he accepted negotiations and asked Yohannis for a delegate. To this the King responded with a request that the Egyptians return to Egypt and a promise to restore the prisoners of war. Ratib was of course not authorized to evacuate and feigned surprise that Yohannis could propose this as long as the conditions for future friendship had not been agreed. [181]

176 Douin, *Ismaïl*, III, 3B, pp. 944–55; Loring, *Confederate Soldier*, pp. 424–7, 434; Dye, *Moslem Egypt*, p. 397.
177 FO 78/2503, fols 7–8, Stanton to Derby, 13 May 1876, reporting that some 10,000 Egyptian survivors passing Suez carried rusty old muskets or no arms at all though they had been equipped with Remingtons when they left.
178 Douin, *Ismaïl*, III, 3B, pp. 951, 956–67. Prince Hasan, at least, complied with a cable reporting 40,000–50,000 Ethiopian casualties (ibid., p. 980).
179 ibid., III, 3B, pp. 955, 978–80; FO 78/2501, fol. 49, Stanton to Derby, 13 Mar. 1876: 'Have just received information that . . . the Abyssinians have been totally routed with heavy loss, and a letter has been received by Prince Hassan from the King asking for peace.'
180 Dye, *Moslem Egypt*, pp. 431–2; Loring, *Confederate Soldier*, pp. 360, 434; Douin, *Ismaïl*, III, 3B, p. 973.
181 Douin, *Ismaïl*, III, 3B, pp. 976–8 (my emphasis). The correspondence between Yohannis and the Egyptians before 15 April is only available in Ratib's reports to Cairo quoted at length by Douin.

The King did not even bother to reply to this, and so Muhammad Rifat and Ratib were obliged to take a new initiative one week later (20 March). But Yohannis would have nothing of Ratib's attempts to explain away Arendrup's and his own expeditions as peaceful enterprises:

> You say that you have come here to examine the aggression committed against your emissaries at Gundet . . . We answer you: O you, great and illustrous men, to whom God has given great intelligence to discern between good and evil, were the emissaries to whom you refer ten or twenty in number and have they come to examine the situation? Is it we who have beaten them because of their small number, or is it not rather so that they were a big army who attacked and penetrated into our kingdom, without any authorization on our part?

After accusing Ratib of having deposed and appointed governors in Ethiopia and of having induced Welde Mīka'ēl to betray his king, Yohannis finally came to his conditions: Reaffirm the ties of friendship which existed before the days of Munzinger and return to your country.[182]

Ratib must have found that he could not win this battle of words and decided to send a delegate, Ali al-Rubi, to Yohannis with Egypt's specific peace conditions. These were: (1) restitution of the arms lost by the Egyptians in the two battles; (2) repatriation of the prisoners of war; (3) free trade between the two countries. Yohannis replied that if the Egyptians really wanted peace, they should restore Bogos to Ethiopia and pay an indemnity for all losses sustained by Ethiopia since its annexation. As for the Egyptian conditions, Yohannis had already promised to repatriate the prisoners of war, and was all in favour of free trade. The captured arms, however, would remain where they were, that is, in the hands of his men. The King excused himself by saying that his chiefs were not willing to hand over the arms.[183] This may well have been true but in that case it was only a more polite way of saying *no*. It is inconceivable that Yohannis himself could have been willing to hand back the arms at the same session as he was demanding an indemnity for losses suffered![184]

To indicate that he was willing to continue the negotiations, Yohannis sent Liqemekwas Mircha Werqē with Ali al-Rubi to Ratib's camp (25 March). For about three weeks the restitution of the arms remained the main issue. The khedive declared that he would be satisfied with part of the arms. Yohannis allegedly became so angry with this foolish talk that he asked how he could possibly be requested to restore any arms as long as the Egyptians occupied Bogos—and Massawa! Ismail nevertheless persisted with advice on how to cajole or dupe Yohannis: if the King showed that he had the power to collect some of the arms from his men, for instance, he would be permitted to regard the others as a gift from the khedive. Ismail's stand on territorial possessions was, if possible, still more absurd. Yohannis should be informed that no Ethiopian

182 ibid., III, 3B, pp. 983–5.
183 ibid., III, 3B, pp. 986–7.
184 Not only Ismail and Ratib but American officers as well (Dye, *Moslem Egypt*, p. 398) seem to have believed that they had convinced Yohannis that he was bound to return the arms if he only could. This was most certainly an underestimation of Yohannis and his advisers.

troop movements could be tolerated in Hamasēn, 'an Egyptian province'.[185] Since Ratib's army had failed to reach Hamasēn and his ally Welde Mīka'ēl had fled the province, there was certainly nothing Ratib could do to prevent the movements of the Ethiopian army there, unless he started a major offensive.

In fact, there was no question of an offensive in spite of the reinforcements that had arrived. Ratib was about to abandon Gura and was afraid that Yohannis's army, which was only eight hours away, might attack him as soon as he left the fort. The Ethiopians had shown some impatience with the delays. Ratib, therefore, wanted to break the deadlock in the negotiations before he undertook the transfer from one fort to the other. He proposed not to mention the restitution of arms or any frontier problems but simply negotiate a treaty of friendship, commerce, and postal relations. Ismail agreed on condition that it was not mentioned anywhere in the document that the agreement was signed on the instructions or on behalf of the khedive. In other words, he wanted to be free to disavow the agreement if he found this to his advantage. Mircha and Ali were sent back to Yohannis on 18 April, the latter with instructions to hold up the negotiations sufficiently to give time for the evacuation of the Gura fort. The plan succeeded and made it possible for Ratib to repatriate some of his troops in the interest of economy.[186]

In the meantime a treaty establishing peace and friendship, trade, and postal relations between the two countries was drafted in Yohannis's camp and sealed by the King. Except for the fact that neither side wanted renewed fighting, the agreement was clearly of more importance to Ethiopia than Egypt.[187] When the negotiators returned to Ratib on 23 April, they brought with them 214 prisoners of war, including seven officers. With these in safety and the evacuation successfully completed, Ratib decided to disavow *his* delegate Ali al-Rubi and not sign the treaty either. If he signed, he felt he would be obliged to evacuate the remaining fortified positions which he had established on Ethiopian territory, and he wanted Egypt to have something to show for the costs in lives and money of his expedition. He therefore suggested to Ismail that the signing could be postponed indefinitely on the pretext that Yohannis had not returned the arms and *all* the prisoners. The khedive agreed and insisted that the treaty should not be signed as long as a single prisoner of war remained in Ethiopian hands.[188]

If Yohannis felt that he had been cheated into handing over the captives present in his camp or understood that the Egyptians were backing out of the agreement altogether, he did not reveal it immediately. To begin with, he did

---

185 Douin, *Ismaïl*, III, 3B, pp. 988–90, 998–1000. It was probably this reference to Massawa that gave rise to reports that the cession of Massawa was Yohannis's first condition for peace (AEMD, Afrique 62, fols 204–9, Cazaux to Decazes, 23 Apr. 1876). From the point of view of prestige the emphasis on the restitution of the arms is understandable; see above p. 329.

186 Douin, *Ismaïl*, III, 3B, pp. 1001–9; ENA, Bahr Barra, Carton 19, nos 140 and 141, Yohannis to Ratib, 15 Apr. and 17 Apr. 1875.

187 Douin, *Ismaïl*, III, 3B, pp. 1011–12; ENA, Bahr Barra, Carton 19, no. 162, Yohannis to Ratib, 23 Apr. 1876.

188 Douin, *Ismaïl*, III, 3B, pp. 1012–15.

not regard prisoners of war as something to bargain with, as he clearly showed after the battle of Gundet when he released all who wanted to leave and sent them to Massawa without any prior negotiations. Those who remained behind that time were only some 'slaves', i.e. Sudanese soldiers, who had refused to return because, as they reportedly said, 'We were bought with money and this was originally our country and no other'.[189] Secondly, all the surviving captives taken at Gura had been returned and the remaining Gundet group, according to Ratib himself, was only thirty-five persons.[190] Yohannis declared that he had already sent for them and would hand them over to anyone delegated by Ratib to receive them. Even Na'ib Muhammad Abd al-Rahim who was not a prisoner of war but 'a traitor to both sides', as Yohannis expressed it, would be released as evidence that the new friendship was sincerely meant.[191]

There was, of course, no way in which Ratib could be satisfied. In early May, he proposed to demand from Yohannis that all the arms, clothes, money, and other property taken from any of the prisoners be restored and that the Ethiopians pay the expenses of the war and in particular blood money for the soldiers massacred immediately after the battle 'under the pretext that the Egyptian government would be obliged to allocate a pension to their families'. This caused Ismail to warn Ratib not to provoke an attack unless he was sure that Yohannis was too weak to stage one. By then the King and his envoy were losing patience. Mircha, who had been detained in the Egyptian camp waiting for Ratib's signature to the treaty, requested his leave on 8 May in no uncertain terms. When he was finally allowed to leave, he took with him Ratib's condition for signing: every single prisoner of war must be repatriated before he could sign the peace agreement.[192] In spite of his earlier disappointments, Yohannis decided to ask once more for European mediation, and an Ethiopian courier managed to smuggle out a letter to the French president in his shoe.[193]

The double standard was, however, so glaring that Yohannis must have arrived at the conclusion that Ratib was not sincere. The release of Abd al-Rahim, for instance, caused no words of appreciation: as an 'envoy' he should never have been arrested in the first place. Whether he was an envoy or a spy when he arrived at Adwa a few days before the battle of Gundet and whether he intended to change sides again or not after having assisted the Egyptians as far as Addī Qwala are complicated questions with no clear answers. Even on the Egyptian side, it was admitted that Abd al-Rahim had some years earlier treacherously transferred his Ethiopian fief of Aylet to Egypt for money and Yohannis called him a double traitor.[194] Kirkham's case, on the other hand, was fairly simple. He had been sent to Massawa after the battle was over,

189   ENA, Bahr Barra, Carton 19, no. 137, Yohannis to Ismail, 13 Dec. 1875.
190   Douin, *Ismaïl*, III, 3B, p. 1016.
191   ENA, Bahr Barra, Carton 19, nos 142–3, Yohannis to Ratib, 28 Apr. and 5 May 1876.
      Douin, *Ismaïl*, III, 3B, pp. 1020–1.
192   Douin, *Ismaïl*, III, 3B, pp. 1021–2, 1026.
193   AED, Protocole C41, Yohannis to Mac Mahon, 3 May 1876, with covering letter, Mailly to
      Mac Mahon, 22 Jun. 1876.
194   Douin, *Ismaïl*, III, 3B, pp. 758, 768–9, 1021; Dye, *Moslem Egypt,* p. 124.

escorting Egyptian captives back to their own base and carrying letters both to Khedive Ismail and to European governments.[195] Nevertheless, it was in vain that Yohannis appealed for the release of his envoy who was seriously ill at Massawa. Ratib had allegedly threatened to 'keep poor Kirkham in prison until finally he should be compelled to feed upon the insects he bred upon his person'. In fact, the governor of Massawa received instructions from Cairo (7 May) to offer Kirkham, who had complained that he did not receive sufficient food, every kind of liquor he wanted, 'to which you shall add a strong dose of pure alcohol'. Six weeks later, Yohannis's general and ambassador reportedly died in delirium tremens.[196]

The question of Welde Mīka'ēl and Hamasēn was an additional cause for irritation. Welde Mīka'ēl had ravaged Hamasēn after the battle of Gura and fled to the lowlands around Aylet.[197] The Egyptians, who did not dare to act themselves, were arming and encouraging him in the hope that he would capture Hamasēn for them as soon as Yohannis returned to Adwa. The attitude of Yohannis on this matter was clear. He had reappointed as governor Welde Mīka'ēl's rival in Hamasēn, Dejjazmach Haylu of Ṣe'azega. Yohannis did not mind losing a governor who had repeatedly been disloyal to him, but the Egyptian government who had accepted the traitor's services would now be held responsible that he did not disturb the peace. It is hardly a coincidence that Yohannis, who otherwise avoided directly pressing for Ratib's signature, did so precisely in the letter concerning Welde Mīka'ēl.[198]

Throughout the negotiations it was taken for granted by Yohannis that both armies would be withdrawn from the frontier as soon as the treaty was signed and that he would, therefore, be able to send home his peasant-warriors to plough and sow in time before the big rains started in June. This explains both his eagerness to collect the scattered prisoners and his irritation over Ratib's insistence that not one remain behind. He had warned Ratib not to allow small matters to prevent the establishment of peace. When he was about to return to Adwa on 30 May, he felt that Ratib had succeeded in doing precisely that.[199]

As soon as Yohannis had returned to Adwa (1 June) and dismissed most of his troops, Ratib began to plan an advance into Hamasēn and the construction of a fortified position there like the one which he had retained with diminished

195 See above, p. 324.
196 ENA, Bahr Barra, Carton 19, no. 145, Yohannis to Ratib, 20 May 1876; Loring, *Confederate Soldier*, p. 348; Douin, *Ismaïl*, III, 3B, pp. 1018–20. Yohannis claimed later in a letter published by his representative in London (FO 407/11, pp. 19–20) that Kirkham had been poisoned.
197 ENA, Bahr Barra, Carton 19, nos 7 and 53, Welde Mīka'ēl to Ratib, n.d.
198 ibid., no. 144, Yohannis to Ratib, 12 May 1876. Welde Mīka'ēl's relations with the Egyptians in March and April 1876 are documented in a number of original letters (ibid., nos 6, 53, 139, 157, to Ratib, Hasan, and other Egyptian officers, n.d.). See also Douin, *Ismaïl*, III, 3B, pp. 982, 996–7, 1024–5, and, for an earlier conflict between Welde Mīka'ēl and Yohannis, above p. 278.
199 Cf. Yohannis to Ratib, 28 Apr. with 30 May 1876 (Bahr Barra, Carton 19, nos 142 and 147).

forces at Kayakor. Ismail did not agree because he did not want a new confrontation with Yohannis. Instead he advised Ratib to furnish Welde Mīka'ēl with arms and money and send him with troops of his own against Haylu. This should be done in such a way that no one would know that Welde Mīka'ēl had acted with Egyptian approval; after Welde Mīka'ēl had captured Haylu, Ratib should write him a letter disapproving his invasion of Hamasēn—for form's sake. In this way it would be possible, Ismail thought, to renew the peace negotiations at the same time.[200]

This time Ali al-Rubi, who had been to Cairo to report, was the bearer of gifts and a letter from the khedive to Yohannis. He was met by his old acquaintance Mircha and escorted to Adwa, where he arrived on 8 July. But his mission was bound to fail. Once again Ismail wanted the captured arms back; in addition, Yohannis should pay an indemnity to cover Egypt's expenses for the war and guarantee the security of the future boundaries by ceding territory, at least Hamasēn, possibly up to the Mereb. In all probability Ismail's letter was not as explicit as his instructions and this led Yohannis to suspect that Ali and Ratib were themselves major obstacles to peace. At any rate, the negotiations were soon over. The King decided to explore the situation by sending a delegate of his own to Cairo, and carried out his decision in a way which offended Ratib.[201]

In the meantime Welde Mīka'ēl invaded Hamasēn and defeated and killed Haylu at Wekī Dibba near Ṣe'azega on 17 July. It was a close battle with many killed on both sides, including one of Welde Mīka'ēl's own sons. That this battle, fought between closely related families and neighbours in Hamasēn, would cause much bitterness was to be expected. In addition, Welde Mīka'ēl was surprised and dismayed to find his action condemned by Ratib: Had he not become the enemy of his king to please the Egyptians; had he not carried out the instructions and fulfilled the desires of the sirdar himself; had he not refused an amnesty and a governorship offered by Yohannis after Gura? He swore 'by the Church and the Cross which is in it' that he had turned down the offer with the words 'The water which has been poured out will not flow back into the jug'. Had he not received the title of ras from Ratib himself? And now the Abyssinians had started to call him Hajj Welde Mīka'ēl. There was much bitterness in this for the head of one of Hamasēn's leading Christian families. Nevertheless, since Ratib was his 'master', he would not say 'God judge you' but 'God stands between you and me'.[202] The extent to which Welde Mīka'ēl was, in fact, carrying out the will of Ratib is best illustrated by the proposals of the commander three days before the battle of Wekī Dibba to abandon Kayakor, which was found difficult to maintain, in favour of three fortified positions in Hamasēn: Asmera, Ṣe'azega, and Debarwa.[203]

200 Douin, Ismaïl, III, 3B, pp. 1028–32.
201 ibid., III, 3B, pp. 1033–5, 1038, 1041; ENA, Bahr Barra, Carton 19, Yohannis to Ratib, 26 Jun. and 18 Jul. 1876, where the increasing distrust is quite evident.
202 ENA, Bahr Barra, Carton 19, nos 7 and 8, Welde Mīka'ēl to Ratib, n.d. See also MT, 1876, p. 105, Pettersson, 26 Jul. 1876; Douin, Ismaïl, III, 3B, pp. 1036–7.
203 Douin, Ismaïl, III, 3B, pp. 1043–5.

All desire to revenge Gundet and Gura with *Egyptian* troops had died. In spite of Welde Mīka'ēl's victory, no Egyptian forces were moved to Hamasēn. Reports that an Ethiopian army was about to attack his ally caused Ratib to abandon the plans. It was only in Cairo that the Egyptian army was in possession of Hamasēn.[204] When the rains were over in September, Yohannis sent two armies to Akkele Guzay and Hamasēn respectively. Ratib abandoned Kayakor in hot haste, and Welde Mīka'ēl fled to Bogos with the army of about 1,500 which he had built up, leaving the Ethiopians in unchallenged possession of those border provinces. Not satisfied with this, Yohannis crossed the *de facto* boundaries created in 1872–73. He personally led an Ethiopian army as far as Keren without, however, attacking the fort. Welde Mīka'ēl refused to accept an amnesty and retreated farther north to Halhal, but Yohannis had the satisfaction of seeing some other minor chiefs return to the Ethiopian fold. Both Ratib and Ismail were sufficiently shocked to fear an attack on Massawa. Yohannis, however, appointed Shīaleqa Alula *ras* and governor of Hamasēn, and returned to Adwa at the beginning of November. The Egyptians continued to evacuate their positions inland. All efforts were concentrated on fortifying Massawa. Financial considerations and Ethiopian refusals to supply the town dictated a repatriation of the bulk of the Egyptian army. Finally in January 1877 the commander was authorized to return to Cairo and the war was ostensibly over.[205]

The total losses for Egypt were reported, by Munzinger's old friend Franz Hassen, as 12,000–15,000 men, 39 cannon, 15,000 rifles, and 40,000 camels and mules.[206] These figures are much higher than the totals reported from the two battles. Even if one takes into account those who deserted or died in skirmishes, from illness, etc., the losses are probably inflated. Nevertheless, with the exception of the transport animals, it was something very different from the march to Meqdela.

The Gordon Negotiations

In two battles, at Gundet and Gura, the Ethiopians had won the war. To win the peace turned out to be a long and complicated process, lasting seven full years. In the meantime a precarious state of 'no peace, no war' with occasional concessions from either side was maintained. The reasons for this are not difficult to discern. The Ethiopians were not overly concerned with the *formality* of a treaty. Whenever negotiations began, however, Yohannis stubbornly maintained certain points: Ethiopia was the aggrieved party; occupied territory should be restored; Ethiopia's access to the sea should be guaranteed. Egypt was unwilling to concede any of this, preferred the status quo in most respects

204 ibid., III, 3B, pp. 1055, 1063–5; FO 78/2503, Cookson to Derby, 7 Aug. 1876.
205 Douin, *Ismaïl*, III, 3B, pp. 1072–7, 1082–5, 1088–9, 1093–4. Important supplementary material on the last phase is found in AECP, Massouah 4, fols 59–62, Carbonnel to Decazes, 10 Dec., 26 Dec. 1876 and 12 Jan. 1877.
206 FO 78/2632, fols 174–84, Wylde to Derby, 23 Apr. 1877. Sabry (*L'empire égyptien sous Ismaïl*, p. 471) accepts these figures without reservations.

and was only concerned whenever there seemed to be a risk that serious fighting might break out again.

Suspicious and disgusted with Ratib and Ali al-Rubi, Yohannis had sent a delegate of his own to Cairo in July 1876 in the hope that this would facilitate negotiations. On instructions from Cairo, Blatta (also Basha) Gebre Igzi'abihēr was allowed to proceed to Egypt, but as soon as he arrived there he was placed under house arrest and nothing more was heard from him for two and a half months. He finally managed to contact the French and British representatives in Cairo, and after several appeals, he was released and returned to Massawa and Adwa with a condescending note which did not even mention the peace negotiations.[207]

The terms Yohannis offered through Gebre Igzi'abihēr were kept secret. Probably Ismail found them so humiliating that he preferred to pretend that they had never been mentioned and imprisoned the envoy to prevent him from talking about them, or the disastrous defeats suffered by the Egyptians.[208] Be that as it may, the experience of Gebre Igzi'abihēr further deepened the conflict. The envoy compared the reception of Ali al-Rubi at Adwa—royal honours, music, decorations—with his own and concluded:

> An Envoy from nation to nation must go not only to those who know God and recognize laws, but also to those who know neither. He takes his message and returns, fearing nothing. But I have been kept in Cairo ninety-five days; the Khedive has not seen me or received my presents; so I ask you to obtain from him my liberty.[209]

Ever since the arrivals of the first Europeans in their country, the Ethiopians had heard much about international law, the inviolability of envoys, etc., and Yohannis was eager to comply.[210] But, somehow it always seemed to work against the Ethiopians, and Gebre Igzi'abihēr was not alone in wondering how one was to deal with someone who recognized neither God nor the law.

From the outset, Yohannis had asked for European mediation. In mid-December 1876, a French traveller and businessman, Pierre Arnoux, arrived in Cairo with the unmistakable message that Minīlik had no intention of becoming an instrument of Egyptian expansion at the expense of Ethiopia. He carried letters from Minīlik and a mandate to ask hard questions.[211] Ismail decided

207 Douin, Ismaïl, III, 3B, pp. 1053–4, 1090–2; FO 78/2631, fols 72–3, Vivian to Derby, 18 Jan. 1877.
208 It was in the autumn of 1876 that the full extent of the Egyptian losses became more generally known and led to exaggerated stories about the precarious situation of the Egyptians even at Massawa. See, for instance, FO 78/2503, fols 203–6, and 2504, fols 6–7, Vivian to Derby, 20 Oct. and 3 Nov. 1876, respectively.
209 FO 881/3192, p. 10, Gebre Igzi'abihēr to Vivian, 29 Nov. 1876. The whole incident of the envoy's detention and release is documented in this volume, pp. 7–11. Gebre Igzi'abihēr was Schimper's son-in-law (MT, 1878, p. 59) and an old hand in Ethiopian politics. For Yohannis's concern and later anger, see ENA, Bahr Barra, Carton 19, Yohannis to Ratib, 23 Oct. and 30 Oct. 1876; BM, Orient. 12913 (c), Yohannis to Gordon, 18 Jun. 1877.
210 AECP, Massouah 4, fols 59–60, Carbonnel to Decazes, 10 Dec. 1876.
211 FO 78/2631, fols 17–27, Vivian to Derby, 6 Jan. 1877, with copies of Minīlik's letter and power of attorney for Arnoux. See below, pp. 368–76 for Minīlik's role in the Ethio-Egyptian conflict generally.

to ignore Arnoux, but no doubt understood the implications. He quickly approved the idea put forward by the British consul general that he entrust his negotiations with Yohannis to a European officer. For the task, he chose one of his most loyal European employees, Colonel (later General) Gordon,[212] who was destined to play the role of chief negotiator until the end of 1879, when he resigned his post as governor general of the Sudan after the fall of Ismail. Soon after his arrival at Massawa in February 1877, he listed the conditions he intended to offer Yohannis as follows:

1. an armistice pending the final concluding of peace;
2. preservation of 'the ancient Frontiers';
3. free trade and free passage for envoys and letters through Massawa;
4. the right for Yohannis to import free of duties 50 pounds of gunpowder, 10 muskets, and 500 percussions caps annually;
5. the sanction of the khedive for the appointment of a new bishop for Ethiopia;
6. an undertaking to stop Welde Mīka'ēl from raiding over the Ethiopian border.[213]

Gordon was confident that Yohannis would accept these terms, particularly 'in view of the differences that had arisen between the King and his Chiefs'.[214] The differences turned out to be very real and on a large scale this time. Two months after the battle of Gura, Yohannis had deprived Ras Welde Sillasē (Wereñña) of his governorship and his liberty, and when Wereñña's son Negash refused to accept this and revolted, Ras Adal was sent to track him down. Adal's victory increased his power and prestige and caused Minīlik to invade Begēmdir in early March. Whether he intended to march on Gonder, as was reported, or not, this unauthorized campaign was a challenge not only to Adal but to the Emperor himself. Just as Gordon prepared to start his negotiations, he found that Yohannis had marched south. Minīlik, who had gone no farther than Debre Tabor, quickly withdrew through Gojjam to Shewa.[215]

At Keren and in Cairo, however, Minīlik had taken Gonder 'at the head of a considerable army', and Yohannis was, consequently, well disposed 'to treat for Peace with Egypt . . . upon the basis of a reduction of Customs Dues at the Ports leading into Abyssinia'.[216] Gordon and the British vice-consul at Jidda, A. B. Wylde, who had joined him, did not believe that Yohannis cared to claim

212 FO 881/3192, p. 12, Vivian to Derby, 26 Dec. 1876.
213 FO 78/2632, fols 11–14, Vivian to Derby, 7 Apr. 1877, citing a private letter from Gordon, 14 Mar. 1877.
214 FO 78/2631, fol. 189, Vivian to Derby, 9 Mar. 1877.
215 FO 78/2633, fols 59–61, Blair to Vivian, 30 Apr. 1877; *Petermann*, 1877, p. 158; BN, Ethiop. 259, fols 22–3. In this early chronicle the connection between these events is quite clear. Gebre Sillasē (*Minīlik*, pp. 72–7) and Afewerq (*Minīlik*, pp. 26–7) on the other hand both fail to mention Yohannis's role, thus suppressing both Minīlik's insurrection and the element of retreat which was involved in the hasty withdrawal through Gojjam. Rather than admitting that the Ethiopians had political scores of their own to settle with each other, a British observer offered the hypothesis that Minīlik attacked in March 1877, instead of 1876, because he had misunderstood the Egyptian instructions he had received (FO 881/3203, pp. 1–5, Wylde to Derby, 23 Apr. 1877).
216 FO 78/2631, fols 248–9, Vivian to Derby, 29 Mar. 1877.

a port of his own. Likewise the Ethiopians were not supposed to care for more arms; thus Yohannis would be satisfied with '50 lbs of powder, 10 muskets and 5,000 caps per annum for his personal use'. The 'ancient Frontiers' were now interpreted as a line between Hamasēn and Bogos, although Alula had declared quite plainly that Ethiopia extended as far as the sea. For Gordon and Wylde the main problem was Welde Mīka'ēl, who wanted Hamasēn and could hardly be expected to keep the peace if he was allowed to govern territory along the new boundary. Gordon believed he had found a solution by offering Egypt's ally a district of his own consisting of the two Maryas and Bēt Teqwē separated from Ethiopia by a corridor from Massawa to Kasala through Keren. Unfortunately Alula, whom Gordon had hoped to meet near Keren, had joined Yohannis. So sure that the King would agree to his terms was Gordon, however, that he dispatched a copy of a signed convention to Yohannis and notified Cairo before going on to Khartoum that he took 'it for granted that the Egyptian terms were accepted provisionally' and that no further negotiations would be necessary.[217]

A few months later there was a first report that Yohannis had, in fact, agreed to the peace conditions, but this was evidently the result of wishful thinking.[218] When Yohannis responded in mid-June, he showed that he was fully aware in whose pay Gordon was. That he answered at all was because Gordon was a Christian and not a Muslim. The King pointed out that in ancient times all rulers had known the boundary of Ethiopia and Egypt, but now people did as they liked. Then he asked with sarcasm what elders had traced the boundary for Gordon so that he could say 'This is it, this is it'. For his part, Yohannis now preferred to leave it to God to judge between Ismail and himself; men would not be able to separate them. To other questions than the territorial, there was no reaction at all.[219]

After the treatment his envoy had received in Cairo, Yohannis seems to have decided not to bother too much about peace negotiations. He felt sufficiently secure to give priority to internal political problems, and it was during the following years, while Ethiopia was still nominally at war with Egypt, that Yohannis made his important contributions towards the creation of a unified Ethiopia. Of paramount importance was the political settlement which he reached with Minīlik in March 1878, the so-called treaty of Liche. Minīlik was forced to renounce his claims to the imperial throne by dropping the title king of kings, and accepting Shewa as a fief from Yohannis. He was to pay tribute, of course, and place his troops at the disposal of the Emperor if they were needed. It is interesting to note, however, that the promise to provide military

217 FO 78/2632, fols 37–45, Vivian to Derby, 16 Apr. 1877, with abstracts from Gordon's private letters; fols 90–1, Vivian to Derby, 2 May 1877; fols 174–84, Wylde to Derby, 23 Apr. 1877; Hill, *Gordon*, pp. 213–21, 304; AECP, Massouah 4, fols 64–5, Carbonnel to Decazes, 5 Mar. 1877, for Alula's views.
218 FO 78/2633, fol. 17, Gordon to Khairi, 2 Jun. 1877; fols 250–1, Vivian to Derby, 24 Jul. 1877.
219 BM, Orient. 12913 (c), Yohannis to Gordon, 18 Jun. 1877, Amharic original. Cf. Hill, *Gordon*, pp. 208–9 and 291, for two different versions of this letter, both inaccurate.

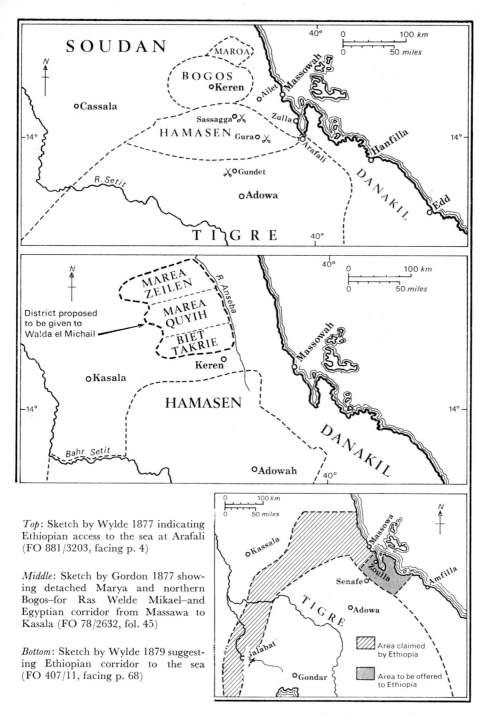

Top: Sketch by Wylde 1877 indicating Ethiopian access to the sea at Arafali (FO 881/3203, facing p. 4)

Middle: Sketch by Gordon 1877 showing detached Marya and northern Bogos–for Ras Welde Mikael–and Egyptian corridor from Massawa to Kasala (FO 78/2632, fol. 45)

Bottom: Sketch by Wylde 1879 suggesting Ethiopian corridor to the sea (FO 407/11, facing p. 68)

MAP 6 *Disputed territories and solutions proposed by British Vice-Consul Wylde and General Gordon*

support was expressed as a mutual obligation: wherever the next attack might come from, it should be met by the united strength of Ethiopia. [220]

In October Gordon decided to return to the Ethiopian frontiers to bring his peace efforts to a conclusion. Convinced that the reply of Yohannis was favourable, he saw Welde Mīka'ēl as the only serious problem. The Egyptians had built up the latter so that he commanded 6,000 men with 3,000 Remingtons. The governor general did not have the troops necessary to deal with him and considered encouraging Yohannis to attack him and thus 'do policeman' for Egypt. Gordon admitted that this solution was 'somewhat dishonourable' and preferred that Yohannis should pardon Welde Mīka'ēl and give him back Hamasēn.[221] The border situation was inflamed and it was not just Welde Mīka'ēl: 'It almost passes belief, but the troops from Amadep [Amideb], without my orders, have attacked a number of the tribes belonging to Johannis beyond my frontier . . . How can I expect Johannis to have any faith in me?' [222]

In a stronghold north of Keren, Gordon found Welde Mīka'ēl surrounded by 'fully 7,000 men'. The Hamasēn chief turned down the suggestion that he ask for pardon. Instead Gordon was obliged to promise him £1,000 a month in exchange for an undertaking not to pillage any longer. If the Egyptians had paid Yohannis, too, for temporarily leaving them in possession of Bogos, as was reported, the annexation was becoming a real drain. In Gordon's opinion 'the territory which Egypt pilfered from Abyssinia' was 'a useless expense' to her, and he would have liked to hand it back immediately if he had had the power and authority to do so.[223] Before the plans for getting rid of Welde Mīka'ēl with Ethiopian assistance had matured, the chief invaded and looted Hamasēn and Serayē. Yohannis's governor Ras Barya'u at Adwa was taken by surprise and wrote to Gordon on 11 May 1878, 'Is this with your permission, [or] has he rebelled against his master? What is the hidden purpose [of this]? Send me the reply quickly whether it is with permission [or not]?'[224] On his return to Massawa from a visit to Harer, Gordon found not only that Welde Mīka'ēl had just killed Barya'u, reportedly in an ambush, but also that his own Egyptian

220   The most specific information about the terms of the agreement was provided by the missionaries Massaja (*Trentacinque anni*, XI, p. 11) and Mayer (Waldmeier, *Autobiography*, pp. 133–4). Minīlik himself publicized the agreement as a reconciliation with his 'father and brother' *Emperor* Yohannis, using *king* as his own title (FO 95/737, no. 176, to Victoria; ASMAI 36/1–6, to Umberto; APR, A 3a, to Leopold II; all 6 Dec. 1878). The chronicles also emphasize the reconciliation element (BN, Ethiop. 259, fols 23–4; Gebre Sillasē, pp. 83–5; Afewerq, pp. 28–9), but the conditions indicate that it was Yohannis who imposed his will on Minīlik, and that was how the message was understood at Adwa (*MT*, 1878, pp. 97–9, Carlsson, 3 May 1878) and Massawa (AECP, Massouah 4, Carbonnel to Decazes, 29 Apr. 1878).

221   FO 78/2634, fols 198–9, Vivian to Derby, 1 Dec. 1877; fols 307–9, Gordon to Vivian, 20 Nov. 1877; Hill, *Gordon*, pp. 289–92.

222   Hill, *Gordon*, p. 303.

223   ibid., pp. 301–4. For the rumoured payment to Yohannis in connection with Bogos, see AECP, Massouah 4, fols 59–60, Carbonnel to Decazes, 10 Dec. 1876.

224   Hill, *Gordon*, p. 305; FO 78/2853, fols 171–4, Vivian to Derby, 9 Feb. 1878; BM, Orient 12913 (E), Barya'u to Gordon, 11 May 1878; *MT*, 1878, pp. 96–7, Hedenström, 18 May 1878.

subordinates had provided liberal supplies of ammunition for Welde Mīka'ēl's new war. He found some small comfort in the fact that Welde Mīka'ēl had captured his correspondence with Barya'u and so knew that he could expect no assistance any longer.[225]

There are some indications that Welde Mīka'ēl had received the ammunition, and other encouragement as well, on orders straight from Cairo. There he was reported to have captured Adwa (which he never attempted), and killed Barya'u as early as March. But Welde Mīka'ēl's success was short-lived. Without reinforcements he could not face Alula who was approaching, reportedly with 20,000 men. He received none, and was quite naturally furious over what he regarded, and not without justification, as a betrayal.[226]

In this situation 'the water that had been poured out returned to the jug': Welde Mīka'ēl negotiated an amnesty with Alula, and in January 1879 he received his pardon from Yohannis at Gonder. About six months later he returned to Hamasēn and Bogos with Alula but all rumours that he would be given a governorship there again turned out to be wrong. He had reached the end of his stormy political career.[227]

The removal of Welde Mīka'ēl was supposed to make a settlement easier; it also made it more urgent—that is for Egypt. Taking advantage of a feeler by the son of Ras Araya who was now Yohannis's governor in the Gonder area, Gordon dispatched W. Winstanley to the court of Yohannis as his deputy. The only thing he offered in addition to the 1877 proposal was the restoration to Ethiopia of the looted crown of Tēwodros. On the other hand, Ethiopia could not have a port, possibly a consul at Massawa, and no restoration of lost territory.[228] Winstanley was kept waiting at the border for two and a half months, and when he finally reached Debre Tabor in mid-April 1879, his reception was far from cordial. According to Winstanley's own account of the audiences, Yohannis told him that he could not say he loved or trusted foreigners, that he resented Egypt's annexations and the arms embargo. As for a port, 'I do not wish a consul at Massowah—I wish Massowah'.[229] On the territorial question, the King reportedly told Winstanley that he would occupy Bogos and Metemma and then make peace.[230]

In a letter to Victoria which he sent with Winstanley, Yohannis was less outspoken or demanding. He declared that he still regarded the Queen as his special friend and would like to act on her advice; otherwise he could easily recapture his lost territory alone. There was, however, also the question of a bishop, and of the freedom to import arms and to trade through Massawa. If

225 Hill, *Gordon*, pp. 313–14; *MT*, 1878, pp. 96–7, Hedenström, 18 May and 12 Jun. 1878.
226 FO 78/2853, fol. 333, Vivian to Derby, 8 Mar. 1878; AECP, Massouah 4, fols 84–90, Carbonnel to Waddington, 25 May, 8 Jun., and 13 Sep. 1878.
227 *MT*, 1879, pp. 25–6, Swensson, 9 Nov. 1878; AECP, Massouah 4, fols 91–2, Carbonnel to Waddington, 10 Nov. and 23 Dec. 1878; Hill, *Gordon*, p. 330; ENA, Registre 52, Abdin, nos 224 and 440, Gordon to Khairi, 10 Mar. and 3 May 1879.
228 Hill, *Gordon*, pp. 330–5.
229 W. Winstanley, *A Visit to Abyssinia. An account of travel in modern Abyssinia* (London, 1881), *passim*, and Vol. II, pp. 242–4, in particular.
230 ENA, Registre 53, Abdin, no. 29, Ala ad-Din to Maia, 5 Jul. 1879.

the British government would arrange this for him he would even be prepared to share the pagan districts around his kingdom with the British, but with no one else.[231] The last statement indicated two things: Yohannis still trusted the British government more than any other; secondly, he was prepared to make some concessions in exchange for a negotiated settlement under British auspices. But this did not mean that he looked only to Britian or was willing to wait much longer. Foreign contacts were again becoming more frequent.

An Italian commercial mission was permitted to proceed to Debre Tabor, and though their reception was rather reserved, they returned to Italy with a letter from Yohannis which indicated possible interest in future contacts.[232] Whether rumours about Russian agents in Ethiopia at the height of the Turco-Russian war of 1877–78 were true or not (they probably were), Yohannis revealed his interest in relations with Russia by taking the initiative of writing to Alexander II at the same time as he wrote to Umberto I. One of the problems where Russia or Greece (but in Yohannis's opinion certainly not Italy) could possibly help was that of a new metropolitan for Ethiopia.[233] More important than any diplomatic activities, was of course the appearance of Ras Alula in the northern borderlands at the head of a large army (30,000 combatants according to Vice-consul Raffray) and with Welde Mīka'ēl as his lieutenant. The Ethiopians overran Bogos, Mensa, and Marya without meeting resistance and demanded tribute from Semhar, Habab, and Barka as well. Alula was reported to have said that he had come to take Massawa and did not intend to go away until he had 'watered his horse in the Red Sea'.[234]

This was the situation in which Gordon undertook his last peace mission. He arrived at Massawa on 6 September 1879 with instructions to maintain the boundaries intact without any financial obligations towards Ethiopia and prevent all incursions and aggression.[235] A last-minute telegram read, 'Give up nothing, but do not fight'. He commented rightly that it was 'not a question of ceding or not ceding the country, but of retaking it'. As far as Egypt was concerned, he went with 'empty hands'. But he had, as he expressed it, told the representatives of France and Britain in Egypt that 'they had interfered to get

231 FO 95/738, no. 297, Yohannis to Victoria, 2 May 1879. Yohannis took the opportunity to write also to his consul, Henry S. King (FO 407/11, p. 25), and his old friend Lord Napier of Magdala (ibid., pp. 26–7), *inter alia* about 'guns, powder and caps'.
232 Giglio, *Etiopia–Mar Rosso*, Vol. I, pp. 172–4; ASMAI 36/1–8, Yohannis to Umberto I, 20 Jun. 1879.
233 FO 78/2634, fols 125–6, Vivian to Tenterdon, 31 Oct. 1877; AECP, Massouah 4, fols 93–104, 123–4, Raffray to Waddington, 28 Jul. and 30 Sep. 1879; FO 407/11, pp. 47–52, Wylde to Salisbury, 20 Oct. 1879. The Emperor had just returned from the church council at Boru Mēda (Gebre Sillasē, *Minīlik*, pp. 86–92) and was as opposed as ever to Catholic influence, or Protestant, for that matter.
234 ENA, Registre 53, no. 29, Ala ad-Din to Maia, 5 Jul. 1879; Hill, *Gordon*, pp. 399, 401; AECP, Massouah 4, fols 93–108, Raffray to Waddington, 28 Jul. and 13 Aug. 1879; fol. 116, Raffray to Monge, 22 Aug. 1879; *MT*, 1879, p. 171, Hedenström, 21 Sep. 1879.
235 Hill, *Gordon*, pp. 397–8. The mention of fees or dues is obscure but may refer to the payment of some kind of tax or rent to Yohannis for Bogos either discussed or promised by Gordon earlier. See, for instance, AECP, fol. 80, Carbonnel to Waddington, 12 Jan. 1878 (for 1879).

sweet things, and now they must interfere to avoid bitter things'. In other words, those who had just grabbed complete financial control over Egypt would have to foot the bill for the war, if it came. He made it quite clear that he intended 'to force France and Britain to intervene in Abyssinia or to give Egypt complete freedom of action (especially financial) to sustain the war against Abyssinia'. To compel a reluctant French government to react more positively, he talked of fomenting a civil war by bringing out Alemayehu Tēwodros from England to fight for Egypt—and indirectly, of course, increase British influence.[236] As a result, gunboats were tracked down for dispatch to Massawa, and cables and letters were sent to Alula and Yohannis.[237]

What kind of settlement Gordon really hoped to reach is difficult to say. Vis-à-vis Britain and France he defended the right of Egypt to refuse all cession of territory; in fact, he maintained that the khedive was bound by his firman (approved ⌊by the Europeans) not to make territorial concessions.[238] In addition to diplomatic support, Gordon evidently hoped that this hard-line attitude—blackmail if you like—would also deliver some hard cash. In a long narrative to his sister which he invited the Foreign Office to read, Gordon admitted that he saw only one solution: the British government had to persuade the khedive to agree to the payment of £20,000 (£1,600 annually for twelve years) to compensate Yohannis for missing taxes from Bogos, and persuade Yohannis to accept this sum; 10,000 rifles out of the 600,000 available at Cairo might replace the money. To offer a port was not necessary, since it was only the Europeans who in their own commercial interest were pushing Yohannis and Minīlik to demand this. On the other hand, permission to import arms and ammunition through a responsible agent would have to be granted.[239] By negotiating a financial settlement, Gordon evidently hoped to avoid the basic question of whose territory Bogos was; likewise an end to the arms embargo would make it unnecessary to discuss a port. At any rate he was prepared to go beyond his instructions. But would it help?

Though he did not reveal it in his official correspondence, where he often sounded optimistic, Gordon nevertheless felt that he had been given an impossible task—and one which presented a moral dilemma. On his way to Alula's camp at Gura on 14 September, he wrote,

> I have sad misgivings whether I can do anything or not . . . Now Johannes will not give me his help for nothing, when I persist in keeping what we have stolen from him . . .[240]

236 Hill, *Gordon*, pp. 399–402; FO 407/11, p. 16, Gordon to Lascelles, 27 Aug. 1879; p. 53, Gordon to Zohrab, (possibly intended for Wylde, see p. 21), 12 Sep. 1879; AECP, Massouah 4, fols 109–10, Waddington to Raffray, 29 Aug. 1879; fols 112–15, Raffray to Waddington, 10 Sep. 1879; fol. 119, Gordon to Raffray, 8 Sep. 1879.

237 FO 407/11, pp. 7, 10, 15–16, Lascelles to Salisbury, 25 Aug., 27 Aug., and 29 Aug. 1879; pp. 16–17, Lascelles to Alula and to Yohannis, 28 Aug. 1879; p. 20, Lascelles to Salisbury, 17 Sep. 1879; AECP, Massouah 4, fols 112–15, Raffray to Waddington, 10 Sep. 1879; fol. 117, to Alula, 8 Sep. 1879; fol. 122, to Yohannis, 21 Sep. 1879.

238 AECP, Massouah 4, fol. 118, Raffray to Tricou, 9 Sep. 1879; FO 407/11, p. 52, Gordon to Zohrab (Wylde), 10 Sep. 1879.

239 FO 407/11, pp. 32–5 'Abyssinie: 1877–1879', dated 15 Sep. 1879.

240 Hill, *Gordon*, pp. 402–3.

His reception at Gura was far from cordial. Alula refused to settle anything but agreed to refrain from hostilities while Gordon travelled to Debre Tabor to meet the King. There was no taking for granted that Yohannis would come to Adwa or accept whatever was sent to him:

> Egypt treated Abyssinia very badly and unjustly, and that is why I do not feel in the least put out at their queer ways of treating me . . . I have abused them; for they (*like us*) want an eye for an eye, and twenty shillings for one pound.[241]

On his arrival at Debre Tabor on 27 October, Gordon soon found that his misgivings were well founded. Yohannis wanted his pound back and knew that he could bargain from strength. Gordon's accounts of the negotiations differ slightly. The most complete list of Ethiopian demands was:

1. the retrocession of Metemma, Shanqilla and Bogos;
2. the cession of the ports of Zulla and Anfilla;
3. a bishop;
4. an indemnity of £1–2 million.

In the course of the negotiations, Yohannis reportedly offered to drop the indemnity and the other ports in exchange for Massawa.[242] According to another version, he demanded 'all the territories taken from him by Egypt, including Bogos and Galabat' and either a port, Zulla or Massawa, *or* £2 million and the right to import arms.[243]

In spite of the fact that Gordon pressed for these demands in writing, he reportedly limited himself to telling the King 'privately' that he would help him to obtain 'an Abouna, free import for arms and letters for himself at Massawa, and Bogos', though the cession of Bogos was very doubtful since he had 'positive orders' not to cede it. There must have been some talk, too, about keeping the peace conditions secret. This did not make sense to Yohannis, for whom an international guarantee was important, and on 8 November Gordon was dismissed with a brief letter to the new khedive, Muhammad Tawfiq:

> You say that it was to make peace that you sent me the letter and the man [Gordon]! You fought me in secret without the kings hearing about it. But the kings shall hear [about it]. Are we to make peace again in secret?[244]

Though Gordon had every reason to expect a failure, as he himself had admitted, he left Yohannis and Ethiopia in anger. He had asked (and was

241   ibid., pp. 403–8; FO 407/11, p. 23, Gordon to Lascelles, 16 Sep. 1879; pp. 35–6, 'Abyssinie: 1877–79 (*continued*)', dated 18 Sep. 1879.
242   FO 407/14, pp. 8–13, 'Abyssinia, 1877–1879', a reconstruction by Gordon of his diary which he destroyed when he feared arrest on his way out of the country; also in Hill, *Gordon*, pp. 412–25, with some variations; AECP, Massouah 4, fols 129–30, Gordon to Raffray, 24 Nov. and 14 Dec. 1879.
243   FO 407/11, p. 77, Malet to Salisbury, 15 Dec. 1879.
244   AECP, Massouah 4, fol. 133, Yohannis to Muhammad Tawfiq, 8 Nov. 1879, copy in Amharic with French translation; also in FO 407/14, p. 26, and Hill, *Gordon*, pp. 415–16, 420–21, with some variations.

allegedly promised) to get Yohannis's demands in writing and had evidently hoped that they would be regarded as sufficiently outrageous to engender support with European governments for a hard-line approach: 'Since I knew through my spies that the King would not lower his demands much, I thought that it would be better not to let him reduce them.' Yohannis was equally disappointed and angry, which already the wording of his letter to Muhammad Tawfiq shows.[245]

About ten days after Gordon's departure, the King took the opportunity to send, with the Greek vice-consul at Suez who had visited him, a number of letters to European heads of state to explain his attitude towards peace with Egypt in general and Gordon's mission in particular. He stressed again that he was not the aggressor: he was not the one who had crossed the sea to fight. He had informed the European powers of the Egyptian aggression eight years earlier. Now he wanted to build a town on the coast to be able to communicate and trade freely with other countries. He accused Gordon of having used language unworthy of a peace emissary and of having tried to make peace in the same secret, underhand way that Ismail had used when he attacked.[246] The attack on Gordon was even stronger in letters to the consuls general in Cairo.[247]

It was no longer possible for the European powers to close their eyes to the fact that Yohannis now—after years of harassment of Ethiopian envoys and traders—demanded territorial and not only functional access to the sea. It was not the first time, of course, but many had argued that Yohannis really did not *want* a port of his own because the Ethiopians did not know how to handle it.[248] Letters from Minīlik revealed the same growing impatience with the embargoes and insecurity for Ethiopians in the coastal towns. He pointed out that it was not the question of conquering Egypt or making war against the khedive. But his grandfather and great-grandfather had used Tajura as their port, and he felt that he had both the right and the might to take it back:

> I am about to die from anger because I have remained without bringing into my country one [new] skill, imprisoned [as I am] by the Egyptian government like a man

245 Hill, *Gordon*, pp. 412–13, 415–20; AECP, Massouah 4, fols 131–2, Gordon to Raffray, 14 Dec. 1879. In this letter to Raffray, Gordon, in fact, exaggerated the demands by including both the three ports *and* an indemnity of 50 million francs. The Greek vice-consul at Suez, D. Mitzakis, who was present at Debre Tabor, maintained that Yohannis's demands were forwarded only as a basis for negotiations (FO 407/14, pp. 56–8, Malet to Salisbury, 20 Feb. 1880).

246 FO 95/738, no. 297, Yohannis to Victoria, 20 Nov. 1879; AAPA, IB 9, Abessinien 2, Yohannis to Wilhelm I, 20 Nov. 1879; AED, Protocole C41, Yohannis to Grévy, 21 Nov. 1879. The text of the three letters is almost identical except that Yohannis added an attack on the Catholic missionaries in the letters to Wilhelm I and Grévy, and declared that he had expelled them. He referred here to the expulsion of Massaja and others from Shewa (AECP, Massouah 4, fols 134–5, Raffray to Waddington, 18 Dec. 1879). The letter to Grévy is available in the diplomatic archives only in a French translation (by d'Abbadie) with the date 21 Nov. probably for 20 Nov.

247 FO 407/14, pp. 46–7, Mahdere Qal to Vivian, 18 Nov. 1879; pp. 49–50, to Monge, same date.

248 See, for instance, FO 881/3203, p. 1, Vivian to Derby, 19 May 1877; Hill, *Gordon*, p. 304.

who has been sentenced to imprisonment for life and prevented from bringing into the country rifles, cannon [and] workers.[249]

If Yohannis and Minīlik did not act against Egypt after their settlement in 1878—and it should be remembered that the hostilities of 1879 were due to Welde Mīka'ēl's invasion of Hamasēn and killing of Barya'u, not to an initiative by Yohannis—this was due mainly to uncertainty about the attitude of the European powers who all seemed to be on such good terms with Egypt. Yohannis, in particular, was bound to conclude that Britain and France were on Egypt's side, whether or not Gordon actually made use of the letters from their representatives to impress the King in that direction.[250] At any rate, Yohannis, who wanted an international guarantee against future attacks, maintained his largely defensive attitude, declaring that he would wait for replies to his letters to Europe.[251] He did not attack Egyptian positions, least of all Massawa. If he had in heated discussions with Winstanley and Gordon claimed the old Turkish port, Yohannis's letters to Europe after Gordon's departure showed that he did not expect to get Massawa but planned or hoped to build an alternative port, at Zulla or Anfilla.[252]

Gordon was not unaware of this. On his return to Massawa, he immediately proposed that Egypt should cede Zulla to Italy. His argument was that the British and French governments would neither recommend the acceptance of Ethiopia's demands nor permit Egypt the financial resources necessary to protect her people. The least they could do, therefore, was to get Italy involved, for, in Gordon's opinion, the cession of Zulla to Italy would 'bring about war between Italy and the King before six months expire, and (will) end in the annexation to Italy of a certain portion of Abyssinia'. There was no need to worry about the outcome: 5,000 soldiers would be sufficient to finish off Yohannis.[253]

The khedive rejected the proposal out of hand. So did the British government, and since Gordon had taken the precaution of sending his 'offer' to the Italians through the British consul general in Cairo, it was never forwarded, officially at least.[254] Nevertheless this last initiative by Gordon—after his attempts to impose a settlement in Egypt's favour had failed—reveals an almost uncanny awareness of the direction which matters were taking. Ethiopia had resisted joint European–Egyptian diplomatic pressure as successfully as it had resisted

249 FO 95/737, no. 176, to Victoria, ASMAI 36/1–6, to Umberto; APR, A 3a, to Leopold II; all 6 Dec. 1878.
250 AECP, Massouah 4, fols 127–8, Raffray to Waddington, 14 Dec. 1879.
251 ibid., fols 145–8, Raffray to Waddington, 16 Mar. and 12 Apr. 1880.
252 The idea of an Ethiopian port at Zulla was supported in England by Captain Speedy precisely when Gordon was making his way back to Massawa. See FO 407/11, pp. 66–8, Speedy to Beaconsfield, 28 Nov. 1879.
253 FO 407/14, p. 38, Gordon to Muhammad Tawfiq, 12 Dec. 1879; pp. 6–7, Gordon to Malet and to De Martino, same date; AECP, Massouah 4, fols 127–8, 134–5, Raffray to Waddington, 14 Dec. and 18 Dec. 1879.
254 FO 407/11, pp. 78–9, Malet to Salisbury, 19 Dec., 30 Dec. 1879, and 3 Jan. 1880; Salisbury to Malet, 20 Dec. 1879.

military aggression. Without a fresh start and a new military provocation there would be neither peace nor war, except on Ethiopia's terms. And these were completely unacceptable, not because the disputed areas were of such vital importance to Egypt, but because the consummation of Ethiopia's victory went against the grain of the political philosophy of the times. An 'uncivilized and savage' African state was supposed to accept European tutelage, as Egypt was doing, not to assert itself and actually increase its power and freedom of action. Gordon foresaw not only that the British government would eventually choose Italy to hold the Red Sea coast but that it would lead to war again. By delaying, however, Britain was ultimately forced to sign the peace treaty herself more or less on Ethiopia's terms and then violate it 'before the ink was dry'.

The Adwa Peace Treaty

In spite of the angry words and the complete failure of the Gordon mission, neither side wanted a military solution. Both reckoned with further tension and border incidents but no all-out war. Gordon was ambivalent. On the one hand, he believed, or argued at least, that the overthrow of Yohannis could be left to the Ethiopians who allegedly hated him even more than they had hated Tēwodros. On the other hand, he wanted the Italians to occupy Zulla and provoke a war with Ethiopia to take the pressure off Egypt, for as he had also admitted, 'You have far abler men to deal with than I had anticipated—men of stern, simple habits . . . a race of warriors . . .'[255] Yohannis continued to pursue a wait-and-see policy. Somehow he hoped that the increasing European influence over the affairs of Egypt would work out in his favour. There was clearly a more liberal attitude towards communications with Europe, and this Yohannis had demonstrated that he was prepared to take advantage of. But the British government was slow to react.

It took almost a full year before Yohannis had the answer to his proposals of May 1879.[256] As usual the reply was evasive. Although it was known that Gordon's mission had failed, the Queen expressed her hope that the negotiations would 'shortly be brought to a successful termination'. She desired that trade be promoted 'without causing danger to the peace of the surrounding countries', a phrase which was included also in a reply written at the same time to Minīlik's 'die-of-anger' letter of December 1878, and which meant, of course, no arms for the rulers of Ethiopia. Victoria concluded her letters, however, with an offer of her 'good offices' to solve the differences with Egypt if necessary.[257]

In his reply, Yohannis concentrated on the Queen's offer of her 'good offices' and immediately asked her to delegate one of her own trustworthy subjects 'to hear the complaints of both sides'. To be sure, he listed his own complaints once more and warned that unless Ethiopia received a sea port of her own, hostilities would eventually break out again; as far as he was concerned, he would, how-

255 Hill, *Gordon*, pp. 413, 417–23.
256 See above, pp. 341–2.
257 FO 95/738, no. 298, Victoria to Yohannis, 12 Dec. 1879; no. 299, to Minīlik, same date. FO 407/11, p. 46, Malet to Salisbury, 18 Nov. 1879.

ever, wait for Victoria's reply. In an accompanying letter to the Queen's ministers, councillors, etc., Yohannis pointed out that the khedive was lying when he talked of his friendship for Ethiopia. Egypt had still not evacuated Bogos (i.e. the fort of Keren) and held other Ethiopian districts occupied as well.[258]

After the rains of 1880, Alula returned to the disputed districts to levy the annual tribute. The Egyptians could do nothing to prevent him, and his soldiers pillaged even in the neighbourhood of the fort of Keren.[259] Since he reportedly had 15,000 men with him, the governor of Massawa feared an attack on the port where the garrison was gradually increased to 9,000 men. Alula denied that he had any designs on Massawa. Nevertheless the situation was very unsatisfactory. The Massawa troops took £51,000 annually and Harer another £33,000 out of a total reserve budget of £100,000 for the whole Sudan, not to speak of the fact that it had been stipulated at Tawfiq's accession that the whole Egyptian army should not be allowed to exceed 18,000 men. The British member of the Dual Control, which in fact governed Egypt, also proposed to the British government that it would be better for Egypt to abandon the Red Sea provinces, at least Harer with its ports, but the British government refused to consider a withdrawal.[260] They allowed the letter which Yohannis wrote immediately after Gordon's visit to go unanswered and delayed the reply to the above-mentioned letters for eight months.

In the meantime (February 1881) Gerhard Rohlfs arrived in Ethiopia with a letter and presents from the German emperor. This was the first response by a head of state to the appeals made by Yohannis after Gordon's visit to Debre Tabor, and the King was naturally very pleased.[261] Wilhelm I assured Yohannis that he would be happy to assist in finding a fair solution to Ethiopia's problems with Egypt.[262] Yohannis responded by asking Rohlfs to be his delegate and conclude peace on his behalf. In his reply to Wilhelm, Yohannis made very extensive territorial claims, based on what he believed to be the ancient boundaries of Ethiopia: the Indian Ocean, the Gulf of Aden, the Red Sea, and in the west Sawakin, Berber, Nubia, Khartoum, Sinnar. In a list of some twenty-five districts and places lost in more recent times, however, the emphasis is on the northern borderlands from Kunama in the west to Asawirṭa (Danakil) in the east—and Harer. In this list Zulla and the Burī peninsula are mentioned but not Massawa. Rohlfs confirmed that his mandate to conclude

258 FO 95/739, no. 216, Yohannis to Victoria, 29 Apr. 1880; no. 217, to the British cabinet, same date.
259 AECP, Massouah 4, fols 156–61, Raffray to de Freycinet, 25 Oct. 1880.
260 FO 403/81A, p. 139, Cookson to Granville, 7 Oct. 1880; pp. 151–2, Malet to Granville, 8 Dec. 1880, with enclosed memorandum by Colvin; p. 153, Granville to Malet, 20 Dec. 1880. For the size and morale of the Egyptian army after Ismail's fall, see John Marlowe, *Anglo-Egyptian Relations 1800–1953* (London, 1954), pp. 114–15.
261 Rohlfs, *Meine Mission*, pp. 40–1, 85–6, 89–92, 206–24; AAPA, IB 9, Abessinien 2, Rohlfs to Bismarck, 17 May 1881, with enclosed report, 16 May 1881. Yohannis was somewhat irritated at this point that an Italian mission which was to bring him certain articles ordered through Matteucci and which had been announced repeatedly from Massawa failed to arrive. See Giglio, *Etiopia–Mar Rosso*, Vol. I, pp. 175–7.
262 AAPA, IB 9, Abessinien 2, Wilhelm I to Yohannis, 18 Sep. 1880.

peace was on condition that the territories annexed after the death of Tēwodros would be restored, and that Ethiopia would receive the Bay of Zulla as an outlet to the sea.[263]

In his reply to Yohannis, the French president evaded the conflict issue completely. Besides flattery, he tendered the advice that the King, in the interest of the progress of his people, should 'offer facilities to the Christians of the West who want to undertake business with him . . .'[264] The only important French undertaking in Ethiopia was a tobacco plantation in Bogos, and tobacco was an abomination to Yohannis.[265]

The British letter was not much more encouraging. Victoria appreciated Yohannis's desire to live in peace with his neighbours and was very pleased with the report she had received from Cairo about friendly communications between him and the khedive.[266] Yohannis was indeed at this time in direct contact with Muhammad Tawfiq about a new metropolitan for Ethiopia. The possibility that Yohannis might otherwise recruit a bishop from some other Orthodox church had made the Egyptians willing to accommodate the Ethiopians in this matter. As usual, it was the question of paying in hard cash, but the negotiations succeeded, and by November 1881 Ethiopia had four new bishops. Yohannis had tested the *détente* by sending money for the purchase of 800 rifles as well.[267] More than two years later he was still reminding the khedive that he wanted the arms he had paid for.[268] When he thanked Muhammad Tawfiq for arranging the matter of the bishops, he expressed his hope that they would soon be able to conclude peace on the basis of the boundaries before the conflict which he had requested the kings of Europe to define and demarcate for them.[269]

The hope of the British government that it would not have to deliver on the Queen's offer of her 'good offices' was clearly premature. At the local level Yohannis did not restrain Alula and his other governors in the north. Their armies moved freely and levied tribute in all the territories lost between 1872 and 1875. The Egyptians remained inside their fortified positions, and the Ethiopians usually left them alone. There was, however, a report that Amideb had been attacked at the very same time as the negotiations for the bishops

263   ibid., Yohannis to Wilhelm I, 17 Feb. 1881; reports by Rohlfs, 16 May and 23 May 1881.
264   AED, Protocole C41, Grévy to Yohannis, 17 Apr. 1880. This letter was first entrusted to two merchants, but some trouble occurred (AEMD, Afrique 62, fols 474–7, memorandum 15 May 1880), and an updated copy with presents was sent to Raffray for delivery to Yohannis about one year later (AECP, Massouah 4, fols 203–8, Raffray to Barthélemy Saint-Hilaire, 14 May 1881).
265   AECP, Massouah 4, 156–61, Raffray to Barthélemy Saint-Hilaire, 25 Oct. 1880, and following dispatches; Hill, *Gordon*, p. 404.
266   FO 95/740, no. 74, Victoria to Yohannis, 8 Mar. 1881.
267   ENA, Sudan, Carton 5/3, Yohannis to Tawfiq, 5 Apr. 1881 and 16 Feb. 1882; AECP, Massouah 4, fols 174–7, Raffray to Barthélemy Saint-Hilaire, 10 Dec. 1880; fols 239–46, to Gambetta, 22 Nov. 1881; FO 95/740, no. 82, Yohannis to Victoria, 4 Nov. 1881. For reports of Ethiopian contacts with Greece and Russia, see FO 407/14, pp. 33–4, Malet to Salisbury, 15 Jan. 1880; p. 42 Salisbury to Malet, 30 Jan. 1880.
268   ENA, Sudan, Carton 5/3, Yohannis to Tawfiq, 17 Mar. 1884.
269   ibid., Yohannis to Tawfiq, 16 Feb. 1882.

started, and when an ecclesiastical mission left for Cairo and Jerusalem in March 1882, Ethiopian armies stood two hours from Massawa and Zulla.[270]

For Raffray, the French vice-consul at Massawa, the French and British letters provided a long-desired opportunity to visit Yohannis. He found, however, both along the way and on his arrival at the King's camp in the Zobel area in August 1881, that he was hardly welcome. He did not improve his relations with Yohannis by insisting that the King pay indemnities to French traders and to the Catholic mission in Akkele Guzay which had recently suffered an attack on its churches by Ethiopian soldiers. There was a tremendous amount of intrigue going on among the Europeans who surrounded the King: the Greek vice-consul Mitzakis, the German Stecker (who had remained behind when Rohlfs returned to Europe), the Italian brothers Naretti, a Spanish envoy named Abargues de Sosten, and Raffray himself. The latter observed on his way to Zobel that all Europeans were despised in Ethiopia. His visit did not improve the situation. By his own account, he was almost chased out of the presence of the King, who accused the Europeans of preventing him from regaining his lost territories. Yohannis seems to have hoped that Germany might give him the moral support he needed for an attack on Massawa; if Raffray succeeded with anything, it was to create suspicion also against this newcomer in the field.[271]

The letters to President Grévy and Queen Victoria which Yohannis dispatched with Raffray indicate how irritated he was over the attitude of the Europeans who pretended that the problems were solved and peace just around the corner. He had himself solved the question of new bishops as it had always been done, but the question of peace was something he had referred to the European kings; he was prepared to have a boundary defined by treaty between his country and Egypt, but he wanted to have the matter settled without further delay. To the Queen, he was particularly blunt: he had shown patience in order to be able to act with her approval; now he wanted a reply, by all means, to his earlier letter.[272] In other words, he wanted an answer whether or not Victoria was willing to send a representative of her own to look into the conflict, listen to both sides, and mediate a settlement.

Yohannis was more correct than he probably knew when he pressed London for the answer, firstly because Bismarck consulted London about Rohlf's eventual peace mission and promised to take action only if Britain wanted him to do so, and secondly because it was the British government that maintained that Ethiopia should not be given a port or facilities to import war materials. Yohannis was restrained from making war only 'by his inability to obtain the necessary supplies of arms and ammunition'. The British agent and consul general in Egypt, Edward Malet, was convinced that Egyptian troops would not stand before the Abyssinians and started to speak of the possibility that Yohannis might come to Cairo with his army! Therefore Rohlfs should be

270   AECP, Massouah 4, fols 174–7, Raffray to Barthélemy Saint-Hilaire, 10 Dec. 1880; fols 258–70, Herbin to de Freycinet, 1 Apr. 1882.
271   ibid., fols 174–270, sundry dispatches from Raffray and Herbin, 10 Dec. 1880–1 Apr. 1882.
272   AEMD, Afrique 62, fol. 538, Yohannis to Grévy, 4 Nov. 1881; FO 95/740, no. 82, to Victoria, same date.

instructed to urge Yohannis to make peace for 'free commercial intercourse (excepting war materials) and the surrender of parts of certain territories captured from Abyssinia by the late Khedive'.[273]

Slowly and reluctantly the Egyptian government and its European 'advisers' realized that Yohannis was not going to give up. Alula saw to it that no revenues from the disputed territories reached Egyptian coffers. With almost no trade, the possession of Massawa itself was a sheer loss, sustained at considerable risk. Though unlikely, the possibility could not be excluded that Yohannis's diplomatic activity would eventually in a crisis situation lead some European government to act in Ethiopia's favour. This situation was, in fact, present in Egypt itself where it was becoming increasingly difficult for the Europeans to govern through the French–British Dual Control. The nationalist movement among the Egyptian officers led by Arabi Pasha challenged the power structure in Egypt, and in the Sudan Muhammad Ahmad had declared himself the Mahdi and raised the standard of revolt. In July 1882 came the bombardment of Alexandria and then the British take-over.[274] To hold on to everything in Ethiopia in this situation was not worth the risks involved. When Yohannis wrote and asked Malet for an *answer* to his letter, it was as if the ghost of Tēwodros had appeared on the stage: 'We might have another Abyssinian war'.[275]

By May 1882 the Egyptian government had started to consider 'territorial concessions to Abyssinia'. But it could only be 'inland territory . . . Egypt could not cede a port'. Malet supported this standpoint:

> I cannot but remain to be of opinion that the possession of a port by Abyssinia would be a danger to Egypt, and that such a cession should not be advocated by England unless our present attitude of protection towards this country becomes changed to one of hostility.[276]

Five months later, with the British in complete control, Sir Charles Wilson proposed 'to restore Bogos and the district near Galabat; to make Massowah a free port; to facilitate the appointments of the Abunas, and to make peace with Abyssinia on these terms'.[277]

In spite of this, it took the British government more than six months to produce one more 'temporizing letter', and another six months before they had delivered it to Yohannis. All it contained was a promise to write again as soon as order had been established in Egypt.[278]

Yohannis did not wait for the letter to arrive, but argued, as if he had never

273 FO 403/81B, p. 39, Granville to Walsham, 27 Jun. 1881; p. 45, memorandum by Malet, 1 Jul. 1881; pp. 80–1, Granville to Walsham, 19 Jul. 1881.
274 Marlowe, *Anglo-Egyptian Relations*, pp. 112–46.
275 FO 1/30, p. 22, Yohannis to Malet, 21 Dec. 1881; pp. 14–20, Malet to Granville, 4 Apr. 1882.
276 ibid., pp. 30–3, Malet to Granville, 1 May 1882.
277 ibid., pp. 40–1, 'Memorandum on the Sudan', 29 Sep. 1882.
278 ibid., pp. 58–63, minutes, October 1882; FO 95/742, no. 130, Victoria to Yohannis, 9 Nov. 1882.

doubted the good will of the British government, 'Now that the Muslim government [of Egypt] has disappeared and the country is in the hands of Christians,
arrange for my country to be returned to me'. He stressed again that he had
never concluded peace with Egypt; Malet had misled the Queen when he said
that the appointment of the new bishops meant that peace had been concluded.[279] When Yohannis received the letter with the new postponement, his
only reaction was, 'The words are very good; but may God prepare the fulfill-
ment'.[280]

That Yohannis was in fact very critical towards the attitude of the British
both between 1872 and 1875 and after the war is evident from a letter he wrote to
Rohlfs in 1882 in which he accused the British of having deceived him by telling
him to keep peace at the same time as they pushed the Egyptians to attack him
and by not keeping their promises to mediate.[281] It was Stecker who was
entrusted with Yohannis's last appeal to Queen Victoria to settle the conflict
with Egypt. He also received an almost identical letter for his own sovereign.[282] Raffray's successor as French vice-consul, who was present at the
King's court in late March 1883 (to obtain satisfaction for destroyed mission
property), was, however, refused a letter for the French government on the
grounds that though France was a great power, whose will the Egyptians were
bound to respect, and though she had a consulate at Massawa, she had done
nothing to prevent the Egyptians from interfering with his mail and confiscating
arms which had been sent to him.[283] Instead of increasing French influence in
Ethiopia, the consulate and the Catholic mission had destroyed the credibility of
France.

An attack by Alula on Aylet and Se'atī in October 1883 indicated that Yohannis would not wait much longer. The following month the British government
had secured the formal request of the Egyptian government to undertake a peace
mission, and had accepted on condition that Egypt was ready 'to agree to such
terms as are likely to satisfy the King of Abyssinia'. The Foreign Office saw only
one problem: the Ottoman government would have to be consulted on the
cession of a port.[284] In fact, this applied only to Massawa, as they would
eventually recall. At any rate the officials in Cairo remained completely opposed
to the cession of a port. They would agree to 'a light duty on Abyssinian
merchandize', but the importation of arms was to be 'absolutely prohibited'. As
for other territory, they would cede Bogos but not Qallabat.[285]

279   FO 95/743, no. 221, Yohannis to Victoria, 9 Apr. 1883.
280   ibid., no. 216, Yohannis to Victoria, 8 May 1883.
281   AAPA, IB 9, Abessinien 2, Yohannis to Rohlfs, 19 Aug. 1882.
282   ibid., Yohannis to Wilhelm I, 9 Apr. 1883.
283   AECP, Massouah 4, fols 350–2, Herbin to Soumagne, 8 Jun. 1883.
284   *MT*, 1884, pp. 2–3, Swensson, 3 Dec. 1883; FO 1/30, pp. 78–80, Baring to Granville, 24
      Nov. 1883; pp. 94–6, Chérif to Baring, same date; pp. 82–5, minutes, 26–7 Nov. 1883; p.
      111, Granville to Baring, 27 Nov. 1883. Much of the correspondence in FO 1/30 and 1/31
      (but no minutes and only a few of the enclosures) appear in the Confidential Print
      (FO 401/6). Where nothing is to be gained by referring to the original correspondence, I
      will cite FO 401/6.
285   FO 401/6, pp. 2–3, Baring to Granville, 29 Nov. and 12 Dec. 1883, Chérif to Baring, 12
      Dec. 1883.

In view of the repeated demands of Yohannis, this was pretty unrealistic. Whatever could be done to smooth the way and impress the King was done. Rear Admiral Sir William Hewett was appointed to head the mission.[286] Attention was paid to proper presents, of course, to the form of the Queen's letter—illuminated vellum with names and titles in red ink and the large signet at the top since that was where the Ethiopian ruler placed his seal—and to Yohannis's title. For the first time Victoria would address him as an equal: 'Majesty' instead of 'Highness'.[287] Lord Napier of Magdala was asked to write a letter to support Hewett and agreed, provided

> we are going to give him any help in return for his forbearance but if our purpose is merely to make him hold his hand now that he has the opportunity of recovering the territory wrestled from him, I should not like to do so. It is an opportunity for Abyssinia, which should not be lost. I therefore sign the letter on the assurance that we are going to recognize him and to hold out the hand of Christian fellowship to him which he has pleaded for so long . . . but if I am mistaken I would respectfully request that my signature may be returned to me.[288]

Napier took it for granted that Ethiopia would receive Zulla and Anfilla and argued that it would only be right to give her Massawa as well, since it yielded no revenue to Egypt and could 'only be of use to her as a means of oppression towards Abyssinia'. In a situation where Yohannis could take anything he liked, Napier felt that he should not be advised to accept anything less than the restoration 'of all the provinces taken from her [Ethiopia] in late years by Egypt' and 'a bona fide, practicable sea-port'. If this was not to be Massawa which 'would be the most just solution', then he recommended that Yohannis be guaranteed communication through Massawa, 'under British protection, free of all duties or any interference', until a new port had been established.[289]

Captain Speedy, who was selected to join Hewett as the most suitable expert on Ethiopia available, expressed much the same views. He did not believe that Massawa, 'a small coral island, destitute of water', was important, but 'the cession of a Seaport would be the only durable solution of the difficulties between Abyssinia and Egypt'. The second best would be 'a Free Port, in the event of its being found wholly impracticable to cede the desired Sea Port'. In either case, it would be 'of the utmost importance that no Egyptian official be permitted to reside at such Port in any capacity whatsoever'. Such a port, whether Ethiopian or 'free' (and British-controlled) should be constructed either between Massawa and Arkiko, or in Zulla Bay. That Metemma (Qallabat) and Senhit (Bogos) would be restored to Ethiopia was taken for granted.[290]

286 FO 1/30, pp. 159–60, Baring to Granville, 12 Dec. 1883; pp. 307–8, Granville to Baring, 27 Dec. 1883.
287 FO 95/744, no. 165, Victoria to Yohannis, 2 Jan. 1884. The presents would eventually include rocket-tubes with rockets, nickel-plated rifles and field guns, etc.; see FO 1/31, pp. 260–2, for a complete list.
288 FO 1/30, pp. 253–5, Granville to Napier, 23 Dec. 1883; pp. 257–9, draft of Napier to Yohannis; pp. 293–7, Napier to Granville, 26 Dec. 1883.
289 ibid., pp. 345–54, 381–93, Napier to Granville, 28 Dec. 1883 and 2 Jan. 1884.
290 ibid., pp. 209–24, 333–42, memoranda by Speedy, 21 Dec. and 25 Dec. 1883.

Consul A. Baker at Sawakin stressed the same point: '. . . in spite of all that is said to the contrary by Egyptian officials and interested traders, the Abyssinians do want a port, and will never be satisfied without one'. He believed that the fear that the Ethiopians would use the port only to obtain arms was exaggerated by the consciousness that Egypt was 'in wrongful possession of Abyssinian territory' and by 'the desire on the part of the traders to retain the present practical monopoly of trading with the Abyssinians under conditions which place the Abyssinians at their mercy as to prices etc.'. With increased security, moreover, trade would increase so that the traders would probably be just as well if not better off than they were under prevailing conditions.[291]

British officers in Egyptian service were less generous; one suggestion included Qallabat *instead of* Bogos and limited arms import through Massawa. In Cairo the Egyptian government was gradually persuaded to agree to the cession of 'a portion of sea-coast' but not Massawa.[292] But then the Foreign Office seemed to feel that they would be giving away too much by authorizing a port: '. . . we have no certain assurance that the King will not accept the lesser benefits if offered by an English Admiral with an illuminated letter from the Queen and a red silk tent, or at least the promise of one'. Would it not be better to ask the King to come to Massawa—in order to avoid any risk of being detained—and tell *what his proposals are?*[293] In the instructions 'an arrangement with him in regard to his frontiers and the use of a sea port' was struck out in favour of 'a territorial arrangement', and Yohannis was to be told that the negotiations had to take place at Massawa because Hewett could not be spared for a journey into the country.[294]

As the situation for the Egyptians in the Sudan deteriorated, a peace agreement with Yohannis became all the more important to prevent the Egyptian garrisons in the eastern Sudan from being caught between hostile Sudanese and Ethiopians. In spite of Gordon's contrary advice, Baring and Granville decided that the mission was becoming urgent. Nevertheless, Granville had still not been able to make up his mind on the question of territorial concessions; instead his vacillation about the coast had spread inland.[295]

This was too much for Hewett. He had been in contact with Alula through a deputy and found out what the Foreign Office had known all along: Bogos and a seaport were Yohannis's demands. By virtue of his rank, Hewett demanded 'the power to settle the business',[296] and was authorized to negotiate a settlement on the following terms:

1. King John to facilitate the withdrawal through his territory of the Egyptian garrisons in the neighbourhood of the frontier.

291   ibid., pp. 463–79, Baker to Granville, 7 Jan. 1884.
292   FO 401/6, p. 8, Baring to Granville, 12 Jan. 1884; pp. 11–12, memorandum by V. Baker, 9 Jan. 1884.
293   FO 1/30, pp. 545–8, 553–61, 605–7, minutes, 19 Jan.–25 Jan. and 9 Feb. 1884.
294   ibid., pp. 567–9, 575–6, Granville to Admiralty and to Baring, 29 Jan. 1884.
295   FO 401/6, p. 15, Granville to Baring, 9 Feb. 1884; pp. 18–19, Baring to Granville, 27 Feb. 1884, with enclosures; p. 21, Granville to Baring, 1 Mar. 1884.
296   ibid., pp. 22–3, Hewett to Baring, 6 Mar. 1884.

2. All differences between Egypt and Abyssinia to be referred to Her Majesty's Government.
3. The King to be at liberty to occupy the district of Bogos.
4. Free transit through Massowah, under British protection, for all goods, including arms and ammunition, from and to Abyssinia.
5. The settlement of the question regarding the appointment of an Abuna.
    The occupation of Galabat by Abyssinia would not be opposed, in the event of such a concession being found absolutely necessary.
    A general reservation with respect to the lawful claims of the Porte should be introduced into the agreement.[297]

Two matters strike one as a bit odd in these instructions. The first is that the question of territory on the coast was passed over in silence, although Baring had confirmed that he saw 'no objection to ceding Bogos *and a portion of seacoast*'. The second is the phrasing of the third clause 'be at liberty to occupy' instead of 'cede'. In the minutes on Baring's cable and in the summary of the clauses 'cession' was used and 'seaport' was listed with Qallabat as an additional concession to be made if necessary.[298]

Hewett was puzzled by the 'general reservation' and asked for instructions. It was agreed in the Foreign Office that the claims were 'ill-defined', and that since Yohannis would not receive 'any *Turkish* territory as distinguished from *Egyptian* territory' and the word 'cession' would not be used, and since 'the title of Egypt or of the Porte was never consummated or confirmed by a Treaty of Peace or by the submission of King John', and since the reservation would be 'so difficult to explain . . . it would perhaps be wiser to . . . strike it out of the instructions, and treat the occupation of Bogos and Galabat as a reconquest by King John, which Egypt has not seen fit to resist'.[299] This is an exceptionally grand example of how complicated the diplomatic issues had become; but nobody seems to have thought of the fact that no article about the territory was necessary at all if the 'cession' was to be regarded as a reconquest—nobody except probably Yohannis!

Fortunately the absurd condition that Yohannis should come to Massawa to negotiate was dropped. Politely but firmly, Alula informed Hewett that the King would himself choose where to receive the mission.[300] On 7 April Hewett left Massawa for Adwa together with the Egyptian governor of Massawa, an American named Mason. Alula met them at Asmera and escorted them to Adwa. Yohannis kept them waiting there for a month, but Alula had instructions to discuss with Hewett and when the King arrived, the negotiations took only a few days. On 3 June a treaty which ended the 1875–76 war was finally signed.[301]

297 ibid., p. 23, Granville to Baring, 10 Mar. 1884.
298 FO 1/30, pp. 755–6, Baring to Granville, 6 Mar. 1884; pp. 778–83, Granville to Baring, 10 Mar. 1884 (my emphasis).
299 FO 1/31, p. 15, Hewett to Baring, 12 Mar. 1884; pp. 37–42, memorandum by Pauncefote, 15 Mar. 1884; p. 47, Granville to Baring, 18 Mar. 1884.
300 FO 401/6, pp. 29–31, Alula to Hewett, 1 Feb. and 12 Feb. 1884; p. 31, Rolfe to Hewett, 12 Feb. 1884.
301 FO 1/31, pp. 2–4, Hewett to Granville, 9 Jun. 1884, pp. 353–6, to Admiralty, same date; for Alula, p. 226, Yohannis to Hewett, 1 May 1884.

The so-called Hewett treaty contains seven articles, of which the three first and most important in the English text run as follows

Article I

From the date of the signing of this Treaty there shall be free transit through Massowah, to and from Abyssinia, for all goods, including arms and ammunition, under British protection.

Article II

On and after the first day of September 1884, corresponding to the eighth day of Maskarram 1877, the country called Bogos shall be restored to His Majesty the Negoosa Negust; and when the troops of His Highness the Khedive shall have left the Garrisons of Kassala, Amedib and Sanhit, the buildings in the Bogos country, which now belong to His Highness the Khedive, together with all the stores and munitions of war which shall then remain in the said buildings, shall be delivered to and become the property of, His Majesty the Negoosa Negust.

Article III

His Majesty the Negoosa Negust engages to facilitate the withdrawal of the troops of His Highness the Khedive, from Kassala, Amedib and Sanhit through Ethiopia to Massowah.

In Article IV the khedive undertakes to facilitate the future appointment of bishops for Ethiopia. Article V provides for mutual extradition of criminals between Ethiopia and Egypt, Article VI for the reference of all differences between the two countries to the British government, and Article VII for ratification of the treaty.[302]

A comparison between the treaty text and Hewett's instructions reveals that the Ethiopians had the upper hand during the negotiations. The two most important issues for Ethiopia were moved to the top, while Yohannis's undertaking to assist in the evacuation of the Egyptian garrisons and to refer differences to the British government were moved down. Much more important, particularly in view of the discussions about 'the reservation with respect to the lawful claims of the Porte' are the changes in Article II. Yohannis apparently did not believe in being 'at liberty to occupy'. He wanted to establish both the fact that Ethiopia had been *robbed of* territory and the obligation of Egypt to *return* that territory. This was taken care of by the phrase 'shall be restored (ይመለስ ፡ ኣል ፡)'. The change from 'the district of Bogos' to 'the country called Bogos', an exact translation of (በጉስ ፡ የሚባል ፡ ኣገር ፡), indicates that the extent of the territory involved was discussed, and the stipulation that buildings, stores, and munitions of war which had to be left behind should 'be delivered to and become the property of' the King further underlines that Hewett and Mason had been obliged to completely abandon the fiction that the whole territorial

302   FO 93/2/2, Treaty between Great Britain, Egypt, and Abyssinia, 3 Jun. 1884; English text printed in *PP. Commons*, 1884, LXXXVII, pp. 1–9; Amharic text of articles I and II published and analysed in my article 'The Adwa Peace Treaty of 1884', *Proceedings*.

ብሔ ፬ ፳ ፡ኛ፡

ፈ ብር ት ፡ ወ ሌ ሪ ሳ ፡ ቷ ፡ የ ሆ ፤ ፡ ኀ ጋ ሠ ት ፡ ቢ ከ ቶ ር ፡ ፈ ኀ ፩ ፡ ነ ት ፡
የ ሆ ፤ ፡ የ ተ ሳ ፡ ብ ር ቷ ኀ ፪ ፫ ፡ የ ኢ ዶ ሳ ለ ፪ ፬ ፡ ኀ ጋ ሠ ት ፡
የ ሀ ሃ ፮ ኬ ፡ ቲ ስ ር ፪ ት ፡ ፪ ቆ ወ ፡ ከ ሱ ር ፡ ሴ ዕ ፡ የ ሆ ፤ ፡ ኢ
ፀ ወ ፡ ኢ ፀ ፯ ፡ ኢ ብ ሔ ር ፡ ኢ ፪ ፡ ይ ሔ ፱ ስ ፡ ኀ ፮ ፡ ሠ ፡ ፬ ፬ ፱ ፡ ኀ ፬
ሠ ፡ ኀ ፱ ሠ ት ፡ ዘ ኢ ት ፀ ቷ ሃ ፡ ወ ክ ሉ ፡ ኢ ፪ ፡ ፱ ፪ ፱ ሃ ፡ ፬ ፬ ወ ፡ ከ
ሱ ር ፡ የ ሆ ፤ ፡ ወ ሐ ፪ ፪ ፡ ተ ወ ሬ ክ ፡ ብ ኅ ፡ የ ፻ ስ ር ፡ ኪ ፪ ዊ ፡
ስ ኢ ተ ፯ ፪ ፱ ፡ ስ ፫ ስ ር ፡ የ ለ ወ ፡ ፡ ጠ ጡ ፡ ሰ ፯ ፩ ፱ ፡ ቈ
ቀ ፪ ወ ፡ ወ ሳ ፡ ኢ ፪ ፬ ታ ፡ ቆ ስ ፡ ኪ ፪ ፯ ፡ ሲ ግ ቡ ፡ ተ ሰ ፺ ወ ፡
ስ ኢ ፯ ኪ ፬ ፯ ፡ ስ ወ ፈ ሽ ቻ ቼ ወ ፡ ስ ተ ክ ታ ፲ ቻ ቸ ወ ፡ ፸ ዘ
፹ ፡ ስ ኢ ፱ ት ፡ የ ፺ ጠ ስ ቀ ፡ ከ ብ ር ት ፡ ሐ ሪ ስ ት ፡ የ ሆ ፤ ፡
፬ ፬ ሠ ት ፡ ቢ ክ ቶ ር ፪ ፫ ፡ ኢ ፱ ፩ ፡ ነ ት ፡ የ ሆ ፤ ፡ ተ ሰ ቀ ፡ ብ ር ቷ
፬ ፱ ፫ ፡ የ ኢ ዶ ለ ሬ ፱ ፫ ፡ ወ ኀ ፬ ሠ ት ፡ ኀ ፬ ሠ ት ፡ የ ፀ ፯ ፱ ኬ ፡
ቄ ስ ር ፪ ት ፡ ሬ ር ፡ ኢ ፪ ፺ ፪ ታ ስ ፡ ሬ ር ፡ ወ ሲ ፹ ፡ ሐ ፪ ወ ት ፡
የ ጠ ር ፡ ወ ፈ ክ ፡ ኢ ሰ ቻ ች ፡ ፈ ስ ፡ በ ሆ ፱ ፪ ፡ ኢ ፯ ር ፡ ፺ ሰ ስ
ሬ ኢ ቻ ወ ፡ ከ ሱ ር ፡ ሴ ዕ ፡ የ ሆ ፤ ፡ ዘ ፪ ወ ፡ ኢ ፬ ዘ ኢ ስ ሐ ር ፡
ኢ ፀ ፡ ይ ሐ ፯ ስ ፡ ፬ ፬ ሠ ፡ ፪ ፬ ፯ ፡ ፬ ፬ ሠ ፡ ነ ፬ ሠ ት ፡ ዘ ኢ ተ ፪
ቋ ፪ ፡ ወ ክ ሉ ፡ ኢ ፪ ፪ ፺ ፪ ሃ ፡ በ ለ ቢ ተ ቻ ወ ፡ ፪ ፬ ፱ ፡ ከ ሱ ር ፡
የ ሆ ፤ ፡ የ ፻ ስ ር ፡ ኪ ፪ ዊ ፡ ፺ ስ ፫ ፡ ቢ ፪ ፫ ፡ የ ጠ ጠ ፱ ፡
፱ ፡ ፻ ስ ሬ ፡ ኢ ፪ ር ግ ፱ ፡ ኢ ስ ዘ ሃ ፪ ፡ የ ፺ ከ ተ ሉ ተ ፱ ፬ ቋ
ስ ት ፡ ኢ ኢ ፪ ፤ ፡ ተ ሰ ፺ ወ ፡ ሬ ተ ፩ ፡ ቆ ስ ፡ በ ስ ፪ ፡ ወ በ ፸ ፤
፪ ፡ ጠ ር ፡ በ ፫ ፻ ፺ ፪ ወ ፪ ሮ ፬ ወ ፪ ፬ ጠ ት ፡ ወ ሐ ፬ ት ፡ በ ኢ ተ ፬ ፬
ሃ ፡ ቀ ጠ ር ፡ በ ስ ፺ ሲ ዙ ፡ ቀ ጠ ር ፡ ኢ ወ ፡ ፯ ለ ፯ ፪ ፡ በ ፪ ፻ ፬
፱ ፡ ፹ ፡ ወ ፬ ፬ ፬ ፺ ት ፡ ወ ሐ ፬ ት ፡ በ ፪ ጠ ቀ ፡ በ ር ፡ የ ፺ ጠ ፺
ፈ ፡ የ ፺ ፬ ፱ ፡ ኢ ፬ ፡ ሀ ሉ ፡ የ ፩ ፲ ፪ ፻ ፡ ኢ ፬ ፡ በ ሆ ፱ ፡ የ ጠ ር ፻
ስ ር ፬ ፻ ፡ ቢ ሆ ፱ ፡ ከ ፺ ፻ ፡ ፩ ፰ ፡ ፪ ፻ ፬ ስ ፡ በ ኢ ፪ ፺ ሲ ዙ ፡
ጠ በ ፯ ት ፡ ፪ ከ ፻ ስ ፪ ፬ ፻ ፡ ፻ ፲ ፡ ፪ ፬ ር ፡ በ ፫ ፻ ፬ ፱
፪ ፡ ወ ፪ ፬ ፺ ት ፡ ፻ ሐ ፬ ት ፡ በ ፬ ተ ሀ ፯ ፪ ፡ ፲ ፡ ጠ ር ፡ በ ፪ ፻
፺ ለ ፲ ፡ ፩ ፱ ር ፡ በ ፫ ፻ ፬ ፪ ፻ ወ ፪ ፬ ፺ ት ፡ ወ ሐ ፬ ት ፡ በ ፪ ፻
ፓ ፡ ፲ ፡ የ ፺ ፪ ፯ ለ ወ ፡ ኢ ፯ ር ፡ ፮ ፰ ፡ ፱ ሀ ፱ ፡ ለ ፯ ፱ ፡ ፺ ፻ ፹ ፻ ፡ ፪ ፻ ፺ ፱
ታ ፡ ፪ ወ ለ ስ ፡ ለ ስ ፡ የ ፻ ስ ር ፡ ኪ ፪ ዊ ፡ ወ ቃ ፪ ር ፡ ች ፻ ፡
ከ ስ ፪ ፱ ፡ ኢ ፻ ፪ ፻ ፱ ፡ ስ ፱ ሐ ፡ ት ፱ ፡ ለ ቀ ወ ፡ ሐ ፻ ፻ ፡ በ
ፁ ፱ ፩ ፡ ፪ ፯ ፻ ፡ የ ኪ ፪ ዊ ፡ ቢ ቶ ች ፡ ኢ ፻ ች ፡ የ ፺ ር ፻
ስ ር ፪ ቻ ወ ፻ ፡ ሀ ሉ ፡ በ ኢ ዘ ሃ ፡ ስ ፬ ር ፻ ፡ የ ፺ ቀ ር ፡
ስ ፩ ፪ ፱ ፪ ፡ ፪ ፻ ፱ ፡ ፯ ፯ ፱ ፱ ፡ ፹ ፪ ሠ ፡ ነ ፯ ሠ ት ፡
በ ከ ስ ስ ፡ በ ኢ ፻ ፲ ፱ ፡ በ ስ ፱ ሐ ት ፡ ፻ ሉ ት ፡ የ ኪ ፪ ዊ ፡
ወ ቀ ፪ ር ች ፡ ፻ ጠ ፱ ፡ ሐ ፻ ለ ሉ ፡ ፪ ፪ ች ፻ ወ ፡ በ ኢ ተ ፻
፬ የ ፻ ስ ር ፡ ኪ ፪ ዊ ፡ ሰ ፲ ፱ ፻ ፱ ፡ ኢ ፱ ፲ ፡ ፪ ፲ ፪ ሠ ፡ ነ ፯ ሠ ት ፡
፪ ሬ ቀ ፪ ር ፡ ቄ ፪ ስ ፪ ፱ ፡ ወ ፪ ፪ ፬ ፪ ፱ ፡ ፪ ፡ ፻ ፡ ከ ፻ ስ ፪ ፯ ፡

ፊጸገሀይ፡ጓጙ፡ሠ፡ንሃሠተና፡ የጸብ ሽር፡ኪጺዊ፡ፁ
ጠቱ፡ፊርቀው፡ካሃዳቸው፡ባዘት፡ወጸፊሃዳቸ
ው፡ባዘት፡ሀሳዊ ሽሩ፡በ ሀሰፆየ፡በጸ ኤጅ ቾዒ፡
ሰልሊው፡ሊሰጠጉ፡ተሰዓመ፡ኗየሀ፡ቃፄ፡ኪጸ
ገ፡ከታተመ፡በ ዒግ፡በ ኤትዮቋየ፡ንጊ ሠ፡ንገሠቱ
ፉ፡በ ሞ ሽር፡ከጸዊ፡ መ ከኩል፡ጠመ፡በ ኒ ፃ፡ ሰኧኅ
ፀልመ ር፡ ኗጓ ሠት፡ ሊ ንጓ ራ፡ ሊ ፊ ሰ ጠ፡ ወ ል ፡ ኧ ጸ ሪ
ጒ፡ ኗ የ ሀ ፡ ቃ ፄ ፡ ኪ ጸ ገ ፡ ወ ገ ወ ተ ፡ በ ተ ሰ ቀ ፡ ጠ ር ተ ጓ ዪ
ዪ፡ በ ኧ ር ል ን ዪ ፡ ኗ ጓ ሠ ት ፡ በ ሀ ዪ ዪ ኪ ፡ ቄ ሰ ር ዪ ተ ፡ ዪ
ጸ መ ፡ በ መ ሽ ር ፡ ኩ ጸ ዊ ፡ ኧ ኗ ዪ ፡ ታ ዪ ቾ ፡ ተ ተ ወ ፡ ቶ ሉ ፡
ዪ መ ፡ ሰ ሰ ል ፡ ሰ ኧ ዚ የ መ ፡ መ ስ ከ ር ን ተ ፡ ፊ ር ፡ ኧ ጸ ወ ራ ፡
ል ፡ ከ ር ፡ ው ሊ መ ፡ ኅ ዪ ወ ት ፡ ሀ ተ ሰ ቀ ፡ ጠ ር ተ ጓ ዪ ፡ ሀ ኒ
ዪ ር ለ ን ዪ ፡ ኗ ጓ ሠ ት ፡ ሀ ሀ ጓ ዪ ኪ ፡ ቄ ሰ ር ዪ ተ ፡ መ ስ ለ
ፊ ፡ ሁ ጓ ፡ ኗ ሀ ሀ የ መ ፡ ጓ ጓ ሠ ፡ ን ገ ሠ ት ፡ በ ሰ ቤ ተ ቸ መ ፡
ከ ቡ ር ፡ ዓ ኧ ጓ ፡ ቢ ዪ ጓ ፡ የ መ ሽ ር ፡ ከ ጸ ዊ ፡ መ ሰ ሰ ፊ ፡ ሁ ፡
ው ፡ ዪ ሀ ጓ ፡ ቃ ፄ ፡ ኪ ዪ ጓ ፡ በ ዪ መ ጓ ፡ ተ ማ ቸ መ ፡ ኧ ተ መ ፡
ኧ ጸ ፉ ፡ ኧ መ ፡ ቋ ለ ሰ ፊ ፡ በ ፲ ወ ፯ ፮ ፯ ፺ ፡ ወ ፱ ፬ መ ተ ፡ መ ሰ
ገ ተ ፡ በ ኤ ት ዮ ፉ ዪ ፡ ቀ ጠ ር ፡ በ ፩ ቀ ም ለ ፤ ፡ ቀ ጠ ር ፡ ፩
መ ፡ ከ ል ፉ ፡ ሰ ዪ ጓ ፡ በ ፲ ወ ፯ ፱ ፹ ፻ ም ፲ ወ ፬ ቀ መ ተ ፡ መ ሐ ረ ተ ፡

W. Hewett

M. ...

arrangement was an Ethiopian reconquest 'which Egypt has not seen fit to resist'.

As for the extent of the Bogos country, the English text permits two interpretations: either the districts of Bogos, Mensa, Habab, the two Maryas, etc., which had been administered and protected directly from Keren (Senhit)[303] or all the territory on Ethiopia's north-western frontiers protected by the three garrisons of Kasala, Amideb, and Keren. The latter might seem unlikely, but the Amharic text makes it very clear that it was the buildings, stores and munitions of war at *all three centres*—በስለሁ ፡ ስፍርት ፡—in *Bogos* that were to become Ethiopian property. Ever since 1872, Bogos had been at the centre of the conflict, and Bogos was often used as the overall name for the disputed areas between Massawa and Kasala. Yohannis made it quite clear that he intended to occupy everything as far as and including Kasala,[304] and one might ask what good the buildings there would do him if he did not. On the other hand, Kasala had not been threatened or claimed by the Ethiopians before the Hewett mission, and giving it up to Ethiopia could hardly be called a restoration. While the mission was in Ethiopia, however, there was great concern that Kasala might fall to the Mahdists, and this is probably why it was included by Hewett, who nevertheless reported that he had told Yohannis that he could not give Kasala to him.[305] After the treaty had been signed attempts were also made to separate the issue of Kasala from that of 'Sanhit and Amadeb with all the frontier'. Finally, the conclusions were that 'Kassala, Amedeb and Sanhit seem to be all included in Bogos' and 'we must go by the Treaty'. On this understanding the treaty was ratified.[306]

The second important issue for Ethiopia was *free transit*. This matter was raised, with the other terms of the treaty, in a letter which Hewett addressed to the King on 24 April while he was on his way to Adwa. Hewett's understanding of *free transit* was that '. . . goods coming out and going into Abyssinia, whether merchandize or munitions of war, may pass free of duty through Massowah under British protection'. Mason, who had not seen this letter beforehand, pointed out that it said more than Hewett's instructions and 'that Abyssinia should be content with the passage of arms, those addressed to the King, free of duty; otherwise, it would be impossible to maintain the port of Massowah'.[307] Hewett was evidently impressed by this argument and decided to forget the offer he had made to Yohannis. In his report on the negotiations he only stated that he had (in the letter referred to) set 'forth in detail the terms which it was

303 This is no doubt what Chérif Pasha had in mind when he wrote (FO 1/30, p. 133) that Egypt was prepared to give up 'the districts of Bogos' (in plural).
304 FO 401/6, pp. 37, 40, Hastings to Admiralty, 29 May and 9 Jun. 1884, quoting Hewett, 18 May and 30 May 1884 respectively. At the time of the mission Qallabat was supposed to be in the hands of the Mahdists and was probably not discussed at all (FO 1/31, p. 427, Mason to Egerton, 12 Jul. 1884).
305 FO 401/6, pp. 37–8, Mason to Nubar, 7 May 1884, Granville to Egerton, 3 Jun. 1884; FO 1/31, pp. 264–99, Hewett to Granville, 9 Jun. 1884.
306 FO 1/31, pp. 371–5, Egerton to Granville, 8 Jul. 1884; pp. 380–404, memorandum by Rolfe and minutes 9–10 Jul. 1884; pp. 417–18, Granville to Speedy, 11 Jul. 1884.
307 FO 401/6, pp. 37–8, Mason to Nubar, 7 May 1884.

proposed to embody in a treaty . . .' but he failed to attach a copy of this important letter though he attached a number of less important ones.[308] With Yohannis, too, the less said the better. Hewett cannot be expected to have brought up the interpretation of *free transit* with Yohannis a second time.

In some roundabout way, judging from Hewett's report, the question of customs duties at Massawa was nevertheless raised and someone (probably Mason) proposed that the revenue, 'after deducting the expenses of the port', should be shared equally between Egypt and Ethiopia. According to Yohannis, it was Hewett who suggested this arrangement but backed down for lack of authorization when he was asked to include it in the treaty. Hewett reported that he had 'pointed out to the King that he could have nothing more advantageous than free transit through Massowah, since he could then establish a custom-house on his own frontier and levy just what dues he pleased'.[309] Ethiopian rulers not only *could* do this but always *had* done it, so this whole discussion does not make sense unless the Ethiopians thought they had been offered a share of the duties collected on goods imported for Massawa itself. Yohannis reportedly asked for some territory on the coast but was told that Hewett was not authorized to grant this. Besides, Yohannis would gain nothing by having 'ports of his own'.[310]

The validity of any or all of these arguments rested entirely on the interpretation of *free transit* given by Hewett before the negotiations started. How could the British negotiator possibly go back on this, or even allow Yohannis to suspect that he considered doing so? The Amharic version of Article I proves not only that Mason reported Hewett's offer correctly but also that Yohannis seized upon an offer which was both clear and sufficiently advantageous to make Massawa as good as an Ethiopian port:

> All goods exported and imported through the port of Massawa, be it the goods of merchants, be it war materials, shall be free from duties (ከግብር ፡ ነጻ ፡), under British protection (ጠባቂነት ፡).

According to Hewett, he had drafted the English text himself and the translation into Amharic was made by the Ethiopian interpreter of the mission who had been engaged at Cairo by Speedy. The latter must have assisted since he was Hewett's political adviser and was at least reported to be 'well acquainted with the language'. A last-minute change in the English text of the final copies indicates both that they had paid attention to Ethiopian requests when they wrote the Amharic text and that Yohannis's own English secretaries Mirça Werqē and his nephew Yohannis Meshesha were checking the English against the Amharic.[311] Hewett had intended *free transit* to go into effect on 1 October.

308   FO 1/31, pp. 264–99, Hewett to Granville, 9 Jun. 1884. The enclosures are indicated in the report, and there is also a list of them (p. 235), but the letter of 24 Apr. is neither listed nor available in a single copy.
309   ibid., pp. 281–3, Hewett, 9 Jun. 1884; FO 95/744, no. 173, Yohannis to Victoria, 25 Jun. 1884.
310   FO 1/31, p. 279, Hewett, 9 Jun. 1884.
311   ibid., pp. 264–99, Hewett, 9 Jun. 1884; pp. 636–7, Hewett to Yohannis Meshesha Werqē, 3 Jun. 1884.

Just before signing, this was changed to 'From the date of the signing of this treaty' which agreed better with the 1 Senē (7 June) of the Amharic text.[312] There is no indication, however, that anyone raised the possibility that *free* in *free transit* could mean anything less than *free from duties*.

Yohannis's letter to Victoria after the treaty had been signed revealed both his gratitude for the concessions with regard to Massawa and his desire to continue negotiations under the auspices of the British government. What he wanted, ultimately, was the complete restoration to Ethiopia of the port 'of his ancestors'. At the Foreign Office in London it was agreed that 'it would be wise to keep him [Yohannis] in good humour by a friendly reply . . . pointing out that H. M. could not do more for him *at present* and that the concession of free transit through Massowah under British protection is one of immense importance to him . . .' etc.[313]

Taken at face value, the Adwa peace treaty of 1884 was a diplomatic victory for Ethiopia comparable to the military ones of Gundet and Gura. The combination of patience and sustained pressure had finally led up to a very favourable moment for negotiations, and the opportunity was not wasted. Ethiopia's lost borderlands were recovered. Massawa was for all practical purposes made an Ethiopian port. There would be no more maltreatment, no more embargoes, and no more customs duties to pay. Yohannis was no doubt disappointed that his claims to the coastline in general had not been recognized in the treaty, but since the issue was passed over in silence and he was not asked to recognize Egypt's claims, it simply meant that this aspect of the problem had been left for the future to solve.

The British/Egyptian authorities were naturally interested primarily in the rescue of their garrisons, and Yohannis and Alula gave their full cooperation in accordance with Article III of the treaty. When it was discovered that Metemma and Girra had not fallen to the Mahdists, Yohannis accepted additional obligations, and these two garrisons were saved together with Amideb and Keren.[314] With regard to the obligations entered into by the British, the situation was quite different. Because the Egyptians did not want to give up Kasala, which was eventually lost to the Mahdists due to postponements, they did not evacuate and hand over Keren either as agreed, though it was the very centre of Bogos. In the opinion of the new governor general of the Red Sea coast, 'The primary object of requesting the Abyssinians to go to Galabad was . . . to divert their attention from Senheit [Keren] and Kassalah . . .'[315] At Massawa harassment evidently continued: '. . . only the other day the Egyptians detained a bell there ordered by King John for his cathedral "simply to annoy" under pretext that custom dues had not been paid'.[316] The very person for whom the

312 FO 93/2/2; FO 1/31, pp. 285–7, Hewett, 9 Jun. 1884.
313 FO 95/744, no. 174, Yohannis to Victoria, 25 Jun. 1884, with minutes; FO 95/745, no. 205, Victoria to Yohannis, 6 Sep. 1884 (my emphasis).
314 FO 95/746, no. 196, Yohannis to Victoria, 28 Aug. 1885; no. 198, Victoria to Yohannis, 8 Dec. 1885. See also Earl Cromer, *Modern Egypt* (London, 1908), Vol. II, pp. 47–9.
315 FO 403/82, p. 180, Baring to Granville, 5 Nov. 1884; FO 78/3799, Chermside to Nubar, 27 Dec. 1884.
316 FO 1/31, pp. 640–1, minute by Granville, [c. 8 Sep. 1884].

extradition clause had most likely been drawn up, Yohannis's own cousin Debbeb Araya, was brought from Sawakin to Massawa for trial—and allowed to escape.[317] In other words, all the three clauses that mattered to Ethiopia were violated within a few months.

These were minor matters. Behind the scenes the real blow to Ethiopia was being prepared. Since the British had their hands full in Egypt and the Porte seemed uninterested in taking effective charge of the Red Sea coast, there was a real possibility that the Ethiopians would move into the vacuum and retake some coastline. If the worst came to the worst, this would have to be accepted in the case of minor ports, for instance Arafalī in Zulla Bay.[318] The problem for Britain was what to do with Massawa. So on 20 October, three months after the ratification of the treaty, Lord Granville sounded Rome's ambassador in London about an eventual Italian occupation of Massawa, which he allegedly did not want to leave to the barbarians (read Abyssinians) or to a rival power (read France).[319] Three months later the matter was settled, and on 5 February 1885 the Italians landed at Massawa.[320]

In the choice between the 'only two possible alternatives, viz., either to hand Massowah over to the King of Abyssinia, or for the Italian Government to take possession of the place', Abyssinia was bound to lose.[321] But the way the choice was phrased is interesting as an indication of how seemingly impossible it had become for the representatives of European imperialism to think straight about African matters. It was to the Italians that Massawa was *handed over*; if the British had been prepared to abandon the place Yohannis would have *taken possession* without diplomatic or any other kind of support.

The Italians soon showed that they had no intention of abiding by the terms of the Hewett treaty. On the contrary, they had come to inherit the estate of the Egyptians, Bogos and all. Yohannis was deeply disturbed that the British had betrayed him in this manner. He had agreed to incur the enmity of the Mahdists on his western frontier, acting as an ally of the British in a defensive operation to save his former enemies, the Egyptians. He had done so for some very important concessions, but as a result of the dishonesty of British diplomacy, he turned out to have traded one weak enemy for two strong ones, the Mahdist state and Italy.

The Main Source of Strength

Emperor Yohannis was an obedient and observant son of the Orthodox church. When he placed his seal with the words 'The cross has conquered the tribe of

317 ENA, Soudan, Carton 3/7, Debbeb to Rashid, 1883/84, and to Muhammad Tawfiq, 1883/84. The dating of these letters is 1876 Eth. cal.; thus they were written within one year after 11 Sep. 1883. See also FO 95/748, no. 194, Yohannis to Victoria, 8 Mar. 1887.
318 FO 403/82, p. 171, memorandum by Fitzmaurice, 28 Oct. 1884; p. 176, Baring to Granville, 2 Nov. 1884; p. 178, Granville to Baring, 4 Nov. 1884.
319 Giglio, *Etiopia–Mar Rosso*, Vol. III, pp. 70–1, Nigra to Mancini, 20 Oct. 1884.
320 The story of the negotiations and the occupation of Massawa is well known. See Giglio, *Etiopia–Mar Rosso*, Vol. I, pp. 335–54, 369–83, and relevant documents in volume III.
321 FO 403/82, pp. 183–7, Baring to Granville, 3 Nov. 1884.

Ismail' (engraved after the battle of Gura) under the peace treaty, it is not likely that he gave much thought to the question of how, precisely, Ethiopia had managed to defeat Egypt. It is not known whether he even considered it as anything remarkable that Ethiopia preserved her independence while Egypt lost hers. Nevertheless the Ethiopian victory which saved the country from nominal Egyptian and *de facto* British rule was under the circumstances a most extraordinary event, more so in some respects than the victory over the Italians at Adwa in 1896. Whether one looks at the conflict from a military or an economic, a political or a diplomatic viewpoint, Ethiopia seems to have been so much at a disadvantage compared with Egypt.

In terms of economic development and financial resources there is no comparison between the two countries. Egypt had for several decades been a main recipient of European capital and technological know-how. That foreign financiers were rapidly driving the khedive's government into bankruptcy does not mean that Egypt lacked resources. For a nineteenth-century government which had managed to pile up almost £100 million in debts over twelve years, one more million for the purpose of preserving Egypt's African possessions, as Ismail put it, was certainly not prohibitive.[322] In Ethiopia neither the subsistence level agriculture nor the foreign trade which, moreover, suffered from the blockade of all the ports could be expected to provide anything comparable to Egypt's resources. The haste with which Yohannis demobilized after both Gundet and Gura has to do with this problem of resources.

Diplomatically, too, Ethiopia was at a very great disadvantage. Ismail had immediate access to representatives of the European powers while Yohannis was at times prevented even from corresponding with them. Hundreds of Europeans and Americans in the service of the Egyptian government provided further channels for making Egypt's views known and accepted. What were Sarzec, a vice-consul who was unable to retain his post at Massawa when Ismail demanded that he be recalled,[323] and Kirkham, a former sergeant without the slightest backing by his own government who was unable to get himself out of Egyptian detention though he carried a British passport and travelled as a diplomatic courier,[324] in comparison with men like Munzinger, Loring, Gordon, and Hewett? Nothing illustrates the advantage of Egypt better than the fact that the British consul general at the height of the conflict over Bogos accepted as *impartial* what the Egyptian governor Munzinger reported.[325]

322 See Marlowe, *Anglo-Egyptian Relations*, pp. 90–1. For Ismail's remark, above, p. 326.
323 AECP, Massouah 4, fols 21–3, Sarzec to Decazes, 30 Sep. 1875. For background, see Douin, *Ismaïl*, III, 2, pp. 422–30.
324 See above, pp. 300, 332–3.
325 Sabry maintains (*L'empire égyptien sous Ismaïl*, p. 466) that Vivian was engaged in an 'impartial inquiry' when he did this. The author, moreover, concludes (pp. 472–3) that 'the second cause of the [Egyptian] defeat lies in the treason of certain missionaries and British and French agents' (the first being the disunity in the Egyptian command at Gura). Of these, he mentions, besides Sarzec and Kirkham, two Hamptons (*sic*), then one of them again under the correct name Houghton with his business associate R. A. Barlow and, finally, a 'French missionary', read Duflot. The only known 'treason' of the Houghtons was that they reported the outcome of the battle of Gundet on their return to England soon after. The only ones even present in the area during the Gura campaign were Kirkham—in

By all tangible criteria except one, Ethiopia was militarily much weaker than Egypt. The exception was sheer numbers. According to Dye, Egypt's regular army in 1875 numbered about 45,000 men,[326] of whom approximately half were in action against Ethiopia. Ethiopia's peasant-warriors were in theory as many as her able-bodied men; of these 50,000–100,000 participated in the war against Egypt, for there were limits, of course, to how many could be brought together at any given place or time. But otherwise, the advantages were all on the Egyptian side: trained soldiers organized into regular units, as against hordes of warriors, relatively speaking without training and without organization; officers with a regular training at Egypt's own staff college and further education in Britain, France, or Germany and foreign officers from Denmark (Arendrup), Austria (Zichy, Thurneyssen, and Möckeln), Italy (Ali Helmi and Sormani), Switzerland (Durholz), and above all veterans of the Civil War in the United States (Loring, Dye, Field, Derrick, Dennison, etc.),[327] as against self-made and self-educated warrior chiefs; Remington rifles, rocket-stands, Krupp steel guns with unlimited supplies of ammunition,[328] as against outdated muskets, matchlocks, and other muzzleloaders, with home-made ammunition.

In terms of 'technical' improvements the situation in Ethiopia had changed very little in the few years since Meqdela. Napier's gift to Yohannis in 1868 was made up of his least valuable arms, and weaponry outside Ethiopia had improved much around 1870. In combination with Kirkham's training efforts and tactical dispositions, the 12 guns, 725 smooth-bore muskets and 130 rifles had nevertheless played an important role in changing the balance of power in Ethiopia at the time. In all probability, however, it was the generous supplies of ammunition, 350,000 rounds for the small arms, that had really made the difference. But Kirkham's own efforts had been limited to a relatively small number of soldiers and he had failed to recruit the right kind of staff to continue the training. Then the Egyptian arms embargo had prevented not only the modernization of the weaponry but also the replenishing of the supplies of regular ammunition.[329] The powder produced in Ethiopia was, as one visitor observed in 1873, 'very weak and bad, but this is perhaps fortunate, as an

---

prison at Massawa—and Duflot, who received the highest praise from Egyptian officers for his intelligence services for Egypt. The real significance of this kind of historiography is that it reflects the attitude at the time of the conflict: *All* Europeans were expected to serve Egypt's interests—otherwise they were traitors—and of course most did.

326 *Moslem Egypt*, pp. 56–9. See also AECP, Égypte 55, fols 231–2, for a detailed list from 1874 adding up to 61,196 men.

327 Loring, *Confederate Soldier*, pp. 349–64; Douin, *Ismaïl*, III, 3B, pp. 826–33. The names include only people participating in the expeditions against Ethiopia.

328 One of Ratib's biggest problems during the evacuation was what to do with all the ammunition in his forts (Douin, *Ismaïl*, III, 3B, pp. 1055–6, 1079).

329 See above, pp. 275–6, 300–1. De Cosson provides an additional good illustration of this (*Blue Nile*, Vol. II, pp. 57–8). When the traveller ran out of ammunition for his own arms, Yohannis persuaded one of his chiefs to exchange a breech-loading rifle with fifty cartridges for a 'double-barrelled fowling-piece . . . which being a muzzle-loader, would be more useful to him than the breech-loader, for which he could not procure ammunition when his fifty cartridges were expended . . .'

ordinary charge of English powder would irremediably damage most of the native guns . . .' As for bullets, they were 'frequently merely pieces of slate cut into a conical shape, in imitation of our rifle bullets'.[330] In early 1875, Arakil learned from a French traveller that the arms of the Ethiopians were 'particularly dangerous for those who make use of them' and as a curious detail that an Italian at Gonder was manufacturing 'shells for the artillery from sardine tins'.[331] Under these circumstances the total number of firearms in Ethiopia is only of marginal interest.[332] Even the estimate by Franz Hassen that Yohannis could probably collect 6,000 *well-armed* 'fusileers' is misleading, at least qualitatively. Certainly the number of swift-firing breechloaders was much less than 6,000.[333]

Further proof that the Ethiopians were still ill-equipped and ill-prepared for gunfire fighting against a modern army is easy to find in the accounts of the battle of Gura. Ethiopian artillery seems to have been in action only on the final day of the battle and only for a few minutes. 'Three or four shells' were fired with one of the cannon captured on 7 March, allegedly by the likewise captured Major Durholz.[334] Musket and rifle fire played some role, of course, particularly in the attempts to take the fort on the final day. But the victory of 7 March was really won in the traditional Ethiopian way: the headlong, relentless attack with spears and swords, on horseback to the extent that horses were available, otherwise on foot.[335]

For the Ethiopians to win this kind of a battle, the Egyptians had to oblige with some poor generalship, blunders, and outright lack of courage, but these are by no means uncommon factors in battles. With the underestimation of the Ethiopians typical of the post-Meqdela period, Arakil wrote nine months before Gundet, '. . . for the conqueror who wants to take possession of Abyssinia, the necessary tools are good maps, some intelligent officers and three or four thousand well-armed men'.[336] The maps and the men (four to five times the number believed necessary) were provided. If the officers with their experience from the wars of the Middle East, Europe, Mexico, and the United States did not manage, and they didn't, it was not because they had underestimated the

---

330   De Cosson, *Blue Nile*, Vol. I, p. 218.
331   ENA, Soudan et Afrique Orientale, Casier 120/73/3, Arakil to Barrot, 12 Feb. 1875.
332   For various estimates, see Pankhurst, *Economic History*, pp. 587–8; for a valuable analysis of the relative importance of firearms throughout the nineteenth century in Ethiopia, Richard Caulk, 'Firearms and Princely Power in Ethiopia in the Nineteenth Century', *JAH*, XII, 4 (1972), pp. 609–30.
333   Dye, *Moslem Egypt*, p. 396. A. Raffray, who visited Yohannis in his camp in December 1873, reported ('Voyage en Abyssinie, à Zanzibar et au pays des Ouanika', *BSG*, 6, X (1875), p. 300) 2,000 poor rifles in an army of 40,000.
334   Douin, *Ismaïl*, III, 3B, pp. 947, 1012. The cannon captured at Gundet were reported to have been deliberately damaged by the captured Sudanese artillerists when they were requested to participate in the campaign (ibid., III, 3B, p. 902, n. 4).
335   ibid., III, 3B, pp. 921–50; AECP, Massouah 4, fols 56–8, Carbonnel to Decazes, 16 Mar. 1876. The more dramatic version that the Egyptians were defeated 'with their own guns and their own Sniders' has nevertheless found its way into traditional Ethiopian historiography (Afewerq, *Minīlik*, p. 24).
336   ENA, Soudan et Afrique Orientale, Casier 120/73/3, to Barrot, 12 Feb. 1875.

arms, training or potential numbers of the Ethiopians. Arakil, for instance, must have regarded a ten to one ratio as acceptable: '. . . the Abyssinian gangs furnished with poor firearms, spears or simply swords amount to approximately 30,000'.[337]

The underestimation concerned more intangible matters. Loring put down the Ethiopian victory to two factors: Yohannis—'the ablest and most renowned African warrior of modern times'; and the Abyssinians—'a desparately brave people'.[338] This would certainly have been labelled chauvinism if it had come from an Ethiopian. The outcome of Gundet produced a genuine shock: 'How was it, in fact, possible', wrote Sarzec, 'to admit that a force of 1,000 men armed with Remingtons commanded by European officers, with four cannon at their disposal, could have succumbed in twenty minutes, not killing from the Abyssinians more than 31 and not wounding more than 55?' His explanation was that the Egyptians had been outmanoeuvred by Yohannis.[339] Was that not what happened once more the same day, and then on a much larger scale at Gura four months later? As for the bravery of the Ethiopians, it was no doubt a quality deliberately fostered and highly valued in Ethiopian society, but then many brave people have lost battles.

The fundamental reason why the Ethiopian people accepted the Egyptian challenge and won their battles lies in the character of the struggle. Loring tells us that when the second Egyptian army saw and listened to the survivors from Gundet, the men grumbled and the officers complained that they had been sent out on an unnecessary war since 'Egypt had more land at home than they could cultivate'.[340] The Ethiopians had been told and were convinced that they were fighting for their land, their homes, and their faith. Out of the feeling that this attack was unfair beyond all reason, the King and his people drew strength and determination.[341] They did not under-estimate the Turks with their terrifying weapons: 'Let alone people, the shells of the cannon and rockets levelled trees and mountains so that a man had nothing to lean against or hide behind'.[342] But they felt they *had to* fight in spite of or rather because of the in-justice of it all.

Basically it was the political strength of Ethiopia that was misjudged. Both before the war and through all the years of the peace negotiations, the Egyptian and European attitude was the same: if we insist, the Ethiopians will yield. Patience was interpreted as weakness; rivalries and disunity as an invitation to dominate. Year in and year out, in report after report, the 'fact' was established that Yohannis stood almost alone. In the north there was hardly a chief, including Yohannis's uncle Ras Araya, who was not reported to have contacted the Egyptians at one time or another. And every such contact was interpreted

337 ibid., to Khairi, 2 Sep. 1875.
338 Loring, *Confederate Soldier*, pp. 410–11.
339 AECP, Massouah 4, fols 39–48, Sarzec to Decazes, 24 Dec. 1875.
340 *Confederate Soldier*, p. 346.
341 See above, p. 321.
342 BN, Ethiop. 259, fol. 21.

as an offer to join the Egyptian camp and live under Egyptian rule. South of Tigrē, the emphasis was for obvious reasons placed more on the independent revolts of major chiefs against the rule of Yohannis. Rases Welde Sillasē of Begēmdir, Adal of Gojjam, and Haylu of Ṣelewa, Lij or Dejjazmach Wibē (also in Begēmdir), Wagshums Teferi and Kebbede, Imam Amedē of Wello, and, of course, Nigus Minīlik all 'wanted' to ally themselves with the Egyptians.[343]

It is neither possible nor necessary to assess the value of all these contacts: whether they were genuine or fabricated by 'messengers' who simply wanted liberal treatment from the Egyptians; and, in the first case, whether declarations of friendship and support were sincerely meant or made with ulterior motives. The fact is that, on the eve of the battle of Gundet, the Egyptians did not find *one* of the King's great vassals taking advantage of the situation to attack him. Likewise, a head count by Ratib two to three weeks before Gura showed that twenty-two 'rases' had rallied to the support of the King and six (or seven) only were opposed to him; it was suggested that the latter *could possibly be induced* to join the Egyptian side.[344]

The *only* chief of any importance to actually take the step was Welde Mīka'ēl. In 1869 Munzinger had played on his ambitions in the hope of setting him up as a French puppet in northern Ethiopia. Caught for his contacts with Napoleon III, Welde Mīka'ēl spent some years in disfavour, occasionally in prison.[345] At Gundet he fought for Ethiopia and received the governorship of Hamasēn in recognition for his services.[346] Exactly when and why he changed sides is impossible to establish. He was reporting the movements of the Egyptians to Yohannis as late as January 1876, but it was probably on the instructions of the Egyptians who wanted to get Yohannis out of Tigrē to meet them.[347] Early the following month when he turned up in the Egyptian camp instead of heeding the summons of the King, it seems likely that he had come to the conclusion that Yohannis would be defeated by the new army and the lands north of the Mereb lost to Ethiopia.[348] No Ethiopian chief had been in a better position to observe the combined European/Egyptian pressures on Ethiopia's northern frontiers and the increasing disintegration as lowland Muslims shifted their loyalties to Egypt and the Catholics of Akkele Guzay and Bogos to the representatives of Europe. There was in this process an element of increasing autonomy for Ethiopia's northern provinces in comparison with the days of Welde Sillasē and Sebagadis, though it is doubtful if Welde Mīka'ēl was aware of this aspect of the drama in which he was involved. Otherwise he seems to have impressed most observers as an intelligent and powerful personality.[349] At any rate, his own fate proves that the time was not ripe. Though Ratib reported that Welde Mīka'ēl had more than 2,000 men with him when he crossed the

343 Douin, *Ismaïl*, III, 2, pp. 361–71; 3B, 703–4, 712–17, 724, 740–2, 761–2, 770–1, 844–9, 889–99, 1029, 1045, 1054–5 (all from the most crucial years 1872–76).
344 ibid., III, 3B, pp. 771–2, 899.
345 See above, pp. 278, 294.
346 BN, Ethiop. 259, fol. 21.
347 Douin, *Ismaïl*, III, 3B, pp. 770–1, 845–9, 876–7.
348 See above, pp. 326–7.
349 Loring, *Confederate Soldier*, p. 386; Hill, *Gordon*, pp. 301–4; Winstanley, *A Visit*, pp. 212–13.

line, Dye and Loring saw 200–300 only,[350] and when the former governor was chased out of Serayē and Hamasēn by Alula seven or eight months later, he took only some 1,500 with him.[351] Armed and ungovernable, Welde Mīka'ēl remained a nuisance and an obstacle to peace for some years. But it was within the Egyptian boundaries that he had his base; neither before nor after Gura did he have more than local significance.

The one ally who would have made a real difference was Minīlik of Shewa. Having claimed the throne before both Tekle Gīyorgīs and Yohannis, he was the obvious alternative to the latter. With his base in Shewa far away from any Egyptian boundary, it was reasonable to expect that he might be willing to give up territory in the north and west to secure the throne. Because he was the natural ally of the Egyptians, and because of the tension between him and Yohannis, it has been taken for granted almost that Minīlik conspired with the Egyptians to open the way for himself to the throne. Because, again, of the tension between Tigrē and Shewa which has prevailed in Ethiopian politics ever since Minīlik succeeded Yohannis, at the expense of the latter's son Mengesha, the question of Minīlik's eventual treason has remained a live issue. European travellers a few years after the events began to publish reports of a conspiracy between Ismail (or Munzinger) and Minīlik to attack Yohannis. Some two or three decades later, i.e. during the last years of Minīlik's reign, Ethiopian authors included references to the matter, Afewerq denying that Minīlik's contacts with Egypt were treasonable, Aṣme Gīyorgīs maintaining that Minīlik did take the initiative to an agreement about attacking Yohannis and was only waiting for the Munzinger expedition through Awsa to reach him.[352]

Minīlik's contacts with the Egyptian government date from late 1872. The coronation of Yohannis seems to have prompted the ruler of Shewa to take some new foreign initiatives. Besides writing a long letter to Queen Victoria implying that he would rejoice (as Jacob over his lost son Joseph!) if the kind of mission sent to Sahle Sillasē would arrive again in Shewa, Minīlik for the first time approached the German and Italian governments. Protestant and Catholic missionaries were the channels, probably the instigators of the contacts; more international recognition, commercial opportunities, and a supply of skilled labour the implied aims. Minīlik's emissary to Rome was an Ethiopian Catholic of questionable character, known as Abba Mīka'ēl.[353] *On his way back*

---

350 Dye, *Moslem Egypt*, pp. 283–4; Loring, *Confederate Soldier*, p. 386.
351 See above, p. 335.
352 See Richard Caulk, 'Menilek and the Ethio-Egyptian War of 1875–76: a reconsideration of source material', *Rural Africana*, 11, 1970, for a review of these sources and of the research position generally on this issue. I have since then done further work on the documentary materials and believe the matter to be sufficiently important to warrant a new exposition based mainly on the documentary evidence, rather than the accounts of travellers of whom many are notorious for their over-indulgence in conspiracy stories.
353 FO 95/731, no. 140, Yohannis to Victoria, 31 May 1872; See Giglio, *Etiopia–Mar Rosso*, Vol. I, pp. 61–2 (notes on pp. 77–8), and Vol. II, pp. 16–17, for the circumstances of Abba Mīka'ēl's mission and references to the documents. Note, however, that the correct date of the letters to Rome is 20 *June*, not *January*. The three letters from Minīlik himself were translated into French, German, and Italian by missionaries before being sent off. They were also sealed with a new seal which must have been made in Europe.

from Rome in November–December 1872, he contacted or was contacted by the Egyptian government. He allegedly told them that Minīlik was disturbed by Yohannis's conquests (of which there were as yet none). There is no evidence that he had any instructions to contact the Egyptian government, and his alleged approval of Egyptian designs on Ethiopia sounds like an echo of the prevailing attitude among influential Catholic missionaries wanting to save their mission in northern Ethiopia. In the meantime, however, Minīlik had forwarded his request for 'scientific books' through Abu Bakr of Zeyla, and thus a contact was established.[354]

That the King of Shewa at this time was primarily interested in opening up his country to European technology and trade is evident from further correspondence in 1873–74. In a reply to Victor Emmanuel on 5 June 1873, he promised that he would protect 'clever men (*bilhateññoch*) and traders' if any would come from Italy.[355] Three months earlier he had responded to a letter from the French trader Pierre Arnoux at Massawa who—influenced, it seems, by Samu'ēl Gīyorgīs—had decided to try his fortune in Shewa instead. Arnoux had, *inter alia*, promised arms through Obok, and Minīlik expressed his satisfaction.[356]

The Shewan king also wrote to Sarzec (31 January 1874) asking him to assist in establishing contact and friendship with all European powers and promising to protect all traders and craftsmen who arrived with a letter from the vice-consul. The intermediary for this contact was the earlier confidant and envoy of Yohannis, Aleqa Birru Welde Gīyorgīs.[357] Samu'ēl had apparently never been in great favour with Yohannis, and Munzinger had for some time kept him under surveillance at Massawa because of contacts with foreigners which the governor found detrimental to Egyptian interests.[358] Birru had shown himself unreliable in some way in connection with the recruitment for Yohannis of a group of foreigners in Egypt, probably including Arnoux, who declared that Birru had accepted money from the Egyptians to make the mission fail, which it did. Birru was still in the service of Yohannis in September 1872, but the King must eventually have discovered his intrigues and so Birru was forced to seek another master.[359]

There can be little doubt that Birru was behind not only the letter to Sarzec of 31 January 1874 but also one to Ismail dated two days later. Again, what

354 Douin, *Ismaïl*, III, 2, p. 363; see above, pp. 293–4, 303. Minīlik's own letter did not reach Ismail (AEMD, Afrique 62, fols 315v.–316r., Ismail to Minīlik, 24 Feb. 1873), most likely because Abu Bakr wanted to word the message his own way; it is possible, too, that it was only a verbal message to begin with.

355 Istituto Italiano per l'Africa, Rome, no. 7323. This seems to be the original of Minīlik's letter. It is written in two columns, Italian and Amharic, and sealed with the same seal as the 1872 letters.

356 AEMD, Africa 62, fols 337v.–338r., Minīlik to Arnoux, 3 Mar. 1873; L. Louis-Lande, 'Un voyageur français dans l'Éthiopie méridionale', *Revue des deux Mondes*, XXX (1878), pp. 877–903.

357 Hiruy has published this letter in *Tarīk*, p. 71. Birru appears as Ri'ise Memakirt Gīyorgīs (see above, p. 280, n. 492).

358 AECP, Égypte 55, fols 286–319, Sarzec to Decazes, 20 Apr. 1874; also above, p. 294, n. 23.

359 AEMD, Afrique 62, fol. 336, Arnoux's report. See also above, pp. 280–1.

Minīlik asked for was 'trustworthy persons having a profound knowledge of arts and crafts'. This was the letter to which Ismail could reply in so general terms that when the answer was by mistake delivered to Yohannis, Arakil felt that no damage had been done.[360] While Ismail's reply to this letter from Minīlik went astray, his response to the message through Abu Bakr eventually reached Minīlik. Accompanied by some minor gifts, it was apparently a very friendly letter with, however, a very strong emphasis on Minīlik's duty to preserve good neighbourly relations. This seems somewhat premature more than two years before the transfer of Zeyla and the conquest of Harer. There was not the slightest hint of any alliance against Yohannis or of the possibility of a war against him.[361]

Minīlik acknowledged the receipt of this letter only in April 1875, expressing his great satisfaction with Ismail's statement that they were neighbours and should live in friendship. In fact, Minīlik used the stricter definition that their countries, Misir (Egypt) and Habesha, had common boundaries, and added, 'I have sent Ras Birru whom I trust and like to Munzinger Pasha to make an agreement for me *about this matter*, so that hostilities do not break out between us [and] the poor do not suffer'.[362] Minīlik of course knew about the Egyptian activities along the coast and Arakil's expedition to the salt plains in the interior, undertaken in February–March 1875.[363] He had every reason to seek an agreement with Egypt about boundaries, trade conditions, and arms import. The difference between him and Yohannis was that he had not suffered any outright military attacks and believed in Ismail's professions of friendship. The possibility of verbal instructions cannot be excluded, of course, but there is no evidence whatsoever that Minīlik was at this point involved in a conspiracy to bring in Egyptian troops to help him fight Yohannis.[364] On the other hand, it is a fact that Minīlik escaped the imminent attack by the army of Yohannis because the latter found it more important to march north and guard against further Egyptian infiltration.[365]

When Yohannis left Wello, Minīlik wrote once more to Ismail. Though he broadened the authorization for Birru to make agreements on his behalf 'on all matters as I myself', there is still no hint that Minīlik was seeking the military co-operation of Egypt to overthrow Yohannis. On the contrary, Minīlik's priority was something very different: he asked Ismail to order the Patriarch to send him a bishop for Shewa. If he received a positive reply to this

360 See above, p. 312.
361 AEMD, Afrique 62, fols 315v.–316r., Ismail to Minīlik, 24 Feb. 1873. According to Arnoux (fol. 315r., to Valfrey, 8 Aug. 1878), Minīlik had given him the originals of the two letters from Ismail that had reached him, i.e., the one just referred to and the letter of December 1875.
362 ENA, Soudan, Carton 5/2/1, Minīlik to Ismail, 1 Apr. 1875 (my emphasis).
363 See above, p. 313.
364 Cf. H. G. Marcus, 'Menilek II', in N. R. Bennet, ed., *Leadership in Eastern Africa: Six Political Biographies* (Boston, 1968), pp. 13–14; idem, 'Imperialism and Expansion in Ethiopia from 1865 to 1900', in P. Diugnan and L. Gann, eds, *Colonialism in Africa* (Cambridge, 1969), Vol. I, pp. 421–2.
365 See above, pp. 309, 313.

request with Birru, he would return to the question of travel arrangements and, when all this was settled, send people to escort the bishop to Shewa.[366] Whether Minīlik took this initiative to strengthen and maintain his independence in Shewa or with the aim of eventually challenging Yohannis in northern Ethiopia, it indicates long-term plans quite different from stabbing Yohannis in the back after having induced the Egyptians to attack him in the north.

All available evidence, in fact, points to Cairo and not Liche or Wereylu (Minīlik's two main residences these years) as the place where the 'conspiracy' originated. Firstly, it is not likely that a wide-ranging plan covering Gordon in Central Africa, McKillop on the Benadir coast, Ra'uf at Harer, and Arendrup in Hamasēn was initiated on the basis of the verbal communications of Birru in Cairo, whatever he might have said. It is far more likely, at least, that the idea to use Minīlik against Yohannis emerged in the process of this planning. Secondly, it was only in Ismail's communications from July 1875 onwards, and only verbally to begin with, that the scheme of a common front against Yohannis appeared. Munzinger was first instructed to establish a governorate at Tajura and open a safe route to Shewa as requested by Minīlik. Birru was given a letter promising Minīlik the bishop and, in response to a verbal request by Birru, 500 rifles, a cannon, and ammunition for the maintenance of peace and security along the trade routes to Zeyla and Tajura. They left Cairo together at the end of July 1875. Some ten days later, Munzinger was instructed to postpone his own departure from Massawa but send Birru on and recommend him to tell King Minīlik to attack Yohannis without delay.[367]

Ismail returned to this matter on 20 August: 'Since we have no interest in fighting with the Abyssinians, we have no objection that you take the steps necessary to *push Minīlik*, the king of Shewa, to attack Kasa [Yohannis] . . . you should *apply all your effort to incite a conflict* between the two so that they attack each other.' A week later he combined, *for the first time*, the attack on Yohannis with 'the offers of service which Minīlik has caused to be made to me', recommending in the same dispatch that one might also make Yohannis *believe* that the Egyptians were about to incite Minīlik against him! It was at this point that Munzinger was instructed to leave matters at Keren and Massawa to his deputy and continue his journey to Tajura and Awsa. He was to judge himself whether he should go on to Shewa or negotiate a commercial treaty with Minīlik through Birru, who had travelled slowly enough to fall in with the governor again. The treaty draft was all in favour of Egypt, but there was an important and, in the circumstances, revealing concession: though the khedive had been obliged, in the interest of public security, to prohibit arms import all along the coast of Africa, he would grant Minīlik all facilities which were not strictly opposed to this objective. In other words, Minīlik, would receive some arms, if he used them in a civil war against Yohannis aimed at paving the way for Egypt's annexation of Ethiopia. He would receive the requested bishop, too, all

366   ENA, Soudan, Carton 5/2/2, Minīlik to Ismail, 22 May 1875.
367   ENA, Registre 2, Ordres supérieurs, Ismail to Minīlik, 26 Jul. 1875; Douin, *Ismaïl*, III, 3B, pp. 721–6.

with the expressed aim of making it known that Egypt recognized Minīlik and his government.[368]

After the attack on Munzinger in Awsa, in which Birru also lost his life, Ismail had to start all over again. In a letter to Minīlik, he reported the disasters of Awsa and Gundet, accusing Yohannis of having caused the hostilities, and went on to say that he had created an army of 15,000 men to take revenge for Gundet, and would raise the number to 20,000 or 25,000 if necessary. After defeating Yohannis, he intended to enforce severe peace conditions on Ethiopia but not take possession of the country, not even an inch of it. As he was satisfied with his own territory, Ethiopia would never tempt him. Finally, he declared that he would be very happy if Minīlik marched to Adwa and established himself there, so that they could sign this peace agreement with each other.[369]

This letter reached Liche on 13 January 1876 and might well have been in the hands of Minīlik in Wello two weeks later. News about the Egyptian invasions and the fall of Harer had arrived in late November, and by the time Minīlik received Ismail's letter, he must also have long known about the Egyptian defeats at Gundet and in Awsa. According to Arnoux, who was in Shewa at the time and received couriers from Minīlik at the end of January, the Shewan army had celebrated Yohannis's victory over the Egyptians for three days.[370] If Minīlik had his heart on the Egyptian side, he took care not to reveal it. It was at this point that he sent his congratulations to Yohannis accompanied by a cavalry force for the continuation of the war.[371] To Ismail he sent nothing for the time being, in spite of the khedive's request for an urgent reply. In a last frantic attempt to get Minīlik involved on the Egyptian side before the battle of Gura, Ismail instructed Ratib (12 February 1876) to contact Minīlik at Adwa (!) or Gonder with the following message:

> Our monarch . . . has ordered us to recognize you as king of Abyssinia . . . We have learned that you have come to Adwa. *If you have come to this town to fight us in agreement with Yohannis*, let us know the truth so that we can inform our noble monarch *the khedive* who *will designate the person whom we are to recognize as the king of Abyssinia* and issue an order to this effect.[372]

Whether this message reached Minīlik before he returned to Shewa at the end of May 1876 is impossible to establish. It is also fairly unimportant since the offer of the throne of Ethiopia was clearly implied in Ismail's letter of December 1875. To this Minīlik finally replied in June 1876, thanking Ismail for the gifts sent with Ibrahim Abu Bakr in 1873 and introducing Arnoux as his new delegate

368 Douin, *Ismaïl*, III, 3B, pp. 731–6 (my emphasis).
369 ENA, Registre 10, Ordres supérieurs, p. 30, Ismail to Minīlik, 6 Dec. 1875. The letter is slightly paraphrased in Douin, *Ismaïl*, III, 3B, pp. 821–4, and in AEMD, Afrique 62, fols 316–17. See also above, p. 325.
370 AEMD, Afrique 62, fols 372–7. This part of Arnoux's report seems to be based on a diary, to which the author added later information. The victory announced and celebrated is obviously Gundet, but the victory described has borrowed much from Gura: the size of the Egyptian army, the presence and capture (*sic*) of Prince Hasan, etc.
371 See above, p. 325.
372 Douin, *Ismaïl*, III, 3B, p. 898 (my emphasis).

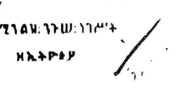

ግባልህ፡ ንጉሠ፡ነገሥት

ዘኢትዮጵያ

ዳግማዊ፡ ሞረለስኬ ንጉሡ ነገሥት ዘኢትዮጵያ ይደርሰ ወደ ክብረ
ክፉ፡ ግላሙ፡ ኢስማኢ ል ባሻ የመጽ ረ ግብፅ ንጉሥ

ከሞ ሰላም

የዘሪ፡ ፍዳመት ከእ ብራ ዟ ም እዙ ስክር ጋራ የስዒ ዴ ል ኝ ፡ በረ ከተ ፈፃ
ዴ ፡ ሰገ ኛ በር ተ መ ታ ጠ ቲ ጀ ዐ ፡ ለ የ ረ ረ ክ ከ ፈ ነ ግ ላ ተ ስ ብ ፡ ፊ ቀ ዴ ፡ ዝ ዩ ግ ለ ተ ሁ
ብ ፡ ረ መ ሐ ረ መ ፡ ግ ላ ተ ስ ብ ፡ ር መ ገ ር ፡ ፩ የ ስ ዴ ታ ፡ ል ዘ ክ ግ ለ ተ ስ ብ ፡ ፩ መ ገ ገ ፍ ፡ ፀ ዥ
ሑ የ ፡ ወ ር ተ ፡ ቅ ዝ ዴ ረ ለ ኝ ፡

ዳግ መ ኛ መ ፡ የ ጂ ኣ ር መ ፡ ዴ ብ ዴ ኒ ፡ መ ሳ ሽ ፡ የ ለ ረ መ ፡ መ ገ ረ ት ፡ ኣ ፀ ኒ ሁ ፡
ዞ ነ ፡ ዴ ግ ሙ ፡ አ ት ፡ ሔ ተ ሮ ስ ፡ እ ር ት ክ ፡ የ ረ ረ ጊ ስ ፡ ነ ገ መ ፡ ወ ዴ ፡ የ ሙ ር ፓ ፡ የ መ ገ ለ ስ ዴ ፡
ገ ፡ አ ር ስ መ ፡ የ መ ጠ ለ መ ፡ ኣ መ ፡ ለ ለ ዞ ፡ የ መ ገ ግ ሡ ት ና ፡ የ ገ ገ ዴ ን ፡ ጉ ዴ ይ ፡ ሁ ለ ፡ እ ገ ዟ
ጀ ር ግ ለ ኝ ፡ አ ገ ጎ ረ ዋ ለ ሁ ፡ ክ ር ስ መ ፡ ዘ ገ ዴ ፡ እ ገ ዴ ዴ ር ስ ፡ እ ከ ዝ ጎ ር ዋ ለ መ ፡ ተ መ ደ ዴ መ
ገ ፡ መ ሮ ጎ ተ ፡ እ ገ ዴ ሃ ለ ረ ዴ ፡ ስ ለ ሁ ስ ተ መ ፡ ሕ ዝ ዴ ፡ ዴ ረ ዝ ከ ተ ፡ የ ጓ ፡ ቅ ር ፡ መ ገ ና ጎ ት
ወ ል ፡ እ ገ ዴ ዴ ር ና ፡ ክ ር ስ መ ፡ አ ጁ ፡ ጥ ቶ ት ፡ የ ጓ ቀ ር ፡ መ ሥ ር ፡ እ ገ ዴ
ወ ን ፡ ዴ ቀ ስ ለ ኝ ፡ ክ ር ስ ፡ ፀ ረ ፡ ጋ ረ ፡ ዘ ፡ ረ ክ ተ ፡ ና ፡ ሀ ፡ ብ ዴ ቤ ፡ ስ ዴ ፡ ፂ ፡ ለ ሃ ለ ሁ ፡ ያ ለ ቸ
ገ ር ፡ አ ስ ዴ ረ ስ ለ ኝ ማ ፡

እ ዘ ነ መ ፡ መ ል ክ ጠ መ ፡ ሠ ተ ር ና ፡ ጥ ለ በ ፡ ገ ዓ ዴ ም ፡ በ ስ ገ ረ ፡ አ ገ ገ ለ ሁ ፡ ዞ ኞ
መ ረ ፡ እ ለ መ ፡ ዴ መ ም ኛ ም ፡ ክ ተ ረ ስ ተ ቶ ና ፡ ክ ፀ ወ ር ፓ ፡ ነ ገ ሠ ት ተ ፡ ወ ዴ ጆ ፡ የ ቅ ር
መ ገ ና ጎ ተ ፡ ወ ል ገ መ ፡ አ ዴ ር ጎ ፡ አ ረ ለ ገ ስ ለ ሁ ፡ ሄ ህ መ ፡ እ ስ ክ ፡ ባ ሕ ር ፡ ፂ ር ፡ ፂ ረ ስ መ
ገ ገ ጄ ን ፡ በ መ ከ ረ ተ ፡ ነ መ ፡

የ ር ስ መ ፡ መ ገ ግ ሡ ት ፡ ጦ ክ ር ፡ ስ ኔ ፡ ሠ ረ ፡ በ ር ገ ፡ የ መ ደ መ ን ፡ መ ስ ለ ኝ ፡
ረ ስ ተ ቹ ን ፡ ሊ ዎ ት ፡ የ መ ጠ ፡ የ ር ስ መ ፡ ወ ታ ዴ ሮ ች ፡ በ ኢ ት ዮ ቅ ያ ፡ ዴ ሁ ብ ፡ በ ዕ ክ ተ ት
ግ ረ ን ፡ ተ ዎ ን ተ ፡ ዘ ረ መ ፡ አ ጎ ረ ፈ መ ፡ ክ ረ ያ ፡ የ ተ ክ ረ ስ ት ፡ ተ ገ ረ ን ፡ ያ ዘ ተ ኣ ፡ ኅ ፡
ሜ ዉ ገ መ ፡ ያ ዘ ተ የ ስ ዎ ን ፡ መ ገ ግ ሡ ት ና ፡ የ ገ ገ ለ ን ፡ አ ገ ረ ፡ ዴ ዘ ፡ የ በ ረ ፡ አ ዴ ለ መ ፡
ሐ ረ ር ገ መ ፡ ክ ር ስ መ ፡ ወ ታ ዴ ሮ ች ፡ አ ጁ ፡ ሆ ል ፡ ዘ ረ ፡ ጠ ረ ፡ ባ መ ገ ገ ቾ ገ ፡ ነ መ ፡ ፩
ስ አ ፉ ና ፡ ሦ ር ፡ በ ከ ሙ ፡ ባ ገ ፡ መ ጥ ተ ፡ በ ጋ ለ ፡ አ ገ ረ ፡ ታ ዴ ዴ ሉ ና ል ፡ በ ሐ ረ ር ጌ ን ፡ በ
ዘ ሠ ለ ብ ፡ የ ወ ጣ መ ፡ ክ ለ ዴ ኛ መ ፡ ሦ ር ፡ ጋ ረ ፡ ጉ ለ መ ኔ ፡ ለ ዴ ፡ እ ገ ዴ ገ ና ን ፡ ተ ቃ ጥ
ያ ል ፡ ዴ ገ ለ ል ፡ ዴ ፡ ሃ ሠ መ ፡ መ ሠ ጠ ር ፡ እ ሁ ዴ ለ ዮ መ ፡ ጉ ፈ መ ጮ ፡ ሃ ሌ ፡ ግ ለ ተ ፡ መ ፡

እሁን ይህን ጦጋ ኅንበለው። የወታደሮትꬂ ሠሪና የወጪቱ፣
የፋቶር፣ የሚያዩ፣ የዲብዲዮ፣ ታል የተከለ እ ይ መስለኝ ጦ። እጅግ፣ የሚ
ያለሪ፣ ነገር። ወ በዚህ ጦ እጅግ አዘነለሁ። ነገር ግን እርስ ጮ ኅለ ነ ጮ
ደጅ ያን እለ ፍ ለለ ጮት እ ለ ለ ሠለ ጋ መ ጦጠ ጮ ይ ወ ተ ኛ ል እ ይ መ ስ ለ ኝ ።
እግሬ ድረ ለ መ ጦ ጮ ። አ ጊ ዜ ለ ፦ ጮ ኅ ላ ዘ ነ ኝ እ ነ ꬁ ... ነ ገር ። ግ ን እ ት ቱ
ያ ፣ በ እ ነ ገ ት ፣ ጦ ር ፣ መ ከ ሰ በ ጦ ነ ጮ ላ ት ይ ገ ግ ራ ል ።

ዘ ሬ ፣ በ ጋ ሕ ረ ፣ ኤ ር ተ ራ ፣ ያ ለ ፣ በ ር ር ት ፣ በ ሕ ዱ ፣ ወ ተ ይ ሮ ስ መ ያ ለ
በ ር ር ት ፣ ወ ደ ፣ እ ኝ ፣ ከ ጮ ረ ት ፣ በ ተ ር ፣ ለ ላ ፣ እ ነ ጸ ይ መ ገ ፣ ከ ስ ከ ሰ ፦ ። ነ ፍ ጥ ፣ ገ ራ ደ
የ ወ ታ ደ ር ፣ መ ሳ ር ይ ፣ ሁ ለ ፣ ለ መ ጦ ጠ በ ቲ ይ ፣ የ ሚ ሀ ገ ን ፣ ሁ ለ ፣ በ ሰ ወ ት ፣ ተ ከ ለ በ
ለ ። የ ግ በ ግ ወ ይ ገ ፣ ጦ ር ፣ እ ገ ፍ ገ ፣ ሁ ለ ፣ ከ በ ለ ወ ። ፕ ቲ ት ፣ ቀ ፦ ት ፣ እ ጥ ሽ ፣ ሊ ገ ፦
ወ ። ክ ኔ ፣ ግ ላ ት ላ ይ ... ይ ህ ፣ የ ሆ ፦ ፣ እ ነ ጸ ዞ ፣ የ ፈ ሬ ቶ ፣ ሁ ለ ፣ ይ ረ ፣ ይ ህ ወ ፣ ለ ር
ለ መ ፣ መ ላ ጦ ት ፣ ይ ግ ገ ል ።

የ ተ ጦ ረ ጦ ር ሁ ት ም ፣ ሁ ለ ፣ ክ ለ መ ሰ ረ ደ ት ፣ ኅ ተ ፣ እ ር ቶ ለ ገ ፣ ሠ ለ ጦ ገ ፣ ለ ገ
ꬂ ። ለ ዲ ፈ ዋ ለ ሁ ፣ ክ ር ለ ጮ ፣ ዘ ገ ፦ ፣ መ ለ ጋ መ ገ ፣ ሓ ሳ ረ ገ ፣ ከ ስ ያ ጮ ሠ ረ ጮ ያ ገ ፣ በ ጮ
ም ። የ ጦ ግ ለ በ ጮ ገ ፣ እ ገ ꬁ ያ ስ ረ ደ ጮ ፣ የ ፋ ቶ ር ። ት ዋ ሪ ፣ ወ ለ ጦ ፣ ክ ር ለ ጮ ፣ ገ ር ፣ እ ገ ꬁ
ጮ ር ክ ለ ኝ ፣ ለ መ ገ ገ ፦ ፣ ለ በ ሬ ፣ ላ ገ ክ ለ ክ ለ ፣ በ ቶ ገ ሪ ፣ እ ጮ ረ ꬂ ፣ ያ ለ መ ሕ ክ
ለ ኛ ወ ። መ ገ ገ ꬁ ፣ በ ማ ክ ለ ፣ እ ገ ꬁ ፣ ር ር ል ፣ ። የ ጸ ገ ድ ም ፣ ቆ ፣ ሁ ለ ፣ ይ ህ ፣ ይ ቀ ር
ላ ይ ገ ለ ፣ ክ ወ ዲ ይ ፣ የ ሚ ጦ ጠ ፣ ሁ ለ ፣ ክ ከ ዚ ህ ፣ የ ሚ ፈ ረ ወ ፣ ሁ ለ ፣ መ ጮ ꬁ ꬁ ር ፣ መ
ም ጋ ት ፣ እ ገ ꬁ ፣ የ ከ ለ ክ ሰ ሉ ꬁ ፣ በ በ ሬ ፣ ሁ ለ ፣ በ መ ገ ገ ꬁ ፣ በ ወ ታ ደ ር ꬂ ጮ ፣ አ ꬁ ፣
እ ገ ꬁ ፣ ያ ገ በ ዝ ፣ የ ꬁ ፣ መ ለ ክ ገ ፣ ለ ታ ደ ፣ መ ꬁ ꬁ ጮ ፣ ያ ꬁ ት ፣ ማ ስ ና ክ ያ ፣ ክ
ꬁ ያ ገ ኝ ፣ ክ ለ ዚ ህ ፣ ኅ ት ፣ እ ር ቶ ለ ገ ፣ ሠ ለ ጦ ገ ፣ ለ ꬂ ꬂ ፣ ለ ዲ ፈ ዋ ለ ሁ ፣ ክ ኔ ፣ የ ተ ፈ
ወ ገ ፣ በ ጦ ጮ ፣ እ ገ ꬁ ፣ ያ ስ ረ ደ ꬁ ወ ፣ ሠ ለ ጦ ገ ፣ እ ለ ወ ፣ ክ ለ ዚ ህ ያ ፣ መ ለ ጋ ጮ ፣ ፍ ረ
ክ ር ለ ጮ ፣ እ ገ ꬁ ያ ገ ኝ ፣ ተ ለ ፈ ፣ እ ለ ኝ ፣ እ ꬁ ኩ ፣ ክ ለ ር ፣ ያ በ ሬ ፣ ለ ም ፣ ፀ ꬂ ꬁ ꬂ ꬂ
ያ ር ዝ ፣ ጮ ።   እ መ ፣ ለ ለ ኔ ፣ ዘ ፲ ፲ የ ꬂ ꬂ ꬂ ፣ ዘ ለ ꬂ ፣ ክ ተ ጦ ተ ꬁ ፈ ።

who was authorized to continue the negotiations for the treaty of commerce and friendship earlier entrusted to Birru. He stressed that he was strongly in favour of such treaties with his neighbours as well as the European powers since he had decided to introduce civilization, technology, and trade to his country and intended to open a safe route all the way to the sea. Then he continued in unmistakable language:

It seems to me that the intention [lit. advice] of your government is to shut the door for my work. Your soldiers who came to fight my neighbours have attacked Tigrē in southern [*sic*] Ethiopia. Even now they have not stopped. Some, told off from them, have seized Tajura and Awsa and the salines. And Adal and Harergē who were ruled by Shewa and by the Galla countries have fallen into the hands of your soldiers. Today the army is close to us. They tell us that a third army has proceeded up the White Nile and has been seen in the Galla country. It is rumoured that the army which has come up via Zeyla and Harergē has an appointment to meet the upper army in Guragē. This is no secret, and Guragē is my country.

Now what shall we say about this? It does not seem to me that the activity of your soldiers and the wording of your letter which indicates friendship and love are in harmony. It is a very frightening matter. I am very sad about this . . .

Now they have prevented everything except cloth from coming to me through the ports of the Red Sea and of the Indian Ocean. Rifles, ammunition [and] all [kinds of] arms which we could use for defence have been deliberately forbidden. The Egyptian armies have encircled the whole country and after a little while they will invade my territory Hawash. If this happens, all I have feared will have come true . . .[373]

Though Arnoux in his own interest was actively involved and stressed his own role in preparing this letter to Ismail as well as a number of other documents including letters to the governor of Aden, the president of France, the king of Italy and the Pope, there can be no doubt that it was Minīlik and his main Ethiopian advisers, Azazh Welde Ṣadiq and Ato (later Ras) Dargē, who were speaking their minds to Ismail.[374] Where Arnoux, for instance, only pointed out, that the salines had provided salt for Shewa and the Galla countries, Minīlik stretched the point and claimed that Adal and Harer had been ruled by Shewa and the Galla.[375] Minīlik had every reason to be as concerned about the Egyptian encirclement as Yohannis. As early as March 1876, an Egyptian agent turned up at Qallabat with emissaries and letters from rulers in Jimma,

373 ENA, Soudan, Carton 5/2/7, Amharic original. This letter is dated 10 Sene 1868 (= 16 Jun. 1876), but was almost certainly written on 10 June, which is the date on the French translation. In his account of the councils and drafting of this and other documents, Arnoux stated (AEMD, Afrique 62, fols 382–4) that the letters were written on Saturday, 3 June, but this must be wrong by one week. Cf. Douin, *Ismaïl*, III, 3B, pp. 1048–50, quoting a French version of Minīlik's letter. The letter was prepared in several sealed copies in both Amharic and French (AEMD, Afrique 62, fols 276–8).

374 AEMD, Afrique 62, fols 382–3, Arnoux's report, and fols 279–81, 286–91, copies of Minīlik to Mac Mahon, 9 Jun. 1876, and various powers of attorney, etc.; IO, Political and Secret Letters from Aden 3, Minīlik to Schneider, 10 Jun. 1876; ASMAI 36/1–4, Minīlik to Victor Emmanuel II, 9 Jun. 1876.

375 Cf. the above text with the French version quoted by Douin or the one in ENA, Abyssinie, Casier 20/9/1.

Innarya, and Goma (districts immediately west of Shewa and the Guragē mentioned in the letter to Ismail). They reportedly asked to be placed under Egyptian rule so as to avoid having to pay tribute to Minīlik.[376] It is indeed difficult to fit a Shewan–Egyptian conspiracy into Minīlik's actions during the war of 1875–76. He continued his campaign against Imam Amedē, the only important Muslim ruler in central Ethiopia, but did not go beyond that in the north. He reached at least a temporary agreement with Ras Welde Sillasē which allowed the latter to join Yohannis, and did not take advantage of Welde Sillasē's or Ras Adal's absence to increase his own territory at their expense.[377] It was only after the war, in 1877, that the internal struggles in Ethiopia flared up in earnest again.[378]

Since the Egyptians spread rumours that Minīlik was on their side, it is only natural that these rumours were repeated and by some eventually believed and stated as facts.[379] It should be noted, however, that the early chronicler of these events, Aleqa Lemlem, who did not otherwise spare Minīlik, accused Aleqa Birru of having betrayed his country, without hinting that Minīlik had any part in it.[380] Birru may well have given rise to or fed the hopes of the Egyptians that Minīlik could be persuaded to stab Yohannis in the back, but he did *not* bring any offer or proposal to that effect from the ruler of Shewa. If he had, there is no reason to believe that the prime minister of Egypt, Nubar Pasha, would not have mentioned it rather than admitting to the French consul general without any extenuating circumstances that Munzinger had been sent to Shewa *to try to excite* Minīlik to attack Yohannis.[381] Though a member of the general staff, first in Cairo and later on the expedition itself, Dye concluded that Minīlik 'had been unsuccessfully approached with Egyptian bribes'.[382] To maintain, in spite of this, that Minīlik conspired with the Egyptians to overthrow Yohannis is not very sound.

The really important point, however, is not that the facts, as far as we know them, exonerate Minīlik, but that they demonstrate the existence of more political cohesion in Ethiopia and a greater awareness of the issues involved than the enemies of Ethiopia foresaw. This does not mean that Ethiopia was a unified and centralized nation-state. On the contrary, Yohannis had, deliberately it seems, accepted the perpetuation of a feudal political structure. In this respect he was, fortunately perhaps under the circumstances, far less influenced by the views of Europeans than Tēwodros. This meant that the provincial rulers were

376 Douin, *Ismaïl*, III, 3B, p. 994.
377 ibid., III, 3B, pp. 898–9. When Yohannis reopened the hostilities by attacking Welde Mīka'ēl in September 1876 (see above, p. 335), Minīlik started a new campaign against the Galla in the south (Gebre Sillasē, *Minīlik*, pp. 70–1).
378 See above, p. 337.
379 For the views of Afewerq and Aṣme Gīyorgīs, see Caulk, 'Ethio-Egyptian War', *Rural Africana*, 11. The Gojjam chronicle of Tekle Īyesus reports the conspiracy story (fol. 83 in the copy available at the Institute of Ethiopian Studies, Addis Abeba) as a fact, but Hiruy (*Tarīk*, p. 67) leaves the question open with a 'God only knows'.
380 BN, Ethiop. 259, fol. 20.
381 AECP, Égypte 56, fols 492–5, Pellisier to Decazes, 20 Dec. 1875.
382 Dye, *Moslem Egypt*, p. 147.

vassals rather than governors, and not only Minīlik but other chiefs as well preferred to let Yohannis carry the main burden of the fighting with his Tigrean army while they kept their own armies in reserve. This is normal in a feudal state, though two almost equally powerful contenders for the supreme position naturally aggravated the risks inherent in the system. It is precisely the fact that the power struggle intensified again after the immediate danger had passed which indicates that Ethiopia was in spite of all one body politic, aware of a common identity.

It was also a characteristic of the feudal system to permit vassal princes to cultivate foreign contacts of their own. Here again, the aim of the vassal was often to strengthen his own position vis-à-vis his overlord or other rivals within the state. This was certainly one of the objectives of Minīlik's foreign contacts though not necessarily the only one. Nevertheless it is not difficult to find also here indications of an awareness of the common identity and destiny. When, for instance, Minīlik was about to 'die from anger' in late 1878, *inter alia* because of the arms embargo, he did not speak of the Bab al-Mandab ports only but of the problem 'from Massawa to Berbera and Harer', which underlines the attitude so forcefully expressed in his letter to Ismail in 1876.[383]

In spite of backwardness, feudalism, and disunity, Ethiopia was a more solid political unit than Egypt. Therefore the attempt to subdue her failed. There were fortuitous circumstances, certainly. But when the British finally came to Adwa in 1884 to sue for peace on Egypt's behalf, it was because Ethiopia had stood the test. It was the mistake of the British to overestimate the 'fortuitous circumstances' and underestimate the determination and strength of the Ethiopian people.

To Ethiopia the war with Egypt was a mixed blessing. It certainly increased the self-esteem of the Ethiopians in general and the warriors of the country in particular. It increased the number of good arms in the country and the awareness that more might be needed—with ammunition, for the new breechloaders required more and better ammunition than the country could provide.[384] It increased the prestige of Yohannis and thereby facilitated his struggle to tie all Ethiopia together under his rule. It taught the Ethiopians that their mountains were not immune to attack and that they should not rely on any assistance, material or moral, whatever Queen Victoria wrote or visiting representatives of European powers said.

But the war was costly, too, above all with respect to its effects on the borderlands in the north. Twelve years of intermittent fighting, raiding, and looting had impoverished the whole area. The peasantry, above all, suffered. Grain and livestock were requisitioned or simply looted, by the regular armies as well as private gangs of robbers. Cultivation was disrupted, and famine and epidemics decimated the population.

As early as March 1877, Gordon wrote, 'The war has pressed very heavily on

383 See above, pp. 345–6.
384 See, for instance, FO 1/31, pp. 361–5, memorandum by Hewett, n.d., but after the mission to Adwa.

the Abyssinian frontier peasantry . . . the soldiery, when they come down to attack us, pillage every one, whether friends or foes. This having gone on for nearly eighteen months, the peasantry are nearly ruined, and are as anxious for peace as even Egypt is.'[385] Year after year, this was the message of the French vice-consuls and the Swedish missionaries alike. To escape hunger and death, the population migrated by the thousands: 'Whole populations have fled towards the west and south of Abyssinia, where abundance and salubrity reign, and have been able to save themselves that way.'[386] Not all of them, however, for one missionary reported that an army of destitute peasants from Hamasēn, in search of land and food, had fought a regular battle with the local population in Wag. Others fled to the lowlands or to Massawa, where much of the early work of the Swedish mission was carried out among destitute refugees from Hamasēn.[387] At one point, when the population of Ṣe'azega appealed for the assistance of Gordon, they stressed that the killing and looting by Welde Mīka'ēl's troops was not the greatest problem, 'but the worst of all is that he passed the rainy season expelling us and saying, "Do not stay in your country" '.[388]

On the political level, intrigue, violence, and family feuds destroyed much of the local autonomy of provinces such as Akkele Guzay, and Hamasēn. Elsewhere Yohannis normally left provincial government to members of the provincial nobility, but in the exposed areas in the north he found it necessary to place outsiders as his governors. In 1875 a *wagshum*, Dejjazmach Gebru, was the governor of Hamasēn. After the battle of Wekī Dibba, neither Hazega nor Ṣe'azega provided a governor there. The responsibility went to Alula from Tembēn who wielded power with an iron hand.

In this situation it is not remarkable that the process of alienation vis-à-vis Ethiopia, initiated by Egyptian/Muslim and European/Catholic influence decades earlier,[389] continued and intensified. The Italians could move in and benefit from the war weariness at the local level to gain a foothold. Thus the Ethio-Egyptian war, which contributed to consolidation and a growth of self-esteem and self-reliance at the level of the Ethiopian state, also contributed, in spite of the victory, to the weakening of the ancient ties between the population of the northern provinces and the remainder of Ethiopia. Somehow, the strength and the wisdom of Yohannis and his advisers was not sufficient to cope with this slow but persistent development.

Massawa to Metemma

For Ethiopia, the replacement of the 'Egyptians' by the Italians meant one more decade of continuous struggle to preserve her integrity and independence. In

385 Hill, *Gordon*, p. 211.
386 AECC, Massouah 2, fols 100–1, Carbonnel to Waddington, 16 Aug. 1875 (*sic*); correct date is 1878.
387 *MT*, 1878, pp. 57–8, Hedenström, 10 Feb. 1878; see also 1877, pp. 40–1, Carlsson, 2 Jan. 1877; 1878, p. 28, Lundahl, 2 Jan. 1878.
388 BM, Orient. 12913 (A), [Those] of Ṣe'azega to Gordon, n.d.
389 See above, p. 171.

Europe, the Powers were busy establishing the ground rules for the partition of Africa. Italy's occupation of Massawa and following attempt to gain complete control over Ethiopia was the kind of mission implicitly expected of her. Backed by the moral support of Great Britain, there was no reason for the Italians to be overly concerned about problems that might arise, in spite of angry protests against the violation of the sovereign rights of the Ottoman Empire. And if these rights, which had caused so much headache at the Foreign Office in connection with the eventual restoration to Ethiopia of places seized only a few years earlier, could now be ignored with regard to Massawa, there is no reason to expect that Italy would be bothered about the historical rights of Ethiopia, whether recognized by an international treaty or not. Besides, the Italians were convinced—without much justification, to be sure—that the Ethiopians regarded them as particularly close and trustworthy friends.[390]

The Italian government had sent missions to both Minīlik and Yohannis in 1883 and offered the facilities of their small colony of Aseb as a means of avoiding the Egyptian blockade. For Shewa, Aseb was a suitable port, and Minīlik signed a treaty of friendship and commerce in May 1883. Yohannis hoped to obtain Massawa and apparently saw no purpose in a treaty with Italy.[391] The landing of Italian troops at Massawa without prior consultation deeply disturbed Yohannis, and it is not likely at all that the two Italian emissaries who visited him to profess Italy's friendship were as successful as they reported, even if Yohannis decided to give them the benefit of the doubt for the time being. One of Yohannis's first actions was to alert Minīlik who immediately protested to both Umberto and his envoy in Shewa, Pietro Antonelli, about their failure to consult the Emperor beforehand about such an important step.[392]

For Yohannis the crucial question was whether the British government had completely abdicated its responsibilities under the Hewett treaty or not. He found it difficult to believe that a pact to maintain peace and friendship 'from generation to generation' should have become invalid within one year. He wanted to know if it was with Queen Victoria's permission that the Italian army had come and if the purpose was to use force and seize his country. The signs were disturbing: consignments of arms for Ethiopia were stopped at Massawa and Italian troops were gradually occupying a number of positions in the hinterland of Massawa, as far as 'the edge of the salt plains'.[393]

390   Battaglia, *La prima guerra d'Africa*, pp. 216–17. This book is the latest Italian work—and a very fascinating one—to cover the whole history of the Italian–Ethiopian relations from the first contacts in the 1850s to the battle of Adwa. Giglio's *Etiopia–Mar Rosso* has reached May 1885 only; the accompanying volumes of documents, however, the end of 1889. Since my purpose in this final chapter is only to bring the narrative to its logical conclusion, the battle of Adwa, and indicate how the earlier experiences of the Ethiopians had prepared them for that event, I will not aim at a complete documentation and only refer to original documents on particularly significant points. The following text is based mainly on Battaglia's work and on my monograph *Wiçhalē XVII. The Attempt to Establish a Protectorate over Ethiopia* (Addis Abeba, 1964) and article 'Adwa 1896: The Resounding Protest' in Rotberg and Mazrui, eds, *Protest and Power in Black Africa*, pp. 113–42.
391   Rubenson, *Wiçhalē XVII*, pp. 42–5.
392   Battaglia, *Guerra*, pp. 217–18, Giglio, *Etiopia–Mar Rosso*, Vol. I, pp. 403–11.
393   FO 95/746, no. 196, Yohannis to Victoria, 28 Aug. 1885.

An evasive answer expressing the pious hope that Yohannis would 'be able to come to a friendly arrangement' with the Italians, and two swords of honour in recognition of the Ethiopian assistance in relieving the garrisons did not satisfy Yohannis. In his reply to this letter the King accepted the argument that he had not been promised Massawa in the treaty. But now the treaty had been violated by Italy. Ethiopian merchants were forced to pay customs duties, and the port was used as a base for aggression against Ethiopia. In conclusion, Yohannis asked the Queen to explain to him how to make friends with the Italians since he did not know how to love them; he did not have the required knowledge or skill for this (የምንፈቀርበትን ፡ ብልሃቱን ፡ አላወቅሁት ፡)![394] This was apparently a difficult assignment, so no answer was sent.[395]

At the local level, the language was clear. Alula was particularly annoyed that Italian troops had come to Se'aṭī, 30 kilometres from Massawa, and hoisted the Italian flag over the small fort when the Egyptians evacuated the place in August 1885: '. . . the country belongs to the King. I cannot dispose of it. Therefore clear out of Se'aṭī.' At this point Kasala was about to fall, and Alula was belatedly urged to march to its relief, which he did—and gained the victory at Kufit on 23 September—in spite of his preoccupation with the Italian threat. But he also made it absolutely clear that he wanted the Italians to 'go home and the sooner the better'. He did not recognize their right to Massawa, much less Se'aṭī, and wondered why the British allowed them to remain and threaten his frontiers.[396]

Yohannis was, in fact, as angry and contemptuous as Alula. Convinced that Ethiopia would soon have to fight the Europeans directly, he wanted to make sure that Minīlik was also aware of what kind of people they had on their hands:

> They [the Italians] are not a serious people; they are intriguers; and all this must be something which the English are doing to me. The Italians have not come to these parts because they lack pasture and abundance in their own country, but they come here because of ambition, in order to aggrandize themselves, because they are many and not rich. But with the help of God, they shall leave again humiliated and disappointed and with their honour lost before all the world. They are not a people who can frighten us; . . . If the two of us always remain united, we shall with the help of God overcome not only the weak Italians, but also the strong people of other nations. As Adam wanted to enjoy the forbidden fruit because of ambition to become greater than God, and instead found nothing but chastisement and dishonour, so it will happen to the Italians.[397]

394   FO 95/746, no. 198, Victoria to Yohannis, 8 Dec. 1885; FO 95/747, no. 151, Yohannis to Victoria, 19 Apr. 1886. For the circumstances of this exchange of letters, see F. Harrison Smith, *Through Abyssinia. An Envoy's Ride to the King of Zion* (London, 1890), pp. 174–223.

395   FO 95/748, minutes on no. 194, 14 Jul. 1887.

396   Battaglia, *Guerra*, pp. 220–1; FO 78/3807, Chermside to Izzet, 24 Jul. 1885; FO 78/3808, Marcopoli to Chermside, 26 Aug. 1885, enclosing an account of a conversation with Alula, same date; Chermside to Marcopoli, 4 Sep. 1885; FO 78/3809, Egerton to Salisbury, 2 Oct. 1885, with extracts from Marcopoli's diary; FO 78/3811, Egerton to Salisbury, 10 Nov. 1885, with enclosures.

397   *AP.DD*, 1889–90, XV, pp. 203–5, Antonelli to Robilant, 26 Nov. 1885. Whether it was Minīlik himself or, more likely, one of his courtiers that leaked this letter to Antonelli is

If Yohannis had hoped that Minīlik would send away Antonelli, he was disappointed. The King of Shewa had much to gain from preserving good relations with the Italians at Aseb and did not feel threatened himself. In that respect the situation was different from 1875–76, and Yohannis may well have felt a bit apprehensive about the loyalty of his main vassal.[398]

Towards the end of 1886 the moves by the Italians to strengthen their position in the hinterland of Massawa increased the tension there. Alula first sent an ultimatum to the Italians to evacuate two positions, Wī'a (just occupied) and Zulla. When the Italian general refused, Alula descended on Se'aṭī, and on 26 January he attacked and almost wiped out a column of some 500 men who had been sent to reinforce the position there. This was the so-called Dogalī massacre, a far stronger protest than the Italians or British had expected.[399]

Yohannis was aware of the seriousness of Alula's action, and wrote to both London and Paris to point out the injustice of Italy's claims to succeed to territories restored to Ethiopia by the Egyptians through the Hewett treaty. Again he asked if the British government had authorized the Italian advances.[400] Though the treaty did not define any boundaries, Yohannis had been promised verbally that Se'aṭī would be evacuated, and the Italians knew this.[401] The clash, therefore, was not due to misunderstanding. The British government agreed with the Italians to try to mediate, but did not improve the chances of succeeding by telling Yohannis that the Italians were 'a powerful nation, with friendly and good intentions' who had been attacked 'injustly by Alula'.[402] A mission headed by Gerald Portal from the British legation in Cairo was sent to negotiate a settlement. The Italian government laid down the terms, and the British Foreign Office warned Yohannis to 'give full credence to all that he [Portal] shall say to you on behalf of the Queen and of Her Majesty's Government'. Italy's terms included an 'apology' for Alula's attack, territory including Se'aṭī, Wī'a, and Aylet, recognition of an Italian protectorate over the Habab and the Asawirṭa, and, jointly with Britain, a new occupation of Bogos with the fort of Keren.[403]

Under these circumstances, Portal's mission was bound to fail. While he was still preparing to go to Ethiopia, Yohannis informed the British government

not known, nor can we be sure, of course, that Antonelli's text is correct. In Ethiopian historiography (for instance, BN, Ethiop. 259, fol. 30) Yohannis is reported to have declared the Italians a cunning and wicked people as early as 1883.

398 Italian authors, also Battaglia (*Guerra*, pp. 224–5), have more or less taken for granted that Minīlik was prepared to betray Yohannis at any time and that he was actually happy that Yohannis was in trouble with the Italians. This is yet to be proved.

399 Battaglia, *Guerra*, pp. 225–42; BN, Ethiop. 259, fols 32–3; *MT*, 1887, pp. 37–8, Winqwist, 21 Jan.–3 Feb. 1887.

400 FO 95/748, no. 194, Yohannis to Victoria, 8 Mar. 1887; AED, Protocole C41, to Grévy, 8 Mar. 1887.

401 ASMAI 36/3–31, 'Istruzioni per la missione d'Abissinia', 7 Jan. 1886.

402 FO 95/748, no. 204, Victoria to Yohannis, 11 Aug. 1887, with minutes.

403 ibid., nos 206 and 207, Victoria and Salisbury, respectively, to Yohannis, 12 Oct. 1887; Gerald Portal, *An Account of the English Mission to King Johannis in 1887*, Winchester, n.d., pp. 7–14; Battaglia, *Guerra*, pp. 287–94.

that he did not believe in the 'good intentions' of the Italians. On the contrary, he believed that they said in their hearts, 'Let us go and fight with Abyssinia, capture it and make Rome and Ethiopia one country . . .' It was precisely to prevent this kind of thing, a repetition of Ismail's aggression, that he had asked for Massawa. By resisting his claim and allowing the Italians in, the British were now responsible not only for the fact that Abyssinian merchants had been forced to pay taxes for three years to the Italians in violation of the Hewett treaty but also for the outbreak of hostilities between two Christian nations.[404] On his arrival in the King's camp at Ashengē, Portal tried to extract an indirect condemnation of Alula's attack by hinting that Yohannis might dissociate himself from the action, but Yohannis replied, 'Ras Alula did no wrong'. As for a treaty with the Italians, there would be no other conditions than those agreed upon at Adwa 1884. In his reply to London, Yohannis went one step farther:

> . . . they [the Italians] wanted to begin the quarrel, they stopped the traders and came to the places in my country called Se'aṭī and Wī'a and fortified them . . . By making me appear to be the offender when I am not, are you not implying that I should give them the land which Jesus Christ gave to me? Reconciliation is possible when they are in their country and I in mine, but now, sleeping with our swords in hand and keeping our horses bridled, are we not with our armies as good as in combat already?[405]

Minīlik, who did not want to be forced to choose between his overlord and his Italian friends, also offered to mediate. He had extended the territory under his rule to the east, west, and south, and had occupied Harer in January 1887, without bothering too much about the attitude of the Italians or any other Europeans.[406] Participation in a war against the Italians in the north was, however, a different matter which would endanger Minīlik's growing trade through Aseb, particularly his import of firearms. Yohannis reportedly showed some interest in Minīlik's initiative to mediate, but the Italians had other plans. Antonelli offered Minīlik 5,000 rifles if he would remain neutral in the war. Minīlik agreed on condition that the Italians undertook not to 'seize or touch a single place on Ethiopian soil'. Since this was their intention and the very reason for their seeking Minīlik's support, the so-called 'convention of neutrality' of October 1887 was meaningless. Neutrality would not, in fact, be of much help to the Italians since Yohannis did not lack troops. His problem was how to operate with a large army in the lowlands long enough to dislodge the Italians from their fortified positions. What the Italians wanted, as the Egyptians before them, was an attack by Minīlik on Yohannis, and Antonelli reported that he had told Minīlik that he could have the promised arms only *after* an accomplished military action. This was not Minīlik's idea of neutrality or of what suited his own

404   FO 95/748, no. 208, Yohannis to Victoria, 26 Oct. 1887.
405   ibid., no. 209, Yohannis to Victoria, 8 Dec. 1887, Amharic text; Portal, *English Mission*, pp. 65–76, 117–20.
406   Richard Caulk, 'The Occupation of Harar: January 1887', *JES*, IX, 2 (1971), pp. 1–19. For attempts by Minīlik to mediate, see also AEMD, Afrique 138, fol. 79, Minīlik to Grévy, 20 Dec. 1887.

interests. As a result, the 5,000 rifles were not delivered within the stipulated six months—or twelve, for that matter.[407]

The return of the Portal mission to the coast was the signal for a new advance to Se'aṭī, which was heavily fortified. In March 1888, Yohannis appeared before Se'aṭī at the head of his army. He exchanged some messages with General Di San Marzano, who made some concessions but maintained the Italian claims to Se'aṭī, Wī'a, and Aylet. There can be little doubt that Yohannis's belligerent attitude had ceased. He knew before reaching Se'aṭī that the Mahdists had defeated the Gojjam army (18 Jan.) and sacked Gonder. He was apparently very worried and even proposed that the Italians join hands with him against the Mahdists. To this the Italian general made no reply. Aware of how difficult it was to capture a fortified position, and probably disturbed by exaggerated stories about an alliance between the Italians and Minīlik, Yohannis decided to leave the Italians alone for the time being, but not without making it clear that he did not renounce his claims: 'Has not Christ distributed [the earth] and made peace? Your country is from the sea as far as Rome, mine is from the sea as far as here; this is Ethiopia. There is no reason for us to quarrel.'[408]

That Yohannis first marched to Se'aṭī and then failed to attack and dislodge the Italians seriously compromised his leadership position. He lost the allegiance of Tekle Haymanot who was humiliated by his defeat and blamed the Emperor for having left him to face an overwhelming enemy alone. Minīlik, who had been ordered to take the field against the Mahdists after Tekle Haymanot's defeat, arrived in the Ṭana region after the Mahdists had retreated. Instead of pursuing them, he agreed to act as a peacemaker between them and Yohannis. Tekle Haymanot was also negotiating, primarily to have his children released and returned from Khartoum.[409] Yohannis had refused to reply to earlier letters from the Mahdi and from Abdallahi, the khalifa, and had probably just received a new one in which he was called a weak slave and exhorted to profess Islam if he wanted to avoid destruction. He cannot therefore have been very pleased to learn that his two great vassals were corresponding with the Muslim generals on Ethiopia's frontier.[410] At any rate, he abruptly ordered Minīlik back to Shewa in May and prepared for a new campaign himself.

In this situation Minīlik and Tekle Haymanot reached some kind of agreement to act in common against the Emperor, should the need arise. For some months Ethiopia was on the verge of a major civil war. Gojjam was in fact invaded by the imperial army, but when it came to Shewa, Yohannis hesitated. He knew that the Italians were now arming Minīlik and pushing him to attack. Belatedly Yohannis saw that the Italians were his worst enemy, and decided to act accordingly. He appealed to the Mahdist general Hamdan Abu Anja to forget the past (also the fact that he had not answered the Mahdi's letter) and unite with

407 Rubenson, Wiċhalē XVII, pp. 46–8, 52–3; Battaglia, Guerra, pp. 283–94.
408 Battaglia, Guerra, pp. 296–302, 313–21; Gebre Sillasē, Minīlik, p. 221.
409 CRO, Mahdia 1/55/16, Minīlik to Idris and Yunis, 3 Apr. and 6 Apr. 1888; Meshesha Werqē (in Minīlik's name) to Abu Anja, 12 May 1888; 1/55/13, Abu Anja to Tekle Haymanot, 28 Feb. 1888; 1/55/16, Tekle Haymanot to Abu Anja, 4 Apr. and 12 May 1888.
410 ibid., 1/55/12, Abdallahi to Yohannis, 1887/1888, not earlier than February 1888.

him against their common enemies, the Europeans and the 'Turks', who would not spare one of them if they managed to conquer the other. Abu Anja's reply left nothing to be desired in terms of frankness:

> All these Ansar . . . If you do not know them yet, you shall know them soon for they did not come to this place [Metemma] for love of money or honour but for cutting you off and all the infidels with you. Awake, therefore from your slumber, get up from your drunkenness and be not deceived by the people of Satan . . . As for your asking for peace with us whereas you are still an infidel, I say that this is an impossibility . . . You are a great fool to ask peace from us before you enter the religion of God . . . You shall know, therefore, that we are determined to fight you, the Italians and all the Europeans, and there could be nothing between us except the sword, unless you believe in God alone.[411]

This did not give Yohannis much choice. Fighting Minīlik would mean weakening Ethiopia with *two* external enemies on the borders. Yohannis chose to deal with the less complicated issue first. He marched against the Mahdists and lost his life at the otherwise successful battle of Metemma on 9 March 1889.[412]

The Treaty of Wiçhalē

The death of Emperor Yohannis finally presented Minīlik with the opportunity for which he had been waiting for almost twenty-five years. He had been a reluctant vassal, and his contributions in defence of Ethiopia's territory and independence had so far been marginal; in fact, they had consisted mainly of his refusal to involve himself on the side of Ethiopia's enemies. This attitude was facilitated, to some extent dictated, by the fact that he had his main power base at a safe distance from both the western and the northern frontiers. Only the Egyptian occupation of the Bab al-Mandab and Gulf of Aden ports and of Harer had been of immediate concern to him as King of Shewa. In the very last year of Yohannis's reign, however, Minīlik came perilously close to allying himself with Ethiopia's potentially most dangerous enemy, Italy. In October 1887 he had promised neutrality, and neutrality only, on condition that the Italians dropped all territorial aspirations. This attitude he seems to have maintained throughout the first half of 1888. The change came when he began to fear that Yohannis would eventually attack him. Now he needed the Italians more than they needed him. He wanted the promised rifles—and more if possible. He undertook to pay for them at Aseb, but was certainly aware that he would be requested to pay in terms of future territorial concessions as well, if he succeeded to hold his own and eventually replace Yohannis as Emperor. It was in this situation that the treaty of Wiçhalē was conceived in Rome in August–September 1888.[413]

411 ibid., 1/55/16, Yohannis to Abu Anja, 25 Dec. 1888; 1/55/13, Abu Anja to Yohannis, January (or 1 February) 1889.
412 For this and the preceding paragraph, see Richard Caulk 'Yohannis IV, the Mahdists, and the colonial partition of north-east Africa', *Transafrican Journal of History*, I, 2 (1971), pp. 22–42; Battaglia, *Guerra*, pp. 347–52; Rubenson, *Wiçhalē XVII*, pp. 48–9.
413 Rubenson, *Wiçhalē XVII*, pp. 49–50, 53, 56, with references cited; Battaglia, *Guerra*, pp. 352–4.

In the draft treaty, these concessions were defined by a line starting at Anfilla on the coast, passing by and including in the Italian colony the villages of Halay, Hebo, Akrur, Asmera, and Ṣe'azega and, after having followed the Anseba a short distance, running in a straight line east to west so that Bogos and most of the other districts once held by the Egyptians would go to Italy.[414] A deviation, loaded with political significance, was also made from the wording of the treaty of friendship and commerce of 1883. The clause by which Minīlik was in 1883 promised the *right* to avail himself of Italian consular authorities, etc. '*for all the letters or communications* that he might want to send to Europe or to the governments with whom the above-mentioned authorities are accredited', was changed into an *obligation* (albeit mildly worded) to avail himself of the Italian government '*for all negotiations of affairs* which he might have with other powers or governments'. Since the option concept was well established by the consistent use of the phrase *sarà in facoltà* in treaty drafts intended for Yohannis and Minīlik from as early as 1879, and verbal similarities, moreover, prove that Antonelli had the 1883 treaty in front of him when he prepared the 1888 draft, the change must be assumed to have been deliberate. As important as the change from option to obligation, was the shift from a 'postman' function to that of a foreign policy guardian. The aim was to control Ethiopia's foreign relations, in other words, do away with Ethiopia's external sovereignty, and it was only logical that the Italian government attempted to use the clause, Article XVII of the treaty signed on 2 May, as a basis for proclaiming a protectorate over Ethiopia.[415]

When Antonelli returned with the draft treaty and the first 5,000 rifles in January 1889, the fear that Yohannis might invade Shewa was subsiding. Once more, the relationship had changed; Minīlik showed no eagerness to discuss any treaty. He had made it clear to Antonelli that he was only prepared to defend himself, while the Italian government expected him to attack Yohannis so that they could expand their colony without running the risk of a new Dogalī. Minīlik, on the other hand, wanted the Italians to do something on the Massawa front so that Yohannis would be obliged to march north after an eventual victory over the Mahdists. In other words, the two potential allies were both waiting for the other party to carry the burden. Who would actually be called upon to do so depended on Yohannis. Whether Minīlik would, in fact, give the Italians active support unless attacked by Yohannis remained (and remains) an open ques-

414 Giglio, *Etiopia–Mar Rosso*, Vol. VII, pp. 117–22, Progetto di trattato . . .
415 Rubenson, *Wiçhalē XVII*, pp. 11–12, 31–2, 40–5, 51–2 (my emphasis). When I wrote this monograph in 1964 (also published in *JAH*, V, 2 (1964), pp. 243–83, 'The Protectorate Paragraph of the Wiçhalē Treaty'), I had no idea that my challenging of Antonelli's 'innocence' and, more important, of the validity of the protectorate claim would agitate Italy's leading colonial historian, to the extent it has done. For our exchange of views, see Carlo Giglio, 'Article 17 of the Treaty of Uccialli', *JAH*, VI, 2 (1965), pp. 221–31; Rubenson, 'Professor Giglio, Antonelli and Article XVII of the Treaty of Wiçhalē', *JAH*, VII, 3 (1966), pp. 445–57, and the exchange of final comments, pp. 541–6; also Giglio, *L'articolo XVII del trattato di Uccialli* (Como, 1967). One of the major reasons why Giglio and I have arrived at different conclusions on the role of Antonelli and the significance of the Italian version of Article XVII is that I have given much more weight to the documentary evidence *preceding* the event while Giglio prefers to build much more on the explanations and interpretations presented *after* the event by those involved.

tion.[416] It is clear, nevertheless, that the Italians had succeeded in driving in a wedge between Minīlik and Yohannis where the Egyptians had failed.

The death of Yohannis at Metemma reduced the equation. Minīlik proclaimed himself emperor and decided to complete the negotiations, thereby reducing Ethiopia's external enemies by one. He was undoubtedly powerful enough to claim the throne without the support of Italy.[417] Even the rifles he did receive were of little use since very little ammunition was supplied and some of that of the wrong calibre.[418] But there was always the possibility that the Italians would eventually support some rival prince or continue to annex territory and establish protectorates if he did not go through with the treaty and contain them within an internationally recognized boundary. Of course, they did both in spite of the treaty, but this he could hardly have foreseen.

On the frontier issue, Minīlik introduced and compelled Antonelli to accept a general reference to the edge of the highlands as the boundary between Ethiopia and Italy's possession. Other important changes in Ethiopia's favour were the substitution of Arafalī for Anfilla on the coast and Addī Nifas and Addī Yohannis for Ṣe'azega on the Hamasēn sector of the boundary. A number of other alterations, *inter alia* some to provide for full reciprocity, indicate that Minīlik was anxious to guard against anything that limited or seemed to limit his sovereignty.[419]

In view of this, it is remarkable that the clause designed to limit Ethiopia's sovereignty in external affairs was not amended. The explanation, however, is simple: the wording of the Italian draft which implied an *obligation* for Minīlik to conduct his foreign affairs through the Italian government was never translated into Amharic. Instead *yichalachewal* (ይቻላቸዋል ፡), a form of the verb *chale* (ቻለ ፡), which was used in 1883 to translate *sarà in facoltà*, was used again. Thus Minīlik *could, had the right or authority to*, request the good offices of the Italian government in matters of foreign relations, if or when he so wanted. Since neither Minīlik nor his interpreter Grazmach Yosēf knew Italian, while Antonelli knew or claimed to know Amharic, the responsibility for not changing the Italian text to conform with the Amharic wording must fall on Antonelli. At any rate, it was the Amharic text that embodied the factual agreement.[420]

---

416   Rubenson, *Wiçhalē XVII*, pp. 53–5.
417   Gebre Sillasē, *Minīlik*, pp. 154–6. It should be recalled, however, that Minīlik, too, was engaged in hostilities with the Mahdists on his own western frontier in Wellega. See Gebre Sillasē, *Minīlik*, p. 150; also CRO, Mahdia 1/55/16, Meshesha Werqē to Abu Anja, 12 May 1888; Alessandro Triulzi, 'Trade, Islam and the Mahdia in Northwestern Wallaggā, Ethiopia', *JAH*, XVI, 1 (1975), pp. 66–70.
418   Giglio, *Etiopia–Mar Rosso*, Vol. VII, 256–62, Antonelli to Crispi, 2 Jul. 1889.
419   Rubenson, *Wiçhalē XVII*, pp. 55–6; Battaglia, *Guerra*, pp. 375–6.
420   Rubenson, *Wiçhalē XVII*, pp. 32–9, Whether Antonelli took a deliberate decision not to change the Italian text or failed to do so from carelessness is impossible to state with certainty and of little importance from the point of view of Ethiopian history. The question of his knowledge of Amharic is more important, and I find the many indications that he knew sufficient Amharic to be able to detect the difference between *chale* (ቻለ ፡) and *ishī ale* (እሺ ፡ አለ ፡)—consented—compelling. It is worth noting that exactly the same form of (ቻለ ፡ ይቻላቸዋል ።) is used twice more in the treaty (Articles VIII and XVI) and translated by *potranno* and *potrà*—'will be able to' (ibid., pp. 67, 69, 74, 76). At first Giglio accepted

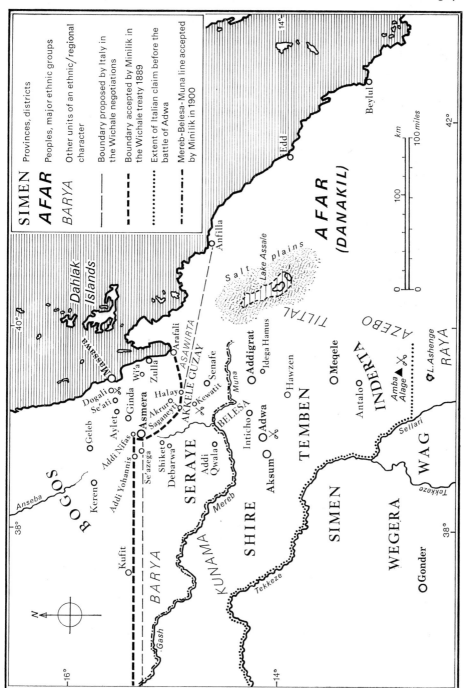

MAP 7 The Italian attack

Antonelli returned to Italy in late August in company with an Ethiopian mission headed by Minīlik's close relative Dejjazmach (later Ras) Mekonnin. Besides the ceremonial task of receiving the ratification of the treaty, its main purpose was to buy arms.[421] For the government of Francesco Crispi it provided an opportunity to follow up the successes (real as well as imagined) of the treaty. In an Additional Convention dated 1 October, it was agreed that the boundary of the colony—to be named Eritrea three months later—should be demarcated on the basis of actual possession ('as of today', zarē, in the Amharic text), that the Emperor could coin his own currency, but in Italy and only after joint decisions as to value and weight, that Minīlik be given a loan of 4,000,000 lire with the customs of Harer as security and the rates laid down there as the norm for all other customs posts, etc.[422]

The paragraph on the boundary was, of course, supposed to supplement, not replace, Article III of the Wiṭhalē treaty. Great care was taken not to arouse Mekonnin's suspicion as to the real purpose of the new formula. Nevertheless, Mekonnin was bothered. He was reported to have said that 'actual possession' did not extend beyond Se'aṭī; so why were the Italians asking for it when they were promised Asmera in the Wiṭhalē treaty? But Crispi went into action to get the Italian commander in Eritrea moving from Asmera to additional localities before Minīlik would arrive in Tigrē; and by the time Mekonnin and Antonelli were back in Ethiopia with the ratification and the new convention, they found the new Italian governor, General Orero, at Debarwa and his Eritrean allies on the Mereb and even beyond. The 'actual possession' clause probably represents the highest level of duplicity reached by the Italians in their dealings with the Ethiopians and certainly indicates that Crispi's statecraft included the principle that it was entirely lawful 'to cheat an African'.[423]

Minīlik was astounded. At Meqele he received the ratification of one treaty in which it was stipulated (Article XVI) that all clauses could be amended after five years, with one year's prior notice, *except* the one on the boundary which was not to be changed under any circumstances, and at the same time another treaty by which his ambassador according to Antonelli's interpretation had signed away all the territory north of the Mereb. Minīlik declared that he would not disavow his relative but that 'actual possession' would have to refer to the date of signature in Rome, the zarē of the Amharic text. This meant that the Italians would be given up to Shiket, some 20 kilometres south of Asmera, but no more. Antonelli agreed, but the military in Eritrea and Crispi in Rome refused; negotiations broke down, Minīlik returned to Shewa, and the Italians remained on the Mereb.[424]

my evidence (*JAH*, VI, 2, p. 228), and in my view his later arguments (*L'articolo XVII*, pp. 27–8, 31–3) are far from convincing. On the decisive point that it was the Amharic text that embodied the factual agreement, Giglio has, however, abandoned the long-standing historical tradition in Italy to the contrary and accepted my interpretation.

421 Gebre Sillasē, *Minīlik*, p. 169.
422 ASMAE, Serie V, Trattati, Etiopia, no. 4.
423 Battaglia, *Guerra*, pp. 379–83, 397–400; ACS, Fondo Crispi, 146/81.
424 Battaglia, *Guerra*, pp. 420–5.

On the boundary issue alone—and this was after all the original reason for the negotiations and according to Antonelli 'the most important' clause—the Wiçhalē treaty had already received a blow from which it would not easily recover. In fact, the illegal occupation of most of Hamasēn and Akkele Guzay and all of Serayē had placed Minīlik in much the same relationship to the Italians as Yohannis had been to the Egyptians over Bogos: a state of 'no peace, no war'. The difference was that Crispi had a second card to play: he believed that Italy could wait, even had better wait, behind the Mereb for other developments to take their course.[425]

On 11 October 1889, as if he had waited for Mekonnin to sign the Additional Convention opening the boundaries first, Crispi notified the signatory powers of the General Act of Berlin that by Article XVII of the Wiçhalē treaty, Minīlik had agreed 'to avail himself of the government of H.M. the King of Italy for all negotiations of affairs which he might have with other powers or governments', and he did so 'in conformity with' Article XXXIV of the General Act. Neither Article XVII nor the notification mentioned 'protection' or 'protectorate', but Crispi's intention that his communication should be accepted as a protectorate claim is evident from the reference to the Berlin Act. Most of the thirteen governments approached had little or no interest in the area and accepted the notification without reservations. The powers who mattered—Britain, France, Russia, Turkey—all had reservations or protested in one way or other. The British found the procedure questionable and asked for a copy of the whole treaty before acknowledging receipt of the notification. But Italy was their ally in the area, and so they eventually swallowed 'the quasi-Protectorate' or 'the so-called Protectorate'. The French acknowledged receipt of the notification but later insisted that they had been tricked linguistically and that they had not accepted the substance of the Italian notification. The Russians had reservations until Crispi finally decided, unilaterally and in vain, that their objections were overruled. The Porte took a deliberate decision not to acknowledge the notification; if the Italians did not respect the sovereign rights of the Ottoman Empire at Massawa, what good could be expected from legal formalities as far as they were concerned? This was the situation in January 1890, and it is difficult to understand how anyone can conclude 'that Crispi had succeeded in his attempt and that everything had come to an end in the best of ways'.[426]

Crispi's first opportunity to test the acceptance of his protectorate claim was the Brussels Conference on slavery, 1889–90, and he decided to take it. On 27 January 1890, the Italian delegate proposed an amendment to open the way for Italy to sign the convention as the protecting power of Ethiopia. The Belgian diplomat Émile Banning, who assisted his colleague Baron C. A. Lambermont in running the conference, commented, 'This would be an indirect sanction of

---

425 ibid., p. 426.
426 Rubenson, *Wiçhalē XVII*, pp. 12–14; for France, also AE(Brussels), Acte Général de Bruxelles, Adhésion I/1, Borchgrave to Lambermont, 22 Mar. 1890. The conclusion is Giglio's (*L'articolo XVII*, p. 75). It seems to me that his eagerness to prove that an Italian protectorate over Ethiopia existed has made him grossly underestimate the strength of the reservations.

article 17 of the Italian treaty'. Therefore it was out of the question; the word protectorate in particular could not be used.[427] Crispi was not at a loss: a request from Minīlik to be a signatory of the convention and a mandate for the Italian delegation to sign on his behalf would at least show that Italy had a special relationship with Ethiopia. Some, hopefully, would regard it as evidence that the protectorate did exist.

Antonelli was instructed through Orero to get a mandate from Minīlik in Tigrē. To mention the 'protectorate' was, of course, as impossible in Meqele as in Brussels. It was unnecessary, too. The Italians had promised Minīlik arms, and he had every reason to co-operate so that Ethiopia would be exempted from the planned restrictions against arms sales in Africa. The message reported from Minīlik was that the Italian delegate should maintain, in Minīlik's name, Ethiopia's interests in all matters that might concern her, but there was no mention of any authorization to sign any agreement.[428] Citing this and the Wiçhalē treaty, together and separately, the Italians tried to get Minīlik's adhesion to the convention on the agenda, stressing how precious and efficient his co-operation would be in the struggle against the slave trade, 'of which there is no longer a trace in the states placed under his dominion'; though Minīlik had unfortunately learned about the conference very late, his 'spontaneous adhesion' should be taken as a welcome indication of the success of the work.[429]

Now the fantastic thing happened that while Ethiopia's support for the convention was regarded as desirable and even necessary, it was found impossible to allow Italy to speak for her even on the basis of the special mandate. The problem was that it might be regarded 'as a first application of article 17 . . .' and in view of the undetermined status of the Italian protectorate, 'any correlation whatsoever with article 17' had to be avoided.[430]

For two months, statesmen and diplomats worked behind the scenes to find a formula which would give Italy some *de facto* satisfaction without implying, however indirectly, any *de jure* recognition of her 'so-called protectorate'. The French and Turkish governments pointed out that questions of this kind were not solved by majority votes.[431] Lord Salisbury, the British foreign minister,

427 AE(Brussels), Acte Général . . ., Adhésion I/1, minute by Banning, 27–29 Jan. 1890.
428 ASMAI 155/1–5, Crispi to Orero, 26 Feb. 1890; Antonelli to Crispi, 3 Mar. and 29 Mar. 1890; Crispi to De Renzis, 19 Apr. 1890; AE(Brussels), Acte Général . . ., Adhésion I/1, De Renzis to Chimay, 7 Apr. 1890. The text of a letter Minīlik to Crispi, 4 Mar. 1890 (Ethiopian dates 1 Mar. or 5 Mar.), delegating the authority is published in *AP.DD*, 1890–91, XVII, p. 6, but Antonelli admitted 29 Mar. 1890 from Massawa that he had only received a verbal mandate. One week later Antonelli forwarded the requested written mandate (Giglio, *L'articolo XVII*, p. 84). There is reason to suspect, however, that the document was not only pre-dated (see ASMAI 36/9–73, minute by Crispi, n.d.) but actually forged. No messenger could possibly have covered the distance from Massawa to Minīlik's camp at Ashengē (Gebre Sillasē, *Minīlik*, p. 171) and back (*c.* 800 kilometres) in the short interval between 29 March and 6 April.
429 AE(Brussels), Acte Général . . ., Adhésion I/1, De Renzis to Chimay, 17 Mar. 1890.
430 ibid., Leopold II to Lambermont, 19 Mar. 1890; Chimay to Vivian, 20 Mar. 1890; ASMAI 155/1–5, De Renzis to Crispi, 25 Mar. 1890.
431 AE(Brussels), Acte Général . . ., Adhésion I/1, verbal notes, the French, undated; the Turkish, 23 Apr. 1890.

agreed that the protectorate claim could not be used, or even mentioned, but supported Italy's right to represent Ethiopia on the basis of the special mandate, as did the German and Austrian governments. The Porte, however, demanded that Italy abandon her proposal altogether or that it be tabled without discussion. Russia suggested and then insisted, with French support, that the only acceptable procedure would be for Italy to communicate Minīlik's adhesion to the Brussels Act *after* the conference so that all could lodge their eventual reservations when notified of the communication.[432] The purpose of this was, of course, to prevent Italy from ever claiming that the conference as such had recognized her right to speak for Ethiopia.

The Italian reaction to the Russian proposal was very strong: 'We are not alone; we are four [the Triple Alliance and Britain]; well, we will band together, and if it becomes necessary to leave the conference, Europe will judge!' But the Russians refused to be moved, and the Italians were obliged to back down step by step.[433] In the end they had to accept reservations by Russia and France even to a simple notification of Minīlik's adhesion made after the conference was over and on the basis of the special mandate only.[434] Instead of demonstrating an internationally accepted Italian protectorate over Ethiopia, 'the Minīlik incident' at Brussels thus revealed how empty Crispi's claims were. The net result was that France and Russia had clarified, in documents deposited with a third party, that they rejected Italy's claims.[435]

Though the reservations of Turkey, Russia, and France cannot be brushed aside as irrelevant to the question of the *de jure* existence (as understood by Europeans) of the Italian protectorate over Ethiopia, neither notifications nor reservations have more than marginal interest from the point of view of Ethiopian history. Firstly, Italy's *claim* alone created the expectation that she would eventually succeed in establishing her protectorate; after a few years everyone would become used to the idea that Minīlik was an Italian vassal and then the formal recognition would be easy to obtain.[436] Secondly, it was not concern for

432 ibid., Leopold [to Lambermont], 25 Mar. and 26 Mar. 1890; Vivian to Lambermont, 26 Apr. 1890; Borchgrave to Chimay, 2 May 1890; Lambermont to Leopold, n.d., with attached 'copy' of Russian reply dated 2 May 1890; Morier to Salisbury, 2 May 1890; ASMAI 155/1–5, De Renzis to Crispi, 25 Mar. 1890; Tournielli to Crispi, 27 Mar. and 28 Mar. 1890.

433 AE(Brussels), Acte Général . . ., Adhésion I/1, [Lambermont] to Vivian, and to Leopold II, 4 May 1890; Greindl to Lambermont, 7 May 1890; [Lambermont] to Greindl, 11 May 1890; Leopold [to Lambermont], 15 May 1890; De Renzis to Lambermont, 10 Jun. 1890; [Vivian to Lambermont], 18 Jun. 1890. These are only a few of the many letters, notes, and minutes which reveal how hard and unsuccessfully Italy fought to get something of political value out of the conference. See also Émile Banning, *Mémoires politiques et diplomatiques. Comment fut fondé le Congo Belge* (Paris and Bruxelles, 1927), pp. 130–2, 137–40, 145, 152.

434 AE(Brussels), Acte Général . . ., Adhésion I/2, contains the notification De Renzis to Chimay, 28 Aug. 1890, and the replies de Giers to de Vinck, 7 Oct., and Ribot to Beyens, 16 Oct. 1890, both with reservations.

435 Cf. Giglio, *L'articolo XVII*, p. 89: 'not a check (*scacco*)' but 'an equivocal recognition of her claims to the protectorate'!

436 AE(Brussels), Acte Général . . ., Adhésion I/1, Greindl to Lambermont, 7 May 1890.

Ethiopia's independence that caused the reservations and protests; if Minīlik had compromised his sovereignty, the alternative to Italy was not independence but some other European power.

With the exception of one intriguing statement from Istanbul that the Porte did not acknowledge the receipt of Crispi's notification of Article XVII, *inter alia* because only Italy and not Minīlik had notified,[437] there were no indications at Brussels that anyone bothered to ask whether Minīlik had really agreed to what the notification said. This is remarkable because Minīlik had written to several of the courts of Europe in the second half of 1889 without using Italy as an intermediary. He even declared to Victoria, 'Today more than ever before, it is my duty to write to all the kings of Europe in order to make you look upon us with the eyes of love and friendship.' He wrote of sending envoys to London and Paris and raised important political matters such as Ethiopia's right to import arms and ammunition.[438]

When Crispi learned about these letters in February 1890, he instructed Antonelli to take Minīlik to task for having violated Article XVII. Though Antonelli replied that he would make 'strong representations', he seems to have done exactly the opposite. In July 1890, however, when the replies of Wilhelm II and Victoria arrived, Minīlik understood that he had been cheated by Antonelli. The Amharic and Italian versions of the Wiçhalē treaty were compared, and the discrepancy between the two texts established. Minīlik's first step (August 1890) was to cite Article XIX, which made the validity of the treaty dependent on the perfect agreement between the two texts, and request Umberto to correct the error in the Italian version and inform the governments to which the article had been communicated about the correction. Predictably, the Italian government did not comply with Minīlik's request.[439] In October, the latter proceeded to notify his other colleagues in Europe of the correct wording of Article XVII, and continued:

> Since the kingdom of Ethiopia is an independent kingdom, we felt, when we heard this rumour [that Ethiopia had become an Italian protectorate], that it was something which degraded ourselves and our kingdom, and have made known the error to you. And, as we all ourselves [have done], we hope that the Italian government has not failed to make known to you the translation error.[440]

Minīlik's audacity called for action. Antonelli was sent to Addis Abeba, but his protracted attempts to make Minīlik accept the responsibility for the imbroglio and some kind of formula under which the 'protectorate' could be maintained all failed. Minīlik informed the Italian government that he would

---

437   ibid., Borchgrave, note for Lambermont, 22 Mar. 1890.
438   FO 95/750, no. 289, Minīlik to Victoria, 14 Dec. 1889; AED, Protocole C41, to Carnot, 14 Dec. and 23 Dec. 1889; AAPA, A, Italienisches Protektorat über Abessinien 1, to Wilhelm II, 14 Dec. 1889. See also Rubenson, *Wiçhalē XVII*, pp. 14–16.
439   Rubenson, *Wiçhalē XVII*, pp. 16–20; Battaglia, *Guerra*, pp. 442–6.
440   AED, Protocole C41, Minīlik to Carnot, 30 Oct. 1890. Minīlik wrote to Victoria, and probably to other heads of state as well, on 4 October; these letters seem to have ended up in Rome. See Rubenson, *Wiçhalē XVII*, p. 20, and Giglio, *L'articolo XVII*, p. 85, n. 64.

not accept the consequences of the personal mistakes of Antonelli; by virtue of Article XIX, he regarded Article XVII as null and void, and he would not accept any obligation whatsoever which limited his independence.[441] Antonelli knew he had been defeated and had no illusions about Minīlik's attitude: friendly relations with Ethiopia required an Italian withdrawal from Serayē and Akkele Guzay and the abrogation of Article XVII.[442] Instead of facing the facts, the Italian government continued to build castles in the air, hoping that European governments would take note of them and thereby make them materialize. They negotiated the two agreements of 24 March and 15 April 1891 with Britain delimiting the boundaries of their would-be protectorate, and made them public on 16 April. The day before, they had dispatched a letter to Minīlik inviting him to believe that 'nothing was closer to the heart' of the King of Italy than to see the Ethiopian crown 'honoured and *independent*'.[443]

Though Minīlik was certainly ignorant of many of the intricacies of European diplomacy and international law, he was sufficiently aware of the political realities to know that he had to act with both firmness and caution. In April 1891, he carried through with an originally Italian proposal that he define the frontiers of Ethiopia. Communicated to the European powers through the Italian government, it would presumably have supported Italy's claims. But Minīlik took care to use no Italian channels when he dispatched his famous circular letter describing Ethiopia as a 'Christian island surrounded by a sea of pagans', and so it arrived more as a denial of Italy's claims to have *settled* the matter than anything else. On the other hand, Minīlik was careful not to make any claims which could be regarded as a failure to honour his agreements. He showed little restraint when he drew the frontiers in the west, south, and east, but in the north he allowed the Italians not only the territory which he had ceded in the Wiçhalē treaty but also the additional places offered in February 1890 to fulfil the 'actual possession' clause and even those discussed in Addis Abeba one year later. It is interesting to note, however, that he maintained Ethiopia's claim to the coast south of Arafalī by virtue of the fact that Muhammad Anfarī was his vassal.[444]

The response was not difficult to foresee. London and Rome replied with copies of their March and April protocols on spheres of influence. Ethiopia was not even mentioned in the protocols, but this did not prevent the Italian government from assuring Minīlik that their purpose was to 'guarantee and protect the

---

441   Battaglia, *Guerra*, pp. 448–57. The letter by which Minīlik announced the failure of the negotiations to Umberto on 11 Feb. 1891 is published in *AP.DD*, 1890–91, XVII, pp. 41–3.

442   *AP.DD*, 1890–91, XVII, p. 36, Antonelli to Di Rudini, 25 Feb. 1891.

443   ibid., XVIII, *Protocolli 24 marzo e 15 aprile 1891* . . .; ASMAI 36/1–21 *bis*, Umberto to Minīlik, 15 Apr. 1891 (my emphasis).

444   FO 95/751, no. 100, Minīlik to Victoria, 21 Apr. 1891; AED, Protocole C41, to Carnot, same date; AAPA, A, Italienisches Protektorat über Abessinien 4, to Wilhelm II, same date; ASMAI 36/13–109, to Umberto I, same date. For the idea of a circular letter, see ASMAI 36/6–52, Antonelli to Minīlik, n.d. (July 1890); for the last territorial concessions discussed before the circular, 36/13–104, Antonelli to Crispi, 31 Dec. 1890; 36/13–106, Minīlik to Umberto I, 22 Jan. 1891; for Awsa, 36/9–74, Salimbeni to Pestalozza, 19 Nov. 1890.

glorious dominions of the Ethiopian empire'.[445] From Paris, on the other hand, Minīlik received assurances that he could continue to count on all the arms and ammunition he wanted and that the governor of Obok, L. Lagarde, would be sent to clarify and settle any differences of opinion about the boundaries between the French possessions in the Gulf of Tajura and Ethiopia in a spirit of friendship and co-operation.[446]

Short of a declaration of war against Italy, there was only one more major diplomatic initiative by which Minīlik could demonstrate his own independence and the emptiness of Italy's pretensions. He had exposed the Italian fraud when he cited Article XIX of the Wiçhalē treaty to establish that Article XVII was null and void. Nevertheless the Italians and their friends in Europe continued to act as if the Wiçhalē treaty had sanctioned Italy's pretensions to a protectorate over Ethiopia. To get out of this situation altogether, Minīlik decided to terminate the whole treaty. On 27 February 1893 he notified the Italian government that the treaty would cease on 1 May 1894.[447] Both dates are significant.

In a more serious attempt to patch up their relations with Minīlik after the breakdown in 1891 and a half-hearted initiative later in the year to use Yohannis's son Mengesha against the Emperor, the Italian government dispatched an emissary, Leopoldo Traversi, to Addis Abeba with 2 million cartridges which Minīlik had bought (and paid for) in Italy under the loan agreement of the Additional Convention. Traversi arrived on 16 February 1893, and Minīlik decided that this was the right moment to inform the Europeans that he now regarded himself as even with the Italians.[448] At the same time he made an attempt to 'fulfil all righteousness' by making the termination of the treaty effective exactly five years after it had been signed, for Article XVI entitled either side to modify all clauses except the one on boundaries after five years, provided one year's notice was given. On the other hand, Minīlik had sufficient experience to know that his unilateral termination would be challenged, and he did not argue his *legal* right to terminate the treaty but his *moral* right to do so, citing as justification Article XVII, boundary infringements, and intrigues with his subjects. In almost identical letters to friends and foes he wrote:

> For it is with much dishonesty that he [Umberto], pretending friendship, has desired to seize my country. Because God gave the crown and the power that I should protect the land of my forefathers, I terminate and nullify this treaty. I have not, however, nullified my friendship. Know that I desire no other treaty than this. My kingdom is an independent kingdom and I seek no one's protection.[449]

When the Italian government ignored the grievances and tried, with the help of Britain and Germany, to convince Minīlik that he could not terminate the

445 FO 95/752, no. 168, Victoria to Minīlik, 18 Aug. 1891; ASMAI 36/13–110, Umberto to Minīlik, 20 Sep. 1891.
446 AED, Protocole C41, Carnot to Minīlik, 8 Sep. 1891.
447 Giglio, *L'articolo XVII*, p. 95.
448 Battaglia, *Guerra*, pp. 507–17, 530–2.
449 AAPA, A, Italienisches Protektorat über Abessinien 5, Minīlik to Wilhelm II, 27 Feb. 1893 (quoted); AEMD, Afrique 138, pp. 340–1, to Carnot, same date; Giglio, *L'articolo XVII*, p. 95.

treaty because Article XVI spoke only of modifications, he returned once more to the matter, and this time he went into considerable detail also with Italy's allies. Italy's refusal to correct Article XVII, her violations of the boundary agreed upon in the treaty, annexations of territory, and arrests of Ethiopian delegates were in Minīlik's opinion sufficient justification for the termination of the treaty. In addition, the Italians had completely ignored clauses on the dispensation of justice and had tried to make secret treaties with his chiefs in the north. Thus the treaty had become a source of enmity and not friendship. Minīlik 'hoped' that he would receive justice from the European governments; the Ethiopians did not want war with Italy, but with God's help they would fight and preserve their independence if the Europeans whom he had trusted and befriended should turn into the enemies.[450]

Obsessed with the 'legality' of their protectorate, the Italian government, led once more by Crispi and with Antonelli as under-secretary for foreign affairs, continued to fight Minīlik in Europe, brandishing the sword of the Wichalē treaty as if everything hinged on its acceptance there and not in Ethiopia. As late as August–September 1895, the Italian government, extending the battlefield to a new state, quoted Article XVII to the Swiss government and demanded a formal reply if, 'yes or no', the Swiss intended to obey 'article XVII of the treaty of Wichalē' in their 'eventual relations with Minīlik'. A new round of diplomatic notes followed to establish who had taken note of what and when. There was still some confusion, but on the whole the European governments saw Italy's claims in terms of Wichalē XVII (not Berlin XXXIV), and it was France, Russia, and Turkey against the rest.[451]

In the climate of the partition of Africa, it was no mean diplomatic achievement of Minīlik to hold out for six years against the forceful and dishonest diplomacy of Crispi in particular.[452] After all, Ethiopia's main ally, France, was not in Africa to practise charity either, and with brokers like Bismarck, Leopold II, and Salisbury, it is rather remarkable that no bargain was achieved. One reason, probably the main one, must have been an awareness or feeling in French circles that Ethiopia, with a little moral and material assistance, would be able to hold her own against Italy. Both Minīlik's circular letter about the frontiers and his termination of the Wichalē treaty were received with considerable satisfaction in Paris. On the latter occasion, the French president encouraged Minīlik with unequivocal statements of 'profound sympathy' for his efforts 'to develop the greatness and the prosperity of the proud nation which has so courageously defended its independence and Christian faith for centuries'.[453]

450 AAPA, A, Italienisches Protektorat über Abessinien 5, Minīlik to Wilhelm II, 13 Dec. 1893.

451 Because Switzerland turned to Brussels for advice, much of the documentation on this last-minute attempt to further isolate Ethiopia is found in AE(Brussels), Conférence de Berlin, Notifications 6, documents 58–70. For Italian actions in 1893–94, see Giglio, *L'articolo XVII*, pp. 95–7.

452 The dishonesty applied to allies as well as opponents. See, for instance, AAPA, A, Italienisches Protektorat über Abessinien 5, Lanza to Marschall, 26 Jan. 1894.

453 AEMD, Afrique 138, fols 368–9, Carnot to Minīlik, 14 Sep. 1893. For the reply in 1891, see above, pp. 393–4. The limitations of Giglio's research on the Ethio-Italian protectorate

That France was looking after her own interests does not exclude a genuine appreciation for the Ethiopian struggle. It is not without significance that the memorandum drawn up when Minīlik's notification of the termination arrived at Quai d'Orsay emphasized that France had certainly not agreed to abide by Article XVII *after* she had been informed of the discrepancy between the Amharic and Italian texts and that there was no reason for her to do so in the future.[454] In fact, official correspondence continued almost until the war with Italy broke out.[455]

Minīlik's contacts with Russia were more sporadic but also more cordial and frank than those with France. This was undoubtedly due to the fact that both Minīlik and Mekonnin, who governed at Harer, were keenly aware that the French could not be relied upon because of their own interests in the area. In March 1892, Minīlik wrote to the Czar, asking for diplomatic support in connection with Article XVII and Italian intrigues with Mengesha, and threatened that the Italians would 'be punished in the same way as their brothers at Dogalī', if they did not stop causing unrest in his country.[456] It was left to Mekonnin to ask for arms and artillery instructors and to explain in no uncertain terms, and making no exception for France:

> We have not found among the Europeans who have become our neighbours any who desire our welfare and independence but those who [want to] deprive us [of them]. The West Europeans in their desire for new land have encircled us; in groups they have crossed our borders to deprive us of our independence, and are causing us trouble . . . Now we have heard and understood [that there is no] Orthodox kingdom except Moscow.[457]

It is evident that the emphasis here is on *West* European as opposed to fellow-Orthodox.

In his relations with France, on the other hand, Minīlik stressed the Ethiopian–Russian friendship at the same time as he expressed his great satisfaction with

issue emerge very clearly from his treatment of these two letters. From a report by the Italian representative in Paris of a conversation with the French minister of foreign affairs, Giglio concludes (*L'articolo XVII*, p. 94) that the first letter, 8 Sep. 1891, amounted to a protest 'against the pretensions of Minīlik'. Of the second letter, 14 Sep. 1893, he states categorically (p. 96), 'France did not reply at all (*affatto*) to Minīlik'. Admittedly no historian can (or should) possibly pay equal attention to all the tens of thousands of documents of more or less relevance for the protectorate issue, but the failure of my colleague to ask himself in this case if and what the French government *really* replied to Minīlik is serious because he uses his ignorance to prove a point which is very important for him, namely, that France was about to give in to Italy's protectorate claims in 1891–93. In this case, as so many others, it is Giglio's deliberate disregard for other sources than Italian (see *JAH*, VI, 2, p. 221, and VII, 3, p. 541, and my replies, VII, 3, pp. 445 and 554) that makes his investigation biased.

454 AEMD, Afrique 138, fols 348–54, memorandum, 12 Apr. 1893.
455 AED, Protocole C41, Minīlik to Faure, 13 Mar. 1895; to Hanotaux, 14 May 1895.
456 AVPR, F. Politarchiv D. 2009, pp. 361–4, Minīlik to Alexander III, 18 Mar. 1892.
457 ibid., pp. 367–8, Mekonnin to Nikolai Alexandrovich, 12 Jun. 1892; pp. 365–6, to the Russian minister of war, same date. Mekonnin's letter to Nikolai, quoted here, is preserved in Amharic; all three letters exist in German translations by an Ethiopian.

the Franco-Russian *entente*.[458] Minīlik knew, of course, that he had to put up with France until Ethiopia had dealt with Italy and her supporters. But the political judgement of Minīlik and his advisers—and in this case it was not the question of the foreigners, Ilg, Chefneux, etc.—was remarkably sound. At the very end, when war was inevitable, the French government gave in to the Italians and promised to stop arms supplies to Ethiopia. This does not mean, of course, that they suddenly accepted the validity of Italy's protectorate claim or Crispi's opinion that Minīlik was 'a rebel and a traitor'. It was the mood of the times, rather than legal considerations, that decided; Paris took the 'European' stand:

> No one here—I have not to take notice of this or that scatterbrained person, or a few habitually malevolent minds—wishes for the success of the Abyssinians at the price of the discomfiture of a civilized nation, from which it is possible to differ in aims and opinions without being supposed to cherish any ill will when that nation is face to face with a brave but barbarous foe.[459]

The Russians refused to be moved. To the dismay of the Italian government, and the delight of the Turkish, an official Ethiopian mission visited St Petersburg and was received as any other diplomatic mission from one friendly sovereign state to another.[460] In July 1895 the Russian stand was summed up in an *Italian* memorandum:

> Russia has just declared, at last, that she regards Minīlik as an independent sovereign and that she has the right, since she does not recognize the Italian protectorate, to have such relations with Minīlik as suit her.[461]

At last, one might say, someone in Rome had seen the light. Not entirely, how-ever, for the problem was still seen only in its European context. Italy was simply suffering for her loyalty towards the other members of the Triple Alliance. Because of this, 'Italy has been declared, first by France and now by Russia, outside European law in matters concerning the rules established for Africa by the acts of Berlin and Brussels'.[462]

It is understandable that Italy stressed the aspect that she was 'losing Ethiopia in Europe'. African territories were supposed to be pawns, so why should anyone bother about Minīlik? Nevertheless the Ethiopian diplomacy undoubtedly played a major role in preventing Crispi from having his way. It is obvious, too, that Minīlik felt the response of France and Russia as valuable moral support. On the other hand, he was far too experienced to believe that he could win the

458 AED, Protocole C41, Minīlik to Carnot, 10 Jan. 1894.
459 Rubenson, 'Adwa 1896', p. 128; cf. Giglio, *L'articolo*, p. 102.
460 Battaglia, *Guerra*, pp. 613–16; SP.HNA, Carton 236/1, Fevzï to Turkhan, 2 Jul. 1895; Husny to Turkhan, 6 Jul., 8 Jul., 9 Aug. 1895; 236/5, Husney to Turkhan, 19 Jul. 1895.
461 AAPA, A, Italienisches Protektorat über Abessinien 5, 'Aide Mémoire, Rome, 12 juillet 1895'.
462 ibid. This memorandum was printed, and though the copy in the German archives is marked 'secret', it would be strange if no copies have survived in the Italian archives.

battle for Ethiopia's independence in Europe. Ultimately, the Ethiopians had to be prepared to fight. Therefore the diplomacy was directed largely towards keeping up a flow of arms and ammunition into the country.

The Ethiopians did not believe in using loans from their enemies to pay for their armaments and showed an extraordinary eagerness to repay the loan contracted by Mekonnin in 1889 as quickly as possible.[463] Other resources had to be found. But the years immediately following Minīlik's accession were exceedingly difficult times in Ethiopia. Tigrē and Begēmdir, in particular, were exhausted from the wars of Yohannis's reign. Then a terrible cattle plague struck Ethiopia in late 1888 and wiped away most of the livestock, according to many reports 90 per cent or more. During the years which followed up to 1892, the Ethiopian people passed through the worst famine of their recorded history. Due to the lack of plough oxen much land went uncultivated and the reported prices of grain and cattle are almost as unbelievable as some of the horror stories told.[464]

It was by continuing to incorporate vast areas in the south, south-east, and south-west that Minīlik increased the financial means of his state, and to a considerable extent also the recruiting base for his army. He taxed the new provinces heavily in gold and ivory and used much of the revenues to purchase arms and ammunition. Though the numbers of arms supplied as gifts by various governments also increased, there can be no doubt that they were only a fraction of the total imports to Ethiopia in the first half of the 1890s. Minīlik simply had the contacts and the financial resources to make the arms traders deliver the goods. Nevertheless there is reason to believe that the quantities involved were often exaggerated by both governments and individual merchants who wanted to stress that what they were themselves supplying was relatively speaking harmless in comparison with what their political and commercial rivals were providing. The biggest *order* reported was for 100,000 rifles and 10 million cartridges from a Hamburg firm in 1893, but this deal was vetoed by the German government. The last Italians to be in a position to report from the Ethiopian capital before the war broke out, Traversi and Colonel Federico Piano, estimated in November 1894 that there were 82,000 rifles and 5·5 million cartridges in the country. In view of the quantities allegedly imported, this would seem to be a very conservative estimate, but the fact is that practically all estimates of total numbers available, even one year later, stop at 100,000–110,000 rifles, some forty cannon, and an undefined number of machine-guns. Nevertheless, the Ethiopian army was armed as never before, for these were up-to-date weapons with proper, if limited, supplies of ammunition.[465]

463 AEMD, Afrique 138, fol. 198, Lagarde to the Ministry of the Colonies, 7 Dec. 1890; Keller, *Ilg*, pp. 80–1.
464 See Pankhurst, *Economic History*, pp. 217–20; Battaglia, *Guerra*, pp. 535, 537, 570. Further information is found in ASMAI 36/11–92, 93 and 36/13–111.
465 See Pankhurst, *Economic History*, pp. 594–602, for a large collection of references to reported orders, deliveries, and position estimates. Note that the same shipments may be, in some cases certainly are, reported more than once. A comprehensive study of these figures and many others which can be extracted from archives in Europe is still to be undertaken.

Adwa: the Seal of Victory

Minīlik's termination of the Wichalē treaty and refusal to even discuss the issue with Colonel Piano, who had been sent to Addis Abeba to salvage the situation, finally convinced the Italians that there would be no protectorate by insisting that Minīlik was bound by Article XVII. Other methods were called for: 'protectorates' could also be established by force, though Crispi's instructions to Eritrea's governor, General Oreste Baratieri, revealed an unmistakable preference for leaving the actual fighting to others:

> Minīlik's inexcusable behaviour compels [us] to prepare from now on a defence plan. As we did with Minīlik against Yohannis, we should now encourage pretenders against Minīlik. Mengesha in Tigrē, Mekonnin in Harer, have, besides personal ambitions, serious grounds [for] hatred [and] revenge against the Emperor. If Minīlik disappears, the empire could be divided into two kingdoms, one in the north, another in the south, under Italy's lofty protection, not to exclude other for us better combinations.[466]

As Crispi himself indicated, this was no new policy, but what he preferred to forget or never bothered to find out was how poorly it had in fact worked, for the Egyptians in the 1870s no less than for his own agent Antonelli in the 1880s. And so the whole story repeated itself. As the Egyptians before them, the Italians dreamed up the kind of Ethiopia which would give them no trouble. To Traversi, she was 'in appearance, a colossus' but without substance; to Piano, she was 'the colossus with feet of clay'. In October 1894, a third Italian in the country, Luigi Capucci, observed: 'No one is satisfied with the actual situation . . . the present empire exists by dint of inertia; with the first clash, everything will go to pieces; a European conqueror . . . will have all the country for himself and the way prepared; soldiers and chiefs will join him for a wager: it is sufficient that he is strong and liberal in the beginning.'[467]

Misled by their own wishful thinking, the Italians saw allies everywhere. No sooner had, for instance, Nerazzini *proposed* from Harer that one might try to win over Mekonnin or *at least compromise him*, than Baratieri reported from Massawa that the governor of Harer, who was also Minīlik's best-informed and probably most trusted adviser and general, had promised to revolt if Minīlik attacked Eritrea.[468]

In actual fact, the year 1894 was characterized by important political events which contributed to the consolidation of the country and not the opposite. First Nigus Tekle Haymanot of Gojjam arrived in the capital to renew his vows of loyalty to Minīlik, and it is clear from the ceremonies on the occasion that it was much more than a routine affair. Four months later, in June, a politically even more important reunion took place in Addis Abeba when Ras Mengesha of Tigrē came with several of his father's great men to receive pardon for his inde-

466 Battaglia, *Guerra*, pp. 572–4.
467 ibid., pp. 570, 622, 580.
468 *AP.DD*, 1895–96, XXIII-*bis*, pp. 5–9, Nerazzini to Blanc, 26 Jan. 1895; p. 21, Baratieri to Blanc, 3 Feb. 1895.

pendent dealings with the Italians in 1891–92. This reconciliation was the outcome of more than one year of contacts and negotiations and meant, in fact, that the Italians, who had encouraged Mengesha's independence to use him against Minīlik if necessary, lost him just as he might have become important as their potential ally. That Alula, too, was present and was reconciled to the idea of serving Minīlik added importance to Mengesha's submission.[469]

In December 1894, the Italians received a warning. Their own governor of Akkele Guzay, Bahta Hagos, unexpectedly proclaimed the liberation of his province from foreign rule. Three days later he was defeated and killed. Baratieri, who suspected—and not without reason—that the revolt had been instigated from south of the Mereb, marched on Adwa but found his forces insufficient and withdrew again. Ras Mengesha pursued him into Eritrea, where an indecisive battle was fought at Kewatīt (Coatit) on 12–14 January. But Mengesha, too, was unprepared for the war and had to make a hasty retreat to Tigrē. Though Bahta Hagos seems to have acted prematurely and mainly because the Italians were appropriating land, there is evidence that Mengesha and Minīlik had started to discuss actions to dislodge the Italians from at least some of the territory to which neither the Wiçhalē treaty nor the offers made later by Minīlik entitled them.[470]

Baratieri and the government in Rome seem to have completely ignored the lesson which they might have learned from the revolt of Bahta Hagos, namely that they did not necessarily command even the loyalty of their own chiefs and allies in Eritrea. The temptation presented by Mengesha's retreat was irresistible. The 'not inactive defence' suggested to Baratieri resulted in the annexation and partial occupation of Tigrē in March–April 1895. Mengesha had no choice but to retreat; other Tigrean chiefs co-operated or pretended to co-operate with the Italians and thus kept their local forces intact. Though some reinforcements were sent from Italy, Italian strategy was based mainly on 'Ethiopian disunity' and Crispi reminded Baratieri, who wanted funds at least, that 'Napoleon I made war with the money of the defeated'.[471]

Minīlik's first reaction was to blame both Baratieri and Mengesha for having precipitated a war which he was still anxious to avoid. As usual he did not fail to ask for international assistance in finding a peaceful solution.[472] But particularly after Baratieri's invasion in March, he must have understood that a major military confrontation was inevitable. Ethiopia's situation was not easy. In the east, the possibility that the British would intervene from Zeyla to support the Italians could not be excluded. Since the French, including Lagarde, had come around to the opinion that the Ethiopians would be defeated, they could only be expected to look out for themselves, and Minīlik's best chance was that the

469 Gebre Sillasē, *Minīlik*, pp. 204–15, 222; Afewerq, *Minīlik*, p. 83.
470 Battaglia, *Guerra*, pp. 594–606; Gebre Sillasē, *Minīlik*, p. 222; Afewerq, *Minīlik*, pp. 86–7.
471 Battaglia, *Guerra*, pp. 606–11.
472 AED, Protocole C41, Minīlik to Hanotaux, 13 Mar. 1895; AAPA, A, Italienisches Protektorat über Abessinien 6, [Minīlik to Nikolai II], n.d. This is an Italian translation without names and date sent from St Petersburg on 24 Jul. 1895, but there is no doubt that it is a translation (more or less correct) of the substance of a letter from Minīlik to the Czar. See also Battaglia, *Guerra*, pp. 611–13.

French and British would neutralize each other so that he did not lose Harer.[473] In the west, nothing had been settled with the Mahdists during the years that had passed, except at a local level. Before marching against the Italians, Minīlik took the precaution of sending an envoy, Muhammad al-Tayib, to the khalifa; the response was not unfriendly but no agreements on neutrality or co-operation were reached before the battle of Adwa.[474]

Minīlik began to prepare for his campaign before the rainy season of 1895, but it was only in September that he issued his famous mobilization order, and the armies began to march. The Emperor declared that the call to arms was in defence of the country and the faith of his subjects against an enemy who had crossed the sea established by God as Ethiopia's boundary. He did not conceal his opinion that the task of fighting the Italians was a difficult one which called for a total mobilization and possibly great sacrifices. His reference to the cattle plague and the famine as factors which had prevented an earlier campaign indicates that he felt a need to explain why he had not acted earlier. There were certainly many in Ethiopia who criticized Minīlik for having been too confiding and too lenient in his relations with the *ferenj*, and it should surprise no one that he made no other reference in a document of this kind to the complicated relations of the past ten years than a comparison of the Italians with moles working underground.[475] The wording of the proclamation implied support for the view expressed by Yohannis and Alula: the Italians should not have come to Massawa to begin with. This does not mean, however, that Minīlik denied his own role in the developments of those ten years or that he went to war to regain Massawa.[476]

Even after the mobilization, Minīlik was willing to discuss a peaceful solution. Negotiations were kept up sporadically throughout the months of the long march to Adwa, and it was only in mid-February 1896 that the final deadlock was reached. That there was never any realistic chance for these negotiations to succeed is another matter. The Italian demands included all Tigrē as far as the Tekkezē and Lake Ashengē or Amba Alagē—'the land where we have planted our flag'—and the notorious Article XVII was to be replaced by detailed treaty obligations which left no doubt about Ethiopia's protectorate status. Leaving aside diplomatic matters which might or might not be settled behind closed doors, it was clearly impossible for Minīlik to give up Tigrē unless he suffered a major defeat. As far as he was concerned, a compromise would have to be found between the Wiçhalē boundary and the Mereb–Belesa–Muna line occupied

473 Battaglia, *Guerra*, pp. 710–13; BN, Ethiop. 269, fols 5–6, Minīlik to Mondon-Vidailhet, 1 Dec. 1895.

474 CRO, Mahdia 1/55/12, Abdallahi to Minīlik, July/August 1895; 1/55/16, Minīlik to Abdallahi, 15 Apr. 1896; cf. Cromer, *Modern Egypt*, Vol. II, p. 83.

475 Gebre Sillasē, *Minīlik*, p. 225; Keller, *Ilg*, p. 94.

476 I find Battaglia's discussion (*Guerra*, pp. 627–8) of a different 'historical truth' in connection with the proclamation a bit far-fetched. To begin with, Minīlik did not say that he had opposed the coming of the Italians to Massawa or their advance inland. The proclamation is held in very general terms and mentions the coast simply as a natural boundary. That the famine would not necessarily have prevented a campaign in 1893 or 1894 is, however, true.

de facto by the Italians since 1890.[477] Minīlik was really not in the right mood for appeasement and did not mind disclosing it:

> I find . . . that the Italians are impossible to deal with. Power is with God. But from now on, no one will try to appease the Italians. I have endured all this until now so that the European powers would know how I have been attacked and not believe me to be the evildoer. This war does not worry me . . . As for them [the Italians], all the people of Europe who see how worried they are will laugh at them.[478]

Ras Mekonnin and Fītawrarī Tekle had brought their largely Galla armies from Harer and Wellega respectively to Addis Abeba in September 1895, and on 11 October the march to the north started with new contingents joining along the route. The armies from Gojjam, Qwara, Begēmdir, and Dembīya, etc., were instructed to march to Lake Ashengē and those from Simēn and neighbouring provinces to make their way to Meqelē.[479] By early December Mekonnin, Mīka'ēl of Wello, and Welē Bitul of Yejju as well as a number of other commanders had reached the southern frontiers of Tigrē with a first army estimated to number 30,000 men. Joined by some Tigreans under Mengesha they fought an impromptu battle against the Italian vanguard at Amba Alagē on 7 December. Outnumbered and outmanoeuvred, the Italians lost more than 2,000 in dead.[480]

Amba Alagē was followed by the long siege and final surrender of the fortified position of the Italians at Meqelē on 21 January 1896. Baratieri had found it impossible to relieve the garrison, and it was saved from complete annihilation only by the decision of the Ethiopians to permit the survivors to leave (with their arms!), possibly in the vain hope that this would pave the way for a complete Italian withdrawal from Tigrē and a negotiated settlement.[481]

During the siege, Minīlik had arrived at the head of additional forces so that the Italians estimated that they were facing 52,000–55,000 men, presumably excluding a number of traditionally armed warriors.[482] Instead of making a frontal attack on Baratieri's fortified positions near Addīgrat, Minīlik turned north-west towards Adwa, thereby forcing the Italian commander-in-chief to leave Addīgrat with the forces at his disposal and march west in order to prevent an eventual invasion of Eritrea through Adwa. By mid-February Baratieri had occupied and fortified a new position about 30 kilometres east of Adwa. The Ethiopians were encamped around the town. The last spell of negotiations ended on 12 February. From then on it became a war of nerves.[483]

---

477 Battaglia, *Guerra*, pp. 636, 642–3, 677, 690, 697–8. How inflexible the Italian government had become is best illustrated by the draft of a peace treaty cabled to Baratieri as late as 18 January 1896 (*AP.DD*, 1895–96, XXIII, p. 98).
478 BN, Ethiop. 269, fols 5–6, Minīlik to Mondon-Vidailhet, 1 Dec. 1895.
479 Gebre Sillasē, *Minīlik*, p. 225.
480 Battaglia, *Guerra*, pp. 635–8, 644–56, 676.
481 ibid., pp. 678–90.
482 *AP.DD*, 1895–96, XXIII-*bis*, p. 190, Baratieri to Mocenni, 13 Jan. 1896. See also ibid., XXIII, pp. 76–7, for an earlier dispatch (26 Dec. 1895) with a breakdown by units of the army which had won the battle of Amba Alagē.
483 Rubenson, 'Adwa 1896', *Protest and Power*, pp. 115–16.

Baratieri had 20,000 men (about 50/50 Italians and Eritreans) with fifty-two cannon at his immediate disposal for a battle at Adwa. He did not expect to increase his force; logistics were difficult enough as it was. He did not intend to take any further initiative because he wanted the advantage of defending himself from his prepared position and hoped that Minīlik would attack—or go away. Minīlik, too, could expect no more troops. All his great vassals except those who had been assigned security tasks elsewhere had obeyed his call. He had roughly speaking 100,000 men with him, probably as many as 70,000–80,000 with rifles, but his artillery was inferior to that of the Italians.[484] He was determined not to attack Baratieri's position: 'They [the Italians] had fortified themselves in an impossible place which was unsuitable for a battle. Though my army was starving, I remained encamped at Adwa . . .'[485]

Provisioning was the problem—for both sides. An army of 100,000 could not live off the same area for long. Minīlik was forced to send foraging parties farther and farther afield. For the Italians the situation was becoming desperate. Their supply lines were increasingly disturbed, and for their Eritrean troops in particular, hunger was reported to be not 'a threatening ghost but a daily reality'. Forced to choose between attack and retreat, Baratieri took his fatal decision on 29 February to attack Minīlik's camp the following morning, a Sunday, and try to defeat the Ethiopians in the open field in spite of all. The race was close: Minīlik had instructed his generals to prepare for decamping on Monday, most probably with an invasion of Eritrea in mind.

Baratieri had counted on the surprise element, on better utilization of the terrain, on superior discipline and concerted action to make up for the discrepancy in numbers, which he did not believe would be so great that day after all. Many things went wrong. Communications on the Italian side got messed up. A faulty map, poor reconnaissance, vague and misunderstood orders left Baratieri with only half of his forces where he had expected them to be. In the end, each of the three brigades (there was a fourth in reserve) fought its own action isolated from the others among the mountains and hills just east of Adwa. The Ethiopian units took little time getting ready for combat. At six o'clock the battle began in earnest, and in a full day of heavy fighting the Ethiopians defeated the Italian brigades one by one until all resistance was broken and the Italian retreat had turned into a complete rout.

The Italians lost approximately 7,000 dead, 1,500 wounded, and 3,000 prisoners of war, or almost two thirds of Baratieri's army. On the Ethiopian side the estimates vary from 4,000 to 6,000 killed on the battlefield and as many as 8,000 badly wounded. Whether or not the Ethiopian casualties exceeded those of the Italians in absolute numbers is of little significance, compared with the fact that Baratieri's army had been completely annihilated as a fighting force, while Minīlik, in spite of the heavy losses, still had an army at his disposal. Once more the Ethiopian soldiers had picked up thousands of rifles and in this case captured *all* the enemy's artillery. The battlefield remained in Ethiopian hands.

In Europe the outcome of the battle produced a profound shock. In spite of all

484 ibid., pp. 116–17.
485 ibid., p. 119, quoting BN, Ethiop. 269, fol. 26, Minīlik to Mondon-Vidailhet, 11 Mar. 1896.

the warnings, it seemed unbelievable that a disaster of this magnitude could have befallen the army of 'a civilized European nation' at the hands of 'an African chief and his warriors'. In Rome, Crispi's government fell amid abuse and street violence. In London, policy on the Sudan was quickly revised. At Adwa, the satisfaction was mixed with regret that the victory had been so costly in human lives. The problem of provisions remained; the road back to Wello, Gojjam, Shewa, Wellega, and Harer was long. As Yohannis had done after Gura, Minīlik accepted the request for a cease-fire and peace negotiations.[486]

It is understandable that Italian historiography—followed by almost all European—has explained the outcome of the Italian attempt to subdue Ethiopia in the 1880s and 1890s primarily as an Italian failure. The reasons for the failure may include any or all of the following elements: political instability in Italy, insufficient financial resources or popular support for a colonial venture, international intrigue against Italy, the vacillation between a 'Shewan policy' (the protectorate) and a 'Tigrean policy' (more territory in the north), quarrels between Italian officers, Crispi's personality and Baratieri's generalship, or lack of it, etc. All this is important, but does not go to the heart of the matter. It must be assumed, after all, that Italy's leaders at the time were not unaware of their own problems. It was in spite of the limitations and contradictions that they pursued their policies. When they achieved so much less than they had planned and expected in their relations with Ethiopia, the main reason was the same kind of underestimation as Khedive Ismail and his advisers had indulged in before them.

This underestimation affected all aspects of the struggle. In the field of international relations, Minīlik was not supposed to understand that Ethiopia's independence was at stake if he accepted the Italian version of Article XVII. If he did understand, he was not supposed to protest. If he did protest, he was not supposed to sustain his protest when those who *made* international law told him that it was too late, that no one had the *right* to listen to him any longer. That the Ethiopians had established an international recognition and gained diplomatic experience before Italy entered the scene was overlooked simply because it was convenient to do so.

The rivalry and disunity in the political leadership of Ethiopia was a cornerstone in Italian planning, as it had been in Egyptian. No serious student of Ethiopian history is likely to deny the existence of centrifugal forces in the Ethiopian state. Rivalry and disunity were, indeed, prevalent factors in the shaping of Ethiopian politics, but so were the considerable skill and political maturity with which these matters were normally handled. Though it might have been difficult for European statesmen to think in those terms, it was Crispi's power base that was narrow and shaky, not Minīlik's. Italy was overextending herself in Africa, rather than Minīlik in the Ogaden or Wellamo.

The mistake of the Italians, as of other Europeans, was to take it for granted that all disunity and rivalry could be used by a foreign power against the

486   For this paragraph and the preceding three, see my article 'Adwa 1896' in *Power and Protest*, pp. 113–29, and the sources and literature cited there.

integrity and independence of the Ethiopian state, in other words that it was *a priori* treasonable. Mengesha Yohannis, who regarded his right to the throne as superior to Minīlik's, might have been willing to co-operate in the overthrow of the Emperor, but there is no reason to believe that he and his supporter Alula would have signed away the independence of Ethiopia or any territory that they could possibly hold on to. Many Ethiopian chiefs were reported to be favourable to Italian rule, but who really showed that he was? To what extent the Italians were deceived by wishful thinking or by the deliberate deceit of some chiefs in the last stages of the conflict is difficult to ascertain. Baratieri admitted that he really did not know at all who would be with him, neutral, or against him.[487]

At the crucial moment, Minīlik commanded the loyalty of every important chief in the country. Old enemies or rivals such as Ras Mīka'ēl of Wello and Nigus Tekle Haymanot of Gojjam were present at Adwa, together with Mekonnin (who might have excused himself with the problem of the security of Harer) and the great men of the north. In fact, the two most important Tigrean allies of the Italians, Ras Sibhat and Dejjazmach Hagos Teferī, defected to the Ethiopian side with 600 men only two weeks before the battle of Adwa.[488] There were even reports that Eritrean 'bashi-bazouks' refused to enter the battle with the excuse that, 'though we eat their money, we will not fight our country and our king'.[489] This statement reflects the positive side of what Baratieri disparagingly described as 'a semblance of the idea of nationhood in the guise of hatred against the whites'.[490] It is not necessary to prove here that this idea or feeling was either widespread or conceived in the terms of nineteenth-century European nationalism. The important fact is that it existed and might well have turned the rank and file against any chief who had decided to collaborate with the Italians in a decisive moment. The removal of Minīlik would not have solved the problem. Behind the leaders was this feeling of attachment to 'country and king' (the order used by Minīlik's secretary, Yosēf of Wiçhalē fame). At Adwa, the Italians finally saw that they had underestimated the Ethiopian people.

It should be mentioned, finally, that there were other aspects of this underestimation of the Ethiopians, connected especially with the Adwa campaign. Though the Italians knew very well that Minīlik could mobilize 100,000 men, they did not believe that he could possibly march more than 30,000 as far as Tigrē because of poor logistics. Traditionally, Ethiopian soldiers as other travellers were supposed to carry with them individually their *sinq*, that is some grain, dried meat, and other food supplies. Even if they had porters and donkeys, this could not last for a campaign of several months. So they would either have to start pillaging or turn back. Minīlik, however, had planned for the Adwa campaign along more modern lines and laid up stores ahead of time along the route. After two months on the march and some 600 kilometres from Addis Abeba, the chronicler commented on the remarkable fact that the *gibbir*, that is the King's feeding of his men, was still complete: '. . . the soldiers have not opened their

---

487 Oreste Baratieri, *Memorie d'Africa (1892–1896)* (Torino, 1898), p. 223.
488 *AP.DD*, 1895–96, XXIII-*bis*, p. 247, Baratieri to Mocenni, 13 Feb. 1896.
489 BN, Ethiop. 269, fol. 36, Yosēf to Mondon-Vidailhet, 31 Mar. 1896.
490 Baratieri, *Memorie*, p. 48.

bags of provisions'.[491] In Tigrē, of course, Minīlik had been prevented from laying up stores, and eventually the soldiers began to run out of food. The return march was very difficult from this point of view. But then Minīlik's army had marched 1,000 kilometres from Addis Abeba and won their victory, having forced Baratieri to attack because he had run out of supplies 100 kilometres from his capital, Asmera. Relatively speaking, again, the Ethiopians were ahead of their reputation.

In purely military terms the same is true. Many Ethiopian soldiers may still have fought like traditional warriors within the limits of their respective smaller units. But all accounts of the battle indicate that firepower, including artillery, was used effectively by the Ethiopians, and that the generals kept an overall view and planned the stages of the battle into the complete victory which Adwa represents. Relatively speaking, again, Ethiopian generalship was not inferior to Italian in the battle that decided the outcome of Ethiopia's struggle for survival in the period of 'the scramble for Africa'.

491 Gebre Sillasē, *Minīlik*, p. 238.

Conclusion

Ethiopia's nineteenth-century contacts and conflicts with other states (or their representatives of one type or another) include too many disparate and conflicting elements to permit a neat and noncontroversial summary. The external influences and interests were many and varied; and in matters of foreign relations Minīlik's Ethiopia was entirely different from Gugsa's and Welde Sillasē's. Some of the most significant developments of the pre-Tēwodros and Tēwodros periods have been summarized at the end of Parts III and IV respectively. In Part V, I have tried to present sufficient material to show *how* the final struggle for survival was fought and won. My closing remarks in response to the question raised in the first paragraph of the introduction to this book can therefore be fairly brief.

Firstly, the geographical features of Ethiopia played almost no role at all in the preservation of her independence. Infiltration from the coast was not only possible but fairly easy at many points from Massawa to Zeyla; in fact it has been a constant theme throughout the long history of Ethiopia. We have also seen that the explorers, missionaries, and early consuls all found the Ethiopian highlands healthy and suitable for colonization. When armies arrived, it actually turned out to be more difficult for the Ethiopians to repel them in the lowlands (Se'aṭī 1888, for instance) than for the Egyptians and Europeans to enter the highlands. True, the deep gorges and narrow mountain passes which abound in northern Ethiopia would have given great advantages to the defender, provided he had used either guerrilla tactics or fortification techniques on a large scale. Because of the element of chivalry in their military traditions, the Ethiopians, however, did not normally engage in guerrilla warfare. This was the trade of the *shifta*, the outlaw. The concept of fortification, on the other hand, hardly went beyond some simple devices to make an individual *amba*, used as a last refuge, a treasury, or a prison, impregnable.

The idea that the Ethiopian highland massif has functioned as a kind of natural fortress for the whole Ethiopian people is clearly misleading. At any rate, it did not function as such in the latter half of the nineteenth century. Napier met with no insurmountable difficulties marching his British–Indian army to Meqdela, and his withdrawal had nothing to do with the mountainous character of the country. The Egyptian armies of 1875 and 1876 had both penetrated beyond the escarpment and the border mountains of Hamasēn and Akkele Guzay when they were attacked and destroyed. The Mahdists pillaged Gonder and the plains of Dembīya in 1887–88, and the Italians had crossed some of the most mountainous country of Ethiopia when they were finally stopped at Amba Alagē in 1895.

Secondly, the notion that Ethiopia somehow survived the 'scramble' because the interest in subduing and exploiting her was weak and sporadic is completely false. The emphasis shifted with the economic and political conditions in Europe, but generally speaking the exportable resources, the potential markets, and the availability of good agricultural land were taken for granted; so was the strategic importance of the country, expressed in terms of the Nile waters and the new seaway to India and the Far East. The French and British pressure to gain commercial control and political influence was almost constant from the eighteen-forties through to the mid-sixties. Rivalry cancelled out many minor efforts but there was nothing unique in this; it happened all over Africa.

The strange case of British withdrawal from all direct involvement in Ethiopia after the successful march to Meqdela and on the very eve of the opening of the Suez Canal, on the other hand, was not due to rivalry in the European camp. It was the result of the resistance which Tēwodros had so stubbornly maintained against the introduction of special rights and privileges for Europeans in his country. Later Britain looked on with 'benevolent neutrality' when Egypt and Italy undertook their major diplomatic and military campaigns to isolate and destroy Ethiopia. Whatever external or internal opposition Ismail and Crispi respectively had to face, it was not this opposition that stopped the Egyptian and Italian armies. In 1875 no less than 1895, there was no lack of determination to subdue Ethiopia, and in the final analysis the Ethiopian people alone prevented it from happening.

Thirdly, the underlying reasons why the Ethiopians succeeded in neutralizing the attempts to partition the country (Wibē v. Ali, Nigusē v. Tēwodros, Minīlik v. Yohannis, *or* Tigrē v. Amhara) or to limit its sovereignty and ultimately subdue it are to be found more in the awareness of a spiritual and national identity than in material resources. The consciousness of a separate identity was part of the heritage from earlier centuries. Minīlik's well-known description of Ethiopia as a 'Christian island surrounded by a sea of pagans' was not invented for his circular letter about frontiers in 1891. Welde Sillasē had used almost the same words to George III in 1810. It was more, however, than just a question of Christianity. From Welde Sillasē's lament to George III that there was in Ethiopia at that moment 'no king Orthodox in the faith' to Mekonnin's observation to Nikolai Alexandrovich in 1892 that there was in Europe no 'Orthodox kingdom except Moscow', the consciousness of Orthodoxy runs like a thread through the dealings with the *ferenj*.[492] This does not mean that the Ethiopians

492 See above, pp. 49–50, 393, 396.

were exclusive or intolerant, for it is also true that from Basha Abdallah and Ali Umar at the Tigrean court in the first decades of the century to Minīlik's envoy to the khalifa, Muhammad al-Tayib, in the last, Ethiopian Muslims found a place as confidants of the rulers, and neither Protestants nor Catholics were *a priori* excluded from counselling the kings. Nevertheless, the undercurrent is unmistakable and could be made to surface in the people at the crucial moments.

Awareness of and attachment to the monarchy, directly or through the hierarchy of feudal lords, also contributed to national consciousness and cohesion, though in all probability to a lesser extent. In spite of the weakness of the Ethiopian state structure during the *first* half of the nineteenth century, both Britain and France recognized the existence of an Ethiopian state with which they took for granted that they should deal on the basis of equality.

As a Christian monarchy with a long history, Ethiopia clearly had certain advantages over most other African polities. Ethiopian political traditions had some affinity with European. A class of literate court officials existed. Often involved in finding compromise solutions to political and ecclesiastical conflicts and entrusted with the recording of endowments and engagements, they were not new to the art of diplomacy.

What really saved Ethiopia from falling under colonial rule was the determination with which this heritage of national consciousness, 'international recognition', and political/diplomatic skill was developed to meet the new challenges. The fact that the first serious threats came from or through Egypt facilitated the unification work of Tēwodros and Yohannis. It was a conflict that was understandable in terms of past collective experience. The attitude towards the Europeans was ambivalent with Tēwodros representing the extreme standpoint both in terms of proud, uncompromising nationalism and humble, personal desire to emulate. But it is important to note that he was unique only in his excesses and his ultimate failure. At the highest levels of the traditional Ethiopian society as well as among the young men who were attracted to the missionaries and other travellers, an educational process of great significance was taking place. In scope it was narrow, of course, but it provided the new insight and skills required in Ethiopia's struggle for survival as an independent nation. It is sufficient to recall that Welde Sillasē and his court after Salt's second visit knew no other way of identifying George III than by associating him with 'the peoples of India' and that Sebagadis's diplomatic mission to Cairo and London was entrusted to an Ethiopian Muslim who knew very little Arabic and an Englishman who had almost forgotten his mother tongue. At the end of the century, leading members of Minīlik's government had visited Europe on important diplomatic and commercial business. At the court there was no problem about calling on French, English, or German-speaking secretaries. And, of course, the old muskets of the sixteenth-century Gran̄ wars had finally been replaced by breechloading rifles, machine guns, and cannon which the Ethiopians knew how to handle.

The irony of the nineteenth-century educational process created by the interaction, peaceful and warlike, between the Ethiopians and their would-be guardians or enemies is that the more racial prejudice and presumption caused the Europeans to look down upon the Ethiopians, the better prepared were the latter to deal with them. By the end of the century, it was an axiom in Europe that 'Africans have no fatherland'. The Ethiopians did not know this, and although they paid dearly by gradually losing Eritrea, neither diplomatic nor military means sufficed to impose foreign rule on the nation as a whole.

Abbreviations

AAPA	Politisches Archiv des Auswärtigen Amts, Bonn
ACS	Archivio Centrale dello Stato, Rome
ADEN	Residency Records, Aden (now at the India Office Library, London)
AE (Brussels)	Archives du Ministère des Affaires Étrangères et du Commerce Extérieur, Brussels
AECC	Correspondance commerciale, Archives du Ministère des Affaires Étrangères, Paris
AECP	Correspondance politique and Correspondance politique des consuls, Archives du Ministère des Affaires Étrangères, Paris
AECP(Brussels)	Correspondance politique, Archives du Ministère des Affaires Étrangères et du Commerce Extérieur, Brussels
AED	Archives diplomatiques (reserved) du Ministère des Affaires Étrangères, Paris
AEMD	Mémoires et Documents, Archives du Ministère des Affaires Étrangères, Paris
AN.AP	Archives privées, Archives Nationales, Paris
Annales	*Annales de la Congrégation de la Mission*
AP.DD	*Atti Parlamentari, Documenti Diplomatici*
APF.SRC	Scritture Riferite nei Congressi, Archivio Propaganda Fide, Rome
APR	Archives des Palais Royaux, Brussels
ASMAE	Archivio storico del Ministero degli Affari Esteri, Rome
ASMAI	Archivio storico dell'ex Ministero dell'Africa Italiana, Rome
AVA	Archivio Vicariato Apostolico, Asmera
AVPR	Archiv Vneschnej Politiki Rossij, Moscow
Basel	Archiv der Basler Mission, Basel
BM	British Museum, London

BN	Bibliothèque Nationale, Paris
BSG	*Bulletin de la Société de géographie*
BSGI	*Bollettino della Società Geografica Italiana*
CML	Congrégation de la mission (Maison Lazariste), Paris
CMR	*Church Missionary Record*
CMS	Church Missionary Society Archives, London
CRO	Central Records Office, Khartoum
DZA	Deutsches Zentralarchiv, Potsdam
EHB	*Evangelische Heidenbote*
ENA	National Archives, Cairo
FO	Foreign Office Records, Public Record Office, London
GS	Geheimes Staatsarchiv, Berlin-Dahlem
HHS	Haus-, Hof- und Staatsarchiv, Österreichisches Staatsarchiv, Vienna
IO	India Office Library and Records, London
JAH	*Journal of African History*
JES	*Journal of Ethiopian Studies*
JSS	*Journal of Semitic Studies*
MM	*Magazin für die neueste Geschichte der Protestantischen Missions- und Bibelgesellschaften*
MT	*Missionstidning, Utgifven av Evangeliska Fosterlandsstiftelsen*
Nouvelles Annales	*Nouvelles Annales des Voyages, de la Géographie, de l'Histoire et de l'Archéologie*
Petermann	*Mittheilungen aus Justus Perthes, Geographischer Anstalt von A. Petermann*
PP.Commons	*Parliamentary Papers, House of Commons*
Proceedings	*Proceedings of the Third International Conference of Ethiopian Studies, Addis Ababa 1966*
RANL	*Rendiconti della Accademia Nazionale dei Lincei*
RFHO	*Revue française d'Histoire d'Outre-Mer*
RO(Paris)	*Revue de l'Orient*
RO(Warsaw)	*Rocznik Orientalistyczny*
RRAL	*Rendiconti della Reale Accademia dei Lincei*
RS	*Revue Sémitique*
RSE	*Rassegna di Studi Etiopici*
SNR	*Sudan Notes and Records*
SOM	Archives du Ministère de la France d'Outre Mer, Archives Nationales—Section Outre-Mer, Paris
SP.BAGM	Başbakanlik Arşivi Genel Müdürlügü, Sublime Porte, Istanbul
SP.HNA	Hariciye Nezareti Arşivi (Archives du Ministère des Affaires Étrangères), Sublime Porte, Istanbul
Spittler-Archiv	C. F. Spittler Privat-Archiv 653, Staatsarchiv des Kantons Basel-Stadt, Basel
TM	*Le Tour du Monde*
Vatican	*Biblioteca Apostolica Vaticana*

Note on Transliteration

There is no widely accepted *simple* system of transliteration from Ethiopian to Latin script, and many so-called conventional spellings of the names of persons and places are by no means well-established. The system used in this book is fairly simple with only two diacritical marks: a dot for so-called 'glottalized' or 'explosive' consonants and a dash for two of the vowels. On the other hand, I have applied the system as consistently as possible for all names except those geographical names where the English spelling is uniform and has in most cases led to a distinctly different pronunciation as well (Abyssinia, Ethiopia, Massawa, etc.). Since most readers will easily recognize the Arabic names and titles found in this book, I have not used any diacritical marks for them and have more readily accepted 'conventional' spellings. My reason for being more rigorous with the Ethiopian names is my desire to write so that Ethiopian readers and others who know the Amharic language may be able to convert the transliterated words back into the Ethiopian originals and recognize sometimes obscure names without difficulty.

Consonants

Where no explanation is given the consonants or combinations of consonants have their normal English pronunciation.

ሀ, ሐ, ኀ, (ኘ)	— h
ለ	— l
መ	— m
ሠ, ሰ	— s
ሸ	— sh
ረ	— r
ቀ	— q (a glottalized k=sound)
በ	— b
ተ	— t

ጭ — ch

ኅ — n

ኝ — ñ (ñ in Spanish *señor*)

አ, ዐ — ' (between two vowels to indicate glottal stop)

ከ — k

ዘ — z

ዥ — zh (*s* in *pleasure*)

ወ — w

የ — y (*y* in *you*)

ደ — d

ጀ — j

ገ — g (*g* in *get*)

ጠ — ṭ (a glottalized *t*-sound)

ጨ — čh (as *ch* but glottalized)

ጰ — p (a glottalized *p*=sound)

ጸ, ፀ — ṣ (a sibilant *t* as in German *Zeit* but glottalized)

ፈ — f

ፐ — p

ቈ — qw

ኈ — hw

ኰ — kw

ጐ — gw

Vowels

Since Amharic vowels are rather difficult to describe in terms of English vowel sounds, the equivalents given here must be regarded as approximations only.

First order **(ለ)** — e (between *e* in *bet* and *a* in *about*)

Second **(ሉ)** — u (between *u* in *full* and *rule*)

Third **(ሊ)** — ī (*i* in *machine*)

Fourth **(ላ)** — a (between *a* in *father* and *u* in *fun*)

Fifth **(ሌ)** — ē (somewhat less open than *e* in *lend*)

Sixth **(ል)** — i (between *i* and *sit* and *girl* but always short and often silent, in which case the *i* is omitted in the transliteration)

Seventh **(ሎ)** — o (as *o* in *lord*)

Glossary

Abun, abune	Bishop, archbishop of the Ethiopian Orthodox Church
Agha	Officer (Turkish) below the rank of *bey*
Aleqa	Chief, commander, head; used without prefix mainly as an ecclesiastical title, chief priest; with prefix as a military title, e.g. *shī-aleqa* = 'commander of 1,000', major
Aṣē, aṭē	Emperor
Ato	Common title of respect (now simply Mr)
Azazh	Commander, chief; usually denoting the head of some unit or office
Baldereba	Official assigned to a visitor at the court for liaison purposes
Balgada	Official in charge of the salt extraction of the Ṭilṭal area
Basha	Arabic and Ethiopian version of *pasha* used in nineteenth-century Ethiopia particularly as a title for higher customs officials and officers in charge of artillery units
Bashi-bazouk	Member of irregular military unit (Turkish)
Bey	Civil and military title second only to *pasha*
Bītwedded	'The Favourite', high court title, often used with *ras*
Blatta	'Page', honorific title normally for court officials
Blattēngēta	'Master of the Pages', prominent court official
Buda	Sorcerer, possessor of the 'Evil eye'
Dawla	Honorific title used by the associate of the *na'ib* of Arkiko
Debtera	Chorister, scribe
Dejjazmach	'Commander of the Gate', general and normally governor, second only to a *ras*
Felasha	Ethiopian 'Jews'
Ferenj	Foreigner (esp. European)
Fiqir kasa	Good will compensation, token of friendship
Fītawrarī	Commander of vanguard
Fukkera	Ceremonial bragging
Gedam	Precincts of a church or monastery
Grazmach	'Commander of the Left'; middle rank military or administrative officer
Habesha	Abyssinia, Abyssinian
Hajj	Someone who has made the pilgrimage to Mecca and Medina
Hulet lidet	'Two births', the strictly Orthodox *Tewahido* doctrine of the Ethiopian Church

Içhegē	Head of the monastic order of Tekle Haymanot, supreme custodian of church property and second in rank to the *abun*
Içhegē Bēt	Residence of the *içhegē*
Itēgē	Queen, empress
Janhoy	Your (or His) Majesty
Kasa	Compensation, indemnity
Kashif	Title used for district governor in the Sudan
Kentība	Mayor, district governor
Kebre Negest	'The Glory of the Kings', Ethiopian literary work embodying, *i.a.*, the legend of King Solomon and the Queen of Sheba
Lij	'Child, son'; honorific title mostly used for members of the higher aristocracy and the royalty
Līq, plur. līqawint	Scholar, prominent churchman
Līqe kahinat	Prominent ecclesiastical official, head of the clergy of a province
Līqemekwas	High official close to the king
Mekonnin, plur. mekwanint	Nobleman, officer
Meridazmach	Traditional title of the ruler of Shewa
Mesfin, plur. mesafint	Prince
Na'ib	'Deputy', title given by the Turks to Ethiopian chiefs on the mainland opposite Massawa
Neggadras	'Head of traders', prominent merchant
Nigus, plur. negest	King
Niguse negest	King of kings
Qēs	Priest
Qum ṣihfet	Traditional Ethiopian calligraphy
Ras	'Head', duke, governor, second only to a *nigus*
Ri'ise debr	Head of a monastery, abbot
Ri'ise mekwanint	Head of the nobility
Ri'ise memakirt	Head of the counsellors
Ṣehafe ti'izaz	Chancellor
Shanqilla	Negro, negroes
Sharif	Honorific title denoting descent from Muhammad
Shīaleqa	Major
Shifta	Outlaw, rebel
Shimagillē	Elder, adviser
Shum	'Appointee', district governor
Sirdar	Commander, esp. commander-in-chief of the Egyptian army
Siyyume Igzi'abihēr	Elect (or appointed) of God
Tarīk	History
Tewahido	Ethiopian Orthodox definition of the nature of Christ
Thaler	Maria Theresa thaler, approx. £. 0.30 during most of the nineteenth century
Wagshum	Governor of Wag province, entitled to special honours because of the royal descent of the family
Wekīl	Representative, agent
Ye-ṣegga lij	'The Son of Grace', deviation from the *Tewahido* doctrine
Zemene Mesafint	The Age of the Princes

Bibliography

SOURCES OR PRIMARY MATERIALS

Unpublished documentary materials

Government archives

AUSTRIA

Österreichisches Staatsarchiv, Vienna
  Haus, Hof- und Staatsarchiv, Politisches Archiv:
    PA VIII, England, Karton 78
    PA XXXI, Ägypten, Italien im Roten Meer, Kartons 48–50

BELGIUM

Archives du Ministère des Affaires Étrangères et du Commerce Extérieur, Brussels
  Archives diplomatiques:
    Dossier 2024/II, Colonisation, Blondeel en Abyssinie
    Afrique 4, Abyssinie
    —10, Égypte
    —13–3, Colonies italiennes
    Correspondance politique, Légations et Consulats, Égypte, vols 2–6
    —Italie, vols 8–13
    —Russie, vols 17–20
    —Turquie, vols 22–4
    Correspondance et Documents, Afrique, Conférence de Berlin, Notifications vol. 6
    Acte Général de Bruxelles, Adhésion I, Adhésion du Roi Menelik
Archives des Palaix Royaux, Brussels
  Fonds Congo, no. 72 Lambermont
  File A 3a

EGYPT

The National Archives, Cairo
  Abdin, Carton 160
  Abyssinie, Dossier Général, Casier 20

Bahr Barra, Carton 19
Soudan, Cartons 3 and 5
Soudan Correspondance Gordon, Casier 118
Soudan et Afrique Equatoriale, Casier 119
Soudan et Afrique Orientale, Casier 120
Sundry registers: Abdin, Maia Sanieh, Ordres supérieurs

FRANCE

Archives du Ministère des Affaires Étrangères, Paris
  Correspondance commerciale, Massouah, vols 1, 2
  —Alexandrie, vols 27, 28
  Correspondance politique and Correspondance politique des consuls, Massouah,
    vols 1–5
  —Égypte, sundry vols.
  Mémoires et Documents, Afrique, vols 13, 61–6, 105–7, 135–8 (these 14 volumes
    comprise Abyssinie, vols 1–5, and Mer Rouge, vols 1–9)
  Protocole, C41 Éthiopie
  Traités, Éthiopie
Archives Nationales, Paris
  Archives privées, 255 Papiers Thouvenel
  Section Outre-Mer, Océan Indien 10/43 and 19/104

GERMANY (FRG)

Auswärtiges Amt, Bonn
  Politisches Archiv des Auswärtigen Amts, Abt. A:
    Die Verhältnisse Abyssiniens, Abessinien, Vols 1–3
    Allgemeine Angelegenheiten Abyssiniens, Abessinien, vol. 4
    Massaua, vols 1–23
    Italienisches Protektorat über Abessinien, vols 1–6
Geheimes Staatsarchiv, Berlin-Dahlem
  Auswärtiges Amt, Restakten

GERMANY (GDR)

Deutsches Zentralarchiv, Potsdam
  Afrika I/24, Die internationale Konferenz in Brüssel zur Unterdrückung des Sklaven-
    handels

GREAT BRITAIN

Public Record Office, London
  Foreign Office Records:
    General Correspondence, Abyssinia, vols FO 1/1–31
    —Italy, FO 45, sundry vols
    —Turkey, FO 78, sundry vols
    Protocols of Treaties, FO 93/2/1, 2 and 3, FO 93/94/1
    Miscellanea, Royal Letters, FO 95/690, 720–53
    Confidential Papers, FO 401/1–7 (on Abyssinia)
    —FO 403/8, 10, 81A–C, 82 (on Somali Coast)
    —FO 407/11, 14, 60–63 (on relations between Egypt and Abyssinia)
    —FO 881/2263, 3058, 3192, 3203 (miscellaneous)

India Office Library, Commonwealth Office, London
  India Office Records:
    Abyssinia Original Correspondence, vols 1–3
    Secret Letters from Aden, vols 26–37
    Political and Secret Letters from Aden, vol. 3
    Home Miscellaneous Series, vol. 456E
    Residency Records, Aden, A1A, vols. 286, 319, 376
    European Manuscripts Section, Mss. Eur. F 103, Rassam Papers

ITALY

Archivio storico del Ministero degli Affari Esteri, Rome
  Trattati, Etiopia, nos 1–6
Archivio storico dell'ex Ministero dell'Africa Italiana, Rome
  Eritrea, posiz. 1/1 to 3/10, 7/1 to 8/3, 14/1 and 14/2
  Etiopia, posiz. 36/1 to 36/18
  Conferenza di Bruxelles, posiz. 155/1 and 155/2
Archivio Centrale dello Stato, Rome
  Carte (Fondo) Crispi, sundry files

THE SOVIET UNION (USSR)

Archiv Vneschnej Politiki Rossij, Moscow
  F. Politarchiv, D. 2000 and 2009

THE SUDAN

Central Records Office, Khartoum
  Mahdia 1/55

TURKEY

Başbakanlik Arşivi Genel Müdürlügü, Sublime Porte, Istanbul
  Misir Iradeleri, sundry files
Hariciye Nezareti Arşivi, Sublime Porte, Istanbul
  Abyssinie, Cartons 236 and 1503

Church, mission, and private archives

Archiv der Basler Mission, Basel
  Brüderverzeichnis
Archivio Propaganda Fide, Rome
  Scritture Riferite nei Congressi, Africa Centrale, Etiopia ecc . . .
Archivio Vicariato Apostolico, Asmera
Biblioteca Apostolica Vaticana
  Carte d'Abbadie
Bibliothèque Nationale, Paris
  Département des manuscrits, Nouvelles acquisitions françaises:
    21299-301 Mélanges historiques et philologiques sur l'Éthiopie, par Antoine
      d'Abbadie
    22430-433 Correspondance et papiers d'Antoine d'Abbadie, principalement
      relatifs à ses voyages et à ses études sur l'Éthiopie

Département des manuscrits orientaux:
  Collection Mondon-Vidailhet
  Dossier sur l'Abyssinie et le Negus Theodoros II & le Consul . . . Lejean
  Fond Éthiopien-Abbadie
British Museum, London
  Department of Manuscripts:
    Aberdeen Papers Add. 19336–19347 (Papers of George Annesley, Viscount
      Valentia)
    Gordon Papers, Add. 51304
  Department of Oriental Printed Books and Manuscripts:
    Gordon Papers, Moffit Collection, Or. 12913
Church Missionary Society Archives, London
  Mediterranean Mission
Congrégation de la Mission (Maison Lazariste), Paris
  Lettres manuscrites de Mgr. De Jacobis
  De Jacobis, Giornale Abissino
Istituto Italiano per l'Africa, Rome
Staatsarchiv des Kantons Basel-Stadt, Basel
  C.F. Spittler Privat-Archiv 653

Published official documents

Atti Parlamentari, Documenti Diplomatici
  1889–90, XV, Etiopia
  —XV-bis, Etiopia
  1890–91, XVII, Missione Antonelli in Etiopia
  —XVIII, Protocolli 24 marzo e 15 aprile 1891 relativi alla delimitazione delle zone d'influenza
    tra l'Italia e l'Inghilterra nelle regioni a Sud, a Ovest, e a Nord dell'Etiopia e dell'Eritrea
  1890–91–92, XVII-bis, Intervista del Governatore dell'Eritrea coi capi del Tigré
  1895–96, XXIII, Avvenimenti d'Africa (Gennaio 1895–Marzo 1896)
  1895–96, XXIII-bis, Avvenimenti d'Africa (Gennaio 1895–Marzo 1896)
Documents diplomatiques français (1871–1914). Paris, 1929–59
Die Grosse Politik der europäischen Kabinette 1871–1914. Berlin, 1925–27
L'Italia in Africa, Serie Storica, Volume Primo. Etiopia–Mar Rosso, II–III, V–VII, Documenti,
  A cura di Carlo Giglio. Rome 1958–72, (cited Giglio)
Parliamentary Papers, House of Commons (BM, State Paper Room Collection)
  1852, LIV, Treaty of Friendship and Commerce between Great Britain and Abyssinia. Signed in
    the English and Amharic Languages, at Ennowga, November 2, 1849
  1868–69, VI, Report from the Select Committee on the Abyssinian War; together with the
    Proceedings of the Committee, Minutes of Evidence, and Appendix
  1870, V, Report from the Select Committee on the Abyssinian Expedition; together with the
    Proceedings of the Committee, Minutes of Evidence, and Appendix
  1876, LXXXIII, Report by Mr. Cave on the Financial Condition of Egypt
  1877, LXXXVIII, Correspondence relative to the Arrest of Messrs. Houghton and Barlow at
    Massowah, and the Return of the Abyssinian Envoy from Egypt
  1880, XLI, Army Estimates: Abyssinian Expedition
  1884, LXXXVII, Correspondence relating to the Mission of Vice-Admiral Sir W. Hewett to
    King John of Abyssinia, and Treaty between Great Britain, Egypt and Abyssinia. Signed at
    Adowa, June 3, 1884
  1890–91, XCVI, Protocols between the Governments of Her Britannic Majesty and of His

Majesty the King of Italy, for the Demarcation of their respective Spheres of Influence in Eastern Africa
1894, XCVI, *Protocol between Great Britain and Italy respecting the Demarcation of their respective Spheres of Influence in Eastern Africa*
Recueil des Traités de la France. 1713–1906. Edited by A. J. H. de Clercq, Paris 1861–1919, (cited de Clercq)

Ethiopian annals, chronicles, and related materials

Manuscript materials

Bibliothèque Nationale, Paris
Département des manuscrits orientaux: Collection Mondon-Vidailhet
Institute of Ethiopian Studies, Addis Abeba
  Tekle Īyesus, *Ye-Gojjam Tarīk*
National Library, Addis Abeba
  Ms. 47, Aṣme Gīyorgīs Gebre Mesih, *Ye-Galla Tarīk*
Universitätsbibliothek, Tübingen
  Berliner Handschriften, Ms. orient. quart. 478, *Ye-Tēwodros Tarīk*
Private Collection of Qēs Badima Yalew
  Hiruy Welde Sillasē, *Tarīke Negest*, (partly in manuscript)
  Tayye Gebre Maryam, *Ye-Ītyopya Tarīk*
Private Collection of Dejjazmach Kasa Meshesha
  Tarīke Negest, (with emphasis on King Tēwodros)

Published Materials

Afewerq Gebre Īyesus, *Dagmawī Minīlik Niguse Negest ze-Ītyopya.* Rome, 1909
Bezold, C., ed., *Kebra Nagast: die Herrlichkeit der Könige.* Munich, 1905
Chaine, M., ed., 'Histoire du règne de Iohannes IV, Roi d'Éthiopie (1868–89)', *RS*, 21, 1913
Conti Rossini, Carlo, ed., 'La cronaca reale abissina dall'anno 1800 all'anno 1840', *RRAL*, 5, XXV, 1916
—'Epistolario del Debterà Aseggachègn di Uadlà', *RRAL*, 6, I, 1925
—'Nuovi documenti per la storia d'Abissinia nel secolo XIX', *RANL*, 8, II, 1947
—'Vicende dell'Etiopia e delle Missioni Cattoliche ai tempi di ras Ali, deggiàč Ubié e re Teodoro secondo un documento abissino', *RRAL*, 5, XXV, 1916
Fusella, Luigi, ed., 'L'ambasciata francese a Nĕgusē', *RSE*, VII, 2, 1948
—*Yaṭē Tēwodros Tarīk.* Rome, 1959, (also in Italian, 'La cronaca dell'Imperatore Teodoro II di Etiopia in un manoscritto amarico', *Annali d'Istituto Universitario di Napoli*, n.s., VI–VIII, 1957–59)
Gebre Sillasē, *Tarīke Ƶemen ze-Dagmawī Minīlik, Niguse Negest ze-Ītyopya.* Addis Abeba, 1966/67, (also in French, Guèbrè Sellassié, *Chronique du Règne de Ménélik II, roi des rois d'Éthiopie.* Edited by Maurice de Coppet, Paris, 1930–31)
Weld Blundell, H., ed., *The Royal Chronicle of Abyssinia 1769–1840.* Cambridge, 1922
Welde Maryam, *Chronique de Théodros II, roi des rois d'Éthiopie.* Edited by C. Mondon-Vidailhet, Paris, [1904]
[Zeneb], *Ye-Tēwodros Tarīk.* Edited by Enno Littmann (English title, *The Chronicle of King Theodore of Abyssinia*), Princeton, 1902, (also in Italian, 'La cronaca di re Teodoro attribuita al dabtarā "Zaneb" '. Edited by M. M. Moreno, *RSE*, II, 1942)

Published private papers, correspondence, travellers' accounts, memoirs, autobiographies, etc.

Abbadie, Antoine d', 'Abyssinia and King Theodore', *The Catholic World*, VII, 1868

Abbadie, Arnauld d', *Douze ans dans la Haute-Éthiopie*. Paris, 1868

Andree, Richard, *Abessinien, das Alpenland unter den Tropen, und seine Grenzländer; Schilderungen von Land und Volk vornehmlich unter König Theodoros (1855–1868)*. Leipzig, 1869

Annesley, George (Viscount Valentia, Earl of Mountnorris), *Voyages and Travels to India, Ceylon, the Red Sea, Abyssinia, and Egypt, in the years 1802, 1803, 1804, 1805, and 1806*. London, 1809, (cited Valentia)

Apel, F. H., *Drei Monate in Abyssinien und Gefangenschaft unter König Theodorus II*. Zürich, 1866

Aspinall, A., see George III

Aubert, Louis Rémy, 'Communication faite à la Société de géographie, par L. Aubert, D.M.P., 1° sur le voyage commercial en Abyssinie et sur la mer Rouge de M. M. Dufey et Aubert; 2° sur les voyages dans le Schoa, l'Efat, et à travers le royaume des Adels, sur Tajoura et Zeïla, ainsi que sur le voyage de Loheïa à Sanah en Arabie, exécutés par M. Dufey seul, en 1837, 1838 et 1839', *BSG*, 2, XIII, 1840

Baker, Samuel W., *The Nile Tributaries of Abyssinia*. London, 1867

Banning, Émile, *Mémoires politiques et diplomatiques. Comment fut fondé le Congo Belge*. Paris and Brussels, 1927

Baratieri, Oreste, *Memorie d'Africa (1892–1896)*. Torino, 1898

Baring, Evelyn (Earl of Cromer), *Modern Egypt*. London, 1908, (cited Cromer)

Bell, John G., 'Extract from a Journal of Travels in Abyssinia, in the years 1840–41–42', *Miscellanea Aegyptiaca*, 1842

Blanc, Henry, *A Narrative of Captivity in Abyssinia*. London, 1868

Bruce, James, *Travels to Discover the Source of the Nile In the Years 1768, 1769, 1770, 1771, 1772, and 1773*. Edinburgh, 1790

Buckle, G. E., see Victoria

Cecchi, Antonio, *Da Zeila alle frontiere del Caffa*. Rome, 1885–87

Combes, E., and Tamisier, M., *Voyage en Abyssinie, dans le pays des Galla, de Choa et d'Ifat*. Paris, 1838

Cromer, see Baring

De Cosson, Emilius Albert, *The Cradle of the Blue Nile. A visit to the court of King John of Ethiopia*. London, 1877

Dimothéos (Timoteos Saprichean), *Deux ans de séjour en Abyssinie ou Vie morale, politique et religieuse des Abyssiniens par le R. P. Dimothéos*. Jerusalem, 1871

Dufey, Jules, and Aubert-Roche, Louis Rémy, 'Abyssinie, Voyage commercial et scientifique', *RO*(Paris), I, 1843

Dufton, Henry, *Narrative of a Journey through Abyssinia in 1862–3*. London, 1867

Dye, William Mc E., *Moslem Egypt and Christian Abyssinia*. New York, 1880

Ferret, Pierre Victoire, and Galinier, Joseph-Germaine, *Voyage en Abyssinie dans les provinces du Tigré, du Samen et de l'Amhara*. Paris, 1847

Flad, J. M., *Notes from the Journal of F. [sic] M. Flad, one of Bishop Gobat's Pilgrim Missionaries in Abyssinia. Edited with a Brief Sketch of the Abyssinian Church by the Rev. W. Douglas Veitch*. London, 1860

—*Zwölf Jahre in Abessinien, oder Geschichte des Königs Theodorus II. und der Mission unter seiner Regierung*. Leipzig, 1887, 2nd edition

Fouyas, Methodios, 'An unpublished document edited and translated into English', *Abba Salama*, I, 1970

George III, *The Later Correspondence of George III*. Edited by Arthur Aspinall, Cambridge, 1962–70, (cited Aspinall)

Girard, Alexandre, *Souvenirs d'un voyage en Abyssinie*. Cairo, 1873

Gobat, Samuel, *Journal of a Three Years' Residence in Abyssinia in Furtherance of the Objects of the Church Missionary Society*. London, 1834

—*Samuel Gobat, Bishop of Jerusalem. His Life and Work*. London, 1884

Gordon, Charles G., *Equatoria under Egyptian Rule. The unpublished correspondence of Col., afterwards Major-Gen., C. G. Gordon with Ismaïl, Khedive of Egypt and the Sudan, during the years 1874–1876*. Edited by M. F. Shukry, Cairo, 1953, (cited Shukry)

—*Colonel Gordon in Central Africa 1874–1879*. Edited by George Birkbeck Hill, London, 1881, (cited Hill)

Graham, Douglas C., *Glimpses of Abyssinia: or, extracts from letters written while on a mission from the Government of India, to the King of Abyssinia in the years 1841, 1842 and 1843*. Edited by Anna, Lady Erskine, London, 1867

Halls, J. J., *The Life and Correspondence of Henry Salt*. London, 1834

Harris, W. Cornwallis, *The Highlands of Aethiopia*. London, 1844

Heuglin, Theodor von, 'Reise der Herren Th. v. Heuglin, Dr. Steudner und H. Schubert im östlichen Theile des Hochlandes von Abessinien, Februar bis Mai 1862', *Petermann*, 1862

—*Reise nach Abessinien, den Gala-Ländern, Ost-Sudán und Chartum in den Jahren 1861 und 1862*. Jena, 1868

—*Reisen in Nord-Ost-Afrika*. Gotha, 1857

—'Th. von Heuglin's Expedition nach Inner-Afrika', *Petermann*, 1861 and 1862

—'Th. v. Heuglin's Reise zu Kaiser Theodoros und nach der Festung Magdala, Februar bis Mai 1862', *Petermann*, 1867

Hill, G. B., see Gordon

Hill, Richard, ed., *On the Frontiers of Islam, Two Manuscripts concerning the Sudan under Turco-Egyptian Rule, 1820–1845*. Oxford, 1970

Holland, Trevenen J., and Hozier, Henry M., *Record of the Expedition to Abyssinia*. London, 1870

Hozier, Henry M., *The British Expedition to Abyssinia*. London, 1869

Isenberg, C. W., and Krapf, J. L., *The Journals of C. W. Isenberg and J. L. Krapf*. London, 1843

Johnston, Charles, *Travels in Southern Abyssinia, through the Country of Adal to the Kingdom of Shoa*. London, 1844

Jonveaux, Émile, *Deux ans dans l'Afrique orientale*. Tours, 1871

Katte, A. von, *Reise in Abyssinien*. Stuttgart and Tübingen, 1838

Krapf, J. L., *Travels, Researches, and Missionary Labours during an Eighteen Years' Residence in Eastern Africa*. London, 1860

Lefebvre, T., and others, *Voyage en Abyssinie exécuté pendant les années 1839, 1840, 1841, 1842, 1843*. Paris, 1845–51

Lejean, Guillaume, 'Gallabat et Gadabhi', *Nouvelles Annales des Voyages, de la Géographie, de l'Histoire et de l'Archéologie*, 6, X, 1, 1864

—'Notes d'un voyage en Abyssinie', *TM*, 1864, I

—*Théodore II. Le nouvel empire d'Abyssinie et les intérêts français dans le sud de la Mer Rouge*. Paris, [1865]

—'Voyage en Abyssinie', *TM*, 1865, II, and 1867, I

Loring, W. W., *A Confederate Soldier in Egypt*. New York, 1884

Louis-Lande, L., 'Un voyageur français dans l'Éthiopie méridionale', *Revue des deux Mondes*, XXX, 1878

Markham, Clements R., *A History of the Abyssinian Expedition*. London 1869

Massaja, Guglielmo, *I miei trentacinque anni di missione nell' alta Etiopia*. Rome, 1921–30, 2nd edition

—*In Abissinia e fra i Galla dalle Memorie del Cardinal Massaja*. Florence, 1895

Munzinger, Werner, *Ostafrikanische Studien*. Schaffhausen, 1864

Napier, Robert, *Letters of Field-Marshal Lord Napier of Magdala*. Edited by H. D. Napier, London, n.d.

Parkyns, Mansfield, *Life in Abyssinia*. London, 1853

Pearce, Nathaniel, *The Life and Adventures of Nathaniel Pearce, written by himself during a residence in Abyssinia from 1810 to 1819*. Edited by J. J. Halls, London, 1831

Plowden, Walter Chichele, *Travels in Abyssinia and the Galla Country*. London, 1868

Portal, Gerald, *An Account of the English Mission to King Johannis in 1887*. Winchester, [1888]

Raffray, Achille, *Afrique orientale: Abyssinie*. Paris, 1876

—'Voyage en Abyssinie, à Zanzibar et au des Ouanika', *BSG*, 6, X, 1875

Rassam, Hormuzd, *Narrative of the British Mission to Theodore*. London, 1869

Rochet d'Héricourt, C. F. X., 'Considérations géographiques et commerciales sur le golfe Arabique, le pays d'Adel et le royaume de Choa (Abyssinie méridionale), par M. C. F. X. Rochet d'Héricourt, *BSG*, 2, XV, 1841

—*Second voyage sur les deux rives de la Mer Rouge, dans le pays des Adals et le royaume de Choa*. Paris, 1846

—*Voyage sur la côte orientale de la Mer Rouge, dans le pays d'Adel et le royaume de Choa*. Paris, 1841

Rohlfs, Gerhard, *Meine Mission nach Abessinien*. Leipzig, 1883

Russ, Camill, [Aufzeichnungen], *Petermann*, 1877

Rüppell, Eduard, *Reise in Abyssinien*. Frankfurt am Main, 1838–40

Russel, Stanislas, *Une Mission en Abyssinie et dans la Mer Rouge 23 octobre 1859–7 mai 1860*. Paris, 1884

Salt, Henry, *A Voyage to Abyssinia*. London, 1814

Sapeto, Guiseppe, 'Ambasciata mandata nel 1869 [*sic*] dal governo francese à Negussié, Degiazmatc del Tigré e del Samièn in Abissinia', *BSGI*, VI, 1871

—*Etiopia. Notizie raccolte dal Prof. Giuseppe Sapeto*. Rome, n.d.

—*Viaggio e missione cattolica fra i Mensa e gli Habab*. Rome, 1857

Shepherd, A. F., *The Campaign in Abyssinia*. Bombay, 1868

Shukry, M. F., see Gordon

Simon, Gabriel, *Voyage en Abyssinie et chez les Galla-Raias. L'Éthiopie, ses moeurs, ses traditions, le Négouss Iohannès, les églises monolithes de Lalibéla*. Paris, 1885

Smith, F. Harrison, *Through Abyssinia. An Envoy's Ride to the King of Zion*. London, 1890

Stanley, Henry M., *Coomassie and Magdala*. London, 1874

Stern, Henry A., *The Captive Missionary: being an Account of the Country and People of Abyssinia*. London, 1868

—*Wanderings among the Falashas in Abyssinia together with a description of the country and its various inhabitants*. London, 1862

Valentia, see Annesley

Victoria, *The Letters of Queen Victoria, Second Series, A Selection from Her Majesty's Correspondence and Journal between the Years 1862 and 1885*. Edited by George Earle Buckle, London, 1926–28, (cited Buckle)

Waldmeier, Theophil, *The Autobiography of Theophilus Waldmeier*. London, 1886

—*Erlebnisse in Abessinien in den Jahren 1858 bis 1868*. Basel, 1869

Winstanley, W., *A Visit to Abyssinia. An account of travel in modern Abyssinia*. London, 1881

Wingate, F. R., *Mahdiism and the Egyptian Sudan*. London, 1891

Wylde, Augustus B., *'83 to '87 in the Soudan*. London, 1888
—*Modern Abyssinia*. London, 1901

Annales de la Congrégation de la Mission. Paris
Blackwood's Edinburgh Magazine. Edinburgh
Bollettino della Società Geografica Italiana. Florence and Rome
Bulletin de la Société de géographie. Paris
Church Missionary Record. London
Evangelische Heidenbote. Basel
Magazin für die neueste Geschichte der Protestantischen Missions- und Bibelgesellschaften. Basel
Missionstidning. Utgifven av Evangeliska Fosterlandsstiftelsen. Stockholm
Nouvelles Annales des Voyages, de la Géographie, de l'Histoire et de l'Archéologie. Paris
Mittheilungen aus Justus Perthes, Geographischer Anstalt über wichtige neue Erforschungen auf dem Gesamtgebiete der Geographie von Dr. A. Petermann. Gotha
Revue de l'Orient. Paris
Le Tour du Monde. Paris

SECONDARY MATERIALS

Abir, Mordechai, *Ethiopia: The Era of the Princes*. London, 1968
—'The Origins of the Ethiopian–Egyptian Border Problem in the Nineteenth Century', *JAH*, VIII, 3, 1967
—'Salt, Trade and Politics in Ethiopia in the "Zämänä Mäsafint" ', *JES*, IV, 2, 1966
Aleme Eshete, 'Une Ambassade du Ras Ali en Egypte: 1852', *JES*, IX, 1, 1971
—*La Mission Catholique Lazariste en Éthiopie*. Paris, [1970], mimeographed
Battaglia, Roberto, *La prima guerra d'Africa*. Torino, 1958
Berkeley, G. F.-H., *The Campaign of Adowa and the Rise of Menelik*. London, 1935, 2nd edition
Budge, E. A. Wallis, *A History of Ethiopia*. London, 1928
Caulk, Richard, 'Firearms and Princely Power in Ethiopia in the Nineteenth Century', *JAH*, XII, 4, 1972
—'Menilek and the Ethio-Egyptian War of 1875–76: a reconsideration of source material', *Rural Africana*, 11, 1970
—'The Occupation of Harar: January 1887', *JES*, IX, 2, 1971
—'The Origins and Development of the Foreign Policy of Menelik II, 1865–1896', Ph.D. diss. (unpublished), London, 1966
—'Yohannis IV, the Mahdists, and the colonial partition of north-east Africa', *Transafrican Journal of History*, I, 2, 1971
Cerulli, Enrico, *Etiopi in Palestina*. Rome, 1954–57
Chaine, M., *La Chronologie des temps chrétiens de l'Égypte et de l'Éthiopie*. Paris, 1925
Conti Rossini, Carlo, *Italia ed Etiopia dal trattato d'Ucciali alla battaglia di Adua*. Rome, 1935
Coulbeaux, J. B., *Histoire politique et religieuse de l'Abyssinie depuis les temps les plus reculés jusqu'à l'avènement de Ménélick II*. Paris, 1929
Coursac, J. de, *Le Règne de Yohannès depuis son Avènement jusqu'à ses Victoires de 1875 sur l'Armée égyptienne*. Romans, 1926
Crummey, Donald, 'Initiatives and Objectives in Ethio-European Relations, 1827–1862', *JAH*, XV, 3, 1974

—'Missionary Sources and their Contribution to our Understanding of Ethiopian History 1830–1868', *Rural Africana*, 11, 1970
—*Priests and Politicians. Protestant and Catholic Missions in Orthodox Ethiopia 1830–1868.* Oxford, 1972
—'Tēwodros as Reformer and Modernizer', *JAH*, X, 3, 1969
—'The Violence of Tēwodros', *JES*, IX, 2, 1971
Darkwah, R. H. Kofi, 'Emperor Theodore II and the Kingdom of Shoa, 1855–1865', *JAH*, X, 1, 1969
—'The Rise of the Kingdom of Shoa 1813–1889'. Ph.D. diss. (unpublished), London, 1966
Douin, G., *Histoire du règne du Khédive Ismaïl. Tome III. L'Empire Africain.* Cairo, 1936–51
Duchesne, Albert, *Le consul Blondeel en Abyssinie.* Brussels, 1953
Giglio, Carlo, 'Article 17 of the Treaty of Uccialli', *JAH*, VII, 3, 1965
—*L'articolo XVII del trattato di Uccialli.* Como, 1967
—*L'Impresa di Massawa.* Rome, 1958
—*L'Italia in Africa, Serie Storica, Volume Primo, Etiopia–Mar Rosso, I, (1857–1885).* Rome, 1958
Hill, Richard, *Egypt in the Sudan 1820–1881.* London, 1959
Hiruy Welde Sillasē, *Tarīke Negest.* [Addis Abeba], 1935/36
—*Wazēma.* Addis Abeba, 1928/29
—*Ye-Hiywet Tarīk.* Addis Abeba, 1922/23
Holt, P. M., 'The Archives of the Mahdia', *SNR*, XXXVI, 1, 1955
—*Egypt and the Fertile Crescent 1516–1922: a Political History.* London, 1966
—*A Modern History of the Sudan.* London, 1961
Izarn, Roger, 'Les documents Arnauld d'Abbadie', *Proceedings of the Third International Conference of Ethiopian Studies, Addis Ababa 1966.* Addis Abeba, 1969
Jaenen, C. J., 'Blondeel: The Belgian Attempt to Colonize Ethiopia', *African Affairs*, LV, 1956
Keller, C., *Alfred Ilg, sein Leben und sein Wirken.* Frauenfeld, 1918
Keller-Zschokke, J. V., *Werner Munzinger Pascha, Sein Leben und Wirken.* Aarau, 1891
La Pradelle, A. de, *Le conflit italo-éthiopien.* Paris, 1936
Longrigg, Stephen H., *A Short History of Eritrea.* Oxford, 1945
Malécot, Georges, 'Les voyageurs français et les relations entre la France et l'Abyssinie de 1835 à 1870', *RFHO*, LVIII, 1971
Marcus, Harold G., 'Imperialism and Expansion in Ethiopia from 1865 to 1900', P. Diugnan and L. Gann, eds., *Colonialism in Africa.* Cambridge, 1969
—*The Life and Times of Menelik II: Ethiopia 1844–1913.* Oxford, 1975
—'Menilek II', N. R. Bennet, ed., *Leadership in Eastern Africa: Six Political Biographies.* Boston, 1968
Marlowe, John, *Anglo-Egyptian Relations 1800–1953.* London, 1954
Marston, Thomas E., *Britain's Imperial Role in the Red Sea Area 1800–1878.* Hamden, Connecticut, 1961
Mathew, David, *Ethiopia. The Study of a Polity, 1540–1935.* London, 1947
Moorehead, Alan, *The Blue Nile.* New York and Evanston, 1962
Morgan, Margaret, 'Continuities and Traditions in Ethiopian History. An investigation of the reign of Tēwodros', *Ethiopia Observer*, XII, 4, 1969
Myatt, Frederick, *The March to Magdala.* London, 1970
Nöldeke, T., *Orientalische Skizzen.* Berlin, 1892
Orhonlu, Cenghiz, 'Turkish archival sources on Ethiopia', *IV Congresso Internazionale di Studi Etiopici.* Rome 1974
Pankhurst, Richard, *Economic History of Ethiopia 1800–1935.* Addis Abeba, 1968

—'Firearms in Ethiopian History, 1800–1935', *Ethiopia Observer*, VI, 2, 1962

—'Popular Opposition in Britain to British Intervention against Emperor Tewodros of Ethiopia (1867–1868)', *Ethiopia Observer*, XVI, 3, 1973

—'The Saint Simonians and Ethiopia', *Proceedings of the Third International Conference of Ethiopian Studies, Addis Ababa, 1966*. Addis Abeba, 1969

—'The Trade of Northern Ethiopia in the Nineteenth and early Twentieth Centuries', *JES*, II, 1, 1964

Perham, Margery, *The Government of Ethiopia*. London, [1947]

Pierre-Alype, L. M., *L'Éthiopie et les Convoitises Allemandes*. Paris, 1917

Rubenson, Sven, 'Adwa 1896: The Resounding Protest', Robert I. Rotberg and Ali A. Mazrui, eds., *Protest and Power in Black Africa*. New York, 1970

—'The Adwa Peace Treaty of 1884', *Proceedings of the Third International Conference of Ethiopian Studies, Addis Ababa, 1966*. Addis Abeba, 1969

—*King of Kings Tēwodros of Ethiopia*. Addis Abeba, 1966

—'Professor Giglio, Antonelli and Article XVII of the Treaty of Wichalē', *JAH*, VII, 3, 1966

—'The Protectorate Paragraph of the Wichalē Treaty', *JAH*, V, 2, 1964

—'Some Aspects of the Survival of Ethiopian Independence in the Period of the Scramble for Africa', *Historians in Tropical Africa*. Salisbury, 1960; also *University College Review*, Addis Abeba, 1961

—*Wichalē XVII. The Attempt to Establish a Protectorate over Ethiopia*. Addis Abeba, 1964

Sabry, Muhammad, *L'empire égyptien sous Ismaïl et l'ingérence anglo-française (1863–1879)*. Paris, 1933

—*L'empire égyptien sous Mohamed-Ali et la question d'Orient*. Paris, 1930

Sanderson, G. N., 'Contributions from African Sources to the History of European Competition in the Upper Valley of the Nile', *JAH*, III, 1, 1962

Tayye Gebre Maryam, *Ye-Ītyopya Hizb Tarīk*. Addis Abeba, 1971/72, 8th edition

Toynbee, Arnold J., *A Study of History*. London, 1934–61

Trimingham, J. Spencer, *Islam in Ethiopia*. Oxford, 1952

Triulzi, Alessandro, 'Trade, Islam, and the Mahdia in Northwestern Wallaggā, Ethiopia', *JAH*, XVI, 1, 1975

Tubiana, Joseph, 'Deux fragments inédits du tome second de *Douze ans dans la Haute-Ethiopie d'Arnauld d'Abbadie*', *RO*(Warsaw), XXV, 2, 1961

—'Le voyage d'Émile Jonveaux en Ethiopie. Effets recents d'une ancienne mystification', *JAH*, IV, 2, 1963

Ullendorff, Edward, *The Ethiopians. An Introduction to Country and People*. Oxford, 1960

Ullendorff, E., and Beckingham, C. F., 'The First Anglo-Ethiopian Treaty', *JSS*, IX, 1954

Work, Ernest, *Ethiopia: A Pawn in European Diplomacy*. New Concord, 1935

Zewde Gabre-Sellassie, 'The Process of Re-unification of the Ethiopian Empire 1868–1889'. Ph.D. diss. (unpublished), Oxford, 1971

Index

This index includes all mentions of persons in the text, but only those in the footnotes which provide factual information about a person, his opinions or activities. Names, of places, districts, provinces, etc., used only for location or identification purposes have not normally been included. References of major importance are indicated by bold-face numerals.

Abargues de Sosten, Juan Victor, 350
Abbadie, Antoine Thomson d', 17–18, 55–6, 71, **75–85**, 88, 113, 122, 152, 157, 166, 169, 182, 206
Abbadie, Arnauld Michel d', 18, 35, 54–6, **75–7**, 79, **83–5**, 87n, 96–7, 100n, 101, 152, 157, 206
Abbas Hilmi Pasha, 135
Abdallah, Basha, 41, 53, 409
Abdallahi Muhammad Turshain, Khalifa, 8, 11, 383, 401
Abd al-Qadir Pasha Hilmi, 258
Abd al-Rahim, *see* Muhammad Abd al-Rahim
Abd al-Rahman Bey, 212–13
Abd al-Razik Bey, 315
Abegaz Se'une, 21–2
Aberdeen, George Gordon, Earl of, 157
Abir, Mordechai, 4, 33n
Abu Anja, Amir, 383–4
Abu Bakr Ibrahim, Sultan, 165n, 274, 303, 369–70
Abu Rawash, 212, 215
Abu Widan (Ahmad Pasha abu Widan), 97–8
abun:
attempts and arrangements to obtain, 48, 50, 62–8, 90–3, 276–8, 290, 337, 341–2, 344, 349–51, 355–6, 370–1

Europeans posing as, 73, 170 position of, 34, 172
Adal, 126, 146, 313, 375
Adal Tesemma, Ras, 307, 327n, 337, 367, 376; *see also* Tekle Haymanot, Nigus
Addī Mengontī, 201, 216 (map)
Addī Nifas, 386–7 (map)
Addī Qwala, 322–3
Addī Yohannis, 386–7 (map)
Addīgrat, 260, 387 (map), 402
Aden, 145, 153, 157, 166, 273–4, 375
Adiyabo, 209, 289–90, 291 (map), 292, 295, 297
Adulis, *see* Zulla
Adwa, 71, 74–6, 325, 402
Adwa (Abba Gerīma), battle of, 3, 402–6
Adwa (Asem), battle of, 275, 282, 322n, 364
Afar, *see* Danakil
Afewerq Gebre Īyesus, 27–8, 337n, 340n, 368
Agamē, 36, 39 (map), 100, 133–4, 167, 191, 205, 278n
Agew, 32
Agewmidir, 31 (map), 98
Ahmad Ghashim, Kashif, 69
Ahmad ibn Ibrahim (Grañ), 57, 96, 163
Ahmad Pasha Manikli, 97–8
Ahmad (or Hammad) wad Mira, Shaykh, 214
Ahmad abu Sin, Shaykh, 215

Ahmad Pasha abu Widan (or Adhan), 97–8
Aichinger, Christian, 55, 65–6, 147, 168
Akkele Guzay, 205, 250, 275, 278, 291 (map), 292–3, 335, 350, 367, 378, 389, 393, 400
Akrur, 385, 387 (map)
Ala ad-Din Bey, 314–15
Alemayehu Tēwodros, 343
Aleme Eshete, 4, 135n
Alemē Gwalu, Dejjazmach, 265–6
Alexander II, Czar, 297–8, 342
Alexander III, Czar, 396
Algaden, 217n, 289
Alī (II) Alula, Ras, 35, 69, 78–80, 83–4, 90, **93–102**, 116, 118, **120–40**, 145, 155, 164, 167, 172, 181–2, 192, 195, 220, 270–1, 408
Ali Faris, Dejjazmach, 270, 274
Ali Goveta, 45
Ali (I) Gwangwil, Ras, 35
Ali Helmi, 364
Ali Khurshid Pasha, 69
Ali ibn Muhammad, Shaykh, 97, 98n
Ali Rida Pasha, 96
Ali al-Rubi Pasha, 330–1, 334, 336
Ali Umar, **60–7**, 150, 165, 169, 409
Aliah Aydu, 102
Alula Ingida (Abba Negga),

Ras, 322, **335**, 338, **341–4**, **348–55**, 368, 378, **380–2**, 400–1, 405

Amba Alagē, battle of, 387 (map), 402, 408

Amba Chera, 216 (map), 305, 312

Amedē Lïben, Imam, 367, 376

Amhara, 31 (map), 34–5

Amideb, 291 (map), 297, 304, 340, 349, 356–9, 361

Andada, 197

André, 277

Anfilla, 39 (map), 44–5, 313–14, 353

   Egyptian occupation, 258, 300–2, 305, 308

   European proposals to acquire, 64, 67, 83, 86–90, 99–102, 112, 121–4, 141–2, 166–7

   restoration requested, 205–7, 344–6

   restored by implication in Wiçhalē treaty, 386

Annesley, Sir George, see Valentia

Annesley Bay, 38, 39 (map)

Antalo, 39 (map), 40, 45, 260

Antonelli, Count Pietro, 3, 17, **379–82**, **385–95**, 399

Apel, F. H., 19–20

Arabi (Ahmad Urabi) Pasha, 351

Arafalï, 339 (map), 362, 386, 387 (map), 393

Arakil Bey Nubar, **310–15**, 319–20, 322n, 365–6, 370

Araya Sillasē Dimṣu, Balgada, Ras, **102–3**, 124–5, 170, 173, 173, 178, 270, 322, 341, 366

Arén, Gustav, 13n

Arendrup (Colonel S.A.) Bey, 315, **318–22**, 324, 326, 330, 364, 371

Arkïko, 30, 39 (map), 51, 69, 166, 228

   allegedly offered to France by Wibē, 112–13

   occupied by the Egyptians, 112, 114–19, 123

   threatened by Wibē, 105–9

Armaçhiho, 31 (map), 98

arms:

   captured in battle, 323, 328–9 335

   embargo, 138, 141–2, 300–2, 310, 337–8, 347, 350–4, 364, 375, 377

   estimated numbers in Ethiopia, 42, 139, 168, 191–3, 365, 398

   Ethiopian arms inferior at Meqdela, 264; at Gundet and Gura, 364–5

   Ethiopians well-supplied at Adwa, 403, 409

   not decisive in internal struggles before Tēwodros's reign, 168

   offers and requests, gifts and imports, 42, 58, 63–8, 74,

83, 86–91, 99–101, 103–4, 127, 138, 149–53, 167–8, 186–7, 192–9, 201, 203–5, 211–12, 221, 275–7, 279, 342n, 349, 364, 369–71, 382–6, 390, 394–8

   production of ammunition, 139, 148, 168–9, 364–5

   production of artillery, 169n, 179, 193, 248–9, 252, 255–6

army:

   British–Indian to Meqdela, 254, 256, 264, 267

   Egyptian, 348, 350, 364–5; Arendrup's for Hamasēn (Gundet), 319–23, 366; Munzinger's for Awsa, 318, 320; for Bogos, 296; Ratib's for Adwa (Gura), 324–9, 335, 364, 372; Ra'uf's for Harer, 317; Welde Mïka'ēl's in Bogos, 335, 340

   Ethiopian, 364–6; for Adwa campaign, 402–3, 405–6; Alula's as governor on the northern frontiers, 341–2, 348; Kinfu Haylu's, 69–70; Tēwodros's, 219, 241, 255–6, 261, 264, 268n; Wibē's, 105; Yohannis's, 319–23, 327–9, 364–6

   Italian for Adwa campaign, 402–3

Arnoux, Pierre, 336–7, 369, 372, 375

Arogē, battle of, 263–4, 285–6

Asawirṭa, 39 (map), 51, 348, 381

Aseb, 303, 316 (map), 379

Asgede Beqla, see Habab

Aṣme Gïyorgïs Gebre Mesih (Aṣmē), 27–8, 368

Asmera, 334, 385, 387 (map), 388

Atbara River as boundary, 215–18, 216 (map)

Aṭinatēwos, Abune, 321

Atish, 31 (map), 69

Aubert-Roche, Louis Rémy, 56, **72–5**, 88, 149, 168

Austria, Austrian:

   mission to Wibē, 138–9

   Kirkham's mission to, 297, 304

Awsa, 31 (map), 35, 303, **313–14**, **317–18**, 325, 372–5

Aylet, 228, 291 (map), 305, 308, 332–3, 352, 381–3

Ayshal, battle of, 136

Azebo, 297–8, 313, 316 (map)

Bab al-Mandab, 145, 258, 377, 384

Badima Yalew, Qēs, 27, 28n

Bahta Hagos, Dejjazmach, 400

Baker, Consul A., 354

Baker, Sir Samuel White, 213–14, 217–18

Banning, Émile, 389–90

Baptist, J., 227

Baratieri, General Oreste, 3, 16–17, **399–400**, **402–5**

Bardel, Auguste, 20, 222, **224–**

31, 234, 237, 241, 252, 254, 267

Baring, Sir Evelyn (Earl Cromer), 354–5

Barka, 39 (map), 215, 292, 342

Barlow, R. A., 363n

Baroni, Raphael, 20, 181n, 186, 193, 197, 198n, 223–4, 233

Barya, 32, 143, 209, **288–90**, 291 (map), **292**, 297

Barya'u Gebre Ṣadiq, Ras, 322, **340–1**, 346

Battaglia, Roberto, 379n, 381n, 401n

Bazēn, see Kunama

Begēmdir, 31 (map), **34–5**, 144, 242, 255, 327, 337, 398, 402

Be'ide Maryam, Emperor, 32

Beillard, Consul C. Chauvin (also Chauvin-Beillard), 190–5

Beja, 215

Beke, Charles T., 85, 121, 167, 169, 213, 218, 246n, 252n, 269

Bekkafa, Emperor, 271

Belgium, mission of Blondeel, 88, **99–102**, 133–4

Bell, John G. (Lïqemekwas Yohannis), 56, 92, 130, 132, 136, 175, 177, **181–2**, 184, **188–9**, 223, 255, 268, 277

Benadir, 317–18

Bender, C., 177, 179, 266, 277n

Beni Amir, 107, 142–3, 215, 216 (map), 289

Berbera, 310, 315, 316 (map)

Bereket, battle of, 173, 216 (map)

Berlin, General Act of, 389, 395

Beshah Wired, see Hayle Melekot

Bēt Gebre Terkē, 296n

Bēt Teqwē, 296n, 338

Betlehem, 68

Beylul, 39 (map), 40, 258, 303

Bezzabih (Bezzu Abba Dekkir), Ato, 173, 241

Biancheri, Mgr L., 137

Bilēn, 107, 296; see also Bogos

Birru Alïgaz, Dejjazmach, 93–5, 116

Birru Goshu, Dejjazmach, 35n, 84, **90**, **93–4**, **97–100**, 116, 125, 129, 136, 270

Birru Pēṭros (of Welqayit), 233, 284

Birru Welde Gïyorgïs, Aleqa, Ras, 277n, **280–1**, 284n, 293, 295n, **320**, 325, **369–72**, 375–6

Bismarck, Otto von, 304, 350, 395

Blanc, Henry, 17, **243–8**, 252, 255, 266, 285

Blondeel, Consul Édouard, 12, 56, 70, 81, 88–9, 92, 97–**102**, **132–4**, 144–5, 167–70

Blumhardt, C. H., 55, 71

Boghos, 317

Bogos, 39 (map), **107**, 114, 184–5, 275, **278**, 291 (map), 335, **338–44**, 363

Bogos—*contd.*
  autonomy and informal 'protectorate' status, 140, **143–4**, 229, 232, 288, 367
  Egyptian annexation, 283, **290–305, 308–10**
  Ethiopian requests for arbitration and restoration, **300–9**, 330, 335, **351–62**
  Italian claims, 381, 385
  taxed and raided by Ethiopians and Egyptians, 106–8, 142–3, 209–10, 250–1
Boru Mēda, church council of, 342n
Bourgaud, 179
Brandeis, F., 178, 227, 254
Brava, 316 (map), 317
Brezka, Martin, 147
Britain, British:
  Antoine d'Abbadie, 81
  attitude towards Ottoman claims to Red Sea coast, 115, 121, 127, 219–20, 258, 285, 352, 355–6, 379
  Cameron as consul, **219–26**, 232–9
  desire to sever relations after Meqdela, 273, 275, 277, 289, 307–8
  Harris's mission, 56–7, 145, **152–9**, 163
  imperialistic policies, **165–6**, 183, **188**, 269, 408
  interest in acquiring a Red Sea port, 36–51, 109, 122–4, 183
  interventions in Ethio-Egyptian conflicts, **69–70**, 76–143, **184–5**, 210, 220–3, 226, 252, 301, **337–62**
  military expedition to Meqdela, 254, **256–68**, 285–7
  Plowden as consul, 120–4, 127–31, 137–8, 143–4, **180–9**, 199, 208, 210
  Rassam's mission, **240–8**
  relations with Minīlik: as king of Shewa, 272, 368; regarding Wichale treaty, **389–95**, 400–1, 404
  relations with Tēwodros embittered, 253–5
  relations with Yohannis: after Meqdela, 279–84; regarding the Bogos crisis, **297–302**, **304–9**; after Gura, 321, 323–4, **326–52**; the Hewett mission and treaty, **353–62**, 377; over Massawa, **379–83**
  Sebagadis's mission through Coffin, **64–5**, 67
  Tēwodros's mission through Flad, **248–9**, 251–3, 255
  Tēwodros's planned embassy, 184, 186–7, **221–5**, 232, 235–40
  'trade, not land', **121**, 144, **166**
  treaties: with Ali, **129–31**, 137, 181–3, 186, 224; with Sahle Sillasē, 144–5, **154–6**, 158, 163; with Yohannis, **354–62**

Valentia and Salt, **36–51**
Wibē's mission through Coffin, **92–3**
British and Foreign Bible Society, 48, 55
Bronkhorst, C., 227
Bruce, James, 217n
Brussels conference, 'Minīlik incident' at, 12–13, **389–92**
Budge, Sir E. A. Wallis, 3
Burī. 39 (map), 40, 44, 348

Cameron, Captain C. Duncan, 10, 17, 20, **219–44**, 255, 263, 266
Campbell, Colonel Patrick, 68–71, 76, 81
Capucci, Luigi, 399
Capuchin Mission, *see* Missions
Carnot, President Sadi, 395
Caulk, Richard, 4, 133n, 365n, 368n
Cave, Sir Stephen, 311–12
Chaillé-Long, Colonel Charles, 317
Chaine, Marius, 24–5
Chefneux, Léon, 397
Cheno, 31 (map), 146, 148
Chrischona Mission, *see* Missions
Christopher, William, 106
Church, Ethiopian Orthodox:
  factions, 34, 49–51, 116, 155, 158, 175
  land holdings, 172, 178, 241
  national identity and unity, 2, 32, 34, 396, 408–9
  opposition to foreign missionaries, 30, 74–7, 91, 103, 118, 158, 175–8, 184
Church Missionary Society, *see* Missions
Coffin, William, 14–15, 19, 45, 48, 56, 58–70, 75–6, 82, 84–6, 91–3, 102–11, 122, 127, 138, 157, 165–6, 168–9, 409
Combes, Edmond, 16n, 56, 72–3, 75, **82–6**, 89, 104, 113–14, 133, 144–6, 149, 152, 157, 166, 168
communications:
  early problems, 52–4, 61–3
  improved conditions for, 169, 171, 284
  obstructed by Egyptian officials, 281n, 324, 352, 363
Congrégation de la Mission (Lazarists), *see* Missions
Contarini, Carlo Teofilo, 92
Conti Rossini, Carlo, 21
Coppet, Maurice de, 26
Coulbeaux, J. B., 3
Crimean War, 183, 221
Crispi, Francesco, 3, 11, 388–92, 395, 397, 399–400, 404, 408
Cromer, Earl (Sir Evelyn Baring), 354–5
Crummey, Donald E., 4, 13n, 33n, 166n, 173n, 175n, 195n, 197n
Currum Chund, 37–40

Dabarki, battle of, 140, 208, 216 (map)
Danakil, Dankali, 31 (map), 44, 51, **146**, 152–3, 303, 306, 309, 313, **318**, 325
Dargē Sahle Sillasē, Ras, 375
Darkwah, Kofi, 4
Da'ud, *see* Qērilos IV
Dawint, 31 (map), 94–5
Dayr as-Sultan, 131–6, 168, 220–1, 236–7
Debarwa, 291 (map), 334
Debbeb Araya, Dejjazmach, 362
Debre Abbay, battle of, 39 (map), 67, 94
Debre Tabor, 31 (map), 35, 341
  battle of, 93–7, 155
  destroyed, 256
  proclaimed capital by Tēwodros, 252
De Cosson, Emilius Albert, 305
Degoutin, Consul A., 89, 92n, **102–20**, 124, 133, 142, 169, 195
De Jacobis, Mgr Giustino, 17, 56, 86–8, 91, **103–15**, 118–19, 122, 125–7, 133, 136–8, 166–9, 173, **175–6**, 180–1, **187–203**, 206–7
Delanta, 216 (map), 260
Delaporte, Consul P. H., 136
Delaye, Consul L., 141, 176, 180
Delmonte, Fr. C., 252, 271
Dembīya, 31 (map), 34, 402, 408
Dennison, Major J. A., 322, 364
Depron, Adrien, 73
Derby, Earl, *see* Lord Stanley
Deres, 169n
Deresgē, battle of, 136, 216 (map)
Derrick, Colonel Clarence, 364
Des Avanchers, *see* Leone des Avanchers
Desē, island of, 42, 200, 202, 207n, 219
Desta, Aleqa, 120
Digsa, 39 (map), 51
Dihono, *see* Arkiko
Dillon (*also* Quartin-Dillon), 84
Dogalī, battle of, 381, 385, 387 (map), 396
Douin, G., 3, 11, 213n, 295n, 302n, 313n
  on Greater Egypt, 311
Dubaina, 217
Du Bisson, Count Raoul, 236, 241
Duchesne, Albert, 88n, 99n, 101n
Dufey, Jules, 56, **72–5**, 88, 146–8, 168
Duflot, 326, 363n, 364n
Dufton, Henry, 213–14, 227, 269
Dunkur, 215, 216 (map), 222
Durholz, Major, 364–5
Dye, Colonel William McE., 322n, 323n, 324, 327, 328n, 364, 368, 376

Edd, 39 (map), 44, **114**, 116, 124, 133, **219**, **258**

education, 172–4, 177–8, 183, 272, 409–10
of Ethiopians abroad, 169, 176, 284
Egypt, Egyptian:
acquisitions along the Red Sea coast, 57–8, 108, **116–18, 250, 258**, 303
'alliance' with Ras Ali, 96–8
annexation of Bogos, 250–1, 283, 290, **292**, **295–300**, 302; Metemma, 303–4; of salt plains, 250, 300, 313
arbitration requested by Ethiopia, **300–302**, **305–10**, 321, **324**, 332, 336, 349–50
border conflicts, **69–71**, 77–8, **98–9**, 184–5, 208–10, **212–18**, **222–3**, 232, 236, 250–1, **289–90**, 294, 297
British attitude towards Ethio-Egyptian conflicts, 69–70, 81, 184–5, 187, 210, 221–2, 224, 250–1, 258, 304–9, 325–6
effects of Ethio-Egyptian war, 377–8
garrisons relieved by Ethiopia, 354, 356, 361, 380
imperialism, 57–8, 289–90, **309–11**, **315–17**
invasion of Habab, 108; of Kunama, 289, 292
peace negotiations, **329–62**
potential strength in relation to Ethiopia, 363–6
relations with Minīlik, 315–17, **368–76**
subversive activities, 251, 258, 290, 294, 302, 315–17, 366–7, 371–2
war, **310–35**
encirclement:
Ethiopian awareness of, 49–50, 298, 393, 408
Egyptian, 298, 316 (map), 317, 375
Eritrea:
Egyptian, 216 (map), 292, 295–7
Italian, 379–83, 385–6, 387 (map), 388–9, 393, 400, 405
Munzinger's role, 278, 283, 292, 295–7
origins of, **140–4**, 171, 209, **250–1**, 278, 288, 367, 377–8, 410
Essler, T., 227, 254
European consuls, consulates, 17, 29, 119, 171, 192, 276
Belgian, 99–102
British, 10, 118, 120–31, 137, 180–9, 219–44, 273
French, 10, 82–3, 89, 109, 112, 115–19, 124–7, 141, 189–96, 199, 202–7, 226–39, 276–9, 281–2, 285, 293, 378
resistance against, 182–6, 188–9, 259, 288
welcome to, 100, 195–6, 199, 202–4, 274

Fala, 260, 263–5, 267, 285
Famaka, 215, 216 (map)
famine, 255, 377–8, 398, 401
Fare, 146
Farīs Aligaz, Dejjazmach, 94–5
Fasīledes, Emperor, 271
Fazughli, 217n, 316 (map), 317
Felasha missions, see Missions
Ferret, Captain P. V., 18, 56–7, 86n, 92, 103, 105, 106n, 170
feudalism, 32–4, 95, 170, 376–8, 409
attempts by Tēwodros to abolish, 172–3
attitude of Yohannis, 376–7
Field, Colonel Charles W., 324, 364
Finn, Consul James, 132, 220–1, 236
Flad, Reverend J. Martin, 22, **176–80**, 186, 211, 224, 230, 232–4, 238n, 242, **247–49**, **251–55**, 262–3, 263n, 265–6, **274**, 307, 319
Flad, Mrs Paulina, 233, 253
France, French:
Antoine d'Abbadie, **77–82**, 166–7
Aubert and Dufey, 73–4
Combes, 82–4
De Jacobis/Delaye/Beillard/ Gilbert/Russel, 176, 180, **189–207**, 219
De Jacobis/Schimper/Degout-in, **103–15**, 118–20, 166
Du Bisson, 236
Lefebvre, **86–90**, 166–7
Lejean as consul, **226–231**
relations with Minīlik, 369, 375, 388–97, 401
relations with Tēwodros, **175–7**, 180, 189, 193, 207, **222–31**
relations with Weldē Mika'ēl, 278, 367
relations with Yohannis, **277–9**, 282, 290, 293, **297–8**, 301, 304, 307, 320, 332, 345–6, **349–50**, 352, 381
Rochet d'Héricourt: Gonder mission, 121–2, 129; Shewa missions, 145, **148–52**, **159–63**
Rolland, **124–7**, 166–7
'treaties': with Nigusē, **201–7**; with Sahle Sillasē, 145, **159–63**, 167; with Wibē, **125–7**, 167
Franz Josef, Emperor, 297–8
frontiers:
before 1870: eastern Shewa, **146**, 153, 370; Egyptian Sudan, **69**, 78, 98–9, **142–4**, **208–10**, 212–13, **215–18**, 216 (map), 222, 232, 250–1, **289**; Red Sea coast, 38, 40, 42, 44–5, **50–1**, 102, 105–9, **171**, 210, 216 (map), 219–20, 232, **250**, **308**
Bogos crisis and proposed solutions, **291** (map), **296–7**,

299–300, **302–6**, 308–9, **339** (map), 342–5, **351–9**, 381
claimed 1881 by Yohannis, 348; 1891 by Minīlik, 316 (map), 393
defined in Wiçhalē Treaty, **385–6**, **387** (map)
further Italian demands, **388–9, 401**
Mereb–Belesa–Muna line, **401–2**
vague concepts of boundaries in feudal Ethiopia, 50, 309
Fusella, Luigi, 24

Galinier, Captain J. G., 18, 56–7, 86n, 92, 103, 105, 106n, 170
Galla (Oromo), **32**, 43, 153
leadership role in Begēmdir, 34–5, 93
resisted Egyptian expedition to Harer, 317, 325
Rochet's plans for, 151
Shewan–Egyptian competition to control south-western, 375–6
troops at the Battle of Adwa, 402
Gamali Pasha, 314–15
Garred Kinfu, Lij, 188–9, 205
Gebre Igzi'abihēr, Blatta (Basha), 277n, 336
Gebre Īyesus, Aleqa, 211
Gebre Īyesus, Ṣehafe Ti'izaz, 106n
Gebre Maryam, 86, 89–90
Gebre Maryam, Içhegē, 66, **132–6**, 139–40
Gebre Maryam Ingida, Basha, 322
Gebre Medhin, 251
Gebre Mika'ēl, Abba, 91
Gebre Mika'ēl Girmu, 27
Gebre Sillasē Welde Aregay, Ṣehafe Ti'izaz, 23n, 26–27, 337n, 340n
Gebriyyē, Fitawrarī, 263–4
Gebru, Dejjazmach, Wagshum, 295n, 320, 322, 378
Gebru Haylu, Dejjazmach, 208
Gedhabi, 222
Gefat, **179**, 230, 237, 247, 252, **254–6**
George III, King, 16, 44, 47, 49–50, 52, 408–9
George IV, King, 14, 59–63
Gerhard, Bernard, 197
Germany, German:
approached by Minīlik, 368; by Tēwodros, 225; by Yohannis, 283, 297–8
attitude towards Bogos crisis, 299, 304
'consul' Hassen, 285
relations with Yohannis after Gura, 345, 348–50; with Minīlik regarding Wiçhalē treaty, 394–5, 398
Gezirat al-Luban, 217
Gigar, Emperor, 32

Giglio, Carlo, 197n, 379n, 385n, 386n, 388n, 389n, 395n, 396n
Gilbert, Consul Théodore, 199, 205–7, 219, 224
Ginda, 291 (map), 310, 314–15
Ginjar, 217
Girard, Alexandre, 277–8
Girra, 361
Giusto da Urbino, Fr., 176
Gobat, Reverend (later Bishop) Samuel, 55, 59, 61, 65–8, 75, 77, 79n, 131–5, 147, 150, 169–70, 177, 195, 237
Gobezē Gebre Medhin, Wagshum, 174, 241, 251, 255–6, 259–61, 268, 270–2, 274; see also Tekle Gīyorgīs (IV)
Godineau, 280n
Gojjam, 31 (map), 34–5, 111, 129, 173, 227–8, 327, 383, 402
Goma, 375–6
Gonder, 30, 33–6, 61n, 128–9, 341
    destroyed by Tēwodros, 241, 252; by the Mahdists, 383, 408
Gordon, General Charles George, 207, 277, 300, 315–18, 337–48, 354, 363, 371, 377–8
Gorgora Bichiñ, battle of, 136, 139
Goshu Zewdē, Ras, 84, 90, 94, 96n, 97–102, 116, 133, 136, 145
Graham, Major Douglas C., 153
Grant, Major A. J., 259
Granville (Granville George Leveson-Gower), Earl, 281, 283, 299–301, 304, 306–7, 354, 362
Greece, Greek, 342, 345, 349n
Gregory XVI, Pope, 77
Grévy, President Jules, 349–50
Gudagudē, see Gundet
Gugsa Mersu, Ras, 35, 41, 46–7, 49, 52, 407
Guizot, François, 113–14, 166
Gundet, battle of, 26, 291 (map), 319, 322–6, 329–30, 332, 335, 361–7, 372
Gur Amba, battle of, 136, 216 (map)
Gura, battle of, 291 (map), 326–35, 361–7, 372
Guragē, 316 (map), 375
Gwalu (Igwale Ṣiyon), Emperor, 32, 41, 47, 52
Gwangwil Sebagadis, 100

Habab (Asgede Beqla), 39 (map), 107–8, 110, 113, 126, 140, 142, 209–10, 232, 291 (map), 292, 296, 305, 342, 359, 381
Habesh, Habesha, Habeshistan, 12, 30, 115, 250
Habte Sillasē, Aleqa, 72, 75, 86, 91, 125, 147, 169
Hagos Teferi, Dejjazmach, 405

Haines, Captain Stafford, 85, 150–2, 158
Halay, 39 (map), 200–3, 385
Halhal, 210, 291 (map), 292, 297, 335
Hall, Moritz, 179
Hamasēn, 36, 39 (map), 102, 107, 143, 193–4, 197, 209, 229, 278, 290, 292, 305, 386, 389
    invasions of, 104, 117, 184, 291 (map), 296–7, 301–2, 314–15, 318–23, 326–7, 331
    rivalry and internal conflict, 294, 333–5, 338–41, 346, 367, 378
Hamdan abu Anja, Amir, 383–4
Hammad Hajj, 40, 53
Harer:
    customs pledged as security for Italian loan, 388
    occupied by Egypt, 310, 317–18, 325, 348, 370, 372, 375, 384
    occupied by Minīlik, 382, 396, 401, 405
Harris, Captain W. Cornwallis, 56, 93, 145, 152–6, 158–9, 163–5, 167–9, 272
Hasan Pasha, Prince, 324, 329
Hasan, Na'ib, 108, 117
Hasan Rifat, 250–1
Hasan Bey Salama Jarkas, 212
Hassen, Franz, 285, 293–4, 302, 327, 335, 365
Haussmann, C., 227, 230
Hawash valley, threatened by Egypt, 317, 375
Hawzēn, 200, 202, 216 (map)
Hayle Maryam Gebrē, Ras, 66
Hayle Melekot, King (of Shewa), 23, 164–5, 173
Hayle Mīka'ēl Sahle Sillasē, Mer'idazmach, 173
Haylu, Kentība, 255
Haylu, Ras (of Ṣelewas), 367
Haylu Goshu, Ras, 101
Haylu Tewelde Medhin (Haylu Habal), Dejjazmach, 72–3, 191, 194, 209, 241, 250–1, 259, 278, 290, 294, 333–4
Haylu (Hayle Maryam) Welde Gīyorgīs, Dejjazmach, 208
Hazega, 294, 378
Hebo, 385, 387 (map)
Heuglin, Theodor von, 136n, 138–9, 214–17, 227
Hewett, Rear-Admiral Sir William, 28, 353–6, 359–60, 363
Hewett treaty (Adwa 1884), 9, 16, 354–62, 379, 381–2
Hiruy Welde Sillasē, Blattēngēta, 144n, 145n, 161, 173n, 309n, 376n
Holland (Netherlands), letter to, 225
Houghton, A. B., and W., 323n, 363n
Hozier, Captain H. M., 286

Ibrahim Ali, 242
Ibrahim abu Bakr, 372

Ibrahim Shehem, Hajj, 164, 165n
Ibrahim Pasha al-Wali, 70
içhegē, 34, 78–9, 98, 116, 155, 173
Idris (of the Ginjar), 217n
Idris, Na'ib, 37, 44
Igwale Ṣiyon, see Gwalu
Ilg, Alfred, 19, 397
Imnetu (Imnete Maryam), Abba, 191, 194n, 195–6, 198–200, 202–6, 278–9
imperialism:
    commercial exploitation, 36–7, 42–4, 48, 53, 73–4, 82–3, 87–8, 99–102, 121, 124, 129, 134, 142, 148–9, 154, 160, 165–8, 181–3, 188, 193, 197, 206, 301, 313
    strategic considerations, 29, 36, 42–3, 81–2, 145
    territorial acquisitions, 57–8, 83, 87–8, 99–102, 124, 134, 206, 219, 250, 289, 296, 303, 311, 315–18, 378–80, 385, 396
Inderta, 36, 39 (map), 259, 326
Ingida, Aleqa, 247n, 266
Ingida, Ras, 263
Ingida Werq Merzē, 265n
Injabara, battle of, 216 (map), 232
Innarya, 316 (map), 375–6
Intịcho, 39 (map), 104, 109, 122
Isenberg, Reverend C. W., 55, 71–6, 103–4, 147, 158, 166, 168
Islam, Muslims:
    confidants and agents of the rulers, 409
    issue in the internal power struggles, 90, 94–8
    revival and spread during nineteenth century, 34–5, 43, 107
    wartime propaganda against, 321–2, 327
Islamgē, 260, 263
Ismail Pasha, Khedive, 3, 236, 250, 252, 258, 285, 290–326, 329–37, 345, 368–76, 382, 404, 408
Ismail Haqqi Pasha abu Jabal, 116–17, 140
Ismail Kamil Pasha, 69
Ismail Sadiq Pasha, 250
Isṭifanos, Aleqa, 78–80
Italy, Italian:
    Adwa, battle of, 3, 363, 399–404, 408
    Gordon's proposal to cede Zulla to, 346–7
    Leone des Avanchers' treaty negotiations, 197
    Matteucci's mission, 342, 348n
    occupation of Massawa, and advances inland, 362, 378–84
    protectorate issue, 15–16, 385–6, 389–99, 401
    relations with Minīlik as king of Shewa, 368, 375, 379–84

treaties: commercial, of 1883, 379, 385–6; 'Convention of neutrality', 382, 384; Wiçhalē, 15–16, 145, **384–99**; 'Additional Convention', 388–9, 394, 398
Iyasu, Emperor, 32
Iyo'as, Emperor, 32

Jacob, Messrs W. and J., 43
Jacobis, see De Jacobis
Jaenen, C. J., 101n
Jaquin, 179
Jenda, 232, 234
Jildessa, 316 (map), 317
Jimma, 375–6
Johnston, Charles, 154n
Jonveaux, Émile, 19
Joyce, Kirwan, 20n, 197–8
Juba River, 315, 317–18, 325
Jumma, Shaykh, 214, 218, 303, 305

Kasa Golja (Abba Kaisi), 293–4, 302
Kasa Haylu, Lij, 116, 129, **135–40**; see also Tēwodros
Kasa Mirçha, Dejjazmach, 259–60, **270–83**; see also Yohannis IV
Kasa Sebagadis (Kasayē), Dejjazmach, 69, 73, 82–3, 85, 91, **173–4**, 191
Kasala, 31 (map), **98**, 107, 232, 289, **356**, **359**, 361, **380**
Katte, Baron A. von, 56, 72–3, 75, 166, 170
Kayakor, 328, 334–5
Kebbede Teferī, Wagshum, 367
Keller-Zschokke, J. V., 315n
Kerans, 235, 237
Keren, 290, 291 (map), 292, **296**, 335, 338, 348, 359, 361, 381
Kewatit (Coatit), battle of, 387 (map), 400
Kibre Negest 33
Kīdane Maryam, Aleqa, 71–2, 75, 77
Kīdane Maryam, Neggadras, 122
Kīdane Maryam, Ras, 255
Kienzlen, G., 177, 179, 229–30, 268
Kielmaier, 71, 75, 150, 168–9
Kilelu, 31 (map), 153
Kinfu, Debtera, 191n, 192n
Kinfu Haylu, Dejjazmach, 69–71, 77–80, 84, 90, 208
King, Henry S., and Company, 280–1, 283, 299, 342n
Kirkham, General J. C., 15, 19, **277**, 282, **297–309**, 314–15, 321n, 324, 326–7, **332–3**, 363–4
Kismayu, 316 (map), 317
Kjellberg, P. E., 289
Kokebē, Dejjazmach, 119
Koso Ber, battle of, 21
Kotsika, Johannes, 183n
Krapf, Reverend J. L., 17, 55,

95n, 103, 147, **150–2**, **154–9**, 162, 164–6, 168, 171, **176–8**, 180
Kufit:
battle of, 380
Egyptian garrison, 209, 236, 289–90, 291 (map), 292, 297
Kugler, Christian, 55, 59, 61, 64–6
Kunama (Bazēn), **32**, 39 (map), **142–3**, 209, **217**, **288–9**, 292, **295–8**, 300, 302, 304–5

Lagarde, Dr, 227, 230–1
Lagarde, Léonce, 394, 400
Lambermont, Baron C. A., 389
Lasta, 31 (map), 34, 174, 241
Lazarist Mission, see Missions
Lee, Samuel, 61n
Lefebvre, Théophile, 17, 18, 54n, 56–7, **84–92**, 99, **102–3**, 113–14, 120–2, 125–7, 138, 144–5, 149–50, **159–63**, 166–7, 169–70, 176, 178, 206
Lejean, Guillaume, 20, 103n, 125n, 214, 217n, 223, **226–34**, 236–9, 250
Lemlem, Aleqa, 24–5, 376
Le Moyne, Consul General A., 133, 135
Leone des Avanchers, Padre, 176n, 186, 197
Leopold I, King, 100–1, 134
Leopold II, King, 13, 395
Lepère de Lapereuse, 195
Lesseps, Viscount Ferdinand-Marie de, 73, 191
Līben Amedē, Imam, 95
Liche, 'treaty' of, 338–40
Littmann, Enno, 22
Loring, General W. W., 311, 315n, 324, 328n, 363–4, 366, 368
Louis Philippe, King, 78, 83, 85, 92, 148–9

Mackerer, Joseph, 193, 252, 254
McKillop (Captain H. F.) Pasha, 314–18, 371
McKilvie, Richard, 252
Mahdere Qal Tewelde Medhin, 176, 244n, 284, 305, 320–1, 323–4
Mahdia, Mahdists, 351, 359, **361–2**, **383–6**, 401, 408
Mahṣene Mīka'ēl (Mahṣentu), Īchegē, 78–80, 116, 132n
Malécot, Georges, 3, 20n
Malet, Consul General Edward, 350–2
Marcus, Harold, 4, 5
Mariyyē Gugsa, Ras, 21, 36, 66–7
Markham, Clements R., 264, 266, 267n, 285–6
Marston, Thomas E., 3, 166n
Martini, Ferdinando, 17
Maru Aklu, Dejjazmach, 21, 66
Marya, Qeyyih and Ṭiqur (Ṣellim), 39 (map), **107**,

209, 292, **296**, 302, 305, **338**, **339** (map), 359
Mason (A. McC.) Bey, 355–6, 359–60
Massaja, Mgr Lorenzo Gugliel-mo, 118, 227, 274, 303n, 345n
Massawa:
administration changed from Ottoman (Hijaz) to Egyptian, 37, 44, 57, 96–7, 108, 115–16, 119, 250
arms embargo, see arms
Britain: alleged 'offers' to, 14–15, 46, 48, 50, 58–9, 64, 128; 'proposals' for acquisition, 106, 121
Ethiopia: importance to and power, 29, 37–8, 42, 44–5, 48, 50–1, 67, 108–9; fear of attack from, 208, 210, 314, 323, 335, 342, 348, 350; proposals to 'hand over', 182–3, 185, 353; requests by Yohannis, 341, 344, 346, 361
Italy: occupation, 362, 379–82
trade: duties and revenue, 40, 42–4, 105, 115, 118–19, 300–1, 351, 353–4; 'free transit', 330, 343–4, 351–2, **355–61**, 380–1; planned diversions from, 38, 40–2, 87–8, 101, 105, 121, 124, 134, 141–2, 346; size, 82
Matteucci, Pellegrino, 348n
May Guba, 216 (map), 217–18
Mayer, J., 177, 277n, 283, 303n
Mecca, *sharif* of, 44, 53
Mek Nimr, 69, 98, 209, 215, 217–18
Mekonnin Welde Mīka'ēl (of Hazega), 292n
Mekonnin Welde Mīka'ēl, Ras, 27, 388–9, 396, 399, 402, 405, 408
Menen Līben, Empress, 79, 90, 94, 98, 101–2, 116, 208
Mengesha Yohannis, Ras, 368, 394, 396, 399–400, 402, 405
Mensa, 39 (map), **107**, **143–4**, 184, **209–10**, 290, 296, 305, 310, 342, 359
Meqdela, 7, **173**, 216 (map), 237, 256, 260–2, 273, 285
battle of, 263–8
significance and myth of, 3, **284–7**, 408
Meqele, 387 (map), 388, 390
Mereb (Gash) River, 98, 319, 322, 334, 387 (map), 388
Merewether, Colonel William L., **249**, 251–2, **254**, **256–9**, 267n, 271n, 306
Merqorēwos, Abune, 48n
Merso Hayle Maryam, Dejjazmach, 94–5, 139n
Merzē (or Meerza), Abba, 273n
Meshesha Tedla, Dejjazmach, 261, 268, 274
Mestewat, Queen (of Wello Galla), 261

434   INDEX

Metemma, 69, **140**, 209, 212, 214, 216 (map), 217, 222, 228, 232, 316 (map), 341, 344, **353**, 361; *see also* Qallabat
battle of, **384**
Egyptian annexation, 303–4
Midre Bahir, 51
Mīka'ēl, Abba, 368–9
Mīka'ēl, Ras (former Imam Muhammad Ali), 402, 405
Mīka'ēl Sihul, Ras, 271
Minīlik II, Emperor, 113, 158–9, 165, 173, **241–2**, 255–6, 270, 272–6, 279, 282–3, 298, 303, 309, 312, **314–18**, 320, 323, 325, **336–40**, 343, **345–7**, **367–77**, **379–409**
Minkullu, 39 (map), 118–20, 123, 125, 127
Mirçha Werqē, Liqemekwas, 177, 244n, 259, **280–1**, 284, 305, **330–4**, 360
Mirraçh Welde Sillasē, 209
missions, missionaries, 13, 17–18, 43, 48, **55–6**, 91, 169, 231, 342n, 368–9, 409
  Catholic: Capuchins, 118, 274, 345n; Lazarists, 15, **55–6**, **77**, 86–7, 98–104, 106, **109–15**, **118–19**, 122, 125, 133–4, 136–8, 143–4, 164, 169, 171, **174–7**, 180–1, **189–207**, 224, 230, 250, 259n, **274–9**, 282–3, 290, **293–5**, 298–9, 326, 350, 352
  Protestant: Chrischona Mission, **176–80**, 185; Church Missionary Society, in Tigrē, **65–6**, 71, **74–6**, 91, 103; in Shewa, **147**, 150, **154–8**; Felasha missions, **178–9**, 224, 230, 232, 234, 237, 274; Swedish Evangelical Mission, 18, **288–9**, 378
Mitzakis, Consul D., 345n, 350
Möckeln, 364
Mogareh, 143
Mokha, 31 (map), 38, 40–2, 115
Mondon-Vidailhet, Casimir, 23–7
Montuori, Fr. Luigi, 98, 118, 164
Mountnorris, *see* Valentia
Moynier, Count de, 241
Muhammad Abd al-Rahim, Na'ib, 228, 240, 294, 312–13, 321, 332
Muhammad Ahmad, the Mahdi, 351, 383
Muhammad Ali Pasha, 2, **57–8**, 68–70, 72, 74, 77–8, 81, 86, **96–8**, 116–17, 127, 145, 148, 217, 290
Muhammad Anfari, Sultan, 318, 393
Muhammad al-Basrawi, 96–7
Muhammad Be'id, Shaykh, 215
Muhammad Loheyta, Sultan, 318
Muhammad Ratib Pasha, *see* Ratib

Muhammad Ra'uf Pasha, *see* Ra'uf Pasha
Muhammad Rifat Bey, 329–30
Muhammad Sa'id Pasha, *see* Sa'id Pasha
Muhammad Tawfiq, Khedive, 344–5, 348–9
Muhammad al-Tayib, 401, 409
Muhammad Yahya, Na'ib, 105, 108–9, **114–19**, 184
Mühleisen-Arnold, J., 156
Müller, J. C., 156
Munzinger (J. A. Werner) Pasha, 17, 171, 209, 241, 250, 257, 259, 269–70, 272, **276–9**, **281–3**, **285**, **289–303**, 306, 308, 310, **313–20**, 323–5, 330, 363, **366–72**, 376
Murray, Alexander, 47
Musa Hamdi Pasha, 213–14, 218, 222–3, 228, 232, 236, 290

na'ib (of Arkīko), **30**, **37–40**, 42, 44–6, 48, **51**, 53, 67, 75, 78, 81, 88, **104–9**, 112, **117**, 119, 121–3, **228–9**; *see also* Muhammad Abd al-Rahim
Napier, Sir Robert (Lord Magdala), **256–68**, 270–7, 279–81, **285–6**, 306, 326, 342n, **353**, 364, 408
Napoleon I, Emperor, 29, 400
Napoleon III, Emperor, 190, 194, 196, 198, 203–5, 222, 225, 228–30, 238, 271, 277–9, 367
Naretti, Giacomo, 277, 350
Negash Welde Sillasē, 337
Nerazzini, Cesare, 399
Nigusē Welde Mīka'ēl (Agew Nigusē), Dejjazmach, 174, 180, 184, 187, **189–207**, 212n, 219, 223–4, 228, 275, 408
Nikolai Alexandrovich (later Czar Nikolai II), 408
Nimrab, 213, 218
Nubar Pasha Boghos, 376
Nus'r Alli, 52
Nöldeke, Theodor, 22

Obok, 145, 369, 394
Ogaden, 316 (map), 404
Orero, General Baldassare, 388, 390

Palmerston, Henry John Temple, Viscount, 65, 78, 85, 121–2, 127, 128n, 152, 166
Pankhurst, Richard, 4, 16n, 365n, 398n
Parkyns, Mansfield H. I., 56, 217
Pearce, Nathaniel, 18–19, 42, **44–50**, **52–3**, 55, 59, 84
peasantry:
  burdens on, 170–1
  hostile towards Tēwodros, 255
  sufferers from the wars in the north, 377–8

Peel, Sir Robert, 157
Peter the Hermit, 198
Petherick, Consul John, 236
Petit, Dr A., 84, 159–60
Pētros VII, Patriarch, 62, 65, 134–5
Piano, Colonel Federico, 398–9
Plowden, Consul Walter Chichele, 10, 15, 17, 20, 35, 56, **118–31**, 133, 137–8, **141–3**, 167, 169, 173, 175–6, **180–93**, 195, 198n, 199, 205, 208, 210–11, 219, 223–4, 233, 255, 269, 286
Portal, Sir Gerald, 381–3
Powell, Thomas, 298, 305
presents:
  to Ethiopian rulers, 44–7, 65, 83, 89, 98, 104, 122, 131n, 152–3, 156, 159, 164, 192, 201, 205, 212, 223–4, 226, 275, 279, 283, 301, 304, 315–17, 353–4, 364
  from Ethiopian rulers, 59–61, 120, 129, 131n, 149, 164, 211, 245, 266, 280–1
Prideaux, W. F., 17, 243, 246–8, 252, 265–6, 283, 285, 296
protectorate:
  Anglo-Egyptian, proposed by Flad, 319
  Belgian, proposed by Blondeel, 100–1
  French, proposed by De Jacobis and Schimper, 109–14; by Rolland, 124–7; allegedly offered by Nigusē, 200–4, 206; assumed by Lejean, 229
  Italian, claimed by Crispi, 385–6, 389–99, 401
  Stella/Munzinger over Bogos, 143–4, 171, 278, 288

Qadarif, 31 (map), 69, 212
Qallabat, 31 (map), **69, 140**, 212, 214, 216 (map), 217–18, 290, 303, 309, **351–5**, 359n, **361**; *see also* Metemma
Qērilos, Abune, 34, 62–3, 66–7
Qērilos IV (Da'ud), Patriarch, **134–6**, 176, 185–6, 189, **210–11**, 240
Qwara, 208, 216 (map), 217n, 222, 304, 306, 309, 402
Qwinzila, battle of, 31 (map), 84

Radwan Pasha, 315
Raffray, Consul Achille, 342, 350, 352, 365n
Raheita, 258, 303
Ras Dumara, 196, 199, 203
Rassam, Hormuzd, 8, 17, 22, 169, **240**, **242–9**, 251–4, 257, 261–3, 265–6, 267n, 285
Ratib Pasha, **324–36**, 364n, 367, 372
Ra'uf Pasha, **317–18**, 325, 371
Raya, 313, 316 (map)

Red Sea coast:
access (possession) lost and reclaimed by Ethiopia, 37, 45–6, 51, 116–18, 250, 258, 297, 300, 306, 308, 335, 345–9, 354–61, 383, 386, 387 (map), 393
claims rejected by Egypt and Britain, 307–8, 341, 343, 350–5
lost to Ethiopia, 362, 388–9, 410
see also Egypt, Eritrea, Italy, Massawa
Reitz, Consul Konstantin, 138–9
René, 277
revenues, mid-nineteenth century:
Begēmidr, 257; Bogos, 343; Hamasēn, 250; salt trade, 250, 313; total, rough estimation, 257
Rizzo, Antonio, 197
Rochet d'Héricourt, C. F. X., 16, 18, 56–7, 121–2, 129, 138–9, 145, 147–53, 157–64, 167–9
Rohlfs, Gerhard, 276n, 322n, 348–52
Rolland, Consul Eugène, 124–7, 141, 167
Rolland et Cie, Étienne, 73, 88
Rosenthal, H., 227, 233, 237
Rouget, Jules, 92
Rüppell, Eduard, 18, 56, 63n, 64n, 68, 147
Rushdy, Major, 322
Russ, Camill, 322n, 323n
Russegger, Jos., 215
Russel, Count Stanislas, 200–7
Russell, Lord John, 220, 224, 238–40, 242–3
Russia, Russian:
approached by Tēwodros, 183, 225; by Yohannis, 283, 297, 304, 342
contacts established after Gura, 342, 349n
relations with Minīlik regarding Wichalē treaty, 389, 391, 395–7
Rustum Agha, 106, 108, 114

Saalmüller, K., 177, 179, 229n, 264, 265n
Sabry, M., 58n, 311n, 363n, 364n
Sahle Dingil, Emperor, 32, 78, 80, 82, 85, 90, 101
Sahle Sillasē, King (of Shewa), 16, 33, 35, 83, 94, 116, 118, 121, 145–65, 167–8, 170–3, 195, 270, 272, 288, 368
Saho, 39 (map), 126, 141–2
Sa'id Pasha, 187, 209–14, 221
Salisbury, Robert Cecil, Marquis of, 8, 390–1, 395
Salt, Henry, 16–18, 37–53, 55, 59, 62–5, 67, 141, 183, 409
salt plains:
attempts by Egypt to occupy, 313, 375

importance to Ethiopia, 142, 219, 300–1, 375
reported revenue, 250, 313
Turkish/Egyptian plans to acquire, 141–2, 250, 300–1
Samu'ēl Gīyorgīs (Samu'ēl bin Ali, Hussein Ali), 150–2, 169, 233–4, 244n, 247, 248n, 263, 266, 284, 369
San Marzano, General Alessandro Asinari di, 383
Sapeto, Fr. Giuseppe, 17, 55, 75–7, 86–8, 147n, 194–6, 200–2
Sarzec, Consul Ernest Chocquin de, 282n, 285, 293, 302, 304, 307, 320, 322–3, 327, 363, 366, 369
Sawakin, 57
Schaffner, 90
Schiller, K., 227, 254
Schimper, Wilhelm, 19, 56, 71, 76, 86, 103–4, 106–18, 125–7, 138, 166–7, 177, 186, 268, 282n, 283, 298
Se'aṭī, 352, 380–3, 387 (map), 388
Ṣe'azega, 294, 334, 378, 385–6, 387 (map)
Sebagadis (Suba Gadis) Weldu, Dejjazmach, 14–15, 36, 45, 58–68, 86, 92, 150, 168–9, 172, 183, 367, 409
Ṣedalu, Aleqa, 78–80
Ṣelama, Abune, 23, 34, 91–5, 111, 116, 118, 125, 132–4, 137–8, 155, 164, 173, 175–8, 180–4, 188–9, 191, 193, 210–11, 233, 238, 240–1, 244, 271
Selim, Sultan, 250
Semhar, 39 (map), 110, 113, 116–17, 209, 308, 342
Senafē, 216 (map), 259
Senhit, 353, 356, 359; see also Bogos, Keren
Serayē, 318–23, 340, 387 (map), 389, 393
Seyfu (Seyfe Sillasē) Sahle Sillasē, 173, 212
Shanqilla, 217, 344
Shendi, 216 (map), 218
Shewa, 34–5, 144–65, 173, 212, 215, 241, 317–18, 327, 338, 368, 371, 376, 379, 383
Shiket, 387 (map), 388
Shirē, 36, 39 (map)
Shotel, 278
Shukriya, 212
Sibhat Aragawī, Ras, 405
Sillasē, 260, 263, 267
Simēn, 34, 174, 184, 190–1, 402
Sinnar, 210, 213
Sobat River, 316 (map), 317
Somali coast, 305, 310
Sormani, 364
Spain, envoy from, 350
Speedy, Charles, 179, 227, 249, 346n, 353, 360
Staiger, W., 178, 227, 254
Stanley, Edward Henry, Lord; Earl of Derby, 262, 272, 308

Stanley, Henry Morton, 286
Stanton, Consul General Edward, 280, 299–302, 306–8
Stecker, Anton, 350, 352
Stella, Padre Giovanni, 143–4, 180n, 181n, 197, 241, 278, 279n
Stern, Reverend Henry A., 18, 178, 189n, 227, 230, 232–5, 237–9, 266
Steudner, Herrmann, 227
Stone, General Charles, 317
Suez Canal, 283–4, 408
Sufi, 215, 216 (map), 217
survival, national:
external threats, 311–12, 378–9, 382, 385, 391–7, 408
geographical factors, 1–2, 407–8
national and spiritual identity, 2, 30–2, 36, 269, 321–2, 327, 366, 408–9
political cohesion and consolidation, 4, 172–3, 269, 338–40, 376–7, 399–400, 404–5, 409
underestimation of the Ethiopian people and polity, 2, 4, 269–70, 285–7, 366, 377, 404–6; see also underestimation
Swedish Evangelical Mission, see Missions
Switzerland, requested to boycott Ethiopia, 395

Tajura, 31 (map), 35, 88, 156–8, 221, 314–18, 345, 371, 375, 394
Taka, 108, 216 (map), 292, 301
Takruri, 214, 217
Tamisier, Maurice, 16n, 56, 72–3, 75, 146
Taranta Pass, 51
Ṭaqayē, Lij, 195–6, 198–9, 205
Tawfiq, see Muhammad Tawfiq
Tayye Gebre Maryam, Aleqa, 27–8
Te'ander, 305
technology (craftsmen and tools):
requests for, 41, 44, 58–61, 64, 87, 100, 123, 128, 139, 146–7, 150, 153–4, 164, 168–9, 174, 177–8, 185, 210–11, 225–6, 237, 245–9, 266, 277, 279–81, 303, 312, 345–6, 368–70
response, 193, 249, 252–3, 312
Tedla Gwalu, 173, 227, 232, 241
Teferi Wessen, Wagshum, 270, 367
Tekle, Fītawrarī, 402
Tekle Gīyorgīs, Emperor, 271, 274–6, 279, 282–3, 290–5, 298, 303, 322n, 368; see also Gobezē Gebre Medhin
Tekle Gīyorgīs, Prince, 75
Tekle Gīyorgīs Fiqir Segged, Emperor, 32–3, 47, 90
Tekle Haymanot, Fr. (of Adwa), 22, 93n

Tekle Haymanot, King (of Gojjam), 383, 399, 405; see also Adal Tesemma
Tekle Īyesus, 376n
Tembēn, 36, 39 (map), 259
Tesemma Ingida, Dejjazmach, 255
Tesemma Welde Mīka'ēl, Dejjazmach, 174
Tēwodros, Emperor, 7, 116, 168–9, **172–200**, **205–77**, 281–8, 290, 295, 303, 326, 341, 347, 349, 351, 407–9; see also Kasa Haylu
Tēwodros myth, 172, 208, 221, 265
Thiers, President Louis Adolphe, 88, 297–8
Thouvenel, Edouard Antoine, 205n
Thurneyssen, 364
Tian, César, 273
Tigrē, **34–6**, 38–9, 41, 51, 59, **67**, 100, 102, 144, 167, **173–4**, **190–4**, **206–7**, 212, 229, 252, 259, 314, **325**, 327, 368, 375, **398**, **400–2**
Țilṭal, 39 (map), 126, 142
Țiso Gobezē, 174, 241
Tora, 305
Touvier, Mgr Jean Marcel, 17, 293
Toynbee, Arnold J., 1
trade:
  'artificial wants' to be taught, 167
  duties and imposts, 118–19, 129, 154, 160, 167, 310
  estimated size, 82, 101, 124, 149
  European initiatives to capture, 36–51, 74, 82–3, 86–8, 101, 112, 121–31, 138–9, 144–5, 154, 157, 159–60, 167–8, 188, 197, 226, 342, 379
  judged to be profitable, 101, 146, 149, 167
  routes, 35–6, 38, 39 (map), 44, 69, 112, 140, 146
  salt currency, 142
  see also Massawa
Traversi, Leopoldo, 394, 398–9
treaties, see Britain, France, Italy
Trimingham, J. Spencer, 1–2
Turkey (Ottoman Empire), Turks
  claims to mainland rejected, 115, 121–4, 127, 140–1
  fictitious suzerainty over Ethiopia, 30, 96, 116, 220, 250
  position on Italy's claim to a protectorate over Ethiopia, 389–92, 395, 397
  relationship to the na'ibs of Arkīko, 30, 37, 44, 51, 112, 116–17
  sovereignty at Massawa violated by Italy, 379, 389 see also Britain, Egypt, Italy, Massawa, na'ib

Umar wad Nimr, 209, 212, 217–18, 222
Umberto I, King, 342, 379, 392, 394
underestimation of Ethiopia and Ethiopians, 2, 4, 366, 377
  as a result of the Meqdela expedition, 285–7
  by Arakil, 365–6; Blondeel, 99–102; Gordon, 346; Hassen, 293; Isenberg, 72, 75–6; Katte, 166; Munzinger, 294
  in negotiations, 330, 366, 404
  on the eve of the battle of Adwa, 399–400, 404–6
Uthman Pasha, 96, 105, 108

Valentia, Lord, Earl Mountnorris (Sir George Annesley), 18, 19, **36–44**, 48, 52–3, 63–5, 67, 72, 124
Valieri, 92n, 169n
Victoria, Queen, 8, 15, 78, 80, 91, 123, 127–8, 132, 134, 164, 186–7, 222–5, 232, 234–5, 237–40, 242–6, 248, 252–3, 268, 272–3, 279–83, 296–300, 303n, 304, 321, 323–4, 341, 347–54, 361, 368, 377, 379–81, 392
Vivian, Sir Hussey Crespigny, Baron, 363n

Wad Kaltabu, battle of, 69, 76, 216 (map)
Wadla, 216 (map), 260
Wag, 174, 216 (map), 327, 378
Waldibba, 291 (map), 305
Waldmeier, Theophil, 18, 22, 177, 179, 226n, 229n, 230–1, 261, 263–6
Wegera, 39 (map), 116, 241
Wehnī, 216 (map), 222, 228, 306
Weiland-Kiepert Map, 215
Wekī Dibba, battle of, 334, 378
Welasma Muhammad, 153, 162
Weld Blundeell, H., 21
Welde Gabir (of Hamasēn), 107, 116

Welde Gabir (bodyguard of Tēwodros), 264n
Welde Gebri'ēl, 21
Welde Gīyorgīs, Abba, 66
Welde Kīros, Abba, 77, 80
Welde Maryam Aleqa, 23–4
Welde Mīka'ēl, Abba, 71–2
Welde Mīkaēl' Selomon (Abba Gomīda), Dejjazmach (Egyptian-appointed ras), 278–9, 290, 292n, 294, 322, **326–7**, **330–1**, 333–5, 337–42, 346, 367–8, 376n, 378
Welde Ṣadiq (Abba Menzir), Azazh, 375
Welde Ṣadiq Mirraçh (Walad Marrag), 209, 218, 241, 251, 289, 297
Welde Sillasē (Wereñña), Ras, 303, 305, 327n, 337, 367, 376
Welde Sillasē Kifle Īyesus, Ras, 19, 21, 33, **36–42**, **44–53**, 59, 61, 63, 67, 92, 102, 141, 168, 271, 288, 367, 407–9
Weldu, Ri'ise Debr, 91
Welē Biṭul, Ras, 402
Wellamo, 404
Wellega, 316 (map), 386n, 402
Wello, 31 (map), 34–5, 173, 215, 241–2, 303, 318, 327, 402
Welqayit, 31 (map), 69, 174, 217n, 241
Wereylu, 316 (map), 371
Werqē, Garabet, 61–2, 169
Werre Hīmenu, 95, 316 (map)
Wi'a, 381–3, 387 (map)
Wibē, Lij, Dejjazmach, 367
Wibē Hayle Maryam, Dejjazmach, 15, 36, 53–4, **66–119**, **122–9**, 132–43, 145, 147, 167–9, 172–5, 181, 183, 189, 191, 195, 212n, 220, 270–1, 288, 408
Wichalē Treaty, see Italy, treaties
Wida, island of, 202
Wilhelm I, Emperor, 282n, 297–8, 348, 352
Wilhelm II, Emperor, 392
Wilson, Sir Charles, 351
Winstanley, W., 341, 346
Wolff, Dr J., 73
Work, Ernest, 4
Wylde, Augustus B., 337–9

Yahya, Na'ib, 104–8
Yejju, 31 (map), **34–5**, 95, 327, 402
Yimam Gugsa, Ras, 66
Yohannis III, Emperor, 32, 90, 94, 98, 189